A Power to Do Justice

A Power to Do Justice

JURISDICTION, ENGLISH LITERATURE, AND
THE RISE OF COMMON LAW, 1509-1625

Bradin Cormack

The University of Chicago Press   CHICAGO & LONDON

The University of Chicago Press, Chicago 60637
The University of Chicago Press, Ltd., London
© 2007 by The University of Chicago
All rights reserved. Published 2007.
Paperback edition 2013
Printed in the United States of America

22 21 20 19 18 17 16 15 14 13   3 4 5 6

ISBN-13: 978-0-226-11624-2 (cloth)
ISBN-13: 978-0-226-06154-2 (paper)
ISBN-13: 978-0-226-11625-9 (e-book)
10.7208/9780226116259

The University of Chicago Press gratefully acknowledges the generous support of the Division of the Humanities at the University of Chicago toward the publication of this book.

Library of Congress Cataloging-in-Publication Data

Cormack, Bradin.
 A power to do justice : justification, English literature, and the rise of common law, 1509–1625 / Bradin Cormack.
   p. cm.
 Includes bibliographical references and index.
 ISBN-13: 978-0-226-11624-2 (alk. paper)
 ISBN-10: 0-226-11624-7 (alk. paper)
 1. English literature—Early modern, 1500–1700—History and criticism.
 2. Law and literature—Great Britain—History—16th century. 3. Law and literature—Great Britain—History—17th century. 4. Law in literature.
 I. Title.
 PR428 .L37C67   2008
 820.9′002—dc22

2007024210

In memory of my father,

GEORGE NOEL CORMACK

CONTENTS

List of Illustrations   ix
Acknowledgments   xi
Note on Citations   xv

Prologue: A Power to Do Justice   1
Introduction: Literature and Jurisdiction   11

PART I CENTRALIZATION

1. "Shewe Us Your Mynde Then": Bureaucracy and Royal Privilege in Skelton's *Magnyfycence*   47
2. "No More to Medle of the Matter": Thomas More, Equity, and the Claims of Jurisdiction   85

PART II RATIONALIZATION

3. Inconveniencing the Irish: Custom, Allegory, and the Common Law in Spenser's Ireland   133
4. "If We Be Conquered": Legal Nationalism and the France of Shakespeare's English Histories   177

PART III FORMALIZATION

5 "To Stride a Limit": *Imperium*, Crisis, and Accommodation in
 Shakespeare's *Cymbeline* and *Pericles*   227

6 "To Law for Our Children": Norm and Jurisdiction in Webster, Rowley,
 and Heywood's *Cure for a Cuckold*   291

Notes   331

Index   387

ILLUSTRATIONS

1 William I, from John Rastell, *The Pastyme of People* (1529) 207
2 Richard I, from Rastell, *Pastyme of People* 207
3 Edward III, from Rastell, *Pastyme of People* 207
4 Henry V, from Rastell, *Pastyme of People* 207
5 Edward IV, from Rastell, *Pastyme of People* 208
6 Henry IV, from Rastell, *Pastyme of People* 208
7 William II, from Rastell, *Pastyme of People* 210
8 William I, William II, and Henry I, from *A Brief Abstract* (ca. 1560) 211
9 Thomas Hood, map of the English headlands (1605) 260
10 Sir Julius Caesar, draft of proclamation on international fishing (1609) 264
11 Frontispiece to William Camden, *Britannia* (1607) 267
12 Map of Great Britain and Ireland, from John Speed, *Theatre of the Empire of Great Britaine* (1611) 268
13 Detail of map of Lancashire, from Speed, *Theatre* 270
14 Detail of map of Warwickshire, from Speed, *Theatre* 271
15 Detail of map of Northamptonshire, from Speed, *Theatre* 271
16 Detail of map of Rutlandshire, from Speed, *Theatre* 272
17 Detail of map of Rutlandshire, from Speed, *Theatre* 272
18 Detail of map of Wales, from Speed, *Theatre* 273
19 Detail of map of Cardiganshire, from Speed, *Theatre* 274
20 Detail of map of Lancashire, from William Camden, *Britannia* (1607) 276
21 Detail of map of Lancashire, from Christopher Saxton's atlas (1579) 277

ACKNOWLEDGMENTS

This book has been a long time in the making, and the debts I have incurred cross many borders. From Stanford, I want to thank David Riggs, Paul Seaver, and Wesley Trimpi for their many insights into my project. My greatest debt is to Stephen Orgel, who nurtured the kind of structured free thinking without which an interdisciplinary project like this one could not have begun to taken shape. More recently, Stephen has been an enthusiastic reader of new chapters and stronger versions of old chapters, an inspired mentor and even better friend. From deeper in my past, I am grateful to three teachers in Edmonton who first introduced me to the sixteenth and seventeenth centuries: Leila Jones, W. J. Jones, and the late C. Q. Drummond.

At the University of Chicago, I have been the beneficiary of a rare level of support from my colleagues in the English Department, who all invested much time in my work. I thank each of them. My colleagues specifically in Renaissance studies have enriched my teaching, thinking, and writing. David Bevington was equally generous with his historical expertise and his enthusiasm for how dramatists think. Carla Mazzio has been an unfailingly supportive interlocutor and an eloquent tester and shaper of ideas. Janel Mueller offered incisive suggestions for my arguments about English nationalism. Michael Murrin took equal care in showing me where to make an argument narrower and where to bring some wider context—though never the whole of the Silk Road—to bear. Joshua Scodel helped me measure more carefully the use of my central terms as a way to make the argument at once more focused and more textured. Richard Strier was marvelously helpful in urging me toward an account of the relationship between the literary and historical particular adequate to my argument about literature's place at the legal table, and law's place at the literary one. I feel fortunate to have been able to complete this book alongside six such scholars and friends.

Outside my field, two colleagues have been especially important for the writing of this book. In scintillating conversation and in extended responses to my writing, Lauren Berlant helped me to think more clearly and confidently about legal and social norms and about the time of jurisdiction. Bill Brown repeatedly energized my thinking about the book's literary and historical objects by opening my sentences onto horizons different from those I could see, thereby helping me find a more meditative book inside the historical one. A number of scholars, at Chicago and elsewhere, read and responded to individual chapters in both early and late drafts. I want to thank Rebecca Brown, Brendan Cormack, Margreta de Grazia, Jacqueline Goldsby, Peter Goodrich, Gordon Harvey, Richard Helmholz, Constance Jordan, Sean Keilen, Julius Kirshner, Loren Kruger, Sandra Macpherson, Jeffrey Masten, Andrew McRae, Eric Oberle, Joshua Phillips, Carolyn Sale, Eric Slauter, Justin Steinberg, and Simon Stern. I have been fortunate to be part of the Project in Late Liberalism, a group whose members offered me new ways to think about intellectual work generally and to track what my book in particular was doing: thanks to Lauren Berlant, Elaine Hadley, Patchen Markell, Mark Miller, and Candace Vogler. At an earlier date, Candace read the whole manuscript and offered a sustaining account of where its interest lay. Among many other scholars and friends who supported and extended my thinking during the book's composition, I am grateful to Danielle Allen, Caroline Bicks, Anston Bosman, Stephanie Brooks, Suzanne Buffam, Colin Burrow, Nora Cain, Edmund Campos, Dipesh Chakrabarty, Beth Ann Day, Ken Fields, Jay Fliegelman, Bill Germano, Christine Holbo, Jinger Hoop, Lorna Hutson, Jonathan Ivry, Oren Izenberg, Rebecca Lemon, Seth Lerer, Saree Makdisi, Helen Mirra, Srikanth Reddy, Ann Rosener, Charles Ross, Katharine Royer, Peter Stallybrass, Goran Stanivukovic, David Thompson, Keith Todd, Robin Valenza, Robert von Hallberg, Luke Wilson, and Diana Young. In addition to his valuable comments on my work, Martin Dimitrov got me to see old things in new light.

Audiences in Cambridge, London, Philadelphia, St. Andrews, Washington, and West Lafayette responded generously to talks based on my work. In Chicago, I have benefited from conversation about my research at the Renaissance Workshop, the English Department Colloquium, and the Chicago Renaissance Seminar. Completion of the manuscript was greatly facilitated by a short-term Francis Bacon Foundation Fellowship at the Huntington

Library and by a fellowship in 2004–5 at the Franke Institute for the Humanities (Chicago). At the latter institution I benefited from weekly conversation among the resident fellows: for their responses to an earlier version of chapter 6, I especially thank Shadi Bartsch, Robert Bird, Jessica Burstein, Jim Chandler, Patchen Markell, Hilary Poriss, Valerie Ritter, and Bill Wimsatt. I also thank my department chair, Elizabeth Helsinger, and two successive deans of the humanities, Janel Mueller and Danielle Allen, for supporting that year's leave.

For their expert assistance across many years, I thank the manuscript curators, rare-books librarians, and staff at the University of Chicago Library, the Newberry Library, the Huntington Library, Stanford University Library, Cambridge University Library, Trinity College Library, and British Library. I also acknowledge Marie Axton, Howard Erskine-Hill, Elizabeth Leedham-Green, and the late Jeremy Maule, who some time ago helped me think about how to use books and manuscripts and the libraries that house them. In different form, a section of chapter 5 was first published as "Marginal Waters: *Pericles* and the Idea of Jurisdiction," in *Literature, Mapping and the Politics of Space in Early Modern Britain*, edited by Andrew Gordon and Bernhard Klein (2001). Excerpts from that essay are reprinted by permission of Cambridge University Press.

Alan Thomas believed in my project from early on, and as my editor he has expertly and patiently shepherded it into print. I am grateful at the Press to Randy Petilos and Kate Frentzel, who helped me with production, and to Lys Ann Weiss for her careful editing of the manuscript. Jeff Rufo helped me compile the index. I want also to register my deep gratitude to the three press readers, whose learned and judicious suggestions made my arguments fuller, clearer, and more nuanced than they could have been without their work on my behalf. Many people have helped me write this book. As poets know too, all errors and oversights belong strictly to the author, not his guides.

My deepest continuous debt is to my family, to Brendan, Maura, Sean, and especially my mother, Margaret Cormack. And to my father, who did not live to see this book finished. On many pages, I am startled now to find him peering back at me from behind words and from under ideas I had imagined to be my own.

NOTE ON CITATIONS

In my citation of vernacular texts in print and manuscript, I retain original spelling but regularize *i/j* and *u/v*. I have also silently expanded contractions and regularized the virgule to a comma. Quotations in foreign languages (Latin and vernacular) are italicized. Titles of works are given modern capitalization. In the case of Shakespeare, I follow standard practice and cite from modern-spelling editions of the plays. Where not otherwise noted, translations are my own.

PROLOGUE

A Power to Do Justice

This book is a study of the intersection of the English legal and literary imaginations from Skelton to Webster. It takes as its subject the cultural meaning of "jurisdiction" during a transitional period when that technical category in law came under peak pressure, in immediate response to specific jurisdictional crises and as part of the long process of centralization and rationalization through which the common law achieved interpretive hegemony. Focusing on law's unstable practices rather than the image of its stability, I analyze the production of English juridical norms in relation to jurisdiction as the administrative principle that orders power as authority by defining the scope of a particular power over a given matter or territory.

Although the book develops several theses about the practical life of the law and its relation to English prose, poetry, and drama, my two central claims are simple. By pointing to a kind of hyper- or metalegality within a single legal system (or, indeed, between systems), jurisdictional variation helps signify for a culture not only the possibility that norms might have more than one source, but also the fact that law is fundamentally improvisational, unfolding into doctrine only as and through practice. My second claim is literary: during the sixteenth and early seventeenth centuries, as English law became more homogenized, literary fictions looked to instances of jurisdictional crisis and accommodation to explore how the fact and principle of jurisdictional heterogeneity specifies the implication of a given judicial order in alternative normative scenes; and to explore, in turn, how that dynamic might help articulate the terms in which literary writers authorize their own representations. In this double engagement with jurisdiction—as a principle that exposes law's provisionality even as it opens a space of intensified literariness and literary authority—this study describes a relatively recent moment in which law and humanistic culture were in a complex but nonoppositional relation to one another. Such a description suggests a way of taking historical-cultural account of the law without depending on the tenacious binaries that, as Julie Stone Peters argues, have limited the interdisciplinary promise of "law and literature" by perpetually casting the relationship as some version of that between law and life, rule and exception, legal formalism and a more ample justice.[1] My book looks to jurisdiction, on the one hand, to counter the idea of a discursive position beyond law, not least because subjection to one or another jurisdiction was in fact the source of those historical rights and privileges that together constituted a free national or civic identity.[2] On the other hand, I am interested in early jurisdiction as an inherently complex rather than simple reality, as one symbol of the possibility of finding within law the mobility that, subject as we are to a narrowed conception of sovereignty, we may too easily locate only in the phantasm of a "life" beyond law.

An uncontroversial historical premise of this book is that English law presented itself to Tudor and Jacobean culture less as a given whole than as, still, a system of shifting jurisdictional realities. Charles Gray, in his procedural history of the judicial writ of prohibition (with which the central common-law courts exercised control over cases being heard in other tribunals), usefully differentiates between two kinds of jurisdictional complexity relevant to early modern law. First, in addition to the central courts of King's Bench and Common Pleas (and to a lesser extent the Exchequer), there was "a considerable distribution of common law jurisdiction among lesser tribunals"; because this was a hierarchical complexity within the common law, however, there were "no serious and persistent problems about such courts' jurisdiction." More significantly for the history he traces, English law also included an array of non–common-law tribunals, including the ecclesiastical courts, equity courts, and High Court of the Admiralty, all of these having, in relation to matters within their purview, "power to compel attendance and apply sanctions as against all the King's subjects."[3] Because they administered law that was doctrinally and procedurally distinct from common law, and because they were staffed by civilians (university-trained lawyers whose expertise in Roman civil and canon law distinguished them from the common lawyers trained at the Inns of Court), these tribunals were the chief locus of jurisdictional tension in England.

From a perspective internal to law, neither of the two species of complexity described by Gray is of any necessary theoretical interest. All authority operates within bounds, and if early modern English law was a heterogeneous field—comprising, among others, the extended system of common-law courts and ecclesiastical courts, the conciliar and equity courts, Duchy courts, Admiralty courts, municipal courts, guild courts, manorial courts, and market courts—it is certainly the case that the various jurisdictions functioned more or less well by functioning more or less together. In this sense, jurisdictional heterogeneity can be understood as a theoretical given, the unremarkable expression of the law's historical evolution, of differences in professional expertise among classes of lawyers, and of the practical realities of administering the law. Accordingly, the limitation of jurisdictional venue in light of the legal matter at hand (or equally a client's choice to follow one or another available jurisdictional venue for reasons of strategy or expediency) could well express a relatively flat complexity in the experience of law, with no attendant apprehension of a relation between venue and legal norm.[4]

And yet administration is not only a reflective cultural phenomenon, but also a productive one: venue shopping is the less theoretical part of the story. The major value of jurisdiction as an object for cultural analysis is that, as category and practice, jurisdiction identifies authority as power produced under the administrative recognition of the geographical or conceptual limits that exactly order it as authority. Jurisdiction amounts to the delimitation of a sphere—spatial (state, city, or manor; domestic, maritime, or foreign), temporal (proximate or immemorial past; regular or market days), or generic (matters spiritual or matters temporal; promise or debt)—that is the precondition for the juridical as such, for the very capacity of the law to come into effect. In relation to jurisdiction understood as that kind of conceptual object, the boundaries between the common law and other English tribunals—the internal boundaries that have been of most interest to historians of English law—can usefully be placed in relation to the more basic but also, technically speaking, less contestable jurisdictional boundaries between different national or sovereign spaces. Of particular interest to me here are the boundaries separating England from Ireland and France—places that for historical, social, and political reasons turn out, with an unsteadiness I take to be paradigmatic of jurisdictional discourse generally, to matter substantially for the internal configuration of the common law. In ways that demand both an inward and outward critical glance, law is inherently a jurisdictional project. Jurisdiction merits the attention of cultural historians and political theorists alike because it belongs to a realm of administrative distribution and organization responsible for reproducing law as a stable form.

Within this dynamic, the literary engagement with early modern jurisdiction becomes exemplary, not (according to a familiar historicist model) because literature supports or resists particular developments in Tudor and Stuart law and governance, but because it is implicated in the same process of shaping unruly practice for which jurisdiction itself stands. In this sense, jurisdiction must be seen as a principle of analysis more than a literary theme or topic per se. Technically, the category of "jurisdictional law" is most coherent as an abstraction upward from a sphere of substantive law when the latter confronts, in practice, the question of its competence over a given case. Correspondingly, the fictions analyzed in this book look to legal vocabularies pertaining to rather different areas of law (including land law, family law, ecclesiastical law, constitutional law, and early international law) and to a wide array of legal scenes and problematics, including bureaucratic feudalism (chapter 1), the concept of equity and the conflict between church and state (chapter 2), the problem for English law of Ireland and France (chapters 3 and 4), and the peculiarly disruptive legalities of the ocean and mercantile city (chapters 5 and 6). If my texts do not share a single topic as legal topics are most often defined (for example, treason, slander, tenure, inheritance, debt, illegitimacy), that is a response to the status of jurisdiction itself.[5] What unites my texts as more than a series of historical engagements with specific legal-jurisdictional events is their shared interest in the impact of the legal threshold on the constitution and configuration of meaning. A century of English literature is more intimately engaged with technical aspects of law than has been understood. (And it is worth noting, anecdotally, that among my authors Skelton, More, and Spenser all had highly charged personal experiences of jurisdictional conflict, whether at Westminster or in Ireland.) The texts I consider provide an intensified apprehension of the law where the status of its norms is most under pressure. Even if jurisdiction is already a principle of distribution that dramatizes the law's operations from within, still it is the fictive encounter with that principle that brings the drama to light and to life.[6] In other words, according to the play of jurisdiction, this literature makes patent, also for the law, the technical preconditions for the emergence of what comes to be expressible as legal ideology.

How might the isomorphism between literary and legal distribution matter for a theoretical account of the relation of law and literature? In Jacques Rancière's provocative formulation, aesthetics can be defined as a "distribution [*partage*] of the sensible," and thus a primary and immediately political mode, among other political modes, of exclusively or inclusively delimiting the phenomenal world for apprehension and possession.[7] "If the reader is fond of analogy," he writes, "aesthetics can be understood in a Kantian sense—re-examined perhaps by Foucault—as the system of *a priori* forms determining what presents itself to sense experience. It is a delimitation of spaces and times, of the visible and the invisible, of speech and noise, that simultaneously determines the place and the stakes of politics as a form of experience."[8] Rancière himself keeps separate the political and juridical orders, most closely identifying the latter with the administrative or "police" function that, for him, never attains the level of (democratic) politics proper—this always involves the disruption of the operative mode of distribution—but instead inscribes a nonpolitical engagement as, strategically, a substitute image of politics.[9] Most compelling for me, a little outside Rancière's argument but within his framework, is the obverse thought that, within the juridical order, jurisdiction has a formal, distributive function that potentially returns the "political" to the administrative reality. Jurisdiction, then, can be construed as the sign under which literary and legal aesthetics are legible in a non-Kantian sense as the system of *posterior* forms "determining what presents itself to experience." Understood from the perspective of jurisdiction, the pertinent cultural-historical question will not be whether literature answers the law's forms by offering something more complex or humane in place of law, but rather how, in the exercise of its own authority, literature makes apparent the potential that, as jurisdiction, resides within the always emergent law *qua* administrative reality. I take as theoretically full, and as pertinent to literature's engagement with law, the definition of jurisdiction offered by the English civilian John Cowell in his 1607 legal dictionary, *The Interpreter*. "Jurisdiction," he writes, "is a dignity which a man hath by a power to doe Justice in causes of complaint made before him."[10] To have jurisdiction is to have "a power to do justice," and in the indefinite article I hear the force of a term of art that remains open to greater or lesser degrees of rationalization: *a* power, because it is, conventionally, a power among others, and because, as such, it entails the fundamental juridical dynamic by which the distribution of a given authority both stabilizes and makes contestable that authority's norms.[11]

THE JURISDICTIONAL NORM

I will suggest in my introduction that the concept of jurisdiction allows for a productive historical perspective on legal ideology and the constitution of the state. Here I want to highlight its even more fundamental importance for the theoretical description of normativity. Jurisdiction makes visible a governing and productive instability in the law, both because a legal norm that emerges within a heterogeneous field can only be provisionally singular, and because jurisdiction marks any norm whatsoever as the recursive expression of an ongoing, practical processing of disorder. For this reason, jurisdiction is more deeply implicated than has been understood in recent political-philosophical discussions of normativity in relation to the impossibility of grounding the juridical order within itself.

In his highly influential essay "Force of Law," Jacques Derrida uses Walter Benjamin's distinction between the positing violence that inaugurates law and the preserving violence that sustains it to describe the groundlessness of law, the purely "mystical foundation of authority" at the law's discursive limit and "in its very performative power."[12] As opposed to this vertical account of a juridical norm deconstructively in search of its origin, my book approaches the problem horizontally, in terms of the activity of law that engenders jurisdiction as a virtual proposition: virtual in the double sense that jurisdiction can be said to have *force* (Lat. *virtus*) but as an *effect* more than substantially. In countering Derrida's model deconstruction of law's legitimacy, I am partly following Giorgio Agamben, who in a brief critique of "Force of Law" suggests that Derrida's description of law's impossibility substitutes one paradox for another. This latter and more urgent paradox that for Agamben structures normativity is the root codependence of norm and exception, a dynamic according to which sovereign power emerges at the limit, or within the zone, between the juridical order and its own suspension.[13] My account of law differs from Agamben's by focusing on jurisdiction rather than sovereignty—this for a historical period in which, certainly, the question of indivisible sovereignty was a matter of debate and concern.[14] For this reason I want to pause briefly over the terms of his argument so as to suggest the implications of my apparent shift to the minor key.

In describing the production of sovereignty at the boundary separating juridical life from the bare life that it opposes, Agamben means to refine Foucault's attempt, in the late writings, to understand the encounter of two regimes of power that are theoretically distinct even if not fully separable historically: the juridical-political regime described by sovereignty, and the field described by the disciplinary and biopolitical technologies of domination exercised on the body. Corresponding to this historical focus on nonjuridical life, Foucault insists methodologically that only by looking past the "the old right of sovereignty" will it be possible to identify, in turn, an elusive "new right that is both antidisciplinary and emancipated from the principle of sovereignty."[15] As Agamben positions himself in relation to this project, the analysis of the juridical exception aims to identify, as the core of sovereignty, the "point of intersection between the juridico-institutional and the biopolitical models of power" as Foucault described them.[16] In contrast to Foucault's desire to move past the horizon of sovereignty, that is, Agamben reconceptualizes sovereignty by identifying within its structure the place where the two Foucauldian regimes fold into one another. To do this, Agamben extends Carl Schmitt's definition of the sovereign as the one who decides on the exception (the suspension of the legal order expressive of the juridical norm).[17] He defines the state of exception as a topological "zone of indifference" (*zona di indifferenza*) that, while "neither external nor internal to the juridical order," in fact produces the possibility of legal order.[18] At the political limit that separates political life from bare life, law constitutes itself in the dialectic between "two heterogeneous yet coordinated elements: one that is normative and juridical in the strict sense (which we can for convenience inscribe under the rubric *potestas*) and one that is anomic and metajuridical (which we can call by the name *auctoritas*)."[19] In this way, Agamben argues, the central distinction underwriting sovereignty emerges from the juridical inclusion of the bare life that in Foucault's account of biopolitics lies beyond the juridical and sovereign order as such: "the inclusion of bare life in the political realm constitutes the original—if concealed—nucleus of sovereign power," Agamben explains. "It can even be said that the production of a biopolitical body is the original activity of sovereign power. In this sense, biopolitics is at least as old as the sovereign exception."[20]

To be sure, the Foucauldian threshold, redescribed by Agamben as generative both of law and of the excluded life form on which sovereignty depends, is far removed from the threshold between complementary areas of judicial competence, which is the legal focus of my book. Indeed, it is notable that neither Foucault nor Agamben (nor Derrida) finds the category of jurisdiction useful for their critical analyses of normative structures. The reason for this is not hard to find: as the infrastructure of the juridical order, jurisdiction is already inside the discourse and technology that critical genealogy means to counter; already captive, one might say, to the order past whose horizon Foucault looks for the shape of a nondisciplinary and nonsovereign power. This book argues that law nevertheless has something to contribute to political theory; that, although jurisdiction belongs to the law in the sense of defining its operations, it remains a powerful index of just how unstable those operations are, and as such constitutes a limit within the law where critique does become imaginable. Nothing is more telling in this regard than the fact that, as the legal scholar Richard T. Ford points out, jurisdictional disputes and ambiguities continue even today to be a source of much "concern and embarrassment" for the law.[21] For the law functions by keeping the source of its authority in fixed view as, insistently, the merely technical (and for that reason discursively unassailable) image of its own jurisdictional scope and operation.

Jurisdiction obliquely encounters the impossibility of grounding the juridical norm by remolding the problem and projecting it onto the manageable—that is, quantifiable—axis of competence or scope. The historian of medieval law Pietro Costa seems to me to get to the heart of the matter in his indispensable survey of medieval *iurisdictio* as a symbol for a complex *process* of power.[22] Most useful in the present context is Costa's account of jurisdiction as it relates to the production of the legal norm in the twelfth-century writings of the earliest scholars (glossators) of the recently rediscovered Roman law. According to Paolo Grossi's account of the medieval juridical mentality, this was a moment in which legal activity, at a certain remove from politics, could be understood always to be an interpretation of a preexisting and coherent order. For that reason, Grossi explains, jurisdiction was a speaking of the law (*iuris dictio*) in the sense that "*speaking* the law means presupposing it as already created and formed, means rendering it explicit, making it manifest, applying it, not creating it."[23] In excess of this fundamental point, however, Costa's insight is that jurisdiction simultaneously functioned to *produce* law in the sense of giving normative formality to the informal equity (*aequitas rudis*) that, as a sustaining principle of ideal justice, chiefly embodied the preexisting order to which interpretation oriented itself.[24] This creative process (creative in the sense of a productive activity, not a creation *ex nihilo*) Costa encapsulates in his description of the emperor's role as judge: "The emperor serves (informal) equity by interpreting it and so translating it into norm."[25] As a speaking of the law, as interpretation, jurisdiction thus grounds the activity of producing normative meaning: "The genesis of the norm passes through *iurisdictio*.... At issue was not a created norm, but a *gathered* norm, reflected from the world's order in a mirror (*iurisdictio*) possessed preeminently by the emperor. *Iurisdictio* is the symbolic locus of a norm that has received, not modified, the given reality.... *Iurisdictio* is nothing other than the place *in which* an informal given comes to be formalized: not changed, but expressed, not created, but mirrored back."[26] Most compelling in this description of what I would term the "jurisdictional norm" is its specification of jurisdiction's force at so comprehensive a level. Although Costa is writing of a particular, and very early, moment in the history of Western jurisdiction, his analysis has broad theoretical implications.

Quite independent of the theological order that underpins the medieval operation of jurisdiction, Costa's description of the historical concept draws an absolute distinction between the activities of creation and of other kinds of making (including interpretation and its functional institution of equity as norm). As his metaphor of the mirror implies, jurisdiction is dependent upon its lateral operation to produce the normative order it expresses. Jurisdiction is the language in which, all but impossibly, a juridical order encloses the world.[27] Allowing Costa's analysis of jurisdiction as a hierarchical process of power descending from the emperor to penetrate even the narrowest and most technical sense of the term, I would put the theoretical point in this way: jurisdiction is the principle, integral to the structure of law, through which the law, as an expression of its order and limits, projects an authority that, whatever its origin, needs functionally no other ground. At the jurisdictional threshold, the law speaks to itself, and in a mirror *reproduces* as administration the juridical order that it simultaneously *produces* as the implicit image back of the form I have called the jurisdictional norm.

My book looks to jurisdiction, then, partly to resist the terms of a conversation about sovereignty that, by excluding jurisdiction as a contributing term, has made sovereignty seem more stable than it is, even in so sophisticated an account of structure as that which Agamben gives. The problem to my mind is that an exclusive focus on sovereignty tends to collapse into a question of origins a conversation that might take place, instead, about the possible relations between the juridical *given*—the necessary conditions for juridical activity—and the juridical *ground*, or supporting frame and symbols for that activity. To put this differently, I contend that jurisdiction helps counter the almost irresistible tendency to make sovereignty have meaning only as political theology, by making it legible, instead, as the real effect of a more mundane process of administrative distribution and management. As the central expression of law's grounding activity, jurisdiction must not be construed as simply another, and minor, name for the limit that separates an already sovereign order from what lies beyond it. It is, rather, the substance of the limit, that through which juridical power, in confronting its own inefficacies, fantasizes itself as sovereignty. In this sense, jurisdiction cannot be fully described from within the juridical conception of power it describes. It belongs instead, I am arguing, to the moment of invention that, in Foucault's terms, allows a nonjuridical regime to issue from the juridical, or to that moment, in Agamben's terms, that folds the zone of indifferentiation (*indifferenza*) into the juridical order precisely *as* sovereignty rather than indistinction. There is no sovereignty that is not enacted in the register of jurisdiction.

Two historical points are important to note here. First, the constitution of jurisdiction changes with the shift from sovereign interest to the more modern regimes of power that Foucault identifies. Second, and more pertinently for the history traced in this book, those later regimes expose within juridical sovereignty's capacity to index its own forms a more complex process of administration and projection than would appear from the law's naturalizing account of jurisdictional order. Jurisdiction half belongs to the law as to a discipline capable, in Foucault's terms, of generating a discourse not of "a juridical rule derived from sovereignty, but a discourse about a natural rule, or in other words a norm."[28] As the primary symbol for the production of legal meaning, jurisdiction works to naturalize the particular juridical rule into norm. This is a process that absorbs the limit at which power begins to cease to function juridically into a fantasy of technical comprehensiveness, which ends by erasing the distinction between rule and norm or by allowing the rule practically to operate as norm.

As the product of a jurisdictional reality that is the virtual proposition and effect of law's operations, the *technically comprehended norm* is itself virtual, spectral in a way that neither Foucault's nor Agamben's divisions fully allow: present, natural, legally efficacious, but also haunted by the image of its own origins in a projected complex of possible beginnings. By exploring the dream of jurisdiction at the place where that category comes under technical pressure, this book thus takes on some of the work that Foucault imagines against disciplinarity and sovereignty, albeit on the wrong side of his line: namely, from within the juridical regime, rather than from the sacred space beyond the walls of that city which Foucault calls "sovereignty" and Agamben, "law." Jurisdiction is an inherent, grounding instability within the configuration of juridical authority. The literary investigation of jurisdictional normativity fits itself to this instability, and this haunting. As a power to do justice in a given case and within a particular sphere, jurisdiction paradoxically takes its critical force, as do the early modern literary texts that formally engage it, from the vistas onto which, already and again, it opens the law.

INTRODUCTION

Literature and Jurisdiction

Jurisdiction may seem an odd category to find at the center of a book of literary history and criticism. Indeed, it is an odd category generally, since it so often comes to function invisibly, under the legal conceptual maps that help order experience. But it is this quality in jurisdiction that has drawn my attention to it as a productive site for thinking about the law and its relation to humanistic culture. As concepts in law and cultural history, jurisdiction and literature are similarly evasive analytical objects. Jurisdiction belongs to law less as a substantive problem for jurisprudential investigation than as the principle and force that makes the investigation possible but which, for that reason, rarely indexes its own potential as an order at law: either we ignore it and get on with the case at hand or we discover, usually at the hands of the legal expert, that the *arcana* of jurisdiction somehow, here or now, preempt the possibility of justice in the case at hand. Literature, for its part, belongs to a given historical culture as part and parcel of that culture, but also as a force that might disrupt the culture's relation to itself. For this reason, the "literary" (the apprehension of what counts as literature, what boundaries produce art) might also be said to be at once central and all but invisible. As part of that general dynamic, literary texts can seem temporally out of joint not only because texts produced for one culture or one moment are constantly being refashioned for others, but also because they offer ways of attending to experience that expose possibilities in the operative historical forms—social, political, and cultural—which they subject to analysis.[1] "We study change because we are changeable," Arnaldo Momigliano writes.[2] A paradigmatic instance of that *ratio* at the heart of historiographic practice would seem to be the study exactly of the forms, at once stable and changeable, that so often are the locus of change as well as its index. A governing thought in this book is that jurisdiction and literature both evade easy analysis because they open the culture in which they function onto more complex orders than those through which they seem to do their work. In the following chapters, I venture to show how deeply engaged early modern literature was with the *technical production* of the legal order, and to define the ways in which jurisdictional topics provoked a metacritical perspective on the management of legal meaning and literary meaning both.

For an initial survey of the scope of this primary relationship between jurisdiction and its literary-fictional analysis, and as an example of my approach to the literary excavation and interrogation of legal form, I turn here to a particular case, a poem written toward the beginning of the historical period treated in this book. In my prologue, I have outlined jurisdiction's importance for the theoretical understanding of the juridical norm. In this more historically oriented introduction, I show the implications of jurisdiction for our understanding of both the temporal logic of legal ideology and the early constitution of the state, and for our very account of the literary and historical object.

THE POEM IN A JURISDICTIONAL FIELD

Shortly after his imprisonment in the Tower in the late 1530s or early 1540s, banished from Henry VIII's court and in internal exile on his estate at Allington in Kent, Sir Thomas Wyatt wrote a verse letter to his friend John Poyntz, putatively in answer to an inquiry over the reasons for his absence from life at the political center:

> Myn owne John poyntz sins ye delight to know
>   the cawsse why that homeward I me drawe
>   and fle the presse of courtes where soo they goo
> Rathar then to lyve thrall under the awe
>   of lordly lokes wrappid within my cloke
>   to will and lust lerning to set a lawe
> It is not for becawsse I skorne or moke
>   the powar of them, to whome fortune hath lent
>   charge over us, of Right to strike the stroke,
> But trwe it is, that I have allwais ment
>   lesse to estime them then the comon sort
>   off owtward thinges that Juge in their intent.[3]

An imitation in the Horatian mode of Luigi Alemanni's tenth satire, and reprinted in Richard Tottel's 1557 miscellany under the title "Of the Courtiers Life Written to John Poins," the poem entered the canon as both a virulent attack on court behavior (as catalogued in the main body of the poem) and an exaggerated performance of Wyatt's personal and political style: the stance of one committed to inward virtue and contemptuous both of "owtward" judgment and of the linguistic, social, and ethical distortions to which the courtier subjects himself.

Adjusting the ethical position from which the poet proclaims his own independence of mind, furthermore, is the suggestion, right at the center of Wyatt's critique and his celebration of rural leisure, that there is something a little paltry in the choice to distance himself from a life of action, especially since that choice seems not to be his at all:

> this maketh me at home to hounte and to hawke
> and in fowle weder at my booke to sitt
> In frost and snowe then with my bow to stawke
> no man doeth marke where so I ride or goo
> in lusty lees at libertie I walke
> And of these newes I fele not wele nor woo
> sauf that a clogg doeth hang yet at my hele
> no force for that, for it is ordered so
> That I may lepe boeth hedge and dike full well.
> (ll. 80–88)

An addition to the source poem in Alemanni, the irritant *clog* that hangs at Wyatt's heel might well be the mud that clings to one at leisure on his own soil. It is also the wooden block attached to the leg to restrict a prisoner's movement, and, as H. A. Mason argued, it almost certainly alludes to the king's continuing restriction of Wyatt's freedom.[4] The passage registers Wyatt's characteristically uneasy engagement with the structures of Tudor power, notably echoing, for example, the poem's programmatic opening gesture, in which Wyatt insistently acknowledges the authority of those to whom fortune has given power over him, so as then to insist, with equal vehemence, that he does not so fully esteem them as others do (ll. 7–12). In the later passage, Wyatt's play of attachment and detachment is effected in the enjambment between lines 87 and 88, a device that allows the reader to hear in the poet a double reaction to his exile. The restrictive clog is of no force, first, in the ironic sense that, as something "ordered so," it is the simple effect of the royal or judicial will, in which, as obedient subject, Wyatt simply acquiesces: "no force for that, for it is ordered so." Second, as one reads past the line-break, the clog is of no force because the restriction that would seem to forestall movement is itself so ordered as to define the very terms in which Wyatt counters the interdiction, allowing him to move, across hedge and dike, in the ways that most matter to his sense of his own liberty: "for it is ordered so / That I may lepe boeth hedge and dike full well."[5]

This "order" that makes the clog available to two complementary narratives dynamically structures Wyatt's weighing of his confinement and liberty, as it gives force both to the power the poem makes its theme and to the poetic stance toward that power. As this book will argue, the best word to describe the order exemplified here is neither punishment nor discipline nor sovereignty, but *jurisdiction*, a familiar term for the juridical administration of authority and for the scope of a particular authority. It is also, as the historian of medieval law Pietro Costa minutely unfolds for a somewhat earlier European context, the controlling symbol generally for a shifting and hierarchical "process of power," one whose life is shaped by the play between authority understood as a static form and authority understood as a processual form: "Jurisdiction is at once the symbol of an ordered power and of the process whereby society orders itself in relation to the one in power [*Iurisdictio è simbolo insieme del potere ordinato e dell'ordinarsi della società al potente*]."[6] This is a sentence to pause over. Like the order of the modest clog that qualifies Wyatt's movement, jurisdiction can be construed globally and locally, as the order power takes and as the topographical expression of that order (here/there; this/that); as the image of an already efficacious order and simultaneously the topological effect that is an order's coming so to express itself.[7] In Wyatt's poem, the clog symbolizes a given power's givenness and reproduces a social world, Wyatt's, in orientation to that power; as juridical matter, moreover, it divides space by limiting movement to a here and not there, even as it folds the speaker's body into the real but not fully coherent expression of that jurisdictional division.

What interests me for the moment is that, from the poem's opening lines, this order should be defined in territorial terms. Poyntz is said to wonder why Wyatt has returned home, in flight from one space to another. And just as Wyatt's sense of himself is powerfully the sense he has of his home in Kent, a principal expression of the king's power is the capacity to order space and control the subject's movement in space, such that Wyatt must feel the force of the king's clogging presence, paradoxically, at the very moment of moving freely within the bounds of his estate. Conversely, when Wyatt asserts his continuous liberty, he expresses his authority as the absence of any person to "marke" the lord's ride or walk over his land. That verb denotes both a watching and the technological work of plotting and setting out boundaries on land (OED *v.* I.1), with the effect that the poet's resistance (always within bounds, of course) takes the form of a prodigiously itinerant relationship to land, alternative to the relationship instituted by the definitions (whether topographic, cartographic, or legal) that underwrite the king's capacity to confine his subject and to say he has confined him.

The poem's attention to the competing claims of overlapping territorial authorities has a logical historical reference to the consolidation of state power undertaken by the first Tudors and extended across Elizabeth's long reign. As the poem begins to suggest, this process of administrative centralization, not fully straightforward in its organization of space, was, abstractly conceived, even more complicated in its re-encoding of various fiscal, legal, and cultural subjectivities.[8] Such a historical-political formulation as this, however, fails to address the delicacy of Wyatt's theoretical apprehension that, according to the very terms of territorialization, the exercise of centralized power can never attain the homogeneity it seeks. Certainly, the authority that emerges in the poem as an alternative to the centralizing fantasy might be understood as a residual form—a traditional way for Wyatt to be on the land, say, that the state or king cannot fully disrupt. But what is most striking in the poem is the sense that it is the attempt itself to organize life through the restricting definition of boundaries that activates the other experience of the threshold, giving meaning to Wyatt's alternative account of his home and land not as something that was fully in place before, but rather as a political form emergent toward a dominant political form that is itself emerging. Kent is local, in other words, because centralization invents it as such.[9] Wyatt's movement is free because the king's restriction of the subject's movement and liberty makes that proposition available and audible as a political and affective reality.

So understood, even the concept of a territorial *alternative* to the dominant construction of royal power, as useful as it may be for describing the limits of centralization, fails to identify what the poem seems finally to be pursuing, which might instead be thought of as a ripple produced within power as an effect of its implementation in time.[10] It follows that the liberty Wyatt experiences on his estate is similarly contested, an aspect of the structural dynamic that finds temporal and affective expression in the poet's statement, already alluded to, that "*no man* doeth marke where so I ride or goo" (l. 83, emphasis added), a sentiment that registers both Wyatt's satisfaction in his liberty and a melancholic regret that the terms of his liberty should, against liberty, preclude the public encounter with which he has been familiar.[11]

The conclusion of Wyatt's poem gives another version of the complexity inhering in the hierarchical process of territorialization. Immediately following the claim that, in spite of the restrictive clog, he yet "maye lepe boeth hedge and dike" on his estate, Wyatt turns from the opposition between central and local to that between alternative centers, national jurisdictions that, predictably enough, all measure up badly in relation to home. "I ame not now in Fraunce to Judge the wyne / with saffry sauce the delicates to fele," Wyatt proclaims, here re-invoking his work as the king's diplomat on the continent; "[n]or yet in spaigne, where oon must him inclyne," nor in bestial "Flaunders," nor, most happily, "where Christe is geven in pray / for mony poisen and traison at Rome / a comune practise used nyght and daie" (ll. 89-99). In the context of the preceding lines, this passage registers, in addition to its fulsome nationalism, the complementary and precisely diplomatic observation that the state over which Henry VIII exercises his territorial power is itself bounded, and in the same way that Wyatt's estate and status are circumscribed by the king's and state's fuller authority.

This layering of territorial realities explains why, when the resolution to Wyatt's nationalist comparison comes, it is not happy England he names but, according to a proverbial phrasing, two alternatives to that national space: "But here I ame in Kent and christendome / emong the muses where I rede and ryme" (ll. 100-102). Rhetorically, we have in the first clause a rather subtle zeugma, in which (near) unlikes are yoked together through a shared preposition. As an answer to the innovative operation of Tudor territorial power, the phrase "Kent and christendom" institutes social identity according to two jurisdictional relationships that neither contradict nor fully conform to the one constituted for Wyatt as the extension of the king's English sovereignty. "Kent" insists, as I have already suggested, on the local identity that the process of centralization newly charges. "Christendom" works somewhat differently and with even greater effect. Insofar as the concept encompasses diverse territories, it disrupts the operative fantasy that English borders are fully real or fully constitutive of the real. Moreover, in announcing a spiritual unity (hence the zeugma), it disrupts the practice of territorialization itself, not by circumventing or suppressing the scope of temporal law, but rather by remembering the scope of canon law, the second of the two textual legacies (along with civil law) that together constituted the *ius commune* and grounded the western European legal tradition.[12] To be sure, this discursive move to include the *ecclesia* in the definition of English space is not the same as

Sir Thomas More's rather more forceful insistence, a few years earlier, that Christendom must be a jurisdictional reality also for England. From within a Protestant ethos and as part of a different jurisdictional event, however, Wyatt can be understood similarly to be invoking an image of Christendom as a functional order against which the claims of the centralizing Tudor state are yet measurable.

Wyatt's attention to false Rome and, then, an authentic Christendom sets up his most surprising and polemical meditation on the territorial structure of the power to which he has been subjected. The poem ends as an invitation—a plea, even, disguised as something more casual—that Poyntz come for a visit. Registering in this way the limits of the pleasure he finds at home, Wyatt also uses the terms of the invitation to counter the state's aggression by unsettling the terms that underlie its practice: "Where if thou list my poynz for to com / thou shalt be Judge how I do spend my tyme" (ll. 103-4). Where the poem has followed the state in expressing authority as a species of power over territory, it thrusts forward as its final word a different category altogether, proposing that the fitting judgment of Wyatt's life and practice will take place not within the order of space, but within the order of time. As familiar as the conceptual move to have time trump space might seem within, say, an Augustinian or Christian-Stoic philosophical framework, the gesture must startle us as a legal move. By remembering time in a poem whose legal-rhetorical argument is structured as an opposition between places and according to the idea of competing, complementary, and overlapping jurisdictions, Wyatt institutes time, too, as a jurisdictional order, positing hypothetically that an authority over time might be authority in the same way as that over space.

How can we understand the status of this peculiar order? First, the temporal might be thought of as a jurisdiction insofar as its production is dialectically coordinate with an intensified territoriality, whose increased visibility has made time available *as* an order. Time is not for that reason, however, merely a metaphorical order, but one that the law creates as supplement, a by-product of its own development and of the changing shape of its efficiencies. Pursuing its own ends, we might say, the law will turn out also to predict alternatives to its own ways of ordering experience. Second, time is presented as the order that disrupts the law's normative claims from within, so that "my tyme" operates at the end of the poem as a reminder that the law, too, has a practical life that the image of a coherently efficacious law does not and cannot erase. Time, here, is not so much an alternative order to law as the principle according to which the law, which works to *place* Wyatt as legal subject otherwise than according to his desire, turns out itself to be out of place, not yet or ever quite where it needs practically to be. In its attention to time, that is, the poem works not as an exposé of the law that collapses its normative claims, but rather as an analytic principle that makes visible the incompleteness of an administrative reality that is always only unfolding toward the image it will turn out to have (and even to have had) of itself.

However strange a temporal jurisdiction must seem, then, time points in Wyatt's poem away from mystification and toward the utter ordinariness of law—a system that in part functions by coming to seem more than ordinary. We can cast Wyatt's move to remember time within the order of territoriality as a particularly potent element in the poem's figuration of a local or minor jurisdiction as against the jurisdictional regime or *imperium* of Crown and Parliament. In retreating from the court to Kent, Wyatt has crossed between spaces that pertain differently to the developing common law, moving as he does from the place of the central, royal law into a place of custom (including, most famously, gavelkind, a mode of tenure and partitive inheritance that, in opposition to common-law primogeniture, was all but synonymous with Kentish law). As the rustic space of the *leges terrae*, the customary usages belonging to the so-called immemorial law (a notion partly invented by the common lawyers to authorize the status of a rationalized central law), Kent does not embody law outside common law, but rather a minor common law within the major one. For royal law grew exactly by absorbing local customs, sometimes voiding them, but most often annexing and internalizing them, acknowledging a given custom so as to control it.[13] Abstractly conceived, this process at the heart of legal centralization means that the time of the dominant law, where historical present meets present history, cannot be single, but is knotted, a complex of temporalities irreducible to one another.[14] Even when acknowledged and controlled by the center, the local will stand apart as a conceptually distinct jurisdiction and temporality, at once constitutive and disruptive of the flatter time of royal law. As I read Wyatt, time enters his poem as a jurisdictional complexity in relation to Crown territoriality because jurisdictional complexity, such as that linking Kent and Westminster, is the legal phenomenon that most powerfully makes the knotted, historical, practical time of the always changing law present to the law.

To take the implications of the poem's disruption of legal order in another direction, I would argue that the muses are with Wyatt in "Kent" for much the same reason as time is. Poetic authority, understood and repeatedly discovered as such, can also be read as the by-product of a legal discourse to which it does not fully belong, but whose changing shape makes its different authority legible, if only imperfectly coherent. In the poem, Wyatt gestures toward this dynamic by spatializing poetry as a sphere of production. Finding himself *among* "the muses where I rede and ryme" (l. 101) means being in a local and local-temporal relationship to them. That representation of literary reception and production is thus in tension with the similarly expressive relationship that Wyatt has disavowed a few lines earlier in his rejection of Spain, "where oon must him inclyne / rather then to be owtewerdly to seme / I meddill not with wittes that be so fyne" (ll. 91–93). The posture of easy conversation with the muses answers this earlier scene, opposing the style of Wyatt's attitude toward literary production to the inclination that, in Spain, doubly disfigures the subject, both as a physical sign of subjection to (absolute) power and as the specific psychological inclination toward seeming rather than being.[15] As opposed to this mingling with foreign wits that are too "fyne" (refined) to weigh in as substantial in the sense that a good English "pownde of witt" is (l. 79), when Wyatt is "emong the muses" he is in a place and scene that not only permits reading and rhyming, but is defined by those activities. For Wyatt to sit "*at* my booke" (l. 81, emphasis added) equates to his being "in Fraunce," "in spaigne," or "at Rome"; like these territorial states, the book is a place of action and a place for judgment according to alternatively comprehensive norms. Even if Wyatt represents his reading and rhyming, in Seth Lerer's phrase, as "private poetic efforts," the point is that this privacy should emerge, in the manner of the state's order, also as a jurisdictional reality, the temporal-spatial projection of an activity into and as a sphere of judgment.[16]

In this light, we can ask how the clog on Wyatt's heel, which orders his free walking across his estate, might be related to the metrical foot that literally measures or "marks" out the space of the poem. I pose this question not for the sake of wordplay, but rather to pause briefly over its methodological implications. If, as part of our evaluation of Wyatt's text in relation to the culture that produced it, we allow the poetic foot and political heel to belong to the same body, we will be saying only that it matters for our history that Wyatt responded to the territorial operation of royal authority upon him by writing a poem, and that the order of the poem—the specific range of its competence—has a central place in the game of orders instituted by the king and taken up by the subject. Wyatt's poetry, in other words, must be seen as a reaction to, and action within, the jurisdictional scene it thematizes.

Helping to specify this relation between poetic competence and political scope is the similarly multivalent force of the "cawsse" that Poyntz asks after at the poem's beginning. This is the term that both structures the poem's extended argument against the court's deformations and produces, as poetic privacy, Wyatt's hyperbolic rejection of the court's norms in favor of the country's: "I cannot I, no no it will not be / this is the cause . . . " (ll. 76–77). This "cause," then, is Wyatt's politico-personal motive for his retreat to Kent. But it is also his story, "cause" in the sense of *causa*, the term used in classical rhetoric for the hypothesis or set of circumstances from which a speech is constructed for judgment.[17] *Causa* is also the substance of the argument itself, such that the author of *Ad Herennium* can speak of the forensic or epideictic or deliberative cause that rhetorical invention helps puts in order (3.1.1); a "cause" therefore in the still familiar legal sense of a "matter for consideration" or "case."[18] By extension into the literary field, finally, the rhetorical cause is the outline of a plot and even the plot itself.[19] Noting this range of meanings in the term, we can see how tightly poetry and politics are intertwined in the text, since the motive Wyatt presents as part of a *political* defense (the "cawsse why that homeward I me drawe") is the matter and hypothesis that the poem subjects to judgment in the very form of the poem.[20] The flexibility of the rhetorical category thus helps Wyatt make the poem available to judgment not only according to courtly reasoning, but also according to those norms proper to it as poetic speech: proper, not because they escape political and legal discourse, or merely analogize it, but because, in an unpredictably ramifying jurisdictional field, they project a competence that, in turn, must look to them for authorization. Wyatt's "muses" name a realm of authority that is the posterior effect of an activity's coming to constitute a sphere.

For this dynamic, time again is of the essence, since, as we have seen, the judgment of the legal and rhetorical "cause" that the poem unfolds is a judgment in time and of time: "thou shalt be Judge how I do spend my tyme." This time is the duration of a life used in one way or another, for social good or ill. But "tyme" is also the basic unit of metrical measurement (OED *sb.*10). Lerer rightly points out that for Wyatt, here, to spend time is "not just to take time reading and writing, but actually to make meters."[21] Spending becomes especially charged as a "metaphor for making meter," he further shows, in the Parker Manuscript version of the poem, where the promise to Poyntz reads as "Thow shalt be judge how I dispende my tyme," a Chaucerian allusion to Harry Bailey's accusation against Geoffrey that in his tale of Sir Thopas "thou doost noght elles but despendest tyme." In the Chaucerian tradition of Tudor courtiership that Lerer charts more generally, Wyatt's satire thus becomes a defense of poetry that justifies "the spending, or the dispending, of time." Generally, time's place in the poem means that Poyntz is being asked, along two axes, to judge, first, whether reading and rhyming are good ways to expend one's time in the political world, and, second, whether Wyatt's spent rhythms specifically measure up, according now to some norm of metrical distribution. But the poem's most striking expression of the peculiarly nuanced loyal contestation that Wyatt invents is that it should bind together, as complements, discourses that may seem to have been posited only as alternatives. For in light of the poem's descriptive extension of the field of judgment, spending time in a poet's way becomes directly political, rather than only indirectly so, a distinct instance and sphere of administration and distribution that is nevertheless cognate with the courtly administration of life from which Wyatt retreats. Even as the poem deploys the traditional division between the active and contemplative orders, there appears in time's relation to the cause of judgment another order underlying both. We can call this last order jurisdiction, the principle in a political world to which poetry also belongs that represents authority to itself as the effect of its management and distribution in time and space.

JURISDICTION AND CRITICAL PRACTICE

I now step back from my reading of Wyatt's poem to reflect briefly on the preceding pages as critical work, since they exemplify my interest, apparent across the book, in the cultural reaction to the configuration of power at the jurisdictional threshold. They also reflect my sense that a close engagement with literary texts can help us track for a particular historical moment the cultural usefulness of the discovery that law is constituted, at limits at once necessary and contestable, as the processing of an unruliness it cannot quite put in order. If we treat the two parts of this summary reflection as one, we can ask why so arcane a subject as jurisdiction might benefit from so differently arcane an approach as close reading. This can be addressed in terms of my claims in this book for the literary and the historical as categories of analysis.

In the study of law and literature, the status of the literary has been problematic for two reasons: first, because literature can so readily be seen merely to reflect the law, understood as a repository of cultural forms whose centrality resides in their social and political instrumentality; second, because the law, as a hermetic discipline protective of its rules of textual production and interpretation, is so conservative in relation to what it takes to be in or out of its orbit. At its worst in practice, literary-legal interdisciplinarity might be fairly emblematized as literature's deference and the law's wry smile.[22] Jurisdiction opens up a more interesting conversation by making law and literature different conceptual objects in relation to one another. The literary texts that, like

Wyatt's poem, have drawn my interest in this book all ponder their relationship to law, and they do so not least by zeroing in on jurisdiction as the locus of the law's own most self-reflexive operations. In this regard, literature might be said to have a heuristic function. The literary is for me primarily a mode of attention, one made possible by opening a space that, like the space of law, is oriented toward an effect (though not necessarily an instrumental one). In offering close readings of texts as familiar as More's *Utopia*, Spenser's *Faerie Queene*, or Shakespeare's *Cymbeline*, I am attending to literary fictions that themselves are attending to how the law, in turn, attends to its operations.

At the same time, literature does not function only heuristically. Wyatt's poem is like the other texts I treat in that, as noninstrumental discourse, it engages and represents the law also by burrowing into forms and categories, such as territoriality, to reflect outward an intensified version of the work that, less audibly, such categories do at law. It is not easy to predict where and how a literary text's orientation toward law will, critically, so express itself as a meditation on the mechanics of legal authority (or of its literary counterparts). My method, consequently, has been to follow texts from within, listening for where their technical and nontechnical vocabularies may be charged by the jurisdictional scene of which they are a part. This is not the equivalent of identifying and unfolding literary allusions to the law, even if an allusion is often the starting point for analysis. Far from being a history of compelling literary reflections of a stable legal reality, my readings are primarily instances of slowed encounter with the complex discourse of law as that was shaped by the shifting effects of jurisdiction. As such, notably, a particular reading does not provide a template for the next one. Because jurisdiction is the book's conceptual object without being, in any narrow sense, its exclusive theme, my readings are best imagined as open-ended engagements with jurisdiction's different horizons. And this legal point is continuous with a literary one: I make no claim that either my readings or the texts that are their objects offer a universalizing account of literature's relation to law. The chapters develop, each along its own trajectory, more local claims about how different kinds of literary production grappled with kinds of legal discourse and legal problems—always, however, in relation and in theoretical response to jurisdiction as a fundamental dynamic for the production of legal-cultural meaning.

Inside my approach is an implicit account, too, of the historical object. Among other things, this book of criticism might be thought of as a minor institutional history of an everyday, a history of legal routine seen through moments of deroutinization (though not of rupture). As such, my argument about jurisdiction resembles a social history of everyday practices that, in Jacques Rancière's phrasing, follows "the barely perceptible movement that tore those activities from the order of routine to throw them into the universe of invention."[23] Far from being mere violations of routine, however, the jurisprudential encounters I am tracking are also subjective encounters with the law, *cases* legible, in Lauren Berlant's terms, as epistemological events in law, marking the place where subjectivity and impersonality are indistinguishable.[24] To adjudicate between the institutional and subjective objects that present themselves to the historical gaze, I employ jurisdiction as one symbol that pries open a hardening institutional reality to make it meaningfully available for subjective encounter. Rancière's notion of his own historical practice as a "poetics of knowledge" is useful here: although my book is not a study, in that sense, "of the set of literary procedures by which a discourse [in my case, law] escapes literature, gives itself the status of a science, and signifies this status," it shares with Rancière's project an "interest in the rules according to which knowledge is written and read, is constituted as a specific genre of discourse."[25] What I resist in the account of his method, however, is the particular mode of privileging the literary as analytical ground, a foundational starting point for thought. Although I spend much time with the particulars of literary texts, and although literature does seem to me to offer a perspective on law's processual life as productive as that offered by jurisdiction itself, my supposition is not that literature is a repository of procedures that either bestowed on law its privileged *status* as science or is able now to return the law to its discursive origins.[26] Like law, literature is for me, rather, the space of an effect compelled by a temporality that (although alternative to that of legal routine) belongs to history, as history. In my readings of poetry's and drama's shifting encounters with law, literature does not detach to become an autonomous jurisdiction, except perhaps metaphorically. Whatever the apparent concession here, my point is thus to insist on poetry's deep centrality to law, and not allow its claim to become only nontechnical. For the time of literature and the time of jurisdiction are, I think, similarly alive to the history of practical knowledge that is the law.[27]

By looking to literature for an intensified account of the practical dynamic through which the law itself emerges, this book presents literature fully as legal matter. The texts I analyze may seem theoretically modest, because essentially nonagonistic in their legal address. But by tracking how literary fictions engaged jurisdiction as the complex scene of the law's own making, I am asking for a view of literature as having direct ethical purchase on law, by being a force *for* and in the law, and not only against it.

JURISDICTION AND LEGAL IDEOLOGY

If certain periods make more available than others the full force of the perception that law reproduces itself as jurisdiction, that is because the root liminality of a given law (and of its norms) becomes most visible when, historically, the law engages a novel question, one to which it has not been fitted, but to which, in response to a changing political or social reality, it must now fit itself: as when, for example, a central court comes under internal or external pressure to hear a matter that traditionally has belonged to another forum; or when a law developed in one country and for one people comes to be applied in and for another; or when, in the face of changing trade practices, a law that binds relationships on and of the land is required in some measure now to control the sea. In the context of sixteenth- and early seventeenth-century England, we can think of the attempts to extend the common law into ecclesiastical and equity jurisdictions, or to extend English law generally over colonial Ireland and over the North Sea fisheries and eastern trade routes. While legal and literary engagements with all such questions necessarily implicated England's status as a nation and empire, they did so chiefly as a problem of technical reason and administration, and thus in a register not exactly favored by recent cultural historical discourse. A study like this one of how jurisdictional authority was imagined during the emergence of the administrative state cannot ignore the reality of ideology, but it can also usefully suggest how ideology itself might emerge, in a reversal of the usual logic of prior and posterior, as the artifact of technical practice.

In its attention to the law as an emergent system, this book departs from an account of legal ideology often given by literary historians. Although students of literature have proven able at troubling the idea of literature as a separate and coherent discursive field, they have often looked to the law of a given historical period as though it were already coherent, whether as a storehouse of categories and norms that the culture at large might re-present by absorbing or resisting them, or as a stable constitutional reality rather than a set of constitutional hypotheses. As I have been arguing, the category of jurisdiction troubles this version of how the law discovers and confirms its meanings. In an extended description and analysis of the ideological claims of jurisdiction, the legal scholar Richard T. Ford argues that *"jurisdiction is itself a set of practices,* not a preexisting thing in which practices occur or to which practices relate."[28] Ford takes as his starting point the covert operation of modern jurisdictions on social identity, and he locates the historical emergence of jurisdiction as a motor for ideology in the conjunction of cartographic technology and the administrative centralization of the state. Arguing that jurisdiction as it is now understood and practiced arose as a "tool" for instituting a modern subjectivity "amenable to a new and more comprehensive form of institutional knowledge, management and control," Ford describes this jurisdictional subjectivity as a new kind of status relationship, one invented, he proposes, just as other status relationships were being displaced, according to Henry Summer Maine's classic thesis, in favor of contract relations.[29]

This is a powerful account of jurisdictional ideology, and its clarity derives in part from its focus on territorial jurisdiction to the near exclusion of, say, a generic-conceptual jurisdiction over a matter at law. Ford focuses the argument in this way, first, because territorial divisions instituted and conditioned the modern political and social identities he is interested in describing. Second, in contemporary parlance the territorial jurisdiction has become prototypical, in the sense that, even when a jurisdiction marks legal authority over a particular kind of question or thing, it will always, in Ford's formulation, "be defined by area": "An entity could, in theory, have authority over 'all oil, wherever it is found.' Such an entity would not be a jurisdiction but an authority of another kind. A jurisdiction is territorially defined."[30]

If this last sentence is tautological as a statement about territorial jurisdiction, in the era of the nation-state it is nonetheless perfectly legible as a conceptual statement about the operation of jurisdiction generally. From a historical standpoint, however, and I think also from a theoretical one, the elevation of territoriality in the description of jurisdiction troublingly narrows the principle by substituting species for genus. In the past, as Ford himself knows, legal authority over a kind of question or thing was not always understood as being modeled on, or secondary to, a territorially defined authority. This notion is difficult for us to contemplate as meaningful, not only because of the relative solidity of our own territorial borders, but also because of the increasing distance of the ecclesiastical jurisdiction, with its special relation to conscience, as a substantive legal reality. In the dynamic of the two laws that grounded Western jurisprudence, the principle that geographical boundaries might be secondary to other boundaries pertained most in the sphere of canon law. The basic point is neatly summarized by Paul Vinogradoff, who, with respect to early ideas of international law, gives prime importance to "the *extra-territorial* jurisdiction of the Canon Law in relations which affect some of the most important sides of social life—e.g. marriage, succession, testaments, trusts, charities, corporations, agreements, &c. . . . The adjustment of the juridical ideas and institutions which had grown up on the extra-territorial soil to the Common Law of England . . . was a task of great importance, productive of incessant conflicts."[31] More abstractly, the legal theorist Pierre Legendre has related this nonterritorial jurisdiction to the later, secular form of the administrative state, pointing to the medieval maxim *Ecclesia non habet territorium* ("The Church does not have a territory") as the canonists' purest expression of an "idea of centralism" energized by the concept of the Church's claim of universal *imperium*.[32] For the impact of this maxim in the temporal sphere, Legendre does not look, as he might have, to the theories and practices of *imperium* through which medieval and early modern temporal authorities protected their borders by restricting the deterritorialized claims of the Church.[33] Instead, and more radically, he links the centralist maxim to an emergent state centralism that, in his account, similarly "instituted the concept of an ideal governance without frontiers," effectively absorbing the Church's jurisdictional claims into an image of the law as a *symbolic* order, rather than essentially a territorial one.[34]

What are the implications of my insisting that one name, jurisdiction, should continue to stand for both kinds of authority, the territorial and the extraterritorial or personal or symbolic? As my opening account of territoriality in Wyatt's verse epistle has suggested, the reason to hold onto a relative amplitude in the concept, and not to conceive of jurisdiction only territorially, is that the theoretical dominance of territorial jurisdiction emerged as part of the ideological process Ford describes so well. At a higher level of abstraction, that is, the hegemony of territorial jurisdiction reflects a further rationalization of the very rationalizing process for which, in Ford's account, the symbol "jurisdiction" *qua* mode of administrative practice generally stands. So understood, territorialization is the limit expression and limit resolution of the normativization of power. While in Ford's view territorialization is a productive cover for the arbitrariness and inequalities of juridical power, I am arguing that it can also be understood in the more mundane but *ultimately* no less ideological sense as one sign of the law's continuous desire to close the gap between its practical efficiencies and its evolving theoretical apprehension of itself.

There is a danger, then, in supposing that jurisdiction is always already ideological. As I have suggested, however, jurisdiction is also the kind of category or principle whose operations can become invisible by coming to seem merely technical, devoid of explicit ideological content. In an attempt to take account of the doubled orientation of the law's practical and administrative life, this book places jurisdiction on a theoretically charged historical axis, investigating it as an ongoing legal process punctuated and motivated by particular moments of crisis. In the long history of English jurisdiction, the sixteenth century was an unusually important period for the rationalization of English common law and the legal system as a whole. This is not to say that the minor jurisdictions disappeared; indeed, most non–common-law jurisdictions at English law were formally incorporated into the common law only with the reforms of the nineteenth century.[35] That said, while at the beginning of the Tudor period it was possible to imagine English law substantially in terms of interrelated spheres of judicial activity, by the mid-seventeenth century the common law of the central royal courts was fully present to the culture as the dominant source of juridical norms. Charles Gray concisely describes the middle period of the sixteenth and early seventeenth centuries in terms of a change in both the content and the felt urgency of "jurisdictional law": "In the pre-Reformation era, the law of jurisdiction was largely concerned with defining and protecting the sphere of English secular courts as against the organs of the international Church. In the 'mature common law' period [the law of Blackstone], compared to the middle stage, the credit of ecclesiastical courts was considerably eclipsed, the structure of the whole non-common law system had been revised by legislation coming out of the mid-17th century revolutionary period, and the dominance of the common law throughout the English legal order was conceived in subtly different terms."[36] Like Gray, I focus on the Tudor and Jacobean periods as a transitional moment in the development of a national law and a rationalized legal discourse, a moment in which, necessarily, the question of jurisdictional heterogeneity was messier than in either the earlier period, when legal orders alternative to the common law were more efficacious, or the later period, when the dominance of common law received more formal expression.

It is essential to the history of this middle period that the common law was Janus-faced. Far from only attacking the scope of alternative jurisdictions, for example, common lawyers and common-law judges were often the ones to delineate the force and scope of an ecclesiastical rule or local custom. There is no paradox here, just as there is none in the notion that, as I have argued in my reading of Wyatt, the idea of the local depends dialectically for its emergence on the emergence of the national or central. For if the common lawyer's delineation of local custom in effect protected a juridical norm alternative to the central law, it also worked to define the former's claim and so circumscribe its legal future. In this period, in other words, the common law came to see alternative legal frameworks as possessed of an authority that could be said to be valid just to the extent that the common law itself acknowledged and controlled those alternatives. Such an account of legal development naturally downplays the a priori ideological significance of the central law's administrative oversight of other jurisdictions, but only so as to locate the production of ideology squarely within a process of administration that might otherwise seem ideologically neutral.

The question remains how one can best track the ideological import of developments that are understandable also in terms of an ad hoc practice. The legal historian and theorist Peter Goodrich provides one answer, arguing that early jurisdiction lies at the center of the history of legal ideology, since it is at the various thresholds where the common law met its rivals that the law's artifice is most visible, and its discourse most clearly in conversation with other, potentially liberatory, discourses.[37] For Goodrich, jurisdictional heterogeneity stands for the possibility of alternative relationships between life and law, and in particular for the possibility that the intimate life, whose complex shape the law continuously restricts in order to produce its judgments, might secure legal status under a jurisdictional order fitted to its particulars.[38] As part of this valuation of the minor jurisdiction, and following the attempts of Legendre to subject legal-administrative discourse to psychoanalytic critique, Goodrich has worked to uncover the "positive unconscious" of the common law: the internalized history of the law's historical encounters with other discursive traditions (such as the civil and ecclesiastical laws, but also logic and rhetoric), as well as the history of irrationality and contingency that the law tends to exclude from the rationalized scope of its self-theorization.[39] In spite of the law's drive to disavowal, Goodrich argues, these engagements through which the law successfully articulated its insular identity remain integral to the law's own logics. In consequence, legal analysis becomes critical by reopening the exclusionary discourse of law onto a more complex scene than that remembered as the image the law produces through and as its own historiography.

Although I adopt neither a psychoanalytic nor a genealogical approach to administrative life, my work is in sympathy with the remarkable and groundbreaking project that Goodrich has developed in dialogue with Legendre. If my historical topic is the middle stages of that centralization of authority through which the modern state emerged, my focus on the jurisdictional limit foregrounds within that process both the tendency away from plurality toward homogeneity, and, consequently, the ordering of life increasingly in terms of a subjection to a single legal order rather than in terms of the relationship among alternative juridical spheres. In this framework, jurisdictional complexity might be said to answer and perform social complexity by giving it expression, by giving priority at law to the relational question of the *respect* in which a person or action or condition is to be understood.[40]

With regard to critical historiography, such a model of jurisdictional complexity means that a given jurisdictional development at common law will potentially belong to diverging stories. Let us take two general examples from the history of the common law's protection of the subject's liberties. In the sixteenth century, the common-law courts moved to grant manorial tenants (that is, tenants in "copyhold," those whose tenures were recorded or copied onto the manorial roll) access to the common law as opposed to those local courts that, falling within the individual lord's jurisdiction, operated in potentially prejudicial ways.[41] More tentatively, in the late Elizabethan and Jacobean periods, the central courts issued prohibitions to protect the subject from evidentiary formalisms associated with the ecclesiastical courts, including both the two-witness rule (on the ground of excessive burden) and, on the ground of self-incrimination, the general, ex-officio oath that ecclesiastical defendants were routinely asked to swear, sometimes without even knowing the scope of questions to follow. Neither jurisdictional process allows us to speak fully of a common-law takeover. In the case of copyhold, the common law essentially absorbed and oversaw bodies of customary law that, in one formulation, were too firmly in place for the central courts to "sweep away" by application of a "uniform system of land law."[42] In the case of ecclesiastical evidentiary standards, Gray shows that the courts were quite restrained in their use of prohibitions (especially during Coke's tenure as chief justice), preferring to delineate the conditions under which a prohibition would stand, rather than asserting the injustice of the alternative standards per se.[43] That said, the cautious technical reasoning everywhere present in the decisions operated with a familiar force, with the common law exercising control over the alternative system by administering the limits of its operation, according, for example, to the criterion of some common-law interest in the ecclesiastical case or the likelihood that the defendant might, under oath, be forced to disclose something to his "shame and infamy."[44] Such tentative jurisdictional moves can and should be understood in terms of the common law's tendency across time to protect the subject against procedures prejudicial to the liberties that the common law itself defines as most relevant to and constitutive of the subject (preeminently, rights over property). At a slight theoretical remove, however, the same jurisdictional changes can be understood as part of the process through which a juridical order, emerging as dominant, came to occupy a more immediate, and necessarily less ironic, relation to its object. The process that allowed the common law to stand as a law-made-more-efficacious-for-life also instituted that law, according to the logic of a consolidating legal formalism, as a substitute for life, as, formally, life-made-efficacious-for-the-law.[45]

This second part of the dialectical story tells how law became preeminently the discourse that, in the interest of legal efficiency, takes cognizance of one sort of fact but not another, agreeing to know something about the life it measures or, alternatively, refusing that acknowledgment. It is not surprising that the common law's own histories have better attended to the first of the narratives to which I point than the second, since case law itself functions instrumentally and as such is dependent for its efficacy on a continuous process of moving past questions of how it became normative.[46] Literary engagements with jurisdiction can fit themselves to both narratives, listening to where the law is going or what the law means to do, but also holding on, for longer than the law does, to the implications of what is being managed and so displaced.

In this last sentence I mean to suggest a final variation of my general theme that literature critically opens law onto the complex temporality that is the scene of the law's own jurisdictional activity. The literature with which this book is concerned might be called the law's prospective or future elegiac mode, not because it exists in a nostalgic relationship to what the law moves past in order to get where it is going, but rather because, by intensifying the apprehension of law's relation to the time of its own production, it construes the activity of the law as always also looking back onto the scene of its own instability. Understood as a spatio-temporal dynamic, jurisdiction can thus be related to the tragic imaginary that Jacques Ehrmann gives in his account of the figuration of exile, flight, and return in Sophocles' *Oedipus Rex* and Racine's *Phèdre*. In his essay, Ehrmann defines the place of tragedy as a dislocation that, within the temporality instituted by tragedy as suspended destiny, disrupts the relative claims of inside and outside. The "structure of tragic thought," he writes, is "the spatio-temporal figure described by the lag, the dis-location of one place relative to another, by the sliding of one place to another . . . connected and separated by a consciousness which, *in order to* live and think them together, as inside and outside, must explode them, thus disintegrating both them and itself. For at the very moment when knowledge becomes *inside*, when it finally is integrated as knowledge, this accumulation of a finally-recovered past causes it to be lost."[47] Put in these terms, the jurisdictional activity that inscribes power as juridical authority is the ongoing process of bringing the law (which is in a lag relation to itself) inside itself as knowledge and acknowledgment, in consequence of which process the law's past is "lost" by being reordered toward its future.

To take this thought a step further, jurisdictional space—a by-product of the jurisdictional process, but one that can be easily conflated with it, such that "jurisdiction" comes to be identifiable with the area over which a law extends—can be seen to function, paradoxically, in the manner of those spaces designated by Foucault as heterotopias. These are the social "counter-sites" (including sacred places, places of representation like the theater and cinema, and colonies) that are real and yet "outside of all places," "absolutely different from all the sites that they reflect and speak about."[48] Although jurisdiction can hardly be said to be outside the dominant order it is responsible for ordering, jurisdictional space does, at a higher level of abstraction, operate very precisely as counter-measure, working like Foucault's heterotopia "of compensation" to "create a space that is other, another real space, as perfect, as meticulous, as well arranged as ours is messy, ill constructed, and jumbled."[49] My point in making this counter-intuitive argument about Foucault's category is not to dismantle the idea of the heterotopic, but to ask whether the possibility of the counter-site might not depend on the dominant site's being itself a fantasy object, real but also different from the real it stands for. Following Ehrmann and Foucault, then, I am suggesting that we might define jurisdiction as the process through which the law aims to reproduce a heterotopic order within or alongside the other real, this by means of an ongoing "tragic" encounter with its own jumbled present.

Implicit in this account of the ideological relation between the law and its own efficiencies is one way my legal and literary projects differ in emphasis from Goodrich's. He locates the continuing promise of law in the historical fact of jurisdictional variation—so that, for example, the "literary" courts of love delineated by Andreas Capellanus and Martial d'Auvergne achieve theoretical importance as a minor jurisdiction, a real forum for the adjudication of the intimate life.[50] In contrast, I identify the promise of jurisdictional heterogeneity with its making vividly present the disorienting practical life of law, along with the recognition that, subject as one may be to the law, the law becomes patent, too, by having subjected itself to an act of containment, an imperfect delimitation. Correspondingly, as opposed to Goodrich's stance toward the law's positive unconscious, my method is more oriented to the description of the historical everyday of juridical deliberation and practice. Finally, while literature or rhetoric for Goodrich points to an order with which the law was once continuous until it disavowed those discourses, the literature I treat is most impressive for registering, precisely in terms of an intensified literariness, a critical potential in the law's own invention, in its capacity both coherently and incoherently to produce through its jurisdictional activity the forms it needs.

THE STATE OF JURISDICTION

As a project in literary and cultural history, this book insists on the visibility of jurisdiction as a significant category in sixteenth- and early seventeenth-century political culture and statecraft. Of course, the legal changes in that period were only one stage in the common law's long rise to ascendancy, and they may most of all have clarified gains the common law had made across the previous four centuries. In this respect, it is unsurprising that medievalists have been at the forefront of recent efforts to make jurisdiction count as a category for English literary and political-cultural analysis. In his formidable study of late medieval literature in relation to the changing conceptualization of "trouthe," Richard Firth Green demonstrates how deeply engaged fourteenth-century literary texts were with the transition from local to central justice and with the absorption of folk-law by king's law.[51] Pushing the question back to the time of Bracton, Bruce Holsinger situates the thirteenth-century *Owl and the Nightingale* in the context of contemporary jurisdictional contestation, especially between the royal and ecclesiastical laws. He decisively unfolds the poem as an instance of what he calls "vernacular legality," a "subgenre of legal writing" that, in addition to exploring "a specialized realm of authoritative legal knowledge" in Latin, helped writers "manipulate and transform the law in the service of vernacular poetics."[52] For James Simpson, who frames his important study of the periodization that divides "medieval" from "early modern" (and "reform" cultural practices from "revolutionary" ones) as an argument, too, about the continuities between the literary and administrative cultures, the jurisdictional plurality that matters is, similarly, medieval, with the Tudors playing the role only of spoiler. "In the first half of the sixteenth century," he writes, "a culture that simplified and centralized jurisdiction aggressively displaced a culture of jurisdictional heterogeneity." "The institutional simplifications and centralizations of the sixteenth century provoked correlative simplifications and narrowings in literature. If literary history and criticism is . . . ancillary to the complex history of freedoms, this is a narrative of diminishing liberties."[53]

Without wanting to challenge the analytical descriptions of medieval jurisdictional complexity in such studies, I do want to resist the picture of Tudor legal or literary culture as, comparatively, only diminished or impoverished. There is, certainly, a positive (and Whiggish) argument to be made that the developments described by Simpson, centralizations though they be, represented measurable gains for due process and the status of the legal subject.[54] My point, however, lies elsewhere. I mean to insist only that the effect of those earlier complexities extends into the later period from which Simpson exiles them, and not just for the formalist reason that Tudor centralization worked, less aggressively than Simpson has it, rather to limit than to displace the earlier, more heterogeneous legal culture. Most pertinently for the present argument, the sixteenth century remains integral to the story of literature's complex response to the jurisdictional field that was English law because the historical pressure of particular crises brought jurisdiction to new theoretical prominence, as the common law's attempt to accommodate new problems continuously underscored the processual nature of legal meaning generally. A juridical dynamic that makes the work of law imaginable, jurisdiction thus became a symbol driven into the culture at large. In literature, I would argue, there was a corresponding increase in pressure: mine is a story of concentration rather than of simplification.

The raising of the theoretical stakes of jurisdiction was in part the legacy of the Reformation, and in a limited sense my book is an account of that event's century-long ripple effect across the whole of English legal culture. One result of the assertion of England's legal and constitutional autonomy from Rome was to give even deeper roots to the idea of a sovereign justice centered in the king and royal courts, a development that was all the more important in light of the disorienting effect of the fifteenth-century wars on the institution of royal justice throughout the realm. With the Reformation, the practice and even idea of interpretation became more centralized, and not just during the few years in the early 1530s when Henry VIII's caesaro-papist construction of his authority seemed a plausible conceptualization of the break with Rome. Most important, statute had a new place in the constitution, and the proliferation of written law in the wake of the Reformation effected a corresponding change in how the central law was understood, since the need to mediate between the unwritten and written law allowed the law theoretically to take on the shape of its own interpretation in the central courts.[55] In Robert Weimann's account of the Reformation generally, the new centering of meaning in scripture allowed textual representation to emerge as the principal source of authority in the European sixteenth and seventeenth centuries: "Modern authority, rather than preceding its inscription, rather than being given as a prescribed premise of utterances, became a product of writing, speaking, and reading, a result rather than primarily a constituent of representation."[56] In the more specialized realm of law, this is the same process that sustained the early Tudor state's increased use of interpretation as the principal means of legal centralization and control. Interpretation became the motor through which the center organized the absorption of the ecclesiastical, the marginal, and the exceptional.

Especially important for the intellectual developments that bound together jurisdictional and interpretive centralization is the work of the early Tudor lawyer Christopher St. German, whose treatises on the status of conscience at common law helped reconfigure conscience as equity, understood as an *interpretive* principle of supplementary justice internal to the law, rather than as an *ethical* principle of exceptional and conscientious justice corrective of the law. J. A. Guy and others have shown the importance of St. German's description of equity as hermeneutic for the future of English jurisdiction: by elevating the status of common-law interpretation, that descriptive shift came, namely, to identify judicial authority with but one of several traditionally integrated judicial spaces. In other words, the reconfiguration of conscience as equity raised the prestige of the common-law courts relative to the courts of extraordinary justice (such as Chancery) and the ecclesiastical courts, the juridical relevance of whose interest over matters of conscience could only decline once conscience itself was refitted in technical terms that allowed for its management at common law.[57]

That the idea of jurisdiction entered Tudor and Stuart discourse more fully than before was a consequence, too, of explicitly professional interests.[58] The growth of the common law in the period involved its extension into legal spheres overseen by lawyers trained in alternative traditions. In relation to ecclesiastical law, R. H. Helmholz explains that, even after Henry VIII banned the study of canon law, the civil lawyers who continued to practice in the ecclesiastical courts retained a distinct identity continuous with their pre-Reformation colleagues: "In 1569 Archbishop Parker wrote to Sir William Cecil about the civilians: 'Sir, I think these lawyers keep but their old trade.' The Archbishop was telling the unvarnished truth. Far from acquiring a 'common law mind,' the Elizabethan and Jacobean civilians remained tied to the traditions of Roman canon law."[59] Civilians were equally protective of their professional identity in the Admiralty court, a second important forum for Roman law in England. The civilians who in the later sixteenth century found their livelihoods threatened by the common-law courts were quick to assert the integrity of the jurisdictions under their management and thereby protect them from the control that the central courts attempted to exercise by prohibition, the legal writ that halted a proceeding in another tribunal by querying the court's competence to hear the matter. The treatise on the jurisdiction of the Court of Requests written by Sir Julius Caesar, a prominent civilian and Master (judge) of Requests, is an example from the 1590s of one such defense.[60] In the early seventeenth century, the reaction to the aggressive use of prohibitions became even more focused, and jurisdiction assumed an even stronger cultural presence. One of the most important legal writers to take up the question of English jurisdiction was William Fulbecke, whose *Parallele or Conference of the Civill Law, the Canon Law, and the Common Law* (1601) delineated the theoretical unity of the three interlocking systems as a way to defuse growing tensions among the courts. Fulbecke's 1603 *Pandectes of the Law of Nations*, a volume whose title deliberately invokes the Justinian *Pandects*, similarly attempted to place English common law within the broader European legal heritage of which the English civil-law jurisdictions were the critical sign and symbol.[61]

In the rise of jurisdiction as a category of importance for Tudor and Stuart culture, the most important factor, perhaps, was the shifting constitutional relationship between king and common law. Along with the Reformation, the early Tudor experiment in fiscal feudalism made the royal prerogative present in a new way, effectively reshaping the prerogative, not by retheorizing it, but by continuously testing its limits as part of the Crown's insatiable pursuit of money. Much important work on the relation between early literature and law has focused on the prerogative as a way to explore the cultural organization of basic constitutional questions concerning the relation of king and state.[62] In such accounts, royal authority is often pitched against that of the common law and Parliament, a discourse of absolutism (as embodied, for example, by King James) against that of constitutionalism (as embodied, for example, by Sir Edward Coke). My understanding of the relationship between king and law differs from such accounts, in that this book describes royal authority and the common law as essentially going hand in hand. This difference, however, seems to me more a matter of historical orientation than a theoretical claim per se for a revisionist legal history as opposed to a progressivist one. In his magisterial survey of the medieval state, Alan Harding describes developments in political theory across the sixteenth century as a dialectical response to earlier legal achievements. "By the end of the middle ages," he writes, "the expansion of royal government from its base in the administration of justice had identified the state of the commonwealth with the state of the king. A number of factors would then start to detach the idea of the state from both legal order and specifically monarchical rule."[63] Within the dialectic Harding outlines, my work can be said to focus on the ongoing centralization of common law as royal justice, attending only secondarily to the ongoing process of detachment that allowed the state, the centralized law, and the king to be imaginable as separate. Although the jurisdictional crises I explore here all question or disrupt the nature of royal power, the narrative I tell concerns the bureaucratic manipulation of the prerogative as part of the law, rather than the pulling of law away from its royal center.

The discourse of jurisdiction does have a place, however, in that second process. Put simply, the complex relationship between royal power and the common law was mirrored in an equally complex relationship between jurisdictional consolidation and royal authority. On the one hand, the king's authority and that of the common law could be seen as coterminous. The prerogative was acknowledged to be part of the common law, and the common-law courts, as explicitly royal courts, intruded on alternative jurisdictions in the service of a more uniform, national law strictly identifiable with the idea of royal justice. On the other hand, Elizabethan and Stuart defenses of weaker jurisdictions against the common law located royal authority most powerfully in the idea of a system of distinct jurisdictions united under the monarch, a move that resists an *exclusive* identification of the king's authority with the central law. One such textual polemic on behalf of England's minor jurisdictions is usefully evocative of the larger constitutional questions that lie mostly in the shadow of the history this book explores.

In his 1607 defense of the civil and ecclesiastical laws against the use of common-law prohibitions, the civilian Thomas Ridley positioned himself as an advocate "for those parts of your Majesties Laws, which are lesse knowen unto your people." His book aimed to "set out" the "whole sum of both the Lawes to the view of the people," in order to redress "such grievances as have bin of late offered by one Jurisdiction unto the other, and in consequence, to all your subjects, who follow any suits in the Civile or Ecclesiasticall Courts."[64] Ridley compares the conjunction of common-law and civil-law jurisdictions to the relationship between two kingdoms: "for now as things are, neither Jurisdiction knowes their owne bounds, but one snatcheth from the other, in maner, as in a batable ground lying betweene two Kingdomes; but so that the weaker ever goeth to the worse, and that which is mightier prevailes against the other: the professors thereof being rather willing to give Lawes and interpretations to other, than to take or admit of any against themselves. For which, the weaker appeales unto your Highnesse, humbly desiring your Majesties upright and sincere Judgement to discerne where the wrong is, and to redresse it accordingly."[65] The association of legal jurisdiction and state territoriality is interesting as part of the process of rationalization I have evoked in my reading of Wyatt, and because it implies as a model for jurisdictional relation an equitable, political accommodation between neighboring kingdoms, similar to that between Scotland and England as that particular relation was being newly effected through their union in James's person, with no correlating union at law. Indeed, the comparison of English courts and royal kingdoms underlines the central feature of Ridley's argument, namely, that common-law writs of prohibition against other English courts derogate from the king's personal authority: "to deny a free course to the Civile and Ecclesiasticall Law in this Land, in such things as appertaine to their profession, or to abridge the maintenance thereof, is to spoile his Majestie of a part of his Honour."[66]

Royal authority, here, is seen to depend on the maintenance of the boundaries that separate distinct spheres of legal activity and legal authority. Thus, in his discussion of the conflict between the common law and Admiralty over marine jurisdiction, Ridley defines the space of law doubly, locating justice metajuridically, first, in the conceptual separation of judicial powers and, then, in the reintegration of those powers within the prince. Law, he remarks, has "set" the "bounds and lymits" of the two jurisdictions: "which they shall not passe: which, as it is the good provision of the Law, so ought either Jurisdiction in all obedience to submit itselfe therunto, for that the diminishing of either of them is a wrong to the Prince from whom they are derived, who is no lesse Lord of the Sea than he is king of the Land."[67] The implication that legal centralization and jurisdictional assimilation are prejudicial to royal authority is fundamental to Ridley's (admittedly defensive) sense of the legal world, as though a greater jurisdictional homogeneity were, for him, allowing the common law to detach itself from the royal authority that alone properly moors it. Such a formulation brings us, of course, back to Harding's observation that political modernity begins with the gradual unraveling of the medieval knot of state and king and royal justice. (And it is interesting that if, as opposed to Ridley's negative construction, we apply a positive spin to his picture of common-law prohibitions against other jurisdictions, we effectively generate the classically liberal account of the strong common law as a safeguard against royal absolutism, understood as an indivisible sovereignty [Lat. *maiestas*] too much split off from the law that alone properly moors it.)

For the conceptual argument of my book, it is especially significant that in Ridley's metonymic figuration of a jurisdiction's "obedience" and submission, he allows England's distinct jurisdictions themselves to absorb the agency of the judges whose pronouncements and prohibitions helped constitute English legal authority. This abstraction of jurisdiction into a function is symptomatic of the larger shift in the political imaginary that Harding describes, and it powerfully underlines the value of jurisdiction as a historical frame for thinking about the realignment of juridico-political meanings. The model of royal authority that Ridley puts on paper is inflected differently from even the centralized power delineated under the early Tudors (most spectacularly by Henry VIII in the early 1530s), insofar as Ridley places the king above the jurisdictional field rather than at its center. This move is possible, I think, only after jurisdiction has hardened as a category, has itself begun to split off from the juridical "process"—the formulation is Costa's—it stands for, a development that correlates with what happens to the associated categories of king and law. In one sense, Ridley's account of a judicial authority's being "derived" from the king is only traditional, jurisdiction being the order of distributing a shared authority that is expressed fully only in the prince. But the formulation Ridley gives to the particular jurisdictional crises his book is addressing suggests also a less traditional understanding of that order: one in which the prince's authority has been fully split off from jurisdiction as process, such that *derivation*, once a concept that signified the process of legal power itself, now links two orders, king and legal jurisdiction, that as *relata* are increasingly fixed and static. As a version of Harding's argument, then, I am suggesting that the jurisdictional compression coincident with the process of rationalization through which judicial authority was consolidated as royal justice paradoxically reproduced the king as an imaginable order external to the state. To that extent, jurisdiction is an indispensable lens through which to track the historical precipitation of those dichotomies—king and Parliament, prerogative and law—that have energized the most tenacious of Anglo-American constitutional narratives.[68]

A LITERATURE OF JURISDICTION

In my prologue and in this introduction, I have argued that, properly understood, the category of jurisdiction usefully disrupts a default account of sovereignty in relation to the genesis of the juridical norm, as well as our critical descriptions of the literary and historical object, the temporality of legal ideology, and the early constitution of the state. Although each of these thoughts informs the literary analyses that follow, my readings do not attempt so much to prove such ambitious claims as to exemplify them by tracking their various inflections in historical time, this by showing how a series of literary texts meditated on jurisdiction as a fundamental principle for the ongoing process of instituting the real. Just as I conceive jurisdiction to be a process of legal order rather than a stable fact, I locate jurisdiction in literature chiefly as a frame for, and enabling principle of, aesthetic production. Through close consideration of textual detail and through a form of cultural analysis attentive to contemporary technical developments at law, each chapter works to disentangle the philosophical or legal implications of a particular literary engagement with an emergent jurisdictional problem. Because of its concentrated textual focus, my work may seem to be principally formalist or rhetorical in orientation. But it is neither, at least not in the usually restricted and instrumental current usages of those terms. When I track the details of a legal argument or a literary one, I am not primarily interested in the rhetorical shape of the argument or in the literary remapping of a technical meaning. I mean rather to reveal the jurisdictional limit at law as a place where legal doctrine is sufficiently destabilized to allow us to see the two discourses, law and literature, as pertaining to a single order and practice of imaginative thought.

This book comprises six case studies in the early history of the literary engagement with the idea of jurisdiction. Organized chronologically, these also present a range of jurisdictional scenes, and in so doing describe a particular arc among the questions under which jurisdiction was confronted in the rapidly changing social and political field of the sixteenth and early seventeenth centuries. The book consists of three parts, each motivated by one of three mutually reinforcing categories—centralization, rationalization, and formalization—that mark desires at law more than achieved realities, none existing except as a tendency or dynamic in search of its own completion. Chapters 1 and 2, on early Tudor political culture, posit two proximate origins for sixteenth-century jurisdictional discourse, looking to the impact on royal law, first, of bureaucratic centralization and, second, of the remapping of ecclesiastical jurisdiction at the Reformation. Chapters 3 and 4 concern the cultural organization of England's encounter with the territorial other, a problem I address in terms of the attempts to rationalize the very different meanings at common law of colonial Ireland and of historical France. Chapters 5 and 6 offer alternative endpoints for the project as a whole, looking to two peculiarly intense legal venues—the zone of the threshold itself and the microlegal space of London—whose organization opens legal culture onto forms alternative to those imagined by a centralizing, rationalizing law.

Chapter 1 treats John Skelton's *Magnyfycence* (ca. 1519–20) as a response to the bureaucratization of royal authority under the early Tudors. Traditionally read as a warning about excessive expenditure in the royal household, Skelton's play emerges instead as an act of political theory, a meditation on the nature of royal identity inside a rapidly evolving administrative culture. This culture abstracted authority from any fully coherent origin and relocated it in a more quantitatively oriented process of management and measurement, the chief sign of which was an anxious proliferation of documentation insufficient to the fantasy of order for which it stood. In my reading of the play's discursive mode, dramatic representation and political representation meet as forms of distribution and embodiment for the consolidation of authority. Skelton describes and analyzes the forms of political delegation in three ways: most simply, he charts the royal household's aggressively bureaucratic pursuit of royal privilege on feudal lands; second, he analyzes legal writing, the material embodiment of delegation, as a site of vulnerability in the state's reproduction and extension of its power; third, he externalizes the idea of royal intention by bringing it in proximity to the idea of equity as a nonarcane principle of legal interpretation and the de facto motor for judicial centralization.

In chapter 2, on Sir Thomas More, I step back from the details of the bureaucratic organization of authority to reflect on the theoretical implications of centralization for the very idea of a legal norm. To elucidate More's general understanding of English law as a meeting of different jurisdictions, I analyze two of his fictions in relation, respectively, to his defense of the ecclesiastical jurisdiction against intrusions by the temporal courts and to his analysis of the fundamental relation between equity and law. More's commitment to the principle of jurisdictional heterogeneity, I argue, points not only to his conservative allegiance to Rome, but also, inside that conservatism, to a potentially critical understanding of the relation between law and life. As a mode of probative hypothesis, fiction works within More's analysis of jurisdiction to expose the same contingency as the experience of jurisdiction does: it casts the normative claim of law back onto a complex of grounds and logics. After briefly treating a parable of the temporal and spiritual orders told by More during his imprisonment in the Tower, I turn to *Utopia* (1516), which I see not only as a philosophical argument about the possibility of worldly justice, but also as a practical and local legal analysis of the procedural relation between English common law and English equity. As such, More's supreme jurisdictional fiction anticipates the work undertaken by Christopher St. German in the 1520s to reconfigure conscience as equity and so subordinate conscience to common law. In the dialectical movement between Books 1 and 2, between worldly and ideal, positive and negative, *Utopia* emerges as a lawyer's analysis of legal rationalization as a process of managing rather than erasing the disruptive potential in law.

Part 2 moves the study forward to the late Elizabethan period and to a different stage in the consolidation of English law, attending to the impact of alternative territorial authorities on an ever more professionalized and nationalistic common law. This shift in the domain of my argument allows jurisdiction to enter more directly into dialogue with the concept of sovereignty as a political reality produced at the jurisdictional threshold between the state and some version of its other. Chapter 3 treats Books 5 and 6 of Spenser's *Faerie Queene* (1596) in light of the Elizabethan attempts to imagine in colonial Ireland a place for English common law. It focuses on the pressure applied by England's colonialist policy on two terms, *common* and *custom*, through which English lawyers celebrated the common law as it operated in England. Early modern Ireland presented a special problem in this regard, in that the customary Brehon law, which the colonizers were eager to displace for both symbolic and practical reasons, had to be imagined in opposition to English common law, whose authority was grounded exactly in its status as custom. Equally, the notion of the "common" that underlay the nationalist construction of centralized royal justice in England was troubled by the very different conception of "common" tenure in Gaelic Ireland. In light of these categorical tensions, which encouraged, as I argue, a strongly positivist account of common-law jurisprudence, Spenser deploys the generic resources of pastoral to rethink the status of property, this being one step in a program to implement the imperfectly coherent law through which English appropriations of Irish land could be rationalized. In the same vein, Spenser's allegorical mode comes to stand for the system of interpretive coercion that transformed law's accommodation of jurisdictional difference into an administrative initiative to identify a distinct Irish legal identity only in order to suppress it.

Chapter 4, on the question of English legal nationalism, turns from Ireland to France, and thus from a legal tradition that the developing common law looked to incorporate to one it needed, rather, to disavow. Grounding the general question of England's relation to France in terms of competing accounts of law French, the much-ridiculed professional language of the common law, I argue that legal Normanism can best be understood as the historical and structural internalization of France in English institutional life and, indeed, in the English language. Legal humanists and common lawyers worked to overpower the potentially embarrassing implications of law French for English national law by relating the common law to an exemplary classical past and, most impressively, by remaking the Norman Conquest itself as its own reiteration and reversal in the Anglo-French wars of the fourteenth and fifteenth centuries. According to this embarrassed legal nationalism, France was positioned jurisdictionally as a space simultaneously external and internal to English legal identity. As engagements with this troped history of conquest and counter-conquest, I argue, Shakespeare's English histories (specifically *Richard III* and the second tetralogy) draw powerfully on their own metadramatic resources to represent France as a continuous historical presence within England, a shadow jurisdiction to the centralizing royal authority they represent in the person of Hal/Henry V. As these plays argue it, national sovereignty, like the power of the stage itself, emerges as the hypothetical projection of jurisdiction in and through its alternatives.

In two chapters, one global in outlook and one parochial, part 3 extends the book's argument by charting out the consequences of jurisdiction for the shaping of legal identity within two zones: the jurisdictional threshold and the nation's mercantile center. Chapter 5 on Shakespeare's *Pericles* (1609) and *Cymbeline* (ca. 1610) turns from a virtual jurisdiction constitutive of national identity (the France that is England's legal past) to another that is constitutive of empire. Shakespearean romantic tragicomedy emerges here as an extended engagement with the idea of jurisdiction as it came under pressure in consequence, first, of the union of the Scottish and English Crowns in 1603, and, second, of the changing status of the ocean as an international space of trade. Shakespeare's plays belong to a moment when transnational authority was imagined as the legal effect not of *dominium* (ownership) but of *imperium*, a jurisdictional relationship and process. Accordingly, I argue, they engage the scene of international politics by taking up the shape of jurisdictional crisis itself, as that is produced at the threshold between sovereign spaces, and as it finds resolution in the reconfiguration or reimagining of the same threshold. Analyzing this highly flexible and unstable language of power as a language of personal relation, I describe the impact of transnational distance both on the subject, whose obligations to the monarch helped constitute *imperium* across distance, and on the monarch himself, who could discover his new authority only when it was projected into a beyond. At the edge of the modern, global *nomos*, these plays reach toward a theoretical account of the jurisdictional principle they thematize, at the same time as they represent, at the temporal and spatial threshold (which the plays distend into the nonspace of the ocean), a deterritorialization of legal identity that transforms jurisdiction into a principle to serve a new kind of power.

Chapter 6, on Webster, Rowley, and Heywood's *Cure for a Cuckold* (1624), returns to the question of jurisdictional complexity internal to English law even as it extends the work of chapter 5 by tracking how the sea's disruptive energies, which are the energies of the limit itself, implode, claustrophobically, into the space of London. Alongside the tragicomic turn to empire, this final chapter on urban comedy thus represents a second endpoint for the book's argument about the practical and theoretical life of the law, finding the legal form of the irrational and unprocessed returned to the center as the law's own contestable image of itself. The subplot of the dramatists' too little known collaboration involves Compass, a sailor who refuses to acknowledge what his neighbors and the law might tell him, that his wife's illegitimate son is not properly his own. Describing Compass's response to the normative order by invoking a labyrinth of complementary jurisdictional orders (including canon law, civil law, common law, manorial law, and municipal law), the play produces in Compass's evasions a consequentialist ethics that is grounded, first, in a splitting off of effect from cause and, second, in the *dramatic* projection of a jurisdictional imaginary capable of sustaining a norm alternative to the law's own jurisdictionally constituted norms. As the logical expression of a process of legal rationalization, the law's authority formally produces in Compass and his odd family the mirror image of its own homogenizing order. With this radically local fantasy, then, the play returns us in a new register to *Utopia* and to More's insistence on the necessarily ironic gap between law and the life that it orders. Structurally, this gap is the topological expression of the plurality that the law encounters and controls in order to function effectively. Legal comedy is the genre that makes visible that topology and the temporal dynamic it continues to represent.

These six chapters on the inventiveness, in the face of legal change, of poetry and drama, romance, pastoral, utopian fantasy, comedy, and tragicomedy, all speak to the resources of fiction as a source of legal-cultural meaning. James Simpson offers an unusually powerful thesis in contending that the jurisdictional centralisms of the sixteenth century produced a cultural field of "diminished liberties" relative to the medieval world.[69] But in light of the literary engagements with law that are the focus of my book, that jurisdictional compression must, I think, be understood rather to have charged the possibility of literature as idea and practice, since it is only against a homogeneous norm, or against the fantasy of such, that poetic or dramatic discourse could claim for itself anything like normative force, only there that literary authority might invent itself *as such* by drafting off its juridical counterpart. The various and provisional literary subjectivities indexed in this book, obliquely rather than directly reactive to the state, are not so much subversive of their juridical-political counterpart as continuous with it: at once by-products, vivid supports, and dialectical partners of the political in formation.

It is not coincidental that, within the jurisdictional framework this book describes, the charged expression of poetic or dramatic authority in relation to the political consolidation of juridical authority can be seen to analogize the growth of temporal authority in relation to the spiritual. In his classic essay on the origins of the modern state, Joseph Strayer points to the Investiture Conflict of the eleventh century as an important event for the emergence of secular authority, since the Church's successful assertion of its independence produced the possibility of new definitions elsewhere in the political culture:

> Like all victories, the victory of the Church in the Investiture Conflict had unforeseen consequences. By asserting its unique character, by separating itself so clearly from lay governments, the Church unwittingly sharpened concepts about the nature of secular authority. Definitions and arguments might vary, but the most ardent Gregorian had to admit that the Church could not perform all political functions, that lay rulers were necessary and had a sphere in which they should operate. They might be subject to the guidance and correction of the Church, but they were not a part of the administrative structure of the Church. They headed another kind of organization, for which there was as yet no generic term. In short, the Gregorian concept of the Church almost demanded the invention of the concept of the State.[70]

Extending, as this book does, the work of jurisdiction beyond the historical and theoretical horizon that state sovereignty seems to mark allows us to see that the dynamic Strayer describes is in reality an ongoing, always shifting process of political and cultural reproduction: one according to which literary texts might, jurisdictionally, emerge as immediately political by reason of their relative autonomy as fiction; or, to take a differently modern example, one according to which a theocratic order might, jurisdictionally, be predicted to reorganize itself within the state as the dialectical response to the incomplete consolidation of state authority.[71] To the question, then, why one now would write a book on the legal and literary negotiation of jurisdiction, a punning answer runs as follows. In cultural history and political theory alike, jurisdiction has been overlooked as a merely technical matter. But exactly as a principle of *mere* distribution—undilutedly [OED a^2, Lat. *merus*, "undiluted"], the administration and management of juridical boundaries [OED sb^2, OE *gemaere*, "boundary"] themselves—jurisdiction holds out for critique all the odd promise of a dynamic that orients us in the world through the disorienting force of its potentiality.

* 1 *

Centralization

CHAPTER ONE

"Shewe Us Your Mynde Then": Bureaucracy and Royal Privilege in Skelton's *Magnyfycence*

Not surprisingly for an early Tudor literary text, John Skelton's *Magnyfycence* has long been identified by critics as primarily a topical text. According to a widely accepted reading espoused by David Starkey, Alistair Fox, and, especially, Greg Walker, the play allegorizes the expulsion of the minions in 1519, when, perhaps with the approval of the king himself, Wolsey successfully rid the Privy Chamber and royal household of various young courtiers and put a group of older counselors in their place.[1] Among those identified as being a corrupting influence on the young king were four royal companions whom Henry VIII in September 1518 had named to the new post of gentleman of the Privy Chamber.[2] Narrative details link Skelton's play closely to these events. Magnyfycence, a prince who hitherto has followed his counselor Measure in ordering his household according to the golden mean, comes under the influence of unscrupulous spendthrifts. Under false names such as Largesse, Consayte, Lusty Pleasure, Good Demeynaunce, Sure Surveyaunce, and Sober Sadnesse, these vice-characters enter his service and, true to their real identities (here, respectively, Fansy, Foly, Courtly Abusyon, Counterfet Countenaunce, Crafty Conveyaunce, and Clokyd Colusyon), bring the court to ruin by stealing the prince's treasure, his character, and his good name.[3] As political morality, Walker shows, *Magnyfycence* thus operates to warn Henry about the consequences of excessive spending in the royal household, and also to praise him for his decisive action in expelling his wanton companions.

When we assign a topical meaning like this to a literary text, we are also describing a literary temporality, in the sense that topicality can usually be said to locate a text's meaning in the time of a particular event and, indeed, in the time of *event* more abstractly conceived. I aim in this chapter to elucidate a more complex version of time's relation to topical meaning, by reading Skelton's play in the context of a fundamental historical shift in the bureaucratic organization of space and, consequent on that shift, in the configuration of early Tudor political-juridical authority. Far from denying the relevance of the historical particular for the literary particular, I will suggest instead how literary topicality might open up complexities in historical time; how the literary text, irreducibly situated in and by the contingencies of history, might work to reveal the event itself as embedded in a complex of forms and practices that destabilize its relation to its own apparent time.

Persuasive as Walker's thesis about *Magnyfycence* is, then, I think it overestimates the degree to which the political meanings in Skelton's play attach themselves to a single moment. David Bevington usefully articulates the general position that politics entered Tudor drama "in terms of ideas and platforms rather than personalities."[4] At that political-philosophical level, certainly, Skelton's play takes up Aristotle's treatment of magnificence in the *Nichomachean Ethics* as a form of liberality, a "suitable expenditure on a great scale" (4.2.1) that is one "mode of observing the mean" (2.7.6).[5] In an attempt to historicize such meanings, John Scattergood demonstrates how Skelton generalized the historical incident of the minions by appealing to the ethical vocabulary found in such royal household books as *The Black Book of the Household of Edward IV* and, from slightly later, the 1526 *Ordinances at Eltham for Henry VIII*.[6] Connecting the play to the codes of behavior in that literature, Scattergood thus unites the play's political and moral meanings: if the play's subject is "the proper management of the royal Household, especially in relation to finance," this was for the Tudor period "not simply a matter of practical politics and economics, but something which had philosophical and moral implications too."[7] As valuable as it is to insist on the place of the general alongside the topical, it is notable that Scattergood's idea of topicality remains, like Walker's, narrowly identifiable with the discrete event, since he identifies that which is general in the play as extra-topical, as "philosophical and moral."

Political topicality can be more generously conceived than this, in terms of the *example*, a genre that bridges particular and general so as to allow topical relevance to lie, in John Wallace's memorable formulation, "in the axiomatic or preceptual middle between the particulars of poetry and the particulars of contemporary history."[8] One effect of such a conceptual structure is that a literary text might be most richly and precisely topical when, with a kind of charged generality, it represents not so much the particular event as the *scene* in which meaning emerges and the event occurs. Thus Seth Lerer posits that *Magnyfycence* eschews "the transparency of topical allusion" to find its political center in its engagement with a Chaucerian paradigm of courtiership and in a broader critique of Tudor theatricality.[9] This argument concerning the impact of literary tropes on the organization of political culture suggests, first, how an allusiveness that falls shy of a transparent, one-to-one correspondence may yet function with immediate topical effect. Second, in his attention to the play's deployment of a literary tradition, Lerer implicitly indexes how in his political work Skelton might be fashioning his own authority as poet and dramatist. This governing impulse in the play has been explored recently by Jane Griffiths, who powerfully argues that across his entire *oeuvre* (and in his self-designations as *orator regius*, laureate, and *vates*) Skelton describes a model of poetic authority that, although responsive to its public origins in the royal court, in literary tradition, and in divine inspiration, is rooted fundamentally in the "improvisatory" and "unpredictable" practice and "process" of writing itself.[10] She shows that *Magnyfycence* expresses that highly reflexive poetic authority most clearly in Skelton's risky association of his own "energiall" poetic craft with the very process of "verbal misrepresentation" responsible for corrupting the princely court.[11]

My argument orients itself to both the political and the literary force of Skelton's text. Like Lerer, I contend that the political meaning of the play extends beyond the local incident of the minions—not, however, through the permeability of the literary and political spheres, but rather in relation to the various administrative levels inside the early modern state. Similarly, the poetic and dramatic authority that for me is most vividly present in the play is one that emerges from that same distribution and performance of office. Skelton's play of royal domestic politics is, I think, most legible as an extended reflection on, and reconfiguration of, what Maura Nolan in her study of John Lydgate identifies as a new form of *public culture*. This public culture, focused on the political center and a narrow social elite, constitutes a "turn away from a Chaucerian vision of the social whole as variegated, multiple, and inclusive, and toward an understanding of the social totality as hierarchical and exclusive, organized around a notion of 'representativeness' that starts with the king as the head of the body of the realm."[12] Skelton's attention specifically to bureaucratic culture as an unstable program of distributing authority makes his particular imagining of that elite public especially apt for the exploration of the Crown's relation to the state, since the "representative" public within his play is made up precisely of those who, as delegates within a bureaucratic culture, represent the king's own "public" authority by projecting it outward.[13] In other words, Skelton's dramatic representation of office—including his own office as poetic interpreter—becomes the formal expression of an emerging representational culture grounded in new modes of managing and distributing power.

In the fifteenth and early sixteenth centuries the domestic politics of the household was not fully differentiated from the politics of the realm. In its analysis of an intimately public court, *Magnyfycence* correspondingly touches on broader national concerns than those associated with the internal household dynamics to which the minions' expulsion most immediately pertains. To put this in terms of the different departments inside the early Tudor household, we must be wary of any interpretation of Skelton's text that emphasizes the Henrician Privy Chamber at the expense of Chamber more generally. David Starkey explains that the medieval household inherited by Henry VII was made up of two departments, the Household, which under the Lord Steward was in charge of "downstairs" offices like the kitchen and buttery, and the Chamber, which under the Lord Chamberlain looked after the "upstairs" and more private rooms. Around 1495 the king made the Privy Chamber a separate subdepartment of Chamber, probably as a means of restricting access to his person and thus minimizing the "direct political pressure of the court aristocracy."[14] Privy Chamber assumed an even higher status under Henry VIII, who filled this most intimate of spaces with his closest companions. In the aftermath of 1519, with the appointment of salaried persons to replace the expelled minions, the Privy Chamber was transformed from a subdepartment of Chamber into "the fully fledged third department of the royal household: much smaller and newer than the Chamber and Household; yet outranking both in prestige, the distinction of its staff, and the level of their remuneration."[15]

When Skelton's prince greets the disguised Abusyon by saying, "Welcom, Pleasure, to our magnyfycence" (l. 1516), Skelton's formula clearly identifies the royal presence in terms of both a royal quality and a set of rooms: by association with its function, Chamber is identified in the Household book of Edward IV as the *domus regie magnificencie*, the household as it pertains to royal magnificence.[16] But which rooms specifically in Chamber does Skelton have in mind? If Henry VIII's Privy Chamber became the keystone in a new politics of intimacy, it is important to remember that the administrative work of Chamber more generally also continued, promoting royal magnificence beyond the household walls through its role, especially through 1520, "as the centre of financial administration" on a national scale.[17] Because the Privy Chamber's "financial activities remained oriented around the monarch's personal interest," that new institution never wholly disrupted the administration of national finance that had been developed in Chamber during its ascendancy under Henry VII.[18] Most important for the national implications of Skelton's play is the fact that Henry VIII, like his father, used Chamber to centralize fiscal control of the royal lands, including both those lands held absolutely by the Crown and those lands held, by the Crown's so-called tenants in chief (*in capite*), immediately of the king as feudal lord, rather than of some intermediate (*mesne*) lord.

Skelton's play is very much about this national scene: Fansy praises Counterfet Countenaunce for being "able to dystroy an hole lande" (l. 513), and in the long list of the various frauds that go under his name, Countenaunce himself boasts that he can "Counterfet maters in the lawe of the lande / . . . In stede of ryght that wronge may stande" (ll. 431–33). At such moments, knowing how Chamber linked the king to a national space allows us to hear a neglected register in Skelton's political argument. Readers of the play have focused on how it critiques excessive household expenditure and promotes a version of magnificence rooted instead in economic frugality. But like the Tudor Chamber it explores, Skelton's play is as concerned with how money enters the household as with how it leaves, as much with the justice of Crown appropriations as with the prudence of Crown expenditure. Richard Halpern, writing of Skelton's satirical poems against Wolsey, emphasizes, particularly in relation to sanctuary, the importance of the idea of legal jurisdiction for the poet's conception of political order.[19] *Magnyfycence* is similarly preoccupied with the question of jurisdictional violation, here as it relates to the program of bureaucratic centralization that, through Chamber, enabled the Crown's potentially intrusive fiscal appropriation of the subject's property. Not through analogy, but as an effect of the emergent administrative culture itself, Skelton's dramatic treatment of the internal disorder that imperils the royal household simultaneously analyzes, on the national level, structures of royal authority that have broad theoretical implications for the constitution of the state.

COUNSEL AND THE ESTATE ROYAL

In an exemplary scene midway through *Magnyfycence*, Skelton reflects on the connection between household service and the question and category of jurisdiction. Foly, who has entered the prince's service under the name of Consayte, tells his master a nonsensical story:

Magn.   What tydynges with you, syr? I befole thy brayne pan.
Fol.   By our lakyn, syr, I have ben a hawkyng for the wylde swan.
   My hawke is rammysshe, and it happed that she ran—
   Flewe, I sholde say—in to an olde barne

> To reche at a rat—I coulde not her warne.
> She pynched her pynyon, by God, and catched harme.
> It was a ronner; nay, fole, I warant her blode warme. (ll. 1805-11)

To paraphrase this self-consciously obscure vernacular, Foly says that his hawk, instead of hunting the wild swan as he intended it to do, flew into a barn in pursuit of a rat, and thus hurt her wing, allowing the rat or "ronner" to escape. Though injured, Foly concludes, the hawk is still alive. (Alternatively, if we take "her" in line 1811 to refer to its immediate antecedent, "ronner," the hawk was injured and the rat got away.) Although the prince dismisses Foly's speech as wordplay—"A, syr, thy jarfawcon and thou be hanged togyder" (l. 1812)—the story is richer in implications than Skelton's characters perceive. It can be read as an emblem for the whole play, a fable about the relationship between authority and jurisdiction, and a warning about the misuse of that authority. Applied to a hawk, "rammysshe" (ramage) means "wild" and, in the words of a seventeenth-century writer on falconry, "coy, or disdainfull to the man, and contrary to be reclamed."[20] In the fool's hawk, Skelton figures both fictional prince and Tudor king. Like the play as a whole, Foly's tale addresses the consequences of unruliness: where Foly's unruly hawk breaks her wing, Skelton's unruly prince is brought through unrule to poverty and despair.

The humor of Foly's story resides specifically in the bathetic substitution of the lowly rat for the swan, a bird that, along with the whale, sturgeon, and wild animals in the royal forests, belonged to the king by virtue of the prerogative.[21] Narratively, that detail underlines the troubling nature of the political relationship between prince and counselor, implying that, in Foly, the prince has granted an undeserving fool the privilege to hunt the royal bird.[22] As emblem, the swan points to the story's even deeper political valence. Instead of following a prey pertaining to the royal prerogative, the hawk has aimed almost impossibly low, and in so doing she has not only lost the lowly prey but also harmed herself in such a way as to prevent her from flying or hunting again. The story functions, therefore, as a warning against substituting the pursuit of a degraded object for the properly royal pursuit of a properly royal privilege.

Given the story's relation to the prerogative, it is all the more important that the hawk hurts herself by flying into an old barn. That jurisdictional transgression fills out Skelton's allusion to royal privilege in literary and political terms. First, by representing a hawk that enters a space in which it does not belong, Skelton is alluding to the history of his own poetic production.

In "Ware the Hauke," an early poem dating between 1503 and 1512, Skelton satirized a worldly priest who allows his hawk to follow a pigeon into the interior of the poet's church at Diss and so pollute that space. The hawking cleric was a conventional and Chaucerian figure, and Skelton's central target in his satire is, generally, the sacrilegious profanation of the sacred. But as Halpern explains in his analysis of the poem in relation to the idea of "cultural territoriality" that organizes Skelton's engagement with the Tudor state, this profanation of the church's "territorial sanctity" also recasts the temporal administration's legal attack on ecclesiastical sanctuary.[23] In Skelton's poetic economy sanctuary can be understood both as a specific jurisdictional privilege and as "the ideological *paradigm*" for those independent jurisdictions that, more generally, were coming under the centralized control of the state.[24]

In light of this response to the state's undifferentiation of the juridical order, it is especially significant that, as part of his jurisdictional critique in "Ware the Hauke," Skelton self-consciously disentangles his own poetic authority, at once announcing it and, as a challenge to the state's own compressions, hiding it. He conceals it in an elaborate Latin puzzle that compares him, as Britain's native-grown laureate, to the equally singular Arabian phoenix of antiquity: "*Sicculo lutueris est colo būraarā / Nixphedras uisarum caniuter tūtātes / Raterplas Natābrian umsudus itnugenus / 18. 10. 2. 11. 19. 4. 13. 3. 4. 1 tēūalet*" (ll. 239–42). Unscrambled, this reads and translates as:

Sic velut est arabu(m)	Just like the phoenix of Arabia,
Phenix avis unica tantum	A bird not like any other
Terra Britan(n)a suum genuit	The Land of Britain has produced
SKELTONIDA *vate(m)*	Its own poetic seer Skelton.[25]

When confronted with these lines, written in or on what the poem's speaker disingenuously calls a "tabull playne" (l. 222), the hawking priest is merely confounded, claiming that "for a crokyd intent, / The wordis were parvertyd" (l. 229).[26] This response is the hermeneutic equivalent of the priest's broader failure to read correctly the jurisdictional order dividing the space for hunting from the space ordered instead by the "spyrytuall law" (l. 156). For in Skelton's play of forms, his scrambled Latinity, if it is to make sense, must be subjected to a process of division (*divisio*) or redistribution of parts, a grammatical exercise that mirrors the politico-juridical division that Skelton perceives to be under threat from those, like the hawker, who no longer care or know how to distinguish among the territorial and conceptual orders that make up the real.²⁷ The "crokyd intent" that the hawking cleric attributes to Skelton's perverse text is, in reality, his own, his attack on Skelton's intentions being but a cover for his lack of skill and for his strategic subordination of the order of the real to his own hawkish desire.

The slightly surprising *content* of the message that the cleric fails to read adds a final cultural layer to Skelton's jurisdictional argument: as the fire out of which British vernacularity springs anew, Latinity becomes the linguistic form that makes Skelton's poetic authority, too, legible as a response to the narrowing territorialization of identity consequent on the present's forgetfulness of traditional orders.²⁸ Skelton's description of himself as *vates*, poet and national prophet, is especially relevant, since that projection of his poetic activity into the future is as much a polemic against the priest's debased present as are Skelton's Latin and his nod to antiquity. The past and future are both orders beyond the expertise of the hawking priest, a fool who, as one said to be "nothynge well *advysed*," (l. 37, emphasis added), remains only disoriented toward the future: "though ye lyve a c. yere, ye shal dy a daw," Skelton screeches (l. 334).

Skelton's reinvocation of the hawk in *Magnyfycence* thus places his dramatic treatment of the prerogative inside his own minor history of a poetic privilege emergent from and reactive to the ongoing process of state centralism. Unlike the hawk belonging to the wayward priest, the hawk that in *Magnyfycence* flies into an "olde barne" violates a purely secular jurisdiction, though one whose age similarly associates it with the customary past. This variation in Skelton's later treatment of territoriality is fully appropriate to the play's fiscal argument. The barn signifies as land or, more precisely, land revenue: it is a "room" that helps convert land from fixed asset into income. Invading the barn to pursue a rat, the hawk figures a prince who, in pursuit of a degraded version of the prerogative, violates a customary space associated with the land. The barn matters in Foly's tale because it links the debasement of royal identity to land, and because as a customary presence it orients past and present toward an implied future. In this last regard, I suggest further that the temporal structure of Foly's story informs the political allegory Skelton imagines. As Foly tells it, the crisis event at the center of the exemplary tale ("it happed that she ran . . . in to an olde barne") is grammatically dependent on a continuous activity in the past ("I have ben a hawking") and on a continuously present state ("My hawke is rammysshe"), even as it is oriented toward the futurity implied by Foly's fear for his hawk ("I could not her warne") and by his supposition as to her present health ("I warant her blode warme"). The hawk's action is a misguided and imprudent bargain with the complex order of time.

The connection among land, Crown identity, and time had been a political commonplace at least since Sir John Fortescue's *On the Governance of England*, a text written originally for the Lancastrian party in the 1440s but recast for presentation to Edward IV after the Yorkist victory of 1471.[29] Like Skelton's play, Fortescue's treatise is concerned with the question of how best to maintain the king's material resources and revenues, and again like the play it is concerned explicitly with magnificence, in both the Aristotelian sense of a liberal expenditure within the mean and the more general sense of glory or splendor in dress and appointments. Under the "extraordinary" or unpredictable expenses of royal life through which the "kynges estate shall alwey be kept unblemyshed," Fortescue describes household costs directly related to magnificence, as, for example, the "grete giftes" that the king must make available as befitting "the kynges magnificence and liberalite" and, more generally, "such tresour, as he mey make new bildynges whan he woll, ffor his pleasure and magnificence; and as he mey bie hym riche clothes . . . juels and ornamentes convenyent to his estate roiall."[30]

The concern to maintain the king's "estate roiall" (*status regis*), a concept roughly equivalent to royal rank or dignity, leads Fortescue to his central thesis, which explicitly links royal dignity to land and ultimately to a quite different kind of "estate"—namely, the interest in land that identifies the temporal relationship of a common-law tenant to the land of which he or she is possessed. The stability and dignity of the Crown, Fortescue argues, depend on the stability of Crown land and landed revenue across time, these being the necessary means whereby the king "mey best have sufficient and perdurable livelod ffor the sustentacion off his estate." To guarantee this stability, Fortescue recommends that there be reserved permanently to the Crown's use a reservoir of land capable of producing a continuous "livelod" for the king.[31] Second, as J. A. Guy explains, Fortescue aimed to "reduce the household element in government, in favor of a council of the principal office-holders in the realm."[32] To that end he recommends that, for the more efficient supervision of his land, the king create a working council with salaried members beholden to him alone, as well as a more efficient royal service run on the principle of "one man, one office," excepting those servants close to his person, for whom it will be permissible to "have in ther contrays a parkershippe ffor ther disporte whan thay come whom [home]."[33]

In their attention to fiscal stability and the shape of royal counsel, the two parts of Fortescue's polemic thus anticipate the argument Skelton makes in negative form through the dramatic representation of wicked servants who disperse a prince's wealth, even as they disperse his authority by concentrating all royal offices in their own hands: "chose out ii., iii., of such as you love best," Colusyon tells Magnyfycence; "Plucke from an hundred, and gyve it to thre" (ll. 1769, 1774). The connection between Skelton and Fortescue goes deeper than having the royal household as their shared polemical target. Fortescue stands at the beginning, and Skelton near the end, of a process that transformed Crown land from an almost ad hoc source of familial and household income into a major source of revenue and, consequently, into the principal site for the adjudication of royal dignity (*status regis*) with respect to the broader public interest (*status regni*).[34] When Skelton asks in his play how a man "may have welth . . . / Ay to contynewe and styll to endure" (ll. 14–15), the problem posed is thus identical in force to Fortescue's attempt to place household finances and royal dignity on a permanent footing for the common good.

In Skelton's play, therefore, the apparently generic and philosophical representation of Fortune, who "can bothe smyle and frowne, / Sodenly set up, and sodenly cast downe" (ll. 2529–30), has precise topical value in that it reproduces a nearly century-old political question of how to stabilize the "estate royal," such that its present health might signify, too, as future health. Similarly, Skelton's treatment of the interaction of the prince and his personified servants resonates with Fortescue's proposals to reform royal counsel. How, the play asks, can Measure have "domynyon" in the palace (l. 120) or Lyberte maintain "Magnyfycence" (l. 157)? How shall Largesse sustain "worshyp" (l. 267), "lordshype" (l. 286), the prince's "noble estate" (l. 308), and the "state ryall" (l. 383)? These are not only allegorical tasks: Skelton's characters are to be understood both as names and as bureaucrats. In these imagined relationships between servants and master, Skelton engages the question of royal status in terms both of the values personified by Magnyfycence's household men (largesse, liberty, measure, and so forth) and of the increasingly formalized relationships through which, as delegates, royal servants in Chamber were coming to govern the royal resources and so sustain the "noble estate" dependent on them. Returning briefly to Foly, we can note that the story he tells the prince establishes a somewhat unstable hierarchy of service, so that the hawk, in her misguided pursuit of the rat, can emblematize both prince and royal servant, just as Foly, as the one in charge of the hawk's royal flight, reads both as royal servant and as an emblem for the prince himself: between Crown and rat, there are three agents (prince, servant, hawk) or, emblematically, only one (prince-servant-hawk). The overlapping of signification is to the point, since the historical extension of the king's prerogative rights on the land depended on the system of bureaucratic representation that Fortescue recommended and the Tudors put in place.

As Skelton's representation of the space of the barn suggests, bureaucratic delegation, as a personalized expression of authority's extension, is closely related to the practice of jurisdiction, since both express authority as a spatio-temporal projection and processing of distributed power. Throughout the play, Skelton highlights the relationship between authority and the innovative territorialization of power, as when Magnyfycence warns Fansy and Lyberte to "loke that ye *occupye* the auctoryte that I you gave" (l. 1456; emphasis added). The implication here that delegation works as the delicate management of conceptual and physical space also underlies Skelton's use of the word *room* to mean "office," since inside the familiar usage Skelton consistently allows his audience to hear the spatial pun. When, for example, Fansy tells Countenaunce that he and Coneyaunce have "pycked out a rome for the," Countenaunce at first understands him to mean a place to live: "Why, shall we dwell togyder all thre" (ll. 508–9). Similarly, Colusyon mocks the gallant Abusyon for his outrageous dress and gestures by asking the audience to give him "rome, syrs. Stonde utter [farther apart]!" (l. 753), a pun in which the physical space of the stage is conflated with the bureaucratic space of the household the gallant stands ready to enter. As Walker has shown, Skelton carefully regulates dramaturgical movement and spatial orientation in the play, in order to reflect the jostling in the household for courtly position, royal favor, and grants.[35]

Most significant, I think, for this regulation and administration of "room" is the fact that Magnyfycence's reconfiguration of office institutes definite court hierarchies. The prince's ruin follows closely on his decision to make Colusyon "supervysour" over Fansy and Lyberte (ll. 1785, 1853), characters to whom the prince has earlier given authority over Felycyte (ll. 1409–56). In these linked hierarchical relationships, on whose peak Colusyon stands as "supervysor" and Conveyaunce as "Survayour" (l. 1862), Skelton carefully replicates the hierarchy of servants on whom the Tudors' fiscal policies depended, the professional officials under the centralized control of "surveyors," themselves the paradigmatic officers of an invigorated Chamber administration. To track the cultural implications of this political gesture on Skelton's part, I turn now to the place of the Chamber hierarchies in the administration of the Crown's landed revenue.

THE BUREAUCRATIC PREROGATIVE

In the early modern period, two kinds of Crown land—land in which the Crown had a direct fiscal interest—generated two distinct kinds of landed revenue.[36] First was the land held absolutely by the king, without his having granted it to a tenant; on such land, the Crown generated revenue by renting it out according to a lease for term of years, or by placing it "in fee farm," a kind of tenure in which the tenant paid only a perpetual fixed rent (without any associated service), in exchange for holding the land heritably or in fee. A second kind of Crown land included those feudal lands held by a subject immediately of the Crown according to a form of tenure that implicated the tenant in some now-obsolete feudal service and, more important, in certain intermittent fiscal obligations, the "incidents of tenure" owed the king as lord and overlord.[37] The Tudor Chamber was intimately involved with the management of both kinds of royal land: with the collection of rents payable to the Crown on the estates it held absolutely, and with the identification and collection of feudal revenues owed on land held by the Crown's tenants in chief. As B. P. Wolffe explains, revenue associated with Crown land had traditionally been directed through the Exchequer, the state office that collected and administered state revenue nationally. Under a system introduced by Edward IV in 1461, and perfected by Henry VII and Henry VIII, however, the Crown began to follow methods of private estate management, so successfully directing its landed revenue into Chamber that by 1509 the household controlled an astonishing 80 percent of all royal revenues and expenses nationally.[38] The great advantage of Chamber was its administrative flexibility. By circumventing the customary legal procedures of the Exchequer, the transfer of Crown lands into the equally centralized but less formal legal space of Chamber allowed both for more efficient accounting and—this was the principal attraction to Henry VII—for a massive accumulation of cash resources under direct supervision of the king, who was able to examine the books drawn up by his treasurer and Council, and approve them personally with the sign manual.[39]

The cultural consequences of the shift in revenue management from Exchequer to Chamber were multiple. Most obviously, it brought a new understanding of the royal demesne. While the demesne had once possessed a social and political value within a patronage economy (with the Exchequer overseeing the circulation of land as it accrued to the king and was then granted away to subjects for services rendered), Chamber policies converted the demesne increasingly into a direct source of revenue for the Crown. Second, Chamber brought with it a new kind of bureaucracy. While the Exchequer assigned revenues through a system of tallies, and relied on local sheriffs for the collection of debt, collection of royal revenue in Chamber depended on a hierarchical system of specialized officials who oversaw the methodical transfer of local revenue into the central treasury. These officials dealt directly with cash, recording the transfer of funds between bureaucratic levels by written indenture. The reeves or bailiffs responsible for manorial accounts transferred the money they collected to regional "receivers," who turned over the funds to the treasurer of the Chamber. The auditing of accounts was similarly structured, local examinations being consolidated into a general summary by a central committee of the King's Council, which under Henry VIII was known as the office and court of the general surveyors and, as such, came to have investigative jurisdiction over Crown lands.[40]

Third and most important, the system of land management in Chamber can be said to have nurtured a new conception of royal agency with respect to the land. In the traditional system, where the Exchequer identified royal lands and revenues for the purposes of distribution, the land forged a relationship between king and subject by mediating the king's agency as grantor and the subject's agency as one bound to act for him into the future. Chamber finance depended on a very different model of agency, one that in its own way was even more personalized. Underwriting the principle that the king should "live on his own," the land now mediated a relationship between the king and himself, between the king and the personal agents or *representatives* on whom he depended as lord to collect, administer, and account for his personal revenue. Like the agency of the subject to whom Crown land might once have been granted, the agency of the receiver and surveyor was necessary to the constitution of royal agency on the land. But whereas in the first case the land constituted a reciprocal obligation between related parties, in the second it created a nonreciprocal relationship in which royal agency was reiterated in the specialized office of royal servant and land agent. There is a paradox here, one shaped by the very idea of a personal bureaucracy. As specialized servants of the Crown, the receiver and surveyor embodied the power of a *centralized* version of royal right—through these servants, in effect, the king was able to claim his own as his own—even as they exposed the fragility of a *personalized* center so wholly dependent on the officer delegate.

Skelton's play about a corrupt royal household, therefore, dates to a period in which royal right with respect to the land of the subject was being institutionalized by means of Chamber's rapid transformation into a national and specialized bureaucracy. Of particular interest in Skelton's representation of administrative culture is the play's attention to the *technical* outlines of Tudor bureaucracy as a way to unfold the ideological import of those administrative developments. The success of the Tudors in bringing about innovative political ends through a traditional vocabulary and traditional forms is clearest in relation to Chamber's control over the second kind of Crown lands, those feudal lands on which the king, as the major part of his prerogative, had certain fiscal claims as both sovereign and lord.[41] Under the program that has come to be called fiscal feudalism, the early Tudors pressed these feudal claims as never before in order to extract money from their tenants in chief; Skelton's play draws its principal energies from this part of Tudor practice.

Two of the most valuable incidents of tenure, primer seisin and wardship, exemplify the mechanics of the program and the place of bureaucratic culture in it. When a capital tenant holding by military service died, the heir being of full age, the king was entitled to full possession of the land, since the heir could have no possession or "seisin" until, "after homage done and relief paid, he formally received his land out of the king's hand."[42] By right of primer seisin, the king received the first year's profit on the land, after which payment the heir could formally sue by livery to be possessed fully of his or her inheritance. If the heir was in his or her minority, the king was entitled to wardship both of the tenant's lands and of the heir's body and sometimes highly profitable marriage. Unlike primer seisin, a privilege pertaining only to the Crown, wardship was a right that all feudal lords could claim when a tenant died, the original theory being that the lord must hold the land until an heir could fully render the obligatory feudal service. The extraordinary value of wardship to the Crown, however, lay in two peculiarities specific to the royal privilege. By virtue of the prerogative, royal claims to wardship superseded those of any other lord from whom the tenant held. Moreover, the Crown was entitled "not only to the wardship of the land held by the deceased tenant of him in capite," a right pertaining to the king simply as feudal lord, "but also to the wardship of all lands the tenant had held by knight service of others."[43] This side of prerogative wardship meant that a large inheritance might come under the king's control even when the Crown had a direct feudal relation to only a tiny piece of it.

Although in theory consonant with a traditional common-law understanding of the prerogative, the scope of Tudor claims on their feudal lands was highly innovative, as was the fervor with which the Crown deployed the newly personalized Chamber bureaucracy to achieve these expanded fiscal ends. The potential legalistically to exploit prerogative rights encouraged Henry VII and Henry VIII to search out their tenants in chief (not always an easy task), and also actively to increase the number of those tenants. At the simplest level, the value of feudal incidents encouraged the continuation of tenures such as knight service that were outmoded long before the Tudor period.[44] A custom developed in Chancery, moreover, allowed tenants to alienate lands held in chief, but required them always to hold onto some small part of those lands. This was a legal maneuver that allowed the Crown to retain the original tenant in chief (over whose entire holdings the prerogative would still extend), even as it brought the Crown a new capital tenant and thus the potential in the future to receive feudal incidents on his or her lands as well.[45] As another way to increase the pool, the early Tudor administrators extended the concept of tenant in chief to include not only those who held *land* of the king, but also those who held heritable but incorporeal rights: Crown offices such as a wardenship, for example, or royal franchises granting them wreck (the rights to goods washed up on shore) or the right to oversee a local market or court-leet.[46]

Nothing was more important for the increased exploitation of the prerogative than the complex chamber bureaucracy that developed to deal with the problem of identifying, pursuing, and maintaining the king's feudal claims. From the first year of his reign, Henry VII sent out formal commissions to identify concealed lands held in chief and to collect such fines and dues as were owed the king according to the prerogative.[47] Departmental specialization followed, with appointments of surveyors, for example, in the newly formed office of wards, to oversee royal wardships and identify lands subject to that prerogative.[48] From 1505 Edmund Dudley, Richard Empson, and Edward Belknap were given the task specifically of collecting fines and taking obligations on outstanding feudal debts to the Crown.[49] In 1508 Henry VII attempted further to rationalize the Chamber administration by appointing Belknap to the wholly innovative office of general "supervisor" or surveyor of the king's prerogative. As W. C. Richardson explains, the office came with a very broad jurisdiction, and Belknap was allowed to appoint under his direct control "as many county surveyors as were needed to assist him"; within a few months, remarkably, the office had "fifteen deputy surveyors, distributed among eighteen different counties."[50]

Upon the accession of Henry VIII in 1509, there were signs that the exploitation of the prerogative might change. Most notoriously, the king had Empson and Dudley executed. Edward Hall, in his chronicle history of Henry VII, identifies these royal servants as particularly enthusiastic "masters of the forfaytures" who enriched their king through confiscations and fines levied unjustly against those whose lands fell within the scope of the royal prerogative.[51] Moreover, Henry VIII suspended Belknap's general surveyorship, formally abolishing it in 1513.[52] In the long term, however, Crown policy did not bear out these early royal initiatives. After 1512 the departmental differentiation of Chamber actually accelerated, going well beyond what Henry VII had been able to achieve. Thus Belknap's bureaucratic responsibilities were simply reabsorbed by the offices of wards and audit that had originally been responsible for them.[53] Across the next decade, for reasons of efficiency, Henry and Wolsey further divided Chamber according to specialized function, so that by the 1520s there were several formal prerogative offices, many of which, in the post-Reformation period, would develop into full-fledged administrative courts of record. Accordingly, the office of audit received statutory recognition in 1512, and from that time was known formally as the office of general surveyors of the king's lands.[54] It expanded quickly, and gave rise to separate departments such as the surveyorship of woods, an office created in 1521.[55] Wards, too, became more fully differentiated. From 1520, the masters of wards were known as "surveyors," a more prestigious title since "a surveyorship commonly carried with it full authority over inferior personnel, as well as responsibility for formulating the policies of the department."[56] Further specialization took place across the 1520s, and in 1540 the administrative court of wards and liveries was created out of the two chamber offices. The administrative court of general surveyors was formed in 1542.

For the landowners of England, the Crown's manipulation of a traditional order meant that a public culture of distributed interest was being transformed into a bureaucratic culture for organizing and managing chiefly one interest. That transition carried very broad cultural implications, since far more clearly than in the case of the Crown's absolute estates, the king's claims on his feudal lands threatened to polarize Crown and public.[57] No longer contained by custom or, as was the case through the fifteenth century, by the king's inability to pursue his claims, the royal prerogative weighed as never before on the early Tudor consciousness, and in a new way. With the bureaucratization of Chamber, the experience of that prerogative was the experience, not of theory, but rather of royal *office* and of those rapidly proliferating officers whose purpose was to extend a spatio-temporal complex of rights centered in the king: rights over particular parcels of land, both now and into the future. Confronted with the local surveyor, the escheator, the royal commissioner, the general surveyor, or the feodary from the office of wards, landowners were made aware, as never before, of the nature of delegated power and of that power's unruly projection into the future as, terrifyingly, an uncontrollable fiscal potential.

Magnyfycence is a play about these royal delegates and the disruptive time of their action. In the context of the Tudor Chamber's administrative work, it is telling, first, that household service in the play constantly drifts toward questions of tenure and land. That slippage in reference governs, for example, Magnyfycence's declaration to Courtly Abusyon, in the language of common-law tenure, that "in my favour I have you feffyd and seasyd" (l. 1536). The association is pronounced, too, in the names given certain of the prince's counselors, since these invoke the bureaucracy that facilitated the Tudors' revenue programs. Crafty Conveyaunce enters the court as Sure Surveyaunce, both names being intimately connected to land. Conveyance (which the play uses primarily in the sense of stealing) denotes the legal transfer of property, usually land, while Surveyaunce—he is also called a "Survayour" (l. 1862)—identifies a general overseer of the prince's land. As we have seen, however, in 1520 the latter name would have been associated specifically with the Chamber officers responsible for the exploitation of the Crown privileges. Rather than identifying Conveyaunce with a particular office in the household administration, the false name "Sure Surveyaunce" bestows on him the paradigmatic Chamber office. Within the national structures of surveillance that grounded the early Tudor prerogative, Conveyaunce/Surveyaunce's names together articulate the specular mechanics through which the Crown, as surely as through legal transfer, was in one construction of its activity able craftily to transfer others' property to itself.

Another of Skelton's names, which depends for its effect on the poet's familiar mixing of Latin with the English and French vernaculars, similarly attacks a royal household whose energies are directed not only inward to the prince's full coffers but outward, too, onto the land that generates Crown revenue and sustains the estate royal. The name "Good Demeynaunce," the identity assumed by Counterfet Countenaunce, implies good behavior, but also the false promise of a well-ordered domain or (in the orthography of law French) "demeyne" or "demesne."[58] Skelton highlights Countenaunce's relation to territorial limits at the very moment he receives his new name from Crafty Conveyaunce:

Cou. Cou.   But then, syr, what shall I hyght? . . .
Cra. Con.   And nowe it cometh to my remembraunce.
              Syr, ye shall hyght Good Demeynaunce.
Cou. Cou.   By the armes of Calys, well conceyved. (ll. 669–75)

There are two jokes here, one spatial and one temporal. First, Calais is Skelton's analysis of the relation of territorial jurisdiction to royal status. In the *Governance of England,* Fortescue includes the "kepyng of Caleis" among the king's ordinary charges for the "yerely mayntenance of his estate."[59] At the margin of royal influence, and as both a fiscal drain and the last remaining part of the Crown's feudal holdings on the continent, Calais territorially symbolizes the extent of royal lands and the difficulties of maintaining royal status through those lands. The oath that Countenaunce invokes as a guarantee of his new name thus pulls to the semantic surface the association of "demeynaunce" with the royal demesne, as well as the point that royal status is being effected on such lands by those who manage the household that Counterfet Countenaunce stands ready to enter and corrupt. Second, Crafty Conveyance says that "Demeynance" is a name that "nowe," suddenly, "cometh to my remembrance." This is Skelton's temporal analysis of the Tudors' administrative construction of what was de facto an innovative demesne inside the remembered form of the old one. For Conveyance's remembrance is really creative practice: in the king's past, we might say, he is remembering the king's disastrous future.

In the Chamber economy, spending is stealing. Thus when Fansy tells Magnyfycence that Clokyd Colusyon has stolen his goods, he says that the prince is "undone with stelyng and robbynge" (l. 1852), meaning both that the vice-characters have stolen from the prince and, with equal plausibility, that the prince's own stealing has finally caught up with him. Skelton encapsulates the link between fiscal expenditure and fiscal appropriation through Adversyte, who, after the prince has come to ruin, identifies the regulation of the household with the regulation of national territory:

> *Adv.* For I stryke lordys of realmes and landys
> That rule not be [by] mesure that they have in theyr handys,
> That sadly rule not theyr howsholde men. (ll. 1938–40)

So a "sad" or serious order within the household is needed to ward off "Adversyte" to the extent that household excess has repercussions across the lord's "realmes and landys." Skelton analyzes this connection between the domestic and national spaces through a pun on "rule." "Mesure" is the virtuous mean by which a prince should exercise his authority, but as a measure that lords "have in theyr handys" it also means a measuring rod or measuring rule.[60] The prince who rules well will rule well. Moreover, the repetition of "rule" in lines 1939–40 creates an appositional structure that identifies the household men whom the lord ought to rule with the very measure by which lords rule or should rule their "realmes and landys." As measurement, the administrative work of the royal household identifies household excess with the household's unmeasured measurement of territory. Magnyfycence finds adversity according to two metrics, by spending too much (money) and by ruling off too much (land).

In the economy of the play, indeed, Magnyfycence's spending is almost secondary to his excessive taking. The prince loses his "felycyte," as Lyberte insists, "Not thorowe largesse of lyberall expence, / But by the way of fansy insolence" (ll. 2114-16), where "insolence" denotes specifically a contempt for inferiors. In other words, the prince's largesse becomes excessive only at the point where it deforms his sense of his status in relation to his subjects. In light of Lyberte's moral, it is notable that Skelton represents the vice-characters' misuse of the prince's wealth almost invariably as the prince's and counselors' conspiratorial theft of another's resources. When, for example, the recently exiled Measure attempts through the offices of Colusyon to reenter the prince's service, Magnyfycence is interested only in whether Colusyon has been paid a bribe for providing access to the royal presence. "Yes," Colusyon replies, "With his hande I made hym to subscrybe / A byll of recorde for an annuall rent (ll. 1666-67). Here instanced is the legalistic appropriation of land revenue into a permanently hobbling future. Elsewhere, the prince's rapacity is even more clearly delineated. Soon after gaining Magnyfycence's confidence, Colusyon tells him:

> *Clo. Col.* With pollynge and pluckynge out of all measure,
> Thus must ye stuffe and store your treasure.
>
> Plucke from an hundred, and gyve it to thre;
> Let neyther patent scape them nor fee; . . .
> For them shall you have at lyberte to lowte
> Let them have all, and the other go without.
> (ll. 1753-54; 1775-80)

Skelton's diction underscores his critique of royal appropriations. "Pollynge," a word for extortion closely linked to the king's or his commissioners' oppression of his subjects (OED 3), and "plucke" both resonate with the unjust appropriation of property by the king. Hall uses the phrase "this pluckyng bancket [banquet]" to refer to the most notorious of the new royal servants, Empson and Dudley, and to their legalistic exploitation of one of the penal laws for financial gain.[61] The ghosts of Empson and Dudley probably also haunt Colusyon's promise to Magnyfycence that he and his "felowes twayne" will do the prince "servyce after your appetite" (ll. 1791-93), "appetite" being here a powerfully personalized expression of the king's fiscal rapacity. For in the contemporary imagination, it was the king's appetite specifically that motivated his two counselors' intemperate exploitation of traditional prerogative rights: "And these twoo persons contented [contended], whiche of theim by mooste bryngyng in myght most please and satisfye his masters desyre and appetide."[62]

The most dramatic example of royal theft in the play involves Felycyte, who, according to the play's personifications, stands for the prince's own accumulated wealth. In the passage in which he is committed to the supervision of Lyberte and Fansy/Largesse, however, he behaves most like an unfortunate subject whose wealth has come within the scope of the prince's too ample intention:

Fan.	What! Shall we Have welth at our guydinge to rule as we lyst? Then fare well thryfte, by him that crosse kyst!
Fel.	I truste your grace wyll be agreabyll That I shall suffer none impechment By theyr demenaunce, nor loss repryvable.
Magn.	Syr, ye shall folowe myne appetyte and intent. (ll. 1414-20)

The various terms in the passage—*guiding, loss, impeachment* (that is, a material injury), *intent*—operate with equal force along two allegorical axes. Fansy/Largesse and Lyberte allegorically embody the prince's unruly appetite, and as such participate in a story of royal spending; but as royal servants, they steal from Felycyte and thus participate in a story about royal taking. A simple insight into the constitution of Crown and state issues from this doubled narrative. When Magnyfycence steals from Felycyte, he robs himself, and equally so whether Felycyte stands for the king's property or for the subject's. As Fortescue also had insisted, Skelton's play argues that the "state ryall" depends both on the king's coffers and, nationally, on the regulation of royal land according to norms that protect the king's status and also that of his landholding subjects.

DOCUMENTARY RECORD AND ROYAL PRIVILEGE

If *Magnyfycence* locates its central political theme in the public impact of Chamber administration and its promotion of Crown privilege, that is because the practical bureaucratization of Chamber had theoretical consequences. As I have already suggested, beyond the landholder's quite appropriate horror of falling within the king's grasp, the Tudor fiscal program entailed also the beginning of a shift in the understanding of the royal prerogative itself. To the extent that the Crown's legal strategies were effective for bringing more and more landholders within the scope of the prerogative, feudal rights such as primer seisin came to attach themselves to the landholding subject more personally and more diffusely than ever before. In the seventeenth-century language of Nathaniel Bacon, Henry "taught the People to dance more often and better to the tune of Prerogative and Allegiance than all his Predecessors had done."[63] Although it speaks to a later, more tumultuous period in the history of the royal prerogative, Bacon's language also captures the crucial point that, whatever its roots in ordinary custom, bureaucratic feudalism made the early Tudor prerogative a felt intrusion of the king and his "state ryall" onto the subject's own estate.

The culture could not but react to the evolving construction of the prerogative. In 1495, for example, as readers at Lincoln's Inn and the Inner Temple, Robert Constable and Thomas Frowyk turned their attention to *De Prerogativa Regis*, the early fourteenth-century document that spells out the traditional rights Henry VII was learning to exploit. Samuel Thorne points out that no readings on *Prerogativa Regis* survive from before Henry VII's accession.[64] This is unsurprising, given that readings were so often motivated by local concerns: they were legal conversations that confronted an emergent issue by reinvigorating some legal text (usually statutory) whose original meanings had been superseded by practice.[65] In much the same way as Constable's and Frowyk's readings do for the legal subculture, Skelton's dramatic engagement with Crown privilege constitutes a cultural reckoning with the process through which the public shape of royal privilege was changing, with the traditional prerogative coming to accrue an untraditional meaning not unlike the personal preeminence that Henry VIII would claim in the early 1530s as he was learning to reimagine his status in relation to the Church. With the work of the new Chamber administration, the public became more centralized, even as the intimate was coopted for the public: at the boundary between Exchequer and Chamber the prerogative was beginning to express itself as the devolution of legal oversight from a formal court of record back onto the king, whose modern authority would now be manifested as the reabsorption of a formal jurisdiction and, then, its controlled and personalized redistribution onto individually vulnerable subjects through executive delegation.

Skelton engages the more theoretical side of this double-edged bureaucratic personalism through his analysis of the impact of writing on the integrity of the royal self. If the early Tudor prerogative was the culture and experience of the commissioners, auditors, and surveyors through whom the king tested his royal privilege, it was also the experience of *paper* (and skin), of all the documentary records through which the king's feudal claims could be queried, noted, audited, acknowledged, or circumvented. Paper in the play is the very language of illicit seizure, the material surface on which the state imagines the form and formula of its next appropriation. Nowhere are the administrative implications of Magnyfycence's surrendering Felycyte to Lyberte and Fansy clearer than in Skelton's focused use of the language of official record. Addressing Fansy, Magnyfycence says:

> *Magn.* Take of his [Felycyte's] substaunce a sure inventory,
> And get you home togyther; for Lyberte shall byde
> And wayte upon me.
> *Lyb.* And yet for a memory,
> Make indentures how ye and I shal gyde.
> *Fan.* I can do nothynge but he stonde besyde,
> *Lyb.* Syr, we can do nothynge the one without the other. (ll. 1445–50)

In terms of the complex function that record-making had in Chamber, this exchange allegorizes the moment of surveillance and appropriation that Tudor landowners most feared. The inventory Magnyfycence requests is a list of Felycyte's (and so, allegorically, his own) household goods, but it is also the list of real and personal property compiled at a person's death; it is the document, therefore, through which the escheator or local surveyor could determine the extent of royal privilege on a tenant's property. An indenture is a deed or contract, executed in duplicate, with each half carrying a notched edge for the purpose of authentication. And as a documentary means of surveillance, indentures underwrote the entire Chamber system, whether in recording the hierarchical transfer of cash to the center, or effecting a commission to act as agent of the prerogative. So the indentures in Skelton's passage contain a commission, formally written out in order to record the precise hierarchy of power. A translation of *memorandum*, Lyberte's "for a memory" alludes to the tag used at the head of specific entries in record books such as those of the Exchequer and Chamber; in the less formal Chamber records, the memorandum was particularly important for keeping track of the formal indentures filed in Chancery. In sum, the passage defines the prince's delegation of authority as a surveillance of the subject (Felycyte) through a bureaucracy (Lyberte and Fansy) that in turn requires formal scrutiny (by indenture). Since the prince has just asked Lyberte to stay and wait on him, the further implication is that Lyberte, corrupted by the vice-counselors, may be requesting the indenture as a way to protect his own interests (and only secondarily the king's) against Fansy. The document here answers the threat of disorder in the sense of guarding against it, but also rationalizes that disorder by giving it formal cover.

The attitude toward the legal document here is fully continuous, therefore, with the late medieval distrust of documents as instruments of legal mischief and signs of a pervasive ethical corruption. M. T. Clanchy identifies this distrust with the problem of forgery and authentication, while Richard Firth Green links it to the proliferation of written instruments, as that caused a depersonalization of contractual relationships and a crisis in the notion of "trouthe" itself, in the sense both of contractual faith and of truth.[66] The production of written documents elsewhere in *Magnyfycence* invariably carries the same negative connotations as the documents that bring Felycyte to ruin. Indeed, Skelton's whole plot depends on Fansy's presenting Magnyfycence with a "wrytynge of recorde / . . . closed under sele" (ll. 309–12), a letter of recommendation purportedly written by the king's loyal counselor Sad Cyrcumspeccyon, but in fact forged by Counterfet Conveyaunce. Conveyaunce's letter powerfully testifies in the play to a new way of imagining legal and social relationships, as Lerer argues when, connecting the forged document to the epistolary politics of Henrician courtiership, he designates it as the "nodal point of privacy and power, diplomacy and desire, for the play."[67] The letter has further and more technical legal resonances: as a record under seal, the letter is strikingly formal, more public than private, a point that Magnyfycence highlights when at the end of the play he remembers the offending document as "a letter sent, / Whiche conteyned in it *a specyall clause* / That I sholde use largesse" (ll. 2435–37; emphasis added). The lesson here is that writing deceives when it becomes specialized through the growth of textual formalism.

In *Magnyfycence*, legal documents are dangerous in ways similar to that of the letter that cannot faithfully be traced back to its sender. So it is worth remembering that in an important sense the two were the same, and that the letter was materially at the very center of English legal culture. The writ (law Lat. *breve*; law Fr. *brefe*) that was issued in Chancery, and through which all proceedings at common law were initiated, was a "thin strip of parchment containing a letter in the name of the king, usually written in Latin, and sealed with the great seal"; in this letter, the king ordered someone (for example, a sheriff or judge) to attend to some particular legal business on his behalf.[68] The document through which Fansy traps Magnyfycence and brings him to ruin is modeled on a royal writ: it is a sealed letter; and apparently it is also in Latin, at least if we take Fansy's calling it a "wrytynge of recorde" seriously. Since legal proceedings became a final and permanent record only when they were transcribed in Latin on parchment rolls, Latin was the principal linguistic sign of a document's status *as* formal record.

This linguistic point casts light on the documentary implications of a remarkable passage later in the play, one of the very few instances in which a vice-character uses Latin. When Foly boastfully proclaims to Conveyaunce and Fansy how talented a scoundrel he is, his language is unusually disorienting:

> *Fol.* For, frantyke Fansy, thou makyst men madde;
> And I Foly bryngeth them to *qui fuit* gadde;
> With *qui fuit* brayne seke I have them brought;
> From *qui fuit aliquid* to shyre shakynge nought. (ll. 1300–1303)

Paula Neuss convincingly glosses "gadde" as "goad" in the sense of torment. But a "gad" is also a measuring rod for land. To paraphrase the passage, Foly is thus saying that he torments men with "*qui fuit*" or, alternatively, that he makes them measure their land with that "who was." In this way, he continues, he brings them from a status of "one who was something" to perfect deprivation.

Taken together, and in a way that has not been understood, the lines are a virtuoso legal joke about the Latin documents through which the Tudors extended their feudal rights on the land. In the insistently repeated "*qui fuit*," Skelton alludes to the legal processes whereby ownership and possession were established at law, and specifically to the legal writ through which the king exercised and exploited his prerogative. When a tenant in chief died, Chancery issued a writ of *diem clausit extremum*, in which the king directed the local escheator to hold an inquisition "to discover exactly what lands he held, of whom, and on what day he died, and who and how old was his heir; this information would enable the seizure of whatever was due to the king as feudal lord."[69] That writ begins by stating both the fact of the tenant's death and the nature of the tenurial and social relationship that has prompted the inquisition. The way it formulaically places the now dead subject in a grammatical past is highly pertinent to Foly's "*qui fuit*": "Because, as we understand it, J. who held of us in chief [*qui de nobis tenuit in capite*] has died [*diem clausit extremum*], we order you without delay to take into our hands all lands and tenements of which the said J. was seised in his demesne as of fee [*de quibus idem I. fuit seisitus in domenico suo ut de feodo*]."[70] An alternative version of the writ was applicable upon the death of a woman whose dower lands (that portion of her husband's estate allowed her for life) included lands held in chief. The resonance with Foly's phrase is more pronounced here: "Because J. who was the wife of B., now dead [*Quia I. quae fuit uxor B. defuncti*] and who held in dower certain lands through inheritance from the aforesaid B, her late husband."[71] In "*qui fuit*" and "*qui fuit aliquid*," Skelton invokes the strategic temporalities of common law, parodying the legal formulas like "*qui tenuit*," "*de quibus fuit seisitus*," and "*quae fuit uxor*" that specified the king's exploitable relationship with his dead subject. The connection between Skelton's Latin and that of the legal writ makes sense of Foly's puzzling boast and its quibble on "gadde." "*Qui fuit*" is both a torment (these are not the words an heir wants to hear) and a surveyor's measuring rod (these are the words by which the Crown craftily stakes its territorial claims). For Foly to bring men from "*qui fuit aliquid*" to nothing at all is thus Skelton's morbid analysis of how Chamber policy exploits the tenant's reduction to material nothingness at death in order to reduce the heir, also, to a state of material deprivation. In Skelton's "*qui fuit*," then, we are hearing how Chamber works to "teach" the past, in Nathaniel's Bacon's phrasing, "to dance more often and better to the tune" of a disjointed future.

Since the written records in *Magnyfycence* invoke a politics of legalistic intrusion and surveillance, it can come as no surprise that the play ultimately teaches the prince to substitute new texts for old. In his penitential interrogation of the ruined prince, Redresse asks Magnyfycence to say more about the letter purportedly sent from Sad Cyrcymspeccyon: "Yet let us se this matter thorowly ingrosed" (l. 2438). The legal point here is that to engross something means to order it specifically by expressing it in a formal legal document (originally, one written in large letters). Skelton thus registers Magnyfycence's testimony before the sage counselors as a legal document, making the prince's repentance a process of substituting for the counterfeit textuality of Fansy's forged letter the reformed textuality of an "ingrossed" matter. Insofar as the textual matter that counters bad writing is spoken, the play is also teaching Magnyfycence to distinguish between kinds of texts, and to eschew writing in favor of a performative speech embodied not least by the poetic speech of Skelton's own play. "Syr, the repentaunce I have no man can wryte" (l. 2392), he tells Redresse, thereby offering a critique of his behavior in relation to the corruptible medium of writing that has encouraged and sustained it. The specialization of writing gives way to living memory and the inexpressibility of conscience.

In a speech to the audience in which he expounds the lesson of the play, Redresse makes just this point, using a legal vocabulary to turn the specialized legality the play has represented once more on its head:

> *Redr.* Unto this processe brefely compylyd,
> Comprehendynge the worlde casuall and transytory,
> Who lyst to consyder shall never be begylyd,
> Yf it be regystryd well in memory;
> A playne example of worldly vaynglory,
> Howe in this worlde there is no sekernesse,
> But fallyble flatery enmyxed with bytternesse. (ll. 2510–16)

"Processe" means both a narrative and a legal proceeding, while to register something is to set it down formally in writing, specifically in a formal collection (such as the register of writs available to the common law). Most important here is the metadramatic energy of the lines. By having Redresse praise the efficacy of "*this* processe brefely compylyd" (emphasis added), Skelton is opposing his own dramatic text, as legal process, to the writing that brings Magnyfycence and the royal estate to ruin. If Magnyfycence is wrong to think that documents protect him from Fortune's "lawys" (l. 1459), Skelton argues that his own play can be trusted as a way to "comprehend" and so order the world of fortune: as James Simpson acutely notes, the play here recommends a "proper balance of discursive freedoms," and insists that "the play itself . . . is the proper thing wherewith to catch the conscience of the king."[72] As opposed to those writings in which Magnyfycence disastrously places his trust, here Skelton's own text is effective because it is registered, through dramatic performance, in memory, rather than on paper: while writing signals a record's inauthentic manipulation of time or space, poetic drama becomes the formal expression of an efficacious juridical process and of a just accounting of time. And it is in just this sense that Redresse can favorably describe his (and Skelton's) process as one that has been "brefely compylyd," a phrase that means both *concisely* ordered (with no undue claim on time) and ordered as a legal brief (Law Fr. *brefe*), the letter or writ, issued out of Chancery, through which one initiated a legal action. As a virtuous representation of action, then, the play finds its authority by functioning itself as writ, as a memorable document that initiates a virtuous action against a political culture that is going wrong.

WARRANTING THE KING

The thesis that memory and conscience are somehow better than writing is as important to the play's configuration of royal authority as is the more explicit thesis that "measure is treasure." But if writing in the play is that which cannot be trusted—the letter is forged; the written record underwrites only legalism, not law—that is for Skelton a point not so much about writing in general as about its effect specifically on the constitution of royal authority. Writing in the play facilitates the delegation or transfer of authority to the royal officer or representative. More generally, it can be said that writing itself is the delegate, the formal expression of an authorizing intention that always resides elsewhere. The imperfection of the written as a vehicle of meaning is that of the centralizing bureaucracy that perilously extends a personalized royal authority outward.

The play locates the connection between writing and the trustworthiness of authority in a term that denotes a kind of legal document and carries a broader ethical significance for the problem of delegation. Skelton uses *warrant* eight times in *Magnyfycence*, only as a verb and always in the colloquial sense "to guarantee as true." Given that he uses the word nowhere else in his work, Skelton's use of *warrant* in *Magnyfycence* is anything but casual, carrying a specific topical resonance important for the overall analysis of the new meaning of royal privilege. A warrant is simply a guarantee, but the relationship among the word's more and less specialized meanings traces, in part, the impact of writing technology on the idea of the guarantee as it relates to trust.[73] As a technical term, it signifies both a superior's or sovereign's command or permission and the token of that permission: a documentary warrant is twice a guarantee, referring to the person or body that authorizes an action and to the external written evidence of that authority or authorization. The warrant thus presents in small the question of bureaucratic and jurisdictional delegation I have been pursuing throughout this chapter: what does it mean to embody authority in an instrument, written or living, beyond the self?

Like writing, the warrant is associated only with Skelton's vice-characters, and since they alone use the word, it comes to carry a connotation opposed to its literal meaning. Their insistence on attesting to the truth of their words variously undermines both their trustworthiness and that of the fact being so warranted.[74] Along with the religious oaths that litter the courtiers' speech, warranting belongs to a rhetoric of trust that expands, then, in proportion to the absence in the speaker of any true ethical center. In his important study of social representations in the fourteenth century, Paul Strohm has analyzed the importance of false swearing for the construction of the public or social sphere. In Chaucer's work, for example, he identifies a given character's propensity for oaths specifically with the debasement of the "trouthe" guaranteeing feudal bonds into the self-interest of those relationships rooted instead in shifting affinities and the cynicism of a falsely "sworn brotherhood."[75] In *Magnyfycence*, Skelton adapts that earlier Chaucerian argument to the language of the contemporary court. An important scene at the end of the play stages the violent rending of language from any honor or action that might give it meaning. After Magnyfycence's fall, and in their final appearance in the play, Colusyon and Conveyaunce come onstage, laughing and gloating over their plot's success (ll. 2160–70). A quarrel breaks out over which of them is the more talented in crime; they exchange increasingly heated words (ll. 2171–97), until Countenaunce enters and attempts to reason with them (ll. 2198–2236). Unity is reinstated only when Magnyfycence, now a beggar, confronts them. They curse him and then, comrades once more, retreat to a tavern, where Skelton leaves them (ll. 2237–76). In the seventy-seven lines before Magnyfycence makes himself known, the quarrelling knaves deliver a total of twenty-two pledges and oaths.[76] Their argument reaches its highest pitch at the point where Skelton juxtaposes oath and warrant in a bravura display of verbal excess:

> *Cra. Con.* Goddys fote! I warant you I am a gentylman borne;
> And thus to be facyd, I thynke it great skorne. . . .
> *Clo. Col.* By God, I tell you, I wyll not be out facyd.
> *Cra. Con.* By the masse, I warant the, I wyll not be bracyd. (ll. 2216–21)

Each of the three religious oaths ("Goodys fote"; "By God"; "By the masse") is paired with a pledge of trustworthiness ("I warant you"; "I tell you"; "I warant the"). This second and redundant pledge works to expose how far the words of the three primary oaths have detached themselves from the faith that apparently guarantees their meaning: as opposed to the trust that should underwrite their speech and action, it is now only their "wyll" that grounds the concept of gentility to which their oaths testify. Part of a language that means only through reference to itself, their "warrants" thus resemble the circular language of Foly, the fool whose words, as Magnyfycence says, "hange togyder as fethers in the wynde" (l. 1818).

Skelton's repetition of *warrant* inevitably allows its legal connotations to surface. To warrant a fact or to warrant land is equally to invoke as guarantee a legitimating ground capable of compassing that which is warranted: when you warrant a fact, you invoke your own trustworthiness; when you warrant land to another at its conveyance, the guarantee comes in the form of the covenant (or "warranty") that binds you to surrender property of equal value in the event that the title should fail. In the early Tudor period, however, the authority that would have paradigmatically been associated with the warrant was the king himself. In the context of the rapid consolidation of legal authority under the Tudors, the warrant was the expression of a central authorizing body. When, therefore, Colusyon proposes that Magnyfycence take money from his subjects in order to enrich his favorites, the audience is meant to hear how odd it is for Colusyon to tell the prince to "use your largesse by the advyse of me, / And I shall waraunt you welth and lyberte" (ll. 1765-66). The unsettling element here is that the warrant is more the prince's than the courtier's; conceptually, it is the prince's to give, not to receive. Colusyon's speech thus emblematizes what principally has gone wrong at court: the process of delegation through which the prince means to protect his estate has allowed his authority to be coopted when it should only be represented. Skelton's characterization of the distorted relationship between king and delegate in terms of warranting is apt; as a guarantee that casts meaning onto an authority resident elsewhere, the warrant, like the courtier, exemplifies the dangers involved in a prince's too trusting diffusion of himself into the mere instruments of his power.

That Colusyon warrants Magnyfycence both wealth and "lyberte" resonates powerfully, too, with the contemporary legal culture. Just as the bill of record, writ, and register signify administrative specialization at the court and in Chamber, Skelton's warrants satirize a specific mode of jurisdictional centralization that became controversial around 1519. In that year, the government issued a general summons of *quo warranto* in Middlesex, this being, in John Cowell's later definition, "a writ that lyeth against him, which usurpeth any *Frawnchis* or libertie against the king... without good title."[77] A franchise or liberty (Lat. *libertas*) is a jurisdictional privilege granted by the sovereign to a person or corporation, and by association the domain or territory over which that privilege extends. The liberty that Colusyon warrants the king can thus be identified with the liberties that the Crown challenged through *quo warranto* in order to recover them from the subjects who held them. More generally, *quo warranto* points us to the jurisdictional subtext of Skelton's representation of his warranting vice-characters.

The writ of *quo warranto* required that the claimant to the privilege produce written evidence that the same was warranted either by letters patent or by prescription (that is, uninterrupted customary use) from the time of King

Richard I.[78] The difficulty of doing so was the point, since that meant the monarch could exploit the writ for his own fiscal ends. Following the example of Edward I, to whose time the statute of *Quo Warranto* (1290) dates, Henry VII revived *quo warranto* proceedings at the beginning of his reign, in order to increase revenue and centralize legal authority. But it was under Henry VIII that the action came fully into its own.[79] As Harold Garrett-Goodyear explains, in a series of *quo warranto* proceedings against individuals, and in two general summonses in 1519 and 1524, Henry VIII used the writ to "challenge the titles by which some Englishmen enjoyed hunting privileges, or held courts, or collected fines imposed by royal judges, or exercised any one of the various rights that were lumped under the label 'franchises and liberties.'"[80] Especially because the king could insist on financial compensation for the past abuse of franchise, the story of *quo warranto* is thus very close to that of *Prerogativa Regis*, in that both exploited the fiscal potential of rights that had been neglected across the previous two centuries. And as with *Prerogativa Regis*, the legal community took enormous interest in the text of *Quo Warranto*, in local response to the Crown's learning to use it anew. In the 1490s, Robert Constable and Edmund Dudley gave readings on the statute; William Marshall followed in 1516. John Spelman's reading of 1519 is of particular interest, since Sir John Fineux attended and took part in it, and it was Fineux who, as Chief Justice of King's Bench, would only a few months later oversee the general summons in Middlesex, whereby all subjects there who claimed any franchise whatsoever were required to appear before the bench and defend their titles.

At the time that Skelton was embodying courtly corruption in his vice-characters' empty warrants, the warrant had become one crucial sign of an accelerating consolidation of royal power. Garret-Goodyear argues that the results of *quo warranto* actions across Henry VIII's reign were patchy at best, not least because the government was ultimately more interested in levying fines than in eliminating private jurisdictions, an administrative attitude wholly consistent with the Crown's fiscal exploitation of its prerogative rights on the land. In 1519–20, however, the motives behind Tudor policy in respect of *quo warranto* were far less clear. As "almost certainly the first general *quo warranto* sessions held in the king's own name since the fourteenth century," the general summons of 1519 made a huge impression on London, both because of its novelty and because among those claiming franchises were "prominent ecclesiastical lords and laymen like the abbot of Westminster, the mayor and citizens of London, and the Archbishop of Canterbury." Londoners found disquieting the prestige of those whose liberties the government was allowing itself to challenge, and they were equally disturbed by the general doctrinal position that Chief Justice Fineux articulated in the proceedings, when he "forced franchise holders in the county to acknowledge the king's stake in their franchises and his right to review their holdings in jurisdiction and other regalian benefits."[81]

Fineux stated the principle underlying this position in a separate but related criminal case from 1519 involving Sir John Savage. The Chief Justice ruled that the state was justified in having removed the accused from his office as sheriff before conviction. Arguing that Savage "held the office on condition that he justify the king's confidence," Fineux seized the chance to extend this point to all offices, privileges, and immunities: "All liberties and all such offices come originally from the king [*a le commencement veygneront del roy*], and for that reason, by presumption of law, all such liberties and offices shall be presumed to be in the king's hands [*en maynes le roy*], and for that reason the king may always put them to their claim: that is, to show by what warrant or right [*quo warranto ou quo jure*] they claim such liberties and offices."[82] In 1519–20 the warrant with which Skelton's royal delegates litter their speech was identifiable with the mechanics of royal control, and with the government's programs to consolidate authority and jurisdiction in a royal center.

In London, the jurisdiction that seemed most threatened by the proceedings was the ecclesiastical, and it is relevant to Skelton's play and to his signal distrust of the "warrant" that the abbot of Westminster was included in the general summons of 1519. Skelton at the time was living within the sanctuary of Westminster, and although ecclesiastical sanctuary was a privilege similar to those falling within the statute, it was only in early 1519 that it became clear that the full pressure of the action could be brought to bear on the status of that particular immunity.[83] The relevant case involved Sir John Savage's son. Accused of murder in 1516, John Savage the younger claimed sanctuary in the Priory of St. John of Jerusalem, whence he was removed by order of the court.[84] At his trial in 1519, Chief Justice Fineux argued that at common law St. John's, like all parochial churches, had a general privilege of sanctuary "for forty days and no more." Rejecting Savage's claim that the priory possessed a particular privilege to have sanctuary beyond forty days, Fineux insisted that sanctuary must be put to the same standard of proof as for any other privilege, so that a privilege would not stand by custom alone without confirmation by an itinerant justice: "usage since time immemorial alone, without allowance in the general eyre, will not serve to have sanctuary." More generally, he argued that such a privilege "is something so much in derogation of justice and against the common weal [*enconter le common byen*] of the realm that it is not allowable by the law."[85]

The implication of this test was startling, since Fineux was asking to measure the validity of earlier grants according to the present order of the law, thereby limiting the efficacy of arguments from prescription or customary use. The lawyer John Caryll highlights this move in his report of the case: "Fineux C.J. Nevertheless, you have claimed such a privilege in times past, and also various other privileges which the king himself could not grant at the present day by the order of his laws [*ne poit graunter a cest jour per lorder de ses leyes*], and therefore cannot have a good beginning, ergo they will not lie in prescription. (Note that. Westminster nevertheless uses sanctuary for debt, but query by what right [*quaere quo jure, etc*].)"[86] As Garrett-Goodyear explains, "Fineux had hit upon an effective basis for destroying sanctuaries. If a general summons [of *quo warranto*] did not exempt ecclesiastical claimants to sanctuary, moreover, not only the sanctuary rights of St. John of Jerusalem but also the privileged precincts of Westminster Abbey and St. Martin's-le-Grand were vulnerable to attack by the king's justices."[87] In the general summons that followed in Middlesex a few months later, Fineux was predictably rigorous in his interpretation of *Quo Warranto*, and he clearly intended to use the statute to destroy privileges and immunities of all kinds, including sanctuary. The other justices were more conservative than Fineux about the statute's reach, preferring to levy fines instead of nullifying the claimant's interest in the jurisdictional franchise, and Fineux's radical conception of *quo warranto* gave way to more practical, short-term ends.[88]

As minor as the word seems for the play as a whole, Skelton's verbal linking of warrant with his vice-characters should thus be understood as a pointed interrogation of the general summons of *quo warranto*, which in 1519 must have seemed a newly vigorous way for the Crown to consolidate the jurisdiction of the central courts against all alternative jurisdictional claims. When Colusyon tells Magnyfycence that he will "waraunt" him "welth and lyberte" (l. 1766), the wicked counselor is guaranteeing the same rewards as those the general summons of *quo warranto* promised to bring the Tudors: wealth, in the form of fines for past abuse of franchises, and, more drastically, liberty, in the form of the recovered franchise. In characterizing Skelton's technique at a moment like this, I would emphasize both how little and how much the topical reference informs the narrative around it. The play is about the royal household, not the Bench, and the narrative of the former is not an allegory for the latter. But taking Skelton's verbal cues seriously also allows us, in the topical *scene*, to follow him as he makes connections across the whole machinery of royal government. And in that light, Skelton's play exemplifies how literary allusion or topicality concerns not only the particular event referenced therein, but also the temporal logic that the event stands for: the diverse and not necessarily linear times that an event like the minions' expulsion or a *quo warranto* proceeding turns out to be describing. Skelton's analysis of the warrant is best seen, I think, as an experiment concerning the shape of emergent political-juridical meanings: a way, in the manner of Fineux's own innovative attempt to use *quo warranto* against sanctuary, to test the connections between one expression of royal authority and another, as these newly gloss the public culture that sustains them.

TOWARD EQUITY

Critical as Skelton is of the royal household and the Crown's programmatic appropriations, I have been suggesting that the play is not so much a polemic against royal privilege per se as a meditation on the value of older and newer versions of authority and self available to the king. For this argument, "intent" is a final and crucial keyword. The play asks what the consequences are for the state at large when royal intention is subjected to the bureaucratic work of writing, of office, of surveyors and masters of forfeit. The indentured courtier, legal writ, inventory, and warrant all enable the royal intention: they are written and living delegates, projections of the sovereign will onto the instruments of its expression and power. In the spatial terms that underwrite the translation of the king's authority into and across jurisdiction, what does it mean for the prince to place his trust in the intending instrument, occupying and residing in it, even as he asks his officer to "occupye" his authority (l. 1456) and be "resydent" (l. 1718) with him? The treatment of intention in *Magnyfycence* is on a continuum with the play's meditation on delegation as it relates to the central administration's exploitation of Crown privileges and reabsorption of jurisdictional privileges.

The character Skelton most closely identifies with the intending royal mind is Lyberte, whose name elides two freedoms, which if taken to excess produce the haughty contempt and prodigality that the play associates, respectively, with the grasping and spendthrift household. First, of course, royal liberty is liberality:

> *Lyb.* For lyberalyte is most convenyent
> A prynce to use with all his hole intent,
> Largely rewardynge them that have deservyd.... (ll. 2117–19)

But liberality is only one of two freedoms in these lines. The second, corresponding to *libertas* rather than *liberalitas*, is that ample intention, the "hole intent" through which the prince is said to practice liberality. "I lyve as me lyst, I lepe out at large" (l. 2080), Lyberte says, and in this sense liberty is the freedom that underlies moral choice generally. In the case of the king particularly, it is the mysterious, unrooted autonomy through which an authority imagines its own constitution.

As against liberality, the play identifies the second liberty with the royal appetite and intention, qualities that the play insistently links to excess and tyranny. When Magnyfycence tells Felycyte that "ye shall folowe myne appetyte and intent," the counselor quite misses the tone of the statement and replies, "So it be by mesure I am ryght well content" (ll. 1420–21), an answer that seems so optimistic as to border on the foolish. And Lyberte says of himself that "in lust and lykynge my name is Lyberte" (l. 2078), a sentence whose tyrannical potential becomes fully present in Abusyon's recommendation that the prince let his "lust and lykynge stande for a lawe" (l. 1607). Similar is Lyberte's own insistence he "is laudable and pryvylegyd from lawe. / Judycyall rygoure shall not me correcte" (ll. 68–69). The "lyberte" that is the king's "hole intent" becomes excessive, then, when it replaces law. The two formulas are near translations, in fact, of two maxims in Roman law that in England were closely associated with political absolutism: *Quod principi placuit legis habet vigorem* ("What has pleased the prince has the force of law") and *Princeps legibus solutus est* ("The sovereign is released from the laws").[89] More powerfully even than the play's allusions to the mechanics of *Prerogativa Regis* and *quo warranto*, the freedom of intention alluded to by Abusyon and Lyberte identifies royal privilege as a theoretical principle. What, the play asks, is the shape of a just or, alternatively, a tyrannical intention?

Already in the mid-thirteenth century, the author of *Bracton* had interpreted *Quod principi placuit* to mean that the king's law was not only his own, not "anything rashly put forward of his own will [*voluntate regis*], but what has been rightly decided with the counsel of his magnates, deliberation and consultation having been had thereon, the king giving it *auctoritas*."[90] In Skelton's analysis of the intentional force subtending the royal law *qua* king's law, the prince's wicked counselors flatter the prince by saying they follow his intention, rather than the reverse. Thus Fansy asks Magnyfycence to "Shewe us your mynde then, howe to do and what" (l. 1435)—this just at the moment before the prince consigns Measure to Fansy's and Lyberte's charge, according to their "mynde," not his. That *showing* is a critical marker of Magnyfycence's failure. For, as opposed to Crafty Conveyaunce, who successfully exploits the fact that his conscience is unreadable—"My inwyt delynge there no man can dyscry" (l. 1356)—the prince is forever exposing just what he thinks. Forever giving his servants the upper hand, he tells Courtly Abusyon that "You shall here myne entent" (l. 1655) and that "Thy wordes and my mynde odly well accorde" (l. 1605).

That Magnyfycence should exhibit this prodigality of intention deepens Skelton's argument about the shape of Tudor royal authority. As part of the political and poetic "processe" of judgment and reformation that ends the play, Magnyfycence correspondingly remakes his royal intention, by asking Redresse and the other counselors how best to direct his intention or "corage":

> *Magn.*   Whereto were most metely my corage to knyt?
> Your myndys I beseche you here in to expresse. (ll. 2479–80)

The difference between this moment and Magnyfycence's interactions with the vices is not simply that between good and bad counsel. Skelton's point, rather, is that a successful prince will not so much show his mind as have others show theirs, in an act of true counsel. As against a chamber bureaucracy that scripts the king's identity by institutionalizing Crown privilege, *Magnyfycence* imagines the royal intention as that which must by nature by kept private. Skelton here extends the argument that where documentary culture becomes a substitute for the authority it embodies, it potentially undermines the estate royal it is meant to protect. To "shewe" his mind is for the prince to make his authorizing intention vulnerable and dangerous in the same way as writing is or can be.

To ask for the shape of sovereign intention is thus to ask *where* it is. What is the place of that intention that makes law possible, the ground from which jurisdiction seems to flow and which jurisdiction, in turn, reconstitutes in its image? If Law in this sense is always beyond, that formulation only rephrases the question.[91] Pretending to plead on behalf of the now exiled Measure, Colusyon hypocritically asks the king to "let pety have some place / In your brest towardes this gentylman" (ll. 1712–13). In invoking the king's body as the source of the regulative norm, Colusyon recalls another maxim of Roman law, which states that the emperor "has all laws in the archive of his breast [*omnia iura in scrinio pectoris*]."[92] Acknowledging the integrity of sovereign intention by placing it inside the body, Colusyon makes pity and severity efficacious *there*, which is to say beyond the place of declarative speech and documentation. But the play dramatizes this construction of law as the fantasy that leads Magnyfycence to think he is in control when in fact he is subject to all manner of manipulation. True authority emerges, rather, in the play of jurisdictional delegation and distribution, which means that the secret place of sovereignty that Magnyfycence longs for and nearly loses is, in reality the always provisional effect of his management of a grounding scene that, misunderstood, his sovereignty seems itself to ground.

The relationship between the king's interiority and his law was a matter of more than theoretical importance in 1519. As a principle of extraordinary justice, royal pity was identifiable with legal equity, which according to a standard definition from canon law was said to be "justice tempered with the sweetness of mercy [*iustitia dulcore misericordiae temperata*]."[93] In technical-jurisdictional terms, Chancery was the court of the king's conscience, the most important forum for the equitable supplementation of the common law. And under Wolsey Chancery's incursions on common-law jurisdiction, most importantly in matters of real property, were foregrounding a technical version of the question Skelton poses in relation to the king's intention: how would an increasingly formalist common law accommodate the concept of conscience as a reserve of justice beyond the institutional law?

The history of early Tudor equity is relevant to *Magnyfycence*'s representation of the prince's sovereign interiority because of the passage, already cited, in which Lyberte frames the relationship between law and freedom:

Lyb. Lyberte is laudable and pryvylegyd from lawe.
Judycyall rygoure shall not me correcte. (ll. 68–69)

Rigor here is a corrective principle opposed to the royal privilege and liberty that, unbounded, stand outside the law. The most notable feature of this equation, however, is that it reverses the usual construction of legal privilege as equity, equity being the correction *of* judicial rigor. In Christopher St. German's formulation from the 1520s, equity is ordained "to tempre and myttygate the rygoure of the lawe."[94] In Skelton, then, Lyberte's juxtaposition of law, correction, and rigor invokes a standard legal formula, even as it upsets that formula. On the one hand, Lyberte's remark construes royal privilege and law as opposed terms; on the other, the vocabulary of equity haunting the lines limns a relationship in which royal freedom emerges as the merciful management of law: without rigor, there is no equity and hence no privilege. In the tension between these complementary constructions of royal intention, Lyberte's maxim springs open in a doubled orientation. Within its rather sinister implication of legal absolutism, it posits an account of the very production of royal law, law here being the dynamic through which, as equity, liberty might be said to correct the legal formalism that potentially corrects it.

St. German's *Doctor and Student*, which I treat at more length in the next chapter, theorizes this dynamic. To counter the perception among certain lawyers that under Wolsey conscience was detaching itself from the common law as a superior principle of justice, St. German argued that conscience was instead a principle of supplementary justice within the law, identical in force to Aristotle's notion of *epieikeia* as a hermeneutic principle rather than an ethical one, less the operation of mercy than the judicial accommodation of a necessarily general law to the particulars of the given case. In St. German's formulation, equity considered "all the pertyculer cyrcumstaunces of the dede, the whiche also is temperyd with the swetnes of mercye"; in this way it followed rather the "intent of the lawe, then the wordes of the lawe." It could thus be seen as the perfection of the law, an "excepcion [that] is secretly understande [understood] in every generall rewle of every posytyve lawe."[95] According to the theory, then, the common law accommodates the potentially arbitrary principle of conscience by formally absorbing it as the law's own secreted intention.

By representing the prince's "lyberte" or sovereign intent as a force that seems both positively and negatively in tension with the formal rigor of law, Skelton delineates the problem St. German would also strive to answer. Although Measure in the play stands for a moderation or temperance that corresponds to the *ethical* construction of equity at law, it is striking that at the same time he embodies equity as a textual *hermeneutic*. Early in the play, chastising Lyberte and Felycyte for the way they are quarreling about the value of royal freedom and restraint, Measure tells them, "Your langage is lyke the penne / Of him that wryteth to fast" (90–91).[96] By comparing their speech with an imperfectly written text, one in which words move faster than their own meaning, royal Measure implicitly identifies in himself the interpretive activity that looks past the illegible letter and imperfections of the written medium. Responding to Measure's criticism, Felycyte correspondingly asks him to fill in what the writing has left out, that is, to provide the equitable supplement:

Fel.   Syr, yf any worde have past
    Me, other fyrst or last,
    To you I arecte it, and cast
    Thereof the reformacyon. (ll. 92–95)

Measure is equity, and measure's place in these lines as a hermeneutic principle underlines how Lyberte and Felycyte, as royal attributes, are on the wrong side of an interpretive dynamic. In debating the discursive order appropriate to the king, rather than embodying it, they resemble nothing more closely than Foly's hawk, which, veering wildly from the properly royal pursuit of the swan, ends up pursuing a textual rat.

This chapter has argued that Skelton's play about the household economy analyzes the impact on the Tudor Crown of the fiscal exploitation of *Prerogativa Regis* and the jurisdictional compressions aimed at through the *quo warranto* proceedings. As a third way in which Skelton imagines the Tudors' innovative constitution of royal identity, equity describes the intention that, in careful negotiation with the written, establishes royal law also as a site of hermeneutic privilege, a "public" interpretation of judicial meaning by the prince himself or, as was historically the case, in a court of royal justice (whether Common Pleas or Chancery). Equity gives us a further way, then, to understand Magnyfycence's fatal error in the play, since it is, disastrously, his own meaning as sovereign *interpreter* that collapses when he gives too easy credence to the letter Fansy passes off as coming from abroad and from a friend.[97] The "processe" that is Skelton's poetic interpretation of court meanings reorients a corrupted and therefore corrupting process of hermeneutic delegation. Writing, whether Skelton's good writing or the royal writing that variously goes awry, is not the place of law, but it gives access to the place of law, and it does so in the same way as jurisdiction does, as one stabilizing sign of the juridical order's processual groundedness. If this writing is to continue to agree with the real it serves, Skelton warns, it must, for the prince above all others, remain the productive imperfection that makes royal interpretation possible and thereby inaugurates, again and only again, the royal self and its royal law.

CHAPTER TWO

"No More to Medle of the Matter": Thomas More, Equity, and the Claims of Jurisdiction

A starting point for any consideration of Thomas More's literary and political career is the turn from the humanist reformer encountered in the work culminating in *Utopia* (1516) to the heretic hunter of the 1520s and 1530s, as found in the official polemics written against Luther and in the increasingly defensive invectives produced against William Tyndale, Simon Fish, John Frith, and Christopher St. German.[1] In this chapter, I will neither repeat nor challenge the standard picture of More's often pedantic and vituperative work for the Catholic cause. In asking after More's relation to jurisdiction, I mean, instead, to describe what I take to be an important and underappreciated continuity between his early and late thought, as a way also of demonstrating, somewhat against the standard view, the central role of More's legal training in his textual production, including his early writing. However substantial the shift from reformer to conservative, Thomas More in one respect consistently thought like the lawyer he was. Across his writings, he kept in view the question of legal jurisdiction's relation to authority and of the boundaries that produce, define, and check power, even as they order experience and judgment. In his analysis of tyranny in *The History of King Richard III*; in his polemical treatises against Protestants and on behalf of the legal procedures, including torture, used against them; in his insistence on the relevance of the general council to the legal order of the English church; and in his appeal to the inviolability of the subject's conscience before the law, More represented political order and civil justice in terms of the different forums that constituted that order and enabled that justice. With a lawyer's attention to the question of judicial competence, he fitted himself, as humanist and religious polemicist both, to the jurisdictional order through which, in his view, laws remain balanced and effective toward their social ends.

This continuity is important, I think, for understanding both the nature of More's legal conservatism and the force of his fiction-making. In light of More's defense, late in his career, of ecclesiastical procedures that violated common-law standards of due process, it is possible to cast him as a kind of legal formalist, as against a legal realism that might allow the law better to fit itself to the person at hand: More justifies his substantive position regarding heresy in part by being a stickler for procedure, for the way things have been done. My first contention is that More's formalism, and hence his legal conservatism, cannot be properly understood in opposition to a category like realism, but only in opposition to a second kind of formalism. More's commitment to legal form rejects a proceduralism that does not look in the first instance to the order or frame inside which a procedure makes sense—a proceduralism, then, that collapses a more complex formalism into a simpler one. Against this procedural formalism, More insists on the priority of forum over procedure, in the sense that a given procedure or convention is not for him measurable as just except within its own jurisdictional sphere, not because that dynamic protects the given procedure—it may of course do so—but because it provides the only way in which any procedure can meaningfully relate to the substantive reality to which it gives form. My second contention is that fiction is one category through which More, both late in his career and in *Utopia*, fashioned a response to the process of centralization through which English law was beginning to stand in a less mediated relation to the life it formally ordered, literary fiction being a mode of expressing the same gap between discursive representation and truth that the jurisdictional distribution of meaning across orders makes visible.

As background, a brief summary of More's legal expertise is in order. It is well known that after his legal training at New Inn (ca. 1494–96) and Lincoln's Inn (1496–ca. 1501) More found himself torn between legal and Christian humanistic study, between his work as a law lecturer at Furnivall's Inn and the monastic life of the London Charterhouse where he lived for three years.[2] The split between these different institutions has rightly been understood as formative for More's thinking. Equally deserving of emphasis, however, is the fact that the legal career he pursued after 1505 was itself anything but uniform, bringing him in touch also with many of the internal divisions that made English law so complex. Even if William Roper's suggestion that "there was at that tyme in none of the princes courtes of the lawes of this realme, any matter of importans in controversie wherein he was not with the one parte of Councell" must count as hyberbole, it is clear that as a successful London lawyer More moved ably among jurisdictions and kinds of law.[3] Coincident with his rise at Lincoln's Inn to positions of increasing prominence for the internal government of the Inn, More was elected to Parliament in 1504 and 1509. He worked as a part-time arbitrator in Chancery, and it seems probable that as part of his practice he would have assisted his father, who as a serjeant at law belonged to the legal elite that possessed the right to argue before the judges of the Common Pleas.[4] In 1509 More was admitted as a member of the Mercers' Company, and from that time acted as counsel for the merchants.[5] His commercial work probably lay behind his appointment early in 1515 to serve as special counsel to Leo X's ambassador in a Star Chamber case involving the confiscation of a cargo of alum on a ship belonging to the pope. More's performance there (in which, as Roper records, he "not onlye declared to thembassador the whole effecte" of the court's opinions, but "also, in defens of the Popes side, argued so learnedly himself" that the forfeited cargo was adjudged restored) brought him to the attention of Henry VIII and Wolsey.[6] Roper's account further implies in More just the kind of expertise at the edges of English common-law jurisdiction that could make a lawyer valuable in continental trade negotiations like the one to which More was appointed in the spring of 1515. That he was admitted in 1514 to honorary membership in Doctors' Commons, the professional society for English civilians, suggests, unsurprisingly, that More had at least some knowledge of Roman law even if he did not number among its English practitioners.[7] Particularly important for the shape of More's legal career was his appointment in 1510 as undersheriff of London, a position that made him judge in the Sheriffs' Court at Guildhall, which had jurisdiction over a wide range of criminal and civil matters. The position of undersheriff also gave More the "right to represent the City in the central courts at Westminster as assistant counsel under the recorder, London's chief law officer."[8]

With More's entry in 1518 into royal service, this pattern of engagement with diverse jurisdictions at English law would continue on a different plane, both in Wolsey's Star Chamber and through his work as a member of the king's attendant council in hearing direct requests for relief from poor suitors.[9] In 1525 More was named Chancellor of the Duchy of Lancaster, a position in which he served as equity judge in the Duchy court, which sat at Westminster and presided within that local jurisdiction over a range of matters "comparable to that undertaken nationally in Star Chamber."[10] More's appointment as Lord Chancellor in 1529 thus brought to a culmination his already decade-long engagement with equity and conciliar justice. The chancellorship itself was marked by his work in the equitable jurisdictions, and also by his fervent engagement with heresy as a legal matter at the boundary between the temporal and spiritual courts. This latter concern is attested to chiefly in the polemical treatises that More wrote, after his resignation, in defense of the ecclesiastical jurisdiction. *The Apology* and *The Debellation of Salem and Bizance*, both printed in 1533, responded specifically to the extended arguments made by the distinguished lawyer Christopher St. German to limit the Church's legal role in matters of heresy and property. As J. B. Trapp explains, although these texts are thematically continuous with the antiheretical treatises such as *The Dialogue concerning Heresies* (1529) and *The Confutation of Tyndale's Answer* (1532–33), they "make a pair apart" in being concerned less with religious doctrine than "with the ecclesiastical jurisdiction in England."[11] As such, the *Apology* and *Debellation* stand as an end point of a private and public career undertaken through and on behalf of the complex jurisdictional field that was English law.

MEDDLING AND THE MATTER OF CONSCIENCE

One of More's best known expressions from the 1530s, a phrase that has come to stand in particular for the terms of his resistance to Henry VIII, captures very well the jurisdictional turn of More's thought. In a letter written from the Tower to Margaret Roper in early May 1535, More recounts that on April 30 he responded to Cromwell's questions concerning the supremacy by saying that he "neyther wyll dyspute Kyngis tytles nor Popys," and that apart from praying for the king, his council, and the realm as a whole, "otherwyse than thus I never entend to medell." He twice repeats the latter verb in his account of the interrogation, telling Cromwell that "I wolde never medle in the worlde agayne," and that "I had fully determyned with my selfe, neyther to study nor medle with eny mater of thys worlde."[12] From the Old French *mesler* and ultimately the Latin *miscere* ("to mingle"), *meddle* in this period carried the two meanings of "mix" and "concern oneself." The word appears in Tyndale's 1526 translation of the New Testament in both senses: in John 4.9, the Samaritan woman at the well wonders how it is that Jesus asks to "drynke of me, which am a Samaritane? (for the jewes medle not with the Samaritans)"; and in 1 Thessalonians 4.11, Paul urges the brethren that "ye studdy to be quyet, and to medle with your owne busynes."[13] In neither usage did *meddle* carry its negative connotation quite so immediately as it does today, even though this narrower sense of "interfere with" was already available and on the way to becoming dominant. In fact, More's usage of the word from the mid-1520s interestingly relates to the longer semantic shift, since in his hands the word tilts toward its negative sense by bringing together its two major meanings, denoting a concern that is also, inappropriately, a mingling. Expressing a fear almost of contamination, the phrase "to meddle with any matter of this world" means to be concerned with the world, but also to attend to it when doing so imperils the integrity of the observer or observed.

Given how for More the verb slips between its two meanings, it is not surprising that during his imprisonment More often used *meddle* in relation to the inviolable privacy of conscience. More produced the most charged version of this repeated claim during a formal interrogation one month before his execution.[14] Responding to the council's exasperated query as to why he should bind himself to his conscience when it was impossible to be fully "suer therein," More insists that the issue is really other, declaring himself sure, not of the truth of his position, but only of having properly informed his conscience. As the obverse to this claim, he insists that "I medle not with the conscience of theim that thinke otherwise, everye man *suo domino stat et cadit*."[15] The allusion to Romans 14.4—"everyone stands or [*aut*] falls by his own lord"—figures the conscience as master, the individual soul as servant. Most interestingly, it strictly asserts the legal status of the internal forum, since according to the metaphor conscience exercises its claim on the soul in the same manner as the temporal lord (*dominus*) exercises his *dominium*. Although this is a fully conventional theological account of conscience, in 1535 it probably worked polemically, too, by answering, in Henry's and Cromwell's own terms, the claims to English sovereign autonomy made, for example, in the 1533 Act in Restraint of Appeals, which declared "that this realm of England is an empire, and so hath been accepted in the world, governed by one supreme head and king having the dignity and royal estate of the imperial crown of the same."[16] More is drawn to *meddle* as a term, I think, because in its semantic flexibility it encapsulated the politics of interference that had dominated the late 1520s and early 1530s: a politics of stepping beyond set boundaries and of inappropriate mingling, whether in relation to *praemunire* and the pope's interference in English affairs or, as More also thought, the king's interference in matters pertaining to the Church.

This connection between meddling and matter goes back into More's antiheretical treatises, where he uses meddling as one term for an inappropriate exegetical interest in the textual matter of scripture. In the *Dialogue concerning Heresies*, published in 1529, More insists that the danger of Tyndale's translation of the New Testament is the potential on the part of readers for "moche medlyng with suche partys therof as lest wyll agre wyth theyr capacytees."[17]

Given that Plato warns against allowing men "to medle moche" in temporal affairs, he writes, "how moche is it less mete for every man boldely to medle with the exposycyon of holy scrypture."[18] In the *Confutation of Tyndale's Answer*, More uses the word in the sense of an inappropriate disciplinary mix, saying that Tyndale and Luther "medle phylosophy with the thynges of god (which is a thynge that may in place be very well done)."[19] Meddling in this latter passage, on its own neither positive nor negative, becomes negative when it involves an interference with, rather than exposition of, a given, inviolable textual reality. A word for attending to a given problem or phenomenon, *meddling* is for More a figure for the mixing that too easily imperils a matter rather than elucidating it; for the kind of speculation that, owing to circumstance or, chiefly, to lack of expertise, threatens not to respect those boundaries that already in themselves define what attention is or is not appropriate for the matter's apprehension.

The important thought that the matter itself dictates the kind of attention appropriate to it informs More's most important use of the phrase, which is in reference to the king. In a letter from March 1534 to Thomas Cromwell, which charts a chronological defense against the charge of having interfered in royal business and blocked the king's will, More recurs so often to the idea of meddling that it becomes the letter's central concept and keyword. Concerning Henry's attempts to obtain a dispensation through Wolsey's legatine court in 1529, More writes "I never medeled therein, nor was a man mete to do, ffor the mater was in hand by an ordynarye process of the spirituall law, wherof I could litle skyll."[20] During his chancellorship, he continues, he read no manuscripts compiled against what he knew to be the king's position; upon offering to return one such book to John Clerk, dean of the Chapel Royal and the book's compiler, More discovered that Clerk had already burned his own copy, "and bycause he no more mynded to medle enything in the mater he desyred me to burne the same boke to. And uppon my faith so did I."[21] Of the king's marriage to Ann Boleyn, More tells Cromwell that he will not "dispute uppon it . . . but with owt eny other maner medlyng of the mater . . . faithfully pray to God for his Grace and hers both."[22] As touching the primacy of the pope, finally, More writes, as evidence of his desire not to "medle in that mater agaynst the Kyngis graciouse pleasure, what so ever myn awne opinion were therin," that in 1533 he had suppressed parts of the *Confutation* that touched on the primacy.[23]

In all these instances, meddling involves the violation of an interpretive boundary drawn around the king's business, in particular the "great matter" of Henry's marriage to Catherine. But to capture the full impact of the phrase as More discovered and repeatedly deployed it, we have to hear inside even his claims on behalf of the sovereign status of royal business an allusion to the meddling that for More had, perhaps, the most importance: the jurisdictional disorder effected by the consolidation of royal power at the expense of the ecclesiastical jurisdiction. In a letter to Cromwell concerning the Nun of Canterbury, also dating to March 1534, More pulls up this topical resonance when he uses the expression to describe Wolsey's engagement with the question of the royal marriage in the legatine court that was convened to produce a judgment favorable to the king. With great indirection (and a degree of plausible deniability), More relates to Cromwell that the Nun spoke to him of a vision involving Wolsey, which she interpreted as referring in part to "the medlinge he was put in truste with by the Kinge, concerninge the great matter of his marriage."[24] This is an extraordinary way for More in 1534 to refer to Wolsey's work as legate in 1529, since it was only when that court failed to produce the desired judgment that Wolsey was charged under the statute of *praemunire* and found guilty of promoting the pope's jurisdiction in England. As opposed to the jurisdictional meddling of the *praemunire* charge, the meddling More attributes to Wolsey in the letter of 1534 is on behalf of the king. But it also glances at the broader jurisdictional framework to suggest continuity between the unjust mixing of jurisdictional authority that justified Wolsey's dismissal and his earlier, official meddling in the king's great matter.

More's rhetorical figure implies a lawyerly and conservative understanding of jurisdiction. Because matters present themselves to judgment with their boundaries in place, interpretation or judgment should fit itself to the matter so defined, rather than the reverse. This, in brief, is the function of jurisdictional heterogeneity. For More, the matter is always stable, and where one's attention or concern is not a priori fitted to that matter (through professional expertise or by recourse to the very idea that human authority is specific rather than generic) and thereby properly oriented to a given place or group or question, it can only meddle, impertinently mixing itself with the essential matter at hand. This chapter traces out the theoretical implications of jurisdictional heterogeneity for two fictions in which More analyzes the claims of conscience in public life. First, in the context of his defense of the ecclesiastical courts in the early 1530s, I look at a parable used by More in 1534 to defend his refusal to swear the oath in affirmation of the Act of Succession. From this more explicit meditation on jurisdiction, I turn to *Utopia*, a book in which More famously embeds his portrait of the ideal republic within a dialogue concerning the relation between public justice and conscientious action. My argument here is that in testing the claims of the ideal on the real world, *Utopia* follows an explicitly jurisdictional structure, using the procedural differences between English equity and the common law to describe the mutually constitutive relation between a legal norm and the particular it orders. Both the 1534 and the 1516 stories are notable for figuring jurisdictional plurality as fundamental to the polity and to those procedures through which its laws are instituted.

CROWN INTEREST AND THE COURT OF PYE SIR WILLIAM POUNDER

In a letter sent in August 1534 to her stepsister Alice Allington, Margaret Roper includes a short fable told her by her father. The letter is cast in the form of a dialogue between father and daughter, and bears a thematic resemblance to Plato's *Crito*, the dialogue in which Socrates lays out why he must abide by the law that has mistakenly found him guilty of impiety. The letter is almost certainly by More himself, written perhaps for circulation among his family and friends as an explanation and defense of his refusal to swear the oath.[25] Nowhere is More's ironic presence more clearly in evidence than in a legal parable that Margaret, pretending to an extreme naïveté about the law, haltingly records for her sister as having been told her by More.[26] As the letter to Alice has it, Margaret has told her father two fables passed on through Alice by Lord Chancellor Audley in the hopes of persuading the imprisoned More not to be so scrupulously wise as in effect to be a fool.[27] In response to these stories, More offers as his explanation of why he cannot swear against his conscience another fable, the story of a certain "Company," a "poore honest man of the countrey" who, finding himself on a corrupt jury, refuses to follow the judgment of the other eleven and in that way "playe than the gude companion" (521–23). Arguing against his fellows that "when we shall hence and come before God, and that he shall sende you to heaven for doing according to your conscience, and me to the devill for doing against mine," the aptly named Company insists that because he does not think "in the matter as you doe, I dare not in such a matter passe for good cumpany" (523). Company's name alludes to the ideal of Christian community, an ideal that stands in tension with the jurors' manufactured and merely illegitimate consensus. In simple terms, then, More uses the story to analogize his situation in late 1534, particularly his resistance to the substitution of one kind of legal consensus for the fuller consensus of the whole Catholic Church.

But the story is not so simple as this. Unsurprisingly for a lawyer's parable, it is most interesting in the semi-technical legal details that "Margaret" treats as almost incidental to the story's main thrust. Through the ironic use of

Margaret's lack of skill in the law, More repeatedly calls attention to this legal vocabulary, which he uses to embed his major argument about conscience within a broader jurisdictional framework, and thereby to articulate a vision of law and of royal authority as depending on the acknowledgment of jurisdictional boundaries. As such, the letter is continuous with the *Apology* and *Debellation* of 1533, texts in which, responding to the arguments mainly of St. German, More had defended the English spiritual jurisdiction against possible encroachments by the common law and parliamentary statute. Indeed, the parable from August 1534 can best be thought of as allegorically reconfiguring and extending those arguments, by demonstrating in terms of the legal system as a whole why More's earlier defense of jurisdictional variegation in relation to the spiritual courts should be understood as good counsel, a defense of the king's authority rather than, as Cromwell's council might construe the matter, an attack upon it. Most interestingly, the parable's status as fiction helps More characterize the nature of truth-at-law. At this more abstract level, where jurisdictional difference emerges as the sign of a law's force and of the limit of Law's reason, fiction comes to stand for the constitutive boundaries around discourse more generally.

The first striking detail in the story as Margaret rehearses it for Alice is that the court in which Company takes his stand constitutes the most minor, perhaps, of all English jurisdictions:

> And with this, he tolde me a tale, I wene I can skant tell it you againe, because it hangeth upon some tearmes and ceremonies of the law. But as farre as I can call to mynde my fathers tale was this, that ther is a court belonginge of course unto every faire, to doe justice in such thinges as happen within the same. This court hath a pretie fond name, but I cannot happen upon it, but it beginneth with a pye, and the remenaunt goeth much lyke the name of a knight that I have knowen, I wis, (and I trowe you to, for he hath ben at my fathers ofte or this, at such tyme as you wer there,) a metely tall blacke man, his name was Sir William Pounder. But, tut, let the name of the courte go for this once, or call it if ye will a court of pye Sir William Pounder. (521)

If Margaret's orthography is skewed, her knowledge of inferior jurisdictions is impeccable. A court of piepowder (Lat. *curia pedis pulverizzati*) was, as J. H. Baker explains, "incident as a matter of common right to every fair" and (after a ruling in 1508) every market, overseeing both civil and minor criminal cases that arose within the fair's or market's confines during the time it took place.[28]

Not formally abolished until the nineteenth century, courts of piepowder operated as courts of record throughout the Tudor period, attracting clients because of the speed with which the court accepted a case, assembled a jury when one was needed, and rendered judgment. (Sir Edward Coke suggests that the court's name, taken from the French *pied poudré*, promises that, "for advancement of Trade, and Traffick," justice there will be as quick "as the dust can fall from the foot, the proceeding there being *de hora in horam*.")[29] Apparently using a hybrid of common-law procedure and the civil procedure associated with the law merchant, the courts were an effective source of justice and even, in certain cases, a continuous one, given that where a market operated throughout the year the attached court was able similarly to extend its temporal jurisdiction. Baker notes, finally, that given the nature of the fair or market, courts of piepowder sat at the boundary between public and private, religious and secular: "No doubt the most active courts were those functioning in market-towns, where they belonged to the borough or city, but there were many markets and fairs in private hands—especially in the hands of religious houses—and they were also supposed to have courts of piepowder."[30]

So More's fiction concerns a jurisdiction inferior to and conformable with the central royal courts whose prestige St. German's writings had promoted, and which under Cromwell's influence were coming with Parliament to be identified as the exclusive safeguard of the subject's and king's interests. In contradistinction to that account of the central courts, however, in More's story it is the minor jurisdiction that must oversee and protect royal right. This becomes clear when Margaret unfolds the case as one involving a rather special defendant:

> But this was the matter loe, that upon a tyme at such a court holden at Bartilmewe fayre, there was an eschetour of London that had arested a man that was owtelawed, and had seased his goodes that he had browte in to the fayre, tollinge hym out of the fayre by a traine. The man that was arested and his goodes seased was a northern man, which by his frendes made theschetour within the fayre to be arested upon an action, I woot nere what, and so was he brought before the judge of the court of pye Sir William Pounder, and at the last of the matter came to a certaine ceremonye to be tryed by a quest of xii men, a jury as I remember they call it, or elles a perjury. (521–22)

The fictional case thus involves an attempt by the northerner and his friends to pervert the natural course of justice, the former by failing to respect the original attainder against him and the latter by initiating an action in the local court against the officer who has attempted to rectify the situation and execute the king's justice. Underlining the jurisdictional thrust of the story are the twin facts that as an outlaw the northerner is formally beyond the protection of English law, and that the king's officer is said forcibly to "toll" the northerner "out of the fayre by a traine," a phrase that emphasizes the narrative importance of the threshold, whether the physical boundary constitutive of the minor jurisdiction or the symbolic boundary between the different laws and systems that together make up England's legal order. The most striking detail, however, is that the story's principal victim, the man forced through fraud to defend himself in the court of piepowder, is an escheator, the legal officer appointed to identify and lay claim to property lapsing or falling to the Crown through a failure in the order of succession or, as here, through attainder, the outlaw being one who, being dead to the law, can have no heir. The case that fraudulently arises in the piepowder jurisdiction, then, ultimately concerns a trial of royal right, a test of the efficacy of the escheator's claim, on behalf of the Crown, to the outlaw's property.

If the minor jurisdiction has the task, indirectly, of doing the king's work, what turns out to be at issue, just as in More's polemical encounter with St. German over de officio proceedings in matters of heresy, is the efficacy of the court's procedure. This is so because, however good in theory it might be, the jury on which the court's operation depends is corrupt:

> Now had the clothman by frendshipp of the offycers, founden the means to have all the quest almost, made of the northern men, such as had their boothes there standing in the fayre. Now was it come to the last daye in the after none, and the xii men had hard both the parties, and their counsell tell their tales at the barre, and were fro the barre had in to a place, to talke and common, and agre upon their sentence. Nay let me speke better in my termes yet, I trow the judge geveth the sentence and the quests tale is called a verdit. They wer skant come in together, but the northern men wer agreed, and in effect all the other too, to cast our London eschetour. They thought they neded no more to prove that he did wronge, than even the name of his bare office alone. But than was there then as the devyll wolde, this honest man of a nother quarter, that was called Cumpany. (522)

As the story narrows the question, only Company's conscientious resistance is able to salvage local procedure, thereby allowing the piepowder court to serve the cause of justice and save the king's officer against those who would malign him. We can see that More is twice figuring himself in the story, as each of the story's two outsiders and each of the king's two faithful servants. Most obviously, in describing the honest juror as a man of simple conscience and a "poore honest man of the countrey," More echoes his sense of himself, after his resignation, as merely a "poore trew man."[31] Second, in the escheator's simple work on behalf of the king's interests, More posits a figure that corresponds to his construction of himself as ever the king's good servant. In spite of his retirement and imprisonment, More asks to be seen as a man like the escheator, one who through circumstance only, not will, has been blocked from doing the king's work.

Beyond the implication that More's conscientious silence is on a continuum with his long service to the king, however, the story begins to define a more general account of the relationship between legal jurisdiction and royal authority. Given the fragility of the escheator's and Crown's ultimate success in the piepowder court, what moral, the story asks, can be drawn concerning the legal protection of royal right? It is notable, first, that the fictive legal crisis arises through the northerners' interference in the centralizing work of a royal officer, as that unconscionable interference is temporarily legitimated by the local court's attention to the matter. So in one reading of the story, it is the intrusion of a local jurisdiction on the king's business that blocks the escheator's work on behalf of the judicial center. Such a reading would correspond to St. German's criticism of the spiritual courts for interfering, for example, in matters of ecclesiastical property that, according to his and the council's account, pertain as such to the temporal sphere. But if More's tale is hypothetically open to this interpretation, it carefully forestalls any critique of the minor court per se. Margaret sets the story up by saying that the court belongs "of course unto every faire," a formulation that accurately and also polemically construes the court's place in the legal system as a given, a necessary incident to the fair in much the same way as the spiritual courts' prosecutorial or criminal jurisdiction was said to be ex officio, pertaining to the bishop by virtue of the office itself. As in his defense of the spiritual jurisdiction, More's parable finesses the question of whether the minor court is maximally efficacious by treating its jurisdiction as a matter of course and custom, and by asking instead whether it is sufficiently efficacious for its prescribed ends.

Far from being only a dodge (which it also is), this move can be seen to apply pressure to More's own position concerning the constitution of English jurisdiction. For by disallowing the accidents of practice to be an adequate measure of a jurisdiction's force, the parable effectively requires an evaluation of judicial procedure in more theoretical terms. The story delivers that defense through analogy to the major jurisdiction against which a minor one might be measured as wanting. At the center of More's polemical engagements with St. German in the *Apology* and *Debellation of Salem and Bizance* had been the comparison of procedures used by the spiritual and temporal courts to discover the factual particulars of a case, whether, respectively, through purgation or by jury trial.[32] More insisted there that the ecclesiastical procedures criticized by St. German have analogues at common law, and that in respect of all procedure pertaining to human justice (the common law included) judicial efficacy can only ever depend on the good faith of those who oversee the procedures and on the public's attribution of that good faith to them.[33] No procedure can be imagined, that is, whether in a local or central court or in any jurisdiction whatsoever, capable fully of securing that forum against abuse and error. Second, even as he emphasized the necessary limits of all human justice, More defended ecclesiastical procedures in positive terms as customary forms, ratified by time and the Council, with which one should not interfere.[34]

In the 1534 parable, Margaret's apparent lack of technical knowledge again indexes the crucial pressure points in More's recapitulation of this double jurisdictional argument. Margaret's doubt as to whether the "quest" of twelve should be called a "jury" or a "perjury" is the least probable of her lapses, a quibble that operates both as a satirical commentary on human willfulness and as a skeptical reflection on the limits of judicial process. It is no accident that More should instance trial by jury as the procedure that potentially limits the judicial efficacy of the local jurisdiction, so much so as to be saved only through the chance presence, "as the devyll wolde" have it, of Company among the twelve. For thinkers like St. German who attempted to limit the ecclesiastical jurisdiction, trial by jury stood metonymically for English due process, the probative procedure at common law against which other probative procedures such as the application of the ecclesiastical oath were measurable as patently unjust.[35] By associating the procedural vulnerability of the local court with the institution most frequently invoked in defense of the central common law, then, More is not attacking that institution as inherently flawed, but rather using the procedural analogy between the local and central courts to make a negative argument concerning the nature of legal procedure per se, as found on both sides of the various jurisdictional boundaries internal to English law.

On the positive side, the parable associates the jury with a second and equally striking term, *ceremony*. Margaret identifies the trial "by a quest of xii men" as "a certain ceremonye" to which the "matter came," that is, in which the matter issued. She uses the same word to frame the parable as a whole, telling Alice that she does not trust her own ability to record her father's story, since "it hangeth upon some tearmes and ceremonies of the law." As a term for a legal convention, *ceremony* is inevitably weighted by its religious connotations, and in a parable that reconfigures More's earlier arguments about the proper relation between the spiritual and temporal jurisdictions, the resonance is of course especially apt. Protestant reformers associated ceremony with what they described as the mere shadows of Roman practice, the outward and material signs of faith that, far from sustaining a true spirituality, instead eroded it. In his 1529 *Dialogue concerning Heresies*, More had defended solemn church practice against such a reading. There, More's hypothetical interlocutor, in sympathy with the author of the iconoclastic *Ymage of Love* (1525), puts forward the reformist position that God favors spirit over the "ostentacyon of outward observaunce" and "rable of suche unsavoury ceremonyes, all whiche are now gone as a shadow."[36] Later, he accuses pilgrims who "put theyr trust in the place or the ymage it selfe" of resembling necromancers who trust in circles drawn on the ground. In response, More offers a general defense of ceremony:

> Whiche two thynges [pilgrimage and necromancy] yf ye wolde resemble togyther, so myght ye blaspheme and have in dyrysyon all the devout rytys and cerymonyes of the chyrch, bothe in the devine servyce as encensynge, halowyng of ye fyre, of the funt, of ye pascall lambe, and over that the exorcysmys, benedyccyons, & holy straunge gesturys usyd in consecracyon or mynystracyon of the blessyd sacramentys, all whiche holy thyngys greate parte wherof was frome hande to hande left in the chyrche, from the tyme of crystys apostels, and by them left unto us, as it was by god taught unto them.[37]

This is a traditionalist's defense of ceremony as deserving respect because it is the present embodiment of a sacred history. When in the 1534 parable More applies *ceremony* to trial by jury, the word's religious valences import into the temporal legal sphere the terms of More's earlier intervention in the debate over religious ceremony. If a jury can be perjurous, More's argument goes, it is nevertheless ceremony, defensible as the historical artifact of a sacred law with whose structures it is best not to tamper.

In light of More's treatment of the piepowder court in ways that both associate it with the central courts and defend its customary status, his representation of the piepowder trial can be seen to replay in highly compressed form, and now in terms of an opposition between local and central, his earlier arguments concerning the comparative legal force of ecclesiastical and temporal forms. In the same way that Company's name makes him part of the full Catholic community, the parable glances at the figure of the heretic himself, in the "northern man" who, though outlawed, continues unlawfully to market his wares in London. As against the "northern men" who make up the jury, honest Company is said to be "of a nother quarter," a phrase that, according to the simplest of geographic logics, implies "not northern" and hence "southern." This spatialization of ethical distinctions allows More to represent himself, in the person of the just escheator, as being "of London" and also, in the person of Company, as being of the south, that is, of Rome rather than Germany. The ecclesiological allegory is further charged by the ominous phrase with which Margaret introduces the jury's decision: "Now was it come to the last daye in the after none, and the xii men had hard both the parties." In its oddly apocalyptic tone, the temporal clause that locates the jury's judgment as belonging to the moment when a liminal day has begun to run toward its end resonates closely with More's sense that in heresy the English church and state were confronting the possibility of end-time.[38] As Alistair Fox has shown, at the end of his public career More carefully deploys apocalyptic rhetoric, as for example in the *Confutation*, in which he anticipates the historical moment "when yt shall come to thextremite" and "Criste shall come downe . . . and destroy the strong captayne of all these heretykes Antichryste hym selfe."[39] If in the piepowder trial the "last daye in the after none" takes on the aspect of this end-time as More had represented it, that allusion serves More's central argument that his choice, like Company's on the jury, involves the time after time when "we shall hence and come before God."

This parable, which works analogically to connect the local and the spiritual jurisdictions, also works nonanalogically as an argument about the value of jurisdictional heterogeneity per se. A story about how a little court protects royal property might, after all, have its own interest for a king. In this respect, the intrusion of a spiritual vocabulary of ceremony and of end-time into the space of the fair allows More to present two related arguments about where the king's royal interests lie in relation to jurisdiction. First, More argues that in pursuing heresy he was, as surely as if he were an escheator protecting the king's revenues, protecting the king's spiritual interests against outlaws looking only to undermine them. Insofar as the story is about a minor jurisdiction, More additionally implies that the protection of jurisdictional heterogeneity against attempts like St. German's to consolidate the central courts also serves the king by protecting that which is properly his. This is the most radical of the tale's implications, because by identifying Crown interest with the law understood as a complex jurisdictional field (including even so minor a jurisdiction as piepowder), it effectively identifies More's adversaries in the debate around the ecclesiastical jurisdiction as unwitting traitors to the king's proprietary interests.

In 1534, to be sure, jurisdictional plurality was anything but central to Henry's account of his legal authority. Simon Fish made his 1529 attack on the ecclesiastical jurisdiction persuasive to the king by associating the spiritual jurisdiction with an outright attack on the Crown: "Did not doctour Alyn most presumptuously nowe yn your tyme agaynst all his allegiaunce all that ever he coude to pull from you the knowlege of suche plees as [be]long unto your hyghe courtes unto an other court in derogacion of your crowne and dignite?"[40] In his reply to Fish, written in his capacity as chancellor, More showed himself to be fully conscious of the threat posed by Fish to the jurisdictional order, aggressively mocking Fish's "grevos" prediction of "the translatynge of the kyngys kyngdome, and the ruyne of the kynges crown."[41] Taking up Fish's implication that the king's dignity resided only on the temporal side of the jurisdictional border, More insisted instead that Fish was slyly working to destroy "the spyrytuall jursydyccyon" by falsely accusing the spirituality of aiming to "dystroy the jurysdyccyon temporall" and of presumptuosly calling "theyr jurysdyccyon a kyngdome."[42] As against Fish, More's traditional account of the prince's relation to law is that, as the head and font of justice, the king protects the jurisdictional order per se. More's 1534 parable is continuous with this account of jurisdiction, his position being that the king's authority resides in the maintenance of jurisdictional boundaries that, far from threatening a fully royal order, are instead its fullest expression.

More is arguing a legal theoretical case almost certainly in the knowledge that politics has moved past the possibility of its being heard as plausible. That said, what underlies the parable's political commitment to jurisdictional plurality is an interesting and radical account of the relation between legal meaning and the forms responsible for producing them. Having said that the jury convened to reflect on their "sentence," Margaret quickly corrects herself: "Nay let me speke better in my termes yet, I trow the judge geveth the sentence and the quests tale is called a verdit." In this quibble, More is directing his readers to reflect on the relation between tale and verdict, a relation that is especially charged since Margaret begins the parable itself by identifying it as her father's "tale." In this double usage More analyzes the necessarily provisional relation between truth and discourse. The verdict and fable are both narratives, tales told in the service of ordering experience: if, etymologically, the verdict or "quests tale" speaks truth (Lat. *verum dicere*), the fictive tale by analogy must do the same, although by other means. Conversely, if a fiction tells its truth only obliquely, the verdict can be seen analogously to be a tale in the sense that its truth too is, obliquely, always only a truth-for-the-law. This is not to say, skeptically, that the courtroom can never effectively probe for truth, but only that the court is structured formally so as always to "know" only that of which it is technically able to be cognizant. God's omniscience aside, truth, including the law's, is always truth in the context of its discovery: jurisdiction constitutes the law's authority by reflecting back the principle that judgment for truth is possible only as the assertion that in *this* case a judgment *here* is appropriate. The impossibility of more firmly grounding human truth (excepting only the pronouncements of the general council, as guided by the Holy Spirit) does not for More invalidate the "truth" discovered in Parliament or at the bar, but it means that such truths become dangerous when they fail to respect their institutional origins. Understood in this way, More's conservative commitment to the Church's absolute account of its authority can also be understood as a commitment to the ironic relation among alternative authorities, as these function in coordination with one another or, when they come into conflict, as they issue in a genuine rather than manufactured conversation among powers. At the place in the 1534 fable where lawyer and humanist meet, More evaluates the law as a story-telling, not in order to disparage it, but to register the gap between life and what law as a discursive system must make of it.

The structural irony of human judgment is at the center of More's invocation of the piepowder court in 1534 and his defense of the spiritual jurisdiction in 1533. Reflecting on the mutual implications of jurisdiction and legal centralization, More's story shows how a doctrinally conservative position might yet hold open a space of potentiality that was in the process of being shut down in the name of protecting the uniformity of royal justice. By protecting the spiritual or minor jurisdiction, More suggests, the king protects both a given power and a whole understanding of what the law means in relation to the real experience and society it orders. Only where a jurisdiction is acknowledged as exerting one kind of claim rather than another, in order to produce one kind of story rather than another (both potentially "true" in the same sense that a fiction might be said to be), is there the possibility also of acknowledging that, however effective it may be toward its end, the legal story must always remain in ironic relation to its own content. The king's province, More insists, is the ongoing, ethical adjustment of the legal story to the content it serves, a jurisdictional task that is unimaginable in a fully homogenized system in which the claims of the legal norm and of conscience become, by definition, indistinguishable. In the piepowder allegory, More counsels the king that, in acceding to St. German's and Fish's accounts of his authority as residing majestically at the center and as being only vulnerable at the edges of the common law, he has ceded, as though to an outlaw, the better part of his English legal patrimony.

AEQUITAS ENGLISHED: CHANCERY JUSTICE AND UTOPIA

More's 1534 parable imagines his resistance to Henry's break with the Church as a form of counsel concerning the complex relation between royal interest and jurisdictional order. But already, in the years immediately preceding More's formal entry into Henry's court, jurisdiction was operating for More along similar lines, as an important frame for thinking about counsel, the order of national justice, and fiction. The chief locus of these concerns was More's *Utopia* (1516). At its center, *Utopia* is a lawyer's book as well as a humanist's. In sympathy with More's late defense of jurisdictional plurality as the dynamic in which human justice is describable, it portrays ideal justice as inseparable from the activity that produces law by formally describing its limits.

At the end of Book 2, in his summary of Utopia's virtues, Hythloday compares Utopian justice with that of other, implicitly European, countries by opposing two words, *aequitas* and *iustitia*:

> I'd like at this point to see anyone dare compare this equity [of the Utopians] with the justice of other nations, among whom may I perish if I find any trace whatsoever of justice and equity.

> *Hic aliquis uelim cum hac aequitate audeat aliarum iustitiam gentium comparare, apud quas disperiam, si ullum prorsus comperio, iustitiae, aequitatisque uestigium.* (238)[43]

We can best translate the Latin *aequitas* not as "fairness" or as a synonym for justice itself, but instead as "equity," a category that in early Tudor England came under pressure as lawyers found it more necessary to give a theoretical account of the common law's authority relative to concepts such as conscience and other legal orders like canon law.[44]

To take full account of Hythloday's opposition, we should note that, having distinguished between the two terms—with equity pertaining to Utopia and justice pertaining to those "other nations"—Hythloday then treats them, at the sentence's end, as if they were equivalents or at least fully continuous with one another. That tension between two accounts of the relation between justice and equity is telling, not only because it foregrounds the irony involved in invoking a "justice" that quite simply is not just, but also because, more technically, it draws attention to More's productive exploration of a flexibility in the meaning of equity itself as a term in legal theory and practice. At the time More wrote, equity was not so much a single category as a rather murky semantic field. As Baker explains, the word had three meanings. In its most general sense, equity was "the source and spirit of all law, an abstract concept of justice." Second, it was a principle of interpretive generosity, a "criterion for interpreting written law according to the true meaning of the lawmaker, on the basis that words were an imperfect vehicle for expressing legislative intention in detail" and for including in advance all possible cases that might emerge. Third, "the classical English notion of equity," which was technically associated with the Court of Chancery, "involved the relaxation of known but unwritten rules of law to meet the exigencies of justice or conscience in particular cases."[45] It is important to emphasize here that in the early Tudor period these were complementary rather than fully differentiated meanings: so long as the relation between theoretical justice and formalist procedure remained an open question, equity was most importantly a way variously to measure the ironic gap between the two.

In 1516, moreover, equity had an immediate topical resonance. A striking feature of More's use of *aequitas* is that the term, used a total of four times, appears only in Book 1 and in the summary encomium of Utopia that concludes Book 2. This is highly suggestive because of the order of *Utopia*'s composition. As established by J. H. Hexter, More wrote *Utopia* in two stages: while on embassy in Bruges between May and October 1515, he composed the opening of Book 1 and the discursive description of Utopia that constitutes the bulk of Book 2; during the nine months following his return to London, he wrote the conclusion to Book 2 and, as Book 1, the dialogue between More and Hythloday on the topic of royal service and the conflict between *otium* and *negotium*, philosophy and courtiership, virtue and action.[46] As a frame for Book 2, Book 1 has rightly been understood as a meditation on the benefits and costs of royal service, as that related to More's personal dilemma, following his return to London, over whether to accept the king's and Wolsey's offer of a position in the royal service along with a permanent pension. This was a situation that More would fully resolve only with his entry into the King's Council in March 1518.[47] In Hexter's account of Book 1 as the externalization of More's political and psychological situation, *Utopia* ironically pits the humanist Hythloday (as a stand-in for More) against a practical and more worldly "More," the character who puts the king's and Wolsey's case in the best possible light.[48] For John Guy, however, who sees More's choice to enter the royal service as a deliberate "act of positive, not negative motivation," *Utopia* tilts distinctly in the other direction, giving the impression that "in 1516, More's desire to enter the King's Council was already strong" and suggesting further that More's central concern in Book 1 was to show how a philosopher such as Hythloday (or the historic More) might without compromise meet his civic responsibilities.[49] Similarly, in one of the most influential recent readings of *Utopia*, Quentin Skinner insists that Book 1 is polemically celebrating "one particular set of humanist beliefs—those of a 'civic' or Ciceronian humanism—and sharply opposing them to a more fashionable and broadly Platonic outlook which was threatening to undermine the element of political commitment in the humanism of More's own time." More should thus be seen not "as expressing doubts about the decision he was himself in the process of making," but "as offering a justification for that decision as the outcome of true understanding of the proper relationship between philosophy and public life."[50]

Extending Skinner's and Guy's positions, my argument is that More's interrogation of *aequitas* is central to his defense of a humanism that is simultaneously philosophical and civic in orientation; and, further, that in relation to the structure or logic of *aequitas*, *Utopia* makes itself available not simply as a book about counsel, but as already a book of counsel, an announcement of More's practical commitments. The immediate political context from the winter of 1515 through the autumn of 1516, the period in which More undertook to frame his discursive account of an ideal republic with the dialogue of counsel, helps explain why More might have turned to *aequitas* as an important structural principle for his book. In September 1515, shortly before More's return to London in October, Thomas Wolsey, Archbishop of York from August 1514, had been elected cardinal. He was so installed on November 17, this only six weeks before he was sworn in as chancellor on December 24. When More returned from Calais, he was returning to Wolsey's London. As chancellor, Wolsey became the highest representative of the king's justice, abstractly the embodiment of his law and his conscience. Practically speaking, he would preside over the conciliar courts such as Star Chamber, as well as Chancery, England's principal court of equity. In light of the Cardinal's rapid consolidation of his position as Henry VIII's chief minister and of his preeminence in relation to the idea and practice of equitable justice, More's decision to introduce *aequitas* into *Utopia*'s frame narrative suggests that his work to reframe the text he had composed in Flanders was an attempt, at least in part, to make it speak to Wolsey.

As we saw in chapter 1, the legal text through which English equity's unruliness came to be tamed is Christopher St. German's *Doctor and Student*, a treatise probably conceived and written in the late 1520s, in the context of Wolsey's decade-long chancellorship and the perception among some common lawyers that, under the name of conscience and through the excessive use of his discretionary power, Wolsey had drawn into Chancery legal business that properly pertained to the common-law jurisdictions.[51] *Doctor and Student* answered the implication that conscience was a dangerously arbitrary category by resecuring its place within and for an increasingly centralized legal system.[52] Following the Aristotelian concept of *epieikeia*, as transmitted through Aquinas and Jean Gerson, St. German described English equity, understood as the legal formalization of conscience, as a principle of interpretive flexibility internal to the law, through which the law realized or perfected itself. He thereby offered a theoretical defense of equity (and a practical defense of Chancery jurisdiction) as being supplemental to, rather than corrective of, the common law, an "excepcion [that] is secretly understande [understood] in every generall rewle of every posytyve lawe."[53]

This account of legal conscience, however, was only the starting point for St. German's principal argument that English law and conscience-as-equity were congruent in such a way as effectively to *limit* the claim of conscience on the law rather than the reverse. We can think of St. German's brilliant achievement as uniting the two maxims for which the book is most famous. On the one hand, St. German writes that "Lawes covet to be rewlyd by equtye" as the principle of justice that "must always be observyd in every lawe of man, and in every generall rewle therof."[54] On the other hand, he insists that where equity follows the law in the traditional theological sense that "conscyence" always looks to law and is "rewlyd by the lawe," this is to be understood not only, as is manifestly the case, "of the lawe of reason: and of the lawe of god. But also of the lawe of man that is not contrary to the lawe of reason nor the lawe of god."[55] In a nutshell, St. German's theory of conscience and equity allowed for the possibility that, exactly to the extent that it was ruled by equity, the temporal law might, as an instantiated expression of reason, itself be the rule against which the claim of conscience was to be measured. Equating the claims of conscience and equity, the common law could thus control conscience, which, if taken as a controlling ethical principle at law, might otherwise seem to circumscribe positive law. By thus subordinating the potentially disruptive category of conscience to the common law, St. German massively increased the prestige of the central courts relative to other jurisdictions, including, most notably, the ecclesiastical jurisdiction.[56]

Far less technical and extensive than St. German's retrospective look at Wolsey's legal policies, More's thoughts on equity in *Utopia* are nevertheless on a continuum with them. In 1516, at the beginning of Wolsey's chancellorship, they can be seen as a lawyer's reflection on the relation between English law and equity, and a lawyer's counsel concerning the office that Wolsey had recently assumed. What, then, does More mean by *aequitas* when Hythloday polemically opposes "this equity [of the Utopians] with the justice of other nations." Hythloday's use of *aequitas* corresponds, first, to what Baker identifies as equity's most general sense, an abstract notion of justice underlying all law. In Hythloday's encomium of Utopian equity, however, this general sense of *aequitas* becomes highly charged through its relation to *aequalitas*, the economic equality effected through the Utopians' elimination of private property. At the conclusion of Book 1, Hythloday celebrates that policy as the sole basis for a good society, arguing that "the one and only road to a general welfare is where an equality of goods is imposed [*si rerum indicatur aequalitas*]." He declares himself persuaded that without the abolition of private property, "there can be no uniform or just distribution of goods, nor any happy government in human affairs [*res aequabili ac iusta aliqua ratione distribui, aut feliciter agi cum rebus mortalium . . . non posse*]" (104). As an index of Hythloday's commitments, More here deploys *res* as keyword: as "matter" and "thing," it connects the commodity to human affairs more generally and thus plumbs the root dependence of government and the *respublica* on the manner in which material goods are distributed.

This relation of political virtue to economic equality (*aequalitas*) and uniformity (*aequabilitas*) governs Hythloday's distinction between equity and justice at the conclusion of Book 2. Just before making that distinction, Hythloday declares that in Utopia, where nothing is private, "men pursue public affairs [*publicum negotium*] seriously," and that public and private interests become coordinate "where everything belongs to everyone [*ubi omnia omnium sunt*]" (238). In this immediate context, it is clear that for Hythloday Utopian *aequitas* must mean economic equity and as such, a kind of justice against which the justice of other nations is exposed as wanting. Turning, then, to those nations that know no equity but only justice, Hythloday asks what sort of justice it can be ("*quae haec iustitia est*") that allows the idle rich to live in luxury, and farmers and laborers barely to subsist. Unfolding the irony of this unjust justice, he declares that it is "an unjust and ungrateful commonwealth [*iniqua & ingrata respublica*]" that "lavishes the bulk of its rewards" on parasites, while making no provision for those on whose labor the republic truly depends (240). This kind of commonwealth is *iniqua*, "unjust," because it is *iniqua*, "unequal." Hythloday's distinction between equity and justice thus recasts what, alongside most readers of More's text, Hexter describes as Utopia's most radical idea: "Community of property and abolition of money are *the only means* for achieving true equality. They are also *only the means*; the end is equality. For the final equations are simple and radical: the equitable is the good; equality is justice."[57] Rehearsing *Utopia*'s fuller argument about distributive justice in terms of the semantic tension among terms, Hythloday construes *aequitas* as a particular species of justice by routing it through *aequalitas*: it is justice in relation to the distribution of quantifiable goods, justice in the aspect of an economic equality that is the source of all civic justice.

Most astonishing in Hythloday's argument is that, in so connecting equality and equity, he reverses the account of those terms as given in Book 2 of Cicero's *De officiis*. This work was an important source for *Utopia* and a text equally important in the Renaissance for its defense of private property and for its investigation of the conflict, so central to Book 1 of *Utopia*, between the moral and the expedient.[58] In an attack on agrarian laws as demagoguery (2.21.73), Cicero insists that a speech concerning the redistribution of property was pernicious ("*capitalis*") in advocating an equal distribution of goods ("*ad aequationem bonorum pertinens*"), for the simple reason that private property is the institution for whose defense governments are chiefly constituted.[59] Those behind such reformist laws, he writes, "weaken the foundations of the commonwealth: harmony, first, which cannot continue when money is taken from some and given to others; then equity, which is utterly abolished when one is not permitted to hold onto one's own possessions [*deinde aequitatem, quae tollitur omnis, si habere suum cuique non licet*]" (2.22.78). According to this argument, although *aequitas* and an *aequatio* in distribution may appear continuous, real equity depends on maintaining that order whose expression is historical inequality with respect to distribution. "How is it equitable [*Quam autem habet aequitatem*]," Cicero asks, "that he who had nothing should have land occupied for many years or even centuries, and he who had that land should lose it?" (2.22.79). The Ciceronian account of equity was current in Henrician England; the author of a treatise on the jurisdiction of English courts, first printed in 1526, defines equity in these terms, when in a concluding paragraph on justice as the theoretical ground for all law he cites Cicero and Macrobius to the effect that "justice is equity, assigning right to each and every thing in proportion to the dignity of each [*Justitia est equitas, ius unicuique rei tribuens pro dignitate cuiusque*]." It is similarly said that "justice preserves for each what belongs to him [*Justitia est servare unicuique quod suum est*]."[60]

In his repeated insistence that *aequitas* looks away from the simple equality of economic equity in favor of a distribution that respects differences in social order, Cicero is following Aristotle's definition, in the *Nicomachean Ethics*, that the just "is therefore the proportionate, and the unjust is that which violates proportion" (5.3.14).[61] So construed, justice does not so much eschew equality as substitute a more complex uniformity for a simple one. Cicero in *De officiis* is helpfully explicit about this substitution in his earlier discussion of *decorum*, the private virtue according to which individuals fit their behavior to circumstance, thereby making the two proportionate. By respecting differences among agents and the situations in which they act, the decorous individual is able to discover a different form of equality. Although *decorum* demands that, whatever we see in others, "we measure our own endeavors by the standard of our own nature [*nos studia nostra nostrae naturae regula metiamur*]" (1.31.110), that respect for difference means that in relation to the individual life, *decorum* is registered not as difference but precisely as an evenness or "uniformity in the whole of a life and in its individual actions [*aequabilitas cum universae vitae, tum singularum actionum*], something you cannot achieve if by imitating the nature of others you neglect your own" (1.31.111). In place of an equality of action among agents and across different situations, *decorum* produces multiple samenesses, each one a uniformity in relation to the private life and the individual's nature.

As with private *decorum*, Cicero's public *aequitas* similarly substitutes a complex equality for the equality of distribution it eschews. In a passage on the origin of kingship and of laws, Cicero identifies the first king as one whose manifest virtue led the oppressed to appeal to him for protection. By reason of that virtue, Cicero continues, he "protected the weaker from wrong, and through the establishment of equitable arrangements [*aequitate constituenda*] checked high and low through a like law [*pari iure*]. And the reason for making laws was the same as for kings: the thing that has always been sought is a right [*ius*] that is uniform [*aequabile*], since it would not otherwise be right" (2.12.41–42). Cicero's *aequitas* here is identified with procedural uniformity or judicial indifference in the application of law. This is an evenness that will express itself, however, exactly in the maintenance of the social differences, like that between high and low, that require the proportionate adjustment in the first place. Economic inequity, in other words, is for Cicero the exemplary difference in historical circumstance according to which a law can be identified as having been equitably applied across cases. Far from contravening *aequitas*, economic inequity motivates and sustains it.

At the most general level, therefore, Hythloday's simpler alignment of equity with equality of distribution is a strikingly direct response, philosophically and semantically, to Cicero's splitting of judicial *aequitas* and *aequabilitas* from the *aequatio bonorum*. *Utopia*'s connection to Cicero, and through Cicero to Aristotle, is suggestive, furthermore, for a second level of meaning in *aequitas* as a particular construction of justice in relation to the written law. Immediately following his attack on the commonwealths for distributing their goods unevenly, Hythloday intensifies the opposition of European justice and true equity by appealing to a second distinction, that between justice and law, specifically written law:

> What's more, every day the rich shave off some part of the daily ration allotted the poor, not only through private fraud, but even through public laws. Consequently, the thing that before was seen as unjust—that those meriting the best from the Republic should receive the worst return—this, they have further disfigured, even transforming it, by promulgation of law, into justice.
>
> *Quid quod ex diurno pauperum demenso diuites cotidie aliquid, non modo priuata fraude, sed publicis etiam legibus abradunt, ita quod ante uidebatur iniustum, optime de Republica meritis pessimam referre gratiam, hoc isti deprauatum etiam fecerunt, tum prouulgata lege iustitiam.* (240)

Having defined the uneven distribution of goods as pernicious, Hythloday here insists that that inequity at least has the virtue of being visible as unjust. Inequity reaches its perfection, rather, at the point where injustice, as a substitute for justice, becomes semantically indistinguishable from it. Hythloday's sentence, one of *Utopia*'s ironic and rhetorical high points, depends for its effect on replicating the social transformation it records: its grammar translates that injustice which is still known as such ("*quod ante uidebatur iniustum*") by means of the published law ("*prouulgata lege*") into a justice ("*iustitiam*") that can be heard with perfect ironic pitch simultaneously as a polity's justice and the injustice named by that justice. While the injustice of distribution is an effect of human willfulness, this second "justice" is an effect of the enacted law.[62]

The sentence in which Hythloday contrasts equity and justice pits Utopian equity also against this second justice. If *iustitia* itself becomes perverse through its expression in the written and promulgated law, then *aequitas* correspondingly must belong to the Utopians as that which instead protects the relation between abstract justice and written law. Equity in this second sense is justice in relation to the public written law, justice in the aspect of the hermeneutic order that grounds the practice of justice. Through his two distinctions—the first between equity and justice, the second between justice and law—Hythloday links two equities, one concerned with the distribution of goods and the other with the written law as a corruptible vehicle for justice. Just as distributive inequity serves private ownership, the gauge that something is inequitable in a written law is that it serves a private rather than public interest. Thus Hythloday declares that, so far as he can see, the world's commonwealths are nothing but a "conspiracy of the rich, who look to their own profit [*suis commodis*] under the name and title of commonwealth" and use law against the public it claims to serve: "These devices [*machinamenta*] become law [*iam leges fiunt*] as soon as the rich decree they are to be observed [*decreuerunt obseruari*], this in the name of the public, meaning of course the poor as well" (241).

The notion that, with respect to the written law, equity looks to public interest was a legal commonplace, one most familiar in relation to legislative interpretation rather than legislative enactment. This equity, taking up Baker's second sense, was the hermeneutic principle or "criterion for interpreting written law," through which a judge could extend or limit a written rule to situations not specifically included in the law, on the theory that the new case was within "the equity of the statute," that is, implicitly within its ambit. As this legal formula implies, the equitable enlargement of a statute was less a conscientious decision than a technical maneuver. The justification for taking the novel case "by the equity" was, first, its similarity to the case imagined by the statute: by effecting uniformity across similar cases, this practical equity preserved the image of a uniform law.[63] Second, jurists could justify the extension of a statute by looking to legislative intention in the sense Aristotle gives in the *Ethics*, where he defines equity (*epieikeia*) as a "rectification of legal justice" in light of its necessary but problematic generality: "When therefore the law lays down a general rule, and thereafter a case arises which is an exception to the rule, it is then right, where the lawgiver's pronouncement because of its absoluteness is defective and erroneous, to rectify the defect by deciding as the lawgiver would himself decide if he were present on the occasion, and would have enacted if he had been cognizant of the case in question" (5.10.3–6).

According to both logics, interpretation comes to look like simply an application of the law, a point made particularly vivid in Sir John Fortescue's account of equity in chapter 24 of his *De natura legis naturae*. There, slightly torquing Aristotle's theory, Fortescue justifies the king's interpretive extension of the law to cover a new case by implying that that case is already included in the very *words* of the statute, only without the legislator having been aware of it: "And often the mind of the lawgiver [*mens latoris*] was not fully conscious [*non persensit*] of that which the words of the law included [*ea quae legis verba amplectuntur*]; and for that reason, the office of the good prince, who is called the living law [*lex viva*], supplies the defect of the written law, which, as though dead, continues always unchanging [*semper immobilis perseverat*]."[64] This is a version of equity that, as theory, is remarkably protective of legal form and formalism. In practice, however, this judicial reconstitution of a grounding intention could still be achieved only according to some measurable norm; as Lorna Hutson has emphasized, the human criterion by which historical legislative intention was measurable was the idea of the public good, the theory being that no legislative act was imaginable that did not have the protection of that good as its end.[65] Against the letter of law, equity looks to legislative intention as measured by the idea of the public good.

Or so the theory goes. For in this context what leaps out in Hythloday's account of the lack of legislative equity in Europe is that legislators there precisely intend the harm they do, which means that any interpretation according to legislative intention is already compromised from within the system. Hythloday's cynicism about the possibility of grounding an equitable account of the written law is continuous with his equally discouraged treatment of *aequitas* as a principle of interpretation in Book 1. In a passage that effectively sets up the moment in Book 2 concerning the inequitable legislator, Hythloday insists that interpretive equity cannot on its own guarantee justice. As he explains to "More," the virtuous counselor who wants to guide the king will get no help from the law, since the law can be twisted to serve the king's interests, and since other counselors will encourage the king to use his judges simply as a means around the law:

> No cause of his will be so patently unjust [*tam aperte iniquam*] that one of them will not discover some chink by which to introduce a legal subterfuge [*qua possit intendi calumnia*]. And if through a disagreement in judicial opinion a thing that is perfectly clear in itself is disputed, and truth brought into question, the king is thereby conveniently [*commodum*] given a handle to interpret the law to his advantage [*pro suo commodo*].... Nor will the judges lack a pretext for pronouncing in favor of the king, since it will suffice for him that equity [*aut aequitatem*]

be on his side or the letter of the law [*aut uerba legis*] or the twisted meaning of the written word [*aut contortum scripti sensum*] or that which for scrupulous judges [*apud religiosos iudices*] outweighs all laws, the indisputable royal prerogative [*principis indisputabiliem praerogatiuam*].

(92)

In Hythloday's account, strikingly, equity is neither more nor less vulnerable to the king's will than the letter it opposes, but simply one among a group of interpretive rationalizations through which the law can be made to do that which is not only unjust but, measured against the law as it stands, illegal, too. The equitable here has become unmoored from the public interest that supposedly motivates its hermeneutics, a point that More underlines through the play inside a term used to refer to the king's private interests: "*commodum*" and "*pro suo commodo*" both stand in tension with a phrase immediately preceding the quoted passage in which Hythloday has spoken of the public welfare as a "*populi commodum*" (92). Commodity speaks to a convenience or fit, a decorous adjustment to circumstance. The irony as Hythloday pronounces it, then, is that the royal will has overpowered the very concept of the convenient, thereby reducing the equitable to the trickery or calumny it supposedly resists. In this sense, the absolutist prerogative is merely a logical extension of equity: as a means congruent with the law to privilege an exception to the law, both equity and the prerogative perilously come, from within the law, to stand beyond the law.

As the word with which Hythloday designates the scandalous misinterpretation of law against the public good, *calumnia* points the reader back to *De officiis*, and to Cicero's treatment of equity as an interpretive principle that resists a too strict interpretation and application of the written law. "Injustices," Cicero writes, "often arise through calumny, from a too skilful and crafty interpretation of the law; and from this there arose the common proverb, 'Extreme law is extreme injustice' [*Existunt etiam saepe iniuriae calumnia quadam et nimis callida, sed malitiosa iuris interpretatione. Ex quo illud 'Summum ius summa iniuria' factum est iam tritum sermone proverbium*]" (1.10.33).[66] As is well known, this adage in which Cicero encapsulates his critique of an only legalistic and inequitable interpretation was extremely popular in early sixteenth-century Europe, largely through Erasmus's treatment of it in the *Adagia*.[67] It enters *Utopia* with Hythloday's first reference to *aequitas*, in a passage that as a whole encapsulates the complexity of the term as I have been charting it out. When Cardinal Morton asks Hythloday to explain why thieves should not be punished by death, Hythloday answers that the punishment does not fit the crime: "it is unjust [*iniquum*]," he says, that "a man's life should be taken away on account that goods were so taken [*uitam eripi propter ereptam pecuniam*]" (72). Here, aptly put, is the idea of *decorum* governing the uniformity that Cicero identifies with equitable justice. Hythloday continues: "And if they say that the punishment is for the offence against justice [*laesam iustitiam*] and the violation of laws [*leges*], and not the money, then is not that extreme law appropriately called extreme injustice [*quid ni merito summum illud ius, summa uocetur iniuria*]" (72). Here, mirroring the Ciceronian and Erasmian adage, is equity as a principle of flexibility for the application of law, a meaning that Hythloday explicates by using the examples of the Stoics and of Manlius (a figure from Livy exemplary of a father's too harsh treatment of a son) to criticize both those laws that are too strict in relation to a given offence and those laws that make no distinctions among offences: "For we should approve neither those Manlian commands that, wheresoever [*sicubi*] they are not obeyed in the most trifling of matters, instantly [*illico*] unsheathe the sword; nor those Stoic decrees that measure all crimes as equal, such that they judge there to be no difference [*nihil . . . interesse*] between someone killing a man and stealing a coin from him, when, if equity means anything at all [*si quicquam aequitas ualet*], there is no similarity or affinity whatsoever [*nihil omnino simile aut affine*] between the two" (72). Having hinted at the equity that longs for just proportion and then the equity that adjusts the written law to avoid the injustice that comes from its too strict application, Hythloday at the end of the passage alludes to the interpretive evolution through which a judge moves between similar cases according to "the equity of the statute." Given the passage's highly compressed account of English equity, Hythloday's angry "if equity means anything at all" reads also as More's reminder that equity, rather than being a fixed principle at law, is the semantic field made up of its more and less technical senses, and that it most productively stands as the ongoing but also unfixed promise of justice through law.

In my account of Utopian *aequitas*, I have only just now touched on the equity that was most closely associated with Chancery, according to which the chancellor might relax given legal rules so as "to meet the exigencies of justice or conscience in particular cases." As Baker explains, "the detailed consideration of particular circumstances, which in England came to adopt the name 'equity,' was more suited to the Court of Chancery than the common-law courts because the Chancery in exercising its bill jurisdiction behaved much more like a jury than a court of law," concerned as it was with the conscientious adjudication of fact rather than technical law.[68] In the context of this relationship between equity and factual circumstantiality, it is notable that in describing the inequity of Manlian laws, Hythloday uses two spatio-temporal adverbs that together give formal expression to the inequity specifically of failing to consider circumstance: "For we should approve neither those Manlian commands that, wheresoever they are not obeyed in the most trifling of matters, instantly unsheathe the sword [*Nam neque legum probanda sunt tam Manliana imperia, ut sicubi in leuissimis parum obtemperetur, illico stringant gladium*]." The play here is between the indefinite and hypothetical *sicubi* ("wheresoever") and the super-definite *illico* ("instantly," "exactly in that place") by which the Manlian edicts respond with strict precision to the infinite contingencies of experience. That is, the Manlian laws—and here, the passage indexes what Baker defines as "English" equity—violate the very idea of circumstance by answering it with a ferociously self-defining limitation upon circumstance.

This grammatical and rhetorical effect is of great interest because of the relation it bears to the title of More's book. *Utopia* is, of course, a nowhere, and as a negative indefinite it is the obverse of the positively indefinite *sicubi* that in Hythloday's sentence stands metonymically for the circumstance that is the proper object of equitable inquiry. Utopia is a place, that is, of a curiously negative circumstantiality, a place in whose particulars circumstantiality exists potentially rather than actually. This means that any concept of justice defined as a convenient fit between norm and circumstance can exist, too, only as a potentiality, but also that legal form for that reason must itself become the vehicle to carry forward the circumstantial potential against which the form might otherwise be measured. Book 1 elucidates this part of More's formalism (which I take to be continuous with St. German's theory of equity's being internal to law and with More's analysis, in the Tower parable, of justice as a jurisdictional tale). In Book 1, I turn now to More's use of legal procedure to bring law and equity into conversation with one another, aiming to show how in light of that dynamic it becomes possible to read the two-book format of *Utopia* as a reflection on the jurisdictionally ironic relation between the common law and the chancellor's law.

PLEADING, TRIAL, AND JUDGMENT: CHANCELLOR MORTON'S DINNER

A*equitas* first emerges as a theme in Book 1 within the story that Hythloday tells "More" about a dinner conversation at the table of John, Cardinal Morton, Lord Chancellor under Henry VII and a man whom More held in high regard, having served as page in Morton's household and having benefited from his continued patronage. As a sign of his respect, More gives Morton a critical role in the argument of Book 1: as host of the dinner and moderator of the debate in which Hythloday engages a pedantic lawyer concerning the justice of English laws, Morton is the principal exemplar in *Utopia* of prudence and judicial virtue.[69] At the time of *Utopia*'s publication in December 1516, Morton would also have played a further role. Hythloday introduces Morton by saying that during his one visit to England he was "much indebted to the Right Reverend Father, John Cardinal Morton, Archbishop of Canterbury, and then also Lord Chancellor of England" (58). For any English reader in 1516, this list of dignities would have suggested an obvious parallel between Henry VII's chancellor and Henry VIII's: with the substitution of York for Canterbury, the list describes Wolsey. This topical connection would have been the more forceful in light of how recent Wolsey's two appointments were.[70] More's portrait of Morton works as ingratiation, representing one chancellor to flatter another, but also as counsel, giving an idealized account of what the new chancellor might become. Indeed, as we shall see, Morton's dinner table describes Chancery itself, thereby portraying for Wolsey the nature of the justice that, as keeper of the king's conscience and as keeper of Chancery, he would now be overseeing. Here again, as in the preceding account of Utopian *aequitas*, the additions of 1516 make *Utopia* Wolsey's book.

Unsurprisingly, the conversation at Morton's table follows the form of a debate, with Hythloday and the pedantic lawyer arguing as to why, in spite of English justice, there are still thieves in England. From its opening, More allows the lawyer and Hythloday to represent the claims respectively of law and equity: while the lawyer celebrates "that rigid justice [*rigidam illam iustitiam*]" with which thieves are punished, Hythloday espouses instead an equitable justice, insisting that punishing thieves by death is "beyond justice and not in the public interest [*haec punitio furum & supra iustum est, & non ex usu publico*]" (60).[71] This thematic opposition is mirrored in the form of the dinner conversation. George Logan has shown that in Hythloday's speech, as in Book 1 generally, More draws on *honestas* and *utilitas*, the central *topoi* of deliberative rhetoric, which, oriented toward the future, concerns itself with the advantages or disadvantages of a proposed policy or action.[72] Logan's reading thus supplements accounts of *Utopia* that have emphasized the book's relation to demonstrative rhetoric, the branch of persuasion that, oriented to the present, considers questions of praise and dispraise, including praise of the city or republic. But for the relation of the dinner scene to the political context of 1516, the most important branch of rhetoric is the forensic, which, oriented to the past, considers questions of truth and falsehood. More structures the dinner scene as a self-contained legal debate, and he does so by looking to English law to follow two of its procedural orders simultaneously. The first belongs to the common law and is exemplary of legal formalism; the second belongs to Chancery and is exemplary of equity's greater procedural flexibility.

In relation to the common law, Morton presides over a formal legal conversation between opposing parties that takes us through all the stages of an action at common law, from pleading through trial to judgment. Hythloday's anecdote opens with pleading, the formal common-law process whereby, originally through oral engagement and later in written drafts, the opposing parties provisionally and hypothetically presented their respective versions of the facts, in order through a process of continuous refinement to settle on the single issue (*exitum*) that was to be decided by the court.[73] At Morton's dinner table, the opposing speakers dispute not the particulars of a single case, but rather the nature of English justice itself, as factually exemplified in the inability of the system to deal effectively with theft. In their pleas, Hythloday and the lawyer counter one another's stories so as to identify where the fault in English justice resides, in order, then, to determine (as in a trial) how to resolve that problem. Here, in More's imagining, the forensic and deliberative fuse.

More replicates the various formal stages of pleading by marking them through a series of verbal cues. The lawyer begins the process by relating ("*narrabat*") that thieves in England "are everywhere punished, with as many as twenty being hanged on one gallows," and then expressing wonder ("*dicebat se mirari*") as to why the country is still troubled by them (60). This move corresponds to the plaintiff's opening declaration, or count, a stage in pleading known in law French as *conte* and in Latin as *narratio*, the term that More alludes to in having the pedant *narrate* his opening statement.[74] In response to the count, a defendant had several options. He might, for example, make a general plea in bar and deny all the facts in the declaration; or he might make what was known as "a special plea by way of confession and avoidance, in which the defendant set out the additional facts on which he relied, and asked the court to adjudge whether, in view of them, the plaintiff ought to have his action against him."[75] This second kind of plea in bar corresponds to Hythloday's entry into the conversation. Daring to speak before the Cardinal, he accepts the "facts" of his opponent's narration, but insists that the lawyer need not wonder ("*nihil mireris*") that the punishments are ineffective, since the thieves steal through necessity, having no other way to make a living:

"there is no penalty [*poena*] so great," he says, "as to keep from stealing those who have no other means of obtaining food [*uictus*]" (60). Here, then, is the avoidance, facts added to the opponent's facts with the purpose of offering an alternative interpretation and thereby of discovering where materially the opponents' stories differ.

Faced with the defendant's avoidance, a plaintiff had, among other options, the option similarly "to confess the avoidance and avoid it, in which case the defendant had to rejoin."[76] This is how the lawyer responds when he replies to Hythloday's objection by claiming that "sufficient provision has been made for this situation [*Est inquit ille, satis hoc prouisum*]" (60). In that "*hoc*," the lawyer "confesses" the fact that Hythloday has described in his avoidance— namely, that thieves steal through hunger—and then adds as his avoidance the further fact that thieves could instead take up farming or one of the mechanical arts to answer the need. Hythloday again counters, and this time More wittily has him identify verbally what the lawyer, according to the science of pleading, has technically just done: "No, I said, you will not *avoid* the matter so easily [*At non sic **euades** inquam*]" (60, emphasis added). The form of Hythloday's answer to his opponent's own avoidance is now predictable: there are crafts and there is farming, Hythloday implicitly confesses, but these will not help, say, a wounded soldier who is prevented by his disability from practicing his own or any other craft, or the idle attendants of rich men, who, once they are forced into the labor market, are fit for neither craft nor labor (60–62). Taking on his opponent's new facts, the lawyer replies that the idle attendants of the rich should be encouraged *not* to farm, since as men of "more exalted and nobler spirit than laborers or farmers," they are more valuable as soldiers (62). Hythloday responds, once again insisting that such social structures rather encourage than discourage thieving.[77] He diagnoses the problem of mercenaries and retainers and, most famously, adduces the enclosures that rob tenants of their homes and livelihood (62–68). He then concludes his argument by recommending legislation to correct, one by one, the structural defects in society whereby honest people are transformed into thieves, treating these in reverse order to that in which he has described them: make laws, he says, to restore enclosed land, limit idleness, restore farming, and restore the art of weaving (68–70).

At the moment he makes these legislative recommendations on the basis of a presentation of the facts that is, after all, still in dispute, Hythloday has in effect preemptively exited the process of pleading. In response, then, to Hythloday's long discourse, the lawyer attempts to reopen the process. He does so by confessing that Hythloday has spoken well enough for a stranger

("*Belle, inquit, dixisti profecto, quum sis uidelicet hospes*"), and then asserting, as his avoidance, that Hythloday's knowledge of the matter under discussion is, as a stranger's, fuzzy rather than exact ("*exacte*"), something the lawyer will now "in a few words make evident [*id quod ego paucis efficiam perspicuum*]" (70). Before he can continue the conversation by detailing his more exact knowledge of the situation, the Cardinal, in one of the scene's rhetorical high points, silences him—"Be quiet [*Tace*]" (70)—and with that brings the process of judicial refinement through pleading to an end.

As he does so, however, More gives to Morton a set of jokes about the legal form that the dinner conversation has to this point encoded. Having silenced the lawyer, Morton promises him that he will have the right to respond at a later meeting:

> which, unless something prevent you or Raphael here, I would like to put off to tomorrow. In the meantime, my dear Raphael, I would gladly hear from you why you think theft should not be punished by death, or what other punishment you yourself would impose as leading more to the public good.
>
> *quem (nisi quid impediat, aut te, aut Raphaëlem hunc) crastinus dies uelim referat. Sed interim abs te mi Raphaël perquam libenter audierim, quare tu furtum putes ultimo supplicio non puniendum quamue aliam poenam ipse statuas, quae magis conducat in publicum.* (70–72)

The first thing to notice here in relation to the scene's legal structure is that the chancellor effects a transition from one question to another. Hythloday and the lawyer have treated the declared fact that the punishment of thieves is ineffective, by probing whether thieves in England steal from necessity; the Cardinal, remaining on topic, changes the terms of the question, asking not how to prevent thieves from becoming thieves, but instead, given thieves, how to punish them more effectively. As such, the chancellor finesses the pleading undertaken by the opposing parties, by settling himself on the issue or *exitum* for trial: since the punishments don't work, his question to Hythloday implies, the flaw is in the punishment: what, then, can be done? Put another way, Morton technically adjourns one proceeding, referring it to a later day, and declares another open. What follows, a second stage of Hythloday's discourse on thieving in which he argues against imposing death for theft, constitutes a *trial*, rather than a process of pleading to produce the question; it is for this reason, indeed, that the chancellor will formally be able to render judgment.

The chancellor thus settles the issue; More signals this stage in the legal process with the dinner party's most startling double entendre, "*abs te*," a phrase through which the chancellor's intervention is transformed into the final stage of the process of pleading. In a pleading, as Baker explains, confession and avoidance could not by itself produce the issue, given that "there was not yet an affirmative and a negative, and so the plaintiff [or defendant] would have to reply to the affirmative matter in the avoidance." After a confession and avoidance, therefore, in order to tender issue, the party had to reply by generally traversing or denying "the whole plea in bar," or by specially traversing the plea and denying "a single material fact" therein. According to legal form, both pleas absolutely required a "negative," a clause in which the pleader identified the material disagreement by directly denying it and so producing it as issue. In the general denial, this was the *absque talis causa* clause, which "traversed generally the affirmative matter (or *causa*) of the justification" contained in the opponent's avoidance; in the special traverse, the negative, which pointed to only one material fact, was the *absque hoc* ("this thing excepted") clause. The essence of the final plea was the negative: "The *absque hoc* clause was essential (though other words could be used), because of the maxim that two affirmatives (though inconsistent) did not make an issue. Another, more technical way of putting it was that an affirmative pleaded against an affirmative was 'argumentative': that is, it implied a denial without denying." Thus "to an averment that someone was dead, it was not sufficient to plead that he was alive, without an *absque hoc* that he was dead." In a plea of trespass for taking goods, similarly, the defendant might plead "that the goods were his own, *absque hoc* that they belonged to the plaintiff."[78] Whatever its apparent redundancy, the *absque hoc* or "without-this" clause formally produced the issue by hypothetically excluding a fact hypothetically included in the opposing plea.

This is what Morton's transition does, with ingenious comic effect: "*Sed interim abs te mi Raphaël perquam libenter audierim.*" As it is usually translated, *abs te* is taken to refer to Raphael, and the passage to mean, "in the meantime, my dear Raphael, I would gladly hear *from* you." But as More has built the sentence, *te* has been used in the clause immediately preceding to refer to the lawyer as against Raphael—"*nisi quid impediat, aut te, aut Raphaëlem hunc.*" So at the moment that Morton tenders the issue by declaring that the relevant question, for Raphael alone, is the kind of punishment used against thieves, More exploits an ambiguity in reference so as to have the chancellor simultaneously dismiss the pedantic lawyer in a moment of brutal legal comedy: "in the meantime, *without* you, I would gladly hear, my dear

Raphael, why theft should not be punished by death." Morton produces the issue for trial not by negating a material fact in the plea, but by negating the material presence of the pleader. The legal quibble is that through the highest formalism at common law Hythloday and the chancellor are able to trump an opponent who embodies legal formalism, a man who "with precision praises that strict justice [*accurate laudare, rigidam illam iusititiam*]" executed on thieves (60), and who claims, against his opponent's amateurism, that his knowledge of judicial matters is "exact [*exacte*]" (70).

Quite apart from the legal wit, More's ingenious joke resolutely turns the scene from pleading to trial. In the section following, the issue having been tendered, Raphael presents a case for relaxing the punishment against thieves, first declaring that the harsh punishment does not fit the crime (72-74), then recommending, in place of so extreme a measure, the punishment used by the Polyerites: repayment of what was taken and, for the thieves, hard labor as "slaves [*servos*]" (74-78). He concludes this stage of his case by recommending a change in English policy, a suggestion that the opposing lawyer answers, so briefly and marginally as to make him seem only defeated by the formal process to which More's legal forms have subjected him: "When I had finished this, I added that I could see no reason [*nihil . . . causae*], why this method could not be used in England, with much more benefit than that justice [*iustitia*] which the legal expert had so praised. At this he—you know, the lawyer [*nempe iurisconsultus*]—replied that such a system could never be established in England, without bringing the commonwealth into the gravest danger; and with that he shook his head, twisted his lip, and fell silent" (78-80). With this, the trial is at a close, and judgment in the hands of the chancellor.

Like the rest of the case as More has presented it, Morton's judgment differs from a standard judgment at common law. Neither for nor against Hythloday, it expresses Morton's prudence as, implicitly, a second adjournment:

> Then the Cardinal said, "It is not easy to predict [*diuinare*] whether the policy would end well or badly [*commodene an secus*], since it has never been tested. But once the death sentence has been pronounced, let the king order a delay in execution and, restricting the rights of sanctuary, try the plan out. Then if the policy were in the event to prove useful, it would be right to establish it as law [*rectum fuerit eam stabiliri*]; if not, carrying out a punishment then against those who are already condemned would be no less to the public good [*e republica*] and no more unjust [*iniustum*] than if it were done now. . . . It seems to me

clear that vagrants, too, could well be dealt with in the same manner, since in spite of many laws against them we have achieved nothing. (80)

In evaluating this careful statement as a judgment, we should note first that, according to the conventional characterization of Parliament as England's highest court, judgment and legislation were far closer in spirit than they are now: indeed, Serjeant Fineux could say in 1492 that "an act of parliament is nothing except *judicium*, and an act is a judgment [*come un jugement*]."[79] Here is a judgment like Morton's, one that, responsive to the past and oriented toward the future, is simultaneously forensic and deliberative.[80] Morton's legislative pronouncement in this light is best thought of as a reservation of judgment. Given the shape of the preceding legal discussion, indeed, it is striking that Morton's speech responds to Hythloday's proposal by adopting an aptly double temporality: first, in light of the deliberative cast of the case at hand, he considers Raphael's recommendation in relation to the future, as a difficulty of predicting what will or will not work; second, in light of the common-law forensics that structures the scene, he anticipates a future from which, in retrospect, the policy could be judged to have succeeded or failed. The shape of Morton's judgment thus mirrors the scene's fusion of a deliberative question to the forensic proceduralism that moves from pleading through trial.

Although highly responsive to the strict form of the common-law case at hand, Morton's judgment is also, notably, equitable, this in a doctrinal and procedural sense. At the level of doctrine, he treats Hythloday's proposal for statutory intervention in terms of the juridical authority involved in the relaxation of the law's norms. First is the dispensation that allows the king to delay execution, a power rooted in the idea of the prince's merciful mitigation of the law. Against this legitimate relaxation of the law, which poses no threat to the legal order, the Cardinal posits sanctuary as a dangerous judicial practice at the edge of the royal law. As touched on in the previous chapter, sanctuary was a right grounded both in the status of the ecclesiastical space as a place of peace and in the claimant's having a legal identity in excess of his or her legal subjectivity under secular law. Although in the early Tudor period sanctuary had become notorious as a way for criminals to avoid punishment and even continue their criminal activity, granting the claimant sanctuary was not in theory to subvert common law, but rather to look beyond it toward criteria other than those that allowed the secular law to function efficiently. In dispensation and sanctuary, then, Morton takes up the profoundly equitable question of *which* exceptions to the law are tolerable to that law. It is relevant, finally, that Morton concludes his statement by extending Hythloday's hypothetical legislation through analogy to include vagrants, since, as we have seen, where a judge equitably extended a statute to include a case not explicitly included therein, similarity was the criterion for so adjusting the written rule. Morton produces against the vagrants the equitable extension of Hythloday's hypothetical legislation.[81]

These doctrinal elements in Morton's judgment cap an important strain in the scene as a whole, insofar as More has inflected the fiction's common-law forms with elements suggestive instead of Chancery procedure. Although Chancery would eventually become as formalistic as the common-law courts, in the early Tudor period Chancery procedure was still marked by a looseness corresponding to the more flexible justice it promised.[82] Indeed, this procedural looseness made its special justice possible. If it was the case that in Chancery "a man will have remedy [*avera remedy*] for those things for which he has no remedy at common law," the capacity of the court to offer that justice depended on its ability to investigate questions beyond where the common law could itself go, bound as it was by its forms and rules.[83] That is, Chancery could take cognizance of facts when the common-law courts were unable to, in the sense of probing for details that the latter courts were bound to find irrelevant, and then admitting them into judicial consideration. This investigative flexibility was answered by greater procedural flexibility for the suitors. An action was initiated in Chancery by bill rather than writ—that is, by a direct address to the court rather than, less conveniently, one of the legal formulas to which all common-law actions were fitted. Once under way, finally, a case in Chancery proceeded less stringently than at common law, a feature of equity justice given prominence in one early Tudor account of the court system: "In this court of Chancery, a man will not be prejudiced through mispleading or because of a fault in form [*pour defaut de forme*] but according to the truth of the matter [*mez solonc le verite del mater*], for an award is made according to conscience and in no way *ex rigore iuris*. And note that there are two powers, ordinary and absolute: the ordinary is in the manner of positive law, and the absolute according to all means [*omnibus modis*] by which the truth of the matter can be known."[84] Just as equity was a mitigation of the law's rigor, so judicial procedure in the equity court was freer than that which rigorously followed the rules.

At key points in Hythloday's account of the dinner conversation, More alludes to this procedural freedom as it relates both to suitor and judge. Hythloday enters the debate by saying that, having heard the lawyer's initial declaration, he "dared to speak freely in front of the Cardinal [*ausus enim sum libere apud Cardinalem loqui*]" (60). The adverb *libere* relates to one the Cardinal uses in reference to himself, when, having silenced the lawyer, he asks Raphael to continue since "I would with pleasure [*libenter*] hear why you think theft should not be punished by death" (70). Both adverbs indicate the mode of argument at the chancellor's table. If Raphael's freedom allows him to speak forthrightly, the Cardinal's pleasure allows him to adjust the parties' forms as they go, in order efficiently to bring to light as many facts as possible. Thus when Raphael, with some impertinence, suggests that, in addition to the logic that links thieves to mercenaries, there is "another and greater reason peculiar to you in England [*est alia magis quantum credo, peculiaris uobis*]," the Cardinal jumps in only to ask for clarification: "And what is that [*Quaenam est ea*]," a question that opens the way for Raphael's novel attack on enclosures, the most famous passage in the dialogue: "Your sheep, I said" (64).

The dinner debate relaxes the procedural strictness of the common law with the greater flexibility of Chancery procedure, thereby answering in form the thematic opposition between the pedant's legal rigor and Hythloday's responsive and equitable justice. But as More's fusion of forms suggests, the debate does not simply dismiss the pedant in favor of the justice that Hythloday recommends. After all, Morton's judgment entertains Hythloday's recommendation to mitigate the punishment of criminals only as a way ultimately to strengthen the law's formal hold through legislation. The interlocking forms of the dinner scene instead analogize the mutual dependence of law and equity on one another. This was the period's standard view of the relation; when the issue was discussed at all, it was less for theoretical reasons than in practical response to the perception that an all-important balance had somehow become imperiled. When Chief Justice Fineux spoke to a new group of serjeants in 1521, for example, and recommended that they practice a balance between equity and law, there was almost certainly in his speech the implication that the former term had become distorted at the hands of Chancellor Wolsey. Treating the lawyers' professional dress as the outward sign of their professional identity, Fineux reminds them that "as your goune (which is close before and not girded unto you) is nother to strayte nother to slake or lowse about you," so the serjeants should in their practice "not be to straight, to rigorus, to extreme yn executinge the lawes, nother yet contrarye wise you should not be to remisse, to slake, to negligent in doinge your duties."[85] A slightly later speech in the same vein similarly allegorizes the lawyers' clothing by unfolding the meaning of the ties descending from the serjeant's coif: "and the one betokeneth the equitie of the law, the other the rigor of the same: meaninge therby that ye may not alwayes stand upon the wordes, which is the very rigor of the lawe, nor yet alwayes upon the intent and equite of the law, but some time upon the one, some time upon the other, as your discretion towarde the persone and necessitye of justice shall require. For as the wise man sayethe, that sometime *extremum jus* is *summa injuria* (that is to saye, that extreme right is extreme wrong)."[86] Both speeches share with More's treatment of equity at Morton's dinner table the conventional and formalist idea that there is in practice an affinity between common law and equity corresponding to the ideal affinity in theory between law and justice.

What is so striking, then, about the loosened proceduralism of the dinner scene, *Utopia*'s most important and fully realized legal moment, is that it shows More to be fully committed to the exigencies of legal practice. I am not suggesting that More's book should be read as recommending specific procedural changes to Wolsey. Rather, he makes the lawyer's habitual argument that the theoretical problem of justice is inseparable from the institutional forms that instantiate it in one or another forum. In this sense, the argument he makes through Morton's dinner is substantively and formally the same as the position he adopted later when, as chancellor, he came to deal with judicial complaints against Chancery injunctions issued to stop proceedings in the common-law courts. More's famous response comes down to us as part of Roper's biography and as a story of another dinner party:

> he invited all the Judges to dyne with him in the councell chamber at westminster: where, after dynner, when he had broken with them what complaintes he had heard of his Injunctions, and moreover shewed them bothe the number and causes of every one of them, in order, so plainely that, upon full debating of thos matters, they were all inforced to confes that they, in like case, could have done no other wise themselfes, Then offred he this unto them: that if the Justices of every courte (unto whom the reformacion of the rigour of the lawe, by reason of their office, most especially appertained) wold, uppon resonable considerations, by their owne discretions (as they were, as he thought, in consciens bound) mitigate and reforme the rigour of the lawe themselves, there should from thenceforth by him no more Injunctions be graunted. Whereunto when they refused to condiscend, then said he unto them: "Forasmuch as your selves, my lordes, drive me to that necessity for awardinge out Injunctions to releive the peoples injury, you canot hereafter any more justly blame me." After that he said secreatly unto me: "I perceive, sonne, why they like not so to doe, for they see that they may by the

verdicte of the Jurye cast of all quarrels from them selves uppon them, which they accompte their cheif defens; and therefore am I compelled to abide thadventure of all such reportes.[87]

More's proposal that the judges themselves do the work of equity looks most like the gamble of a legal expert who knows what the answer will be. As Norman Doe has written, conscience in the late medieval period was not the sole preserve of the chancellor, since the judges at common law, legislators, and jurors all knew themselves to be bound by conscience and appealed to it as a "mode of justification in the courts of common law."[88] As evidenced by St. German's careful coordination of conscience and law so as to circumscribe the former, however, the meaning of this continuity between the common-law and equitable jurisdictions was rapidly evolving. Thus Baker argues with respect to More's offer to the judges that, if it was not genuine, that was because it had already become impossible to turn the clock back on changes in the central administration of justice that were increasingly binding the common-law courts to a procedurally regulated account of justice—so much so that, astonishingly, "by 1566 it would be an indictable offence to say that the King's Bench was a court of conscience."[89] Sincere or not, the moment at More's dinner table is thus metonymic for what is certainly the century's most important jurisdictional development: "by declining the invitation the judges finally settled the role of the Court of Chancery for the next three hundred years as a separate court of equity."[90]

The justice that More portrays at Morton's table is the same as that he defended in himself as chancellor (and which he recommended to the judges who nevertheless, as More interprets the matter, chose to stick to the law and leave the judgment of fact to the jury). Fitted to the forms of strict law and strict procedure, this equitable justice is identifiable only as a procedural relationship, constituted for More not as an ideal, but as two orders of a single law brought into productive jurisdictional conversation. Even though the pedantic lawyer is humiliated by Hythloday's speech (and by More's witty legal forms), More's proceduralist text reminds us that what Hythloday says and the chancellor hears depends on the pedantic lawyer, too, for its utterance.

JUDICIAL IRONY AND THE FORM OF THE LEGAL PARTICULAR

The two books of More's *Utopia* are similarly dependent upon one another for their meaning, and between them More charts what I want to call the play of judicial circumstantiality. A defining feature of Utopian society as presented in Book 2 is its tendency to uniformity, the governing instance of this being, of course, the distribution of commodities "evenly [*aequabiliter*] among all" (146). The island carries this all-important uniformity in a carefully ordered series of outward signs. The island's fifty-four cities are "precisely the same [*prorsus ijsdem*] in language, customs, institutions, laws, the same [*idem*] in location and, to the extent permitted by the spot, the same [*eadem*] in appearance" (112). To know one city, each of which is divided into "four equal parts [*aequales partes*]" (136), is, Hythloday says, to know them all, "since they are exactly similar [*omnino similes*] in so far as the nature of the place permits [*quatenus loci natura non obstat*]" (116). The houses are identically fine, each with a front onto the street and a back door onto a garden (120), as are the clothing and food that the citizens consume. The cities' populations are controlled through the transfer of children between families and of adults between cities and colonies, so as to keep these uniform where a quota has been exceeded ("*plus aequo*") for a given city or the state as a whole (136). Although individuals pursue different trades, everyone practices agriculture without exception (124). In terms of law, all are expert in the few laws that Utopia has, and the laws are so promulgated as to be understandable by all (194). In various ways, individual lives are regulated from above according to imposed norms. Indeed, in direct correlation with the uniformity of the city and the uniformity of individual lives across time, pleasure itself is defined as the body's being in a uniform state ("*aequabili corporis statu*") (172). Nor is it incidental that eggs in Utopia are hatched not by the individual hens that laid them but by farmers who incubate them at a uniform ("*aequabile*") temperature (114).

Most readers feel that there is something unpleasant, even inhumane, in the manufacture of this *identity*.[91] James Simpson associates Book 2's emphasis on similarity and uniformity with the tendencies of the Tudor state to dismiss or process the contingencies of history, culture, and the body. In his reading, More is in thrall to the absolutist fantasy of Book 2, and *Utopia* becomes one example of the diminution of imaginative possibility that for Simpson is consequent on the bureaucratic centralization of the early Tudor period.[92] I agree with Simpson's description of the basic cast of Book 2, and of the relevance of Tudor centralization for its representation, but I would nonetheless characterize the island's uniformity differently, in relation both to More's attitude toward the fantasy republic and to the place of the particular in the fantasy. In light of More's treatment of justice in Hythloday's frame narrative, the uniformity of Utopian society, I think, can best be thought of in legal-philosophical terms as the relative absence of that variation in circumstance that allows, in one construction, for the practice of equity.

Already by the spring of 1516, More would have known that Wolsey had made parity before the law a central part of his program for legal reform through the conciliar courts. In a "notable and Elegant Oration in Englishe" delivered to the king in Council on May 2, 1516, the Cardinal made the imposition of "indifferent Justice" throughout the realm the central priority of his administration, a proposal to which the king assented by declaring in turn that "his moste desyer and comforte" was in "thindifferent ministracion of Justice to all personnes as well highe as lower which be to him in semblable Regarde."[93] Although this legal parity is, along with all the other uniformities, a reality in Utopia, it is notably effected there without the equity of circumstantial interpretation. Hythloday's account of Utopian legal procedure foregrounds neither an abstract justice against which positive laws might be measured, nor the interpretive measures that might ensure justice, but instead various safeguards that make the problem of equity disappear up front. To prevent undue confusion or an outright manipulation of law, Hythloday says, there are few laws in Utopia, no lawyers, and a hermeneutic system according to which "they consider the most obvious [*crassa*] interpretation of the law to be the most just [*aequam*]" (194).[94]

If this is fair, it is also merely rigorous—by which I mean that the society, equitable though it be, is also one in which there is no equity. At the center of More's philosophical meditation on the meaning of particularity for law is the fact that, although Utopia has ample characteristics, the details of daily life with which More fills the pages of Book 2 are simply not circumstances in the legal sense of those variations across lives to which the human judge might appeal as motivating or mitigating factors for past action. Utopia is instead the fantasy of an absent or negative circumstantiality. It is as if the channel that King Utopus excavated and the sea he caused to flow "around the land [*circum terram*]" (112) had together excluded the possibility of any mundane *circum*stance other than the island's singular identity, thereby recasting the latter as the obverse of the half-empty and half-full circumstantiality of Book 1's "wheresoever [*sicubi*]." The French legal humanist Guillaume Budé plays with this aspect of More's book in a letter to Thomas Lupset first included in the 1517 Paris edition of *Utopia*. Attending closely in his letter to the theoretical relation between justice and equity, Budé writes that he has heard that Utopia is also known as Udepotia, this name a "never" to answer More's "nowhere" (10). As Budé activates More's title, the two names together constitute a negation of the spatiotemporal circumstance to which Aristotelian equity can be said to attend.

The legal paradox of Utopian society is that the Utopian equity praised by Hythloday depends on the lack of that circumstance which grounds the English equity of Chancery. This is a real paradox, and it cannot be disposed of simply by declaring More either the adherent of a Utopian version of things or, alternatively, its satirist.[95] If the social ground of distribution in Utopia—*aequitas* in Hythloday's anti-Ciceronian sense—appears to minimize the need for interpretation by minimizing difference, it is also true that this relative lack of difference is what makes the system vulnerable to its own codes. One way to understand the Utopians' disturbingly rigorous treatment of the slave class or the brutality of their response to nonnormative behavior like adultery and to threats from outside the normativized state, is as the logical unfolding of a distributive *aequitas* rather than (as in Cicero and Aristotle) an *aequitas* that is a proportionate adjustment of norm to circumstance. Legal norms function as law by becoming embedded in circumstance, and in this sense—the thought is at once idealistic and distressing—Utopia might be said to have norms but not, properly speaking, realized law. Although Utopia itself barely has courts, the island thus allows us to identify the epistemological principle that subtends England's plurijurisdictional system, in which different courts function by not collapsing into one another either their procedures or their matters. Particularity and circumstantiality are not synonymous. Rather, the circumstance is the particular in its general aspect, and as such it answers an image of the jurisdictional norm as the general in its particular aspect.

We miscast the book's question by asking whether More meant his Utopia seriously, because, according to the play of equity in *Utopia*, that question substitutes for the legal reality he is delineating an account both of the normative order and of the particular it organizes as being already in place, when in fact each depends on the other for its shape. As he has constructed *Utopia*, More insists instead on a juridically ironic movement between the two equities—the equity of distribution and that of decorous adjustment—as a way of measuring, not least for the new Lord Chancellor, the jurisdictional relationship of English equity, as law's variegated promise, to the common law it is said to mitigate. This open, difficult relationship, which is also that of particular and general, is expressed in the relation of *Utopia*'s two books. The whole of *Utopia*, indeed, resembles the dinner conversation that Morton formally and liberally oversees at his judicial table. As in that conversation, the story that Hythloday unfolds in the garden at Antwerp ends with a judgment, one in which "More" shows himself to be judiciously self-distancing in just the way Morton has been when he reserves judgment of Hythloday's legislative proposals: "I frankly confess that there are many things in the Utopian republic that I can more properly [*uerius*] wish for [*optarim*] in our states [*ciuitatibus*] than hope [*sperarim*] to see" (246). As prudent counsel, *Utopia* is suspended between the fullness of that wish and the peculiar emptiness of this hope. Devoid of circumstance, the Utopia of Book 2 is a place that is productive by remaining indefinite. If we follow the double legal structure of the chancellor's dinner and ask, then, what it might mean to mitigate this fiction whose norms are ordered by the absence of circumstance, we will find ourselves in Book 1, the place of difference and disagreement where Utopian negativity takes shape ethically and circumstantially as critique, as Hythloday's constant testing of the fallible discursive order of law in the world. If we start in Book 1, we must, conversely, end up in Book 2. Alone, neither book institutes justice. Each is a power. The norms of Book 2 pertain there as to an imaginary, but they belong also to the historical particulars of Book 1, in the mode of potentiality.

So a philosophical paradox concerning the relative priority of the experiential particular and the general norm is implicit in More's jurisdictional analysis of equity. In one account of that category, the particular is prior because it is the measure of the law that comes to encompass it; in another, the legal norm is prior as, itself, the pertinent measure of experience. But for More, and in Utopia's two-book structure, neither is prior: the particular and general are understandable only as sibling participants in the form that produces each of them, and which, in the world of human adjudication, gives each of them meaning. Utopia's negative circumstantiality is productive because it allows a particularity to emerge released from a prior, singular content, this as a mirror of a generality released from a prior, empty universality.[96] And circumstantial form (as ordered matter and as the careful formalisms of careful jurisdictional activity) holds these twin indefinites together. In the gap between the two books of More's fiction, the justice that is equity emerges as a continuous negotiation between the formal possibility of the general norm and the formal potentiality of the particular circumstance. For the lawyer who wrote *Utopia* and counseled the new lord chancellor who hovers over the book, this is an equity that, to produce its meaning, may well appeal to criteria like the *bonum* and *aequum* of ideal justice or the *ratio* that is a law's intending principle. But this equity knows, too, that law is law only when it acknowledges the ironic gap between norm and experience and so fits itself, as jurisdiction and as decorous institutional form, to the exemplary matter—specific and general, historical, limited—that turns out to have called the law, and its particular limits, into being.

* 2 *

Rationalization

CHAPTER THREE

Inconveniencing the Irish: Custom, Allegory, and the Common Law in Spenser's Ireland

We now turn from the Henrician court to late Elizabethan England, in order to explore the literary reaction to a somewhat different stage in the development of the common law. The legal changes of the early sixteenth century were important for giving the common lawyers an increased institutional confidence concerning the place of their law in the fashioning of national identity. In the following chapters, I therefore move from inside to outside so as to address the impact of legal centralization on England's status relative to alternative territorial jurisdictions that, although intimately tied to England, were not yet fully rationalized at common law. Here I look across the Irish Sea to consider England's jurisdictional relation to Tudor Ireland, as that influenced Edmund Spenser's allegorical representation of the colonial enterprise in *The Faerie Queene* (1590/1596). This work, as numerous literary and cultural historians have shown, is deeply rooted in the poet's experience as an undertaker in the first Munster plantation (1585-98) and as a minor official in the Irish colonial government. I am concerned here with only a limited question—namely, Spenser's reaction to the reconfiguration of English law in response to its contact with Ireland and to the congruent deformation of the native Irish or Brehon law. In sympathy with recent work on the legalization of conquest in Spenser's Ireland, my analysis focuses on the impact of that jurisdictional meeting on two categories—the common and the customary—that lie at the center of the English law's institutional and political identity.[1] My first argument is that the stories Spenser tells about tenure in the pastoral worlds of Books 5 and 6 are allegorical interventions in a historical political scene structured by the conflict between private and common ownership. Second,

I argue that, as Spenser deploys them, the pastoral and allegorical modes are themselves legible as the expression of a customary law brought to its vertiginous edge by England's colonial policies. At the end of his poem, Spenser reflects on the colonial enterprise of which he was a part by adjusting literary genre to answer the pressure exerted by jurisdictional complexity on the forms of insular law.

STRUCTURING THE COMMON IN COLONIAL IRELAND

Early in 1572 Sir Thomas Smith, then ambassador in France and soon to be appointed principal secretary, published *A Letter Sent by I. B. Gentleman unto His Friende Maystser R. C. Esquire* in support of his ultimately unsuccessful plan to colonize the Ards peninsula and parts of Clandeboye in eastern Ulster.[2] The argument is presented through a complex dialogic structure in which the said I. B. reports to the young and impoverished R. C. the contents of an earlier conversation between I. B. and the younger Thomas Smith, the organizer of the expedition. I. B.'s plea centers on the promise of land: "Adventure therfore boldely with him [Thomas Smith, Jr.], as for your portion of Lande, I knowe that his Father and he are bounde to her Majestie by a Covenant... that they shall distrybute to all ayders heerein according to the rate before mentioned."[3] In the hierarchy of distribution descending from Elizabeth through her councilor and his son to "all the ayders heerein," Smith constructs a colonial program from which the commonwealth as an integrated whole stands to benefit. At the same time, he promotes the project as serving the interests of a select group, those whose money the adventure promises to transform into property. Offering 255 English acres of arable land to each foot-soldier, and 510 acres to each mounted one, Smith requires in return that each soldier-adventurer be responsible for his own military furnishings, and that toward the cost of common provisions each foot-soldier contribute ten pounds, and each horseman twenty.[4] Smith makes even clearer how uncommon a part of the commonwealth he is addressing when he extends his offer to those who cannot go themselves, but are willing to contribute even larger sums in support of mercenary proxies.[5] The project comes out of the same practical economics as found in the 1581 *Discourse of the Commonweal* attributable to Smith, luring those whose private interest in acquiring land, as opposed to any broader commitment to the public weal, mirrors Smith's own interests as a private adventurer.[6] In a peculiarly frank moment, I. B. reports the younger Smith's response to the objection that "men are more moved by peculiar gaine: than of respecte they have to common profite."

Rather than disavowing private profit, Smith exuberantly links the colonial adventure to its logical endpoint in piracy or conquest: "Mary answereth he: they shal have their peculiar portions in that frutefull soile, being but as a bootie to be devided amongs them."[7] England's Ireland is a fantasy of a distinctly uncommon profit.

The susceptibility of R. C. to the project is linked to his status as "Esquire," which was applied in the period as a generic honorific equivalent to "gentleman," such that Sir Edward Coke could write that "there is small difference between an esquire and a gentleman; for every esquire is a gentleman, and every gentleman is *arma gerens*."[8] In his treatment of the category in *De republica Anglorum* (ca.1565; pub. 1583), however, Smith somewhat nervously preserves a greater degree of distinction among the commonwealth's orders, identifying various levels of gentlemen within the ruling part of the commonwealth, and so treating "esquire" after the *Nobilitas maior* and *Nobilitas minor* (knights), but before the even more generic "gentleman": "Escuier or esquier (which we call commonly squire) is a French worde, and betokeneth *Scutigerum* or *Armigerum*, and be all those which beare armes. . . . These be taken for no distinct order of the common wealth, but do goe with the residue of the gentlemen: save that (as I take it) they be those who beare armes. . . . and by that had their name for a dignitie and honour given to distinguish them from a common souldier called in latine *Gregarius miles*."[9] As esquires, Smith's potential colonialists belong, but only just, to the governing nobility in the commonwealth. Smith's definition is most interesting for simultaneously differentiating and conflating the orders of esquire and gentleman. As if to substitute for the vanishing distinction between these, the passage foregrounds a second tension, that between a "common wealth" constituted by and as "distinct" orders and the generic commonness of a "common souldier," against whom the esquire's position remains definable and measurable even in the absence of any absolute distinction between the specific "esquier" and generic "gentlemen." Commonness fixes social hierarchy at the same time as it marks the necessary counterpart to social prestige.[10]

Smith's dual construction of the common carries traces of Sir Thomas Elyot's explicit polemic, in his *Boke Named the Governour* (1531), against the name of "commonwealth" as a serious mistranslation of the Roman concept of *respublica*: "A publike weale is [a] body lyvyng, compacte or made of sondry astates and degrees of men whiche is disposed by the ordre of equitie, and governed by the rule and moderation of reason. . . . Wherfore hit semeth that men have ben longe abused in calling *Rempublicam* a comune weale. As they which do suppose it so to be called for that, that every thinge shulde be to all men in commune without discrepance of any astate or condition, be therto moved more by sensualite than by any good reason or inclination to humanite."[11] Smith is far less anxious than his predecessor about the class implications of a common order, and he defines the commonwealth as "a society or common doing of a multitude of free men collected together and united by common accord and covenauntes among themselves, for the conservations of themselves as well in peace as in warre."[12] That said, the program for Ireland similarly expresses a tension that allows commonness to mark both solidarity and difference, as when Smith analyzes how the adventurers will establish and defend a common frontier. Marking social difference, he reassures his investors that "great numbers of the Husbandmen which they call Churles [will] come and offer to live under us, & to ferme our grounds," delineating within this group of laborers "both such as are of the Cuntry birth, and others, bothe out of the wilde Irishe and the Englyshe pale."[13] Because it adds a language of racial differentiation to that of class differentiation, Smith's colonialist agenda thus offers an unusually powerful instance of Elyot's anxiety that a commonwealth might, after all, be common. In the Ards that Smith imagines, the adventurer's private interest is paramount, and it pertains less to a singular English commonweal than to the commonwealth in miniature fashioned at and by the frontier separating a New English population from a native population (whether "wilde" Irish or gaelicized English) figured not as indigenous but instead as imported labor, a population whose movement in space promises to naturalize the colonial community as itself indigenous. Commonness in Ireland is the place where cultural integration is fantasized as sovereign ownership, and English ownership as the guarantee of a *genuinely* common order for Ireland.

Before 1541, when the Irish Parliament passed a statute declaring Henry VIII to be king of all Ireland and the Irish his legal subjects, bound to him in the same way as the English, the Gaelic Irish had no legal protection at common law: with the exception of members of the so-called five septs (or clans), to whom rights had been conceded by writ for reasons of royal blood, this was an alien population beyond the limits of the common weal and common law. Far from disappearing after 1541, the problem of legally accommodating the Gaelic Irish assumed a new form. If the individual's status as subject had in theory been confirmed, the practical question still remained of bringing under centralized control both the traditionally autonomous Gaelic lordships and the heavily gaelicized Old English lordships beyond the Pale. In the absence of such control, Ireland remained only fictively under English sovereignty, and the Irish subject only nominally within the common law and commonweal. In

1612, Sir John Davies makes this point in terms of jurisdiction and its relation to conquest: "For, though the Prince doth beare the Title of *Soveraign Lord* of an entire country (as our Kings did of all *Ireland*), yet if there bee two third parts of that Countrey wherein he cannot punish Treasons, Murders, or Thefts, unlesse he send an Army to do it; if the Jurisdiction of his ordinary Courts of Justice doth not extend into those parts to protect the people from wrong & oppression; if hee have no certaine Revennew, no Escheats or Forfeytures out of the same, I cannot justly say, that such a Countrey is wholly conquered."[14] By the 1580s, confronted with the fact of the Irish chiefs' ongoing recalcitrance, the English already understood how precarious any claim through conquest was, since throughout Elizabeth's reign native Irish magnates resisted both the shiring of their lands and the introduction of judicial officers as representatives of the legal order.

Irish resistance to English justice thus revealed an operative gap between theory and practice, and between two legal concepts: *dominium* in the sense of "possession," to which the English Crown had, according to its own theory, a claim through conquest, and *imperium,* or "sovereignty," which in large parts of the island the English manifestly lacked. The English attempts to close the gap between these two can be understood to adjust one or the other of the terms. Policies that envisioned a gradual introduction of English sovereignty into the lordships, and aimed at a more ample accommodation of the native Irish, adjusted the second. Included here is the use of seneschals, English government officials who were "intended to stabilise the lordship during the delicate opening phases of its contact with English government" and who were by their presence "in time expected to exercise a powerful cultural influence over the clansmen."[15] With respect to land, native Irish tenures would remain stable, but through a process of surrender and regrant, undertaken from the 1540s forward, the customary landholder could cede his lands, then receive them back directly from the Crown, to be held according to the now visibly sovereign common law. Such gradualist policies were a spectacular failure. Adjusting the other side of the *ratio*, the process of New English colonization exemplified in the Munster plantation adjusted *dominium*, positing a brutal solution so little accommodating to the Irish as to constitute reconquest.[16] Through a process of confiscation and redistribution, ownership was to be reinvested in the Crown and then by charter grant in New English settlers, who would carry English justice and sovereignty with them as part and parcel of their tenures. In the case both of a policy of surrender and regrant and of colonization, the constitution of the common—of commonwealth, the common law, and the ideal of an Irish subject continuous with the English one—was thus reframed as a technical question of ownership, of substituting New English tenures for Gaelic or gaelicized landholding.

The traditional patterns of Irish landholding are complex, and never more so than in the later sixteenth century, when the Irish chiefs adeptly played off the traditional and English structures against one another. Drawing on Kenneth Nicholls's indispensable picture of Gaelic clan organization and landholding customs in the late medieval and early modern periods, I wish here to isolate certain general features taken by the New English writers as representative of the system they aimed to replace.[17] The Gaelic lordship pertained to the extended clan, a political unit that might include subordinate lines themselves constituting clans within the larger group. In a given clan, then, there generally existed an overlord and a group of subordinate chiefs or "petty captains" under whom there might be vassal lords in yet another degree of subordination.[18] The overlord did not directly control the land of the subchiefs, unless these were tenants at will; more usually, they were possessed of the land as freeholders, but paid a customary tribute to the overlord according to how far the latter held actual power over them.[19] That tribute came as regular rents or exactions on the land, in the form of money, food, and service, or, irregularly, as "coyne and livery," a system, in Nicholls's words, "of free entertainment for the lord, his troops, servants and hangers-on" when the lord traveled through the subordinate's lands. Failure to pay the exactions could result, through a system of "pledges" or mortgages, in the transfer of a subordinate lord's lands to the overlord, such that the exactions were often in practice a means for the overlord to extend his direct tenurial holdings.[20]

The New English attacked the brutal system of rents and extortions imposed by the overlord on subordinate clans and landholders, but their central objection to Gaelic tenure was to the relationship between lord and land within the local branches of the sept, including the overlord's. Gaelic land was held corporately by the extended kin-group. Neither overlord nor petty chief owned the land within his lordship; the system of tribute I have outlined was in theory a relationship between collateral branches of the clan, rather than between the chiefs of those branches. The English identified this corporate aspect of Gaelic tenure specifically with modes of succession and inheritance, respectively "tanistry" and "gavelkind." The Gaelic word *tanist* means "second," and tanistry refers to the practice whereby, during the chief's lifetime, the clan elected as his successor or "tanist" the "eldest and worthiest" in the clan. As Nicholls explains, the "weakness of the system was, of course, the conflicts which inevitably arose over the succession.... In practice, more often than not, perhaps, there was a bloody conflict for the succession ending in the accession of the strongest or most unscrupulous."[21] *Gavelkind*, a term adopted by the English from the Kentish custom, referred to a system of partible inheritance opposed to common-law primogeniture.[22] In Kent, the deceased's land did not pass to the eldest son, but was divided among all his legitimate sons. John Davies defines the peculiarities of the Irish custom as against this Kentish one: "And by the Irish Custome of Gavellkinde, the inferiour Tennanties were partible amongst all the Males of the Sept, both Bastards and Legittimate: and after partition made, if any one of the Sept had died, his portion was not divided among his Sonnes, but the cheefe of the sept, made a new partition of all the Lands belonging to that Sept and gave everie one his part according to his antiquity."[23] Certainly, the potential for violence when the new partition was made was one of the custom's ill consequences. Davies also identifies the practice of redistribution within the sept as the cause generally of the deplorable state of the Irish countryside: "For, who would plant or improove, or build uppon that Land, which a stranger whom he knew not, should possesse after his death? . . . And this is the true reason why *Ulster*, and all the Irish Countries are found so wast and desolate at this day; and so wold they continue till the worlds end, if these Customes were not abolished by the law of *England*."[24]

The English objected to tanistry and gavelkind for reasons deeper, also, than the intermittent and real chaos the practices occasioned. The two customs came to seem the main obstacle to English sovereignty in Ireland because they helped constitute a form of ownership in which the sept had the kind of temporal relation to the land that in English law was reserved for the Crown. Kin-ownership was kin-sovereignty and thus incompatible with English sovereignty in Ireland. This was not a matter only or even chiefly of legal theory, since the impermanence of personal tenures consequent on Irish gavelkind made any English project of centralizing authority a practical impossibility. A consequence of tanistry, for its part, was that Gaelic chiefs refused to be bound, as an heir would be, by the obligations of their predecessors. Thus, for example, in his *View of the Present State of Ireland*, Spenser describes as a legalistic trick the refusal of Elizabethan Irish lords to abide by their predecssors' acknowledgment of Henry VIII's sovereignty in relation to their land:

> *Eudox.* Howe cane they soe doe justlie? Dothe not the Acte of the parent in anye lawfull graunte or Conveyaunce binde his heires for ever theareunto, Since then the Ancestours of these that now live yelded themselvs then subjectes and Leigemen shall it not tye theire children to the same subjeccion.

Iren. They saie noe for theire Auncestors had not estate in anye theire Landes, Segniories or hereditamentes longer then duringe theire owne lives, as they Alleadge, ffor all the Irishe doe houlde theire Lande by *Tanistrye* which is saie they, no more but a personall estate for his life tyme that is *Tanist.* by reasone that he is admitted theareunto by eleccion of the Countrie.[25]

(It should be noted that Spenser here misconstrues the term *tanist* as referring to the office of chief rather than successor; his understanding of the elective system and its implications is otherwise accurate.) For all the power actually wielded by the individual lords, gavelkind and tanistry marked ownership within the lordships as common and thus as disastrously unstable. As the English saw it, the matter of land in Ireland was doubly troubled in relation to the common. Invested commonly in the kin-group, Irish tenure opposed a common-law system in which all tenures descended temporally from the Crown; as such, Irish landholding patterns preempted the extension and projection of an English commonweal according to common law. Temporally and spatially, one kind of commonness opposed itself to another.

ALLEGORIES OF TENURE I: COMMONNESS IN BOOK 6 OF THE FAERIE QUEENE

The Faerie Queene is similarly troubled by the diverse claims of the common, nowhere more so than in Spenser's representation of ownership in the peculiarly complex pastoral world of Book 6. In canto 9 Spenser returns the reader to the adventures of Calidore, whom he has abandoned in canto 3 in favor of Serena and Calepine. In a stanza meant to bring Calidore's story summarily up to date, Spenser says that Calidore's pursuit of the Blatant Beast has taken him progressively deeper into the rural: "from court . . . to the citties," "from the citties to the townes," "from the townes into the countrie," "from the country back to private farmes," and "thence into the open fields" (6.9.3–4).[26] The progress can be understood, first, as a reverse passage across time and the stages of human civic development, and, second, as a synchronic map of the civic landscape within which Irish colonialists like Spenser moved.

The tension between "private farmes" and "open fields" is important for both the synchronic and diachronic axes, since private tenure was the legal cornerstone for English sovereignty in Ireland. According to the mythic account of human origins told most famously by Ovid in Book 1 of the *Metamorphoses*, private ownership marked the transition from the ages of gold and silver, when all things were held in common, to the age of bronze: "The careful surveyor marked with the long boundary line the earth that before had been common in the manner of the sun's light and the air [*communemque prius ceu lumina solis, et auras / cautus humum longo signavit limite mensor*]" (1l.135–36).²⁷ In his influential commentary on the *Metamorphoses*, Jacobus Pontanus glosses these lines by noting a passage from Cicero's *De officiis* that was central to the early modern legal conception of the natural world. Especially pertinent to the Irish context is Cicero's attempt to map the complexities and contradictions of postnatural *dominium*: "Nothing, however, is private by nature [*Sunt autem privata nulla natura*], but either through long occupation [*vetere occupatione*], as when at one time a people entered into unoccupied lands [*qui quondam in vacua venerunt*], or by conquest [*victoria*], as when they acquired the land in war, or by law, by contract, by agreement, or by allotment [*aut lege, pactione, condicione, sorte*]. Thus the lands of Arpinum are said to belong to the Arpinates, the Tusculan lands to the Tusculans" (1.7.21).²⁸ Conquest is a legitimate way for a people to acquire dominion over lands, even when, implicitly, long occupation has first given dominion to another group. The conflict between the claims of prior occupation and conquest suggests how little helpful arguments from the state of nature are for sorting out ownership in the postnatural world. This becomes even clearer when Cicero compares, within the postnatural context, a nation's possession to an individual's: "The division of private possession is similar. Thus, because each individual came to hold as his own some of that which by nature had been common [*quia suum cuiusque fit eorum, quae natura fuerant communia*], each person should retain only that which was his lot [*quod cuique obtigit, id quisque teneat*]; and it follows that if someone strive to obtain more for himself, he will violate the law of human society [*si quis sibi appetet, violabit ius humanae societatis*]" (1.7.21). Cicero's highly conservative account of ownership (continuous with his account of *aequitas*, as explored in my second chapter) might well make a Munster settler nervous. Even though he acknowledges the right of conquest, the weight of Cicero's analysis falls against the kind of appropriation colonialists like the English in Ireland sought to achieve. It is to answer the implications of accounts like Cicero's of the transition from a state of natural to postnatural *dominium* that Spenser deploys pastoral. His point in doing so is not to reinforce the rights of conquest, but to dismantle the idea of the common integral to Cicero's vision of the natural state. More precisely, the version of pastoral he gives in Book 6 substitutes for a natural or pre-civic commonness of ownership a natural but simultaneously civic commonness of political consent.

When Spenser opposes "private farmes" to "open fields," he seems to suggest that Calidore's journey is taking him into a world beyond (and before) private *dominium*, but the poem immediately undoes the suggestion. Indeed, the reader who succumbs to Spenser's temptation to read Calidore's journey in this way can be seen to make the same error as Calidore himself does when, mistaking Meliboe's and Pastorella's world for an ideal world, he dons a shepherd's clothes and abandons his quest of the Blatant Beast. In Spenser's unfolding of the story, the lawless Brigants (6.10.39), who destroy the pastoral community and lead the shepherds into captivity, dramatically expose both Calidore's error and the true nature of this pastoral world. As Andrew Hadfield has argued, the narrative reinvokes the uneasy pastoral of *Colin Clouts Come Home Againe*.[29] Colin's comparison in that poem of (English) pastoral ease and (Irish) pastoral danger offers a devastating picture of the Munster Plantation and the lives of its New English settlers, subject as they are to "bloodie issues," "leprosies" and "griesly famine," to "nightly bodrags" (raids), "hue and cries," "ravenous wolves," and "outlawes fell" (ll. 310–19).[30] Like Colin's Irish pastoral, the natural world in Book 6 is the opposite of golden.

In representing the shepherds' polity as already part of the postnatural, fallen world, Spenser means to provide a starting point for Irish political discourse: like the political treatises or plats that argued from a body of empirical evidence for particular political action, Spenser's pastoral is a polemically nonidealizing *description* of the colonialist experience.[31] Central to this picture is Spenser's emphasis on the place of private ownership in the constitution of community. His shepherds are economic individualists: "each his sundrie sheepe with severall care / Gathered together, and them homeward bare" (6.9.15), where "severall" repeats the equally blunt social implications of "each his." Even when the shepherds "their labour share," moreover, they do so in confirmation simultaneously of their economic (and erotic) separateness: "To helpe faire *Pastorella*, home to drive / Her fleecie flocke; but *Coridon* most helpe did give" (6.9.15). Calidore explicitly identifies the underlying principle of the community when he refers enviously to Meliboe's happiness in "this small plot of your dominion" (6.9.28), where "plot" identifies both Meliboe's land and the work of surveying on which his ownership or dominion rests.[32] Meliboe clarifies the nature of his dominion when he contrasts the "yearely hire" of the years he spent at court working "in the Princes gardin," (6.9.24) with his present freedom: "I from thenceforth have learn'd to love more deare / This lowly quiet life, which I inherite here" (6.9.25). Meliboe's freedom and dominion is grounded in the principle of inheritance.

Dominion and inheritance are most powerfully linked in the figure of Pastorella, and not only because as Meliboe's heir she signifies the centrality of private ownership to the pastoral world. Her connection to Meliboe as adoptive father also signals how a commonness alternative to common ownership operates amid these pastoral privacies:

> He [Meliboe] was to weet by common voice esteemed
> The father of the fayrest *Pastorell*,
> And of her selfe in very deede so deemed;
> Yet was not so, but as old stories tell
> Found her by fortune, which to him befell,
> In th'open fields an Infant left alone,
> And taking up brought home, and noursed well
> As his owne chyld; for other he had none,
> That she in tract of time accompted was his owne.
> (6.9.14)

Both the verbal echo of the "open fields" that earlier opposed "private farms" and the spatio-temporal pun on "tract" signal that Pastorella's adoption is in complex ways a matter of dominion. Most important here is that the shepherds' "common voice" should give Meliboe patriarchal dominion over Pastorella, twice designated here as "his owne." Meliboe's paternity seems to be ratified in two ways: both as a fact "in tract of time accompted," that is, confirmed in the manner of a custom; and as a fact formally assented to, "by common voice esteemed." Imagining his pastoral world in one further sense as a commonweal according to the English pattern, Spenser grounds pastoral ownership in the quasi-parliamentary consent practiced by the shepherds.

Although Calidore partly understands the nature of the political group he has entered, he fails to appreciate how the productive privacies of the pastoral world render it vulnerable to the destructive desire of those beyond the boundaries instituted by the private. In canto 10, a band of Brigants/brigands erases from the pastoral landscape all signs of the civic and private:

> It fortuned one day, when *Calidore*
> Was hunting in the woods (as was his trade)
> A lawlesse people, *Brigants* hight of yore,
> That never usde to live by plough nor spade,
> But fed on spoile and booty, which they made
> Upon their neighbours, which did nigh them border,

> The dwelling of these shepheards did invade,
> And spoyld their houses, and them selves did murder;
> And drove away their flocks, with other much disorder.
>
> (6.10.39)

The shadow world of the brigands stands in opposition to the shepherd community, and in ironic relation to the classical golden world. Spenser places the brigands in caves, a negative version of the homes they destroy. They dwell "in a little Island," he says, "Covered with shrubby woods": "For underneath the ground their way was made, / Through hollow caves, that no man mote discover / For the thicke shrubs, which did them alwaies shade / From view of living wight, and covered over" (6.10.41–42). As Hadfield points out, the passage implies a specifically Gaelic barbarism: a fortified island served Hugh O'Neill, for example, very well in the Nine Years War.[33] It is equally important that in Ovid's account of the ages of man caves set about by thick trees pertain to the golden age, with homes originating only in the silver: "Then for the first time they entered houses; caves had been their homes, and dense shrubs and branches joined with bark [*tum primum subiere domos; domus antra fuerunt / et densi frutices et vinctae cortice virgae*]" (*Met.* 1.121–22). The major point is that, within a postnatural order, the brigands' "golden" age is necessarily a perversion, one that subverts the civic by its false adherence to a superseded past. The true golden age can be instantiated only in the civic polity of the shepherds, and that polity remains safe just to the extent that it resists the brigands' false sense of the golden. In this sense, Spenser's ironic invocation of Ovid's golden world can be seen to pull to the surface the major narrative drive of the *Metamorphoses* itself, in which the decline from a natural world is simultaneously legible as a history of civic progress.

The critique of an outmoded natural order extends to the golden ideal of common ownership, which Spenser aligns in the brigands' shrubby world with the Irish tenurial practices of tanistry and gavelkind. Meliboe's patriarchal "ownership" of Pastorella finds its distorted equivalent in the brigands' capture of her, and also in their desire to hold her in common. Pirate merchants arrive at the wooded island, and the brigands lead them to their captain: "And therefore prayd, that those same captives there / Mote to them for their most commodity / Be sold, and mongst them shared equally" (6.11.10). But the captain, who has fallen in love with Pastorella, refuses to share her equally:

> Therewith some other of the chiefest theeves
> Boldly him bad such injurie forbeare;

> For that same mayd, how ever it him greeves,
> Should with the rest be sold before him theare,
> To make the prises of the rest more deare.
>
> (6.11.15)

The ensuing quarrel, in which the captain, most of the captives, and sundry brigands are killed, allegorically realizes what for the English seemed the chaos implicit in so impractical a system of tenure as kin-ownership and partible inheritance. In the contrast between the brigand "captain" and "other of the chiefest theeves," Spenser is, furthermore, identifying the peculiar dangers of the Gaelic sept, in which subordinate lords, according to the custom of gavelkind, always potentially threatened the overlord and the stability of the land divisions authorized under him.

The brigands' desire to share Pastorella is an echo of an earlier moment in Book 6 when Serena, Calepine's beloved, is captured while asleep by a "savage nation" in all respects like the brigands and the English stereotype of the Gaelic Irish.[34] This nation, too, wants to share their prize:

> Then when she wakt, they all gave one consent,
> That since by grace of God she there was sent,
> Unto their God they would her sacrifize,
> Whose share, her guiltlesse bloud they would present,
> But of her dainty flesh they did devize
> To make a common feast, and feed with gurmandize.
>
> (6.8.38)

Cannibalism was conventionally troped as one among many Gaelic vices, continuous with the image of American cannibalism as represented, most famously, by Montaigne.[35] Of particular interest for the present argument is the degenerate implication of "common." Like the proposed sale of Pastorella, the feast the cannibals propose is a ghastly version of native Irish tenure. Their appeal for justification to the "grace of God," moreover, is Spenser's perverse invocation of natural law, a representation in the extreme case of reserving possession, as Cicero recommends, to those into whose hands nature or God delivered it. Hadfield convincingly interprets Serena as one more of Spenser's unflattering allegories of Elizabeth, and Christopher Highley similarly identifies Pastorella as "a tantalizing figure of the queen or at least an attenuated re-embodiment of the nurturing and civilizing powers to which she laid claim."[36] It seems clear, however, that Serena and Pastorella are also versions of Ireland itself. In the attempts by the respective bands of savages collectively to own or consume them, Spenser allegorizes the Gaelic and gaelicized lords' use of kin-based ownership to subvert the civic work of commonwealth and common-law tenure.[37]

Another moment in Book 6 makes clear that what marks these alternative tenures as subversive is their relation or, better, nonrelation to inheritance. In canto 4, having rescued a male infant from a ravenous bear, Calepine courteously surrenders the child to Matilda, a "lamentable Dame" whose childlessness, Calepine learns, is the cause of her unhappiness. In language that explicitly repeats the terms of the English claim to dominion in Ireland, she tells the knight that she is "wife of bold Sir *Bruin*, who is Lord / Of all this land, late conquer'd by his sword / From a great Gyant, called *Cormoraunt*" (6.4.29). Crucially, the vocabulary of conquest gives way immediately to the technical language of common-law tenure: "So is my Lord now seiz'd of all the land, / As in his fee, with peaceable estate, / And quietly doth hold it in his hand, / Ne any dares with him for it debate" (6.4.30). So Sir Bruin holds his land in the manner of the New English landholders, as an estate in land.[38] We can note here how precisely the passage recasts the conventional formula for legal possession at common law, according to which the possessor was said to be "seised" or possessed of the land "in his demesne as of fee," this being the equivalent of the law French "*fuit seisie en son demesne come de fee*" and Latin "*seisitus fuit, in dominico suo ut de feodo*." In his 1628 commentary on Littleton's *Tenures*, Coke connects demesne to the hand: "*in dominico suo* . . . which is as much as to say as *Demeine* or *Demain*, of the hand i.e. manured by the hand, or received by the hand."[39] Matilda's description of her husband's claim thus splits apart the two parts of the legal formula: Bruin holds "in his hand" that of which he is seised. Given how closely Spenser follows the legal formula, it is interesting that in its overall effect the passage should also seem so anxious about Sir Bruin's tenure. What can it mean, for example, that Sir Bruin avoids debates that patently concern claims other than the giant's already superseded one, or that Matilda's "peaceable" and "quietly" comes off as a little too insistent, more fantasy than simple reality?

The suppressed unease of the lines brings out an ambiguity, too, in the conventional legal formula itself: by using the phrase "As in his fee," Spenser allows the reader to hear how oddly close formal legal possession is to a mere similitude of possession. One of Coke's glosses on Littleton's *Tenures* limits the semantic range of the phrase in order to control the same ambiguity: "*Ut de feodo*. Where (*ut*) is not by way of similitude, but to be understood positively that he is seised in fee. And so it is where one pleads a descent to one *ut filio et haeredi*, that is to Jo[hn]. S[tyles]. that is son and heir, *& sic de caeteris*, where (*ut*) *denotat ipsam veritatem*."[40] Coke's gloss restricts the semantic range of the formulaic *ut* in order to shut down the possible implication of a gap between seisin and fee, present possession and the quality of heritability that extends possession into the future. Conversely, Spenser imports the language into the poem in order precisely to pull up a submerged uncertainty in the form and formula that gives Bruin his claim to a territorial possession and to the future of that possession.

The equivocation is exactly appropriate to the Irish situation, and Spenser uses the Matilda episode to allegorize the technical legal problems associated with New English tenures in the Munster Plantation and in Ireland more generally, since the tenures through which the English intended to introduce English sovereignty proved remarkably unstable. To take the signal example of the Munster plantation, in which Spenser received a seignory of 3,028 acres, that project was made possible by the confiscation of lands pertaining both to the rebel Earl of Desmond, attainted in 1579 and killed four years later, and to his Gaelic and Old English supporters.[41] But these confiscations turned out to be ineffective through a lack of fit between the Irish and English patterns of holding land. Since only those lands of which the attainted lord was fully possessed legally reverted to the Crown, it was imperative to identify who at the time of attainder was possessed of which land. This was difficult to do. In the case of Gaelic lands, the problem was that the chief could not be said to be seised of all lands pertaining to the extended kin-group; the legal question was, instead, whether those subordinate landholders who paid him tribute were to be understood, according to the English pattern, as freeholders or merely as tenants at the lord's will. In the case of those Old English lords like Desmond, who exacted Gaelic tribute throughout their seignories, the situation was no less complex, as is clear from the perplexing status of "chargeable land," which the English in Ireland defined as being "subject to burdens at the will of the lord."[42] A report from Munster in 1589 on this tenurial category clarifies why the problem posed by gaelicized feudal tenure was all but indistinguishable from that posed by Gaelic communal tenure: "it could never be decided whether the chargeable lands were the traitor's inheritance that had the rents and spending thereof, or whether they were the lawful inheritance of such the tenants whose ancestors had enjoyed the possession thereof of many descents.... It is probable that in the beginning some of the tenants were freeholders and others but tenants at will to Desmond, but how to distinguish them, wanting the Earl's evidences and rentals, we know not."[43] In summary, then, the problem in the case of Gaelic lands was to identify the equivalents of English tenure, and in the case of gaelicized lands to identify estates now so "degenerate" as to give them fully the aspect of clan possession.

Within the original or ideal feudal system that underlay the common law, property marked a relationship between lord and tenant; as J. H. Baker describes it, "once a feudal contract was entered into, neither the lord nor the tenant owned the land absolutely." Instead, they possessed shared interests in the substance of their relation, the fee (or *feodum*) of which each was, differently, possessed or "seised." "The lord was seised 'in service,' and the tenant was seised 'in demesne' (*in dominico suo*)."[44] A plausible solution, then, that might have accommodated the complexities of Gaelic tenure to the English system was the legal hypothesis that chief and tenant were in some sense *both* seised, the former holding the land as a fee in service and the latter, ultimately possessed, holding it as a fee in demesne. But as Nicholls explains, this solution was unavailable, not because it was a fictional construction of the Gaelic system of kin-ownership (although it certainly was that), but because of *English* law. The difficulty was that the statute *Quia Emptores* (1290) had declared that thereafter land could be alienated only by substitution of one tenant for another, thereby abolishing the process of subinfeudation whereby a vendor (himself directly or indirectly a tenant of the Crown), might have made the purchaser his tenant in turn.[45] Since the statute prevented the introduction of any further such mediate (mesne) tenures, this meant that new tenures could only be held directly from the Crown. "Caught in the trap of *Quia Emptores*," Nicholls writes, the English in Ireland were thus "unable to postulate a tenurial solution" to the complexities of Irish landholding, with the result that, in the commissions established across Ireland to negotiate claims within Gaelic and gaelicized territories, the common lawyers "came in general to regard the occupiers with subordinate interests in the land as 'freeholders' and the lord's rights as no more than a rent-charge, where indeed they were not dismissed as mere 'Irish exactions.'"[46] Gaelic tenure, which combined ultimate kin-ownership and a diffusely theorized relationship between chief and tenant, could only imprecisely be accommodated to the more rigid English sense of common-law ownership.[47] Without the possibility of mesne tenure, the presence of alternative claims on land in the unassimilated lordships presented an irremediable problem. With respect to the policy of surrender and regrant, it was unclear who in the first place should be the beneficiaries of the grant. Similarly limited was any forfeiture by attainder, even though attainder might seem on the surface a fully certain means of reinvesting land in the Crown.

This is the theoretical problem that Spenser takes up in the Matilda episode, specifically in relation to Munster and Cork. The Munster planters were from the start plagued by lawsuits brought by Gaelic and Old English constituents claiming to have held, and still to hold, the freehold or its equivalent on lands confiscated by attainder.[48] The situation meant, in Anthony Sheehan's formulation, that "the only clear legal principle subscribed to by everyone, Irish and English, was that possession was nine points of the law."[49] There were subordinate lords who argued that their tenancies had vested in them, and not the earl or his associates, the fee or its equivalent. That freehold, they said, had not been disrupted, and at most "the chief rent which was previously due to the earl would now be payable to the crown or the principal plantation proprietors."[50] Then there were those who claimed to hold leases or mortgages on attainted lands.[51] The Gaelic Earl of Clancare, Donal MacCarthy Mor, was astonishingly successful in two different kinds of claims. In western Munster, he argued that lands confiscated as the Earl of Desmond's were in fact part of his lordship, the landholders there being but tenants at Clancare's will. Even more interesting, however, is his partial success in western areas pertaining to septs traditionally subordinate to his, since, as Michael MacCarthy-Morrogh points out, such claims tacitly asked that the Crown recognize that even after he "had surrendered his former titles on his creation of Earl," he nevertheless continued to exercise "'jurisdiction and dominion' over these areas."[52] In effect, for reasons at English law, the Crown was recognizing the very gap between England's supposed possession, or *dominium*, and its jurisdiction, or *imperium*, that the policy of surrender and regrant aimed to close by visibly investing tenure in the Crown. Against the advice of her New English officials, who understood the implications of all such claims for the stability of the plantation, Elizabeth insisted that the native Irish be allowed as her subjects to proceed in their claims. Many of these were successful, resulting in the return of lands included in the planters' original grants to native Irish subjects. The figures are remarkable: in Spenser's Cork, the undertaker Hugh Cuffe lost most of the 12,000 acres in his seignory to Ellen Fitzedmund Gibbon and James MacShane; MacCarthy-Morrogh estimates, generally, that by 1611 "about one-third of the whole plantation area had been returned to the local inhabitants."[53] The New English response was predictable. According to one account of the Munster commissions, the queen saw "the hartes of your assured subjects daunted, dismaied: your enemies strengthned: your state in that contry weakened: faithfull subjects supplanted, rebelles placed, your majestie unlawfully dispossessed of your lands."[54] In the suggestive formulation of the principal undertaker Warham St. Leger, Elizabeth had rewarded "a company of hollow-hearted papistical wretches and disinherited her loving and natural English subjects."[55]

In this context, Sir Bruin's capacity to suppress debate of his tenure emerges as the keystone in Spenser's treatment of tenure in the Matilda episode.[56] Conquest or colonization solves one problem—Bruin defeats the giant Cormoraunt—but only to introduce another. Like the new Munster landholders, Sir Bruin holds the land in fee (and from the Crown), but his estate can remain peaceable only to the extent that he can ward off claims unaffected by his victory over the giant. Hence Bruin's suppression of those claims ("Ne any dares with him for it debate"), and hence, too, the hint of impermanence in his being said to hold the land "as in his fee." Ireland makes apparent that where ownership is a relationship or, better, the trace of a relationship between Crown and tenant, tenure remains to that extent conditional, the threat of any alternative relationship being paramount. From the perspective of the Munster colonists, the declaratory force of the queen's grant remained dangerously subject to a process of historical investigation into alternative and prior claims. Since the queen allowed her own grants to be challenged, furthermore, the structures of possession at common law could themselves be understood to readmit the very system they replaced. The legal forms by which Sir Bruin holds his land after Cormoraunt's defeat allows for Cormoraunt's return in diffuse form.

What solution does Spenser provide to the practical and theoretical impasse? Sir Bruin and Matilda's estate is perfected when Calepine provides them with an heir, a son *"gotten"* but not *"begotten"* (6.4.32) who can be counted on finally to overthrow the rival giant (6.4.33). Significantly, Matilda is said to accept the baby "As of her owne by liverey and seisin" (6.4.37), that is, according to "[de]livery of seisin," the formal procedure for transferring possession, by conveyance of a clod of earth or other token from vendor to purchaser. The baby is both token and possession: Spenser's pun on the technics of common-law possession generates the thesis that to possess an heir to one's land is in effect to be seised of it in the fullest sense. The importance of an heir to Sir Bruin's successful control of Cormoraunt's land is implicit also in the giant's name. The cormorant's familiar association with rapacious greed is only part of Spenser's meaning; etymologically, the cormorant is the "cor marin," the sea raven or *corvus aquaticus*. In the *Hieroglyphica*, Piero Valeriano finds meaning in the raven's impatience with its own young. In a 1576 French translation, the relevant passage reads: "The figure of the raven denotes the man who disinherits his children or expels them from his house [*Le pourtraict du Corbeau denotoit signamment l'homme qui des-heritoit ses enfans ou les chassoit de la maison*]."[57] Pierre Dinet confirms the association: "The raven stands finally for the father who treats his children badly, and disinherits them [*Finalement le corbeau est indice du pere qui traicte mal, & desherite ses enfants*]."[58]

Emblematically, therefore, the giant Cormoraunt rejects the idea of succession and inheritance on which the future of Sir Bruin's tenure depends. As we have seen, a Gaelic tenure grounded in kin-ownership likewise rejected both heir and the idea of the heir, in favor, first, of the elected tanist and, second, of a kind of succession that impaired continuity by releasing the customary chief from a predecessor's contractual obligations. So Cormoraunt opposes not only Sir Bruin's dominion, but also the whole pattern of landholding that Sir Bruin has with "sweat and swinke" (6.4.32) imposed on the land, emblematizing the long-standing Irish resistance to common-law inheritance. And Spenser's argument is that the successful settlement of Ireland will depend on the suppression of all traces of that resistance: on the eradication of tanistry and gavelkind, to be sure, but also on the suppression of those Gaelic claims that manipulate the common law in order slyly to reintroduce the marks of Gaelic ownership.

Another episode can profitably be read in the context of Spenser's use of pastoral to argue that English sovereignty in Ireland depends on the suppression of Gaelic practice. This is the passage in Book 6 in which Pastorella is reunited with her real and noble mother. After rescuing Pastorella from the few brigands surviving their self-slaughter, Calidore brings her to the castle Belgard, home to Lord Bellamour and the Lady Claribell. Spenser provides a brief family history. Claribell is the daughter of the now deceased "Lord of *Many Ilands*"; when, in the past, she refused to marry "the Prince of *Picteland* bordering near" (6.12.4) and instead wed Bellamour, her father consigned the couple to prison, where Claribell conceived and bore a child, Pastorella, and where the two lovers remained "till that her syre / Departed life, and left unto them all" (6.12.10).[59] Pastorella's family is thus associated with the northern aristocracy or even, in one reading of "many islands," with the Hebrides. As Richard Neuse suggests, however, the details of Pastorella's and Claribell's lives allows each to signify as Elizabeth.[60] Given in particular the Irish subtext of Book 6, the royal connotations of "Lord of *Many Ilands*" are hard to overlook once we remember the statute of 1541 that declared Henry VIII king of Ireland as of England. The detail of a daughter who inherits a father's estate is also suggestive. As Pastorella's mother, to be sure, Claribell cannot in any easy sense stand for the childless queen, though it is pertinent that Pastorella's conception and birth are accomplished in secret and that Claribell immediately surrenders the child "for hyre," to be "fostred under straunge attyre" (6.12.6), with the result that the mother remains childless to public view.

In light of Spenser's earlier representation of Pastorella as Ireland, a meaning for the passage surfaces that is highly critical of Elizabeth's policies. Given

Spenser's sly use of "seisin" and "fee" elsewhere in Book 6, there is something productively ambiguous in the description of the erotic union between Bellamour and Claribel: "And *Bellamour* againe so well her pleased, / That of her love he was entyrely seized, / And closely did her wed" (6.12.5). The erotic charge here derives from an ambiguity of active and passive rooted in the pun on "seized" and "seised." At the same time as Claribell's love seizes Bellamour, makes him hers, Bellamour comes to possess, to be seised of, her love. The implications of Bellamour's name for so closely wrought and claustrophobic an erotic structure are double-edged. What does it mean for a ruler like Claribell to love and be loved by love itself? In what will such a union issue? If Pastorella stands here for Ireland, as she plausibly does in her earlier encounter with the savage brigands, Bellamour comes to look most like Elizabeth's political self-love. Spenser's historical argument is that the queen in surrendering to Bellamour has managed to produce in Pastorella only an orphaned Ireland and, as its poetic correlative, a genre that must endlessly revisit the conflicting claims of private and common, feudal and communal. In due course in the Claribell episode, we arrive at the story we already know: the abandoned child is found and raised by a shepherd, now explicitly described as Irish, being "in his mantle wound" (6.12.9). Allegorically, Meliboe turns out to have been Elizabeth's viceregal authority, a foster father to Elizabeth's alienated kingdom, but one who unwittingly subverts her sovereignty there, insofar as he proves unable to protect his "owne" daughter against the Brigants' alternative and communal claim on her.[61]

As Spenser uses Pastorella's family to allegorize English policy in Ireland, he figures Elizabeth's failure in her second kingdom as a double failure. First, in the representation of shepherds having to live next to thieves bent only on the destruction of pastoral order and pastoral property, Spenser allegorizes the consequences of the queen's too scrupulous extension of her laws to her uncivil Irish subjects in relation to their claims against the tenures of New English settlers. Read against the Matilda episode and the argument there connecting *dominium* and inheritance, Spenser seems, furthermore, to allegorize the consequences for English sovereignty in Ireland of Elizabeth's refusal to marry a real lord, to produce a real heir, or even (allowing for a broad interpretation of Claribell's rejection of a Scottish suitor) to name a real successor. At issue here is that in the absence of a successor the Crown must lack the chief sign of its own extension through time. But in Ireland, where sovereignty depended on incorporating the lordships as common-law estates, the Crown had most of all to be a corporate entity capable of challenging the presumptive corporate sovereignty instituted by Gaelic landholding patterns.

Spenser's tenurial meditations posit that in the absence of an heir England is symbolically deprived of the very ground for common-law sovereignty it seeks in Ireland. Elizabeth's second failure, her childlessness, is thus the symbolic equivalent of the first failure, her weak interpretation of conquest and her perverse desire to defend in her native Irish subjects a sovereignty alternative to her own.

The final canto of Book 6 is thus a daring criticism of Elizabeth's failure, as queen of Ireland, to counter the destructive logical force of a not fully rationalized common law. Pastorella's return home is a fantasy of Ireland's longed-for and long-deferred integration into an English commonweal, and it depends exactly on Calidore's eradication of the savages whom Elizabeth variously accommodates. If pastoral irony allows Spenser in Book 6 to negotiate the tension in natural law between the claims of conquest and prior possession, the anger of the final canto makes clear that he thinks that task should have been redundant. In other words, if pastoral rather than epic is for Spenser the necessary poetry of Elizabethan politics, that is the consequence of a royal courtesy that makes heirs only of brigands and thus forces poets endlessly to theorize the accommodation of the barbaric to the civic. The poetic concessions of Book 6 are those, in effect, of an *Aeneid* in which Turnus is spared and invited into the future. Spenser's Irish pastoral arrives at its comic ending, all the time remaining a thorny reminder that another genre altogether is more appropriate by far to the story of sovereignty that England longs to tell.

UNCOMMON LEARNING: CUSTOM IN DAVIES'S REPORTS

I have been arguing that the construction of a commonness exclusive of common tenure was essential to England's legal conquest of Ireland. Such rhetorical maneuvers are seldom unidirectional, however. To explore the obverse pressure imposed on English common law by the Irish jurisdiction, I now turn to a second and equally powerful semantic equivocation in England's legal rhetoric. The English appropriation of the common for ideological ends is equivalent to the contemporaneous siege on the idea of the customary, a category that, like commonness, contained meanings to be fashioned and meanings to be forgotten in order to make conquest seem a natural continuity. We can enter this part of my argument by looking forward from 1596 to one of the most important documents in the history of England's "legal imperialism" in relation to the Irish colony.[62] In 1615 Sir John Davies, James I's Attorney General in Ireland, published in Dublin the first collection of printed Irish legal reports.[63] In an important introduction addressed to Lord Chancellor

Ellesmere, Davies writes himself into Irish and English legal history, by signaling the book's jurisdictional innovation even as he follows the model of Sir Edward Coke's introductions to the several volumes of his English reports, which had been published across the preceding fifteen years. With exemplary clarity, Davies's introduction celebrates both the antiquity and the customary nature of the common law in a manner reminiscent of Coke and, more generally, of what J. G. A. Pocock has famously termed "the common-law mind": "The *Common lawe* of England is nothing else but the *Common custome* of the Realme," Davies writes, and as such, it is the "most perfect, & most excellent [law]... to make & preserve a commonwealth." In contradistinction to a written law "imposed uppon the subject before any Triall or Probation made, whether the same bee fitt & agreeable to the nature & disposition of the people, or whether they will breed any inconvenience or no," a "*Custome* doth never become a lawe to binde the people, untill it hath bin tried & approved time out of mind" (∗2r).[64] The appeal to the antiquity of an immemorial past is so familiar in the English context as to be a commonplace; unsurprisingly, in extending the encomium across the introduction, Davies everywhere follows Coke's lead in the several volumes of his reports. He proclaims the superiority of the customary common law both to statute and to the civil and canon laws; rehearses the myth of an ancient constitution adopted rather than supplanted by William the Conqueror; defends the continued use of law French as expressing more perfectly than English or Latin the terms of art necessary to the law; contrasts the certainty of the common law to the uncertainty of a civil law glutted with gloss and commentary; asserts the efficiency of English law relative to other systems of law; and defends the integrity of the learned "professors" of the law—all this in order, ultimately, to praise the chancellorship and Ellesmere's exemplary performance in that office.

So close is Davies's defense of English law to Coke's that we can easily forget his argument's particular occasion, its unavoidable jurisdictional resonances: these are, after all, Irish reports. In a real sense, however, it is Davies's argument itself that forgets its own occasion. In his elaboration of the virtues of English customary law, Davies does not once address the theoretical questions of how, legally or otherwise, nations meet, or whether customs "tried & approved time out of mind" with respect to one nation will necessarily "bee fitt & agreeable to the nature & disposition" of another nation, or "whether they will breed any inconvenience or no." Structurally, the question can be evaded because Davies wholly circumscribes the particular occasion of his book, treating of Ireland, in the manner almost of a parenthesis, only at the beginning and end of the lengthy introduction. He dedicates the first two paragraphs to his Irish context before turning to a general encomium of the common law. Nineteen pages later, Davies returns in five concluding paragraphs to Ireland: "it remaineth that I present unto your Lordship the rude collection of a fewe selected Cases, which since the beginning of his Majesties raigne have bene argued, resolved, & adjudged in this Realme of Ireland" (∗11r). Even when Davies finally comes to the point that there is a special body of law in Ireland that must be taken account of, he carefully provides an institutional version of his introduction's near-total displacement of James's third kingdom: "these Cases being resolved and adjudged in the Courts of Justice in Ireland, are not collected & published by mee, to encrease the number of the bookes of lawe in England, or to interrupt the better studies of the Students there, by reading of this collection, but principally for the use and benefitt of our practisers heere in Ireland" (∗11v). Here, then, is the conventional modesty *topos* filtered through the lens of a legal nationalism impervious to the notion that an alternative and subordinate jurisprudence might have something to say to the center.

If Davies's introduction works to marginalize the local claims that Ireland makes on a theoretical account of a time-refined common law, that is in part because the book operates, in respect to Ireland, in something of an institutional vacuum. Davies himself makes the point: "But all the arguments & reasons of the judgements & resolutions given in the Courts of Ireland, have hitherto beene utterly lost & buried in oblivion" (∗1v). Since there is no textual history of reporting in Ireland, the necessary context for his Irish reports is the English report. But the scope of Davies's book suggests a second and tactical reason for his occluding a theoretical account of how jurisdictions meet and national differences come to be accommodated. His is a surprisingly slim volume; the nine cases and two resolutions he includes are concerned with the consolidation of English power in Ireland following the defeat of the Gaelic lords at the beginning of James's English reign. As Hans Pawlisch has shown in his bracing study of Davies's political manipulation of Irish jurisprudence during the first decade of James's reign, the reported decisions constitute a kind of radical jurisprudence to effect that consolidation. A brief summary of some of the judgments will give a sense of the political project underlying and unifying the several cases: municipal rights to customs duties, formerly granted by charter, collapse in the face of a centralized national law; fishing rights pertaining to a Gaelic lordship give way to an extended royal prerogative; a debased Irish coinage, in spite of the evident gap between its assigned and "natural" values, is held according to the terms of a royal proclamation to be legal tender; a Catholic priest is convicted of treason according to the English statute of *praemunire*; an ecclesiastical jurisdiction in matters of bastardy is ceded to the secular jurisdiction.[65] The two most critical reported decisions are the case of tanistry and the resolution concerning Irish gavelkind, whereby the customary landholding patterns alternative to common-law descent were finally declared void at law. The story with which the book is concerned, then, is neither accommodation to custom nor the antiquity and continuity of custom in Ireland, but rather the creation of what can best be thought of as proximate origins, legal moments from which henceforth an Irish legal history will be told, and told precisely in the absence both of preexisting local concessions to the native population and of alternative Irish customary systems. To the extent that the book celebrates the moment of English law's *becoming* effective across Ireland (a marker, that is, of true imperial sovereignty), the antiquity of English law is irrelevant to the way it will operate on the island. Davies's defense of the customary common law as if were operating in an exclusively English context corresponds to the strategic forgetting of difference on which the common law's sovereignty in Ireland was to be grounded.

The radical beginning constituted by Davies's volume of reports must, however, seem natural rather than artificial, continuous rather than innovative. Davies asserts such a continuity with an Irish legal past when, at the beginning of his introduction, he accurately dates the presence of English law in Ireland back to the time of Henry II and King John (∗1r). He notes, also, that records of legal proceedings have been kept since that time, and that a good many of "these aunciente recordes" survive "as faire & authentique, as any I have seene in England" (∗1v). At such moments Davies can be seen to be making a traditional rhetorical claim: in a different kind of introduction or book, the vocabulary of authenticity and antiquity could be seen easily to lend authority to the work at hand. In a book, however, that initiates the practice for Ireland of printing reports and, more important, limits its historical scope to the ten years preceding publication, that vocabulary has chiefly a symbolic value. The antiquity of legal records to which the reporter has access loosely adheres to his recent reports, in spite of their irrelevance to the recent cases or to the book's occasion, purpose, and effect. Through a similarly mobile iconic value, Davies's lengthy consideration of the common law as *English* custom comes to be relevant to a book of Irish reports, just as more broadly yet, a customary law perfectly fitted from "time immemorial" to one nation comes to seem perfectly and necessarily fitted to its colony. If Davies can be said here to make the iconic legally efficacious, I mean specifically that, under the pressure of the colonial context, "custom" detaches itself from the national and local (English) circumstances that exactly define the customary, and thereby assumes a rhetorical weight wholly at odds with its usual meaning as a legal term. The customary, in other words, opposes itself to custom.

The peculiar tactics of Davies's theoretical inclusions and occlusions come more sharply into focus when we remember that such arguments about the antiquity of customary law were developed in response to just the kind of national difference that he is keen to efface in relation to Ireland. Useful here is Pocock's analysis of the appeal to antiquity as found in Fortescue's foundational text for English law, the *De laudibus legum Anglie*. As Pocock points out in relation to this defense of English custom and statute, Fortescue apprehends that the *particular* character of a nation's law is unrelated to its deducibility from rational principles.[66] In response to that extra-rational legal core, Fortescue argues for the superiority of English law to all other laws by claiming that English customary law, predating even the Roman conquest, is the oldest among all surviving systems and for that reason "not only good but the best."[67] As Pocock explains, the argument from antiquity allowed Fortescue and the common lawyers who followed him to get around the problem of saying, for example, why "English law suits the English better than Venetian law suits the Venetians." It does so by appealing to brute quantification: "If the laws of England are indeed older than those of Venice and have been longer in continuous usage, then more men, in more years and more situations, have testified silently in their favor; . . . Such is the rationale of the argument from antiquity."[68] When Davies alludes to the unmatched antiquity of English customary law, then, he is appealing to a legal theory grounded in and responsive to national circumstance and local contingency. Conversely, when he marginalizes the claims of Irish jurisdiction on his theoretical account of the customary common law, he is suppressing the claims of particular national contingencies in order to make coherent the inconsistencies between English legal theory and the practice of English law in Ireland.

We might with equal accuracy say that he *represses* those Irish claims and Irish circumstances. Peter Goodrich has powerfully probed the texts of early modern common law for the "positive unconscious" of that law, the symptomatic traces of vocabularies and jurisdictions that were sacrificed in the professional manufacture of the common law.[69] Goodrich's analysis of English law attends to a history of legal failures in the early modern period, of "texts and traditions that were interpreted out of existence by the ascendant doctrinal writers."[70] He focuses on the critical attempts by civilians and antiquarians like Abraham Fraunce, Sir Robert Wiseman, and John Cowell to reform the common law by bringing the methods and texts of the civil-law tradition to bear on the English law and institutions.[71] But Davies's

Ireland, constituting as it does a site of erasure for legal meanings alternative to those that will become dominant, presents an especially clear instance of the historical process elucidated by Goodrich. Davies's casebook carries the traces both of the repressed (Irish) alternatives and of the mundane technics of the act of repression, testifying as it does to the efficacy not of customary law, its purported subject, but of radical jurisprudence, an institutionally imposed law no less positive in its character than statute. In Davies's reports, more clearly even than in Coke's, the judicial decision *writes* itself into law, overpowering the unwritten even as it attempts to assume the aspect of the unwritten.[72] As a whole, the book operates to mask as continuity the substitution of custom and the suppression of national difference at law. The conflicting claims in Davies of dominant and suppressed customs, of "English" and "Irish," of written and unwritten, of the antique and the innovative, are thus versions of the tension that emerges within the idea of the "common" at the moment of its deformation inside a colonial common law and commonweal. If the "common" in Ireland was refitted as a narrow ideological quantity, so too the customary became the interpretation that the dominant law ascribed to its own power: an institutional form fictively assumed by the imperial and by the statutory.

SPENSER AND THE PROJECT FOR STATUTORY REFORM

In the coercive force of their erasures, the judicial decisions recorded in Davies's casebook have the shape of statutory rather than customary law: they can best be understood as a quasi-legislative substitute for a long-deferred parliamentary intervention in Ireland. When Lord Deputy Chichester convened the Irish Parliament in 1613, it had not met for nearly thirty years, a period twice as long as any other hiatus during the preceding century. But Parliament had once seemed far more central to England's legal agenda in Ireland. In the 1530s Thomas Cromwell reinvigorated the Irish Parliament, shaping it, as Brendan Bradshaw has observed, into "an active instrument of English government," a means of providing "his programme of reform in [the Irish colony] with legislative underpinning."[73] In the 1541 Parliament in which Ireland was by statute declared a kingdom and the Irish his legal subjects, Lord Deputy St. Leger invited into the upper house Irish representatives from the lordships beyond the Pale, thus transforming the Parliament "from a localised institution into a nationally representative assembly." St. Leger's intention in so doing was that the assembly should reflect "the constitutional change effected by the act for the kingly title . . . and the inauguration of a single polity of subjects composed of Englishry and Irishry alike."[74]

Even though St. Leger's model for the Irish Parliament disappeared as early as the 1550s, the program of bringing Ireland under the control of English institutions continued to be allied in theory to the idea of statutory reform. Practically, however, it became clear to the Dublin authorities during Elizabeth's reign that Parliament was an ineffective and even dangerous instrument for the reform of the Irish nation.[75] The long gap between Elizabeth's last Irish Parliament (1585/86) and James's first marks, indeed, the final stage in a shift from reform by statute to a more coercive and brutal agenda of plantation and reconquest. Certainly, the Nine Years War, waged between 1594 and 1603 against Hugh O'Neill in Ulster and other magnates across the island, rendered at least temporarily irrelevant any continuation of reform through legislative means. In the years following the war, as Pawlisch shows, Davies coordinated in place of statute a set of judicial resolutions with almost statutory authority. But with the Ulster plantation, begun in 1608 in response to the 1607 flight of the Ulster lords and the resulting appropriation of their lands for the purpose of new English settlement, the government was in a position to consolidate its authority once again through statutory means, all the more so because the king constituted, in Ulster and in the older Munster plantation, eighty-four new borough seats, thus extending New English representation in the lower house for any future Parliament, and so circumventing the traditional problem of an antigovernment Old English majority.[76] At stake, then, in the radical retreat from statutory reform was only a deferral of statute's legislative authority, a displacement of statute's "written" hermeneutic onto alternative sites for positive and coercive law.

Spenser's *View of the Present State of Ireland* argues in favor of such a deferral. Irenius, the Anglo-Irish spokesman for practical reform, explicitly repudiates the position of his more theoretical English interlocutor, Eudoxus. The latter wonders why the law cannot at once be used to effect reform. The reason, Irenius answers, is that English laws are not, as they ought to be, "fashioned unto the manners and Condicion of the people to whom they are [in this case] mente" (*View*, 54). Not least because of an Irish addiction to "the sworde" (*View*, 55), English statutes are at best ineffective and at worst wholly counterproductive. To the question posed by Eudoxus, "Howe then doe ye thinke is the reformacion ... to be begonne yf not by Lawes and Ordinaunces," Irenius replies, "Even by the sworde," where the sword stands not only for reconquest but also, as Irenius says in an improbable gloss, for "the Royall power of the Prince which oughte to stretche it selfe forthe in her Chiefe strengthe to the ... Cuttinge of ... evills ... and not of the people which are evill" (*View*, 147–48). Irenius's program comes in two parts, then, the violence of reconquest moving always toward a new accommodation of the Irish to the law. Once the people have been "humbled and prepared" (*View*, 198), laws will appropriately reassume their centrality for civil reform. And when that time comes, Irenius notoriously says, it will not be "convenient" to change all the laws: "Therefore sithens we Cannot now applie Lawes fitt to the people as in the firste institucion of Comon wealthes it oughte to be we will applie the people and fitt them to the Lawes as it most Convenientlye maye be" (*View*, 199). Irenius's version of political accommodation involves a reform of the people by the law, a law able to operate, as Hadfield points out, only because of institutional underpinnings established through force.[77]

Spenser is not imagining a fit that accommodates Gaelic law. Henry VIII, however, had imagined just such an accommodation. Writing to the Earl of Surrey in 1520, the king had urged his commander to ask of the Irish Brehons, the judges or arbitrators at Gaelic law, "under what manner and by what laws they will be ordered and governed; to the intent that if their laws be good and reasonable they may be approved, and the rigour of our laws, if they shall think them too hard, be mitigated and brought to such moderation as they may conveniently live under the same."[78] Seventy years on, Spenser's sense of accommodation is more coercive than this; as reformers had done during the intervening decades, he aims to eradicate Gaelic law by so imagining that law as to make the coercive act appear natural. Central to this strategy is the identification of Gaelic law with Gaelic custom. In the *View*, Irenius differentiates three kinds of evils "hurtefull to the [Irish] Common weale": "the firste in the Lawes the second in Customes, the laste in religion" (*View*, 45). The category of custom refers here to nonlegal practices such as semi-nomadic pasturing, bardic poetry, the wearing of the mantle and of the glib. But in the first section on laws, when speaking of the clash between the Gaelic and English systems, Irenius and Eudoxus characterize the Brehon law also as custom, "a certaine rule of righte unwritten" (*View*, 47), and tanistry as "Custome" (*View*, 50), a "daungerous Custome" (*View*, 52), and one among the "ill Customes" of the Irish (*View*, 52). Given that the tripartite structure of Spenser's analysis insists on the distinction between custom and law, it is striking that the term *custom* so easily drifts into a section to which it nominally does not pertain. Spenser's designation of the Brehon laws as custom identifies them as unwritten, but also places them on a plane with the wearing of the mantle or glib.

This conflation of law and custom dates back at least to the 1366 Statutes of Kilkenny, which, in order to prevent the further gaelicization of the Anglo-Irish living in the Pale, racialized the Gaelic Irish in terms that denigrated their customary appearance, dress, language, and law. One of the statutes refers to the "Brehon law, which by right ought not to be called law but bad custom [*lei . . . de Breon que par reason ne doit estre nome lei eins malveis custume*]."⁷⁹ In two treatises written in the early seventeenth century, John Davies quotes the phrase in alternative translations from the French: the Brehon law was deemed, he says, no law, "but an evill Custome," and "noe lawe but a lewd custome."⁸⁰ Within the language of sixteenth-century reform, the elision became something of a commonplace. At work principally was the predictable strategy of opposing a reasonable English law to an unreasonable Gaelic one. Thus, in a treatise from 1571, Rowland White condemns the continued use by the native Irish throughout Ireland of the "Brehons Lawe as they dyd before the conquest which custome they . . . doo meyneteyne and use the same contrary to God his lawe and also repugnant to the Quenes Majesties lawes and all other good civill orders."⁸¹ What interests me here is not the designation of Irish law as contrary to reason or natural law, but rather the degree to which Brehon practices came, as for Spenser, semantically to be identified with *mere* custom, custom as opposed to law. In his 1594 *Solon His Follie*, Richard Becon calls for a "mutation of auncient laws & customes," but refers to persistent Gaelic practices such as tanistry only as "custome" that should be "abolished by lawes."⁸² A passage from another treatise by White, this one from 1569, is particularly interesting in this regard. In a densely structured passage, he refers to Gaelic tanistry first as "a customary Lawe" repugnant to English law, then as "That custome" and "This Lawe and custome," finally as "this said custome of the brehonnes" and "this unlawfull use and custome."⁸³ The clustering of these alternative formulations works, as did the Kilkenny formulation, serially to disengage the Gaelic practices from any pretension to authentic legal status. According to the rhetorical opposition of law and custom, then, the New English criticized Brehon law, not just as evil custom or bad custom, but as custom pure and simple. This is interesting because it is a singularly odd and dangerous argument for the English to make, given that the usual argument about *English* law was that as custom tested across time and found useful or fitting to the people, it was superior to imposed written law. It is certainly true in the legal arena that, as Ciaran Brady has more generally observed, "the Tudors were, for the most part, remarkably incurious about Gaelic Ireland."⁸⁴ Faced with the problem of construing the eradication of one customary law in favor of another, the English most often appealed bluntly to the right of conquest. The semantic pressures I have been analyzing, through which the meanings of both *custom* and *common* were narrowed for political ends, points to a similarly incurious identification of accommodation with coercion.

But the story is not a story only of force, since the same semantic pressures testify to the felt peril of suppressing meanings so close to one's own. Confronted with a jurisdiction in which customary law is not common law, nor Gaelic commonness English custom, the twinned concepts of customary and common split apart, and not only for Ireland. The attempt to configure as natural the law's extension into an alternative jurisdiction requires, again as if naturally, the refitting of the dominant law itself. At the moment of legal suppression, the suppressed meaning also shapes a version of English law useful to the colonial institution and enterprise. If English law could not logically be imposed as customary law, it could logically be imposed as sanctioned statute law. The emphasis laid in the early reform literature on the autonomy of the Irish Parliament, and on its competence throughout the whole kingdom of Ireland, already implies the centrality of positive sanction to the imagined imposition of law, as indeed does the energy behind the Tudor programs for statutory reform. It is true that, in practice, statute was to be less frequently invoked in Ireland than in England, where Thomas Cromwell's articulation of Parliament's omnicompetence made statute the driving force behind the development of public law.[85] In Ireland, nonetheless, we can identify a particularly intense version of the relationship between statute and the law of which it is a part, and so hear rise the ideological pulse under the practical skin. When, in Spenser's dialogue, Irenius claims that English laws themselves have inadvertently led to evils in Ireland, Eudoxus asks whether he means "this by the Comon lawe of the realme or by the Statute Lawes and Actes of parlamentes." To which Irenius answers, "Surelye by them bothe for even the Comon Lawe beinge that which *William of Normandye* broughte in with his Conquest . . . with the state of Irelande . . . dothe not so well agree" (*View*, 46).[86] So Spenser here uses the myth of the Norman Yoke to create a highly centralized, royalist, and public view of the law. Like Spenser, and in opposition to those who argued that the common law drew from a source of legal right in place before the Conquest, Sir Francis Bacon and King James would both use the myth to argue for a similarly centralized view.[87]

My argument is not that Spenser formulates an innovative theory, but that in his case the theory takes hold peculiarly in response to the local pressure exerted by Ireland. Irenius invokes the theory within a discussion of why statutory reform has been so ineffective in Ireland, but in his formulation common law in general assumes the character of statute: positive sanctioned law is constituted as the hermeneutic by which to understand the whole of the common law. It is but a step from here to Davies's radical, because binding, jurisprudence. One critic has said in relation to the passage just cited from the *View* that Spenser did not trust the common law because he believed not in the ancient constitution, but in the Norman Yoke.[88] But this is to reverse cause and effect, and to misconstrue the operation of ideology in the political sphere. The point is not that Spenser criticized the project of legal reform because he believed in one story of legal origins over another, but rather that he invoked a particular story in order to argue for a particular course of reform. If the passage exposes the need for a deferral of statutory reform until the Irish are ready to be brought "to agree" with the laws, it also highlights why at that point sanctioned statute was imagined as a legal template for law and for the imposition of civil order. The positivist construction of the common law in Spenser's tract serves him because it circumvents the problem of justifying the imposition of one customary law on another, by allowing for the far simpler opposition between sanctioned law and primitive custom.

ALLEGORIES OF TENURE II: CUSTOM IN BOOKS 5 AND 6 OF THE FAERIE QUEENE

Spenser's allegory in Books 5 and 6 of the *Faerie Queene* is concerned in the deepest sense with this manufactured opposition between present sanction and primitive custom. In Book 4, "custome" neutrally signals a pattern or behavior preserved for its ancient character (4.1.9–11, 4.6.44). But in the narrower Irish context of Books 5 and 6, as we might expect, custom takes on an exclusively negative valence, opposing itself to Artegall's and Calidore's law. In the two most important relevant passages, Spenser represents an unjust tax or imposition as a customary practice to be eradicated by law. The quibbling identification of custom both as tax and habitual behavior is not accidental, since Spenser is targeting for criticism exactly those customary exactions on Gaelic land through which the native lord was able to exercise authority throughout his seignory.

At the beginning of Book 6, the returning Artegall tells Calidore, who is pursuing the Blatant Beast, that "since the salvage Island I did leave / . . . I such a Beast did see" (6.1.9). If these lines imply that, like Artegall, Book 6 too will abandon the savage Irish landscape of Book 5, Calidore's first adventure rapidly undoes that implication. The Knight of Courtesy meets a squire, bound "hande and foote unto a tree" (6.1.11), who alerts him to an evil suffered by local travelers:

> Not farre from hence, uppon yond rocky hill,
> Hard by a streight there stands a castle strong,

> Which doth observe a custome lewd and ill,
> And it hath long mayntaind with mighty wrong:
> For may no Knight nor Lady passe along
> That way, (and yet they needs must passe that way,)
> By reason of the streight, and rocks among,
> But they that Ladies lockes doe shave away,
> And that knights berd for toll, which they for passage pay.
> (6.1.13)

The mysteries of this custom are, the squire explains, erotic. Briana, the proud lady of the castle, perpetrates the "shameful use" (6.1.14) for love of the equally proud Crudor,

> ... who through high disdaine
> And proud despight of his selfe pleasing mynd,
> Refused hath to yeeld her love againe,
> Untill a Mantle she for him doe fynd
> With beards of Knights and locks of Ladies lynd.
> Which to provide, she hath this Castle dight,
> And therein hath a Sensechall assynd,
> Cald *Maleffort*, a man of mickle might,
> Who executes her wicked will, with worse despight.
> (6.1.15)

The defeminizing/effeminizing Gaelic mantle is only the most explicit of the many Irish allusions here. Pauline Henley relates the name Briana to the Irish Brian.[89] But the name also suggests "Brehon," a meaning underlined by Spenser's invocation in "custome lewde and ill" of the Statute of Kilkenny's negative characterization of Brehon law. Briana's castle is on a rocky hill, furthermore, a topographical site closely associated with Gaelic practices. Spenser's Irenius identifies "rounde hills" and the "Rathe or hill" as the tradition place for a clan to meet and "parlye" (*View*, 128).[90] More significant is that hills and stones figure in Irenius's description specifically of the ceremony by which, after election, the tanist was invested with his office: "They use to place him that shalbe theire Captaine uppon a stonne allwaies observed for that purpose and placed Comonlye uppon a hill" (*View*, 50). Briana's strange exaction stands for Gaelic custom generally.[91]

The Briana/Crudor episode matches a passage in Book 5, in which another customary exaction allegorically renders Irish custom, specifically the customary charges on Gaelic land. Like Briana, the Sarazin Pollente and his daughter Munera occupy a castle from which, as Artegall learns, they tyrannize the surrounding country by exacting a monetary toll from all those wishing to cross a particular bridge, justifying this practice according "to the custome of their law" (5.2.11). A "groome of evill guize" (similar to Briana's senechal) taxes the poor, while Pollente himself "uppon the rich doth tyrannize," both by claiming the passage money and, in certain cases, by stealing the "spoile" of knights sent to their death through trapdoors on the bridge where the tyrant "custometh to fight" (5.2.6–8).[92] These customary practices, wrongs which Pollente daily "encreaseth more" (5.2.6), have made him a magnate, "Having great Lordships got and goodly farmes, / Through strong oppression of his powre extort" (5.2.5). So the terms of enrichment here correspond to the native Irish lord's extension of his power and tenures by means of exactions and extortions imposed on land pertaining to subsidiary lordships within the larger seignory.

Artegall and Calidore confront two versions of the same customary wrongs. The difference between the outcomes of their meetings registers Spenser's complex sense of what might constitute an accommodation of Gaelic custom to English law. With the help of Talus, the Knight of Justice brutally kills Guizor, Pollente, and Munera, and reforms the "wicked customes of that Bridge" (5.2.28). The absolute lack of accommodation here exemplifies Spenser's use of Artegall/Talus to represent the interdependence of justice and force; allegorically it renders the argument in the *View* that English sovereignty depends on a military suppression of native Irish power. At the hands of the Knight of Courtesy, in contrast, Briana and Crudor fare much better than their counterparts with the Knight of Justice. Calidore does kill Briana's seneschal, justifying this action in language that reinvokes the opposition between law and custom: "it is no blame / To punish those, that doe deserve the same; / But they that break bands of civilitie, / And wicked customes make, those doe defame / Both noble armes and gentle curtesie" (6.1.26). Having eliminated the servant, however, the knight spares the noble lovers who devised the wicked custom. After overcoming Crudor, Calidore stays his "mortall hand" (6.1.40), and instead presides over the union of Briana and the hitherto unwilling knight: "So suffring him to rise, he made him sweare / By his owne sword, and by the crosse thereon, / To take *Briana* for his loving fere" (6.1.43). At issue in the responses of Calidore and Artegall to their respective antagonists is, of course, the difference between courtesy and justice. But, as Elizabeth Fowler acutely argues, *courtesy* is itself a legal term, referring to the "Latin *Comity*, the principle upon which conflicts of law are decided."[93] Calidore's courteous behavior toward Briana and Crudor represents, then, the kind of legal decision-making that must be deferred but will become possible after a just force such as Artegall's has imposed order on Ireland.

Accepting the terms of Spenser's general thesis about law across the two books, we are able to see why Calidore must kill Briana's seneschal. The office has a specific historic resonance for Ireland. As Brady explains, the term *seneschal*, which referred originally to the major-domo in a feudal household, was from the mid-sixteenth century used in Ireland to refer to the proto-constables authorized by the English administration to establish and maintain order in the hitherto unassimilated lordships.[94] The seneschal system was a failure, so much so that the seneschal came, along with the Old English magnate, to represent for the New English reformers a hybrid identity more dangerous even than the Gaelic. Rather than bringing a civil and English order to the lordships, the seneschals tended themselves to become gaelicized: since they were not required to follow the common law, they tended to use a mixture of English law, native Gaelic law, and martial law. This meant that, far from consolidating Crown interests, they aggravated the existing situation by assuming a highly personalized power, which itself "rested upon their continuing willingness to ignore or condone a certain level of violence within their territories."[95] When Calidore kills Briana's seneschal, therefore, Spenser is allegorizing the New English argument that Anglo-Irish comity, the meeting of English law and Irish custom, depends on eliminating the influence of the Old English presence. In doing so, Calidore facilitates the unmediated accommodation of the customary Gaelic elements represented by the lovers whom he spares.

Although this meeting is less brutal than Artegall's confrontation with Munera and Pollente, Calidore's solution registers the de facto lack of courtesy underlying Spenser's comity. Spenser provides the English colonist's fantasy of accommodating the colonized without the cost of accommodation. First, out of simple gratitude, Briana surrenders her castle to Calidore, who in turn gives it to the squire and "his damzel" as recompense for the wrong they suffered at the hands of the seneschal. In the context of Spenser's concern with land ownership elsewhere in Book 6, this outcome is instructive: Irish land comes into English hands and within the scope of English inheritance. More significant are the terms of Crudor's surrender to the English champion: he is made to accept Briana, "Withouten dowre or composition; / But to release his former foule condition" (6.1.43). As an image of any agreement imposed on the native Irish by the English, this is both coercive and implausible. By the 1590s New English reformers had abandoned the gradualist notion that native Irish lords would surrender their customary rights simply to conform to English practices (and leave their "former foule condition"). In the term *composition*, a technical word drawn from the sphere of Irish fiscal policy, Spenser alludes to a principal strategy underlying the failed gradualist policy, composition being the process through which customary exactions, like coin and livery, on Gaelic or gaelicized land were converted to a stable annual rent-charge payable by landholders both to the Crown for the defense of the province and to the overlord in lieu of the traditional exactions.[96] Already subject to his military conqueror, Crudor receives from Calidore the benefit of no composition. When Crudor promises the other his "true fealtie for aye" (6.1.44), and abandons the custom that he has imposed on Briana, and she on the countryside, Spenser is imagining a negotiation between Irish custom and English law in which the native lord will be compensated only by the love (in Briana) of the "Irish" and the diffuse good will of his new and real lords.

In Books 5 and 6, Spenser argues that the common law must suppress custom, just as it must also suppress commonness. The two aspects of that legal equation merge in the allegory of the egalitarian Giant, which directly follows that of Pollente and Munera. The juxtaposition of the two episodes is not casual: Pollente's monopolistic exactions sit at one end of a spectrum, the Giant's egalitarianism at the other.[97] After executing Pollente and Munera, Artegall and Talus come upon an (Irish) rock, on which a Giant holding a set of scales is attempting to "weigh equallie" (5.2.30) the whole world, in order to reduce to equal shares the sea and earth, the fire and air, heaven and hell. Within the local context I have been elucidating, the Giant's program to treat legal and political equity in quantitative terms can be understood to combine the Gaelic "extra-legal" appeals both to commonness and ancient custom: "And so were realmes and nations run awry. / All which he undertook for to repaire, / In sort as they were formed aunciently; / And all things would reduce unto equality" (5.2.32). The Giant's communism appeals to ancient custom to revive the ideal of equality in ownership. Annabel Patterson rightly associates the "great assembly" (5.2.29) listening to the Giant with the Gaelic assemblies that Irenius sees as potentially dangerous to the commonwealth.[98] I would argue further that the communism espoused by the Giant renders the perceived dangers of a Gaelic tenure understood both as kin-ownership and as customary pattern. The giant's plan to "equalize" not only political communities but also a topography of plains and mountains (5.2.38) will erase all visible signs of difference, and as such approximates both the leveling accomplished by the brigands who destroy the pastoral community in Book 6 and the effect of Irish gavelkind, as described by Davies, in rendering the Irish landscape "wast and desolate" with none of the differentiation that accompanies the civic.

What interests me, in the context of an Irish policy in which the interpretation of English and Irish legal orders had become politically paramount, is that the episode moves so quickly from a concern with the structure of political ownership to an analysis of interpretation as a secondary mode of legal coercion. Artegall insists that for true understanding of the world's order the Giant needs to look beyond "things subject to thy daily vew" to their underlying "causes" and "courses" (5.2.42), which are hidden in God's inscrutable will. Opposing the Giant's theory of vision, Artegall installs a theory of interpretation that has more to do with the relation of words to meaning. If "thou be so wise," he tells his opponent, use your scales to weigh the wind, the light, or thought: "But if the weight of these thou canst not show, / Weigh but some word which from thy lips doth fall" (5.2.43). Artegall is laying a trap: redefining the point or issue to be debated, he shifts from the material to the immaterial, from the quantitative to the qualitative.[99] From the sphere of distributive justice, that is, Artegall moves to legal interpretation: "Which is (sayd he) more heavy then in weight, / The right or wrong, the false or else the trew?" (5.2.44). Predictably, and with irritation, the Giant sees his attempt to answer the question fail: "the winged words out of his ballaunce flew" (5.2.44). When the Giant fails equally to measure the concepts of right and wrong, true and false (5.2.45–46), Artegall is poised to admonish his frustrated opponent according to the new terms he has engineered:

> Be not upon thy balance wroken:
> For they doe nought but right or wrong betoken;
> But in the mind the doome of right must be;
> And so likewise of words, the which be spoken,
> The eare must be the ballance, to decree
> And judge, whether with truth or falsehood they agree.
>   (5.2.47)

The debate is over, and when, in anger, the Giant thrusts away "the right," Talus drowns him by throwing him from the rock into the sea.

As so often in Book 5 (and in Ireland), reasoning gives way to a violence rationalized by and as judicial interpretation. Constructing the Giant as a naïve reader for thinking in quantitative terms, Artegall insists on a flexible relationship between words and truth or words and law. Dissociating Spenser from his knight's violence toward the Giant, Elizabeth Fowler powerfully argues that Artegall's understanding of that relationship is "woefully corrupt" both as "a definition of what a judge does and as a theory of equity."[100] Artegall locates justice wholly within a narrowly private and authoritarian ethical sphere, she argues; according to him, "not only the specialized, discretionary aspect of the common law, but *justice itself* is subjective: it lies in the mind and ear, a position quite alien . . . to English jurisprudence in general." But this is not a fully convincing characterization of Artegall's argument, which seems to me, rather, traditional in the way Fowler defines the tradition. Artegall says, first, that the "doome," the pronouncement (OED *sb.* 2), of "right" must be in the mind; and, second, that the ear is the qualitatively oriented balance that judges how closely words agree or fit "with truth or falsehood." It is not justice that is here subjective, but the pronouncement of justice and the interpretation or application of a verbal or written law. Artegall is thus articulating the work of equity in two ways, or for two closely related, and ultimately inseparable, spheres of legal activity. Where, given the particular circumstances of a case, the word of law would generate a too strict judgment, the judge in his decree cannot depend on any absolute definition of legal right and wrong, but "in his mind" equitably mitigates the word of law in favor of the spirit.[101] Second, and in the realm of textual and statutory interpretation, equity fits the words of a statute to the spirit of the law, in order, once again, to avoid injustice or legal inconsistency: the "ear" judges how far the words "agree" with truth or falsehood, and fits the words to the former.

When I say that Artegall's equity is traditional, I am not disputing Fowler's accurate sense that Artegall's justice is peculiarly centralized and "self-serving," nor do I mean simply to restate Patterson's equally cogent argument that the debate between Artegall and the Giant stands for "a confrontation between two ways of conceptualizing justice, the abstract and the applied."[102] Rather, I emphasize that Artegall's verbal victory resides in his effecting an institutional deformation of the debate he finds himself in: the historically relevant point is not that he mischaracterizes equity, but that he should redefine an ethical issue of distribution as one of judicial and statutory interpretation. Artegall's attack on how the Giant *sees* the world is relevant here. Customs are seen and followed, laws read and interpreted, and where customs are interpreted, they lose their essential character. When Artegall reconstrues the Giant's argument about the claim of antiquity's order as a matter, instead, of words and their agreement with truth, he thus frames his legal victory in two ways, as a local intervention and as a methodological one. The maneuver is familiar to us: Artegall is the New English proponent of legislative and statutory intervention against custom; he is also Davies's judge, whose decisions, with all the force of statute, eradicate custom by asking what its reason is and how it fits into a law whose own written and institutional reason already excludes it. Artegall is Spenser's and England's bureaucratic hero.

ALLEGORICAL CONVENIENCE AND THE ABSENCES OF STATUTE

To explore further Spenser's sense of how the statutory function might help distance England from a Gaelic law whose articulation as theory would bring it rather too close to the common law intended to replace it, it will be instructive to reexamine the Pollente episode by placing it alongside a second passage from Book 5, one only indirectly concerned with the reform of the Irish. Taken together, the two passages extend Spenser's treatment of judicial interpretation in the debate between Artegall and the Giant, exhibiting on the poet's part a simultaneous engagement with the interpretive status of allegory. The first passage addresses the manufacture of signs, the second their interpretation.

We have seen that, having dispatched Pollente and Munera to their deaths, Artegall reforms the "wicked customes of that Bridge" (5.2.28). He also manufactures cultural memory, by making the former practitioners of those customs into exemplary patterns: Pollente's headless corpse is "carried downe along the Lee, / Whose waters with his filthy bloud it stayned"; and his head is "pitcht upon a pole . . . / To be a mirrour to all mighty men, / In whose right hands great power is contayned" (5.2.19). Talus likewise chops off Munera's hands and feet, and nails them "on high, that all might them behold" (5.2.26). Spenser alludes here not only to actual exemplary practices in Ireland (as explicitly signaled by the Lee), but also to a mode of historical poetry alternative to his own allegory—namely, the mirror literature exemplified by William Baldwin's *Mirror for Magistrates* (1559) and, in Ireland, by John Derricke's 1581 work, *The Image of Irelande*.[103] In the conventional manner of that poetry and to argue that Irish rebellion is neither just nor viable, Derricke brings the rebel Rory Og O'More (d. 1578) onto his poetic stage, in order to have him in his own words warn others against following him into rebellion. "Suppose," Derricke tells his readers, "that you see a monstrous Devill, a trunkelesse head, and a hedlesse bodie livyng . . . [the head] mounted uppon a poule (a proper sight God wot to be holde) vanting it self on the highest toppe of the Castell of Dublin, uttering in plaine Irishe the thynges that ensewe."[104] In his account of Artegall as the shaper of political memory, then, Spenser means to absorb into his own poetic structure this earlier model of poetic counsel.

Allegory, however, is more complex than the older exemplary mode. In addition to making Pollente and Munera into bloody examples, Artegall imposes another sign on the Irish landscape by burning Pollente's misgotten goods and razing his castle, "That there mote be no hope of reparation, / Nor memory therof to any nation" (5.2.28). So, even as he reproduces his English authority by deforming the Irish body, Artegall erases the memory of an earlier (Irish) authority alternative to his own. As political strategy, the second gesture is strikingly at odds with the exemplary mode. To say that Artegall wants his own power memorialized and another's erased does not account for the deliberate violence of Artegall's histories. Responding to the problem of evil custom, Artegall *institutes* cultural memory through the exemplary mirror of Pollente's punishment, and he *erases* cultural memory by imposing a significant absence on the landscape.

We can better understand the dissonance between these two modes that colonial authority takes by looking to a second passage from Book 5, this one concerned with the reading of signs. In canto 7, Britomart rescues Artegall from the castle of the Amazon Radigund, whom Artegall has failed to defeat because of his misplaced sense of equity. Radigund has effeminized her prisoner by dressing him in women's clothes and setting him to women's work. When, therefore, Britomart discovers Artegall, she is "abasht with secrete shame" to find him "deformed" by his "disguize" (5.7.38). Here Spenser refers his reader to the *Odyssey*. Britomart's astonishment at his clothes, he says, was greater even than that of Penelope, who failed to recognize Odysseus upon his return. The reason is that Odysseus was so changed that "she knew not his favours likelynesse, / For many scarres and many hoary heares, / But stood long staring on him, mongst uncertaine feares" (5.7.39).

But Spenser's version of Homer is not fully accurate as to the reason Penelope fails to recognize her husband. His passage conflates two different meetings with the changed hero. In Homer, Penelope is uncertain whether she recognizes her husband because he is clothed as a beggar, which means that the *Odyssey* offers a closer parallel than the imperfect one that Spenser draws between Artegall's clothes and Odysseus' scars. The *Odyssey*'s scar, furthermore, belongs famously to an earlier moment in the story, when the old nurse Euryclea, as she washes the stranger's feet, suddenly recognizes him as her master, not in spite of, but exactly because of, a scar on his thigh. Spenser's intertextual conflation of the two Homeric episodes creates a powerful model of allegorical interpretation, since the reader who remembers Homer will confront the "scarres" that mask Spenser's Odysseus as, also, the scar that reveals Homer's hero. Put generally, the sign that allows for recognition or memory also mars it. Put differently, the sign that prevents recognition allows for it. The scar is a veil; in the terms Spenser applies to his own allegory in the 1589 letter to Ralegh, it is a "darke conceit," promising meaning even as it causes unease by withholding it: the passage becomes an allegory for allegory.[105] A scar, additionally, marks something that is no longer there, an absence made significant by the presence of the substituting sign. Implied, then, at the level of interpretation is the relationship between sign and meaning articulated in the Pollente episode when Artegall aims to produce a political culture through the simultaneous memorialization and erasure of an (Irish) customary past.

The signs manufactured and interpreted in these episodes are allegories for an allegorical mode that presents and obscures meaning, and exists always as the negotiation between the present sign and a corresponding significant absence. This is important for Spenser's analysis of Irish legality because it allows us to see how the reforming signs that Artegall leaves on the landscape are also statutory. The idea that the laws shaping a culture's memory are constituted by means of obscuring linguistic signs, in negotiation with something *not* there, was integral to the idea of the sanctioned written law that was meant ultimately to replace Irish law and custom. The distinction at work in the legal sphere is the equitable one between letter and spirit.[106] In his 1571 collection of reports, the lawyer Edmund Plowden writes of a judicial decision concerning the interpretation of statute: "And first they said that acts of Parliament are positive laws [*leyes positive*] consisting of two parts. The first is the words [*parolles*] of the act, and the other the sense [*sence*], for the letter without the sense is not the law [*car le letter sans le sence nest le ley*]. But the letter and the sense together are the law. And anyone who wants to be learned in the positive law must be aware [*doit aver intelligence*] of both."[107] For William West, the letter and the reason of the law correspond to "the fleshe and soule," the "kernel and shell."[108] The author of *A Discourse on the Exposicion and Understandinge of Statutes* (ca. 1565) draws out the implications of this for the equitable interpretation of statute: "For synce that wordes were but invented to declare the meanynge of men, we must rather frame the wordes to the meanynge then the meanynge to the wordes."[109]

As a poetics that locates meaning in half-obscuring signs, allegory seems an apt way to frame a program of reform dependent on statutory language that must itself be half-obscure. What are we to make of this? The connection I am drawing here between Spenser's central poetic strategy and his legal argument in the second part of *Faerie Queene* speaks to the broader culture of textual interpretation generally.[110] But it has particular relevance for the Irish situation. Like allegory, the law Spenser is working to imagine for Ireland is a half-empty vessel. In addition to eliminating Irish custom, the judicial marks that Artegall imposes on the landscape refashion the idea and possibility of custom, by displacing it onto a kind of writing and legislation that contains the past and imagines the future through the production of significant obscurities. As in his confrontation with the Giant, Artegall's victory against Pollente is marked as interpretive, eradicating both his "wicked" customs and the hermeneutic space in which custom is able to assume its authority in the first place. Michael Murrin has emphasized the importance for allegorical theory of the epistemology that, influenced by neoplatonism, actually "requires opaque allegory" in order adequately to "intimate" an infinite and "nameless reality."[111] In a similar way, but on a local and political level, Spenser's obscuring judicial signs are responses to an Irish reality he sees as resistant to analytical capture except through a hermeneutic carefully oriented to its particular content.

Given the coercive aspect of interpretation in Spenser's Ireland, it is unsurprising that in the *View* Irenius's program for Irish legal reform should sound so like the governing rule for statutory interpretation just cited from the mid-sixteenth-century *Discourse for the Exposicion of Statutes*. The two relevant passages define closely related kinds of legal accommodation, which turn out, however, to be opposites:

> For synce that wordes were but invented to declare the meanynge of men, we must rather frame the wordes to the meanynge then the meanynge to the wordes. (*A Discourse*, 140)

> *Iren.* Therefore sithens we Cannot now applie Lawes fitt to the people as in the firste institucion of Comon wealthes it oughte to be we will applie the people and fitt them to the Lawes as it most Convenientlye maye be. (*View*, 199)

The first of these recommends the interpretive adjustment of law in light of the intention behind the law; this is equitable interpretation, the judicial consideration of circumstance through a negotiation between word and intention. For Irenius, in contrast, the "people" are to be accommodated and shaped to the law. I juxtapose the two maxims in order to isolate what I take to be the radical implications of Irenius's odd formula for the legal accommodation of the Irish. Spenser is here imagining the subordination of the colonized through a coercive force that, in the manner of Artegall's engagements with Pollente and the Giant, can be rationalized as interpretation. Specifically at issue, however, is the nature of the disagreement between English law and Irish person that so worries Irenius. *Convenience* is the critical, and easily misunderstood, term for that relationship, and it comes from the sphere of judicial, especially statutory, interpretation.

The idea of convenience and inconvenience dominates the passage in which Irenius articulates his legislative proposal. He begins by saying that he does "not thinke it Conveniente (though now it be in the power of the Prince) to Chaunge all the Lawes"; he then recommends, as we have seen, that the people be fitted to the laws "as it most Convenientlye maye be." He concludes by saying that the "lawes . . . shall abide . . . onelye suche defectes in the Comon lawe and inConveniences in the statutes as in the beginninge we noted . . . maye be Changed by some new actes . . . to be by a parliament theare confirmed" (*View*, 199). Derived from the Latin *conveniens*, the law French terms *convenient* and *inconvenient* mean, respectively, "suitable, meet, fitting" and "absurd, unfitting, logically inconsistent, unnecessary, undesirable."[112] As a category of legal solecism, an inconvenience resembled a repugnancy, that is, an inconsistency between two clauses within the same legal document. An inconvenience referred, however, to a repugnancy or lack of agreement between two different texts, or between a text and the law as a whole.[113] Inconvenience was a technical inconsistency at law, and in the early year books, as J. P. Collas points out, "its technical nature is often emphasised by the addition of *de lei*"; in the reign of Edward II, for example, we find the following: "semble a moy qe ceo est graunt *inconvenient de ley* (trs. it would be a great absurdity in law)."[114] Thus, as F. W. Maitland argues, the legal maxim that "the law will suffer a mischief rather than an inconvenience" originally meant that "it will suffer a practical hardship rather than an inconsistency or logical flaw." Maitland adds, however, that "already before Coke's day a change in the usage of the word *inconvenience* obscured the meaning of this maxim, and therefore it could be glossed by the introduction of the words *private* and *public*."[115] It is in that sense of a private versus a public wrong that the distinction between mischief and inconvenience survives today.[116]

I would argue that this shift in the meaning of inconvenience from a logical absurdity to a public wrong reflects the parallel growth of public-law ideas out of a private-law construction of justice. Samuel Thorne shows in his analysis of statutory interpretation in the sixteenth century that a judicial departure from the word of statute was theorized as interpretation only with the development of the twin notions that all subjects are "bound by acts of Parliament," and that statutes form a cognate group requiring "rules for their general application."[117] Before the maturing of these doctrines across the Tudor period, a judge's alterations of a legislative enactment "were not regarded as [interpretive] interferences with legislative power... but instead as an integral and in no way exceptional part of the judge's task, which had for its objects the reaching of legally sound results and the proper administration of justice between litigants."[118] Under the earlier private-law model, the absurdity or inconvenience consequent upon a statute's application carried no public-law implications, but was judged to be undesirable only for the damage or prejudice—the inconvenience—it might cause a private litigant.[119] Under the public-law model, however, the lack of agreement between a statute and the law assumed the aspect of a public wrong, since its existence called into question the coherence of law as a public, sanctioned, and cognate body. According to the new paradigm, an inconvenience *"de lei"* was no longer a technical matter, but instead challenged the common reason and sanction underlying the law as a whole. It is in this context that "inconvenience" comes to assume the narrowed modern meaning of a wrong inflicted on the public at large—a definition that, taken out of its historical context, obscures the still resident implication of an absurd lack of agreement.

This semantic history helps to explain why *convenience* is so useful a term for Spenser's analysis of the Irish problem at law. The insurmountable theoretical problem for the English in Ireland was the lack of fit between the Irish and an English customary law they resisted as the chief sign of the colonizing presence. Like the technical inconvenience caused by the inappropriate use or interpretation of a law, the cultural lack of fit between Irish and English constitutes for Spenser a logical absurdity. Irenius points out that someone who transferred the laws of the warlike Lacedaemonians to the people of Athens would "find a great absurditye, And inconvenience" (*View*, 54). Similarly for Ireland: although the common law is "of it selfe moste rightefull and verye Conveniente" for England, he says, it is unsuited to Ireland, since "if those Lawes of Irelande be not likewise applied and fitted for that realme they are sure verye inconvenient" (*View*, 65–66). An improper text or interpretation creates a technical inconvenience by opening a gap between the law and the reason implicit in or imputed to that law; analogously, when Spenser uses *inconvenience* to refer to the lack of fit between a law and a people, the gap is between the law and a national character imagined to operate with the same logical force as legal reason.

Spenser's culturally deterministic construction of Irishness explains why in the colonialist context he finds the coercive reshaping of character to be so necessary. To apply and fit the English common law to the Irish realm would be to localize in the contingencies of Irish society and character the reason according to which a law can be judged as fitting or as void. But Irenius proposes the opposite: "we will applie the people and fitt them to the Lawes, as it moste Convenientlye maye be." That is, Irenius's maxim confronts the possibility that another people's reasons or *reason* may not be one's own, not by accommodating that difference, but by substituting a manufactured and institutionalized reason as the standard against which logical coherence or absurdity can interpretively be measured. Irenius's dictum is disorienting, because it invokes the interpretive position that legal reason remains reasonable by being flexible in the face of (national) circumstance, only then to reconstruct that reason as the inflexible and institutional reason of a fully normative Law. The language of convenience and inconvenience in Spenser is the rhetorical motor at law that allows a positivist rationale to overpower reason. In the face of English law's own incapacities in relation to a supposedly English kingdom, Irenius's maxim rationalizes legal unreason by racializing Irish reason and then, simultaneously, by figuring as a matter of interpretive coherence the diminution of the claim of Irish character on law.

Spenser's notion of inconvenience as both a political and interpretive category thus captures in miniature the major argument of this chapter. The suppression of Gaelic custom and commonness in favor of English categories can be seen as part of the growth in England of a public-law scheme, a construction of institutional justice that at its most rigid sees variation as subversive, and responds to it through the coercive violence of interpretation that erases the force of alternative jurisdictions. Artegall's justice imprints the landscape with significant absences whose purpose is to establish, as a proximate origin for a future politics, the possibility of logical coherence at law. Confronting the problem of jurisdictional difference in Ireland, the English similarly affirmed that legal meaning there would be carried forward as a productive absence internal to the legal sign, which is to say as the strategic forgetting that, in Spenser's telling, inheres in statute and in the allegorical mode he allows to serve that hermeneutic. For Ireland, this was not the generous dynamic, familiar in England, by which an empty center circumscribed by the word might be equitably replenished according to the needs of the future. In Spenser's coercive Irish universe, the statutory and allegorical sign, whatever its apparent flexibility, was the instrument only of institutionalized rigor and the site of unnatural deformations disguised as reason.

CHAPTER FOUR

"If We Be Conquered": Legal Nationalism and the France of Shakespeare's English Histories

In 1576, in London, Claudius Holyband (Claude de Sainliens) published *The Frenche Littelton*, an introductory textbook for students of French.[1] A Bourbon Huguenot who had settled in England in the 1560s and who for two decades ran the most successful French school in London, Holyband showed himself from the start of a lengthy publishing career to be a canny marketer of his own talents; that the book was printed thirteen times between 1576 and 1630 attests to his success. Holyband's textbook is arranged as a series of dialogues, printed on facing pages in English and French. In an early dialogue (inevitably, a conversation about learning languages), the father of a boy headed to school speaks highly of his teacher, a "M. Claude De sainliens" who runs a school "Au cymitiere de Sainct Paul, près l'enseigne de la Lucrece." The teacher's address is likewise included in English on the title page as "in Paules Churchyarde by the signe of the Lucrece."[2] In that simple way, the book advertises Holyband's school, which was his principal means of support. That moment of self-promotion mirrors Holyband's dedication of the book to Robert Sackville, son of Lord Buckhurst, a strategy that broadcasts, in terms of a client-patron relationship, the author's preexisting integration into the community from which he is most likely to draw his students.

The most striking marketing gesture of all is the book's title. In his preface, Holyband explains why he chose so unusual a name for his primer: "That as everie student applying himself to the knowledge of the lawes of this Realme, doth commonly travaile in the booke called Littletons tenures, to learne at his first entrie the ground of the Law for the matter therein handled: so everie persone purposing to have any understanding of the french tongue myght (for his first labour, and as his readiest way to come to the knowledge of the ground of the same tongue) beginne with this present booke."[3] The explanation is adequate on its own terms, but it masks the extent to which the title's allusion to the fifteenth-century legal treatise isolates and attracts a particular constituency for Holyband's textbook and, ultimately, his school. The students at the Inns of Court, for whom "Littelton" would have been particularly resonant, had varied and compelling reasons to learn French. For those students who went to the Inns for sophistication more than for law—who went, that is, to be noticed—a knowledge of French was, like the ability to write poetry, just the kind of literary and cultural marker that might attract the attention of a powerful patron in need of a secretary.[4] Equally, French was important to the more narrowly professional or institutional life of the Inns, since, as the language of formal pleading and reporting, Norman French (law French) was the language of learned conversation and English legal precedent. In relation to Holyband's textbook, it matters that law French was the language of Littleton's *Tenures* itself. At a time when publishers issued English translations of Littleton's treatise aimed at nonspecialists and recalcitrant law students, a *French Littelton* could be taken to refer with equal accuracy both to Holyband's text and to the original lawbook on whose title Holyband improvises.[5] His title can best be seen, then, as an inside joke about England's French, about that language's simultaneous internalization and otherness in sixteenth-century English, and specifically legal, culture.

On the verso of the prefatory leaf that presents a dedicatory sonnet written by George Gascoigne, there appears an anonymous sonnet on the status of France and French in England:

> *Anglois, tu as esté separé du Françoys:*
> *Et toy aussi, Françoys, de l'Anglois qui t'embrasse*
> *De langage divers, plus long temps que de Race,*
> *Tu l'as esté de foy, & quelque temps de Loys.*
>
> *Les Loys n'ont empesché, ô Françoys, que l'Anglois*
> *Ne t'aye ja receu, Car Foy t'a mis en grace.*
> *Foy qui tous les ésleuz enfans de Dieu ramasse*
> *En un corps avec Christ, l'Eternel Roy des Roys:*

> *Il ne reste donc plus que le divers langage.*
> *Mais voicy* Hollyband, *qui faict un mariage,*
> *De tous les deux, sus donc, lisez-le d'un accord.*
>
> *Si qu'en langage, en race, en Foy, & Loys unis,*
> *Viviez en double paix, de vray amour munis:*
> *Et le monde vaincrez peché, satan, la mort.*
> Pax in bello[6]

The poem celebrates the political unity of Anglo-French Protestantism—although in the Jacobean printings of 1609 and 1616, it could have been taken to evoke King James's efforts to convene an ecumenical council that would bring Catholics and Protestants together.[7] It is most striking for representing the relationship between French and English as paradoxical, the Latin tag "*Pax in bello*" (in imitation of Gascoigne's emblem "*Tam Marti quam Mercurio*") being only the most explicit expression of the oddly tense relation between the two peoples. In a poem that in multiple and specific ways attempts to erase the differences between the two nations, for example, it is notable that the penultimate line should insist on a "*double paix*," a phrase that defines the reciprocal accommodation of French and English in terms of an ineradicable difference. The poem's first stanza presents the obverse quibble: even as it categorizes national difference according to four criteria, it implies through the language of separation a unity chronologically prior to that disunity. The representation of an Anglo-French history that fluctuates between unity and difference thus matches the poem's account of a contemporary unity grounded in doubleness. If the poem praises Holyband's work by associating it with an international Protestantism that joins the French Huguenot and English Protestant as the "*ésleuz enfans de Dieu*," it also registers the longer history of Anglo-French relations extending from the Norman Conquest, the historical event that ultimately underlies the poem's uneasy stance toward its own representations of Anglo-French unity and Anglo-French difference. As the sonnet's equivocations register the effect of the Conquest on national identity, to be English is at once and with equal force to be and not to be French. This chapter concerns the cultural management at law and in drama of that deep jurisdictional paradox, approaching it in terms of the status of Conquest as a historical problem that, for cultural reasons, refuses historicization and so opens the space for a different account of event from that which history usually gives.

It is an important accident that the language of English common law replicated the cultural complexity of England's relation to France and to French. In order to teach its English audience a new tongue, Holyband's *Littelton* prints on opposite pages French and English versions of the same conversation. The law French in which Sir Thomas Littleton, like the sixteenth-century lawyers who followed him, wrote wedded the two languages by quite other means, as the opening sentence of his *Tenures* shows: *"Tenant en fee simple est celuy que ad terres ou tenements a tener a luy et a ses heires a touts jours."*[8] Equally typical is Sir Edward Coke's description of a proclamation in which *"le Roy E. 3. in le 39 an de son raigne . . . command le exercise de Archerie et Artillery, & prohibite le exercise de barres & le hand & foot balles, cockfighting, & alios ludos vanos."*[9] In his 1588 *Lawiers Logike*, Abraham Fraunce referred to this particular mix of French, Latin, and English as "that Hotchpot French, stufft up with such variety of borowed words, wherin our law is written."[10] Fraunce articulates in relation to the lawyers' professional jargon a version of the paradox staged by the preliminary sonnet in Holyband's own "legal" textbook. For Fraunce, the language of English law is caught between a French that is borrowed to the extent it is used in England and the French that, as he says, is itself stuffed with borrowed words from Latin and English. As a critique of English law, therefore, his argument denies even as an ideal or lost original the possibility of a stable linguistic ground that is itself not already doubled through borrowings. The linguistic paradox can be formulated generally in terms of a question about the culture of English common law: what does it mean that the principal marker of a nation's legal autonomy, even insularity, should be a language that speaks so powerfully of accommodation and assimilation and even a prior hybridity?

To the extent that the complex linguistic situation, for which I am asking the title of Holyband's volume to stand, is understood as the historical trace of an event or events in England's past, our question points to the manufacture at common law of the insular history that the law needed and the lawyers desired: a legal past made in light of the institution's own and always compelling present. Under such a historical model, law French could operate partly outside history, as merely an institutional given. One could tell this story of England's relation to France in terms of the fate of the Norman Yoke, the constitutional theory espoused in variously inflected ways by late Tudor and Jacobean thinkers to contextualize the impact of the Norman conquest on England's institutions, sometimes to counter the potentially absolutist implications of the claim that the rights guaranteed by English common law were an effect only of conquest.[11] Rather than focusing on the ideological and political implications of that theory, however, I look to the problem French posed for English legal nationalism as a way to unfold at the microlevel the odd pressures involved in representing the crisis of Conquest so as both to embrace and disavow its meaning. How did the representatives of an emergent legal nationalism deal with the historical jurisdictional reality that, in light of conquest, England was also elsewhere, and an elsewhere also England? In the institutional defense of law French, I argue, conquest came to be emptied of content through the record of its reiterations and, most important, its reversals: the Conquest was saved for English common law by becoming an iterative structure more than a discrete event. In this reading, iteration is the eruption precisely of the nongivenness of law French and of Conquest into a historical story that might construe them merely as givens.

The historical drama I treat is similarly divided against itself. This part of my argument starts with the observation that the Shakespearean history plays that tilt toward and away from Henry V's invasion of France are as deeply concerned with the trope of reiterative conquest as they are with the idea of linguistic estrangement. In Steven Mullaney's masterful reading of Hal's self-education in 1 and 2 *Henry IV*, learning the language of power is the theatrical process both of fitting oneself "toward" the other and of "rehearsing" without affirming that which in speaking you re-present.[12] As a dramatic way to come to terms with France, however, the rehearsal of the moment of Conquest is exactly affirmative, in the sense that it functions to reintegrate crisis into the historical time the crisis has disrupted. The history play, then, is for me a genre for thinking about a historical crux's resistance to historicization. Like the discursive iteration at law of an event such as the Conquest, historical drama reflects the eruption of crisis into a homogeneous narrative that is not fully adequate to its historical material. One reason why Shakespeare's dramatic analysis of the wars that produced Tudor history and Tudor Englishness is so deeply concerned with the testing and absorption of other tongues is that English military nationalism itself was unimaginable except as a version of the Conquest in 1066 that made English and the very idea of it newly capacious. So far as the legal subculture is concerned, the quarrels about law French were, after all, always also quarrels about a specific *English* vernacular, one cognate with the dominant English vernacular that sixteenth-century writers similarly attacked as barbarous, impoverished, and impure. While the law worked to overpower the cultural meaning of law French by making it stand as pure English, the representation on stage of conquest as an iterated cultural form pulls France into the interior of England's insular jurisdictional identity. And it does so as an affirmative act of historical imagination that grounds or, better, regrounds all that ideology might rehearse.

CONQUEST AND THE EMBARRASSMENT OF NORMAN FRENCH

In 1903 F. W. Maitland formulated a position regarding law French that anticipates the question I have posed concerning the language of the common law: "We have known it put by a learned foreigner as a paradox that in the critical sixteenth century the national system of jurisprudence which showed the stoutest nationalism was a system that was hardly expressible in the national language. But is there a paradox here? English law was tough and impervious to foreign influence because it was highly technical, and it was highly technical because English lawyers had been able to make a vocabulary, to define their concepts, to think sharply as the man of science thinks." Might it not be exactly the case, he asks, that the "Englishry of English law was secured by 'la lange francais qest trope desconue.'"[13] Maitland's answer, brilliantly convincing on its own terms, also sets up an alternative question. Maitland interprets a broadly cultural paradox about the relationship between legal language and national identity as purely institutional in scope, within which scope the paradox disappears into the thought that the institution simply found the language it needed. Notably, in its appeal to imperviousness and technicality, his answer repeats arguments put forward by the early modern common lawyers when they defended law French as resistant to change because of its archaic forms and technical precision. There is, to be sure, no outright contradiction in an insular language's being said to serve an insular law, but a tension or pressure may yet arise from a law's so staking its institutional claims, however rational those claims are on their own terms. By appealing to *techne*, Maitland comprehends the "foreigner's paradox" in effect by getting around it, and he does so in the way the law itself controls that of which it takes cognizance or, alternatively, that which it places beyond its scope. Left uncharted in arguments that accept legal reason as reason is the anxious effect of rationalization that also accompanies such meetings.

Historically, the use of law French in early modern England can be seen simply as an artifact of the history that had placed a Norman on England's throne; the professional language of law inherited by the later lawyers was theirs for the simple reason that the common law they practiced as a national law had originally served a small Norman elite in circumscribed royal courts served by speakers of Norman French. This is not, however, the story that the lawyers with whom we are concerned could tell or wanted or needed to tell. For the representatives of an emergent legal nationalism, the common law was first and foremost English law, and there was a felt awkwardness in linking it too closely to a Norman past; in their alternative stories about England's legal history, they found ways to meet that awkwardness. One reason the Elizabethan and Jacobean lawyers were able to imagine more suitable historical explanations than conquest for the potentially embarrassing fact that English law's technical vernacular was more theirs than it was England's is that the early history of law French was rather vague.[14] Although the "catastrophe" of the Norman Conquest provided the ultimate historical cause for the "indelible mark" of French on English law,[15] the history of the two centuries following 1066 was sufficiently obscure to allow for variously inflected stories to be told about the impact of conquest. Particularly important in this regard is the gap between descriptions of the written law and descriptions of oral proceedings in the courtroom.

In the sixteenth century the written languages of English law were three: Latin for the formulaic writ book and the final transcription of the plea roll; English for statute; French for the legal report. The emergence across the previous five hundred years of these three idioms speaks more to a tension between Latin and the vernacular than to any battle waged between the "native" English and Norman French vernaculars. Indeed, the impact in 1066 of the French language on the written law was minimal: until the thirteenth century Latin was the sole language of record—for statute as for writ and the plea roll. French entered English law as a written language only in the mid-thirteenth century, when the first collections of reports appeared, precursors to the so-called year books, which first appear at the end of the century. The reports, professional records of oral argument before the bench, would continue to be written in French for the next 450 years.[16] At the same time as the reports emerged, French began to replace Latin as the language of the statute rolls, an association fully in place by the reign of Edward III and continuous until the time of Richard III and Henry VII, when English finally replaced French as the language of enacted law.

Left implicit in this sketch of linguistic change is the impact on the written law, and thus on the evidence of past practice, of the language spoken in courtroom pleading. The history of the spoken language is inevitably more obscure than that of the written, not least because formal records such as the Latin plea roll were translated from the language of oral proceeding. The moots and readings held in the Inns of Court as pedagogical exercises and lessons were conducted in French from their earliest recorded appearance.[17] The use of law French in the thirteenth-century year books supports the implication here that by the time of Henry III, and certainly of Edward I, French was firmly in place both as the language in which lawyers thought about the law and as the language of pleading in the central courts.[18] It is also clear that in the years immediately following the Conquest, French would have been spoken in the *curia regis*, the court that served the king's own vassals and thus used the language of the immediate royal circle.[19] From this, one theory about the later use of French emerges. If across the two following centuries French gradually became more generally the norm for pleading, Maitland argues, that is because plaintiffs dispossessed of their freehold found particularly helpful the "assize of novel disseisin," an innovative action available to them from 1166, but only in a royal court, one identifiable through its ultimate connection to William's *curia* as "a French-speaking court."[20] The dramatic increase in those courts' business would have led, then, to the broader acceptance of their procedural and linguistic practices. Under this model of institutional development, there is not so much a directly motivated change in linguistic usage as an extension of usage through jurisdictional accident.

This jurisdictional hypothesis concerning the emergence of law French as the dominant language of pleading has been challenged by George E. Woodbine on the grounds that it is impossible to say which language the law courts "which had sprung from the original *curia regis*" used once they lost their personal character and began, through a process of absorbing local county and hundred-court jurisdiction, to serve "all England and not merely . . . the king's own vassals."[21] Rejecting the notion that the Norman Conquest had much to do with the documentable rise of French as the language of written law two centuries later, Woodbine points rather to a significant change in the legal culture's broader attitude to French in response to the marriage of Henry III to Eleanor of Provence, the subsequent tensions throughout his reign between "English" and "French" factional interests, and the triumph, finally, in 1265 at Evesham, of "the royal party and its French adherents over the English barons."[22] Notably, this model for linguistic change depends as much on external catastrophe as does a theory of an immediate Norman impact in 1066: for the first and distant Conquest, Woodbine substitutes a second and proximate one. At stake in the differences between Maitland's and Woodbine's hypotheses is not so much the national character of early English law as the nature of that law's resistance to the encroachment of nonnational elements. Different as the two stories about twelfth- and thirteenth-century law French are, each in its way protects Englishness from the implications of an internalized French: Woodbine's theory, by arguing that in the local courts,

"If We Be Conquered" 185

and possibly the central courts, English may have remained the language of law long after the Conquest's imposition of foreign rule; and Maitland's theory, by imagining the triumph of law French to be only the accidental consequence of the central law's extending to everyone the protection of his freehold—a consequence, that is, exactly of that most powerfully English sense of the law's "*meum* and *tuum*." Both stories reject radical hybridity at law as the implication of Conquest and the continuity of law French. The Conquest is seen, rather, to have had only a formal effect and to have been quickly absorbed into an identifiably English paradigm.

The modern legal historical accounts of the law's resistance to French have precursors in the early nationalist explanations for the uncomfortable presence of French inside English law. But for the sixteenth century, far more than for Woodbine or Maitland, the Norman Conquest loomed large as the *direct* causal explanation for the fact of law French. Sir John Fortescue in the fifteenth century is responsible for the association. The discussion of the law's three languages in chapter 48 of his foundational *De laudibus legum Anglie* constitutes the earliest historical theorization of England's French. The passage is so important to later Tudor and Jacobean discussions that I quote it here in full; for ease of reference later in my discussion, I assign in brackets a number to each stage of the argument. Fortescue, as chancellor to the Lancastrian court in exile, is here explaining to the Prince of Wales why the laws are taught at the Inns of Court rather than in the universities. Significantly, he invokes the history both of written and oral practice:

> The chancellor: 'In the Universities of England the sciences are not taught unless in the Latin language. But the laws of that land are learned in three languages, namely, English, French, and Latin; in English, because among the English the law is deeply rooted; in French, because after the French had, by duke William the Conqueror of England, obtained the land, they would not permit the advocates to plead their causes unless in the language that they themselves knew, which all advocates do in France, even in the court of parliament there [1]. Similarly, after their arrival in England, the French did not accept accounts of their revenues, unless in their own idiom [*in propria idiomate*], lest they should be deceived thereby [2]. They took no pleasure in hunting, nor in other recreations, such as games of dice or ball, unless carried on in their own language [*in propria lingua*] [3]. So the English contracted the same habit from frequenting such company, so that they to this day speak the French language [*linguam Gallicanum*] in such games and

accounting [4], and were used to pleading in that tongue [5], until the custom was much restricted by force of a certain statute [6]; even so, it has been impossible hitherto to abolish this custom in its entirety [7], partly because of certain terms which pleaders express more accurately in French than in English [8], partly because declarations upon original writs cannot be stated so closely to the form of these writs as they can in French, in which tongue the formulas of such declarations are learned [9]. Again, what is pleaded, disputed, and decided in the royal courts is reported and put into book form, for future reference, always in the French speech [*in sermone semper Gallico*] [10]. Also, very many statutes of the realm are written in French [11]. Hence it happens that the language of the people in France now current does not accord with and is not the same as the French used among the experts in the law of England [12], but is commonly corrupted by a certain rudeness [13]. That cannot happen with the French speech used in England [*infra Angliam usitato*], since that language is there more often written than spoken [14]. In the third language above mentioned, in Latin, are written all original and judicial writs, and likewise all records of pleas in the king's courts, and also certain statutes [15]. Thus, since the laws of England are learned in these three languages they could not be conveniently learned or studied in the Universities, where the Latin language alone is used.'[23]

Fortescue's account and implicit defense of law French is an account principally of pleading. It falls into two parts: a history of the introduction of French as a spoken language in pleading (at 1–5); and an explanation of the tenacious hold of French on courtroom practice, as grounded in its technical character and, critically, its impact on the law's written language (at 7–14).

In exploring the sixteenth-century fate of this analysis, we can follow Fortescue's own lead by noting that the two sections of his argument pivot around his one-clause account (at 6) of "a certain statute" that "much restricted" the Norman-sanctioned custom of pleading in French. Fortescue is referring here to the 1362 Statute of Pleadings (36 Edward III cap. 15), a document that for the following centuries was, along with the year books' more indirect testimony, the principal trace of the law's early linguistic history. Written itself in French, the statute attempted to legislate the substitution of English for French as the language of formal legal debate. In its official Tudor translation, it attributes the failure "commonlie" to hold and keep the realm's "lawes, customes, and statutes" to the fact that "they be pleaded, shewed, and judged in the french tongue, which is much unknowen in the saide realme [*en langage fraunceis que est trope disconus en le dit royalme*] so that the people, which impleadeth or be impleaded in the kings court, and the courts of other, have no knowledge nor understanding of that that is saide for them or against them by their serjeaunts and other pleaders." Declaring it reasonable that the "lawes and customs the rather shall be perceived and knowne and better understoode in the tongue used in the saide realme," the statute enacts "that all plees . . . shall be pleaded, shewed, and defended, aunswered, debated, and judged, in the English tongue [*en la lange engleys*], and that they be entered and enroled in Latine. And that the lawes and customes of the same realme, termes, and processes be holden and kept, as they be and have bene before this time, and that by the auncient termes and formes of the declarations [*par les aunciens fourmes & termes de countre*] no man be prejudiced, so that the matter of the action be fullie shewed in the demonstration and the writ."[24] Given the rhetorical momentum of the statute's reforming impulse, it is notable that two of the three enactments are wholly conservative. Not only does it affirm Latin to be the appropriate language for the formal record of the plea rolls, but, as Peter Goodrich emphasizes, it explicitly preserves the law French of the "auncient termes and formes" of the declarations, these being the formal "counts" or opening pleas that were pronounced in the central courts in "French set forms."[25]

This conservatism has much to do with the statute's utter lack of effect on the linguistic course of English law. As Fortescue himself implies (at 7), the statute was in practice less watershed than waterlogged, exemplary in its failure: it was "a documentary record of the degree of resistance to the administrative use of law French, but as substantive law it was equivocal, inconsistent, and ineffective."[26] From an institutional perspective, the statute's real meaning is its sense that law French was already indispensable. Fortescue seems to have recognized that the statute's failure was itself necessary to the law he knew and practiced. Even though he mentions the abolition of law French as a desirable end (at 7), overall he underplays the nationalist implications of a document whose stated intention was to elevate the English vernacular over another vernacular said no longer to relate to the country's national character.

Fortescue provided the terms in which, at the beginning of the seventeenth century, Sir Edward Coke responded to law French as a mark of the Norman Conquest. The meaning of that response, its institutional function and strategies, can best be understood by examining how Coke carries forward selective elements both from Fortescue's general analysis and from the statute to which it alludes. We shall see that, while Coke's account everywhere reveals its debt to Fortescue, its reordering of detail foregrounds a gap, only nascent in Fortescue, between what we might call national and institutional interests or identities.

Coke first addresses law French in 1602, in the preface to the third volume of his *Reports*. While for Fortescue the history and meaning of the language was a matter principally of oral pleading, Coke is concerned with law French as the *written* language that he himself uses as reporter. In part, this is a consequence of how pleading had in the sixteenth century shifted from a tentative oral process before the bench to the more formal exchange of written pleas. Law French was for Coke even more a written language than it had been for Fortescue.[27] That said, when in 1628 Coke refers to law French as a language that is "most commonly written and read, and very rarely spoken, and therefore cannot be either pure or well pronounced," he has in his ear Fortescue's remark (at 14) that French at law "is there more often written than spoken."[28]

In 1602, Coke's greater emphasis on the written allows him to downplay Fortescue's central argument about the Conquest. Even as he lays out the institutional centrality of law French, Coke erases the historical account through which Fortescue made sense of that centrality. He begins his account of the "tongue wherein these Lawes are written," by noting the Latin of "all judiciall Records," of *Glanvill* and *Bracton*, and "divers of our Statutes."[29] French is introduced in reference to Edward I. Conspicuously, Coke's point of origin for the introduction of law French into England is not, as in Fortescue, the Norman Conquest, but rather English Plantagenet claims in France: "In the raigne of him and his sonne many Statutes are indited in the Latine: (as some also of the Statutes of *Richard the second* be). And divers also be enacted in French, for that they had divers territories and Seignories that spake French within their dominion, & in respect thereof the better sort learned that language." Coke now turns to the French specifically of legal reporting, saying that by publishing his reports in that language he has only followed the precedent of former reporters and authors. And here, too, Coke reverses Fortescue's story by reversing the direction of national influence: "And the reason that the former Reports were in the French tongue, was for that they begun in the raigne of King *Edward the third*, who as the world knowes had lawfull right in the kingdome of Fraunce, and had divers Provinces and Territories thereof in possession; It was not thought fit nor convenient, to publish either those or any of the Statutes enacted in those dayes in the vulgar tongue, lest the unlearned by bare reading without right understanding might sucke out errors, and trusting to their own conceipt might endammage themselves, & sometimes fall into destruction" (E1r). Coke's account of the law's languages, then, writes French out of English history except as the consequence of English sovereignty in France: Edward I's French territories explain the French statutes, and Edward III's French territories explain the reports. Moreover, when Coke places the origin of reporting in the reign of Edward III, he is remembering the English monarch whose invasion of France began the Hundred Years War and who for the first time styled himself King of France, a title used by all subsequent monarchs until George III.[30] The reason underlying that tenacious but at best optimistic construction of English honor in France comes sharply into focus in light of Coke's erasure of Fortescue's account of law French: like Coke's imagining law French as historically a language emblematic of English sovereignty, the claim to the French throne has power as a response to the uneasy pressure of 1066 on English consciousness.

In light of Coke's reconfiguration of language and sovereignty to downplay the cultural awkwardness of law French, it is not surprising that, at the beginning of the passage on the law's languages, Coke recalls the statute of 1362 that aimed to abolish the use of law French only as evidence that Latin is the language of record: "all judiciall Recordes are entred and enrolled in the Latine tongue: As it appeareth by an Acte of Parliament in Anno 36.cap.15" (E1r). This is not quite historical misrepresentation, but by focusing on the statute's conservative pronouncement rather than the reform it enacted, Coke recasts the statute as marking not, as for Fortescue (at 5–6), the English vernacular's resistance to French, but rather the simple integration of a learned tongue into the fabric of English law.

In one further way Coke's argument invokes Fortescue even as it forgets his details. Fortescue explained law French as the expression of public law, as the language the French imposed on the advocates as (at 1) "the language that they themselves knew." Remarkably, Coke reverses this account of how, in the sphere of pleading, law French emerged in England as a shared *public* language, by construing law French as an *institutional* form intended to exclude "the unlearned," lest "by bare reading" they might "sometimes fall into destruction."[31] In the hypothetical figuration of these unlearned subjects, law French is wrested back from Fortescue's history of England's Norman past. For in one sense, of course, even the lawful right that Edward had in the "kingdome of Fraunce" would be irrelevant to the decision not to publish the law in the "vulgar tongue," since it is only the English unlearned who would find themselves troubled by the obscure secrets of that particular substitute language. The point, then, is that law French here serves an English audience, not a French one. In Coke's refashioning of Fortescue's argument, a public language becomes an institution's learned, private language in order to keep it English, with respect now not only to the sovereign said to have introduced law French, but also to the audience that received it.

As almost a coda to his history of law French, Coke finally introduces Fortescue's William the Conqueror, though he does so for his own purposes:

> And it is verily thought that William the Conquerour finding the excellencie and equitie of the Lawes of England, did transport some of them into Normandie, and taught the former Lawes written as they say in Greeke, Latine, Brittish, and Saxon tongues (for the better use of the Normans) in the Normane language, and the which are at this day (though in processe of time much altered) called the *Customes of Normandie*: So taught he Englishmen the Norman termes of hunting, hawking, and in effect of all other playes and pastimes which continue to this day; And yet no man maketh question but these recreations and disports were used within this Realme before the Conquerour's time. (E1r–v)

This is perhaps the most striking moment in Coke's reception of the earlier text. Fortescue (at 3–4) appeals to the English use of French names for hunting and gaming as a point of comparison (at 5) for the simultaneous adoption of French pleading. Coke uses it as evidence for the contrary point that the English did not receive their laws from the Normans, but rather gave their laws to them. One can certainly read this moment as Coke's hijacking of Fortescue's earlier text in service of the insular account of legal antiquity for which, following Pocock's classic exposition of English legal historicism, he is usually made to stand.[32] A more generous interpretation does more justice, however, both to the spectral presence of Fortescue in Coke's text and to Coke's late Tudor history-making. If Coke's and Fortescue's stories differ, what remains most striking is that the Conquest should be the fulcrum on which the differences are weighed. Indeed, Coke's appositional account of William the Conqueror pertains to his main discussion of written law French more than at first appears. Coke's bizarre argument that William imported only the names of leisure pastimes will seem beside the point (and typical of Coke's ahistoricism) only if we fail to see that Fortescue's Conqueror already directs the progression of the earlier part of Coke's argument, which so deliberately excludes him. To replace William I with Edward III—that is, to reverse the direction of Anglo-French conquest—is to struggle for control of a story or a structure so fundamental to national identity that its invocation alone is more potent, affectively and cognitively, than either the particular conquest or the particular interpretation ascribed to it. Historians have described the various uses to which seventeenth-century factions put the theory of the Norman Yoke, which grounded English law, rights, and institutions in the fantasy of a pre-Conquest history.[33] However, to see the Norman Yoke as central to early modern historiography because it allowed for a *particular* legal interpretation of the Conquest is to neglect the complexities involved in the culture's shared sense that there were compelling reasons for so formulating the question. Coke resembles Fortescue not only because he everywhere invokes his ghost, but also because he takes from Fortescue the fundamental trope and fact of conquest as determining the nation's and law's character.

We can analyze the consequence for English legal nationalism of remembering Fortescue straight by turning to Sir John Davies's defense of the common law in the 1615 volume of his Irish *Reports*. In some respects, Davies's account resembles Coke's. But if it is likewise indebted to Fortescue, both the Irish context of Davies's argument (as explored in chapter 3) and his greater allegiance to the fifteenth-century text place his version of the argument under a different and exemplary pressure. Davies's discussion of law French comes in the context of his defense of English common law as customary law, which he defines as "the most perfect, & most excellent, and without comparison the best, to make & preserve a commonwealth," since, in opposition to the written law that is "imposed upon the subject before any Triall or Probation made," a "Custome doth never become a lawe to binde the people, untill it hath bin tried & approved time out of minde."[34] As part of the argument, Davies is driven to address the crisis of the Norman Conquest, and asks, "But uppon what reason then doth *Polidor Virgill* & other writers affirme, that *King William the Conqueror* was our *Lawegiver*, & caused all our lawes to bee written in French?" (*3r). In response, Davies appeals to the theory of the Norman Yoke in order to preserve the law's immemorial and thus English character. It is to the point that in posing Polydore's question, Davies compresses two distinct propositions, since Davies's answer is to deny the first proposition, that William gave England its laws, by accommodating the second, that William gave England the *language* of its laws. In order so to split legal language from the essential meaning of that which it records, Davies accounts for the use of written French by appealing, as Fortescue had done, to the history of pleading:

> Assuredly, the *Norman Conqueror* found the auncient lawes of England so honorable, & profitable, both for the Prince & people, as that he thought it not fitt to make any alteration in the fundamentall pointes

192 *Chapter Four*

or substance thereof: the change that was made was but *in formulis iuris*: he altered some legall formes of proceeding, & to honor his owne language, & for a marke of Conquest withall, he caused the pleading of divers Actions to be made and entred in French, & sett forth his publique Ordinances & Acts of Counsell in the same tongue: which forme of pleading in *French* continued till 36 *Edw.* 3. when (in regard that the *French* tongue begann to growe out of use, which for many yeares after the *Norman Conquest* was as common as the English among the Gentry of England) it was ordained by Parliament, that all pleas should bee pleaded, debated, & Judged in the English tongue, & entred, & enrolled in *Latine*. (∗3r)

The argument that the substance of law was preserved even through a change in form is certainly elegant. But insofar as Davies addresses the *writing* of French (Coke's topic, too) by taking over Fortescue's account (at 1–5) of the French *spoken* in pleading, we can see that his answer is also somewhat inelegant in relation to Coke, who perhaps saw that the one was not going to explain the other.

The difference between Coke's history of a proximate reverse conquest and Davies's history of an incomplete conquest is not ideological (even though the theory of the Norman Yoke had certainly become more available in political discourse between 1602 and 1615 as a way to establish the long continuity of English law and customs, including the customs of Parliament itself). Both writers are attached to the idea of an immemorial law; and Coke too invoked the theory as part of his story of English sovereignty with respect to France and French. The difference between Coke's and Davies's rhetoric speaks, rather, to a change in the configuration of Anglo-French relations. If one story allowed Coke to control the implications of law French by displacing it onto a more favorable conquest, and the other allowed Davies to articulate an operative difference between form and content, that shift means that by 1615 one conquest would suffice.

Davies's relative lack of anxiety about 1066 is brought into even sharper focus at a later stage in his account of law French. Like Coke, Davies writes as a reporter. Speaking of the legal genre his own book exemplifies, he notes that since Henry VII only "our *Reports* ... have ever untill this day beene penned & published in that *mixt* kinde of speech which wee call the *lawe French*" (∗3r). To explain why French should still be appropriate in 1615, Davies goes to Fortescue, who had pointed out (at 8) that certain terms are expressed "more accurately in French than in English" and further that, although modern French "is commonly corrupted by a certain rudeness," law French as effectively a dead language could not so change (at 12–14). Davies adopts these arguments, based respectively on the technical character and the immutable character of a static language: "And this is the true & onely cause, why our *Reports* & other books of the lawe for the most part, are not sett forth in *English*, *Latine* or the *moderne french*, for that the proper & peculiar phrase of the common lawe cannot bee so well exprest, nor any case in lawe bee so succinctly, sensibly, & whithall so fully reported as in this speech" (∗3r). It is remarkable that in this argument for law French as a technical language Davies should even imagine *modern* French as a possibility for the seventeenth-century English report. In the fifteenth century, Fortescue's point (at 8) concerned only the advantage of law French over English, and in 1602 Coke reinvented and reversed the Conquest in order to wrest even Old French from France.

As in this argument from technicality, Davies alters also Fortescue's argument from immutability, arguing that law French differs from the "*French* tongue, as it is now refined and spoken in *Fraunce*, as well by reason of the words of *Art* and *forme*, called the *Tearmes* of the lawe, as for that wee doe still retaine many other old wordes & Phrases of speech which were used four hundred years since, & are now become obsolete & out of use among them, but are growne by long & continuall use so apt, so naturall, & so proper for the matter & subject of these *Reports*, as no other language is significant enough to express the same, but onely this *lawe french* wherein they are written" (∗3r–v). Where Fortescue spoke of the corruption and "rudeness" of modern French, and the consequent advantages of a dead language, Davies speaks, instead, of refinement. The tiny emendation registers a powerful shift in the legal discussion of the Norman Conquest and its impact on England. As against Fortescue and even Coke, it is only to the extent that the Frenchness of law French was not at issue that Davies can even hypothetically imagine an English law written in modern, refined French. The Conquest has been domesticated. While the Conquest had for Coke elicited geographical nationalism, for Davies it elicits a historical nationalism, marking not a break and crisis but a basic continuity from 1066 forward: if law French is advantageously immutable by reason of its age, it is technically apt through the process of having "growne by long & continuall use." Here Davies returns to his central concern with immutable custom as that which in time "groweth to perfection" (∗2r).[35] When Davies speaks of Conquest, it is the idea of English custom and no longer the idea of the Channel that dictates the turns of his argument.[36]

LEGAL HUMANISM AND THE ERASURE OF NORMANISM

Far more than in Fortescue's fifteenth century, then, an anxiety of remembering underlies the law's self-construction at the beginning of the seventeenth, generating versions of its own autonomy by reiterating, circumscribing, and absorbing the Conquest. If France and the language that marked its English internalization were powerfully sources of legal institutional anxiety, that is a consequence in part of an earlier sixteenth-century reformist response to the Conquest and its English legal legacy. I want briefly to turn to these humanist appeals for legal change to fill out the common lawyers' account of the relation among their vernaculars with arguments about the relation of those vernaculars to Latin. The critiques of the common law by Thomas Starkey, Sir Thomas Elyot, and Sir Thomas Smith are, in the manner of the common lawyers' later construction of law French, primarily defenses of that law. In various ways, these critiques aimed to reveal the paramount virtues of English law by removing its impurities, and to delineate its logical order by countering the obscure idiosyncrasies of English practice relative to its civilian counterpart on the Continent. Here, I will focus only on a shared sense that law French was undesirable because it distanced the law, not from the English vernacular, but from the Latin through which English law could be linked to an authoritative classical past. These texts associate the erasure of an antiquated Norman heritage with the recovery of a linguistic purity that belongs to England, not in an alternative historical account of the law's origins, but as an exemplary *pattern* for law.

The second book of Thomas Smith's *De republica Anglorum* (pub. 1583) is, like Fortescue's treatise a century earlier, overtly concerned with the comparison of English and continental institutions according to the legal reason underlying them. Even though Smith's comparison is surprisingly moderate relative to Fortescue's condemnation of French absolutism, French law remains an always externalized point of comparison. In this context, Smith constructs the language of English law, not as the trace of the Norman past, but as a mark of its distance from the classical world. Indeed, he disparages law French by focusing on the debased Latin integral to it, as, for example, when he distinguishes the continental and English meanings of *placitum*: "All pursuites and actions (we call them in our English tongue *pleas*) and in barbarous (but now usuall) latine *placita*, taking that name *abusive* of the definitive sentence, which may well be called *placitum* or *aréston*. The French useth the same calling in their language, the sentence of their judges *areste* or *arest* . . . but we call *placitum* the action not the sentence, and *placitare* barbarouslie, or to pleade in englishe, *agere* or *litigare*."[37] The passage measures the quality of *placitare*, a legal neologism at English law, equally against the English *plea*, Latin *placitum*, Greek *aréston*, and modern French *areste*. The testing of England's mixed language against a desirable classical purity extends to Smith's account of visibly Norman words in the English law. Thus when he frames his discussion of pleading in the chapter following, he places the English "writ" and its equivalents from Greek ("*graphé*") and the Roman civil law ("*actio*" or "*formula*") on a single linguistic plane, adding only at the end that "in our barbarous latine we name it *breve*."[38] Similar to this construction of English law's "hotchpot" jargon in relation to classical Latin is an important passage written by Coke in 1602 that also privileges the classical world over the continental. In an account of England's distant Druidic past, Coke glosses a line from Juvenal's fifteenth satire, notably allowing a classical influence on English law so as explicitly to avoid a nearer and more historical alternative debt: "*Gallia caussidicos docuit facunda Brittanos*: Not that the French men did teach the Lawyers of England to be eloquent . . . but that a Colony of Grecians residing in France as *Strabo* saith, *Gallia* was said to teach the professors of the Lawes of England, being written in the Greeke toong, eloquence."[39]

Coke's appeal to Greece for the origins specifically of legal *eloquence* makes sense in terms of the earlier humanist program. In *The Boke Named the Governour* (1531), Sir Thomas Elyot includes a remarkable chapter on the education of the common lawyer, in which he proposes that students should proceed first through a nontechnical education, and only then into the study of law, a discipline whose innate dryness is dangerously compounded by its being "involved in so barbarouse a langage, that it is not onely voyde of all eloquence, but also beynge seperate from the exercise of our lawe onely, it serveth no commoditie or necessary purpose, no man understandyng it but they which have studyed the lawes."[40] Elyot's proposed reform, whereby the laws might be "in englisshe, latine, or good french, written in a more clene and elegant stile," is directly associated with his desire to return English law to classical rhetoric. He argues that a program of classical education cannot but make English lawyers "men of so excellent wisdome, that throughout all the worlde shulde be founden in no commune weale more noble counsaylours," insofar as England's laws are themselves grounded in "most excellent raisons" and are "gadred and compacte (as I mought say) of the pure mele or floure syfted out of the best lawes in all other countrayes." When, later in the chapter, he again asserts that the laws need to be in a "pure latine or doulce french," the sweetness of that reformed tongue echoes his insistence that the "swetnesse that is contayned in eloquence," far from being a distraction for the young student, is necessary to the perfection of legal practice. Since good laws come in a refined tongue, linguistic reform is but part of the broader modeling of English practice on the purity of classical law. Thus, to clinch his argument that eloquence has a place in English law, he appeals to "Quintus Scevola, whiche being an excellent autour in the lawes civile, was called of all lawiars moste eloquent"; to Crassus, "of all eloquent men the beste lawiar"; and to Servus Sulpitius, who "was nat so let by eloquence, but that on the civile lawes he made notable commentes... by all lawyars approved." This celebration of the classical fusion of law and eloquence reaches a high point with the claim that the Pandects and Digests of the civil law exemplify the finest style in their time. Elyot's reform of the law's languages would return the law to a clean elegance and sweet purity, just as training in classical rhetoric would bring to the law a formal quality equivalent to that of Roman law.[41]

In Elyot, as in Smith, the humanist representation of linguistic barbarism as a failure to live up to a Roman model disengages English law from the vernacular culture of which France and Norman French are constitutive parts. This need to distance England from its proximate Norman past is at times made more explicit. At the beginning of his 1553 *Arte of Rhetorique*, Thomas Wilson offers the following as an example of a question that contains the general in the particular: "If I shall aske... whether it bee lawfull for William the Conquerour to invade England, and win it by force of Armour, I must also consider this, whether it bee lawfull for any man to usurpe power."[42] In a book that famously extends to great lengths Elyot's association of English law and Roman forensic rhetoric, the example suggests an underlying anxiety about the nature of English historical and legal identity. Thomas Starkey's *Dialogue between Reginald Pole and Thomas Lupset* unpacks the point. Written in the 1530s for presentation to Henry VIII, Starkey's dialogue makes wholly explicit the link between a return to Roman legal forms and the rejection of Norman ones. The continued use of French is, in Lupset's words, "ignominious, and dishonour to our nation, forasmuch as thereby is testified our subjection to the Normans."[43] For Pole, law French is a "barbarous language," the crucial point being for him, too, that the language undoes claims to English political autonomy. Indeed, Pole's central point is that the common law itself, and not simply its formal expression, carries the taint of Normanism. Thus, at one point, he associates the custom of wardship with "the time... of the Conqueror, or tyran" William; by looking "a little higher" to a principle of the ideal commonwealth, he then opposes the tyrant's (and England's) injustice to the reason embedded, rather, in "the time of nature."[44]

In a particularly fierce passage, Pole suggests that the problem posed for England by Norman continuities can be solved through the reception of "the civil law of the Romans to be the common law here of England with us":

> Who is so blind that seeth not the great shame to our nation, the great infamy and rot that remaineth in us, to be governed by the laws given to us by such a barbarous nation as the Normans be? Who is so far from reason that considereth not the tyrannical and barbarous institutions infinite ways left here among us, which all should be wiped away by the receiving of this which we call the very civil law?—which is, undoubtedly, the most ancient and noble monument of the Romans' prudence and policy, the which be so writ, with such gravity, that if Nature should herself prescribe particular means whereby mankind should observe her laws, I think she would admit the same.[45]

The embarrassment of Norman French again drives the legal reformer back to the time of "Nature," but this is a nature rooted firmly, now, in classical example as much as in any utopian hypothesis.

One final version of English legal nationalism deserves mention, this one in some ways a midpoint between the arguments of Fortescue and the classically oriented humanist arguments I have been discussing. In the preface to his 1519 translation of the abbreviated pre-Tudor statutes, the great legal writer and publisher John Rastell asks "whi the said lawes of englond were writin in the french tong."[46] The question is similar to Coke's and Lupset's question about the language of the law's reports, but not identical, since Rastell is asking only about enacted law, and thus about an already obsolete practice, the language of Tudor enacted law being English, not law French. In answering his question, Rastell notes, as Fortescue does (at 1 and 11) that the Conqueror imposed French, first, as a way of including the French-speakers "as wel gentilmen as other that cam with him." Turning to more overt political strategy, Rastell writes that William and his counselors "perceivid & supposid that the vulgar tong which was then usyd in this realme was in a maner but homely & rude nor had so greate a copy and haboundaunce of wordys as the frenche tong than had nor that vullgare tonge was not of itself suffycyent to expound & to declare the matter of such lawis & ordenaunces as thei hade determined to be made for the good governaunce of the people so effectually and so substauncyally as they cowd indyte them in the french tong."[47] In its attention to the linguistic qualities of English relative to another language, Rastell's position here identifies him with humanist legal critics like Smith or Elyot.

Unlike them, however, Rastell is able easily to counter the unpleasantness of the Norman past by appealing to a legal present wholly amenable to his English nationalism:

> But yet... our late sovereyn lorde kynge henry the vii. worthye to be called the seconde salomon... concyderynge and well perseyvynge that our vulgare englissh tong was marvelously amendyd & augmentyd by reason that dyverse famous clerkys & lernyd men had translate and made many noble workys into our englisshe tong wherby there was moch more plenty & haboundaunce of englyssh usyd than there was in tymys past. & by reason therof our vulgare tong so amplified & sufficient of itself to expound any lawys... ordeynyd and causyd that all the statutys and ordinauncis which were made for the commyn welth of this realm in his dayes shulde be indyted & wryttyn in the vulgare englyssh tonge & to be publysshyd declaryd and imprintid.[48]

Rastell authorizes his own translation of the statutory *Abridgment* by celebrating the earlier translations of "famous clerkys & lernyd men" and by identifying translation as the very source and ground for linguistic nationalism. Like our other humanist writers on the law, Rastell weighs linguistic rudeness against eloquent abundance, but because he is speaking of a discontinuity between the Norman past and English present, he is able to associate legal English with the eloquent rather than, as Smith or Elyot must for England's law French, the rude and barbarous. Rastell's case is of interest, then, both because of his proximity as translator to the mechanics of a humanist legal nationalism, and because the relative simplicity of the history he is able to tell highlights for us the rhetorical complexities required of humanists and lawyers confronted with the embarrassment of Norman continuities.

Among the writers who critique the continuity of law French within English law, Starkey is unusually vehement in his insistence on the Conquest's ongoing embarrassment for English culture: when Pole urges the adoption of civil law, manifestly a marker of legal antiquity, he leaps over the tyranny of Conquest by wedding English legal identity to a Roman past. Even though the other humanist critiques we have examined anticipate no reception of Roman law per se, they similarly fit the law into a classical and Latin model. When Elyot and Wilson foreground the relationship between English law and classical rhetoric, and when Smith constructs law French as a distortion of Latin, they are using as the descriptive *exemplum* for England's present the distant legal past that Pole, more polemically, would substitute for the proximate Norman past. This provides a final perspective on the ways in which later common lawyers imagined law French. As we have seen, Coke and Davies answer the embarrassment of the Norman Conquest by reinventing or reimagining its terms. Given that Starkey's text, more powerfully than any other we have read, invents its legal nationalism in response to Norman France, it is to the point that his answer should so differ from theirs. When Coke and Davies imagine a national law that is, institutionally or by custom, its own model, they are answering the implications, not only of the French presence internal to English law, but also of an earlier humanist rhetoric that, against France, had preserved the integrity of national law by defining its connection to an alternative non-English model. Thus two responses to Conquest, one of them also a response to the earlier response, deliver two constructions of the common law. It is not easy to identify which, as history, is the more conservative in its goals, since each shapes the past in order to reject Anglo-French hybridity as a theoretical presence operative within the national law. Where the common lawyer preserves the hybrid language by reiterating it as English, the humanist follows the integrity of a lost linguistic model—Greek, the purity of Latin, even Elyot's sweeter/classical French—and so also counters the history of France-in-England. As the shared ground for these differently articulated legal nationalisms, France thus determines two modes of nationalist historiography that equally conserve English identity, the one by means of reiteration, the other by means of example.

ENACTING CONQUEST IN HENRY V AND RICHARD III

Shakespeare's English histories place France within England in ways evocative of both the humanist's and the common lawyer's responses to Normanism in English law.[49] Scholars have long been interested in how the first and second tetralogies construe the fifteenth-century history of the houses of York and Lancaster through the lens of England's military engagements in France. Beyond their obvious appeal to national pride and prestige, certainly, England's military victories across the Channel were compelling to an Elizabethan audience for the parallels they offered to the explosive Irish situation of the 1590s. As Christopher Highley argues, *Henry V*'s construction of English identity in opposition to French culture replays the Tudors' alienation and disavowal of the Irish, by coopting "an elusive 'Irishness' for the English," a fantasy that speaks to English hopes for Essex's success in his Irish campaign.[50] At the same time, Philip Schwyzer notes how closely tied Englishness is in the plays to the problematic English ideal of a fully incorporated Wales.[51] For the plays' analysis of national identity, furthermore, France does not operate only as analogy. Leah Marcus connects 1 *Henry VI* to the English Protestants' participation in the French wars in the 1590s; David Womersly demonstrates how deeply engaged *Henry V* is with Henri IV's pretense to the English throne, a claim taken fully seriously in the England of 1599; and Deanne Williams argues that the plays represent a late stage in the cultural process through which, responding to 1066, English culture fetishized France in order both to control and disavow it.[52] Like Williams, and in opposition to accounts of how Englishness or even a highly complex Britishness was articulated in simple opposition to France, I am interested in the long and diffuse claim of 1066 on England's national identity. The dichotomy of self/alien or national/foreign fails to comprehend the complexities of the Anglo-French relationship, one whose ambivalence allowed it more easily to be performed than categorized.[53]

Henry V and *Richard III* both respond to the Conquest through the representation of conquest as a reiterative structure, one the plays uses to *enact* identity, at the moment of its performance, as a relational form. At issue, first, is the surface continuity between Shakespeare's reading of Anglo-French conquest in *Henry V*, where Agincourt in 1415 replays Edward III's victory at Crécy in 1346, and Coke's use in 1602 of Edward's claims in France as a way to counter the implications of the Norman Conquest for English law.[54] As at law, the dramatic iteration of conquest as a formal and narrative structure points to an important ripple in how England's relation to France was coded. If these conquests are structurally the same event, that is so because as versions of 1066 they also define that formative moment as exemplary of a fully hybrid Englishness.

The repetition of conquest *reverses* the Conquest by acknowledging that, far from being a simple other, France is a pressure internal to and generative of English identity.[55] In arguing that a structure's iteration might enact a meaning that cannot quite be spoken, I mean to relocate rather than deny the complexity of cultural rehearsal—the process, as described by Mullaney, through which a culture's or self's identity emerges, ironically, as the practiced disengagement from what is spoken in self-representation. As one way to ground a process of self-fashioning that might otherwise result only in an iterative subversion of itself, the idea of identity as a performative enactment allows for the possibility that an unstable identity, such as that which ambivalently issued from England's historical relation to France, might acquire stability in relation not to a particular ideological position, but rather to the regime or relational field in which identity gets to be imagined in the first place. As I use the term, *enactment* is the declaratory performance of identity as scene and situation rather than content. Shakespeare's plays enact the Englishness that is France, which is to say, they represent the form in which the story of Englishness can be told.

That the plays are less anxious than Fortescue's or Coke's legal histories about registering France as an already internalized presence within English culture is highly suggestive for the specifically dramatic register of their engagement with a national past. Just as the law ultimately overpowered its anxiety about Normanism through the manufacture of a more comprehensive institutional identity for English law, Shakespeare looks to the theater's own forms and strategies to represent the enactment of Englishness. Enacting identity, in other words, is no less a dramatic structure than its rehearsal. Famously, *Richard III* and *Henry V* both theorize kingship in terms of acting: following Sir Thomas More's characterization of Richard, *Richard III* identifies tyrannical kingship with bad acting, power's unconvincing performance of its authority. Perhaps in response to that earlier argument about theater, *Henry V* represents kingship in terms of the actor's delicate capacity to invent his authority by so captivating the audience as to see his authority mirrored back to him as though from that other place. In this dynamic, authority is a collaborative, virtual projection, in which the authorizing audience (itself, in part, the projection of the actor/sovereign) comes to resemble the authorizing time of the past, which legitimates the political present when it is cast as the particular historical form necessary for that present. Alongside the strangeness of seeing a single event and year repeated across historical *time*, at stake in Shakespeare's representation of Anglo-French conquest is the theater's capacity also to reconfigure *space* and so bring the strange place onto familiar ground. Particularly in *Henry V*, the thematization of theater's own jurisdictional violations powerfully reconstitutes the play's thematic argument about the nature of England's historical conquests, enacting as drama the long reiteration through which England's defeat was absorbed and imagined as its own sovereignty.

Henry V construes conquest as example, a structure in which the particular and general are in dialectical tension. In the prologue to Act 5, the Chorus asks the audience to imagine Henry being brought in stages back from Agincourt "home" to "London " (5.0.35, 37): first to Calais (5.0.6–7), then across the channel to the English coast (5.0.8–13), thence to Blackheath (5.0.16) and, finally, to the City itself, where "The Mayor and all his brethren, in best sort, / Like to the senators of th'antique Rome / With the plebeians swarming at their heels, / Go forth and fetch their conqu'ring Caesar in" (5.0.25–28). The comparison of Henry to Caesar famously introduces a second comparison of

Henry/Caesar to the Elizabethan "General of our gracious Empress," whose victorious return from Ireland the Chorus now asks the audience to project and, in a hypothesis, celebrate (5.0.29–34). The topical reference is usually understood to be to Essex's Irish campaign of 1599, although recently Richard Dutton has put forward a powerful argument that the passage was added for the 1602 revival and refers to Charles Blount, Lord Mountjoy, who, after the English victory at Kinsale on December 24, 1601, would indeed have seemed to be on the cusp of victory in Ireland.[56]

In this deliberate layering of its histories, the passage practices humanist exemplarity by exposing the historical thickness that makes examplarity so powerful as historic practice but also ineffective as a fully stable frame for ethical judgment.[57] The phrase "their conqu'ring Caesar" registers in small that epistemological ambivalence, in its inflated tone and by slyly suggesting the impermanence of any *particular* Caesar or conquest or, correspondingly, any particular invocation of Caesar. The implicit critique of humanist practice thus mirrors the earlier lampooning of Captain Fluellen, whose allegiance to the exemplary model of Roman military discipline (as at 3.3.3–9, 3.6.6–15, 4.1.66–74) is brilliantly shown up as pedantry relative to the *praxis* of war. That said, the play's skepticism is directed as much against the practical or pragmatic self as against the scholar-pedant, as shown by Fluellen's most notorious *exemplum*, his comparison of Henry to "Alexander the Pig" (4.7.12), a pun that Shakespeare directs equally against humanist pedagogical practice and the brutal reality of the English king's victory at Agincourt.[58] When the Chorus designates England's returning Henry as "their conqu'ring Caesar," that phrase thus compactly weighs and undoes two arguments concerning the origin of authority: Fluellen's exemplary mode, according to which the conqueror conquers by becoming Caesar; and Henry's exemplary action, according to which Caesar becomes Caesar through the bare fact of conquest.

The timing of the play's comparison of Henry to Caesar disrupts the emblematics of English conquest in a further way. While Fluellen seems comically off the mark for comparing the topography of Henry's and Alexander's respective birthplaces in Wales and Macedon (4.7.20–28), the Chorus more carefully choreographs the comparison of Henry to Julius Caesar, whose "*Veni vidi vici*" made him the archetypal conqueror of France and thus Henry's military progenitor.[59] But it is only when Henry enters London after his victory that the play deploys the example of Caesar, the narrow terms of the comparison being Caesar's triumphant entry into Rome. By means of that deferral, then, the passage remembers Caesar's entry not only into Rome but also into Britain, a historic event duly noted, for example, in *Cymbeline*: "When Julius

Caesar /... was in this Britain / And conquered it" (3.1.2–5). In the context of this geographic irony, the full temporal irony of "their conqu'ring Caesar" emerges, since by invoking Caesar's Roman triumph, the Chorus has grafted onto the representation of Caesar's and Henry's French conquests the quite inappropriate memory of Caesar's conquest of England.[60] In general, the point of this temporal-spatial irony is that, as history-making, the exemplary mode always carries forward the forgotten detail, too, the detail that, through extension, may be waiting to undo the example's intended story.[61] But it is especially apt that in a play about a fifteenth-century English invasion of France, Caesar's conquests of Britain and France should be evoked together. To think of conquest in an Anglo-French context is to remember not an event but rather a pattern, a history of invasion and counter-invasion extending from the Norman Conquest of 1066 and including the long and complex history of English gains and losses on the Continent. If Shakespeare's exemplary invocation of Caesar allows him, contrary to the ideal workings of humanist example, to remember, inside the story of Henry's conquest of France, an earlier pattern of England itself being conquered, that moment of subversion is itself incomplete, since with respect to English identity the Conquest at least of 1066 is equally constitutive as destructive of Englishness.

We can explore an early stage in Shakespeare's reiterative history-making by turning to *Richard III*, a play that, though concerned with struggles internal to England, places the struggles that bring the Tudors to the throne in the context of a remembered Norman past. Conquest is the play's principal term for Richmond's military engagement with King Richard. The ghosts that appear in Act 5 to disturb Richard's sleep and comfort Richmond on the eve of battle repeatedly conceive of Richmond as conqueror: Henry VI's ghost urges Richmond that "Virtuous and holy, be thou conqueror" (5.4.107); Hastings's ghost encourages him to "Arm, fight, and conquer for fair England's sake" (5.4.136); and, in a formulation that binds military victory to the workings of conscience, the ghosts of Rivers, Grey, and Vaughan predict that "our wrongs in Richard's bosom / Will conquer him" (5.4.123–24). In his battle oration on the day following these several visitations, Richmond encourages his soldiers by saying that if they are fighting for their wives, "Your wives shall welcome home the conquerors" (5.4.239). The term is twice applied also to King Richard: by the Duchess of York, who hopes that he will die "Ere from this war thou turn a conqueror" (4.4.174); and, in a passage first printed in the 1623 Folio, by Richard himself, who seeks the hand of Elizabeth of York by promising her mother that he will "lead thy daughter to a conqueror's bed" as "Caesar's Caesar."[62]

In one sense, it is unsurprising that Richard or Richmond should imagine himself or be imagined as conqueror, since the term can simply designate one who claims victory or country by force of arms. Perhaps because it is technically only a country or a people that can be conquered, however, the term carries the further connotation, as for Alexander or Caesar or the sixteenth-century *conquistador*, of the victor's entry from beyond the conquered territory. Certainly, this is the word's force when used to designate William I, a king who can without ambiguity still today be referred to simply as "the Conqueror." (When Joseph Hall writes in one of his satires of a bore who "tells how first his famous ancestor / Did come in long since with the Conquerour," the image of coming into England from a beyond is inseparable from the idea of conquest.)[63] With respect to this further connotation, conqueror and conquest sit far less easily with *Richard III*'s representation of 1485. At issue, first, is a bitter historic irony, isolated by the Duchess of York when she laments that her sons "themselves, the conquerors, / Make war upon themselves, blood against blood, / Self against self" (2.4.64–66). Her lines summarize the history that has turned England from real conquest in France to factional disputes between the houses of Lancaster and York, and finally to the quarrels internal to the Yorkist line. The ironic force of her term *conquerors*, that is, depends on our registering as part of its immediate semantic history the increasingly domestic delineation of external and internal, self and other. In such a context, what can it mean for Richmond or Richard to be conqueror?

Put simply, 1485 is 1066. The English civil wars are conflated with the idea of external conquest so that the coming of the Tudors to England from exile in Brittany can end those wars by reenacting the foundational moment of Englishness as a recurring complexity in England's national identity with respect to France. In his speech to his soldiers on the day of battle, King Richard makes the association audible, although, crucially, not to himself. In its expository progression, the speech powerfully consolidates the semantic resonance of all the play's earlier allusions to conquest:

> What shall I say more than I have inferred?
> Remember whom you are to cope withal:
> A sort of vagabonds, rascals and runaways,
> A scum of Bretons, and base lackey peasants
> Whom their o'er cloyèd country vomits forth
> To desperate ventures and assured destruction. . . .
> And who doth lead them but a paltry fellow,
> Long kept in Bretagne at our mother's cost,

> A milksop, one that never in his life
> Felt so much cold as over shoes in snow?
> Let's whip these stragglers o'er the seas again,
> Lash hence these overweening rags of France,
> These famished beggars, weary of their lives,
> Who, but for dreaming on this fond exploit,
> For want of means, poor rats, had hanged themselves.
> (5.5.43–60)[64]

Throughout the passage Richard constructs Richmond as an invading adventurer, foreign, beggarly, crudely ambitious, unambiguously an aspiring conqueror. And at the climax of his increasingly passionate argument, Richard makes exactly that point: "If we be conquered, let men conquer us, / And not these bastard Bretons, whom our fathers / Have in their own land beaten, bobbed, and thumped, / And in record left them the heirs of shame" (5.4.61–64). Crudely patriotic, Richard opposes an authentic English self to the foreign others coming into England from Brittany.

In transforming an Englishman into a Breton, however, Richard foolishly also transforms Richmond into William. The latter association is underlined in the phrase "bastard Bretons." In Richard's generic insult against Richmond and his followers, Shakespeare alludes to William's illegitimate descent from Robert, Duke of Normandy. William's bastardy is invoked, too, in *Henry V*, where the Duke of Bourbon deprecates the English invaders as "Normans, but bastard Normans, Norman bastards"(3.5.10), and the dauphin imagines the children of French women and English soldiers as "bastard warriors" (3.5.31). If the French thus construe Agincourt as a tragic reiteration, in reverse, of 1066, Shakespeare is allowing his audience to celebrate, against the French, the curiously virile identification of Englishness with bastard Normanism. Something similar happens in *Richard III*. In Richard's speech, Brittany is not Normandy, of course, but that is secondary to the crude simplicity of its being "France" (5.4.57). Indeed, the geographical conflation of Brittany and Normandy underpins the historical argument of the passage. Attempting to tap into the memory of England's most patriotic moment, Richard describes the bastard Bretons as in the past, to their recorded shame, having been defeated by Englishmen, namely, those who served under Henry V in his French campaigns. But the Agincourt of 1415 relates to Brittany in just the way Normandy does, as part of a generic north of France. Metonymically standing in for all of France, that northern margin becomes the site for the sequence of Anglo-French conquests, each of which is locked into the memory of the other.

At the moment of Richard's invoking Henry V's conquest in France, who, then, is more English, Richard or Richmond? The point is that the tyrant king has chosen an extraordinarily clumsy way to denigrate his enemy, since by inadvertently connecting Richmond to William he not only predicts the conqueror's victory on Bosworth Field, but also makes Richmond English in as deep a sense as the Henry who in 1415 had already reiterated, in reverse, William I's originary conquest. Shakespeare's passage acknowledges, in ways that Richard himself cannot hear, the hybridity of Anglo-French identity and the peculiar relation of Englishness to the idea of conquest. The richest joke against Richard thus depends on hearing the force of his subjunctive: "If we be conquered," Richard urges, "let men conquer us," his point being that the possibility of conquest lies in the future, but not at the hands of such as Richmond. What he cannot hear is that they *are* conquered, and that it is conquest itself that has made possible the Englishness he attempts to mark in "we." All that awaits him in the field is the declaratory iteration or enactment of this foundational structure.

Like William's Conquest, however, Richmond's conquest of England must finally become English in order, then, to be England's conquest, too. What iconography of conquest, what form taken by Conqueror or conqueror, can allow him to be incorporated into English history? A set of royal woodcuts from the early Tudor period usefully frames the question. In Tudor iconography, by and large, William the Conqueror is notable principally for his absence.[65] But in the 1529 *Pastyme of People*, a chronicle history of "dyvers realmys and most specyally of the realme of Englond," John Rastell prints a full-page woodcut portrait for each English king from William the Conqueror to Richard III.[66] William is shown with sword and orb (fig. 1); through these iconic symbols of a conqueror king, the book specifically associates him with the following kings: Richard I, John, Edward I, Edward III, Henry V, and Edward IV.[67] Additional iconographic information differentiates among the conquerors who were responsible for the various foreign conquests central to English nationalism: as absent crusader, Richard holds no orb, but wrestles a lion (fig. 2); Edward III carries two crowns on his sword, the second representing his conquest of France and his claim specifically on the French throne (fig. 3); more simply, an aggressive Henry V is shown in dynamic left profile, knees bent, as though charging beyond the picture's frame into his story (fig. 4).[68] The kings known for their military victories within England are more generic in their representation. But here certain omissions seem telling: given that Edward IV carries a sword (fig. 5), for example, why does Henry IV not carry one (fig. 6)? The impression one has from these portraits is of the

FIGURE 1 William I. Woodcut from John Rastell, *The Pastyme of People* (London, 1529), A1r. London, British Library, C.15.c.6. By permission of the British Library.

FIGURE 2 Richard I. Woodcut from Rastell, *Pastyme of People* (London, 1529), B1v. London, British Library, C.15.c.6. By permission of the British Library.

FIGURE 3 Edward III. Woodcut from Rastell, *Pastyme of People* (London, 1529), C5r. London, British Library, C.15.c.6. By permission of the British Library.

FIGURE 4 Henry V. Woodcut from Rastell, *Pastyme of People* (London, 1529), E1v. London, British Library, C.15.c.6. By permission of the British Library.

FIGURE 5 Edward IV. Woodcut from Rastell, *Pastyme of People* (London, 1529), F2v. London, British Library, C.15.c.6. By permission of the British Library.

FIGURE 6 Henry IV. Woodcut from Rastell, *Pastyme of People* (London, 1529), D6r. London, British Library, C.15.c.6. By permission of the British Library.

constitutive differences among conquerors who, as conquerors, nonetheless significantly resemble one another. When, we might ask, can a conquering king be represented as conqueror? Does Rastell write a Lancastrian history by representing only Yorkist Edward IV, and not Lancastrian Henry IV, as taking England by force? Or is the point that Henry IV is not a conqueror, but just a traitor to Richard II? Equally, do the representations of Henry V and Edward III mark them as conquerors in a different sense from Edward IV or, indeed, William I?

The portrait of William, which identifies him alone as "Conquerour," already implies the iconographic questions I am asking about the portraits later in the series. In addition to the sword William carries, the woodcut shows, in the negative space around the king, a spear, three arrows, and an axe, additional symbols that speak to the particular significance of this inaugural violent conquest. The arrows are the most striking feature, since directly opposite William's portrait, which makes up the first page of Rastell's post-Norman English chronicles, is the text that closes the earlier Saxon history with an account of the Battle of Hastings and King Harold's death as a result of an arrow wound: "In the bygynnyng of which fyght the englishmen kept them in good aray lyke to venquysh the normans wherfore duke wyllyam causyd his men to giff bak as though they fled wherby the Englishmen folowyd and brake theyre aray & the normans cam fyersly uppon them & in conclusyon had the vyctory where that kyng harold was woundyd wyth an arow in the left eye & therof incontenent dyed and so was there slayne . . . & was buryed at waltham which was the last that reynyd in Englond of the blood of the Saxons."[69] The juxtaposition of the textual and visual arrows registers the uneasy implication of William's Conquest for a later English historical consciousness. The anonymous mid-sixteenth-century *Breviat Cronicle* displays a similar unease about William when, avoiding altogether the designation of "Saxon," it records that William reigned "with greate cruelnes towarde the Englysh men" and that his Norman "governers . . . greatlye oppressed the Englyshe men."[70] By so powerfully distinguishing between the "English" and the invaders who, nevertheless, help constitute a later Englishness, the *Cronicle*, like Rastell's representation of the fateful and heroic arrow, demonstrates how William I inaugurates the ambivalent representations, later in England's history, of versions of royal conquest that look both outward and inward.

Another set of pictures helps us see how the culture attempted to resolve the problem William posed for an emerging English nationalism and for the representation of his descendants. Soon after 1502, Henry VII commissioned for the great hall of his palace at Richmond a series of portraits of English kings. As Gordon Kipling argues in his account of these pictures, the underlying principle for the series was less genealogical than exemplary: the artist intended to "portray the Tudor monarchy as a font of magnificence, the chief of the Burgundian virtues. The artist has included in the portrait series only those kings who have achieved fame as conquerors and warriors." The sequence portrayed "bold and valiant knights," extending "from Brute and Arthur, to Richard the Lionhearted and Edward III." Given the thematic argument of the sequence, Kipling notes that "one is surprised to see William Rufus instead of William the Conqueror."[71] Indeed, since William Rufus historically maintained his hold on his father's English crown only by paying his elder brother, the Duke of Normandy, not to invade England, his inclusion in a group of conquerors does seem as anomalous as his father's exclusion.

But the paradox Kipling points to is also its own solution, since it is exactly the substitution of son for father, I think, that makes sense of the father's

FIGURE 7 William II. Woodcut from Rastell, *Pastyme of People* (London, 1529), A2v. London, British Library, C.15.c.6. By permission of the British Library.

omission. Because 1066 marks the conquest of England, the first William cannot be absorbed as an English historical presence as easily as an Arthur or Richard or even Brutus. As progenitor of all later kings, William must, however, be absorbed. The artist's inclusion of the son thus indicates that, whatever its immediate damage to English prestige, the Conquest allows for Englishness as a filial legacy. (Not incidentally, this identifies the mechanics of legitimation used by Henry VII when, by marrying the daughter of Edward IV and niece of Richard III, he guaranteed that, although he had no claim on the throne, his children would have one through their mother.) Prototypically and symbolically, William the Conqueror is the historical moment that, as limit, is both inside and outside the construction of national prestige, while William Rufus is the moment at which the limit is reabsorbed into national history and national time.

William Rufus is incorporated into history as the king his father cannot be, and this in two senses. First, he absorbs his father's conquest of England into his own pacific Englishness: Rastell's portrait of William Rufus shows him with scepter rather than sword, his expression benign rather than fiercely stern (fig. 7).[72] Two sequences of printed royal portraits from later in the century—Thomas Talbot's 1597 royal portrait book and the anonymous abstract of royal genealogy printed by Gyles Godet around 1560—repeat that

FIGURE 8 William I, William II, and Henry I. Woodcut from *A Brief Abstract* (London, ca. 1560). London, British Library, G.6456. By permission of the British Library.

basic iconography.[73] In Godet's volume especially, William Rufus's scepter, kingly robes, and pitying expression vividly answer the Conqueror's military furnishings and general ferocity (fig. 8). *A Breviat Cronicle* similarly signals Rufus's greater incorporation into "England" when it reports that, in response to a rebellion of "dyvers Lordes in England," he "vanquished the traitours and chased them out of hys realme."[74] The language of treachery and expulsion makes England William II's proper domain in a way quite unavailable to the Conqueror: in the *Cronicle*'s account of the Exeter Rebellion against William I, it is said simply (and more neutrally) that Exeter and Northumberland "rebelled" and were "subdued and after grevously punyshed."[75] So William Rufus rewrites the Conquest itself by domesticating it. The collection of portraits printed by Godet includes verse histories of the various kings, and it is recorded there that William Rufus managed to "subdue" the Welsh and "slewe their king," with the effect that "Ther was never king sins that tym raigning."[76] This is a rather optimistic account of William Rufus's engagements in Wales, not only because William I had himself made inroads into Welsh territory, but also because it was not until the reign of Edward I that the princes and independence of Wales were suppressed, and not until the 1536 Act of Union that Wales was constitutionally incorporated into England. The poem's celebration of William II's relatively minor achievements in Wales is the inaccuracy whereby the second Norman king might redirect the Conquest in service now of a pan-British Englishness. By doing so, he marks the extent to which, as opposed to his father's absorption of England, his England has already absorbed its Norman past. This is the context, also, in which to construe the oddity of the poem's insisting on the permanent demise of Welsh kingship, given that the Tudors were a Welsh dynasty. If William Rufus becomes English by absorbing Wales and thus his Norman past, Henry of Richmond at Bosworth Field is able symbolically to become king by coming from two beyonds, each of them internal to the country he, in turn, conquers. One way to state the structural response to Conquest is that if 1485 is 1066, Wales is for that reason also France.

Richard III thus sets out the representational paradox of England's conquests that Shakespeare explores in the second tetralogy, in relation to the Lancastrian conquest not only of France, but of England, too. When he lands at Ravenspur on his way to becoming Henry IV, Bolingbroke reiterates the historical crux of 1066, a point made in *3 Henry VI* when, to solidify his own claim to the crown, King Henry registers Bolingbroke's deposing of Richard II, not as "rebellion," but as a version of William's right: "Henry the Fourth by conquest got the crown" (1.1.133). Henry V's conquest of France, moreover, is explicitly compensatory for his father's conquest of England: "to waste the memory of the former days," Henry IV urges his son, "my Harry, / Be it thy course to busy giddy minds / With foreign quarrels" (*2 Henry IV*, 4.3.342–45). If *Richard III* makes the point that the English are more English for Richmond's conquering them, *Henry V* is the text that probes that paradox by asking how the son resolves crisis and makes the father's conquest English again.

At the simplest level, Henry's wars in France reverse the direction of the father's conquest. In Canterbury's speech concerning the Salic Law, taken nearly verbatim from Holinshed, the play marks Henry's war as compensatory not only for Henry IV's but also, symbolically for William's.[77] The speech is multiply critical of Henry's wars. The archbishop's argument that the law barring succession through the female line does not pertain in France depends on the law's extending across a narrower territorial jurisdiction: "the land Salic is in Germany, / Between the floods of Saale and of Elbe, / Where, Charles the Great having subdued the Saxons, / There left behind and settled certain French / Who, holding in disdain the German women / . . . Established there this law" (1.2.44–50). But this is an argument for only *generic* English claims in France. For the particular occasion, it is merely specious, since the archbishop's logic actually promotes Yorkist Mortimer's lineal claims, rather than Henry's. Furthermore, an English play that remembers a great French conqueror subduing Saxons and settling certain French in the conquered territory is also remembering its own history. Against the example of Charlemagne's Saxon conquest, the play places Henry in an exemplary line of conquerors, alluding to Richard the Lionheart (1.2.124) but most especially to Edward III, whose 1346 victory at Crécy explicitly prefigures Henry's territorial triumphs. Thus Canterbury urges him to invoke the "warlike spirit" of Edward III and "your great-uncle's Edward the Black Prince, / Who on the French ground played a tragedy" (1.2.104–6), a sentiment that looks forward to the French king's description of Crécy as "our too-much-memorable shame" (2.4.53). If Agincourt repeats the exemplary pattern of Crécy, however, it also iterates the exemplary, foundational, and unspoken event that stands under Ravenspur. Behind Agincourt-as-Crécy stands the less easily assimilable structure of Ravenspur-as-Hastings.[78]

It belongs to Henry V, as to William Rufus, to incorporate his father and his father's conquest. In his deathbed speech to Harry, Henry IV imagines this structure of absorption in terms of the absorption of his own body into the ground:

> God knows, my son,
> By what bypaths and indirect crook'd ways
> I met this crown ; and I myself know well
> How troublesome it sat upon my head.
> To thee it shall descend with better quiet,
> Better opinion, better confirmation,
> For all the soil of the achievement goes
> With me into the earth.
>
> (2 *Henry IV*, 4.3.313–20)

The "achievement" or conclusion Henry alludes to is his illicit taking of Richard II's crown, a conquest which, for that reason alone, is no sure conclusion but only a contestable one. "Soil" has a double register, and the pun figures the mechanics of the temporal process Henry is describing. First, soil is the stain that conquest places on the Lancastrian crown, and which Henry V's "better confirmation" will erase, but it is also the soil or territory claimed by Henry upon taking Richard's crown. At the moment Henry's body is taken into England's earth, that is, England becomes coextensive with the conqueror's body. In the full argument, England's soil goes with Henry into the earth not as something thereby lost to the son, but as something for the first time fully absorbed for the son into the royal body he will now inhabit. Territorial incorporation marks sovereignty, and it is in this sense that Henry V will say of the territories over which he now, and speciously, claims sovereignty that "we have now no thought *in* us but France" (*Henry V*, 1.2.302, emphasis added).

When Henry IV concludes his deathbed oration by advising the future king to "busy giddy minds / With foreign quarrels," he defines as the ultimate resolution to his stained history the events that, in the definitively English conquest of France, his son will make into *his* history. The crisis of national conquest can be absorbed, but only in time (by the son) and only by wresting the nation's spatial boundaries to bring the conqueror within them. In a fine essay on Shakespeare's English histories in terms of Derrida's understanding of a center that is inside and outside, always elsewhere from the totality of which it is the center, Rowland Cotterill identifies "England-with-France" as the critical term in the plays' treatment of English kingship and nationhood.[79] I would describe the paradoxical character of Englishness Cotterill indexes somewhat differently, not as "England-with-France," but as "France-in-England"—an analytical category rooted not so much in the contemporary politics of Anglo-French relations as in a continuous cultural development extending from 1066 forward. For how shall we characterize the force of the plays' remembered conquests for the Elizabethan culture that saw them enacted? In the movement from *Henry VI* to *Henry V*, Cotterill sees a shift "from fantasy to reality," the substitution of a historical sovereignty for an unreal projection.[80] Understood within the history that extends beyond 1415 and even 1346 back to 1066, however, it is not cultural fantasy that is at issue, but rather the imaginary that makes France resident as a structural presence fully inside Elizabethan English nationalism. This is a France enacted for and in the cultural memory, not as fantasy or as fetish, but as the regime, though not the content, of national identity.

SPEAKING APART

Henry V delineates this regime—the condition of possibility in which Englishness can be thought—by meditating on the resources of drama itself as a mode of hypothesis that generates linguistic meaning and action that, in different ways, are in excess of their content. The play looks, first, to the pun as a place in the language that carries forward, in ways not quite inaudible, the lingering impact of France on England. To consider these turns of phrase returns us to the strange place of the French language in English law.[81] In disguise on the eve of Agincourt, Henry meets Pistol, who twice asks his identity:

Pistol:	*Qui vous là?*	
King Henry:	A friend.	(4.1.36–37)

Pistol:	What is thy name?	
King Henry:	Harry *le roi*.	
Pistol:	Leroi? A Cornish name. Art thou of Cornish crew?	
King Henry:	No, I am a Welshman.	(4.1.49–52)

Both exchanges are jokes about England's French, and each depends on a translation. In the first, Henry must hear through the sentry's ungrammatical challenge, which translates doubly as "Who you/comes there."[82] This odd elision of the king's person with his coming thus identifies Henry with the activity of his coming or conquest, this being a version in small of the dynamic that sees Henry put forward his claims to France as a way to legitimate his royal persona. The second joke depends on Pistol's hearing Henry's French as English, an error that, inside the translation from French, hides a translation from France as well. In the same way as Brittany functions as the north coast of France, Cornwall here stands for the southern coast of England: "Leroi" sounds Cornish to Pistol to the extent that it sounds French, which is to say that Pistol hears the name as an old Norman name. The exchange thus constitutes in miniature the tetralogy's analysis of Conquest/conquest as a trope long constitutive of English kingship. Henry's reply that he is Welsh, not Cornish, concisely reformulates the theme of absorption treated in 2 *Henry IV*, according to which the royal name and lineage is placed beyond the reach of a French past by being reconstituted within a more capacious England.

Henry's displacement of Cornwall and its implications onto Wales (and his Welsh ancestry) might remind us especially of William Rufus's military engagements in that country as given in the portrait book printed by

Godet, since to be Welsh is semiotically for Henry to be English and a conqueror. When, in Act 5 of *Henry V*, Pistol refuses to eat the leek Fluellen has offered him, his oath "Not for Cadwallader and all his goats" (5.1.25) contributes another version of Henry's and Godet's point about filial kingship, conquest, and Wales. The king whose name he disparagingly invokes is not, as Gary Taylor suggests in his gloss, merely a "famous seventh-century Welsh warrior king," but the figure who stands in the chronicles and portrait books as the last Briton king before the inauguration of the Saxons whom William will ultimately defeat in 1066.[83] Even as it alludes to an early moment in the history of "English" domination over Wales, Pistol's insult introduces an even earlier historical threshold parallel to the Conqueror's, thereby instituting a complex British hybridity by insisting once more on the priority of the iterated scene of conquest over its particular content.

In Pistol's linguistic encounter with his French prisoner, Monsieur le Fer (4.4), Pistol's translation of le Fer's French into English is marked by an even greater overdetermination in the performance of Britishness. The scene's principal joke (in which gunpowder substitutes for the crossbow that actually gave Henry his victory at Agincourt) is that "le Fer" must stand a very poor chance against a Pistol. With his English, too, Pistol everywhere overpowers his opponent. Given that Wales is at issue in Pistol's encounter with Henry, it is notable that, as Taylor points out, Scots, Irish, and English usage together direct Pistol's translation of le Fer: le Fer's "moi" becomes Pistol's "moy," (4.4.12–13), a Scots term for a measurement of corn; his "qualité" becomes "Calin o custure me" (4.4.3–4), itself an "English corruption of the Irish refrain *cailin og a' stor*' ('maiden, my treasure')"; and his "bras" becomes "brass" (4.4.16–17).[84] As translator, Pistol imagines French as versions of an English that has already internalized other national tongues. In Pistol's reinterpretation of what he hears, England's conquest of Wales and Ireland, and its imagined incorporation of Scotland, become versions of France-in-England, a culture absorbed and transformed through its absorption into the distinct form that is reiterated as English. Mistranslation or lack of linguistic fit means, we might say, that although Pistol's crazed vernacular places him apart from the interlocutors he seeks to engage, it also allows him to speak a part in the scene of a more capacious English than he can fully hear himself inhabiting.

More than any other sequence in the play, the marriage negotiations at the play's conclusion construe the national relationship as a linguistic turn, one that orients the national present toward its own history. Given that marriage and political accommodation are at issue here, it is unsurprising that Queen Isabel should speak of the marriage between Henry and Catherine as mutually and reciprocally incorporating one nation into the other: "So be there 'twixt your kingdoms such a spousal . . . / That English may as French, French Englishmen, / Receive each other. . . ." (5.2.347–52). In its wedding imagery and chiastic structure, this is highly reminiscent of the dedicatory sonnet to Holyband's *French Littelton*, and like the French used at English law, Isabel's metaphor recodes an accommodation of France to England that is dictated more by institutional need than reciprocal feeling. Immediately preceding the French queen's perhaps too optimistic slant on things, the practical and watchful Exeter has insisted that King Charles subscribe to a final and telling article (which Shakespeare found in Holinshed) before the negotiations can conclude:

> Exeter: Only he hath not yet subscribèd this: where your majesty demands that the King of France, having any occasion to write for matter of grant, shall name your highness in this form and with this addition: [reads] in French, *Notre très cher fils Henri, Roi d'Angleterre, Hériter de France,* and thus in Latin, *Praeclarissimus filius noster Henricus, Rex Angliae et Haeres Franciae.*
> (5.2.321–27)

This is political resolution enacted as a linguistic effect of the languages used to describe the resolution.

Notably, of course, English is absent from the document. One critic has suggested that "the document does not include the conqueror's language: the French tongue, it would seem, will not stoop to England's will."[85] But the meaning of the passage seems to me to lie elsewhere, since in its doubling of French and Latin forms, the treaty precisely replicates the institutional practice of English law. First, the document is legible in terms of the central courts' practice of translating the French forms of the opposing parties' written pleas into the final Latin form of the plea roll. Alternatively, the document can be read in terms of the lawyers' professional literature and as a kind of case report. Although the traditional year books, through which lawyers had long transmitted their common learning, were written in law French, the authoritative named reports first printed under Elizabeth transmitted the law very consciously as a combination of Latin and French, more or less to the exclusion of English. This is because Edmund Plowden gave his foundational 1571 *Comentaries* (on which Coke modeled his own, even more influential reports) a double structure, as both a collection of reports and a pedagogically useful book of entries, the formal pleadings through which the parties isolated the issue for trial.[86] For each of the cases he records, Plowden begins with the Latin of the plea roll, then proceeds with the analytical account, in law French, of the court's reasoning on the point of law at issue. Reading the two parts of the report together was, and still is, a matter of hearing one form of speech at English law translated into another. As a legal instrument, Henry's treaty replicates the doubled documentary and professional record of English legal practice; in its Englishness it records the underlying legal paradox of England's French and England's France.

Earlier in Act 5, Henry and Catherine's courtship has similarly evoked legal practices internal to England. The scene fits Henry to Catherine, and France to England, through an accommodation of French to English, English to French. I am interested here, as in my earlier analysis of names in the play, in the syllabic effect of the international courtship:

King Henry: *Je quand suis le possesseur de France, et quand vous avez le possession de moi*—let me see, what then? Saint Denis be my speed!–*donc vôtre est France, et vous êtes mienne.*
(5.2.176–79)

Catherine: Your majesty 'ave *fausse* French enough to deceive de most sage *demoiselle* dat is *en France.* (5.2.210–11)

Catherine: *Les dames et demoiselles pour être baisées devant leurs noces, il n'est pas la coutume de France.*
King Henry: (*to Alice*) Madam my interpreter, what says she?
Alice: Dat is not be de *façon pour les* ladies of France—I cannot tell vat is *baiser* en Anglish.
King Henry: King Henry: To kiss.
Alice: Your majesty *entendre* bettre *que moi.* (5.2.249–56)

Syllabically, the interweaving of French and English here is remarkably close to the intrusion of English into law French. This is particularly true of Alice's speech, perhaps because she is, after all, the professional whose task it is to teach the French princess the nature of England's constitution.[87] The similarity between the play's and law's mixing of English and French underlines the broader structure of the play, which at its opening and conclusion frames the story of military conquest with alternative appeals to the language of law rather than might. For the Salic Law that in Act 1 is said potentially to exclude England from France, Henry in Act 5 substitutes a marriage treaty that brings England and France into one another; for the sophistication of Canterbury's interpretive gloss on the Salic Law, he substitutes the sincere pleading (in its legal sense, too) of a "plain king" who wants to marry (5.2.125).

In this context, Henry's, Catherine's, and Alice's macaronic versions of English are part of a serious legal game. That the Anglo-French marriage should be marked by the fusion of French and Latin, French and English, as found in English law, reminds us that the resolution between countries that the play enacts (now in the strictest meaning of that word) already inhabits English law as France's inescapable and repetitive historical presence. In these various scenes of productive linguistic interference, the performance of identity (whether by Catherine, Henry, or Pistol) works as the observation that language carries a hidden history alongside its patent one. These dramatic enactments of how languages meet or do not meet one another make audible a part of English national identity that, for example, Coke's rationalization of law French means instead to circumscribe. As history-making, the interlinguistic pun or macaronic exchange reaches beyond the vernacular's immediate temporality to open it onto its own history and so make the vernacular differently available to itself as history and culture.

Closely related to the temporal effects of this linguistic work in *Henry V* is the play's description of drama's capacity to violate spatial jurisdiction. This is the second way in which the play draws on its own resources as drama to enact the regime of national identity that is its theme. In *2 Henry IV*, Shakespeare represents Henry IV's death by importing a geographical quibble from Holinshed's account of the reign:

> *King Henry:* Doth any name particular belong
> Unto the lodging where I first did swoon?
> *Warwick:* 'Tis called Jerusalem, my noble lord.
> (4.3.362–64)

Jerusalem is not a city, but a chamber, the room in which Henry will die and so fulfil the prophecy that "I should not die but in Jerusalem, / Which vainly I supposed the Holy Land" (4.3.367–68). The king's error is a matter of having supposed that he would traverse space whereas, as the play stages it, distance itself is overcome through England's national space becoming uncannily plural.[88]

The king's mistaken supposition thus anticipates in reverse the work of hypothesis that *Henry V* enacts and celebrates in its metadramatic account of the relation between theater and sovereignty. Most famously, it is the Chorus who meditates on theater's ability to overcome its own material circumstances, this through the expansion of its institutional resources to include the audience it enthralls:

> Suppose within the girdle of these walls
> Are now confined two mighty monarchies,
> Whose high upreared and abutting fronts
> The perilous narrow ocean parts asunder.
> Piece out our imperfections with your thoughts:
> Into a thousand parts divide one man,
> And make imaginary puissance.
>
> (1.0.19–25)

Theater's promise here is the promise that through the hypothetical disruption of time, space, and circumstance, fictive action might become efficacious: "Linger your patience on," the Chorus tells an audience impatient to see Harfleur and Agincourt, "and we'll digest / Th' abuse of distance, force—perforce—a play" (2.0.31–32). Promising eventually to get to France, the Chorus here asserts that the play's own making depends on its reconfiguration of jurisdictional space, the very space that generates the crisis represented in the play. To digest the abuse of distance is, as Taylor notes, to "set in order" the play's "disregard of the unity of place."[89] And the Chorus can revel in that disregard because it only takes to a logical extreme drama's dependence generally on the hypothesis that one place might be two.

If, while the audience is forced to wait for something to happen, the king remains at Southampton and thus at only a proximate remove from the south bank of the Thames, that is a temporary deferral of the truly virtuosic disorientation the play celebrates when it asks its audience (absent the groundlings, note) to become continental travelers:

> There is the playhouse now, there must you sit,
> And thence to France shall we convey you safe,
> And bring you back, charming the narrow seas
> To give you gentle pass—for if we may
> We'll not offend one stomach with our play.
>
> (2.0.36–40)

The dramatic and hypothetical disorientation of space that allows Henry V's victory in France to be staged answers Henry IV's converse failure to recognize that spaces are folded into one another, not only by importing the alien into England, but also by replicating the mechanics of Henry V's mode of authority. Most simply, of course, the Chorus transforms the audience into the army that gave the king his victory in France. "Follow, follow," the Chorus urges when introducing the scene at Harfleur: "Work, work your thoughts, and therein see a siege" (3.0.17, 25). Here the audience can become soldiers only because, as the play represents 1415, Henry's soldiers themselves become effective soldiers by becoming an audience, the productive mirror of the authority Henry needs in order, not quite tautologically, to have authority over them.[90] This is the play, of course, that begins by lamenting the absence on stage of a king real enough to be himself:

> O for a muse of fire, that would ascend
> The brightest heaven of invention:
> A kingdom for a stage, princes to act,
> And monarchs to behold the swelling scene.
> Then should the warlike Harry, like himself,
> Assume the port of Mars. . . .
>   (1.0.1–6)

It then represents a king whose authority is the actor's. The political meaning of the double identification by which the king becomes an actor so that the Elizabethan actor might be adequate to his role is thematized in the Chorus's appeal to the audience that they "Into a thousand parts divide one man / And make imaginary puissance" (1.0.24–25), a formula as valid for Henry's authority at Agincourt as for the theater, insofar as the king becomes effective by reinventing or rediscovering his authority beyond himself, displacing it onto an extended military body capable of reflecting his authority back unchanged.[91]

Shakespeare leaves it to a soldier to characterize the relation between authority and its constitutive extension in space or time: royal jurisdiction becomes a legal reality, as the play construes it, where it is hypothesized into efficacy. Following the battle at Agincourt, Williams discovers to his peril that the soldier he quarreled with on the eve of battle was and is the king. In his defense, he casts Henry's identity in exactly the Chorus's terms:

> *King Henry:* It was ourself thou didst abuse.
> *Williams:* Your majesty came not like himself. You appeared to me but as a common man.
>   (4.8.48–50)

Williams's point is that his erroneous supposition on the eve of battle must be taken as valid in a way that the real cannot be: "I beseech you take it for your own fault, and not mine, for had you been as I took you for, I made no offence" (4.8.52–54). According to Williams's erroneous supposition and the counterfactual he now asks Henry to accept, the king was not quite the king. Notably, this follows the same logic that allows the king to become his royal self through the power of supposing himself to be that self and of being supposed so.

What especially interests me is that Williams should reject "abuse" as a description of his earlier interaction with Henry, given that, as we have seen, the Chorus has figured drama as a mode of hypothesis that works by digesting the "abuse of distance." To digest the violations of distance is to make it productive or effective by putting it in order (as though through a process of textual digestion such as commonplacing, which ordered diverse textual particulars under selected topics or "places" for a reader's later use).[92] Williams's argument digests his abuse of the king in just the way that the play is said by the Chorus to digest the abuse of distance by folding one place, France, hypothetically into another, the Globe. Like the theater and like England, the king acquires meaning by being in two places at once. And through dramatic hypothesis, the historical stage does the cultural work of relating, and accommodating to one another, those two opposing terms. This is equally so in the case of the distinct territorial jurisdictions (England and France, but also Ireland, classical Rome, Jerusalem) that turn out to be integral to national identity, and, relative to the Crown, in the case of those different *persons* we might describe as the common man who happens to be king and the king who is king.

The ordering of these places that are the king's places or England's places thus describes the mechanics of sovereignty itself, which comes into political existence as an imaginary, projected. In this account of what it means to exercise control over others, the sovereignty that the play thematizes (and which Henry imagines to be coterminous with legal identity) is the effect of a jurisdictional hypothesis that so distributes place as to allow for a functional distinction between places without, however, fixing it. The secret history of jurisdiction is that jurisdictional authority is produced as an ongoing, serial, ad hoc encounter with its own limits, and therefore depends on the virtual projection of its alternatives. For that reason alone, the alternative—France, the unrationalized past living in the present, the local inhabiting the already centralized—must evade, even at the moment of its capture, the kind of indivisible sovereignty that Henry fantasizes as both the source and securing of his political legitimacy. This is to say, too, that in "digestion," the process of orienting matter toward its practical use, Shakespeare invents a figure for what I have called the enactment of identity, the process through which in the plays formal repetition affirms the impossible or unconscious history—the France that is already in England, the conquest that is not only defeat, the self that is here by being elsewhere—as henceforth, and again, the condition of national possibility.

3

Formalization

CHAPTER FIVE

"To Stride a Limit": *Imperium*, Crisis, and Accommodation in Shakespeare's *Cymbeline* and *Pericles*

Part 2 of this book has explored how deeply the manufacture of English legal identity depended on the accommodation of alternative territorial jurisdictions that remained as yet unrationalized at common law. The case studies that make up part 3 treat the consequences of that unrationality or irrationality for the formal configuration of the jurisdictional threshold and of the legal norms that emerge from it. In this chapter, I turn to the first decade of James VI and I's English rule, and to two late plays in which Shakespeare further tested England's relation to the international scene by exploring the fragility of authority or *imperium* across distance. Critics of Shakespeare's tragicomedies—a category including *Pericles*, *Cymbeline*, *The Winter's Tale*, and *The Tempest*—have shown how these plays variously record the cultural impact of the Stuart accession to the English throne, in terms, for example, of the dramatic treatment of the royal family as a newly prominent cultural idea,[1] or in relation to the plays' representation of tyranny as a response to the suddenly more pressing distinction between absolutist and constitutionalist rule under the Stuarts.[2] In sympathy with such work, but adopting a more technical perspective, I approach Shakespeare's tragicomedies as engagements with the idea of jurisdiction at a moment when the category came under new pressure as a consequence of the political union of 1603 and in response to a still evolving construction of *imperium* as a specifically supranational authority.[3] Tracing the ways in which the legal construction of international distance deployed the natural bodies of the monarch and subject, I argue that *Cymbeline* and *Pericles* treat the question of political and legal accommodation as a problem of the

IMPERIUM AS CRISIS AND ACCOMMODATION

Empire in 1603 was a contested term. The first royal proclamation after the accession of James VI of Scotland to the English throne declared him "the onely Soveraigne Lord and King of these Imperiall Crownes." But the proclamation's title refers in the singular to "the Crowne of the Realmes of England, Fraunce and Ireland."[4] A subsequent proclamation of 16 May 1603, "for the uniting of England and Scotland," speaks of the "Imperiall Crowne of England," while that of 20 October 1604, in which James makes known his intention to adopt the style of "king of Great Britain," declares that England and Scotland are now united "under one Imperiall Crowne."[5] Did James possess one imperial crown or two, then, one empire or two? The apparent ambiguity in the idea of empire reflects the constitutional point that Scotland and England, though united after 1603 in the person of the king, remained constitutionally distinct.[6] Most important, it speaks to a productive flexibility in the idea of *imperium* itself, a term that David Armitage has usefully mapped for the early modern period in relation to the original Roman legal category: "The Roman legacy of *imperium* to medieval and early modern Europe was threefold. It denoted independent authority; it described a territorial unit; and it offered an historical foundation for claims to both the authority and the territory ruled by the Roman emperors."[7] First, then, James could claim multiple imperial crowns in the sense that each of his kingdoms was possessed of independent *imperium*, a concept that in England was most famously found in Henry VIII and Cromwell's Act in Restraint of Appeals (1533), which "declared and expressed that this realm of England is an empire."[8] Whatever its polemical force against Rome, this claim was the opposite of novel, since it was a commonplace in England and across Europe to define and defend national sovereignty in the Roman vocabulary of empire: as the dictum had it, *rex in regno suo est imperator*.[9] Second, after 1603 James could (under a single imperial crown) claim *imperium* "in the form of a composite monarchy, linking disparate realms and territories under a single, supreme head."[10] More visibly than in the case of political and jurisdictional independence, this authority related to the *imperium* possessed by those "supranational polities" such as the Holy Roman Empire and the papacy "that claimed both universal authority in the present and descent from the Roman Empire in the past."[11]

As Armitage emphasizes, the two principal meanings of *imperium*, one pointing to national independence and the other to supranational authority, were not necessarily in conflict. A king's claim to independent *imperium* "did not suggest any intention to compete with the emperor or the pope for supremacy."[12] Nevertheless, the polemical force of the claim to independent *imperium* partly resided in the fact that it looked back to Rome just as surely as did the claim to supranational or universal authority. In J. H. Burns's telling formulation, claims to independent *imperium* were "fragmented" versions of Rome's *liberum imperium*, and as such always bore some relation to the idea of a supranational order, particularly as that was embodied by Rome's most visible successor. "Yet *the* Empire was still there," Burns writes, "and, for the jurists who shaped so much of the political discourse of the fifteenth century, that empire still provided the essential context for the deployment and discussion of ideas about political authority."[13] In Spanish discourse, as Anthony Pagden has shown, colonial holdings in the New World were conceived as an analogue to the late Roman empire, not least because the papal bulls from 1493 ratifying Spanish possessions were justified as a donation "analogous with the Donation of Constantine."[14] The ideological force of the imperial comparison was enormous, and Pagden suggests that it explains the stubborn reluctance of Spanish writers well into the seventeenth century to question the Donation of Constantine, "a document which had been shown to be a forgery as early as 1440." For the same reason, he notes as unsurprising that "Philip II should have considered taking the title of 'Emperor of the Indies' to compensate for the loss of the imperial title itself, or that, by the seventeenth century, the king of Castile was being referred to in semi-official publications as the 'Emperor of America.'"[15] Even though, constitutionally, *imperium* transparently identified the jurisdictional independence of the national monarchy, its most potent ideological force resided in the evocation of transnational authority.[16]

In the English context, James's accession to the English throne made the central tension in the concept of *imperium*, as well as the word's complex prestige, newly audible and available for political discourse. Brian Levack notes that James's dual monarchy was "often referred to as an empire," as, for example, in a 1603 panegyric by Jonson and Dekker that distinguishes between kingdom and empire ("And then so rich an Empyre, whose fayre brest / Contaynes foure Kingdomes by your entrance blest") or in a tract on the union by John Thornborough: "many Shires [make] one kingdom, many kingdomes one Imperial Monarchy."[17] As James was to discover in the first years of his reign, empire in the more expansive sense had far less to do with the law, under which England and Scotland would remain constitutionally separate for another hundred years, than with imagination. In the first place, the vocabulary of *imperium* was useful for measuring James's relative prestige both in Europe and in a developing and competitive global mercantilist economy; second, *imperium* would be a kind of shorthand for the tricky project of imagining the relation among James's kingdoms. Here the relation between Scotland and England was paramount. Wales had been integrated into the English constitution; Ireland remained, if uneasily, both colony and dependent kingdom. James's vision of two fully independent kingdoms united under one name was something other, and to realize it James required a supranational *imperium* that would not disturb the independent *imperium* of the constituent states. For English culture after 1603, Scotland embodied the tension between the two complementary aspects of empire that together looked back to the authority of Rome.

As a meditation on Stuart Britain and on the relation between England and Scotland, nation and empire, autonomy and expansion, Shakespeare's *Cymbeline* (ca. 1610) reproduces the tension within early modern *imperium*.[18] In terms of its immediate topical appeal, the play uses the historical question of Britain's jurisdictional independence from the Roman empire in order to interrogate the relationship, internal to James's Britain, between the king's discrete kingdoms and the imperial whole. In its claims to supranational authority, *Cymbeline*'s Rome looks as much like James's Britain as Cymbeline's Britain does. The play presents not one but two versions of the *translatio imperii* that transmitted Roman prestige westward, as well as two ways, correspondingly, of construing royal authority with respect to the subject. The play is structured around a series of doublings: two imperial rulers; two cultural milieus, Augustan Rome and the world of Renaissance merchants; and two plots, a political one taken from Holinshed and a domestic one taken from Boccaccio. Although in tragicomedy, as in tragedy, the familial is always political, *Cymbeline*'s plots are unified not only through analogy between those two spheres, but also through their shared concern with jurisdictional space, as that is produced by the threshold that both creates political conflict and makes political accommodation imaginable. Shakespeare's proposition in *Cymbeline* is that the territorial threshold dividing kingdoms from one another or a kingdom from an empire cannot be understood separately from the temporal limit that divides time into past, present, and future. And the play argues that, if constitutional crisis emerges from a mischaracterization of the spatio-temporal threshold, resolution itself can emerge only when the threshold is acknowledged as itself a constitutive unreality, a productive fiction.

To unfold this thesis, *Cymbeline* moves around two jurisdictional and interpretive crises, one for each of the plots. In the story of Imogen and Posthumus, Iachimo invades Imogen's chamber to counterfeit the evidence of seduction and so win his wager. In the more overtly political story, Rome invades Britain, the two sides having embraced war as a way to decide Britain's constitutional status relative to Rome. The tensions within *imperium* underwrite and even produce both crises. In the debate at Cymbeline's court over Britain's refusal to continue paying tribute to Rome, the king and Caesar's ambassador, Lucius, invoke the two complementary constructions of empire as irreconcilable alternatives, and in this way effectively speak past one another. On the one side, the king argues that Britain is free, possessed of independent *imperium*, and that the tribute demanded by Caesar is groundless at law, an effect merely of violence: "Till the injurious Romans did extort / This tribute from us, we were free. Caesar's ambition / . . . Did put the yoke upon's" (3.1.46–50).[19] To establish his historical claim to "ful jurisdictioune and fre impire within his realm," Cymbeline appeals to two legal precedents, the first from Britain's royal past:[20]

> Our ancestor was that Mulmutius which
> Ordained our laws, whose use the sword of Caesar
> Hath too much mangled, whose repair and franchise
> Shall by the power we hold be our good deed,
> Though Rome be therefore angry.
>
> (3.1.53–57)

Related to this historical precedent for Britain's freedom is the contemporary precedent of two Balkan peoples: "I am perfect," Cymbeline tells Lucius, "That the Pannonians and Dalmatians for / Their liberties are now in arms, a precedent / Which not to read would show the Britons cold" (3.1.71–74). If Britain's jurisdictional independence can be traced back to an ancient legal past, this passage identifies its "liberties" also as a common European legal inheritance and as part of the broader *ius gentium*. As against Cymbeline's double legal argument, Lucius speaks for universal empire, this in terms that precisely deny to Cymbeline and all others the possibility of independent *imperium*: "I am sorry, Cymbeline, / That I am to pronounce Augustus Caesar— / Caesar, that hath more kings his servants than / Thyself domestic officers—thine enemy" (3.1.60–63). That Lucius here *pronounces* Caesar's enmity toward Cymbeline is significant in light of his most forceful declaration of war, a sentence that also defines the mechanics of Augustus's empire: "Let proof speak" (3.1.75). The supranational empire conceives itself as speaking, sustaining itself through the experience of a repeating and thus potentially eternal present. Cymbeline's national sovereignty, in contrast, is imagined through the application of precedent, by *reading* the texts both of its own origins and of comparative politics. As the play figures the two modes of empire or *imperium*, they parallel complementary modes of textual production (writing/speaking) and reception (reading/hearing).[21]

Out of these various oppositions, the play at its conclusion manufactures a political consensus that historically alludes both to the *pax Augusta* and to the diplomatic projects of James I, a king whose motto was *Beati Pacifici*.[22] Answering the play's symbolic configuration of the imperial crisis as an opposition between speech and writing, imperial consensus is described *visually*, with the new peace projected onto the play's final image of "A Roman and a British ensign" waving "Friendly together" (5.4.481–82), as well as the seer's politic reinterpretation of the Roman eagle that "Lessened herself, and in the beams o'th' sun / So vanished; which foreshadowed our princely eagle, / Th'imperial Caesar, should again unite / His favour with the radiant Cymbeline, / Which shines here in the west" (5.4.473–77).[23] This turn from textual to visual representation coincides with the play's representation of political accommodation as something different from one of the two sides simply capitulating to the other. In this regard, what matters most is that each side becomes the spokesman for the position the other has occupied earlier. Thus Lucius's seer gives Cymbeline's empire a kind of precedence when, having the Roman eagle diminish in joining with the sun, he presents a version of the *translatio imperii* in which Britain absorbs and overpowers the universal authority to which it nominally submits.[24] It is similarly important that Cymbeline is the one to substitute a more recent precedent for those he had earlier used against Rome, voluntarily "promising / To pay our *wonted* tribute" (5.4.462–63; emphasis added).

More than the fact that each side thus concedes something to the other, this representation of diplomatic accord underlines the point that crisis and consensus emerge from the same ground and in the same vocabulary, this being a consequence in part of how claims to *imperium* have supported both sides of the debate. Shakespeare has earlier encapsulated this peculiar linguistic drift between the opposing positions when Cloten, asserting national sovereignty, disputes the relevance of Britain's having in the past been conquered by Rome:

"There be many Caesars / Ere such another Julius," he tells Lucius; "Britain's a world / By itself, and we will nothing pay / For wearing our own noses" (3.1.11–14). The whole problem of *imperium* as it dramatically issues in crisis can be put in Cloten's way: Britain may be a world, which is Cymbeline's point, but it is not the world, which is Lucius's. For Cloten not to hear the implication of his own language for his opponent's argument as well as his own means too that he is unable to hear the capacity of such language to negotiate between empire's two meanings and to accommodate empire's apparently incompatible spaces to one another. Having represented *imperium* in terms of distinct, related, and competitive political orders, the play concludes by finding consensus in a language that allows both orders to function separately, within spheres or jurisdictions that need not collapse into one another. For all their differences, Lucius and Cymbeline share the sense that jurisdiction is the starting point for political discourse. As the play describes it, political (as opposed to military) resolution seeks not to undermine the relevant boundaries between imperial powers, but exactly to enforce them by reimagining them in response to the crisis that the boundary itself precipitated.

Shakespeare's second plot, taken from Boccaccio's story about an Italian merchant's wager on the chastity of his wife, similarly exploits the idea of the productive boundary or threshold. No less than in the explicitly political plot, this is a boundary between competing imperial jurisdictions. Since Imogen is everywhere identified with Britain, both symbolically and in her capacity as heir, Posthumus's decision to trust the Roman Iachimo as opposed to his wife, wholly conventional in terms of the gender alliances of romance plots, is also a choice between two imperial cultures.[25] Iachimo's deception and Posthumus's response to it are represented in the same terms that associate British and Roman accounts of empire with writing and speaking, with Posthumus having to choose between Britain's history and the vivid presentism of Rome, which is to say the two textual methods by which *imperium* diversely constitutes itself. Posthumus has the precedent of Imogen's legal vows, her letters, and, most important, the history that has encouraged him to take up Iachimo's challenge in the first place. Overpowering these precedents is the story that Iachimo manufactures for him based on the corporeal signs he has gathered in Imogen's bedchamber:

> Ah, but some natural notes about her body
> Above ten thousand meaner movables
> Would testify t'enrich my inventory. . . .

> A mole cinque-spotted, like the crimson drops
> I'th'bottom of a cowslip. Here's a voucher
> Stronger than ever law could make.
>
> (2.2.28–40)

In response to these signs, which as evidence (and notably as *blazon*) substitute a textual reality for a lived one, Posthumus adopts in relation to Britain the same position that Lucius does. In the letter instructing Pisanio to kill Imogen, Posthumus writes, "I speak not out of weak surmises, but from proof as strong as my grief and as certain as I expect my revenge" (3.4.23–24). Echoed here are both Luciuis's spoken pronouncement and his proof. Simultaneously legal proof and a proof that is nothing more than Posthumus's experience of his self-absorbed grief, it is cognate with Lucius's earlier narrowing of Cymbeline's historical evidence to presentism and force: "Let proof speak" (3.1.75).

Iachimo draws Posthumus away from Britain by speaking in Augustus's way in the sense, also, that the evidence by which he undermines Posthumus's own version of the past works through its irreducible presence. First, it is present physically as the stolen bracelet, the material sign of Posthumus's and Imogen's fidelity. Once stolen, the bracelet enters a different and parodic economy: as a commodity carried by a merchant beyond Britain's borders for the purpose only of undoing Britain's prestige, it reverses the ideals of national mercantilism. Second, Iachimo makes his evidence present to Posthumus in the rhetorical sense of *energeia*, which Aristotle associates in the *Rhetoric* (3.11.1) with speech that brings the thing represented vividly before the hearer's eyes.[26] It is as speech that Iachimo makes Imogen's secret mole persuasive in the case against her. More specifically, his rhetoric makes the signs vivid by drawing Posthumus into the memory of his own desire, his sexual dissatisfaction—Posthumus will lament of his wife that "Me of my lawful pleasure she restrained" (2.4.161)—and his secret distrust of Imogen's virtue:

> If you seek
> For further satisfying, under her breast—
> Worthy the pressing—lies a mole, right proud
> Of that most delicate lodging. By my life,
> I kissed it, and it gave me present hunger
> To feed again, though full. You do remember
> This stain upon her?
>
> (2.4.133–39)

Iachimo's evidence persuades because, as imperial pronouncement, it delivers in speech vivid textual versions of the case—the desire, satisfaction, and the guilt—that it pretends only to be reporting.

THRESHOLD SPACE, THRESHOLD TIME

When Iachimo steals into Imogen's bedchamber to manufacture his case against her (2.2.10–51), his violence differs from Lucius's violence toward Britain in being cowardly subterfuge rather than an open and declared invasion. And yet as violations of British jurisdiction, the two acts are imagined according to remarkably similar topologies. The play represents Iachimo's jurisdictional intrusion by means of the trunk out of which he enters the scene and into which he exits it. The trunk functions in two ways. First, its presence on the stage visually imports Rome and Italy into Britain, thereby representing (and in different terms even effecting) Rome's invasion of Britain, which as public crisis brings Posthumus home only to transform him, in a subjective jurisdictional crisis, into a traitor. The trunk also stands, however, for the kind of resolution that the play ultimately discovers: supposedly containing gifts in silver for the emperor, this room within a room is a powerful symbol of the ultimate absorption of Rome into Britain, as represented by Lucius's seer in the image of the eagle who "Lessened herself, and in the beams o'th'sun / So vanished" (5.4.473–74). Like the categories of empire or jurisdiction themselves, the trunk is doubly the locus, then, of crisis and accommodation. Iachimo supplements this visual argument when, returning into the trunk at the scene's conclusion, he says how eager he now is for morning to come: "To th' trunk again, and shut the spring of it. / Swift, swift, you dragons of the night, that dawning / May bare the raven's eye! I lodge in fear" (2.2.47–49). "Lodge" is an ethical and political term: the trunk houses him, but in fear; alternatively, it is fear itself that houses him. To lodge in fear is to be accommodated, but not quite. Iachimo's trunk thus becomes a parodic symbol of that political accommodation whose structure the play pursues so doggedly. As the instrument that effects the rift between Posthumus and Britain by lodging Iachimo in Imogen's chamber, it is, quite literally, political *accommodation* constituted as crisis rather than resolution.

The trunk is the play's most powerful signifier of outside and inside. As Iachimo's lament suggests by linking jurisdictional space to fear, the trunk invokes the *time* of threshold as well as its space: to lodge in fear is to live antiheroically in relation to time, not so much in the present as in useless orientation to the future. Shakespeare fills in the description of fear's scope in his treatment of Belarius and the king's two sons, who in pastoral Wales live at the limit of Cymbeline's legal jurisdiction. Being outside the law means for them having one of two relationships to time and to heroic virtue (Lat. *virtus*, "power"). Misinterpreting Cloten's appearance as a sign that Cymbeline is pursuing him, Belarius tells the boys that "I fear some ambush. / ... We are held as outlaws" (4.2.67–69). For Belarius, the law is fully constitutive of his family's life, his fear being an expression of that subjection. Guiderius provides a different account of what being outside the law means for time, eschewing his foster father's fear for the practical work of the present:

> The law
> Protects not us, then why should we be tender
> To let an arrogant piece of flesh threat us,
> Play judge and executioner all himself,
> For we do fear the law? What company
> Discover you abroad?
>
> (4.2.126–31)

According to this argument, fear must extend only as far as the law's limits, in the sense, first, that those outside the law's protection are not bound to respect it, to hold it in fear, to tolerate a threat like Cloten's merely because of his law. Second, the law works by instilling a fear of consequences, and thus meets its own limit in its capacity to work, or not, on the subject in that way. Fear, Guiderius argues, pertains to the future, not to the present: Cloten's arrogant threat is real only to the extent that the outlaws, out of fear for what the law might do, grant him as judge a jurisdiction that need not belong to him.

Guiderius again connects time and virtue in response to Belarius's wild imagining that, should the three of them join battle against the Romans, Cymbeline's men "may drive us to a render / Where we have lived, and so extort from's that / Which we have done, whose answer would be death / Drawn on with torture" (4.4.11–14). Guiderius pulls the old man out of these futures back into the radical present: "This is, sir, a doubt / In such a time nothing becoming you / Nor satisfying us" (4.4.14–16). As Guiderius imagines the time of heroism here, his father's doubt "in such a time" is not only unworthy of the old man, but unbecoming, too, in the special sense that it unmakes Belarius by placing him outside the time and present in which, exclusively, becoming happens.

As Guiderius has it, the present only is the place of action and of being. By means of a set of puns involving Iachimo's trunk, Shakespeare grounds this fundamental thesis for the play in a metaphysical account of the temporal threshold. After Iachimo has convinced Imogen to keep safely the plate and jewels intended as a "present for the Emperor," he tells her that he is consigning the trunk in which they are stored "only for this night," since he must leave the following day (1.6.187,198). Imogen protests, but Iachimo replies that the delay caused by coming to see Imogen has already put him behind schedule with respect to the timing of the gift: "I have outstood my time, which is material / To th' tender of our present" (1.6.207-8). The curious "outstood"— the OED gives this passage as the first use of "outstand" in the temporal sense of "stay to or beyond the end of"—works here chiefly through the exclusion of its implied opposite. Iachimo has overstayed his time in the sense that he now stands *outside* it rather than *inside* it; he stands outside his time, therefore, insofar as he no longer inhabits it as an *instant*: he is no longer present to his own present. (In a different register, this is fully cognate with Guiderius's objection to Belarius that, in time, the present rather than the future is what matters, and that to live in the future is not to *be* in time at all.) The second half of the statement Shakespeare gives to Iachimo repeats the first, now in terms reminiscent of Book 11 of the *Confessions*, where Augustine accounts for the present as a threshold that the mind, capable of anticipation and memory, oversees as the limit between past and future, a temporal reality without temporal extension.[27] Shakespeare recasts this philosophical point through two puns on *tender* and *present*. Time, he tells Imogen, "is material / To th' tender of our present," that is, relevant to the offer of the gift. But time is material to the present also in a philosophical sense, since although time comprehends past, present, and future, it subtends only the present. In an Aristotelian metaphysics, matter is the substratum of that which form brings into being; by analogy time is material to "our present" in the sense of materially supporting only the present, since it is only the present that exists at all, the past having ceased to be and the future having not yet come into being. Taking "tender" to mean "tendering," therefore, we can hear that the temporal present is being said to offer something for which time is material. And through a substantive overtone linking "tender" to "tender state" (OED *sb.*[3] B1), the present for that reason itself becomes tender. "Th' tender of our present," that is, expresses with great precision the fragility of the Augustinian instant, the thread that gives us reality and, subtended by time, divides time into its two unreal kingdoms. To outstand time, as Shakespeare's metaphor has it, is to leave the present and instant for a time that, extended into past or future, is only unreal.

Philosophically speaking, the threshold present counts because it alone is real. The whole plot of *Cymbeline* unfolds this insight as a politics of accommodation, according to which the past and future are equally threatening or irrelevant, and the present alone efficacious; and according to which, also, the spatial fiction that is the territorial threshold disappears into its own irreducible substantiality. What, the play asks, is the spatial shape and temporal shape of political crisis and political accommodation? In declaring war over the meaning of a territorial line and the relative importance of past and present for defining a constitutional relationship, Cymbeline and Lucius fix the reality of lines that might, alternatively, function most effectively for peace by remaining undefined. Once crisis has defined the threshold (and made it solid), however, the content of the two sides constituted by that boundary becomes oddly secondary to the threshold reality. This is why the play so insistently locates the possibility of accommodation only in the threshold that has produced the crisis. Politically speaking, the threshold comes to count when jurisdictional crisis has constituted it as the singular reality.

The play analyzes the political efficacy of the threshold for dealing with crisis in terms of lines that limit or divide and lines that connect. In their first appearance in the play, the Welsh outlaws once again lay out the main terms of the argument. Reconfiguring the pastoral *topos* of hill and dale, high and low, Belarius praises the life led away from the world of princes and royal service, in terms of visual perspective:

> Now for our mountain sport. Up to yon hill,
> Your legs are young; I'll tread these flats. Consider,
> When you above perceive me like a crow
> That it is place which lessens and sets off. . . .
> (3.3.10–13)

This is an argument that for Belarius cuts only one way. Turning the father's spatial argument on its head, however, Guiderius points out that only Belarius is able to make the comparison: "Out of your proof you speak. We poor unfledged / Have never winged from view o'th' nest, nor know not / What air's from home" (3.3.27–29). This is to say that Belarius, though speaking from the vantage point of his experience ("proof"), is really speaking from *outside* that experience rather than within it: in praising only the rural, Belarius has stepped outside his experience in the same way that, as an outlaw, he has stepped beyond the law. To be true to the claims of his two lives, the argument goes, Belarius needs to speak from the place where he literally can "view" both.

Guiderius fills in what this means when he concludes his speech by comparing Belarius's "quiet life" (3.3.30) to a prison whose walls are as virtual as they are real: whatever this life is to Belarius, "unto us it is / A cell of ignorance, travelling abed, / A prison for a debtor, that not dares / To stride a limit" (3.3.32–35). If honor or virtue here is a matter of testing the threshold that divides one space from another, the interesting point is that "stride" suggests two relationships to that threshold line. First, Guiderius is insisting that, as opposed to the debtor, he and Arviragus should "step over" (OED *v.*4) the limit, which after all is a kind of fiction that depends for its force on their being afraid of it. (This is the spatial version, then, of his later argument that Cloten's threatening presence is only as real as the outlaws allow it to be.) Second, "stride" hints at the act of walking the limit, in the sense of striding along a line and so measuring it (OED *v.*5). To stride a limit involves daring to test its efficacy in the world, but also to ask after the nature of its extension. The limit is the place and vantage point from which one can see all that the limit divides.

The political meaning of Guiderius's claim is tested and materialized in the battle with the Romans, where victory comes to Cymbeline only when the Welsh outlaws, in stopping the Britons' terrified retreat, teach them a proper relation to the threshold line. "This was strange chance," as a Briton lord puts it, "A narrow lane, an old man, and two boys" (5.3.51–52).[28] With Iachimo's trunk in the domestic plot, the lane is the play's most important symbol for the substantial threshold. "Close by the battle, ditched, and walled with turf" (5.3.14), it is in two ways the extended version of the limit that Guiderius desires "to stride." First, its topography is such as to give "advantage" (5.3.15) to Belarius who *bestrides* the line in order to block it: "Athwart the lane / He with two striplings . . . / Made good the passage" (5.3.18–23). Second, when the Romans are routed and made to return up the "strait pass" they have earlier "damned / With dead men hurt behind" (5.3.11–12), their strides (now *along* the limit) measure their defeat, just as earlier their strides seemed to measure victory:

> forthwith they fly
> Chickens the way which they stooped eagles: slaves,
> The strides they victors made; and now our cowards,
> Like fragments in hard voyages, became
> The life o'th' need. . . .
>
> (5.3.41–45)

In obverse relation to the Romans, the once cowardly Britons here notably *become* their own lives, in the same sense that allowed Guiderius earlier to accuse Belarius of expressing an unbecoming doubt, a doubt that, by forfeiting the present, negates the possibility of being.

The space of the lane thus offers the Britons victory also as a temporal threshold, an answer to Belarius's way of being in time or, equally, to Iachimo's when he tells Imogen he has "outstood" his time in Britain. The lane narrows time to the present or instant, the time of heroism or cowardice. Indeed, *stand* is the word that both wins the day and emblematizes the mechanics of the productive threshold. Repeated ten times in Shakespeare's doubled presentation of the battle as staged action (5.2.11–18) and as Posthumus's report of that action (5.3.1–63), the Britons' courageous "stand" geometrically opposes their earlier and cowardly "lengthened shame" (5.3.13), "stand" being a *point* that is at once spatial, temporal, and ethical. Those layers coincide in Belarius's threat to the retreating Britons: "Stand, / Or we are Romans, and will give you that / Like beasts which you shun beastly . . . / Stand, stand" (5.3.25–27).[29] Emphasizing the efficacy of the word in relation to place, Posthumus insists that it is "With this word, 'Stand, stand,' / Accommodated by the place, more charming / With their own nobleness" that the trio successfully won the soldiers back (5.3.31–33). Just as Iachimo's trunk unheroically lodges him in fear, here the threshold limit—the extended lane and the narrowed instant—accommodates the heroes, and in so doing returns those who through fear had "turned coward" (5.3.35) to their proper place and time and virtue.

Recalling how the anonymous lord describes this moment—"This was strange chance: / A narrow lane, an old man, and two boys" (5.3.51–52)—we can see that Shakespeare further elaborates the metaphysics of the temporal and spatial threshold that is the play's major theme by connecting it to the distinction between native and foreign. In a play so concerned with representing the political alien, why might chance, too, be called strange? Once "banished" from Britain (1.1.8) and so placed, like the Welsh outlaws, beyond its laws, Posthumus can in Italy be only "stranger" (1.4.27). In Britain, conversely, it is Iachimo who is foreign, a status Shakespeare puts under comic pressure in the scene in which Cloten learns of the merchant's presence at court:

First Lord:	Did you hear of a stranger that's come to court tonight?
Cloten:	A stranger, and I not know on't?
Second Lord (aside):	He's a strange fellow himself and knows it not.
	(2.1.30–34)

The pun links Iachimo's foreignness to Cloten's comic lack of self-knowledge concerning his own strangeness or unaccountability. Shakespeare again tests the word's two meanings against each other when Belarius declares that he does not know what Cloten's presence at the imperial margin means for the outlaws: "Yet still it's strange / What Cloten's being here to us portends, / Or what his death will bring us" (4.2.182–84). If Cloten is strange because he is in some way alien to himself, here Cloten's presence is strange for being as yet unreadable, strange because its significance really belongs to the future but already, weirdly, inhabits the present. In this context, the anonymous lord's "strange chance" takes on a highly charged meaning as a description of the British victory in and on the lane. Politically, a stranger is not merely an outsider, but an outsider who for the moment finds himself or herself inside. By analogy to that spatialized category, chance is temporally strange. When Lucius insists to Cymbeline that Britain won through "chance of war. The day / Was yours by accident" (5.4.75–76), his formulation works by compressing the whole day into that fall and instant; the seer will similarly speak of the "stroke / Of this yet scarce cold battle" (5.4.469–70). Chance or accident is strange because it compacts temporal extension into an instant, making time foreign to itself by bringing an extraneous future into the radicalized present, as something that is there without fully belonging.

Chance or "hazard" (4.4.46) opens the way to accommodation because it reconfigures the threshold that issued in crisis. Time can heal, however, only as extension, not as threshold. This is why at the play's conclusion Cymbeline casts peace not as an event in the present, but as a state that joins the present and future, going forward as act, promise, and memory:

> My peace we will begin; and Caius Lucius,
> Although the victor, we submit to Caesar
> And to the Roman empire, promising
> To pay our wonted tribute....
>
> (5.4.460–63)

We can note how as diplomatic speech, political accommodation here answers an earlier moment that similarly linked the past, present, and future, but which there marked political crisis. After Lucius has declared war on behalf of Caesar, and pronounced Caesar Cymbeline's "enemy" (3.1.63), the British king responds in language that, though fastidiously diplomatic, seems also curiously generous: "I know your master's pleasure, and he mine. / All the remain is, 'Welcome'" (3.1.83–84). The welcome, which as "well come" is a declaration about the immediate past, *remains* because it has yet to be said, and only enters the present (at the precise moment of "is") when Cymbeline utters it. In this mixing of temporalities, Cymbeline's gesture recasts the clumsier and more explicitly threatening charge to Lucius that Cloten has just spoken: "His majesty bids you welcome. Make pastime with us a day or two longer. If you seek us afterwards in other terms, you shall find us in our salt-water girdle" (3.1.76–78). The temporal joke here is that Cloten's welcome (issued under the dominant sign of his threatening "afterwards") would have Lucius in the future make a present time into *past* time. While these welcomes emblematize the compression of time into crisis, Cymbeline's declaration of peace at the end of the play designates it as something that has a beginning, thereby folding the radicalized present back into an extended temporality and continuous time.

ROBERT CALVIN AND THE LIGAMENTS OF EMPIRE

To extend *Cymbeline*'s analysis of jurisdiction as a threshold that crisis makes substantial, and from which accommodation and resolution must issue, Shakespeare looks to the category of allegiance as that which connects persons across jurisdictional distance. If, with respect to a threshold reality, the play asks what allows for continuity and what threatens it, this is also to ask, in a different register, after the nature of constancy. I mean constancy in the ethical sense that Cymbeline's queen has in mind when she angrily identifies Pisanio as "thou that stand'st so for Posthumus" (3.5.56). In the context of the play's usage elsewhere, "stand" here figures Pisanio's continued allegiance to his exiled master as both a temporal and spatial state of being. And as the queen points out when trying to tempt Pisanio to betray his master, that places his allegiance in an apparently antagonistic relation to his master's status in exile:

> Return he cannot, nor
> Continue where he is. To shift his being
> Is to exchange one misery with another,
> And every day that comes comes to decay
> A day's work in him. What shalt thou expect
> To be depender on a thing that leans,
> Who cannot be new built nor has no friends
> So much as but to prop him.
>
> (1.5.53–60)

The question the play raises through Posthumus's exile is whether allegiance and fidelity can transcend distance. Does the servant remain bound to the master across distance? More centrally, how does Posthumus remain bound to Imogen as husband and subject once he leaves the kingdom with which she is identified? In terms of the queen's rebuke to Pisanio, is the exiled Posthumus a leaning house or, just possibly, a leaning compass?[30] Thus the story of Posthumus's exile and its impact on him and on those who remain at home relocates the imperial threshold in those structures that bind across distance or fail so to do. This is an *imperium* constituted not just by the line dividing kingdom from empire but also by the lines through which autonomous *imperium* is transformed and extended into its transnational counterpart.

As the warp and weft of empire, these two lines came together around the legal issue of the union of Scotland with England, specifically in the case of the *Post-Nati (Calvin's Case)*, a land case brought forward in 1608 and decided in the Exchequer Chamber before an assembly of all the high court judges. In this test case engineered by the Crown, it was resolved that those of James's Scottish subjects born after his accession to the English throne were born also within the allegiance of the king of England, and were thus capable of inheriting land there. In an important reading of *Cymbeline*'s self-conscious topicality in relation to the politics of Union, Leah Marcus links Posthumus Leonatus through his name with the Scots and specifically the *post-natus* of 1608, arguing that his "beleaguered marriage" and exile figure James's "faltering national union."[31] Extending her account of the case's importance for *Cymbeline*, I shall look at the arguments underpinning the decision, in order to show how, by casting the problem of *imperium* in terms of the conjunction of a temporal and a territorial threshold, they produced, like the play, a model of political continuity grounded in ethical constancy.

The *post-nati* at the center of the case were those born in Scotland after the accession of James to the English throne. As Sir Edward Coke formulates it in the seventh part of his *Reports*, the "question of this case as to matter in law was, whether Robert Calvin the plaintiff, being born in Scotland since the crown of England descended to his majesty, be an alien born, and consequently disabled to bring any real or personal action for any lands within the realm of England."[32] The judges' decision for the plaintiff (and the Crown) allowed James to achieve judicially some of what he had aimed at through a full constitutional union of the two kingdoms, a project the Commons had failed to ratify in 1607. Since an alien was defined as one "born out of the ligeance of the king, and under the ligeance of another," the critical question was whether after 1603 James was, with respect to the allegiance owed him, one king or two.³³ As Sir Edwin Sandys put it at the Great Conference on Union held between the two houses of Parliament on 25 and 26 February 1607, did "subjection to one king make all the people born within the places of that subjection to be naturalized over all places of that king's subjection"?³⁴ In that the crowns of Scotland and England remained legally distinct and yet united in the single person of the king, how was the relation between allegiance and law to be construed? Arguing for the plaintiff, Francis Bacon noted for the court that "the depth of this question" was "whether this privilege and benefit of naturalization be an accessary or dependency upon that which is one and joint, or upon that which is several."³⁵

The first thing to note here is that, although the implications of the legal decision in *Calvin's Case* were allowed in Scotland, there was never a reciprocal case argued there explicitly to guarantee the rights of the English *post-nati* in Scotland. At a practical level, the reason was that the urgency of the question was felt much more in one direction than the other. In terms of legal theory, moreover, the Scots would have had *ab initio* less difficulty in imagining the claim of the English *post-natus* than did the English common law in relation to the Scottish *post-natus*. On the one hand, insofar as Scottish custom construed dominion less in terms of physical territory than in deep relation to the king's power as *dominus*, a change in the extent of the king's dominion would seem logically to pull along, as it were, the subjects in all territories pertaining to him.³⁶ At common law, on the other hand, in which the kingdom was imagined so powerfully as territory, the spatial limit between kingdoms was necessarily more critical for the constitutional account of allegiance after Union.

As in *Cymbeline*, the legal case revolved around two distinct threshold realities. So Bacon opened his speech on behalf of the plaintiff by pointing to the case's singular importance whether measured by "place, that reacheth not only to the realm of England, but to the whole island of Great Britain" or by "time, that extendeth not only to the present time, but much more to future generations."³⁷ In relation to the first, Lord Chancellor Ellesmere eloquently argued for the impossibility of dividing allegiance into two, by reflecting on the territorial limit as a fictive legal reality that should not be construed as being more real than the king:

> Nay shortly, Can any man bee a true subject to king James as king of England, and a traitor or rebel to king James as king of Scotland? Shall a foote breadth, or an inch breadth of ground make a difference of birth-right of subjects borne under one kinge? Nay, where there are not any

certen bounds or limits knowne at all, but an imaginary partition wall, by a conceipted fiction in Lawe? It is enough to propound these and such like Questions, whereof many more might bee remembred: they carry a sufficient and plaine answere in themselves: *Magis docet qui prudenter interrogat* [He teaches more who asks questions intelligently].[38]

Second, as the name *post-natus* suggests, the legal consideration of Union involved not only this line between Scotland and England, but also the further threshold that divided James's subjects into the two temporal domains of before and after. Because the two parties came to issue on the status only of the *post-natus*, it is unsurprising that the court attended principally to the relation of sovereign authority and subjection to the jurisdictional and territorial threshold between James's distinct kingdoms. That said, I will argue that where the temporal limit was theorized in relation to the distinction between the *ante-* and *post-natus*, the lawyers and judges confronted an irrationality or gap in their reasoning, without fully resolving it.

To reach the conclusion that allegiance does not follow national contingencies, the court defined it as variously belonging to nature. At the Conference in 1607, the attending judges laid out the legal infrastructure according to which allegiance and laws could be detached from one another. Allegiance, for example, was said to be "before laws," since "if a heap of people meet together so near, that they appoint a king, there allegiance is before they have laws proclaimed or prescribed."[39] This was Bacon's argument, too, that natural law is prior to human, and that, by analogy with the natural and "original" submission to a father's authority, the operation of human law could not "evacuate or frustrate" the claim exerted by allegiance on those it bound.[40] Similarly, allegiance was said to be "after laws" in the sense that it does not change as laws change, such that if "the king be expelled by force and another usurps, yet the allegiance is not taken away, though the law be taken away."[41] This same reason underlay the court's logical but astonishing resolution that those born under "one natural obedience" as natural subjects of the two kingdoms would retain their status in the event that the two kingdoms should, according to the laws of descent, be divided again by a failure of James's line, "for that naturalization due and vested by birth-right, cannot by any separation of the crowns afterward be taken away."[42] Allegiance was furthermore said to extend beyond law, since "[i]f the king go out of England with a company of his servants, allegiance remaineth amongst his subjects and servants, although he be out of his own realm, whereto his laws are confined"; similarly, it "extends as far as defence, which is beyond the circuit of laws."[43]

The most important among these positions was that "allegiance followeth the natural person, not the politick."[44] This was powerfully argued in terms of the "connexion" constituted by a subject's implicit or explicit oath of allegiance in exchange for the king's oath of protection. In Coke's formulation, allegiance was the ligament that connected minds or souls to one another, a *"vinculum fidei,"* a *"ligamentum, quasi ligatio mentium"*: "As the ligatures or strings do knit together the joints of all the parts of the body, so doth ligeance join together the sovereign and all his subjects, *quasi uno ligamine* . . . for as the subject oweth to the king his true and faithful ligeance and obedience, so the sovereign is to govern and protect his subjects . . . so as between the sovereign and subject there is *'duplex et reciprocum ligamen.'*"[45] Allegiance is the connection between minds as that also binds together the state's body. But as it emerges here, this latter body is something other than a body politic, since it is a body made up of radically personalized bodies bound to one another through allegiance.[46] For the connection constituted by the reciprocal oaths could exist only between natural bodies, as Ellesmere argued in relation to the subject: "This bond of Allegeance whereof we dispute, is *Vinculum fidei*; it bindeth the soule and conscience of every subject, severally and respectively, to bee faithfull and obedient to the King. And as a Soule or Conscience cannot be framed by Policie; so Faith and Allegeance can not be framed by Policie, nor put into a politike body. An oathe must be sworne by a naturall bodie; homage and fealtie must bee done by a naturall bodie; a politike body cannot doe it."[47] In relation to the relative claims of the king's distinct laws and his single person, the important point here is that the subject's natural body can be in relation only to the king's natural body, which alone is capable of receiving the oath of allegiance and offering the oath of protection. The governing distinction at issue—between James's diverse kingdoms and the single person in whom their crowns were united—was recast in terms of the distinction between the king's two bodies.[48]

Bacon invoked that theory to answer an objection raised first in the 1607 Conference, and then by the respondents in the case of 1608. According to the civil-law rule of *duo jura* concerning the relationship between person and office, it was argued, the allegiances to James as king of Scotland and as king of England were to be treated as distinct: "when two rights do meet in one person, there is no confusion of them, but they remain still in the eye of law distinct, as if they were in several persons [*cum duo jura concurrunt in una persona aequum est ac si essent in diversis*]."[49] Repeating what the judges had said informally in 1607, Bacon claimed that however valid this was as a rule not only of the civil law but also of "common reason," it faltered where the mortal body somehow affected the nature of the artificial one, that is, "in cases where there is any vigour or operation of the natural person." Although in corporations generally, "the natural body is but *suffulcimentum corporis corporati*, it is but as a stock to uphold and bear out the corporate body," this was profoundly not true for the Crown, in that between the king's natural and artificial bodies there was a "mutual and reciprocal intercourse . . . that these bodies have the one upon the other."[50] Most familiar is the impact of the politic body on the natural, such that, for example, the former "induceth the natural person of the king with these perfections: that the king in law shall never be said to be within age; that his blood shall never be corrupted; . . . that his body in law shall be said to be as it were immortal; for there is no death of the king in law, but a demise as it is termed."[51] As raised in *Calvin's Case*, however, the question involved the obscurer impact of the natural body on the politic: "But on the contrary part let us see what operations the king's natural person hath upon his crown and body politic."[52] The "dignity of the natural person of the king" operated, for example, to cause "the crown to go by descent, which is a thing strange, and contrary to the course of all other corporations." Similarly the king's natural body enabled the law to say "it is treason to compass the death of the queen or of the prince," even though "[t]here is no part of the body politic of the crown in either of them," the categories of wife and son being "*nomina naturae.*"[53] The king's mortal body here assumes political importance in opposition to the corporate body. Because the natural body not only supported a legally effective corporate identity, but also was itself legally efficacious, Bacon and the judges avoided the implications of *duo jura*, a rule grounded in the absolute distinction between person and office.

One of the most interesting ways in which the court described the nature of the ligament or string connecting king and subject was by analogy to the family, which in Coke's report comes powerfully to stand for the inviolable relation between noncorporate bodies that are naturally bound to one another. Having shown that allegiance is due the king by the law of nature, Coke is concerned to show why "*jura naturalia sunt immutabilia*," unaffected by local or municipal law, and thus why allegiance to a natural person extends beyond even national boundaries.[54] He argues that the bond of allegiance is inviolable in ways analogous to the familial bond. If a man is outlawed, for example, the king will have his property, including all wardships, except where the ward is the outlaw's own son or daughter, "for nature hath annexed it to the person of the father," a status in nature that the law cannot take away.

Similar priority is given at law to the natural bond between husband and wife:

> Now if he, that is attainted of treason or felony, be slain by one that hath no authority . . . in this case his eldest son can have no appeal, for he must bring his appeal as heir, which being *ex provisione hominis*, he loseth it by the attainder of his father; but his wife, if any he have, shall have an appeal because she is to have her appeal as wife, which she remaineth notwithstanding the attainder, because *"maris et foeminae conjunctio"* is *"de jure naturae."* . . . So if there be a mother and daughter, and the daughter is attainted of felony, now cannot she be heir to her mother for the cause aforesaid; yet after her attainder, if she kill her mother, this is parricide and petit treason; for yet she remaineth her daughter, for that is of nature.[55]

The distinction between the legal categories (ward, heir, outlaw) and the natural ones (son, wife, daughter) is interesting in light of a play like *Cymbeline* that, at the level of plot, so carefully weaves together familial and political allegiance. In the legal discourse as reported by Coke, we see the court appealing to the family in order to ground (from natural law, but for common law) the legal principle and political argument about allegiance that, in reverse order, the play encodes in its representation of Posthumus's unsettled relation to the royal family.

To return briefly here to Shakespeare, *Cymbeline*'s analysis of the threshold reality responds to the theoretical problem posed by the territorial threshold that legally separated James's imperial kingdoms by measuring its impact on political subjectivity. The judges' description of allegiance as the reciprocal *ligamen* connecting minds and bodies powerfully resonates with *Cymbeline*'s account of Posthumus's exile. Posthumus's physical departure from England is the subject of an exchange between Imogen and Pisanio. When he tells her that his master remained on deck "so long / As he could make me with this eye or ear / Distinguish him from others" (1.3.8–10), the play is inviting the audience to speculate on whether Posthumus will or can remain distinctly himself in his new surroundings. Imogen also raises this question when she worries lest the "shes of Italy should . . . betray / Mine interest and his honour" (1.3.30–31). Given the play's conflation of Imogen and Britain, and its description of Posthumus in relation to her royal status, Posthumus and Imogen are both implying the territorial question asked in *Calvin's Case*: does allegiance trump distance or distance, allegiance? If Posthumus should remain loyal, it will be, as Pisanio says, through his soul remaining linked to Britain in a way that transcends physical distance: "how slow his soul sailed on, / How swift his ship" (1.3.13–14).

Most remarkably, the play casts this representation of allegiance in terms of perspectival distance. In response to Pisanio, Imogen provides a visual emblem of the force binding her husband to her, figuring his departure in terms of the lines that represent and compress depth onto a plane. She imagines herself on England's shore:

> I would have broke mine eye-strings, cracked them, but
> To look upon him till the diminution
> Of space had pointed him sharp as my needle;
> Nay, followed him till he had melted from
> The smallness of a gnat to air, and then
> Have turned mine eye and wept.
>
> (1.3.17–22)

Imogen's imagery links the lovers through lines that have their source in her eyes and meet in Posthumus's body. Taken together, Pisanio's and Imogen's images figure the plot in terms of a limit that mirrors the shore as threshold: will the fragile line connecting the two bodies even to the sharp point of diminution and disappearance be sustained across distance, or must it crack, too, like Imogen's "eye-strings"? These strings are the ocular muscles that "crack" under severe strain, but they are also the strings or lines of connection, which threaten to break at the moment the viewed object melts "to air." The visual mechanics here, which repeat the scene's ethical argument, answer the *ligatio mentium*, the ligatures and strings of allegiance, as the structure that may or may not adequately bind persons across distance. In the image of persons bound to one another, *Cymbeline* is here capturing not just the problem of uniting James's kingdoms, but also the fragility of the legal forms that in 1608 subtended that imperial vision of Britain.

The argument that allegiance trumps law applied only to the *post-natus* and not the *ante-natus*, the subject born under allegiance to James at the time he was king of Scotland only. Certainly, political reasons underlay the decision to try the case in the form in which it was brought forward, since the English feared the possibility of Scottish interference in the economy, and may have been chiefly concerned with the generation of Scots that accompanied James to London. As a case involving a three-year-old, *Calvin's Case* would have seemed less immediately threatening. In the view of Sir Edwin Sandys, however, who spoke in Parliament against the legal claims of the *post-nati*, the distinction between the *ante-* and *post-nati* was theoretical nonsense: "for the subjection is now all one. Therefore, the law that should make a difference is not reasonable; and because the law is confessed to be, that those before born be not naturalized, therefore the law must also be, if it retain the same reason, that those born after are not naturalized."[56] Sandys's syllogism might, of course, have worked in reverse, applying the fact that the *post-nati* were naturalized in England to derive the conclusion that the *ante-nati* were, as well. In the event, another logic than his was followed.

As the judges ruled the matter, the temporal threshold was as essential to the shape of a given person's political subjectivity as the spatial one. Coke reports as the court's decision that there are three "incidents" that make for a subject born: first, that "the parents be under the actual obedience to the king"; second, that "the place of his birth be within the king's dominion"; third, that the "time of his birth is chiefly to be considered; for he cannot be a subject born of one kingdom that was born under the ligeance of a king of another kingdom, albeit afterwards one kingdom descend to the king of the other."[57] Clarifying the reason underlying this last point, Coke adds that time is "of the essence of a subject born; for he cannot be a subject to the king of England, unless at the time of his birth he was under the ligeance and obedience of the king. And that is the reason that Antenati in Scotland (for that at the time of their birth they were under the ligeance and obedience of another king) are aliens born, in respect of the time of their birth."[58] Underlying this near tautology is the double claim that political subjectivity is possible only as allegiance to some king, and that natural allegiance must remain always singular, it being impossible to be born under the allegiance of more than one king. The allegiance of a Scot born during Elizabeth's reign was not transferable to the new English king, because natural allegiance, fixed at birth, neither shrinks nor grows in response to the accidents of time. Thus, where Ellesmere invokes the inscrutable limit between jurisdictional territories to argue for the absurdity of dividing the king's allegiance against itself, Bacon looks to the equally radical *instant* as the threshold that binds the law by producing a distinction that goes beyond law: since the "law looketh not back: and therefore cannot, by any matter *ex post facto*, after birth, alter the state of the birth," the law may privilege only "those which drew their first-breath under the obeisance of the king of England."[59]

Whatever the apparent logic of these arguments regarding the *ante-nati*, they are not fully compatible with the arguments concerning the *post-nati*. With respect to the latter, the court ruled that allegiance is due by natural law to the king in his natural capacity and not to the king in his political capacity: those born into the allegiance of James of Scotland at the time he was king of England were thus born subjects also in England. With respect to the former, the court ruled that descent of the English Crown to James could not make the *ante-natus* "subject to that crown to which he was alien at the time of his birth," which is to say that the king's natural capacity was circumscribed by his political capacity.[60] It is not incidental, then, that here the language of subjection turns from the person of the king to the Crown. That turn makes visible a certain irregularity in the court's metaphysics. Insofar as those born on both sides of 1603 continued equally to owe allegiance only to one sovereign, why in the case of the *ante-natus* should allegiance due the king in his natural capacity be trumped by the legal or political capacity? Why, in other words, was the question put in terms of the *ante-natus*'s subjection and allegiance to the political Crown, when that construction of allegiance had to be purged from the account of the *post-natus* in order for the court to resolve the case in Calvin's favor?[61] The terms in which the 1608 case was brought forward obscured this fundamental gap in the court's treatment of the relative efficacy of natural and legal categories in relation, respectively, to the territorial and temporal thresholds. To put the anomaly in terms of the king's body, the court's account of the *ante-natus* in the context of its main decision regarding the *post-natus* meant this: the natural body that trumped the *territorial* threshold between kingdoms was itself trumped by the *temporal* threshold that, in time, divided the natural from the natural-political.

This is significant for *Cymbeline* because of the play's construction of royal subjectivity in terms of the temporality of the heir, that is, the heir's relation to the threshold moment that separates a natural from a political identity. The play insistently conflates the national and personal in the figures of Imogen and, as the final scene unfolds, of Guiderius, too. Importantly, the heir is constitutive of kingship itself. In chapter 19 of his *Leviathan* (1651), Thomas Hobbes gives classic formulation to the paradoxical situation in which the child thus creates the father, saying that there can be "no perfect forme of Government, where the disposing of the Succession is not in the present Soveraign."[62] In Hobbes's account of elective kingship, the general implications of this become clear, since if the elective king "have Right to appoint his Successor, he is no more Elective, but Hereditary. But if he have no Power to elect his Successor, then there is some other Man, or Assembly known, which after his decease may elect a new. . . . If it be known who have the power to give the Soveraigntie after his death, it is known also that the soveraigntie was in them before."[63] In *Cymbeline*'s representations there is the similar argument that the heir is a future absorbed into the present and that sovereignty, as a promise of continuity across time, must therefore reside in the capacity to make one's heir. This is one reason why Cymbeline is so threatened by his failure to control Imogen's marriage. It also underwrites Cloten's comment to Imogen that her marriage is no contract at all, since she and Posthumus lack the capacity, without her father's permission, to "knit their souls" (2.3.114) as others do: "Yet you are curbed from that enlargement by / The consequence o'th' crown" (2.3.117–18). Here space and time intersect in the same way as in *Calvin's Case*, with a temporality of kingship (the "consequence") undoing the natural body's capacity for the "enlargement" effected by the strings that "knit" souls together in the "self-figured knot" of reciprocal fidelities (2.3.116).

When resolution comes, it is through the operation of time, which by revealing Guiderius's and Arviragus's true identities gives Cymbeline a new heir and thereby saves Imogen's marriage from the gap between the space of "enlargement" and the time of "consequence," a gap that makes the marriage valid and yet illicit. When she is disguised as Fidele, Imogen experiences life with her friends as the fantasy of brotherhood that the play ultimately delivers: "Would it had been so that they / Had been my father's sons, then had my price / Been less, and so more equal ballasting / To thee, Posthumus" (3.6.73–76). Here is the promise of accommodating souls to one another by erasing political capacity and returning the natural person to herself.

In his restless analysis of how *imperium* brings identity and subjectivity under pressure, Shakespeare also represents the contrary process: as opposed to Imogen, who only thinks she is heir, Guiderius is heir without knowing it. And in a remarkable passage that, once again, makes Guiderius the unknowing voice of the play's most sophisticated language, Shakespeare describes this second way of being in the world by asking what it is for a natural body to be in waiting for a political capacity. After decapitating Cloten, Guiderius shows the foolish prince's head to his family. Belarius reacts in terror:

> *Belarius:* What hast thou done?
> *Guiderius:* I am perfect what: cut off one Cloten's head,
> Son to the Queen, after his own report,
> Who called me traitor, mountaineer. . . .
> (4.2.118–21)

"I am perfect what." Guiderius speaks more truly than he realizes. Perfectly certain what he has done, he *is* also "perfect what," perfectly a particular in waiting for the shape of its own definition, which, as it turns out, will arrive only at the threshold moment of the king his father's death. To be "perfect what" is to be a *quodlibet*, and to occupy what Giorgio Agamben calls a "whatsoever" reality, a space of particularity that through the lack of its own specificity holds the general within it as the negative space of potentiality.[64] Guiderius is royal identity caught by a temporality that continues to keep the political form separate from the natural body. If as imputed sovereign and *post-natus*, Imogen and Posthumus figure the relation across jurisdictional distance between those bodies knit together by the ligaments of empire, Guiderius grounds the play's description of the *ante-natus*, not because Guiderius allegorizes the *ante-natus*, but because as heir he gestures toward the *sovereign*'s natural body in relation to the *ante-natus*: a sovereign body that, perfectly itself and perfectly singular, is at the same time politically unformed and undifferentiated, held by time toward the threshold instant of its fulfillment.

MARKET PLACES

In her account of *Cymbeline* in relation to the world of the *Aeneid*, Heather James has noted the anachronistic mixing of Augustan Roman and Boccaccio's Italian merchant milieus as one of the play's most striking features.[65] Similarly, Patricia Parker argues that, in the final scene, Iachimo's submission to Posthumus necessarily complicates the politics of Cymbeline's submission to Augustus, especially since Iachimo is so closely associated with a post-Roman Italian culture essentially contemporary with that of Jacobean England.[66] In the context of the play's fascination with the limits that dynamically structure political encounter, this mixing of time and genre comes more sharply into focus. Boccaccio's characters inform the dynamics of the play, not simply as figures anachronistic to the classical context, but also as merchants. In Boccaccio's original story, trade is the narrative strategy through which the distances dictated by the romance plot can be crossed, so as to allow for narrative resolution in the form of long-separated characters being reunited. Focusing as it does on the question of Posthumus's allegiance to a highly personalized royal authority, *Cymbeline* carries the traces of Boccaccio's merchant narrative. As a traveler in foreign parts, a subject who must be both subject and no subject, the early modern merchant, like Posthumus, functioned imaginatively to extend the sovereign's *imperium*. This was necessarily provisional. As J. G. A. Pocock notes, empire in opposition to *regnum* was throughout the period "a term which tended to move towards lower levels of organization," to looser forms of political control.[67] As we have been seeing, this was so in part because early British empire had less to do with territory than with the unquantifiable lines connecting prince and subject: like the gullible Posthumus and like the *post-natus*, the merchant was the too-weak instrument for the extension of the royal body across distance.

Even more powerfully than in *Calvin's Case*, allegiance across national boundaries was at issue in the 1606 case of Impositions (*Bate's Case*), which Constance Jordan has usefully linked to *Cymbeline* in terms of the relation of the prerogative to the dangerously unstable operation of conscience.[68] My interest is in its delineation of an imperial subjectivity split within itself. In the case, James sought legal justification for imposing duties beyond the traditional poundage on goods imported into the realm through his royal ports. The question was whether the royal prerogative gave the king the right to impose on currants imported from Venice an extra "5 *s*. a hundred for impost," over and above the poundage imposed by statute.[69] John Bate's overriding argument, repeated in the 1610 parliamentary debates over new impositions, was that the common law prevented a subject from being taxed without consent of Parliament. "[F]or if there be a right in the king to alter the property of that which is ours without our consent," one member of Parliament in 1610 declared, "we are but tenants at his will of that which we have."[70]

Even though some of the presiding judges in *Bate's Case* expressed astonishment that "any subjects would contend with the king, in this high point of prerogative," they did not argue that that the king's prerogative was in fact above the common law.[71] As Glenn Burgess has stressed, the question was formulated instead as a matter of jurisdiction: "The king's right to impose customs duties was a matter of *absolute* prerogative, not because this gave the king rights over or against common law, but because it gave him rights outside it."[72] This argument depended on being able to construe the relationship between Bate and the king in such a way that it fell outside the common law. Representing the Crown in the 1610 debates, Francis Bacon thus made a distinction between two kinds of duty: "the question is *de portorio*, and not *de tributo*, to use the Roman words for explanation sake; it is not, I say, touching any taxes within the land, but of payments at the ports ... where *claves regni*, the keys of the kingdom, are turned to let in from foreign parts, or to send forth to foreign parts; in a word, matter of commerce and intercourse, not simply of carriage or vecture."[73] In another formulation he declared that "the reason for the imposition is whatsoever concerne the government of the kingdome as it hath relation to forrayne parts."[74] One way in which the case could be turned toward foreign parts and thus toward the prerogative was by thinking of the law *de rebus*, rather than *de personis*. Chief Baron Fleming's judgment is explicit on this: "That the king may impose upon a subject, I omit; for it is not here the question, if the king may impose upon the subject or his goods; but the impost here is not upon a subject, but here it is upon Bates, as upon a merchant, who imports goods within this land... and at the time when the impost was imposed upon them, they were the goods of the Venetians, and not the goods of a subject, nor within the land."[75] Fleming sets out, in relation to two kinds of threshold, two ways in which the imposition does not involve a subject's property. First, until the duty is paid, the currants that Bate bought remain foreign, the property of the Venetians. Second, and more remarkably, Bate the subject is divided in himself from Bate the merchant.

Fleming's distinction between Bate and Bate, not dissimilar to that drawn in *Calvin's Case* between, for example, a natural son and a legal heir, is the more striking in that an alternative interpretation runs through the judges' statements. Under the hypothesis that the currants did belong to the subject Bate and were a subject's property at the time of imposition, the judges made the case follow the prerogative, rather than the common law, by figuring Bate as subject only in a circumscribed way, bound in this instance exclusively to the king's person. Justice Clark draws a distinction between the case at hand and a possible precedent involving a patent for playing cards: "And for the case of Darcy, for the monopoly of cards, it is not like; for that is of a commoditie within the land, and betwixt the patentee and the king, and not between the king and the subject."[76] The distinction here is between personal and legal capacities. A patentee is bound to the king in a legal relationship, as though between offices. But like Robert Calvin, so Clark's argument goes, John Bate is bound to the king in a personal subjection, and not according to an artificial construct such as the patent connecting grantor and patentee (or, to invoke *Calvin's Case*, a political relationship involving the king as king of England).

Relevant here is Clark's earlier allusion to the "recompense and valuable satisfaction" which the merchant receives in return for the payment of duties: "for he hath the king's protection within his ports, and his safe conduct upon the land, and his defence upon the sea."[77] Fleming expands the latter point: the king "is also to defend the merchants from pirates at sea in their passage. Also by the power of the king they are to be relieved, if they are oppressed by forraign princes, for they shall have his treaty, and embassage."[78] Subject or no subject, then, there is a payment owed the king that, according to the operation of the reciprocal oaths of allegiance and protection, remains outside the strict scope of common law, yet within the king's jurisdiction. In 1610 Yelverton makes explicit the nature of the merchant's relation to the common law: "Wee are where the common lawe cannot judge. The merchant... is not under the protection of the lawe, thoe under the protection of the King.... He is under the jurisdiction of the King by the lawe of nations.... The King [is the] onely lord of the sea."[79] When he imports the currants, Bate is a subject bound by an allegiance not to the king's laws but purely to the king's person.

To bring Bate's property under the royal prerogative, the court thus specified Bate paradoxically as both a subject bound to a personalized king, and as no subject but only a merchant. We must not do away with the tension between these two parts of the judicial decision. Discrepancies in the reasoning of the different judges are to be expected, especially given the court's desire to cover all possible legal angles and so treat the question in terms, for example, of both *res* and *persona*. Most important, the merchant's structurally ambiguous position within early imperial culture enables his complex legal subjectivity to emerge in the case. Necessary to a politics of expansion, of empire, and even of diplomacy, the merchant both fashions and potentially threatens expanded *imperium*, exactly by crossing into a space where allegiances become muddy and possibly subversive. How far should we take the implication of currants that at law belong to the Englishman Bate and simultaneously to Venice? In terms of Shakespeare's representations, what are the implications of a Posthumus who repeatedly trades Italian and English clothes? In other words, what does an imperial subjectivity look like? Like Guiderius, whose subjectivity is in waiting and therefore bridges a temporal threshold, Posthumus Leonatus and John Bate become subjects when the imperial spaces they move between are internalized and reproduced as distinct capacities experienced as a fracture in the legal constitution of the self.

WATERMARKS

The judicial insistence in *Bate's Case* that the king protects the merchant subject from pirates identifies the sea as an important space for the articulation of empire: *per marem* but not *ultra mare*—beyond the scope of English common law, but not yet within another national jurisdiction. I now turn to this space as a special instance of the threshold reality, in order to explore how the ocean as limit emerges as the protagonist of romantic tragicomedy. Like *Cymbeline*, Shakespeare's *Pericles* is deeply concerned with political crisis and accommodation, specifically with the impact of alternative powers on a sovereign authority. *Pericles* interestingly extends *Cymbeline*'s engagement with the jurisdictional threshold by focusing on the ocean as the most visible space on and through which international relations are forged. What is the nature of this distended limit? Cognate with *Cymbeline*'s analysis of the thin bonds between the bodies that make up an imperial polity, *Pericles* represents the process by which maritime distances between states disrupt the integrity of sovereign authority itself, in order ultimately to enable its production in a new form. In this way, Pericles's journeys on the Mediterranean replicate attempts by James VI and I to imagine on the sea the legal basis for an authority functional beyond Britain's territorial limits. Although the sea was the most powerful of all marks of jurisdictional difference, it remained itself an ambiguous legal quantity and thus enabled the blurring of distinction necessary to the transformation of a national identity into an imperial one.

For practical and strategic reasons, the mapping of the ocean's contestable space was as fluid as the ocean itself. In 1613 William Welwood, professor of civil law at St. Andrews, included in his *Abridgement of All Sea-Lawes* a response to Hugo Grotius's *Mare liberum* of 1609, in which Grotius had argued that the sea was common to all, thereby defending the Dutch East India Company's right to trade against the Portuguese claim of *dominium* over the marine trade routes. Grotius's argument had implications for English commerce in that James was eager to restrict Dutch fishing off the English and Scottish coasts.[80] Arguing against Grotius and in support of the extension of territorial jurisdiction into proximate or coastal waters, Welwood repeats Grotius's scoffing remark that any pretense to private possession of the seas must rest, finally, on marine boundaries established neither by nature nor by the hand of man, but simply and ridiculously by "an imaginarie or fantastick line."[81] With such lines, Grotius had hypothesized, a geometer or astronomer could lay claim to all the earth and heavens. Welwood, however, finds the imaginary more persuasive. He concedes the point that islands like Guernsey or sands or rocks or other "visible marks above water" most explicitly index the "bounds (or laying-out the limits) of the divisible parts" of the sea, and thus most efficiently enable possession. But God, he says, has also endowed men with understanding and allowed them with "the helps of the compass, counting of courses, sounding, and other waies, to find forth, and to designe *finitum in infinito*, so farre as is expedient, for the certain reach and bounds of seas, properly pertaining to any Prince or people."[82]

The navigator's fantastic lines become effectual only if human intention can, of itself, underwrite real extension. And Welwood claims this is so: on the land, he notes, possession is sufficiently marked by entry onto one part of it "with a minde to possesse all the rest thereof, even to the due marches." The same principle can be applied to possession on the sea, even to its natural limits: "And what can stay this to be done on sea, as well as on land?"[83] But the obvious problem with so employing the imaginary or the intentional is that it might not correlate with the real. In a response to Welwood written around 1614, but printed only in 1872, Grotius writes that imaginary lines, precise though they be, cannot effect appropriation except in conjunction with a "corporeal act" of possession: by a fleet, in other words, or (in narrowly adjacent waters) by coastal guns.[84] As the truism has it, possession is nine-tenths of the law. Welwood himself is closer to this eminently practical position than his rhetoric sometimes implies; thus, having defended a theory of intentional sovereignty, he must finally suggest what the actual limits naturally due a prince or people are. He invokes the classic formulation from the civil law: "Which bounds *Bartolus* hardily extends and allowes for Princes & people at the sea side, an hundreth miles of sea forth from their coasts, at least; and justly, if they exercise a protection and conservacie so farre."[85] In that final qualification, we are back to Grotius's de facto subordination of jurisdiction to force. Welwood's reference to the need for "protection and conservacie" does not undo his theoretical assertion that coastal seas pertain really to the adjacent territory, but it helps to formulate the crucial problem for a national representation of the sea: how to designate a space that can be intended as sovereign, but is manifestly open to the operation of alternative powers.

Although no answer can satisfactorily exclude the primacy of force, in the early seventeenth century James attempted to identify a less skeptical ground for authority by linking marine sovereignty with the natural continuity of the king's natural person. From the perspective of national law, the terms of the attempt are hardly surprising: given that the common law is the law of the *land*, it was only through the king's natural capacity that a norm could be imagined that might comprehend the sea as a legal space. The critical question for James's program, however, was how the prerogative associated with the king's natural body might operate on the sea with respect not only to national law, but also to international law. For only in that sense could the royal person circumvent the problem of alternative corporate claims on the ocean and thereby generate a version of sovereignty able to subvert the ocean's contestability. We can trace James's program to extend British sovereignty onto the sea in two proclamations concerning marine waters proximate to the British coast. On 1 March 1605 James issued a proclamation "for revocation of Mariners from forreine Services" in the hope of preventing his subjects from disrupting the peace recently negotiated with Spain in the Treaty of London (19 August 1604) through their "warlike Services of any forraine State upon the Sea."[86] Included here were the privateers who, carrying letters of marque against Spain, had retreated after 1604 to the United Provinces and were aiding the Dutch in their ongoing encounters with Spain. Since Spain and the Provinces were still at war, the proclamation also laid down certain principles to be followed by royal officers and subjects in cases where ships belonging to the two nations came into conflict. Specifically, it was James's concern to delineate as neutral water his "Ports, Havens, Rodes, Creekes, or other places of our Dominion, or so neere to any of our sayd Ports or Havens."[87] To aid his officers in enforcing that neutrality, he "caused to be sent to them plats [charts] of those Limits, within which we are resolved that these Orders shall be observed."

There was nothing innovative in this declaration. The maritime historian T. W. Fulton writes that areas of the sea in close proximity to a country "were recognised as belonging to it, in the sense at least that hostilities of belligerent men-of-war or the capture of prizes were forbidden within them; they were 'sanctuaries' under the jurisdiction and protection of the adjoining territory."[88] The plat to which the proclamation refers was a broadside engraved by Thomas Hood, which had been prepared by the Trinity House at the request of Sir Julius Caesar, judge in the High Court of Admiralty (fig. 9). Along with an explanatory textual "schedule," it was formally presented on 4 March 1605, after which both map and schedule were circulated by the king's printer, Robert Barker, under the title *Of the Head-lands of England*.[89] Used in conjunction with the textual explication, which identified twenty-seven crucial headlands, the map demarcated twenty-six areas of neutral water, defining those reserved waters as "all the Sea coasts within a streight line drawn from one Headland to the next Headland, throughout this Realme of England." Like their fantastic counterparts invoked a decade later by Welwood, these straight lines—imaginary also, even to the extent of not appearing on the Trinity House chart—marked a sovereignty in the sense that they designated the waters as being under the jurisdiction of the adjoining territory. As a material artifact, then, and not least because of its clotted record of coastal place names (a cartographic feature most familiar from the portolan charts or rutters that served coastal navigators), the chart is remarkable for representing England as an edge, projected outward onto a spectral and even elastic beyond.

The areas delimited by the imaginary lines between headlands were known as the "King's Chambers." John Selden noted the intensely personal character of James's claim to these waters in his *Mare clausum*, a treatise on sea sovereignty written in part around 1618 as a response to Grotius, but published only in 1635 at a time when Charles I was pushing his claims over the sea farther even than his father had done.[90] Thus Selden personalizes the chambers by transforming them into domestic space: "Wee have very great

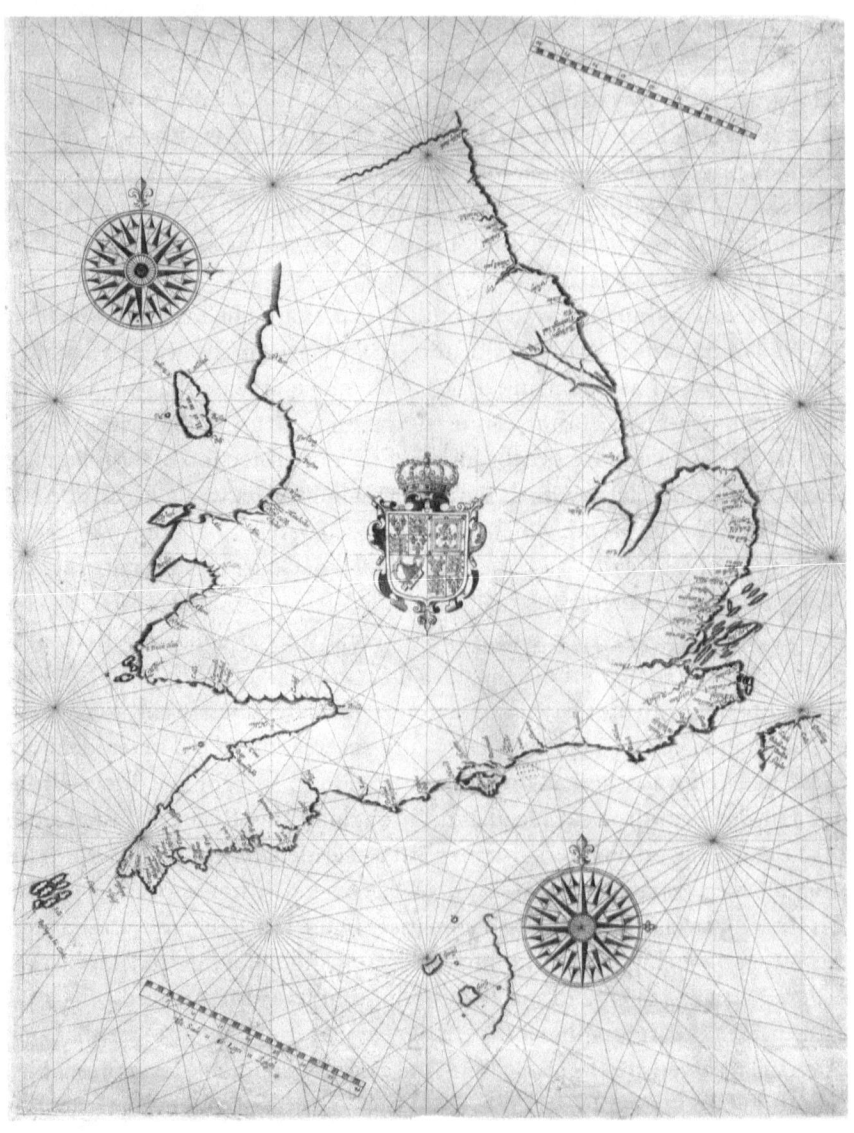

FIGURE 9 Thomas Hood, map of the English headlands. From [*A Note*] *of the Head-lands of England* (London, 1605). STC 10019.5. By permission of Houghton Library, Harvard College Library.

Creeks of Sea cut off by these lines from the Sea round about, which they call *Regias Cameras* THE KINGS CHAMBERS, and the Ports Roial. Even as in an hous the inner private Rooms, or Chambers, or Closets, which in barbarous Latin are wont to bee termed *Camerae*, are reserved for the Master."[91] The chambers, set off by "these lines," are private rooms, and controlled not by the law but by the king's person.

Most important for the present argument, Selden's use of the 1605 proclamation clarifies the nature of James's policy concerning marine jurisdiction insofar as it deforms a central aspect of that policy, transforming a carefully constructed royal authority into a more absolute but also less flexible power. For Selden, the proprietary nature of the chamber metonymically implies the king's dominion over an extended territory: "and as the Citie of *London* hath of old been called in our Law the *Chamber of the King of England*, whereby the rest of his Dominion round about is set forth [*dominio eius . . . designato*], as it were by the use of a more narrow Title: So these Creeks, though very large, beeing called by the like name and limited at the pleasure of the Kings of *England*, do in like manner shew his Dominion [*dominium*] over the rest of the Sea."[92] In arguing that James's invocation of the Chambers' "more narrow Title" implied "in like manner . . . his Dominion over the rest of the Sea," Selden is arguing that the king has property in the northern seas. But this was retrospectively to read James's project as more radical than it was, since nowhere had James claimed in respect of the waters more than imperial jurisdiction (*imperium*). By circumventing the operative distinction between *imperium* as the reach of legal authority and *dominium*, to which pertain the most direct and absolute rights of use (including the critical right of exclusion), Selden is able to use the Jacobean proclamation to claim for Charles a sovereignty "of the most absolute kind," a sovereignty carrying with it the broader rights pertaining to *dominium*.[93]

James's less absolute claim in 1605 was no less strategic for being so modest in comparison with Selden's version of things. Understood in the context of the *arcana imperii* and of James's deliberate mystification of the royal prerogative as a way exactly to enlarge his rights, his marine program is notable in that the personalized language of royal jurisdiction exclusive of *dominium* was sufficiently flexible on the sea to instantly and incontrovertibly compass not only Spain and the United Provinces within British waters, but all the world, though only in a circumscribed way: so long as a ship of "what Nation soever . . . bee within those our Ports and places of our Jurisdiction, or where our Officers may prohibit violence," it was "understood to be under our protection."[94]

The potential scope of that traditional and theoretically unremarkable claim became clear in 1609, when James attempted to encourage English fishing by imposing restrictions on the massively more successful Dutch fishery. In May of that year James issued a "Proclamation touching Fishing," resolving that "no Person of what Nation or qualitie soever, being not our naturall borne Subject, bee permitted to fish upon any of our Coasts and Seas of Great Britaine, Ireland, and the rest of the Isles adjacent, where most usually heretofore any Fishing hath bene, untill they have orderly demaunded and obtained Licenses from us."[95] Although reminiscent of a traditional Scottish tax, the so-called "assize-herring," the 1609 tribute was innovative in being applied to foreigners.[96] James justified his action by declaring that foreign fishing had disrupted not only his royal prerogative but also the relationship of allegiance between him and his subjects:

> Whereas we have bene contented since our comming to the Crowne, to tolerate an indifferent and promiscuous kinde of libertie to all our friendes whatsoever, to fish within our Streames, and upon any of our Coastes of Greate Britaine, Ireland, and other adjacent Islands, so farre foorth as the permission or use thereof might not redound to the empeachment of our Prerogative Royall, nor to the hurt and damage of our loving Subjects, whose preservation and flourishing estate wee hold our selfe principally bound to advance before all worldly respects: So finding that our connivence therein, hath not onely given occasion of over great encrochments upon our Regalities, or rather questioning of our Right, but hath bene a meanes of much dayly wrongs to our owne people that exercise the trade of Fishing . . . Wee have thought it now both just and necessary . . . to prevent those inconveniences, and many others depending upon the same.[97]

Coastal jurisdiction here is marked as the affirmation, first, of the prerogative, and second, of the bond between king and subject, according to which the king is "bound" by an oath of protection, and the subject by an oath of allegiance. As we have seen, the legal relationship thereby constituted, the double *ligamen* connecting king and subject, had already served James well, both in *Bate's Case* and in *Calvin's Case*.

As against those earlier instances of allegiance's legal efficacy, however, in the proclamation of 1609 the weight of James's personal bond with his subjects fell exactly on foreign fishermen, on those who were not his subjects at all, and would thus normally be bound only within the geographic confines of a territorially conceived *dominium*. Here was the crux. To make plausible a shift of obligation from subject to alien, to allow *imperium* to operate with the force of *dominium*, James emphasized in phrases like "our Coasts and Seas" the idea of a geographical limit to his claims, even as he kept the precise extent of the limit strategically vague.[98] The proximate sea is constructed, then, as a space that enables a personal relationship independent of place to operate in an unusual way. Through a delicate balancing act, a sea that is not property generates, because of the king's obligations to the subject, a further obligatory relationship between the king's person and the foreign. This is, in part, how the royal chambers had operated in the earlier proclamation from 1605: foreign ships, because of their geographical proximity to the coast, could be "understood" to be under the king's protection and so within the scope of an otherwise irrelevant personal relationship.[99] Understood or imagined to be. Along with the conceptual lines or "strings" connecting the king's mind to other minds, the geographical lines demarcating the royal chambers (and, more loosely, the proximate seas) jointly provided a way to think of the sea as a site where, through the operation of a personalized royal authority, obligatory international relationships could be generated as radically natural.

The strategy did not convince those who did not want to be convinced. In the long negotiations that ensued between Britain and the United Provinces, it was clear from the beginning that the legal position adopted by James would never satisfy the Dutch. Unsurprisingly, in his answer to the claim that James could exclude foreigners from his coasts as from his land, Grotius focused exactly on the distinction between *dominium* and *imperium*, in order to expose the pretensions of the English claims in the North Sea.[100] The *imperium* that James claimed was moot, Grotius argued, and since it was absurd to claim *dominium* over water, it was absurd also to exclude foreign fishing. In the context of this kind of argument, grounded as it is in the operative legal distinction between the two central terms, James's invocation of a geographically charged *imperium* seems at the level of legal theory remarkably astute, even if rather too optimistic.

A document preserved in the papers of Sir Julius Caesar provides important evidence for supposing that the king and council developed a jurisdictional argument exclusive of *dominium* not through lack of foresight, but as a deliberate choice. Written in Caesar's hand, "Notes touch. the Fisshing uppon the costs of great Britaine" appears to be a memorandum drawn up in council on 12 April 1609 (fig. 10).[101] As T. W. Fulton points out, it lays out the principles that would find formal expression in the proclamation James issued a month later.[102] Fulton, however, neither transcribes the text nor notes that in several

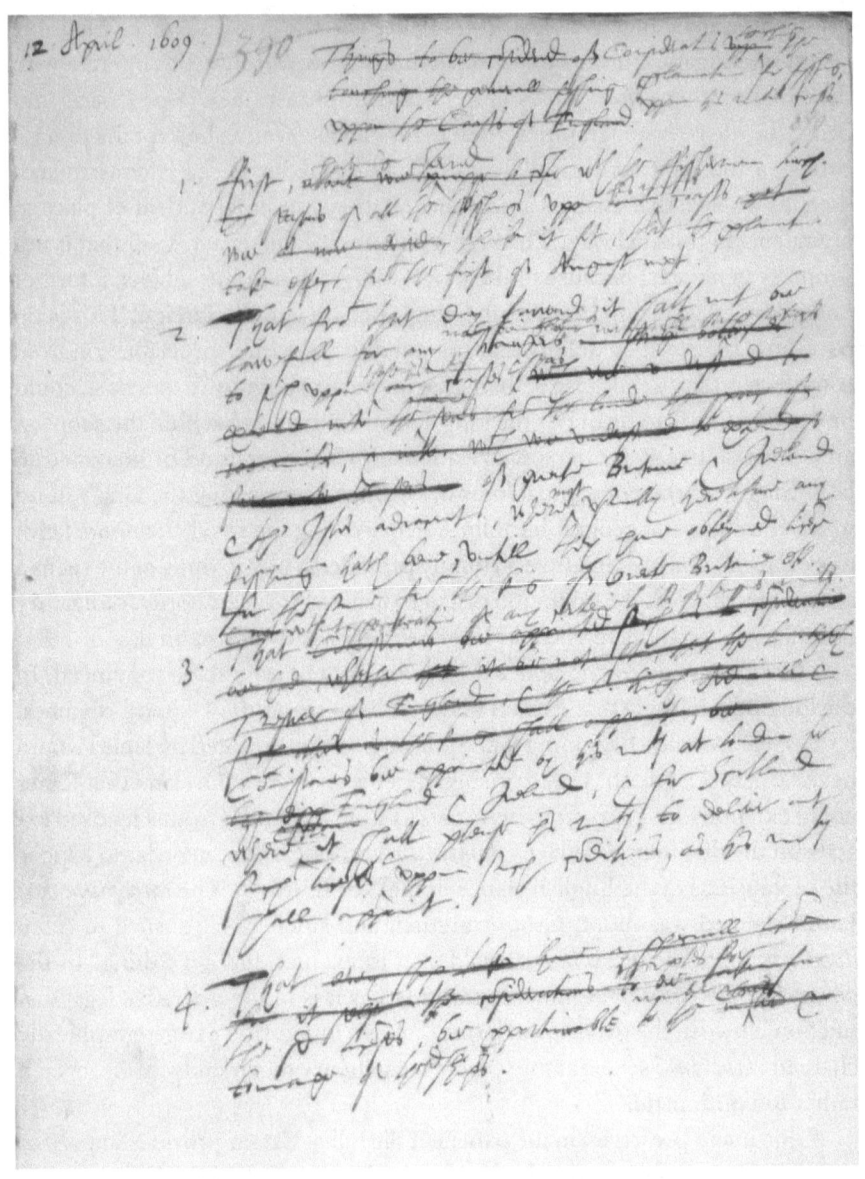

FIGURE 10   Sir Julius Caesar, draft of proclamation on international fishing, April 1609. London, British Library, Lansdowne MS 142, sig. 379r. By permission of the British Library.

places it has been emended, also in Caesar's hand. These emendations are important not only because they make their way into the final text of the proclamation—to this extent, the memorandum can best be thought of as a draft of the central part of that later document—but also because they record how James's jurisdictional strategy emerged at a given point in the council's discussion and was chosen over alternative formulations in which the role of the king's person and prerogative was far less visible. I shall highlight the most important emendations by quoting the document first in its earlier version, then in its revised form.

The first major emendation gives us a useful sense of the document's own history. In the first draft of the first article, Caesar writes: "First, albeit we purpose to confer with the Fishermen touch. the seasons of all the Fisshings uppon our coasts, yet wee al nowe advise, thinke it fit, that the proclamation take effect from the first of August next." With emendations, the article read as follows: "First, having confered with the Fishermen touch. the seasons of all the Fisshings uppon his majesties coasts, wee think it fit, that the proclamation take effect from the first of August next." Given the shift in time and mood between the two versions, it seems clear that Caesar originally wrote the notes before the conference with the fishermen was held, that he continued to use the document, and that the major revisions date to just after that conference was held.[103] As I read the document, then, it records changes across a relatively short period of time in the council's thinking about how best to make the argument for excluding foreigners from waters near the English coast.

The other emendation of substance in the first article hints at a change in policy, since in the shift from "our coasts" to "his majesties coasts" the argument against the foreigners is more forcefully located in the king's person. The changes to the second article of the memorandum seem to be similarly motivated. In the first version of the second article, Caesar notes that, according to the proposed proclamation of 1 August: "from that day forward it shall not be lawefull for any strangers or strange bottoms to fish uppon those our coastes & seas which we understand to extend into the [*illegible insertion*] seas from the lande the space of 100 miles, & into which wee understand to extend so farr into the seas of greate Britaine & Ireland & the Isles adjacent, where usually heretofore any fisshing hath bene, untill they have obteyned license for the same from the king of Great Britain etc." With corrections, this article read as follows: "that from that day forward it shall not be lawefull for any strangers not being the kings naturall borne subjects to fish uppon those his majesties coastes & seas of greate Britaine & Ireland & the Isles adjacent, where most usually heretofore any fisshing hath bene, untill they have obteyned license for the same from the king of Great Britain etc. without specification of any certeine limits of leagues or miles." Again, "our coastes" becomes "his majesties coastes." "Strange bottoms" is struck out, probably to emphasize that the issue at hand is the presence of persons, and only incidentally of their vessels. The personalization of the argument is underlined through the additional qualification of "strangers" as "not being the kings naturall borne subjects," a phrase that stands behind the final wording of the printed proclamation, which orders that no person "being not our naturall borne Subject, bee permitted to fish." (The May proclamation also preserves "most usually heretofore" as opposed to the earlier draft's "usually heretofore").[104]

Most interesting in the April memorandum is that the emended version omits the attempt in the first draft to specify the extent of national waters to 100 miles, this being a rule imported from Bartolo da Sassoferrato (Bartolus), the fourteenth-century jurist and commentator on Roman civil law. That change leads to the addition of the explicit statement at the end of the article that the seas should be named "without specification of any certeine limits of leagues or miles." Although it is possible to read this last qualification as a hyper-compensatory emendation, it seems more likely that it is Caesar's "extra-textual" reminder to substitute a generality about the prerogative for the greater certainty of Bartolus's rule. All in all, the document tells the story of how one model of asserting England's claim over the ocean gave way to another. Turning from a model of right grounded in measurable distances and national interests to a politics of vagueness centered in the king's personal bond with his subjects, the document records the discovery of a highly fluid and, as Grotius would insist, highly unstable means to place the law in the space beyond which it pertained.

Richard Helgerson has delineated in chorographical descriptions of England the gradual displacement of royal authority onto an idea of Britannia as the land itself, as, for example, in the maps of Drayton's *Poly-Olbion* (1613) or the Ditchley portrait of Elizabeth (ca. 1592), which shows her standing on a map of England.[105] In my argument, we are seeing the mechanics whereby royal authority was simultaneously relocated onto the ocean, as a central part of the ideological belief, explored by Armitage, that Britain "was an empire of the seas."[106] We can think, for example, of the frontispiece to Camden's 1607 Latin and 1610 English *Britannia* (fig. 11). This is an imperial image: the four parts of James's British dominion, England, Scotland, Wales, and Ireland, are each represented, as they are in the quarterings of his royal coat of arms. They are, moreover, materially linked through the lines extending outward from the compass rose. Such compass markings were critical to both the production

FIGURE 11 Frontispiece to William Camden, *Britannia* (London, 1607). By permission of the University of Chicago Library, Special Collections Research Center.

and use of marine charts, since through the loxodromes, or oblique windlines extending from the compass rose, mariners were able to discover for any point the available winds, and so set a course. As David Waters explains, a working chart showing the winds radiating from a group of related compasses would appear "to be covered with a medley of criss-cross lines" until it became clear

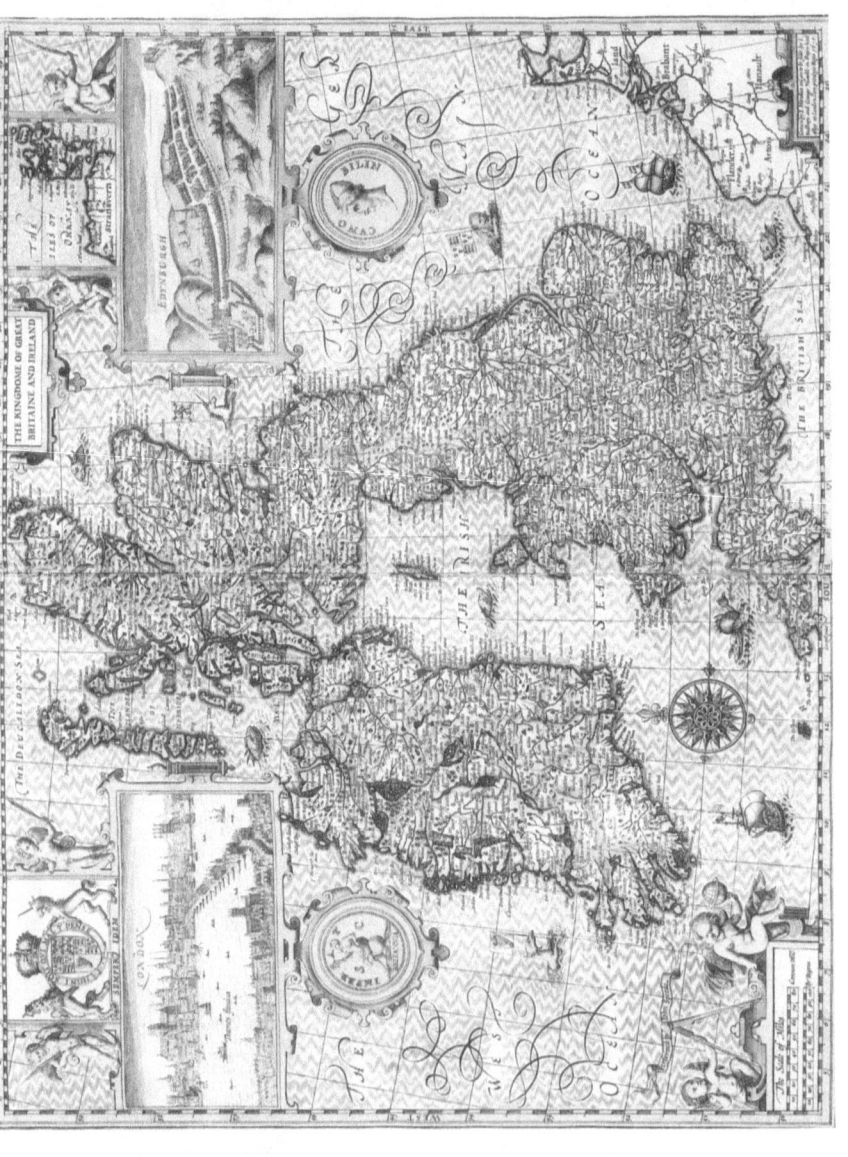

FIGURE 12 Map of Great Britain and Ireland, from John Speed, *The Theatre of the Empire of Great Britaine* (London, 1611). London, British Library, G.7884. By permission of the British Library.

that each of those lines "was a rhumb or wind."[107] But as a set of imaginary lines thus corresponding to a natural phenomenon, the loxodromes could also represent a political argument, expressing jurisdiction across the water as prior and natural rather than artificial.

Not surprisingly, then, the compass rose on Camden's map strongly resembles the sun, another symbol of James's British and transnational authority. In one of his treatises on the union of Scotland and England, for example, John Thornborough compares the idea of political union to "the Sunne in the middest of heaven, among the Stars; and as the Stars take light of the Sun, so al blessings of Weale publique proceede from this sacred, & thrice happy union into the name of great Brittaine, whose glorious light shineth to all."[108] In Ben Jonson's "Panegyre, on the Happy Entrance of James," the king similarly becomes the "the glory of our western world," whose "thousand radiant lights ... stream / To every nook and angle of his realm" (ll. 3–6).[109] In another of Thornborough's treatises on Union, finally, the sun analogizes the relationship of the king to his diverse subjects, in a manner that highlights the powerful connotations of lines that, as in a compass rose, emanate from a center: "Do not divers Sunne beames come from one Sunne, and all they of one nature? Are not divers lines drawne from one Center, and all be of one fashion? ... And may not divers people under one Prince, though they are devided in persons, yet be united in lawes?"[110]

The symbolic connection between the compass rose and a mapped politics of jurisdiction is beautifully embodied in John Speed's 1611 atlas, *Theatre of the Empire of Great Britaine*. The atlas guides the reader on how to read the compass rose as an emblem of royal *imperium*. In the general map of James's whole kingdom, Speed represents four medallions, three of which are manifestly imperial: in the upper left, the royal coat of arms; midway down, an imperial Britannia in emulation of a Roman medallion; on the right, an image taken from a coin pictured in Camden's *Britannia* and representing Cunobilis, the original Cymbeline and the first king to unite all of Britain (fig. 12). Grouped as it is with these three, the fourth medallion, the compass rose, absorbs their imperial significance. To extend this initial association, the atlas manipulates the symbol in a variety of ways. The compass rose is shown, for example, in a map of Lancashire next to the portraits of the four Lancastrian kings, themselves embedded in a rose-emblazoned frame (fig. 13). Above them, James's personal motto, *Beati Pacifici*, is translated into English. The compass rose can be seen here as James's more imperial version of the union of the white rose and red by Henry VII. In a map of Warwickshire, Speed includes in the left margin an image of the compass rose

FIGURE 13 Detail, map of Lancashire, from Speed, *Theatre of the Empire of Great Britaine* (London, 1611). London, British Library, G7884. By permission of the British Library.

"To Stride a Limit" 271

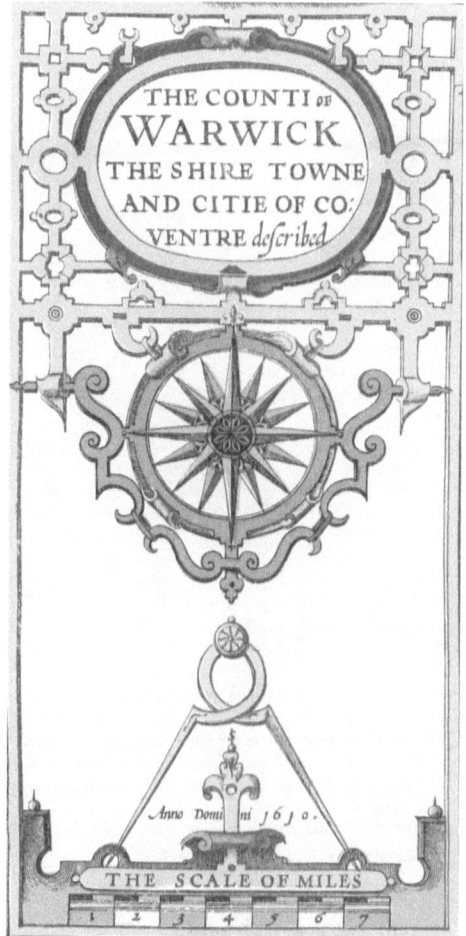 

FIGURE 14 Detail, map of Warwickshire, from Speed, *Theatre of the Empire of Great Britaine* (London, 1611). London, British Library, G.7884. By permission of the British Library.

FIGURE 15 Detail, map of Northamptonshire, from Speed, *Theatre of the Empire of Great Britaine* (London, 1611). London, British Library, G.7884. By permission of the British Library.

suspended from a decorative frame above a geometer's compass (fig. 14). In the following map of Northamptonshire, the frame and geometer's compass have stayed, but the compass rose has been replaced with what can therefore be considered to be its equivalent: the royal arms (fig. 15). Similarly, in the map of Rutlandshire, Speed includes on the left margin a highly stylized

272 Chapter Five

FIGURE 16 Detail, map of Rutland-shire, from Speed, *Theatre of the Empire of Great Britaine* (London, 1611). London, British Library, G.7884. By permission of the British Library.

FIGURE 17 Detail, map of Rutland-shire, from Speed, *Theatre of the Empire of Great Britaine* (London, 1611). London, British Library, G.7884. By permission of the British Library.

compass rose, recognizable through the fleur-de-lis that traditionally marked north (fig. 16). In the right margin of the same map and in the same framing device, he substitutes the royal arms (fig. 17). The symbolic conflation of the compass rose and the royal is firmly in place by the time we reach a dazzling example of the point in the general map of Wales (fig. 18). Here the compass rose, emptied of all its traditional marks other than the loxodromic lines, has become identical with the royal arms that now occupy its gutted center. In a heraldic table conveniently and strategically printed at the beginning of the atlas, Speed designates these arms, generically identifiable as royal, as belonging specifically to the ancient Welsh princes.[111] In a map of Cardiganshire in Wales, a medallion suspended from a frame and hovering

FIGURE 18 Detail, map of Wales, from Speed, *Theatre of the Empire of Great Britaine* (London, 1611). London, British Library, G.7884. By permission of the British Library.

FIGURE 19 Detail, map of Cardiganshire, from Speed, *Theatre of the Empire of Great Britaine* (London, 1611). London, British Library, G.7884. By permission of the British Library.

over the Irish Sea makes the same political point (fig. 19). Here represented is a compass rose obscured by the superimposed Welsh Crown. Since Henry had been created Prince of Wales in 1610, the year preceding the publication of the atlas, the rose in the Welsh maps thus describes both James's imperial authority and Henry's widely admired commitment to the extension of British influence through exploration, trade, and military force.

Speed's atlas provides a lesson in the transformation of a mariner's cartographic tool into a symbol of imperial sovereignty. That representational fluidity is appropriate since the compass rose itself transforms the sea. It does so symbolically, and to the extent that, through its imaginary lines extending from a center, it delineates the central logic of early British empire, a jurisdictional strategy through which contestable space beyond the law could be structured as natural possession. Under the influence of writers like Grotius and Selden, we think of *dominium* as the ultimate ground for international relations. But James's invocation on the sea of a jurisdiction exactly exclusive of *dominium* should not be understood as some still imperfect version of the more exacting argument ultimately made by Selden on behalf of James's son. A map depicting Lancashire from Camden's 1607 *Britannia* makes the point (fig. 20). Here is the compass rose operating as it does in Speed, subtended by an impressively large geometer's compass. Camden's map indicates that it has been reengraved from the original designed by Christopher Saxton for his 1579 cartographic collection; crucially, however, that earlier map shows suspended over the Irish sea, not a compass rose, but Elizabeth's arms (fig. 21). The presence in the later map of the compass rose, rather than King James's arms, may relate simply to the relative cost of engraving the two symbols. But as transmitted material artifacts, Saxton's and Camden's maps embody also gently competing ideologies. As a representation of royal authority, the rose is both more indirect and more powerful than the arms. The overriding fact for British imperial thinking in the Tudor and early Stuart periods was the absence of *terra nullius*, uninhabited territory over which, according to natural law, a discoverer could press a national claim to mere *dominium*.[112] To move out beyond national borders was necessarily to move into alternative jurisdictions or into spaces like the sea in which direct containment was impossible. Empire was a matter, instead, of meeting the foreign with sufficient art to "naturally" accommodate it without loss of advantage or prestige.

DISPLACING SOVEREIGNTY

First printed in 1609, Shakespeare's *Pericles* is now accepted as a collaborative work with George Wilkins, author *of The Painefull Adventures of Pericles Prince of Tyre*, a prose redaction of the story printed in 1608 (in advance of the Quarto) to capitalize on the successful production of the play earlier that year.[113] The most striking dramatic feature of the play (and one reason, surely, for its popularity in the decades following its first production) is its virtuoso fracturing of action across so many state boundaries.[114] As a journey across the eastern Mediterranean, the play is both a tour and a *tour de force* of exoticism. This structure is thematically crucial, since *Pericles* represents

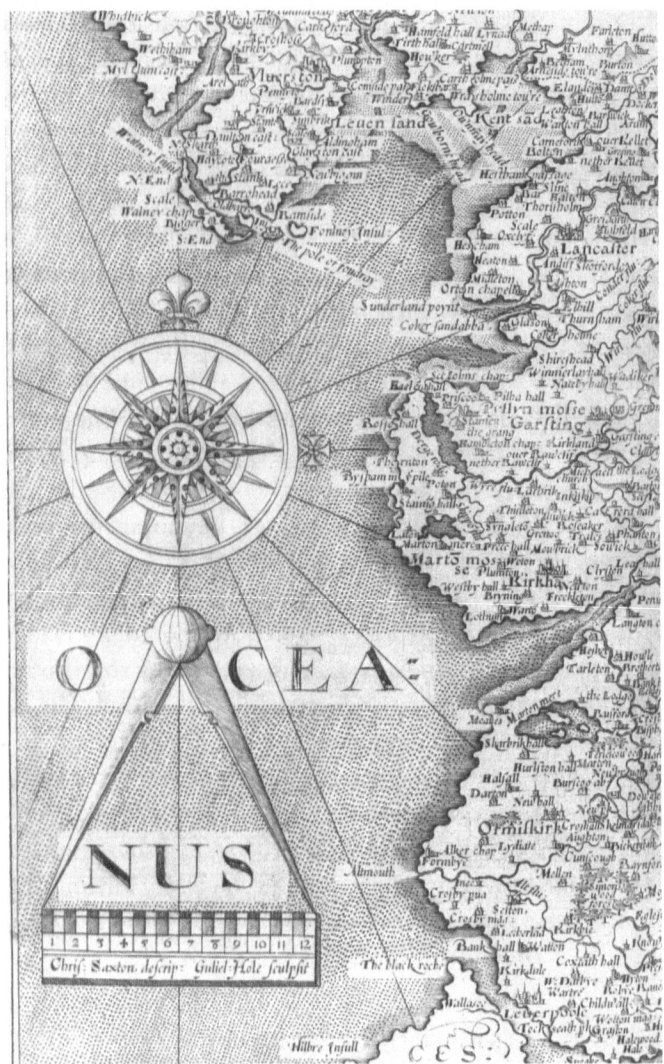

FIGURE 20 Detail, map of Lancashire, from William Camden, *Britannia* (London, 1607). By permission of the University of Chicago Library, Special Collections Research Center.

the extension of authority across distance, the agent of that extension being the sovereign himself, cast by the contingencies of tragicomedy into territorial jurisdictions other than his own. Most important, Pericles is cast onto the sea, the marine distance separating his own territory from those alternative ones. Destabilized by his journeys, Pericles refers to the sea itself as a "watery

FIGURE 21 Detail, map of Lancashire, from Christopher Saxton's atlas (London, 1579). London, British Library, G.118.e.1. By permission of the British Library.

empire" (2.1.49), a place itself of only unstable sovereignty. This small detail points to how the play finds political significance in the liminal shore and liminal ocean themselves, rather than only in the spaces they separate.[115] Geographical detail serves a topological argument: what chiefly matters in the proliferation of Mediterranean territories is that they all have coasts.[116] As facilitator of Pericles's story, and as the play's political arena, the sea is both place and nonplace, a negative place that is productive as the source rather the site of meaning and action.

The hero's name speaks to the play's engagement with the idea of the ocean. In earlier versions of the story, including John Gower's *Confessio amantis* and Laurence Twine's mid-Tudor *Patterne of Painefull Adventures* (reprinted 1607), Pericles is known as Apollonius of Tyre. The change of name points us to North's Plutarch, from which, as Macdonald P. Jackson notes, Shakespeare took "all six of the Greek names in *Pericles* which do not derive from Gower—Pericles, Cleon, Philemon, Escanes (or Aeschines), Simonides, and Lysimachus."[117] The argument that Shakespeare used Plutarch because Pericles there exemplifies a kind of patience, a virtue that Shakespeare's character embodies more fully than Apollonius does, is surely right but not quite sufficient.[118] Read against King James's attempts to consolidate and theorize Britain's legal control of its proximate waters, Shakespeare's use of Plutarch takes on another dimension, since Athenian Pericles was remembered in early modern Europe, not only for his funeral oration, but also for a speech in which he strongly promoted Athenian naval power and identified the state with that power. Prince Pericles's exemplary patience thus assumes political content as the affect of the sovereign in waiting for his imperial destiny.

Thirty years before the play's performance, John Dee used Pericles in his *General and Rare Memorials Pertayning to the Perfect Arte of Navigation* (1577), a treatise arguing that Queen Elizabeth should establish a "Pety-Navy-Royall" as a means to secure the coastal seas for English merchants and fishermen, and thereby protect the "*Publik-Weale*, of this Kingdom."[119] Throughout the text, Dee refers to Pericles's speeches on behalf of marine power, thereby making him an active spokesman for a revitalized Tudor *imperium*: "What wold that Noble, Valiant, and Victorious Atheniensien PERICLES, say, yf, now, he were lyving, and a Subject of Authority, in this Brytish Kingdom? . . . Who, taught by word, and proved in effect, *Vnam Pecunia parandae rationem putandam, Naues quamplurimas habere* [that the one method of obtaining money which should be considered is having many ships]."[120] A page later, Dee explicitly makes Pericles an exemplar for the "Subject of Authority" whom Dee imagines to have the power to effect political change: "*O Pericles*, thy life (certainly) may be a pattern and Rule to the higher Magistrates (in very many points) most diligently, of them, to be imitated."[121] Dee's most forceful use of the Greek orator comes late in the treatise, when he appeals to some "Brytish, or English Pericles" to put his political platforms into effect, probably intending this title for Christopher Hatton, to whom the treatise is dedicated.[122] Ultimately, Dee was thinking of the queen herself, but Elizabeth, ignoring the platform laid out in the *Memorials*, pressed no jurisdictional claim over the northern seas, probably because of her concern to protect her subjects' trade and fishing interests by opposing all foreign pretensions to *mare clausum*.[123] In the event, Dee's call for a "Brytish, or English Pericles" would be answered only by the Stuarts and not, at least initially, by recourse to a stronger navy. Dee's text is highly suggestive for Shakespeare's play: like Plutarch's orator and Dee's British hero, and like King James himself who was in the process of constructing a useful version of the sea by tracing on it the lines of an elastic authority, Pericles uses the sea in the service of a delicately balanced *imperium*. Shakespeare's new name speaks to the play's interest in the new authority fashioned on the sea.

As in *Cymbeline*, the central terms of *Pericles* are jurisdictional. At the end of Act 2, Pericles faces one in a long line of adventitious obstacles the play throws in his way. King Simonides of Pentapolis plays a trick on the recently shipwrecked prince, whom he believes to be simply a knight and gentleman of Tyre. Although he wishes the knight and his daughter to marry, Simonides accuses Pericles of having "bewitched" his daughter Thaisa into an inappropriate desire. Pericles protests. The terms of the following exchange between the two sovereigns embody the play's jurisdictional theme:

Simonides: Traitor, thou liest.
Pericles: Traitor?
Simonides: Ay, traitor.
Pericles: Even in his throat, unless it be the king,
That calls me traitor, I return the lie.
(2.5.53-55)

Pericles's personal honor is at stake. His sword, he says, will prove that anyone who accuses him of being a "rebel to [Thaisa's] state" is "honour's enemy" (2.5.60-62). In the double meaning of "state," however, and particularly in the juxtaposition of "traitor," "rebel," and "enemy," the prince converts his honor into a political argument about the continuity of his jurisdiction. Francis Bacon would have understood Pericles's position. In his speech on behalf of Robert Calvin, Bacon presented the mirror image of the same point: a Scotsman "subject to the natural person of the king, and not to the crown of England," could by law be no enemy to the king or to the subjects of England. "Or must he not," Bacon continues, "of necessity, if he should invade England, be a rebel and no enemy, not only as to the king but as to the subject?"[124] By insisting that he is no *traitor*, Pericles calls Simonides on the matter of legal categories, thereby defining his allegiance as his own, and marking his "state" and authority as independent of the jurisdiction within which he now finds himself through the accidents of romance. In this light, Pericles's qualification, "unless it be the king," assumes a sly second meaning. Here Pericles acknowledges that there are sovereign authorities before which matters like private honor become necessarily negligible. But to the extent that he can himself be the king referred to, Pericles is articulating the ground precisely of a public but secret resistance to that alternative authority. In a moment of high diplomacy, Pericles protects his life by saying that he will not, in this particular case, give the lie, even as he preserves his own sovereign integrity by secretly doing so. Submitting to Simonides, Pericles marks his submission in part as a reconfirmation of Tyre's own sovereign *imperium*.

The plot of *Pericles* is "marked by a series of disasters at the local level which are somehow righted by the play's larger design."[125] As a special instance of this pattern, the play repeatedly demonstrates how an apparent concession on the part of the prince preserves and even extends his sovereignty. When Cleon of Tarsus, for example, is told that Pericles's ships have been sighted off his coast, he misreads the fleet as an emblem of war and thus the bluntest form of international engagement:

> Some neighboring nation,
> Taking advantage of our misery,
> Hath stuffed the hollow vessels with their power,
> To beat us down, the which are down already,
> And make a conquest of unhappy me . . .
> (1.4.64–67)

In fact, Pericles's ships, stuffed with grain that will feed the starving population, stand for a subtler bond, one grounded in beneficence and, on the other side, in gratitude and deference; as Tarsus's savior, Pericles will speak not of legal debt, but of love and the kind of reciprocity central to natural rather than artificial law: "We do not look for reverence, but for love, / And harbourage for ourself, our ships and men" (1.4.97–98). That said, in one respect Pericles's request is no request at all. The allusion to harborage recalls an important passage in Book 1 of the *Aeneid*, where Ilioneus complains to Dido about her treatment of the sea-weary Trojans: "What race of men is this? What country is so barbarous as to permit this custom? We are denied the welcome of a dry beach [*Quod genus hoc hominum? quaeve hunc tam barbara morem / permittit patria? hospitio prohibemur harenae*]" (1.539–40).[126] These lines were a *locus classicus* for early discussions of natural law and the *ius gentium*; in his defense of the freedom of trade and navigation, for example, Hugo Grotius turned to Virgil's passage as an embodiment of "that law of hospitality which is of the highest sanctity" and as evidence that all nations hold the seas in common.[127] When Pericles asks for harborage, he is asking for something that cannot really be refused him, in which case Cleon's favor generates no real obligation in the receiving party. As in his verbal exchange with Simonides, Pericles himself remains free even as he enters the political union.

However informal the bond between Pericles and Cleon, it constitutes a highly charged and unequal relationship, an effect of the play's erosion of the boundaries among the political, diplomatic, economic, and military. When Pericles returns to Tarsus to deposit Marina there, his language of princely love seems newly inflected as politics.[128] Cleon refers to his "duty" (3.3.23) toward Pericles as a kind of inevitable logic binding Pericles's princely intentions and thought to Cleon's thought for Marina:

> Fear not, my lord, but think
> Your grace that fed my country with your corn—
> For which the people's prayers still fall upon you—
> Must in your child be thought on.
> (3.3.18–21)

Speaking of Marina, furthermore, Pericles tells Cleon that "Here I charge your charity withal, / Leaving her the infant of your care" (3.3.14–15), where "charge" and "charity" both expose the complex economic realities that underlie the idealized political alliance that Pericles has put in place through his generosity. In Twine's *Patterne of Painefull Adventures*, one of Shakespeare's two principal sources, Apollonius's wheat is even more explicitly implicated in the realities of exchange. There the prince initially sells his stored wheat to the starving inhabitants for "no more than I bought it for in mine owne Countrey, that is to say, eight peeces of brasse for every bushell."[129] The really telling point is that Apollonius can be so precise as to price. As Steven Mullaney notes, Twine's text is explicit on the need to expel the implications of money's having so entered the diplomatic equation: "But Apollonius, doubting lest by this deede, hee should seeme to put off the dignity of a prince, and put on the countenaunce of a merchant, rather than a giver, when he had received the price of the wheate, hee restored it backe againe to the use and commoditie of the same Cittie."[130] As gift returned, "the brass coin effaces the course of its circulation and restores Apollonius's princely countenance."[131] The circle of exchange disguised as nonexchange completes itself when the civic population transmutes the brass coins into a brass statue representing Apollonius in a military chariot, "holding corne in his right hand, and spurning it with his left foote."[132] As Mullaney argues, the "flurry of brass coins serves to remind us that a gift is never merely a gift."[133] That as commodity or gift Apollonius's wheat is literally repaid in the same coin emblematically links diplomacy and trade, making both of them versions of that conquest which Cleon feared and the chariot emblematizes. Although *Pericles* erases Twine's blunter demystification of princely sovereignty, the shape of Cleon's obligation to Tyre's prince remains similar. Indeed, Cleon's initial reading of Pericles's ships turns out to be just shy of prescient: sixteen years on, Pericles is poised to launch a marine invasion of Tarsus, in response to Cleon's lack of gratitude (5.1.239-40). Only Diana diverts him to Ephesus.[134]

Cleon's passivity in the face of his fear of conquest acknowledges that legal authority is inevitably a matter of strength as much as of any theoretical claim to jurisdiction. Like Cleon, Pericles experiences a melancholic fear of Antioch: though Antiochus's "arm seems far too short to hit me here," he says, "Yet neither pleasure's art can joy my spirits, / Nor yet the other's distance comfort me" (1.2.8-10). As the play ultimately has it, however, Pericles is the one to stretch his imperial arm across the water. Extending his authority outward from Tyre more subtly than through conquest, he will encompass Tarsus as a kind of subordinate confederate, as well as Pentapolis and Mytilene, which enter the circle of his authority through his own and Marina's marriages.[135] Romantic delay and dispersion turn out to be politically strategic. If the play begins with Pericles's disastrous choice to bind himself to Antiochus and to the terms of Antiochus's riddling wager, it presents thereafter a series of subtler negotiations between the prince's authority and his subjection to the foreign. As we have seen in his exchanges both with Simonides and with Cleon, the same physical displacement that threatens to disperse his goods and his royal identity enables the reproduction of that identity in an altered form. Pericles imposes his imperial authority on the Mediterranean not by conquest but by making the right marriages, and most of all by moving across the water, often with the trappings of a merchant: with wheat or with the "full bags of spices" that he places in his wife's casket before consigning it to the ocean, and which seem a treasure to those in Ephesus who discover them when the casket or chest is tossed up on their shore (3.2.64). In light of King James's enabling extension of the prerogative across Britain's proximate waters, and in light of the judgment in *Bate's Case*, the political efficacy of Pericles's marine exile can thus be understood to recast the place of the king's natural body in the structure of trade relations and of British *imperium* more generally.

In representing the political consequences of Pericles's trials on the sea and in states other than his own, Shakespeare and Wilkins make the prince's accommodation of the jurisdictional other seem both aggressive and deferential. A final instance of that dynamic involves the play's interest in the alternative names available to authority: prince, king, regent, governor. At the end of the first scene in Act 5, Pericles offers Marina in marriage to Lysimachus: "for it seems you have been noble towards her" (5.1.248). Ironically elided in Pericles's formulation is Lysimachus's earlier attempt to coerce Marina into prostitution: "Come, bring me to some private place. Come, come" (4.5.95). It is also true that a governor may not be quite the best match for a princess. But when Pericles introduces his future son-in-law to Thaisa, he renames him: "This prince, the fair betrothed of your daughter, / Shall marry her at Pentapolis" (5.3.72–73).[136] Central to this deferential elevation is the nature of the contract required by Pericles to preserve his own prestige, even as he recognizes and accommodates in Lysimachus a useful alternative to his own royal self. To the extent that the new designation of Lysimachus comes to seem natural, it constitutes a symbolic resolution to the confusion that generates the play's action, the misnaming at the heart of Antiochus's incestuous relationship with his daughter: "*He's father, son, and husband mild; / I mother, wife, and yet his child*" (1.1.69–70). Rejecting this initial confusion of names as unnatural and unlawful, Pericles embraces the second mixing of names as necessary to the legal constitution of his new authority.[137]

At issue in the marriages that bring Pericles two of his kingdoms, and in the play's close concern with naming, is the acknowledgment that international bonds are forged less through natural law than according to contract, whereby named parties enter into a named and stable relationship. At the same time that James was trying to exercise an innovative jurisdiction over the northern seas, England was engaging the United Provinces on the matter of access to the East Indian spice trade, over which the Dutch had by now a virtual monopoly. In this debate, curiously enough, the English came to occupy a position directly opposed to the one articulated in respect of the northern fisheries. Arguing from the natural freedom of commerce, as set forth in *Mare liberum*, they insisted that, whatever the Dutch role in liberating the Indian seas from the Portuguese, the English were now as much entitled as they to trade in the islands. At a London conference in 1613, Grotius himself answered the charge. The issue was not the natural freedom of the seas, nor the natural freedom of commerce, but rather, he said, the exclusive nature of the trading contracts that the Dutch East India Company had made with the island sovereigns, contracts that the English could not legally impede. According to these, Grotius said, the island princes had granted exclusive trading rights in exchange for Dutch protection against the Portuguese.[138] The terms of this commercial contract correspond closely to those of the natural bond between king and subject, as articulated by James in 1609. But the shift in emphasis from natural law toward an artificial obligation allowed the Dutch a more certain solution to the problem of competing interests than had been available to James (and a more rigid one, perhaps, than he would have entertained).

Grotius's discursive shift to contract clarifies the importance of naming for the early trade empires. For a nation's success in trade depended not so much on the extension of the sovereign self as on its proliferation, the identification and designation of the alternative sovereign parties who could effect the stabilizing and advantageous agreement. The acts of naming in *Pericles* are contractual, but they show how the stable contract becomes the site also for the more flexible construction of relative international prestige. And that is a delicate matter. To put the problem in the symbolic cartographic terms we have earlier mapped out, even if the compass rose describes the natural extension of a national authority, it remains unclear what happens when lines from two roses intersect. Partly, names happen. At times these names seem explicitly strategic, as in one complaint made by English merchants about their Dutch republican competitors in the Indies:

> [A]s they [the Hollanders] hinder our trade, so they forbeare not (which I cannot but write with stomacke) the honour of our King and kingdome, as presuming somtimes to call themselves *English*, and pretend Embassage, and presents from his Majesty, which they did to the King of *Siam*. In other places calling the Crowne and State of *England* into comparison, which made the King of *Achem* ask captaine *Best* whether the King of *England*, or the King of *Holland* were the greater Monarke.[139]

If the point here is that the Dutch become more successful traders by becoming English, that is so because the names available to the English monarchy more effectively or efficiently mirror the king of Achem's authority than do the Dutch republican names. Equally, of course, the meeting of nations was shaped by the names belonging to the Eastern sovereigns. In 1607 the English East India Company requested from James royal letters to the various Eastern princes, each written according to his own particular style: "The most puissant Prince ... of Suratt"; "The Highe and Mightie Kinge of the Molloccos"; "The Right Honorable the Sabander of Luntor."[140] The differences between such names mark the priority of the local for the mercantile encounter. Unsurprisingly, this concession to the local was often controlled even as it was articulated. When James sent a letter in 1604 to "the greate and mightie kinge of Bantam, & of the dominions and territories adjoyning," he was acknowledging in that name a sovereignty like his own, a royal identity necessary to British trade. But James did not, as he would in the case of Spain or France, refer to this royal alternative as brother, an omission whose significance is noted at the bottom of a copy of the letter preserved in the first Letter Book of the East India Company: "Note that the Kinge writeth him not brother."[141] The familial is too prestigious, perhaps, or too perilous a mark. Like Prince Pericles's recognition as suitor that the names Antiochus offers him are dishonorable, or like his elevation of his future son-in-law Lysimachus, James's linguistic negotiation established, as favorably as it might, the terms of the contractual, imaginary line that was to serve a newly complex *imperium* by preserving an integrated sovereign self across distance, even as that self was dispersed.

MARINE EFFECTS: LIMIT BELONGING

In the plot that sees Pericles's submission to alternative powers reinscribe the source of his own authority, water is both medium and actor. When he abandons Tyre, his delegation of authority to Helicanus is mirrored by his abandoning land and law in favor of a sea and nature to which even kings are subject: "Wind, rain and thunder, remember earthly man / Is but a substance that must yield to you, / And I, as fits my nature, do obey you" (2.1.2–4). Yet the waters that here bereave Pericles "of all his fortunes" (2.1.9) also return to him the armor (already rusted) that admits him to Simonides's court and ultimately to a royal and international marriage. If the sea becomes the deep source of Pericles's reconfigured authority, it is also the narrative engine for the romance plot, in the sense that the sea delivers onto the play's coasts the various devices that allow the plot to advance: Pericles's waterlogged body and then his armor in Pentapolis; Thaisa's coffin in Ephesus; the pirates that rescue Marina from Tarsus only to transport her as a slave to Mytilene's brothels. The margin of the sea is the play's most potent topographic symbol and topological reality, marking, for example, the place Dionyza intends to use against Marina: "O'er the sea-margent / Walk with Leonine" (4.1.25–26).[142] In the poem that Pericles includes in Thaisa's coffin, he meditates on the place where sea and land meet: "*Here I give to understand / If e'er this coffin drives a-land / I King Pericles have lost / This queen, worth all our mundane cost*" (3.2.67–70). Cost is Pericles's worldly fortune, but also his coast. And the message means that Thaisa's death is deterritorialization in the extreme, the sea's overpowering of the very idea of that land he imagines the coffin reaching.

The play thematizes the coast or liminal shore according to a legal vocabulary that organizes the indefinable limit between land and sea by distinguishing among kinds of property derived from the sea. When Cerimon's servant says of Thaisa's coffin that the sea "Did . . . toss up upon our shore this chest; / 'Tis of some wreck" (3.2.50–51), his supposition that there has been a shipwreck identifies the chest itself as *wreccum maris*, goods that John Cowell notes belong by common law to the monarch: "This wreck being made, the goods that were in the shippe, being brought to land by the waves, belong to the King by his prerogative. And thereupon in many bookes of our common lawe, the very goods, so brought to land are called wreck."[143] At common law, in other words, it is not so clear as Cerimon suggests that the gold he hopes to find in the chest is his at all: "If the sea's stomach be o'ercharged with gold, / 'Tis a good constraint of fortune / It belches upon us" (3.2.56–58). Fortune is, perhaps, what one makes of it.

The second point is that the sea is said to "toss up" the chest, an important detail in light of the decision in *Sir Henry Constable's Case* of 1601, in which Constable brought an action of trespass against one Gamble. Constable had inherited from his father a grant of wreck (by letters patent) in a manor on whose shore goods, comprising twelve shirts and five cloaks, were found between the high and low watermarks ("*inter fluxum & refluxum maris*"). The goods had been seized by Gamble on behalf of the Lord Admiral, and the question was whether these fell under the Admiral's jurisdiction or, as Constable argued, the common law's (and thus, according to the grant, his). As reported by Coke in 1605 in the fifth part of his *Reports*, the court defined *wreccum maris* exclusively as those goods driven onto the shore by the sea (over which consequently the Admiral had no jurisdiction)—this in contradistinction to those goods that did pertain to the Admiral as, variously, *flotsam, jetsam*, and *lagan* (or *ligan*). The distinction among these other categories involves the nature of the sailors' intention for the goods, *flotsam* being goods that float off a wrecked ship; *jetsam* being goods thrown overboard in an effort to save them, notwithstanding which the ship perishes; and *lagan* being goods that would sink to the bottom of the sea, so "*ponderous*," as Coke writes, "*que ils sink al bottom, & les maryners al intent de eux reaver [re-avoir] lye a eux un boye, ou corke, ou auter tiel chose, que ne voet sinke, issint que ils poient trouver eux arrere.*"[144] Thus when Cerimon notes that the chest is "wondrous heavy" (3.2.53) and closely "caulked and bitumed" (3.2.59), and asks "Did the sea cast it up?" (3.2.53), his remarks seem to depend on the distinction between wreck and, specifically, lagan. The scene further complicates the coffin's proximate legal history when, having discovered Thaisa's body within, Cerimon wakes her, since neither wreck nor floating goods were said to be forfeit should any living creature at all escape the wreck and reach shore alive: "*si home, chien, ou chate, escapes vives.*"[145] In waking Thaisa, Cerimon is undoing the basis of the property claim that up to that point has energized the coastal scene and the characters' shared fantasy.

As opposed to Thaisa's chest, Pericles's armor is brought onto the shore in a net by fishermen in Pentapolis, and thus, oddly, as both a kind of lagan and wreck. Through their labor, the fishermen blur the boundary between wreck and floating goods, converting the latter form of property into the former. In so doing, they become imperial agents in the manner of John Bate, whose imported currants could similarly be said variously to *belong* according to where they variously were. In a familiar imperial move, after identifying the armor as his own, Pericles nevertheless defers to those who recovered it, and instead of claiming it by right—he is alive and the armor was his—indicates that he means to "beg of you, kind friends, this coat of worth" (2.1.132). One fisherman gladly surrenders the armor, but another makes a strikingly direct ethical claim that, in light of the difficulty of categorizing property at the shore's edge, seems also to be a legal one: "Ay, but hark you, my friend, 'twas we that made this garment through the rough seams of the waters. There are certain condolements, certain vails. I hope, sir, if you thrive you'll remember from whence you had them" (2.1.144–48). Finally, in one of the play's most cogent legal moments, as the pirates steal Marina from the "sea-margent" where Leonine means to kill her, one of them shouts, "A prize, a prize" (4.1.89), thus technically claiming her according to the laws of war and the *ius gentium*. The point here is not only that Marina is made into property, but also that the pirates are claiming jurisdiction at the sea's margin, just as the Admiralty had done in *Sir Henry Constable's Case*. (In that case the decision, against Constable, was that between the high and low water marks, although the soil pertain to the manor, the common law and the Admiral have "*diversum imperium*," sharing jurisdiction "*interchangeablement*" depending on the ebb and flow of the sea.)[146]

The shore is a place, then, whose topography vividly makes belonging a difficult problem for adjudication. The play's analysis of the difficulty reaches its culmination in the representation of Marina's political and ethical subjectivity, the play's most complex achievement. If Pericles's travel disrupts the clarity of jurisdictional boundaries, Marina, born as she is on the ocean, resists legal categorization altogether. Shakespeare makes this point in topographical terms in Marina's riddling response to her father's question as to her origins:

Pericles: You're like something that—what countrywoman?
Here of these shores?
Marina: No, nor of any shores.
Yet I was mortally brought forth and am
No other than I appear.

(5.1.93–96)

To be born on the sea is to belong to no shore. Marina here posits an identity split off from the categories that territorial law requires to make sense of the world. In Pentapolis, Pericles is repeatedly designated as foreign, a "stranger" (for example, 2.2.41, 2.3.65), but it is Marina who is the play's most perfect stranger, in the sense that, strictly speaking, the circumstances of her birth make her foreign to place in general. To Pericles's question, "Where do you live," Marina replies, with general force, "Where I am but a stranger. From the deck / You may discern the place" (5.1.105–6).

The ocean is a place, but not. Caught between a double negation—no, not from Mytilene nor from other shores—Marina is unable to express her origins because her origin is a place of nonbeing. That is why she can punningly say that she was "mortally brought forth," this being a direct reprise of Lychorida's sense, at the time of Marina's birth in the storm, that the sea, for those who can sense it, is for dying: "Here is a thing too young for such a place, / Who if it had conceit would die" (3.1.15–16). Yet Marina's claim that nevertheless she is "no other than I appear" insists on an integral identity in spite of her territorial and ontological estrangements. Like the ocean itself, Marina poses a problem for law's normativizing account of belonging even more extreme than that posed for the common law by the liminal space of marine ebb and flow. Politically, Marina is her father's daughter, and, even more than he does, she stands for a relation to place antithetical to that instantiated by the play's various sovereign authorities. Take, for example, Lysimachus, Marina's future husband, and his response to Helicanus's request that he identify himself:

Helicanus: First, what is your place?
Lysimachus: I am governor of this place you lie before.

(5.1.17–18)

In addition to the quibble on office and geography, the exchange indexes the sovereignty effected through territorial division only so as then to subordinate it to the topological relation of place to *non*place, of Mytilene to the sea that, in contrast to Lysimachus's place, Helicanus and Pericles are said to occupy. It is this latter space (which is, we might say, always "before" or "this side" of place) that Marina radicalizes as the source of her own strange identity.

On land, the tragicomic brothel reconstitutes for Marina the sea's displacing energies. Marina's charged relation to her estrangement in these rooms is nowhere clearer than in Lysimachus's failed seduction of her. Eager only to possess her, Lysimachus urges Marina not to fear his power and position, and instead to split his natural from his political body, not least because, as the play teasingly implies, those bodies are differently sensed and one of them is fully unequal to the occasion: "my *authority* shall not *see* thee, or else look friendly upon thee. Come, bring me to some private place. Come, come" (4.5.83-95, emphasis added). But these comic lines are also exceptionally dark. "Place" works here as a generic, a lexical cue for the scene of prostitution that the law both puts in place and disavows. The play repeatedly designates the brothel in this way, with a cumulative pressure that makes the placedness of the word disappear into emptiness, a frightening particularity that is also empty of specific content: "such a place as this" (4.5.2); "a place of such resort" (4.5.84-85); "this unhallowed place" (4.5.104); "this place" (4.5.183). Lysimachus asks, furthermore, for privacy, a category that in relation to place functions for him as the promise that here, in this place, his desire to possess her can be fulfilled, but for Marina as the danger of entering a zone of *privation*. Marina refuses. As the source of her identity, nonbeing is exactly not its site. In this equation she resembles her father, whom the generative sea is forever returning to the places of his story. The small exchange between Marina and her future husband thus parodically amplifies Marina's self-absenting from shore and territorialized space as the very condition of her integral self-belonging.

Displaced and yet in space, Marina is a creature of the limit itself. To say, as she does to her father, that she lives "Where I am but a stranger. From the deck / You may discern the place" insists on her liminality as foreigner but also on the foundational liminality of her origins. For the act of discernment that allows Pericles to locate the "honest house" where she now teaches the citizens of Mytilene is not reversible, given that the place of her birth on the water must remain, from whatever perspective, indiscernible and undifferentiated. In the terms I have charted out in *Cymbeline*, where the spatio-temporal threshold is the place from and on which to gain perspective, here the *distended limit* of the ocean is that which, conversely, cannot be seen. No one in the play inhabits space (although not place) more fiercely and privately than Marina, for the reason that the public belonging against which Lysimachus measures his idea of the private is not hers. Child of the sea as she is, this lack is also the source of her peculiar authority, a relation to self and ground that identifies her as exemplary daughter to her father, whose sovereign reach is similarly produced as the limit disruption of a singular identity and, insistently, its reintegration as sovereign potential.

It is not coincidental that the *literary* authority represented in the play is similarly produced out of the negative: "To sing a song that old was sung / From ashes ancient Gower is come" (1.0.1–2), the play's choric ghost announces. Mullaney locates in Gower's old tale, "forever timely and uncontaminated by historical or cultural contexts," Shakespeare's attempt to define a theater that is itself "free from history and from historical determination."[147] Locating the same vivid authorizing energy in culture itself, Jeffrey Masten has excavated the play's complexly patriarchal account of literary and political authority, as both are fashioned in tension with the erotics of family and friendly dramatic collaboration.[148] I want to bring these two accounts of Gower's authorizing presence together by noting how dramatic authority in the play is imagined as a radical potential inside Gower's poetic authority: as with Marina's impossibly deterritorialized identity, to come from ashes is to come, phoenix-like, from a version of mortality that is yet rich with potential. *Pericles* identifies jurisdictional heterogeneity as the source of the prince's reconfigured and tragic *imperium*, as the source of his daughter's comic resistance to the dangerous houses she falls into, and as the source of the deterritorialized identities that the play constitutes in Pericles as his waiting and in Marina as the privacy of her estrangement. In negotiation with the concept of jurisdiction that everywhere subtends the play's thematics, the same plurality through which authority and ontology are destabilized so as to find themselves in newly concentrated form makes "Gower" possible, makes possible the poet's flight across distance onto a *stage* enlivened, as by an author, by the play of history against the space of what remains unseen.

CHAPTER SIX

"To Law for Our Children": Norm and Jurisdiction in Webster, Rowley, and Heywood's *Cure for a Cuckold*

The preceding chapter argued that in the late tragicomedies Shakespeare conceives of dramatic action both in terms of the distances between distinct jurisdictions and in terms of the threshold reality separating them. In so doing, he stages the legal equation by which imperial identities emerge as themselves a threshold reality: selves newly reconstituted by the geographical, political, or ontological limits that seem to define them but which more precisely determine their potential. As these plays present the jurisdictional point, which corresponds to the historical invention of a new English *imperium*, there is no place beyond law, but only a productive metalegality that follows from a place or person or category becoming unstably subject, in theory or in fact, to more than one norm. I turn now from the transnational context back to the question of jurisdictional plurality internal to English law, and from the vast distances of romance to those circumscribed by urban comedy. In self-consciously shifting my focus from the global to the parochial, I aim to show how the charged legality produced as an effect of jurisdictional plurality could sustain not only the quietly coercive accommodations of King James or Prince Pericles or Cymbeline's odd family, but also a comic freedom constituted jurisdictionally as one formal norm's response to another. If legal romance is the dramatic genre of an early imperial context in which extraterritorial authority was imaginable in terms of a jurisdictional effect, and of a belonging, separate from place and ownership, then the legal comedy I treat here might be said, conversely, to stage the scene in which property itself remains productively open to more than one description, grounded as it is in an idea of jurisdiction inseparable from the fact of jurisdictional plurality. Indeed, as we will see, legal resolution in the city depends on a fully global imagination, such that the distinction between narrowly local and broadly global does not quite make sense. Like the unruly nonplace of the ocean and of the threshold line, comic London is a place, at the very *center* of common law, in which the legal form opens onto the time of its making and thus onto a potential for discovering competing legalities and other forms. This is an argument, therefore, about literary representation's special relation to the extreme case.[1]

Put the case, then, of a sailor Compass, who returns after four years at sea to Blackwall, a London suburb some few miles east of St. Paul's, to discover that Urse, his wife, now has a son aged three months. Instead of blaming her and disavowing the boy, Compass answers the implication that he has been cuckolded in the simplest manner possible: by denying it, by thanking his wife for her labor, and by laying claim to the child as his *own*. This, in brief, is the premise for the subplot to *A Cure for a Cuckold*, a provocative and too little known play written in 1624 by John Webster, William Rowley, and John Heywood.[2] As against the claims of the biological father, Franckford, a childless merchant who wants the child partly for legal reasons involving his purchase of land, Compass defends his claim on the child, first, by proposing irrationally that he is the biological father—the child is his flesh and blood, he will say—and second, by so challenging the force of Franckford's claim as to split the question of legal paternity from the disciplinary force of biology, a move at once familiar from the common law's way of ordering experience and somewhat in excess of it. The case between the two fathers eventually goes to law in a scene played out in a tavern. There, against the arbitrators' initial ruling, Compass scores his victory over the merchant by promoting Urse's right to her son—a child she has borne effectively as surrogate for the wealthier childless couple—and by annexing his own hyper-patriarchal claim to hers.

The play tests Compass's claim—his attempt to legitimate the child—in terms of competing legal and discursive orders: pitting the mother's rights against the biological father's, for example, but also natural law against human law, central law against local and municipal law, English common law against the Roman civil and canonical orders that together constituted the *ius commune*.[3] The play's fascination with jurisdiction and with semi-technical distinctions within and between legal orders speaks to the continuing importance of the Inns of Court as sponsors and knowing audience for theatrical and literary production. It also emerges in response to the historical fact that illegitimacy lay at the jurisdictional border between the temporal and spiritual laws, and could be diversely accounted for depending on the legal discourse brought to bear upon it. In terms of doctrine, for example, those two laws differed in their attitudes to legitimation by subsequent marriage, a doctrine in canon law that was soundly rejected at common law. A second point of doctrinal difference, and one especially relevant to *A Cure for a Cuckold*, is the difference between the two laws in relation to children born to a married woman but through an adulterous relationship. While canon law bastardized such issue, the common law from as early as the twelfth century operated under the strong "presumption that a child born in wedlock is legitimate."[4] Principally to prevent the intrusion of other laws in matters of inheritance, the common law was highly protective of its jurisdiction over illegitimacy, a matter that in other European countries was treated as essentially spiritual. As John Brydall explains in the *Lex Spuriorum* (1703), a text that rehearses doctrine and procedures that had been long in place, suits to prove bastardy or legitimacy had to be moved first in a temporal court and only then "transmitted to the Ecclesiastical Court, by the King's Writ to be examined, and tried there, and thereupon the Bishop is to make a Certificate to the King's Court."[5] That is, the central royal courts acknowledged the ecclesiastical jurisdiction over bastardy, but strictly controlled it, even to the extent that a suit "commenced in the Ecclesiastical Court, before any Question be moved of such matter in the Temporal Court" would for that reason alone be open to a common-law prohibition.[6]

Nor did the common law merely control the transmission of cases from the temporal to the spiritual jurisdiction. For example, to avoid a potential doctrinal embarrassment, cases in which legitimation by subsequent marriage was at issue were tried at common law *without* referral to the ecclesiastical judge. The common lawyers gave the name "Special Bastardy" to these cases, in which "the Marriage is confessed, but the Priority or Posteriority of the Nativity of him whose birth is in question, is controverted"; here the question "shall be tried by the Country and not by the Bishop. But generall Bastardy alledged, shall be tried by the Certificate of the Bishop."[7] A similar reasoning kept out of the spiritual courts cases involving possible illegitimacy within wedlock: from as early as 1234, as R. H. Helmholz explains, when "bastardy because of adultery was alleged, the matter would not be sent to the bishop."[8] With respect both to doctrine and procedure, the idea and practice of jurisdiction dominated the treatment of illegitimacy at common law.

In the attention it pays to different jurisdictional orders, *A Cure for a Cuckold* thus refracts a relevant historical, legal, and cultural context.[9] But the play's argument, I think, should be understood more in theoretical than in sociological terms, as a meditation on the nature of legal identity at a historical moment when, as we have seen throughout this book, the process of legal centralization and rationalization was giving ever greater prominence to the common law's configuration of legal identity. The play engages in jurisdictional analysis as a way to reflect critically on the nature and production of legal normativity. In the context of jurisdictional instability, Compass's irrational (because absolute) claim to be the child's father is legible not as an extralegal act of resistance to the rational order that would name the child a bastard, but rather as an attempt to constitute for himself an alternative *juridical* identity, one that is more knowing about the place of jurisdiction in the constitution of legal authority than any fully rationalized account of the public law's relation to its norms would make visible. The play refuses to offer a utopian fantasy of an order of justice beyond law. Instead, by representing the possibility that not one but several norms might be at stake, Compass's critical construction of his family effectively privatizes jurisdiction, even as it exposes the public legal norm to the complex practices that produced it.

The opening scene of Shakespeare's *King John* (ca. 1595–96) provides a useful dramatic context for the specifically legal orientation of Compass's argument. After dismissing the French ambassador who urges, against John, the claim of Geoffrey Plantagenet's son Arthur to the English throne, John and his mother are interrupted by a pair of brothers who present before them a legal case that Essex describes as "the strangest controversy / . . . That e'er I heard" (1.1.44–46).[10] Against Philip, the elder son of the deceased Sir Robert Faulconbridge, the younger brother, Robert, claims his father's lands as the latter's son and true "heir" (1.1.56). The plaintiff's argument, in apparent contravention of primogeniture but in accordance with the terms of the father's declared will (1.1.109), is that the elder brother is not the son of Faulconbridge, who at the time of Philip's conception was on embassy in Germany: "But truth is truth," Robert says in feigned embarrassment; "large lengths of seas and shores / Between my father and my mother lay, / As I have heard my father speak himself, / When this same lusty gentleman was got" (1.1.105–8). In this argument, Philip (who, as it turns out, is the issue of King Richard) is illegitimate and thus incapable of inheriting the Faulconbridge estate. King John's ruling leaves no room for doubt as to the legal speciousness of the argument:

> Sirrah, your brother is legitimate;
> Your father's wife did after wedlock bear him.
> And if she did play false, the fault was hers,
> Which fault lies on the hazards of all husbands
> That marry wives. Tell me, how if my brother,

> Who as you say took pains to get this son,
> Had of your father claimed this son for his?
> In sooth, good friend, your father might have kept
> This calf bred from his cow from all the world;
> In sooth he might.
>
> (1.1.116–24)

To a contemporary audience, John's decision would have been heard both as familiar and as involving a set of spatial and temporal equivocations.

As already noted, the legal presumption that a child of a married woman was the legitimate child of the husband was indeed fundamental at common law, working to stabilize the transmission of property by subordinating, in cases of doubt, a possible biological reality to the operative fiction of legitimacy. There were, however, exceptions to the general presumption, where, as Sir Edward Coke outlines, it was flatly impossible to get around the sexual scandal: "if the Husband be within the four Seas, that is, within the Jurisdiction of the King of England, if the Wife hath Issue no proof is to be admitted to prove the child a Bastard, for in that case, *Filiatio non potest probari*, unless the Husband hath an apparent impossibility of procreation; as if the Husband be but eight years old, or under the age of procreation, such Issue is a Bastard, albeit he be born within marriage."[11] First, a husband's impotency or inability to procreate undermines the presumption of legitimacy. Second, and more relevant for Compass (though his insistence on his paternity *could* be read as his protest against the implication of impotence), legitimacy was measured along the axes of geography and time. As Helmholz explains, the "four seas rule" precipitated out of the lawyers' long insistence on presuming legitimacy even in cases of notorious adultery:

> Common lawyers were led to make some extravagant arguments in favor of a position that so clearly violated common sense. For instance, it was said that if a husband was in France at any time when conception could have taken place, the child was legitimate, no matter how clear the adultery. The reason: the husband might have slipped across the Channel at night. Only if he were as far off as the Holy Land was the result otherwise. Finally, the even more mechanical test of the four seas—that is, the limits of the kingdom—was settled on as the dividing line. And when called upon to produce an argument for legitimacy, the pleaders of the fifteenth century retreated to the homely analogy, "Whoso bulleth my cow, the calf is mine."[12]

In relation to *King John* we can note, first, that John supports the ruling in Philip's favor with the same proverb that the lawyers imported into their reasoning. It is also significant, though, that Sir Robert's mission in Germany placed him beyond the four seas at the time of conception, an argument that Robert makes when he insists that Philip could be his father's only if he arrived fully "fourteen weeks" early (1.1.13). And although John's ruling ignores the possibility of an exception to the presumption of legitimacy for reasons of geographical distance, Philip's subsequent decision to acknowledge his royal father and formally "bequeath" the Faulconbridge lands to his half-brother in order to follow his grandmother Eleanor to France (1.1.148–54) may inscribe, as a further legal act and as his own geographical displacement, the possibility that the law might well, under the right circumstances, swing against the husband's paternity rather than for it.

Time, however, works quite clearly against Philip's claim. Coke's summary of the four seas rule interestingly skirts the question of time, since he neglects to say *when* the husband must be beyond the four seas for the strong presumption of legitimacy not to pertain. The doctrine ultimately points to the time of conception, but here too the lawyers worked hard on behalf of their version of reason. In his lengthy treatment of the topic, the nineteenth-century lawyer Sir Harris Nicolas reports that as early as the time of Bracton it was held that for a child born in wedlock to be deemed illegitimate, the husband must not have had "access" to his wife "for one, if not two years at the least before the birth."[13] In a case from 1440 Serjeant Markham posited, in a most impressive temporal extension of the doctrine, that presumption of legitimacy could be overturned if it could be proved that the husband and putative father of the child "for three years before his birth, and for three years after, was beyond the sea"; Serjeant Ayscough suggested that the father must be "beyond the seas six years before his birth."[14] These, however, are more extreme temporal specifications than the common law seems ultimately to have accepted. Coke's omission of a temporal specificity commensurate with the geographical one speaks to a greater lack of clarity in relation to the former, especially as regards the requirement for a husband's absence after the birth of a child. In the case of *Done and Egerton v. Hinton and Starkey* from 1617, for example, the judges ruled only "if the wife of a man who had been beyond the sea for such time, before the birth of the issue which the wife had in his absence, that the issue could not be his, it is a bastard."[15]

According even to this relatively restrained pronouncement as to time, it is clear that in the case of Philip Faulconbridge, born fourteen weeks late but *after* his father's return from Germany, the common law would have presumed legitimacy.[16] Things are not so clear for Compass, whose family presents an even messier spatio-temporal situation than the Faulconbridges. The relevance of the Shakespearean scenario for *A Cure for a Cuckold* is multiple, then. First, the child at the center of that play's subplot is in a similar situation to Philip. Indeed, Compass's basic claim rests on the same grounds as those that John attributes hypothetically to Sir Robert in response to Richard's hypothetical claim over Philip: like Sir Robert, Compass is a husband who, even against a known biological father, might at law logically claim his wife's child as his own, as a "calf bred from his cow." In this sense, the common law itself might be seen to ground, through its patriarchal reckoning of the force of marriage, the variable construction of paternity that Compass seeks; within that construction of the question, the play is thinkable as a fiction that dramatizes the common-law fiction presuming legitimacy. Except that *A Cure for a Cuckold* seems designed explicitly to prevent the common-law presumption. If Sir Robert's geographical displacement in Germany makes his legal paternity more ambiguous than King John's ruling implies, it is even more vividly the case that Compass's otherwise unassailable claim as Urse's husband (and thus the baby's father) founders, according to the law that could have supported the claim, by his having been beyond the seas during conception and gestation both.

As with the argument I made in chapter 5 concerning the extension of the sovereign presence across international distance, one question is whether a subject engaged on diplomatic or commercial business can meaningfully be said to be beyond the king's *jurisdiction* merely through distance. In relation to Compass, in particular, it might playfully be asked why, inside a mercantile economy, the "four seas" that underwrite the exception to the common-law rule must be taken to refer, as though this were the only natural construction of the phrase, to the waters around Britain rather than the oceans that English merchants were charged with making their own. In a reading of the phrase perversely responsive to an emergent globalism (and, less perversely, to the legal-formal extension of royal jurisdiction across distance), there would be no way for a husband ever to be beyond his paternal rights or obligations.

This is not, however, the argumentative direction taken by *A Cure for a Cuckold*, which instead presents the issue under the aspect of the extreme case. The play eschews the givenness of a husband's legal paternity by going so far as to place Compass at the critical moment on the other side of the *world*, and not for one or two years but for four. It then goes on to ask how he might nevertheless at law make his a child who is not his. In other words, the question posed by the play is this: what does law look like when it goes beyond even the common law's own impressive fiction-making? My reading of *A Cure for a Cuckold* falls into three parts, unfolding in order of increasing technical complexity the play's analysis of the necessary incompleteness of law's forms. I consider first, across the main plot, the play's analysis of name and place as formal sources of stability for the legal order. The configuration of norms is also a matter of names, and to claim a name (like father) alternative to one (like cuckold) that specifies your place in a given order disrupts that order by subjecting its names to a critique of their operation, pushing even further than the law does the priority given property over procreation. (In Compass's case, he means to make the child *his* quite in excess of any fiction that would allow the child to be his for reasons of inheritance.) Second, I shall return to the subplot and to Compass's story in order to trace how, as an instance of law's speaking, the playwrights model the enunciatory and *dramatic* production of legal authority generally. Finally, I will look to the play's use of jurisdictional tensions inside the forms of common-law action to identify Compass's stubborn argument as a kind of proceduralist intervention that might be said not to subvert the common law's incomplete logics, but, indeed, to complete them.

THE ORDER OF NAMES

In the world of *A Cure for a Cuckold* names and identities, whether natural or civil, achieve meaning in relation to place. In accordance with the conventions of city comedy, the main plot explores this, its major theme, through the double lens of marriage and of the various professions that make up its richly textured urban scene. With respect to both gender and professional relation, the play understands naming as a technical practice that, like jurisdiction itself, stabilizes a social and legal order by identifying as prior what might be understood instead as the posterior effect of mundane practice.

Because the play is not well known, let me summarize the main plot. *A Cure for a Cuckold* opens at the wedding of Bonvile and Annabel, with Lessingham urging Clare to marry him and so "follow" the example or "president" (1.1.10–11) laid down by their friends. But Clare, who is secretly in love with Bonvile, rejects the advance, telling Lessingham that the "onely road" (1.1.55) to her affection is to discover and execute the meaning of a riddle she poses in a letter to him: "*Prove all thy Friends, finde out the best and nearest, / Kill for my sake that Friend that loves thee dearest*" (1.1.101–2). Interpreting the letter as a challenge to test his love, Lessingham pretends to need a second for a duel in Calais, in order thereby to discover who is his best friend. Bonvile alone is willing to risk his life. Much to the confusion of the bride and her family, the two friends depart in secret for Dover. Once in Calais, Lessingham reveals his real motive for luring Bonvile there, by showing him Clare's riddling letter. But Bonvile extricates himself from the duel, proposing that Lessingham has already fulfilled the terms of the challenge in killing the friendship between them, by killing him *as* friend: "We now / Are severed: thus hast thou slain thy friend, / And satisfied what the Witch thy Mistriss bad thee" (3.1.123-25).

Meanwhile, a puzzled Annabel has attempted to follow Bonvile to the ferry that takes the friends across the Thames and so onto the Dover road. On the path, she is accosted by Rochfield, a poor gentleman and younger son who has just that day turned thief. Unable to unlock the wedding necklace and bracelet that Rochfield wants to steal, Annabel promises instead to give him the equivalent value in money. Guiding him home, and introducing him to the wedding guests as Bonvile's kinsman, she fulfills that promise, only then to encourage Rochfield to surrender the money to Annabel's father, Woodroff, a merchant adventurer looking for co-investors: in this way, Rochfield realizes, Annabel "has fisht for her Gold back, and caught it; I am no thief now" (2.4.154-55). Rochfield's fortune is made when, joining the sea adventurers, he is responsible for saving the ship in a confrontation with three "Spanish men of War," and for helping to capture one of these as "our prize" (3.3.89), under the authority of a "*Letter of Mart* [marque]" (2.4.138), the license granted by the king authorizing a subject to act privately, and hence de facto as a pirate, in the capture of an enemy merchant ship.

When Lessingham returns to England and tells Clare that he has slain his friend, Clare replies that he has misinterpreted the meaning of her riddle, by which she had intended only to solicit Lessingham's assistance in her suicide, supposing as she had that she was his "best esteemed friend" (4.2.16). Learning that Bonvile is the friend he has slain, however, Clare turns from despair to joy, declaring that she will now marry Lessingham since, in slaying the man she loved without hope of reciprocation, he has slain "my deerest friend, / And fatalest enemy" (4.2.41-42). Horrified by her fickleness and his own treachery toward Bonvile, Lessingham abandons her. Bonvile enters, explaining to a surprised Clare how Lessingham has only "kill'd me for a friend" (4.2.126). When Clare reveals her love for him and the true intention of her riddle, Bonvile insists that Clare repent and marry Lessingham. The play's concluding act sees Lessingham suddenly turn villain in a conventional revenge plot. Attempting to avenge himself on the world, he accuses Annabel of having adulterously given the tokens of Bonvile's love to Rochfield, and he attempts to turn Annabel against Bonvile by revealing Clare's secret love for the groom. Order is restored only when Clare confesses the part her riddle played in the plot's "Labyrinth" (5.1.280) and when Rochfield reveals how Annabel has saved him from a highwayman's life. Bonvile and Annabel are reconciled, as are Lessingham and Clare: when he confesses to the "wilde distractions" (5.2.76) that have driven him to seek revenge, she replies, as the play's second reformed villain, by repenting her "peevish will" (5.2.82).

As my summary suggests, *A Cure for a Cuckold* is, like the plays explored in chapter 5, a text deeply interested in topography and in how place or position variously determines meaning. In this sense, the dramatic use of Calais, a place favored for dueling because it lay beyond the jurisdictional reach of English laws against the practice, is on a continuum with the play's impressive mapping out of London, in terms of its references to suburbs (Bethnall Green, Wapping, Limehouse, Shadwell, East and West Ham, Bow); streets (such as Tuttle Street in Westminster); and symbolically important administrative centers, such as Guildhall. As important as such places are both thematically and as sites for dramatic action, even more important is the movement *between* places. It is notable, for example, that, as with the ships that are so central to Shakespeare's romantic tragicomedies, this play indexes both the "Ferry" (2.1.33) that takes Bonvile and Lessingham across the Thames and the "Barque" (3.1.147) that sails from Calais back to England. Dividing the space of the play, the water of the Channel is an important marker for the play's representation of English identity and an important symbol for the in-between, a zone the play effectively thematizes.

In part, this zone is a place of danger. After the "death" of his friendship with Lessingham, Bonvile refuses to travel in the same ship as the latter, wryly noting that "you know 'tis dangerous living / At Sea, with a dead body" (3.1.148-49). And when Rochfield reports that Woodroff's ship met the Spanish men-of-war when it had "Scarce . . . reacht to *Margets* [Margate]" (3.3.53), the play is identifying as the place of military danger the north-east corner of Kent, a liminal point just where the Thames estuary might be said to open fully onto the Channel. In the symbolic economy of the play, the ships meet just at the edge of the edge of home. David Gunby rightly identifies the "way" and "path" as a major theme through which the play treats the idea of the troubled "path of life."[17] Even more than at sea, the play identifies movement on land as being fraught with danger, most notably in relation to the path with which Annabel is "not well acquainted" (2.1.44), and which Rochfield turns to his own topographic use by seizing the opportunity to rob her there and so claim her as his own: "whoever owns her, she's mine now: the next ground has a most pregnant hollow for the purpose" (2.1.47-48).[18]

But if the path or middle place is dangerous, it can also, if turned to advantage, become the means and symbol of upward mobility. As the play's heroine, Annabel has the role of bringing Rochfield to safety, both in the literal sense of leading him from the highway to her home, and in the figurative sense of initiating his movement up a social ladder by giving and then taking back the money he nominally steals from her. At sea, too, the waters that encompass Britain are similarly a place for making good. The play revolves around characters like Compass, Franckford, and Woodroff, whose place in the world depends on ocean trade. (As a major port, notably, Blackwall was closely associated with the East India Company.) Thus, in the play's main example of social mobility, when Rochfield helps to capture the Spanish ship, the merchants' *prize* stands metonymically for the profit of moving between places, for a general economy of the in-between. Similarly, Woodroff's letter of marque, which lends legitimacy to the merchants' *almost* extraterritorial act of aggression against the Spanish ships, stands for the law of this zone, the normativizing letter through which danger is turned to profit.

The theme of social mobility underwrites the play's broader fascination with the language of professional and trade life. Nowhere is that connection clearer than in the confrontation between Rochfield and Annabel on the deserted path. In this scene, Rochfield comically places thievery in discursive proximity to the legitimate practices from which his birth has, he argues, excluded him. First, he figures the thief as tradesman or shopkeeper: "The place will serve for a yong beginner, / For this is the first day I set ope shop" (2.1.17–18). But when he protests to Annabel that as an "honest thief" (2.2.7) he will not "violate your Chastity, / (That's no part yet of my profession)" (2.2.14–15), he turns from trade to professional life and metaphorically begins the social ascent that Annabel will help him achieve literally. As the scene unfolds across Rochfield's inept attempts to unlock Annabel's jewelry, the play's language elevates thieving to each of the three learned or "bookish" disciplines in turn. First, Rochfield speaks of his lack of skill as that of a novice student of law, saying that "These picking Laws I am to study yet" (2.2.41). Then he transforms himself into physician, telling Annabel that she is "the best Patient for a young Physician, / That I think e're was practis'd on" (2.2.47–48). And when Annabel manages to steal his sword and use it against him, she continues the game by converting Rochfield into an unlearned "clerk," a generic term for scholar, but also the term within the English church for one in holy orders or, as seems equally plausible given the play's professional banter, for the lay parish clerk who assisted in parochial duties: "You a Thief," Annabel chides, "And guard yourself no better? No further read? / Yet out in your own book? A bad Clerk, are you not" (2.2.52–54).

The comedy of the scene depends on the conventional notion that thieving is a little world of its own, subversive because it too is a guild with a set of professional codes. The further point is that thievery here discursively absorbs the most attractive among those professions open to younger sons. In this way, the play is turned comically into a perverse version of handbooks like Thomas Powell's *Tom of All Trades* (1631), which promised to lay out for its young readers alternative paths by which they could advance (and so avoid falling into a life like that Rochfield means to follow).[19] The play uses the language of professional advancement against itself, converting thievery into book learning, just as it makes ocean trade into sanctioned piracy. A parody of the literature of making good, the scene's brilliant march across the professions thematizes how names function to differentiate among social practices that another system of naming might bring closer together.

Appropriately enough, then, the second act begins with a play on professional names that permeates the drama as a whole. Rochfield enters, meditating on the meaning of his familial and social status:

> *Rochfield:* A Younger Brother! 'Tis a poor Calling
> (Though not unlawful) very hard to live on. . . .
> (2.1.1–2)

The joke is double. First, it mixes the natural and civil, inappropriately defining brotherhood as a "Calling." But the point is also that a professional vocation or calling is just that, the name by which one is called, and so not far from a category like "brother" at all. The line levels out the distinction between natural and civil by subordinating those categories to the idea of name on which both depend. In extending the notion of what can be considered a name, the play interrogates the work categories do in the production of knowledge and identity, challenging the notion that any category, including those that belong to "nature," might be a merely empty form waiting to be filled by some other, more specific identity. Categories are always full and determinative.

This relation within naming between particular and general is thematized when Annabel first meets Rochfield. Asking him to identify himself—"Defend me goodness! What are you?" (2.2.3)—she receives in reply a name that is so general as not to be useful and so close to nature as not to seem a name at all. "A man," he says. Annabel wants specifics, and their following conversation moves according to a beginner's logic by narrowing the generic designation to approach the self she is asking after. To Annabel's probing "An honest man, I hope" (2.2.4), Rochfield replies that he is instead "an honest thief" (2.2.7), an alternative that evades Annabel's question by making clear that "honest" may be as appropriate a starting point for logical partition as "man" is. Annabel declares Rochfield's second self-definition unnatural. If he has earlier insisted that the natural kinship of younger and older brothers issues in names and vocations that are neither neutral nor merely natural, Annabel holds onto the notion that names should be so, pointing out that Rochfield's substitute for his "proper" identity is so far from producing a natural name as to invent an artificial and monstrous one, a name whose parts are ill fitted in the sense of not belonging to the same linguistic *family*:

> *Annabel:* Honest and Thief hold small affinity,
> I never heard they were a kin before,
> Pray Heaven I finde it now!
> *Rochfield:* I tell you my name.
> *Annabel:* Then honest thief, since you have taught me so,
> For Ile enquire no other, use me honestly.
> (2.2.8–12)

Rochfield's answer to Annabel's charge, in which he finally names the category of "name" that subtends the whole passage, is instructive because it insists, against Annabel and in accord with his own view of the status of younger brother, that the kind of natural kinship that Annabel seeks may not be the most effective gauge for assessing identity. In saying that she can trust the name he has assigned himself, he accuses her of having a prejudicial account of what a name can be. And his point is that a name like his ill-fitted one might be valid not as something natural or *already* coherent, but as that which action produces as its effect. His "I tell you my name" means just "Wait and see."

Rochfield's claim that "honest thief" names him disrupts the apparently neat distinction between proper name and category. So, too, with the play's names generally, which in their punning references to place encode and even materialize the "property" of the proper name. In a play about moving between kinds of places, and in which characters squabble about who owns whom, it is striking that Bonvile should carry a town in his name and that in Lessingham's name the suffix *-ham*, which can mean "meadow" and "home," should both parallel the place built into Rochfield's name and speak ironically to how Lessingham will be so little at home in the play's erotic and social stories. As part of the play's ongoing questioning of natural and artificial categories, proper names begin to look just like nouns among other nouns, even as "man" and "honest thief" become names like other names. An important point in this regard is that the scene between Annabel and Rochfield represents not only the conventionality of the name, but also the mechanics whereby the convention becomes effective and to that extent valid. For Rochfield's ability to claim "honest thief" as his name ultimately depends on Annabel's assenting to that name by allowing it to be sufficient for the action to proceed: "Ile enquire no other, use me honestly." As with the play's parodic exploration of the social ladder, the scene probes in perverse terms the familiar structure whereby, for example, one's consent to treat another as doctor or lawyer or priest allows those names to do the work required of them. Names are productive in this sense because they are already relational.

The play's representation of Annabel genders the account of professional naming that frames its analysis of Rochfield. The scene in which Annabel and the wedding guests are first introduced is structured to emphasize the role that names have in placing persons in social relation to one another.[20] In response to those who wonder why Clare has absented herself from the feast (she is, the audience knows, lovesick for the groom, Bonvile), Woodroff suggests that the unmarried woman is envious of his daughter's new name.

> *Woodroff:* Sick of the *Maid* perhaps, because she sees
> You Mistriss Bride, her School- and Play-fellow
> So suddenly turned Wife.
>
> (1.1.122–24)

What follows this list of identities for Annabel is an exchange of names between bride and groom that comically defamiliarizes name and person even as it offers alternative accounts of the hierarchical relation between the two persons whose marriage is being celebrated:

> *Raymond:* Nay Mrs. Bride, you shall along with us;
> For without you all's nothing.
> *Annabel:* Willingly,
> With Mr. Bridegrooms leave.
> *Bonvile:* Oh my best Joy,
> This day I am your servant.
>
> (1.1.134–37)

In response to Bonvile's here taking on the name of servant, Woodroff punningly exploits the way the name his new son carries on his wedding day already implies that class status: "Onely this day a Groom to her service, / For which the full remainder of his age / He may write Master" (1.1.139–41). Groom is a contractual name in the same sense as husband or master or servant, but also in the special sense that it identifies the contract*ing* personality. And the temporal specificity of the category helps underline the play's broader point that names are powerful because they function, in practice, to determine place and to locate the position from which a person comes to act or speak.

Insofar as marriage ritualizes the exchange of terms by which a Woodroff can be said to "have bestowed" his "one Daughter" (1.1.149) on a Bonvile as "Wife," the wedding scene depends on the idea that, with respect to place, names are perfectly substitutable, such that a "Maid" can "turn" wife and a "daughter" cede the primacy of that familial relationship to the marital one. That substitutability is the promise of social order. But as we have seen with Rochfield's being an "honest thief," *A Cure for a Cuckold* is interested in what happens when categories that do not belong together nevertheless come to exist in the same person (or place) at the same time. Annabel shares with Rochfield the productive ambivalence through which, naming himself, he manufactures his identity. In their encounter on the path, Rochfield makes this connection between the two explicit, by asking after her identity in the same way she has asked after his: "Be you Wife or Virgin?" (2.2.16). And when she answers that she is "both, Sir," he makes the right inference:

> *Rochfield:* This then it seems should be your Wedding-day,
> And these the hours of interim to keep you
> In that double state.
>
> (2.2.17–19)

The double name here marks, in respect of time, an "interim" state structurally identical to the interim space of the path.

Like the path or the sea, a "double state" is thus at once dangerous and full of possibility. Indeed, this doubleness engenders the action of the play. If Rochfield's strange names are strategic for him, Annabel as heroine perceives that she can follow him in using his names, so as to turn him—here is the story—from one to the other and make him *fully* "honest." For her part, Annabel's status as both wife and maid produces action in the sense that it is simultaneously a state of suspension and a way to act: she is able to become the play's heroine because, no longer her father's and not yet her husband's, she can here be fully an agent. The doubleness, finally, produces dramatic possibility itself, constituting dramatic time as the temporal unfolding or distensions of the threshold moment of "turning" from one category to the other. When Rochfield speaks of "these the hours of interim" that keep Annabel "in that double state," he is referring also to the hours of the play's performance, since the comic space of the play is made possible by and as the suspension that Rochfield's and Annabel's names let them inhabit.

Given this relationship between name and dramatic action, it is no surprise that Annabel saves Rochfield by assigning him a new name and by appropriating for herself a second pair of names. In a scene that provides one of the play's crucial keywords, she brings Rochfield home in order to give him the money he wished to take from her. There, she introduces him to the guests as "a loving kinsman of my *Bonviles*" (2.4.51), a fiction she repeats when she refers to him as her "deer Cousin" (3.3.44). Giving herself yet another name, she tells the guests that Bonvile's unexpected absence now requires her to "*personate* both Groom and Bride" (2.4.54, emphasis added) in the sense of welcoming the wedding visitor on his behalf. In an alternative formulation, she will say of her husband's and her roles that she "must, I see, supply both *places* still" (2.4.87, emphasis added). Annabel personates the roles of bride and groom, meaning that she acts her "own" role as well as Bonvile's. These personated roles, as the play's language makes clear, are "places," too, in the way Calais is thematically a place: a site for action and a frame within which a particular action or judgment becomes possible.

The efficacy of Annabel's strategic name for Rochfield cannot hide that it is also false. In the play's final scene, Woodroff revives Annabel's point that *thief* and *honest* are words that lack kinship, by turning the "natural" affinity of words against her. When Rochfield confesses that to protect him Annabel chose "to call me Cousin" (5.2.55), Woodroff says that it is Annabel who, in mixing up names, has made herself cousin to the thief:

> *Woodroff:* Call a thief Cousin? Why, and so she might,
> For the Gold she gave thee, she stole from her husband,
> 'Twas all his now, yet 'twas a good Girl too.
>
> (5.2.56–58)

If Annabel turns Rochfield's theft into something else, part of the reason her theft can also be double (and not merely theft) is that when the money exchanged hands she was personating Bonvile too: the money at that moment is hers because in performing his role she becomes the husband into whose identity, paradoxically, marriage will in the end dissolve her legal identity. But Woodroff (as her father and the play's justice of the peace) points us in a different direction. Having given judgment against Annabel by declaring the money "all" her husband's, he adds "yet 'twas a good Girl too," a formula that suggests, as against qualification, a *supplementary* weighing of the action according to criteria other than those that make her a thief.

What might Woodroff's "too" mean, then, for critical legal history? As a mode of action, Annabel's personation exploits the possibility that one might simultaneously occupy more than one role or place; this mode of being involves resisting, too, any account of an action that would reduce it only to an account of its origins. In Woodroff's "too," that is, the play supplements an intentionalist ethics with a consequentialist one, with Woodroff at this moment measuring Annabel's action in terms of the good that issued from it rather than from the knot of intention (hers and Rochfield's) that led up to it. This ethical switch is integrally part of the play's thematic argument because, at the most conceptual level in its treatment of space, the play uses topography and distance to analogize the space of action itself, the distance internal to action that leads from intention to consequence. It does so in order to delineate two ways of construing the ethics of an action, and so to test, in the same way as it tests the validity of a given name, the criteria according to which a normativizing judgment is made.

In his important study of legal performance in relation to practice, Luke Wilson demonstrates how far early drama conceived of action in terms of the complex temporality emergent from the forensic reconstruction of intention, as that was being theorized at law in the areas of intentional homicide and, at contract, the action of *assumpsit*.[21] Written within the tradition Wilson maps out, *A Cure for a Cuckold* construes action in terms of a distance between places and in terms of the different ways of getting from one place to the other. The play opens, for example, by spatializing action, with Lessingham urging Clare that the marriage of Annabel and Bonvile is a "noble president / Me thinks for us to follow" (1.1.10–11). Like the "president," which is a starting point from which an action flows toward its end, intention is an action's starting point and as such the category most often invoked in the valuation of action. The play thematizes intention in terms of the problem of interpreting written texts, of reading through them to the motivating intention behind. To take the most important example, the action of the main plot spins messily out from Clare's letter in directions other than the intended one. (In this sense, her name parodies her dramatic function as a source only of obscurity.) The difficulty of reading Clare's text is that the intention behind the injunction to Bonvile to kill his dearest friend seems unnatural and therefore not to be granted. When Lessingham asks, "What might her hidden purpose be in this" (1.2.13), he is insisting on going behind her words on the presupposition that their apparent meaning cannot, according to the norms of nature and reason, be their real meaning.²² The play thus offers multiple ways of saving Clare from her own words. Lessingham suggests that the injunction is not murderous because she supposes in "some fantasie" that "the name Friend" is "worn out of the world" (1.2.14-17). When Bonvile proves that hypothesis wrong, Lessingham supposes that "she loathes me, and has put, / As she imagines, this impossible task, / For ever to be quit and free from me" (3.1.79-81). Bonvile for his part suggests simply that she is mocking her suitor:

> *Bonvile:* Upon my life, she does Equivocate:
> Her meaning is, you cherish in your breast
> Either self-love, or pride, as your best friend,
> And she wishes you'd kill that.
>
> (3.1.75-78)

What unites these reactions, as they look to intention in order to bypass or explain away the apparently irrational and unjust meaning, is the attempt to fix the meaning of a word, "friend," by applying it to a world of other signs. The play's chief dramatic crux emerges as a relationship, impossible to read, between a name or category and the intention beneath its surface.

The characters' determination to account for Clare's action in terms of a hidden intention makes all the more striking Annabel's quite different conception of action. As if resisting in Annabel not only Clare's imperative to fix reference but also Clare's intentionalism, the play turns out to be singularly uninterested in Annabel's motivation in bringing Rochfield home and in giving him Bonvile's money. Her purpose, as is repeated several times, is simply to make good on her promise to him: "By all the Vows which this day I have tyed," she declares, "I will deliver you in ready Coin, / The fullest and dearest esteem of what you crave" (2.2.72, 78-79). Again, when she gives him the money, she says only that she has fulfilled her obligation: "See sir, my promise, / There's twenty Pieces" (2.4.112-13). Like Clare's text, Annabel's action constitutes a riddle, but one that the play resolves in terms of consequence rather than intention. Annabel is good, not because of an intention the play stages in her (however seductive the possibility of inferring one in her), but because her theft is readable, in Wilson's sense, not only forward from Woodroff's reconstruction of some malicious intention on her part toward her husband, but backward, too, from its consequences.

The consequentialism that the play registers in the character of Annabel is ultimately a version of the impersonation it also approves in her. For to play a role *as* a role is to ask that judgment follow the role's effect rather than any intention in which the action might, retrospectively, be said to have its origin. As the play's topographical analysis has it, the fixed name or fixed place is the fiction grounding an action whose meaning, however, may also be its effect in the world. Like the dramatics of the interim, the path and middle way and in-between are ethically productive because, Janus-faced, they look forward and backward to two places in which judgment can originate. In so doing they disrupt a normativized account of action as rooted only in the place or *topos* of intention, this in favor of an ethics that in one further way acknowledges the constitutive role of position for meaning: not just the position that a physical place, proper name, professional vocation, or kin relation gives you, but the positions, also, from which and toward which an action proceeds, and from which an evaluation of action might, therefore, derive.

THE IRRATIONAL BEYOND: JURISDICTION'S SURFACES

I want now to return to the story of Compass's paternity with which I began the chapter. If the riddle of Clare's letter cannot be understood except through appeal to her intention, the riddle in the subplot about Compass's nonnormative family is, like Annabel's theft, understandable in terms of consequence. As the title announces, the play promises to show how, as cure, the action of cuckoldry can be made inconsequential. Given that that action has *issued* in a visible effect, that is, Urse's child—the pun connecting child and consequence underwrites the whole of the play's action—the riddle of the title is the same as that which Compass makes his own when, in sympathy with the common-law presumption of legitimacy, he insists that the child is his. Even more than Annabel, Compass is the play's principal guide.[23] If Rochfield, Lessingham, and Bonvile have proper names that place them territorially, Compass's name, equally responsive to place, corresponds rather to the very *process* of placement and direction, the imposition of order on the arbitrariness of experience.

Challenging the account of Urse's action that would assign her child to the biological father, Compass becomes the play's topographical hero by disrupting its various topographies. In the manner generally of theater's practical man or woman of the world, he is a guide to a more ample ethics, one in this case associated with the sea, as opposed to the land and to the law of the land. The first thing to say in this regard is that Compass enters the play (and England) from a conceptual beyond, the dramatic counterpoint to the play's representation of the dangerous and productive in-between. In the main plot, notably, *beyond* is an important keyword that the dramatists use to signal the psychological and moral boundary between the rational and irrational, and so to index the state of being outside the bounds of virtue. Thus Lessingham tells Clare that " I have loved you / Beyond my self" (1.1.28–29); Clare says in relation to Bonvile that she has loved "Not as I ought, but as a woman might / That's beyond reason" (4.2.55–56). This horizontal topography of reason's sphere is opposed in the play to measurement along a vertical rather than horizontal axis. It is along this second axis that the play measures male-male friendship, which Lessingham finds to be "far beyond the love of man to woman" because it is "more near allied to eternity" and "transcends all" (3.1.48–51). In this alternative map, even Bonvile's support of his friend is vertically oriented: "But you," Lessingham tells him, "stand by my honor when 'tis falling, / And nobly under-prop it with your sword" (3.1.52–53).

Compass effectively brings together the horizontal and vertical axes or maps according to which virtue is measured. He rescues the irrational beyond by identifying his desire for a child who is "not" his own, *not* with unreason, but with an alternatively rational and alternatively legal norm more adequate to human behavior than is the norm of any law that would deny him the child. The account he gives of his family is irrational, then, to the extent that it is a fantasy against and beyond the reason that imposes categories like bastard or cuckold. Giving priority in his account of action to the "issue" rather than the cause, Compass interrupts a causal narrative that would give priority to Franckford's paternity, by means of a supplementary narrative that posits as a stable given the very end he desires as a way to move the story of his family forward: of the order of law, he says, "I will yield to nothing but my Childe" (4.1.147). In this sense, Compass's account of the act issuing in the child is simply pragmatic, a prudent way to accommodate the past by directing it toward the future. Asserting the right to determine the flow of meaning from cause to effect and from effect to cause, he becomes, in the play's terms, dramatic path and moral compass.

Compass's challenge to law's ordering of experience is a multilayered re-description of time and space. As his first strategy, he manipulates what we know about time and geographical distance. Upon his return to Blackwall, two local boys, Jack and Rafe, tease him by saying his wife's son must have been "long a breeding" since it is "four year ago since you went to sea, and your childe is but a Quarter old yet" (2.3.32–35). In response, Compass explains that the length of a pregnancy might vary according to "soyl," "Horizon, and the Clime" (2.3.38–39) or even more local differences, such that "it varies agen by that time you come at *Wapping, Radcliff, Lymehouse*, and here with us at *Black-wall*, our children come uncertainly, as the winde serves" (2.3.48–50). Supplementing the temporal argument, Compass brings the Indian port of Surat into impossible proximity with the East India Company's home base and shipyards near Blackwall:

> *Compass:* ... sometimes here we are supposed to be away three or four year together, 'tis nothing so; we are at home and gone agen, when no body knows on't: if you'l believe me, I have been at *Surrat* as this day, I have taken the Long-boat (a fair Gale with me), been here a bed with my wife by twelve a Clock at night, up and gone agen i'th morning and no man the wiser, if you'l believe me.
> *Jack:* Yes, yes Gaffer, I have thought so many times, that you or some body else have been at home; I lye at next wall, and I have heard a noise in your chamber all night long.
> *Compass:* *Right,* why that was I, yet thou never sawst me.
> (2.3.50–59)

Part of the point here is that Compass's outrageous geography, a parody of the common lawyers' arguments for the presumption of legitimacy, merely makes substantial the virtual proximity of home and away that underlies a mercantilist economy. Compass delivers a version of the same spatio-temporal joke to Urse. When she tries to conceal that she has a son, he asks her if "my boy's well," "the boy I got when I came home in the Cock-boat one night, about a year ago! You have not forgotten't, I hope" (2.3.107–11).

Such comic language can be understood as a kind of bawdy aggression toward Urse and as bluff, comic speech that nonetheless has the practical purpose of dealing with a problem that has presented itself. The passages are most impressive, however, for destabilizing categories at law by asking, in a critique of knowledge, that an irrational belief be taken seriously. Empty of content, Compass's story nevertheless can mean something if measured in terms of its suppositional effect rather than its suppositional origin. In this sense, it is notably like the belief that dramatists demand when they ask their audience to imagine that France lies in the Globe or Blackwall on a stage in Clerkenwell. It is also like the belief that compels the law itself when, to effect a desired end, it gives assent to a legal fiction, as when it presumes a husband's paternity or, to take another example equally pertinent for the play, when English courts allowed the plea that a place outside England where a commercial contract had been sealed was also situated *within* England. This meant that a deed might be pleaded as having been made "at Harfleur in the county of Kent" or at Lyons "to wit in the parish of St. Mary le Bow in the Ward of Cheap."[24] Like the dramatic or legal fiction, Compass's warped geography assumes force to the extent that it is assented to. The most striking part of Compass's remarks to Jack, then, is the repetition of "if you'l believe me," a conventional formula that also works to expose the relationship between truth and belief. More pointedly, Compass's insistence that Urse not *forget* the event that his language is only in the process of calling into being invites similar assent, an irrational suspension of what is temporally known for the purpose of reaching a given (and presumably more just) end.

The central importance of communal assent to the production of truth is magnificently thematized at the end of the fourth act when, in order fully to bury the name of cuckold, Compass and Urse theatrically stage their divorce and deaths, so as then to personate themselves (as Annabel does) and woo and remarry as "a fresh new man" and new woman (4.1.221). In the wooing scene, they meet one another as recent widower and recent widow (each, as their stories have it, with a young son—but this is, of course, the same baby). The performance is witnessed by Compass's friends, on whom Compass significantly imposes silence: "I beseech you, silence and observation," he says (4.3.13). This silence functions dramatically as an implied assent to the elaborate fiction that the couple performs. When Raymond interrupts the irrational wooing of husband and wife with the aside "Some what sententious" (4.3.29), his comment thus threatens to break the fictional world. The play here impressively parodies Ben Jonson's metatheatrical inclusion of critics within his plays, those characters who comment from the sideline on the decorum of the unfolding drama. But in opposition to Jonson's more knowing theater, which instructs by testing the boundary between theater and audience, the fiction that Compass and Urse compose must be protected as theater if it is to work at all. This point Eustace makes bluntly clear to Raymond after the latter's outburst: "Oh silence was an Article enjoyned," he chides (4.3.30). To a second interruption, Eustace again insists, with telling force, "Nay, will you break the Law?" (4.3.40). As the acknowledgment of those boundaries that protect and legitimate the fiction that Compass and Urse speak together, this law of silence is nothing other than the law that allows the comic and irrational ritual to take on normative meaning in the world.

The epistemological critique implicit in Compass's fictions is matched by an ethical critique similarly figured in terms of the need to respect discursive and jurisdictional boundaries. The story Compass tells Jack, Rafe, and Urse of his having crossed impossible distances to be present at the child's conception can be read symbolically as upsetting, through the application of a sailor's perspective, a land ethics that for its part takes insufficient account of time or place—no account, that is, of a Blackwall or a sailor's "three or four year" absence. When Compass responds to Urse's request for forgiveness by asking, "Forgive thee, for what? For doing me a pleasure?" (2.3.135), the code that sustains his alternative and more generous norm is one in which the past toward which forgiveness might have been oriented has already been absorbed into the presentness of pleasure. In opposition to vengefulness or regret, pleasure here is what allows the past to remain in the past. In relation to space rather than time, Compass identifies his recoding of the world with the ocean, telling the boys that the mysteries whereby a sailor in Surat can father a child in London are something "you'l understand when you go to sea" (2.3.39–40). Most impressively, a maritime ethics underlies his saying that in Blackwall "our children come uncertainly, as the winde serves" (2.3.49–50). Although the formulation indexes the supposed uncertainty of any Blackwall child's legitimacy, it does so only to identify the question of legitimacy as strictly a landsman's concern, since according to the qualification "as the winde serves," the uncertainty of the birth is simultaneously predictable, though only for those sailors who both serve and are served by the wind. According to the full metaphor, those who know how to follow the winds will appropriately read a birth's uncertainty by reading through it in order to make it certain again.

In the wooing scene, Compass again enrolls the winds as part of his defense of an alternative sexual norm, one, as he asserts, by which mariners' wives specifically should be judged if through some sexual "slip" during their husbands' absence they should become subject to landsmen's slander. Such slander, Compass assures Urse, is unjust and unskilled, since "land and fresh-water men never understand what wonders are done at Sea" (4.3.74–75):

> *Compass:* Then if they knew what things are done at sea, where the Winds themselves do copulate, and bring forth issue, as thus: In the old world there were but four in all, as Nor, East, Sou, and West: these dwelt far from one another, yet by meeting they have ingendred Nor-east, Sou-East, Sou-West, Nor-West, then they were eight; Of them were begotten Non-Nor-East, Nor-Nor-West, Sou-Sou-East, Sou-Sou-West, and those two Sows were Sou-East and Sou-West's daughters, and indeed there is a family now of 32 of 'em, that they have fill'd every

	corner of the world, and yet for all this, you see these baudy Bellow-menders when they come ashore, will be offering to take up women's coats in the street.
Urse:	Still my husbands discretion!
Compass:	So I say, if your Land-men did understand that we send Windes from Sea, to do our commendations to our wives, they would not blame you as they do.

(4.3.83–97)

Compass's amusing parable takes on particular resonance in light of the play's thematization of the pathway, since the winds that Compass names are the wind and rhumb lines that make sailing and navigation possible. Unlike the unruly path that Annabel and Rochfield find themselves on, the wind line is a rationalized way, an abstraction on which, because it is a line, there is room neither for the "pregnant hollow" that serves Rochfield's thievery (2.1.48) nor for Annabel's uncertainty as to "where I am" (2.2.1). Except, of course, that the sea's lines are also notoriously *unclear*, not because they have unruly borders but because they are so hard to read. The wind line is both rational and irrational, according to one's position and depending on whether one knows how simultaneously to serve and master it.

In this passage, Compass disrupts a land ethics by upsetting a rationalized account of agency, the wind in his account being both actor and medium for the sailor's agency. Where an action is, as here, a confluence of forces, there can be no absolute origin, but only a model of horizontal service in which wind and sailor accomplish their practical end by serving and being served, reciprocally. Not coincidentally, this picture of a practical doing is a version of the quietly disruptive collaboration between Rochfield and Annabel, according to which Annabel is able, on the unruly path, to guide Rochfield home only because he leads *her*:

Rochfield:	Come, you know your path back?
Annabel:	Yes, I shall guide you.
Rochfield:	Your arm, Ile lead with greater dread than will....

(2.2.100–101)

Like Compass's parable, this is an account of doing as practice, in which it is impossible to isolate a singular intention as an adequate account of an act. Challenging a normativizing account of mastery, Compass's bawdy story of how sailors use the winds to impregnate their wives is both the fantasy of an agency so complex as to allow him to be supremely patriarchal and an irrationally practical assault on an order that identifies the patriarchal with a merely rationalized origin. To put this in terms of the wind parable, landsmen get lost at sea because they do not understand that when the winds "bring forth issue," what counts is where the winds end up and not, as the category of bastardy might have it, where they come from. And sailors for their part are those who identify *what* home is by where it is, rather than the reverse.

At its simplest, Compass's claim that sailors are always already masters of the winds that reach their wives insists that a truly ethical judgment depends on acknowledging variation among persons and circumstance. The corollary to this equitable principle is that true judgment must involve a heightened awareness of division, a concept the play identifies in the *discretion* that Urse praises in her "two" husbands: "still my husbands discretion." Urse here looks forward to Rochfield's defense of Annabel when, as he puts it, she "in her own discretion thought it meet, / For cover of my shame to call me Cousin" (5.2.54–55). From the Latin *discernere* ("to divide"), *discretion* becomes an important keyword in the play because it locates judgment in a differentiation among cases rather than in their coordination. At the same time that the play construes discretion as the capacity to determine what is right or wrong in one's own conduct, it also nods toward the public meaning of the word: discretion as the power of a judge or court to determine, within the limits of the law, the punishment or remedy appropriate to a given case. In this sense, Compass and Annabel can be said to inhabit discrete legal spheres, to the extent that the play constructs in them the kind of jurisdiction to which discretion at its most technical belongs.

The private forum that the play imagines as ethical discretion is jurisdictional in more than a metaphorical sense, since, according to the play's account of action and issue, the categories among which discretion distinguishes belong to the space that an action *is* or *becomes* when it is subjected to one or another kind of ethical or juridical evaluation. In two ways, Compass pursues a model of action that will allow Franckford's role in begetting the child to be acknowledged without its becoming determinative. First, he measures action as labor and labor as a diversely relational form. Speaking to Urse, he lays claim to the product of her labor by arguing the analogy of the theater, where according to the "Law amongst the Players . . . a fellow shall have his share though he do not play that day," so he will not "loose my share" simply because "I was out o'th way": "Will not you labor for me as I shall do for you," he asks (2.3.128–33). The notion, according to a relationality built into the legal construction of labor itself, that Compass is entitled to the product of Urse's labor is reconfigured in his later confrontation with Franckford in front of the house where the child has been put out to nurse. The scene subjects Compass's legal claim to the forms of legal pleading whereby parties at law isolated the issue or "state of the question" to be tried.[25] As it emerges here, the pertinent issue is not one of fact (whether or not Franckford helped conceive the child), but one of law, involving specifically the impact of different intentions on legal possession. Compass bawdily insists to Franckford's wife that labor is the lens through which to view intention's scope, an argument that swings in Urse's favor and thus his: "what tho your husband lent my wife your distaff, shall not the yarn be mine? Ile have the head, let him carry the spindle home agen" (3.2.84–86). In response to this argument, Franckford tenders issue by confidently fixing the terms of the legal question as he imagines Compass has just laid it out: "The Law shall show which is the worthier Gender: a Schoolboy can do't" (3.2.94–95). But this is not the whole of Compass's point, which is also that a father's labor is simply not equivalent to the mother's. As the actor who, metaphorically, merely facilitates productive work, Franckford is represented as a kind of accessory to the action that belongs fully to Urse as principal. Although in felony law accessories were understood as agents and "received the same judgment as principals," their agency was legally circumscribed, acknowledged at law only in relation to a primary agency, such that an accessory, for example, could not be convicted without a principal.[26] The priority of the principal is suggestive for Compass's argument, which works to split the accessory doing (represented as merely the mechanical precondition for action) from that in which the action issues. Franckford's labor to get the child (3.2.59) may be labor, but it is not quite action: in prying open the distance between intention and consequence, Compass's spinning metaphor works to cut off Franckford's pathway to the child.

A second way that the play represents action as a surprisingly productive form involves action's dependence on the dramatic enunciation and performance of meaning. For this argument we can turn to the subplot's representation of Compass and Urse's marriage, through which the play's various characters are newly accommodated to one another and so reoriented toward a shared future. In the play's final scene, after Compass's legal victory against Franckford, the merchant is reintegrated into the sailor's family, not as father to his biological child, but as father to the bride in the fictive marriage that Urse and Compass celebrate as the new source and sign of their unity. This, as Compass delights in telling Woodroff, the play's befuddled justice of the peace, means that Compass is Franckford's son, and that the baby—Compass's son—is both Franckford's "Grand-childe" and, given who the birth father is, Compass's "elder brother" (5.2.112–13). When a confused Woodroff replies to Compass that it seems that Franckford "begat this" baby "before you," the sailor avoids the consequence by punning on temporal and geographic extension: "Before me? Not so sir, I was far enough off when 'twas done; yet let me see him dares say, this is not my Childe" (5.2.14–16). To which Bonvile replies, "You cannot see him here, I think sir" (5.12.17). This is the play's thesis at its most extreme, the moment when the facts of geography (the site of Compass's first attempt to disrupt English norms) and of Franckford's role in the child's conception (the site of Compass's second attempt to disrupt English norms) are accommodated to the story of Compass's paternity, because they can be registered as irrelevant to the end he effects by applying a norm just "far enough off" to be rationally useful for the case at hand.

Most important, this performance of a norm that is partly enabled by Franckford's legitimation of the marriage replicates the mechanics whereby public norms, too, come into effect. As justice of the peace, Woodroff challenges Franckford for taking on a role in what, after all, might be considered a sham marriage. In doing so, however, Woodroff paradoxically manages only to define the terms of the marriage's legitimacy:

Woodroff: Brother, you are a helper in this design, too?
Franckford: The Father to give the Bride, sir.

(5.2.109–10)

Just as Franckford, here called brother, is Woodroff's brother-in-law (Franckford is married to Woodroff's sister), so Franckford is not so much "Father" as the "Father-to-give," an artificial father or father-in-law, according now to the very law he helps "design" by allowing that new law to present itself in a scene of self-legitimation.[27]

Another performance of a supplementary jurisdictional competence to that of public law occurs earlier in the play, in the wooing scene between Compass and Urse, which, as already noted, is made to depend upon the silence of those who, in witnessing it, thereby testify to the productive efficacy of its rituals. What remains to be excavated is the deliberately legal character of the performance. For when Eustace chastises Raymond for interrupting the scene by asking, "will you break the Law" (4.3.40), his language is most striking for converting what was on Compass's part only a request—"I beseech you, silence and observation" (4.3.13)—into juridical norm. What does a law like Eustace's, so trivial on the surface, mean for our understanding of Law? Compass's request becomes law for no reason outside the scene witnessed by the one who declares it law. That is, Eustace's "Law" comes into being by transforming the place of Compass's and Urse's speech into jurisdictional space and, as it so marks it, by generating the curious result that jurisdiction can then double back and constitute as law the law that constituted it. The temporal suspension or lag between Compass's request and Raymond's law is thus essential to the scene's meaning, since it points to the dynamic internal to legal jurisdiction whereby a temporal phenomenon or speech act (a *iuris dictio*) comes to take on the aspect instead of the scene of authority, its space and competence. Like the marriage that concludes the play, the scene of Compass and Urse's wooing stages the mechanics of jurisdiction itself. For in exposing the relationship between authority and the performance of assent to that authority, the scene makes prior as norm a law that is the posterior effect of its own practical extension in space and time.

By theatricalizing the force of jurisdiction, the two scenes of wooing and marriage that I have been describing make legal jurisdiction available for appropriation by one like Compass, whose legal claims must be all the more radical for confirming rather than subverting the logic of a normative, public law. I mean that for the play there can be no difference between the official law that declares Urse's child a bastard and the theatrical law that is produced by Compass, Urse, and their witnesses against that law. At the conclusion of Act 5, Woodroff, once again spokesman and unmaker of the Law's singularity, skeptically asks of the newly remade husband, "What Marriage call you this" (5.2.104), and wonders if the marriage is not just "a new trick" (5.2.108). His question allows Compass to reply, "Yes sir, because we did not like the old trick" (5.2.109), an uncanny response that alludes to the trick of cuckoldry performed against him, but also unveils the old trick of law that his and Urse's legal performance has supplemented as, itself, both trick and jurisdiction. As Compass brings to the surface of his own and law's management of their respective norms, jurisdiction is the administrative process through which law dynamically orders the world by producing the legal reality it must also serve.

COMMON LAW: JURISDICTION'S DEPTH

Compass's alternative jurisdiction emerges within the play's direct encounter with a traditional legal account of conflicting orders of power. I turn now to the play's use of this more recognizably technical vocabulary, which although cognate with the play's treatment of the legal force of names and its analysis of the dramatic enactment of juridical legitimacy, has particular importance for the text's legal work. First, it foregrounds the institutional context for the

"To Law for Our Children" 319

play's broader ethical argument, in that it follows a vocabulary available primarily to the members of the Inns of Court who were able to hear it. Second, it defines according to the common law's own terms the play's broader juridical critique of the idea that a legal norm is, essentially, single. In its encounter with the common law's specialized forms, the play references the histories inside common-law procedure as a way to identify, from inside out, the jurisdictional tensions that open the legal order onto the kind of alternative Compass imagines. My argument takes up two scenes in which Compass formally defends his claim on the child.

The scene in which Franckford and Compass resolve that the pertinent question in their case is the relative worthiness of the two genders puts in Compass's mouth the play's most powerful sentence about the impact of legal rationalization on the relation between law and life: "must we," he asks "go to law for our Children now a days?" (3.2.102). If he must do so, the point is that the scene has made unusually messy the question of which law he means, since it has fractured law into the different jurisdictions that together constituted England's legal order. As the scene opens, Compass confronts the nurse with whom Franckford has placed the child. Refusing to surrender him, the nurse presents the law as interdiction, saying she has "no authority to deliver, no not to let you see the Childe; to tell you true, I have command unto the contrary" (3.2.1–3). From this first strike, the exchange follows the form of legal pleading through a back-and-forth adjustment of the case at hand. It quickly moves, as from depth to surface, from the vertical question of legitimation to the horizontal question of jurisdictional competence.

Compass: Command! From whom?
Nurse: By the father of it.
Compass: The father! Who am I?
Nurse: Not the father, sure. The Civil Law has found it otherwise.
Compass: The Civil Law! Why then the Uncivil Law shall make it mine agen. Ile be as dreadful as a *Shrove-tuesday* to thee, I will tear thy Cottage but I will see my Childe.
Nurse: Speak but half so much agen, Ile call the Constable, and lay Burglary to thy charge.

(3.2.4–12)

Bypassing the philosophical question of the law's origin in the idea of the "father" to whom the nurse appeals for legitimacy, the passage has Compass and the nurse meet instead around the technical question of which legal forum might be appropriate to the case, with each of them attempting to gain the jurisdictional upper hand. The nurse's "Civil Law" is in excess of what she intends to say, because it refers both to the made law of a given polity and also, specifically, to Roman civil law, as practiced on the Continent and as followed procedurally by English civilians in jurisdictions such as Admiralty. Compass's "Uncivil" law is correspondingly multivalent. In his impolite threat to use force, his phrase legally invokes an irrational order that counters what law's reason find against him, but he can also be heard to insist on an "Uncivil" law in the sense of placing the case under the jurisdiction of the common law, rather than the civil law. It is thus exactly to the point that the nurse turns this move against him by insisting that the common law, as embodied now in the constable, more clearly favors her side.

Having settled in this way on the appropriateness of a common-law jurisdiction, the two parties parry by diversely framing the legal question in terms of the common law's ordering of land possession. The nurse opens the second stage in their pleading by insisting that, since Franckford has given her money to look after the child, it is "to his use I keep it" (3.2.16). The legal joke here is that "use" refers also to the legal use (Lat. *opus*, "benefit"), an early form of trust by which much of the land in early modern England was held and transmitted. A. W. B. Simpson describes the basic form of the use: "The essence of such a transaction is that lands are conveyed to a person or persons (called the feoffee or feoffees to uses) with a provision that they be held for the benefit (*ad opus*) of a beneficiary. The beneficiary is described in law french as 'cestui a que use le feoffment fuit fait,' and from this obtains his curious title 'cestui que use.'"[28] In the nurse's speech, then, she makes herself the feoffee to whom Franckford has conveyed, to his own use, the father's interest (or fee) in the child. Following his opponent's legal maneuver, Compass replies that the father's interest is not the only one that pertains, asking (with "bastard" working only apparently against his own interests), "Why thou white Bastard-breeder, is not this the mother," a point the nurse concedes: "Yes, I grant you that" (3.2.17–18).

Quibbling on the nurse's "grant," Compass overpowers her common-law argument by converting that word of concession into a word of common-law conveyance, as though she had just acknowledged Compass's claim and granted him possession. In this discursive context, alongside "use," Compass introduces a second kind of landholding:

Compass: Dost thou? And I grant it too: And is not the Childe mine own then by the wifes Coppy-hold?

Nurse: The Law must try that.
Compass: Law? Dost think Ile be but a Father in Law? All the Law betwixt *Black-wall* and *Tuttle-street* . . . shall not keep it from me, mine own flesh and blood! Who does use to get my children but my self?

(3.2.19–25)

According to the syllogism, Compass argues for legal possession of the child by virtue of the major premise that a wife's possessions are legally the husband's and the minor premise that the child is hers by copyhold. Paul Clarkson and Clyde Warren usefully gloss the legal allusion by writing that the play uses copyhold doubly: "The child is admittedly Compass's wife's . . . so he refers to it as her likeness, hence her Coppy-hold. At the same time, he likens the child to land held by his wife by copy of court roll."[29] Having answered the nurse's claim over the boy by substituting one way of holding land (copyhold) for another (the use), Compass at the end of this passage undoes the nurse's own argument by directing her term, *use*, against her: "Who does use to get my children but my self." In the context of the nurse's common-law claim, this implies that the child is his because, whatever the begetting, the use of the child is his; against the nurse's construction of the situation, Compass makes himself the beneficiary, the *cestuy que use* of Franckford's begetting.[30]

What makes the linguistic play on *use* and *copy* so interesting for the scene as a whole is that both terms point back, now from inside the common law, to the concept of jurisdictional difference with which the scene opened in opposing "civil" and "uncivil," natural and human, Roman and English. In the two puns, that is, the dramatists engage the plural history of common-law norms themselves. In the case of historical copyhold, the central common-law courts began to recognize copyhold tenures and to exercise a jurisdiction over them only from the middle of Elizabeth's reign. As a form of possession, copyhold grew out of villein tenure, according to which a tenant held land, most often within the confines of the lord's manor or estate, by the custom of the manor and more or less at the will of the lord. This highly unsettled title was recorded on the roll of the lord's court, the practice that in time gave to this lowest form of tenure the name of "tenure by copy of court roll," hence copyhold. In this essentially private arrangement governed by manorial custom and overseen by the customary courts pertaining to the different manors' seigniorial lords, the central common-law courts did not originally involve themselves. Since the legal interest (or fee) around which the common law was organized remained fully in the lord, not the copyholder, there was no technical means for the common law to acknowledge the latter's customary interest. In the fifteenth century, however, copyholders began to seek and receive protection in Chancery, as a court of equity and conscience. The theory was that this court looked not to the legal matter of the fee, but rather to conscientious behavior: "since it was unconscionable for a lord to flout the customs of his manor, a copyhold tenant might complain to the chancellor if the lord failed to do right."[31] Eventually, from around the 1570s, copyholders began to have recourse also at common law when the judges, probably in response to the rise of copyhold actions in Chancery, found in the law of trespass a way to allow the action. The common law thus came to accommodate within itself the differences that had found expression as a distinction, initially, between central and local justice, and subsequently, between common law and equity: "Coming so late in to the royal courts the copyholder brought with him a body of customary law which it was quite impossible for the common lawyers to sweep away. They thus adopted the principle that the rules governing the landholding of a copyholder were to be found in the custom of the manor concerned. These rules varied from place to place, and so copyholders were never subjected to a uniform system of land law; there never grew up anything which could be called a common law of copyhold."[32]

A striking point about this legal history in relation to the scene I am describing in the play is that the history of the legal use looks so similar to it. As with copyhold, the use was held until the sixteenth century to be beyond the jurisdictional scope of the common law; as with copyhold, those who found themselves cheated, for example, by the feoffees to use to whom they had conveyed the fee had no recourse at common law, since the law was technically able to look only to the question of who was seised/possessed of the fee (and this of course was the feoffee). From the mid-fifteenth century, as with copyhold, landholders began to seek and find relief in Chancery, where the chancellor enforced the use as binding the consciences of those who entered such agreements. Finally, in the sixteenth century, as a result of the 1536 Statute of Uses, the matter of uses came uneasily within the common-law jurisdiction that had originally excluded it.[33] In consequence of these developments, the Elizabethan and Jacobean common law came to be much occupied by the question of whether, having brought copyhold and the use into the law from outside the tenurial system of seisin and fee, the two modes of holding land (but especially the use) should follow or diverge from the common-law norms for possessing land.

The important point for the cultural meaning of copyhold and uses is that both categories pointed to a history of jurisdictional accommodation recent enough to be fully present *as* history for early seventeenth-century lawyers, a group that, to be sure, lacked a refined sense of the common law's long history. In a legal reading on uses delivered in Grays Inn in 1600—although printed only in 1642, the text circulated in manuscript within the Inns of Court across the intervening decades—Francis Bacon connected the two categories precisely in terms of their analogous histories:

> I have sought likewise whether there be any thing which maketh with them [uses] in our law; and I find that Periam, Chief Baron, in the argument of Chudleigh's case, compareth them to copyholders. And aptly for many respects: First, because as an use seemeth to be an hereditament in the court of chancery, so the copyhold seemeth to be an hereditament in the lord's court [the manorial court]; Secondly, this conceit of imitation hath been troublesome in copyholds, as well as in uses.... And thirdly, because they both grew to strength and credit by degrees; for the copyhold at first had no remedy at all against the lord, but was as a mere tenancy at will; afterwards it grew to have remedy in chancery, and afterwards against the lords by trespass at the common law.... So no doubt in uses, at the first the chancery made question to give remedy, until uses grew more general, and the chancery more eminent; and then they grew to have remedy in conscience: but they could never maintain any manner of remedy at the common law, neither against the feoffee, nor against strangers; but the remedy against the feoffee was left to the subpoena, and the remedy against strangers to the feoffee.[34]

Having articulated this apparent difference between copyhold and use, Bacon here turns to the matter of his reading, the statutory intervention of 1536 that worked to bring the matter of uses within the common law.

That Bacon could provide a historicized account of the analogy between use and copyhold is highly suggestive for the dramatist's use of the law in *A Cure for a Cuckold*, since as historical categories both terms offer in compressed form the broader jurisdictional argument that the play makes by variously linking judgment and place. That Compass and the nurse frame the question of the child's paternity in terms of these two modes of holding land reflects the fact, as outlined earlier, that questions of illegitimacy often arose in property litigation in the common-law courts, and were thence transmitted to the ecclesiastical courts for trial and certification. *A Cure for a Cuckold* remakes this jurisdictional relationship in terms of modes of possession that themselves sat at the jurisdictional boundary between common law and equity. If Compass's and the nurse's quick march across jurisdictions comically reifies a father's interest in his son, it also constitutes a critique, through legal analogy, of how the norms that measure a life emerge. The norm arises, first, within one jurisdiction among others, each one of which is potentially the source for an alternative norm. Within a given legal discourse, furthermore, the norm arises as a function not of singularity but, rather, of the law's internalization and accommodation of historical difference. Like the name that a person carries or accepts, the norm that makes one a particular kind of subject is always historical, not natural; at the moment it is constituted, it points beyond itself. To put this in the play's terms, Compass's claim to be the child's father looks less like whimsy and more like law when the normative law, according to which the sailor's practical wisdom might seem whimsical, is marked even in its singularity by irreducible difference. A source of sophisticated humor for the legal insider, the play's representation of jurisdictional jockeying also gives Compass and Urse their legal voice, a juridical identity more knowing about the place of jurisdiction than a rationalized law would tend to allow.

The identity that opens up for Compass is neither the rights-bearing subjectivity of liberalism nor a romantic subjectivity grounded in some fantasy of standing beyond the law's reach. His legal subjectivity is highly traditional, even if the play also marks it as new for having come under the new historical pressure of the common law's jurisdictional success. Compass proceeds at law by acknowledging the force only of his own claim, but instead of rejecting legal analysis he appropriates the law's buried history against itself. The violence he does the law is a function of the law's having offered him a position unified and stable enough to stand against, but also, in equal measure, of the law's not being discursively single at all, but sufficiently incoherent to allow a resistance such as his to assume the shape of normativity. Law in the play—and in the version of history that the play stages for its audience—is at once stable enough and flexible enough to make Compass a hero against and for the law.

The dramatic production of resistance as normative also structures the second of the play's scenes to make use of a semi-technical legal vocabulary, this being the tavern scene in which Compass finally scores a legal victory before his judges. The two opposing parties sit at separate tables, Compass and Urse with "Pettifog, *the Attorney*," and Franckford and Luce with "Mr. Dodge, *a Lawyer*." They come together to hear the judgment delivered by two arbitrators who, off-stage, have been considering the case: an unnamed counselor and Woodroff, Annabel's father and so the hinge character for the primary and secondary plots. As the lawyers' names suggest, the scene works conventionally by satirizing the legal profession and in particular its attachment to obscure language, to paper, and to fine distinctions. Early in the scene, Franckford reveals that the reason he is so eager to be recognized as the father of the illegitimate child is that "I made a Purchase lately, and in that / I did estate the Childe, 'bout which I'm sued, / Joynt-purchaser in all the Land I bought" (4.1.39–41). This narrowing of an ethical question to one of legal tactics finds an equivalent in the lawyers' love for the *stuff* of their profession, a material manifestation of the not always happy displacement of justice onto procedure. As Pettifog sits down, he "*pulls out papers*" (4.1.st.dir.) as the critical marker of his vocation, even as Dodge assures Franckford that the merchant will be proved the "true Father" through Urse's "Affidavit" and Dodge's own texts: "Look you sir, here's the Answer to his [Compass's] Declaration" (4.1.33–36).

This satirical portrait of the law's fussiness looks to jurisdictional difference as the principal source of legal confusion. The scene is particularly impressive in its treatment of Compass's lawyer, refracting the socio-legal reality around illegitimacy in terms of three separate kinds of jurisdictional tension relevant to English law. First, Pettifog appeals both to common law and the rival civil law when he reassures Compass of victory: "The childe is none of yours: what of that? ... for *partus sequitur ventrem*, says the Civil Law: and if you were within compass of the four Seas, as the common Law goes, the childe shall be yours certain" (4.1.72–76). That the civil-law principle is irrelevant to common-law legitimacy, and, most important, that Compass was exactly beyond the four seas that surround England and mark its jurisdiction, makes the satirical point, even as the comparison works also to place English law within a broader legal discursive context.

Second, the play's representation of Pettifog points to tensions *within* English law, since he is associated with Guildhall, the administrative center for London and the home to several local and municipal courts, such as the courts of assistants, which had jurisdiction over matters internal to the London guilds. Even though the municipal and central courts usually operated harmoniously, procedural differences could give rise to jurisdictional tensions. Indeed, Compass's friend Lyonel levels against Pettifog the standard complaint made by the common lawyers, namely that in following civil-law procedure, such minor jurisdictions managed to subvert justice by circumventing the safeguards built into common-law procedure. "You," Lyonel says accusingly of Pettifog and Guildhall lawyers generally, "are in effect both Judge and Jury your selves" (5.1.79). The lawyer counters this description by saying, "That's ordinary, sir: you shall have the like at a *Nisi Prius*" (4.1.83).

In attempting to diminish differences between the civilian and common-law procedural orders, this reply has just the shape of the standard defenses made on behalf of minor jurisdictions when they came under pressure from the central courts. With *nisi prius,* furthermore, the play introduces another layer to the jurisdictional field, since, as the play's editors point out, this was "the legal formality determining that an action might not be heard at Westminster 'unless beforehand' (legal Latin) it had been tried at the court of assizes in the county where the cause originated."[35] Just as Guildhall speaks to the jurisdictional tensions between common law and other English jurisdictions, so *nisi prius* speaks to the tensions between central and local justice as that also defined the practice of the common law.

The most interesting instance of jurisdictional pettifoggery in the scene is the lawyer's jarring response to Compass's "And what do you think of my Suit, sir" (4.1.64). The lawyer replies by clearing the legal decks and rehearsing the admitted facts of the child's conception in terms of a bawdy legal pun: "Why, look you, sir: The Defendant was arrested first by *Latitat* in an Action of Trespass" (4.1.65–66). The play's editors explain the humor of the line: "The comedy lies, first, in the typical lawyerly jargon about which legal form has been, or should be used in a particular instance; second, in the introduction of common-law terminology (Latitat and Action of Trespass) into a subject that would never normally be a matter for the common law; and, third, in the concept of Trespass (with its many legal meanings) to describe seduction."[36] Apart from the line's major effect, which is the humor of describing Franckford's sexual encounter with Urse in terms of an inappropriate lurking (Lat. *latitare*, "to lurk"), the lawyer's description is interesting for again framing the case of legitimacy in terms of a jurisdictional tension, this one between the two central common-law courts of King's Bench and Common Pleas.

In the writ of *latitat,* Pettifog refers to the notorious legal fiction by which King's Bench, from the mid-fifteenth century, and with spectacular success across the Elizabethan and Jacobean periods, brought within its jurisdiction much of the civil litigation involving debt or property that Common Pleas traditionally oversaw. The maneuver depended on the fact that King's Bench had a general jurisdiction over anyone held in custody of the marshal as a prisoner of the court of the Marshalsea. The court could therefore assert its jurisdiction over a given action by entering the defendant on the court rolls as being in the marshal's custody. A plaintiff wishing, for reasons of speed, to pursue debt or property litigation in King's Bench could file a so-called bill of Middlesex, in which it was fictitiously alleged that the defendant was guilty of a trespass by force and arms in Middlesex, an offense that did fall within the court's jurisdiction.[37] Even when the defendant was known to reside outside of Middlesex, the court then directed the sheriff to produce the defendant to answer the plaintiff's charge. As W. S. Holdsworth explains, once the sheriff declared (of course) that the defendant could not be found, the court extended its arm by inventing fictitious reasons as to why a nominal resident of Middlesex might be found in the county where he actually resided: "[A] writ of latitat was issued to the sheriff of an adjoining county. The writ recited the bill of Middlesex and the proceedings thereon, stated that the defendant 'latitat et discurrit' [lurks and runs about] in the county, and ordered the sheriff to catch him. The trespass and the proceedings thereon were fictions invented to give the court jurisdiction. Thus when the defendant did not live in Middlesex it was clearly a waste of time to start with a real bill of Middlesex. Such a bill was supposed, and the issue of a latitat was the first step taken in the action."[38] The final stage of this ingenious maneuver, one of the great moments of legal invention in English legal history, involved bringing the defendant formally under the marshal's custody, after which the court could proceed in the civil action that had all along been at issue.[39] The effect of this fiction and of litigants "shopping for the most advantageous forum" was to create in the sixteenth and seventeenth centuries the appearance of "an internecine struggle for business between the common-law courts themselves."[40] The second important point is that, as with use and copyhold, the history of the jurisdictional tension that made "Latitat in an Action of Trespass" so effective a procedural shortcut was well known *as* history. This is witnessed by John Cowell, who concludes his entry under *latitat* in his legal dictionary of 1607 with an account of the particular professional motives that had motivated the jurisdictional maneuver: "I have bene enformed," he writes, "that the bringing of these actions of trespas so ordinarily to the kings bench, was an invention of Councelers, that because onely Sergeants may come to the common plees barre, found a meanes to set themselves on worke in that Court."[41]

With respect, then, to the boundaries between English law and Roman law, the boundaries between the common law and other English jurisdictions, and the boundaries within common-law jurisdiction itself, Pettifog stands for the jurisdictional confusion that gave English law its identity. The main effect of the play's representation of all this jurisdictional white noise is to emphasize the maddening complexity of a system made up of overlapping jurisdictions. It leaves the audience unable to determine which law is being represented as having jurisdiction over the case. Far from using such language allegorically to identify the tavern as ultimately equitable, say, or ecclesiastical, the play is rather indexing the centrality of jurisdiction generally for law, and in that way mapping any given jurisdictional domain as only one among those available spaces where a problem or an identity might be structured. Enter Compass.

When the arbitrators return with their decision, they initially declare that Franckford should logically have possession of the child, according to the analogous (and more typical) case of a father trying to *avoid* responsibility for his issue:

> *Councellor:* A childe that's base and illegitimate born,
> The father found, who (if the need require it)
> Secures the charge and dammage of the Parish
> But the father?
>
> (4.1.151–54)

And where the earth brings forth fruit, the arbitrators continue, "who but the lord of it / Shall pluck the Apples. . . . / 'Tis still most cleer upon the Fathers part" (4.1.163–66). To this argument, Compass presents the apparently antipatriarchal argument that will allow him to become patriarch on his own extreme and expanded terms. His argument, which convinces the arbitrators to reverse their judgment, foregrounds his resistance to one legal order and simultaneously commits him to a law of multiple discursive orders:

> *Compass:* All this Law I deny, and will be mine own Lawyer. Is not the earth our Mother? And shall not the earth have all her children agen? I would see that Law durst keep any of us back, she'l have Lawyers and all first, tho they be none of her best children. My wife is the mother, and so much for the Civil-law. Now I come agen, and y'are gone at the Common-law: suppose this is my ground, I keep a Sow upon it, as it might be my wife, you keep a Boar, as it might be my adversary here; your Boar comes foaming into my ground, jumbles with my Sow, and wallowes in her mire, my Sow cryes *week*, as if she had Pigs in her belly, who shall keep these Pigs? He the Boar, or she the Sow?
>
> (4.1.67–76)

What interests me, of course, is that Compass's ethical rejection of "all this Law"—and if we want to put Compass's situation in the conventional way, he is confronting the fact that he is married to an adulteress who is mother to a bastard—should end up wanting so much to look *like* law.

In light especially of Compass's earlier reflection on the ethical differences between land and sea, the speech is important for inventing a new *land* law, one that he defines as being organized on behalf of the land (and "Mother") by a different guild from that which oversees the normatively patriarchal law: "she'l have Lawyers and all first," he says of England's territory, "tho they be none of her best children." Dismissing Pettifog as his legal representative, Compass includes himself among this professionalized underclass when he insists that he "will be mine own Lawyer." This means that, according to the norms of his fantastic jurisdiction, he now advances professionally in a way exactly reminiscent of Rochfield's rise as thief through the learned professions. And in contradistinction to the winds that disrupt land life from the outside, here Compass, both rationally and deferentially, subverts the law fully from inside its own rational way of ordering the world's surfaces. This is possible, as the dramatists argue the point in their complex meditation on legal normativity in relation to the jurisdictional production of status and law, because legal jurisdiction itself means always and only as practice and as history.

In the play of jurisdiction represented on and as their stage, the authors of *A Cure for a Cuckold* find for Compass a legal paternity greater even than that which the common law tended fictively to locate in the husband as an extension of his patriarchal relation to the household. It is crucial to note that they do so in a manner that extends rather than overturns the law's own logics, so that the play can end by overlooking adultery and attributing paternity to the husband in recognizably the same way as the common law strove to do. But if Compass perfects rather than overturns the law's patriarchal ordering of experience, the mechanics of his intervention point us to radical jurisprudence, a jurisprudence that looks within the law for what the law does not see.

So I conclude my account of the sailor's story by asking his question in terms that I have most closely associated with the main plot. What's in a name, whether mother, father, cuckold, bastard, or even Compass? To be sure, the law is in the name. In sympathy with Webster, Rowley, and Heywood's comic production of the scene of jurisdiction, however, I have argued, here and throughout this book, that jurisdictional practice inevitably has priority over the fact of sovereignty. And that means that the law is less coherently inside its names than we suppose. The proposition that we are the law's subjects, therefore, gives the law too much, unless, with common, practical Compass, listening for how the law goes about doing what it does at the limit of its competence, we come to hear also all that it also lets in.

NOTES

PROLOGUE

1. Julie Stone Peters, "Law, Literature, and the Vanishing Real: On the Future of an Interdisciplinary Illusion," *PMLA* 120 (2005): 442–53. On literature's ability to disrupt law's disciplinary autonomy and its formalism, see the related exchange between Peters and Peter Brooks in *PMLA* 120 (2005): 1645–47. For another account of the impasse in law and literature, see Jane Baron, "Interdisciplinary Legal Scholarship as Guilty Pleasure: The Case of Law and Literature," in *Law and Literature*, ed. Michael Freeman and Andrew D. E. Lewis (Oxford: Oxford University Press, 1999), 21–45.

2. For a study of early modern subjectivity in relation to territorial, social, and economic displacement, see Patricia Fumerton, *Unsettled: The Culture of Mobility and the Working Poor in Early Modern England* (Chicago: University of Chicago Press, 2006). For a description of the university student as one whose travel linked him to two jurisdictions, rather than to none, see Julius Kirshner, "Made Exiles for the Love of Knowledge: Students in Late Medieval Italy," in *Bartolomeo Cipolla: Un giurista veronese del Quattrocento tra cattedra, foro e luoghi del potere. Atti del Convegno Internazionale di Studi (Verona, 14–16 ottobre 2004)*, ed. G. Rossi (Padua: Cedam, 2007). The classic modern account of the relation of liberty to juridical identity is Hannah Arendt, *The Origins of Totalitarianism* (New York: Harcourt Brace, 1951).

3. Charles M. Gray, *The Writ of Prohibition: Jurisdiction in Early Modern English Law*, 2 vols. (New York: Oceana Publications, 1994), 1, viii.

4. Among legal historians, Daniel Burnham has argued for the impact of client demand on the shaping of jurisdictional boundaries. See his "Jurisdictional Competition and the Evolution of the Common Law: An Hypothesis," in *Boundaries of the Law: Geography, Gender and Jurisdiction in Medieval and Early Modern Europe*, ed. Anthony Musson (Aldershot: Ashgate, 2005), 149–68. See also the essays collected in Shaun McVeigh, ed., *Jurisprudence of Jurisdiction* (New York: Routledge-Cavendish, 2007). Published as my book reached proof stage, this volume

shares, from within legal studies, my focus on jurisdiction as both the condition of normative order and a source of law's potentiality. Our converging interests highlight jurisdiction as an important category and frame for social, political, and cultural work across various disciplinary boundaries.

5. Important analyses of early modern law and literature have of course been organized around more narrowly defined legal topics. Among recent studies, see, for example, Karen Cunningham, *Imaginary Betrayals: Subjectivity and the Discourses of Treason in Early Modern England* (Philadelphia: University of Pennsylvania Press, 2002); Elizabeth Hanson, *Discovering the Subject in Renaissance England* (Cambridge: Cambridge University Press, 1998); Rebecca Lemon, *Treason by Words: Literature, Law, and Rebellion in Shakespeare's England* (Ithaca: Cornell University Press, 2006); Charles Ross, *Elizabethan Literature and the Law of Fraudulent Conveyance: Sidney, Spenser, and Shakespeare* (Aldershot: Ashgate, 2003).

6. Luke Wilson's work on intention similarly insists on the continuity between legal and literary discourse. Triangulating law and literature with concepts of practice, Wilson incisively uncovers the complex temporality of action that was figured on stage and in homicide law and contract law (chiefly in actions of *assumpsit*). See his *Theaters of Intention: Drama and the Law in Early Modern England* (Stanford: Stanford University Press, 2000).

7. Jacques Rancière, *The Politics of Aesthetics: The Distribution of the Sensible*, trans. Gabriel Rockhill (London: Continuum, 2004).

8. Ibid., 13.

9. See in particular Jacques Rancière, *Disagreement: Politics and Philosophy*, trans. Julie Rose (Minneapolis: University of Minnesota Press, 1999). Gabriel Rockhill's "Glossary of Technical Terms," printed as Appendix 1 in *The Politics of Aesthetics*, helped orient me in Rancière's broader project.

10. John Cowell, "Jurisdiction," *The Interpreter* (Cambridge, 1607), Oo4v. Beneath Cowell's sense of jurisdiction as a dignity (*dignitas*) that an officer "has" is the question, long debated in medieval law, whether administrative officers possessed *imperium* by right or always only by delegation. Relevant in this regard is the medieval distinction between *ordo* and *iurisdictio*. In the period leading up to the conciliarist moment, the limitation of the former to a sacramental function allowed canonists to limit the bishop's claim to possess a jurisdiction equivalent to the pope's. See Constantin Fasolt, *Council and Hierarchy: The Political Thought of William Durant the Younger* (Cambridge: Cambridge University Press, 1991), 203–4. More generally, Fasolt's book gives an exemplary account of the intersection of the local, national, and ecclesiastical forces underwriting late medieval discourse around jurisdictional plurality. For *ordo* and *iurisdictio*, see also Brian Tierney, *Foundations of the Conciliar Theory: The Contributions of the Medieval Canonists from Gratian to the Great Schism* (Cambridge: Cambridge University Press, 1955), 25–36, at 32–33.

11. When scholars in law and political science today speak of norms in relation to law, "norm" is usually understood, in opposition to the force of a judicial rule, as an informal code of behavior that emerges in the sphere of practice as a source

of legitimacy complementary to that of law. See, for example, the essays collected in *Norms and the Law*, ed. John N. Drobak (Cambridge: Cambridge University Press, 2006). My study concentrates on norms in the sphere of *judicial practice* itself, but "norm" in my usage should not for that reason be narrowly understood as a synonym for judicial rule. On the contrary, my focus is on the normalization of an as yet unsettled sphere, whereby a genuinely open question at law gets closed in practice by jurisdictionally fixing the question, by shaping it anew, and, in the very process of making it legible, naturalizing it. Normativity is not a fact, but the process of giving contingent practice retrospectively and in effect the aspect of necessity.

12. Jacques Derrida, "Force of Law: The Mystical Foundation of Authority," in Derrida, *Acts of Religion*, ed. Gil. Anidjar (New York: Routledge, 2002), 241–42.

13. Agamben responds to Derrida's reading of Benjamin's essay in two places. See, first, Giorgio Agamben, *Homo Sacer: Sovereign Power and Bare Life*, trans. Daniel Heller-Roazen (Stanford: Stanford University Press, 1998), 64. In a fuller critique, Agamben points out that the very phrase "Force of Law," which in Derrida speaks to the impossible ground of law's authority, is not accurately applied to the law at all, but rather to the nonlegal order that operates as though with the force of law; it belongs, that is, to the state of exception. See Giorgio Agamben, *State of Exception*, trans. Kevin Attell (Chicago: Chicago University Press, 2005), 37–39.

14. See preeminently Jean Bodin, *Les Six livres de la république* (Paris, 1576). The first English translation is that of Richard Knolles, *The Six Bookes of a Commonweale* (London, 1606). The chapters most central to Bodin's conception of indivisible sovereignty can be found in Bodin, *On Sovereignty: Four Chapters from The Six Books of the Commonwealth*, trans. Julian Franklin (Cambridge: Cambridge University Press, 1992). On Bodin's thought in the constitutional context of the Huguenot revolution, see Quentin Skinner, *The Foundations of Modern Political Thought*, 2 vols. (Cambridge: Cambridge University Press, 1978), 2:239–301.

15. Michel Foucault, *"Society Must Be Defended": Lectures at the College de France, 1975-1976*, ed. Mauro Bertani and Alessandro Fontana, trans. David Macey (New York: Picador, 2003), 40.

16. Agamben, *Homo Sacer*, 6.

17. Carl Schmitt, *Political Theology: Four Chapters on the Concept of Sovereignty*, trans. George Schwab (Cambridge, Mass.: MIT Press, 1985). On Shakespeare in relation to political theology and especially the religious, social, and juridical construction of citizenship, see Julia Reinhard Lupton, *Citizen-Saints: Shakespeare and Political Theology* (Chicago: University of Chicago Press, 2006). See also Deborah Shuger, *Political Theologies in Shakespeare's England: The Sacred and the State in Measure for Measure* (Houndmills: Palgrave, 2001).

18. Agamben, *State of Exception*, 23. The translator's "zone of indifference" does not adequately render Agamben's *zona di indifferenza* in the original: *Stato di eccezione: Homo Sacer, II.1* (Turin: Bollati Boringhieri, 2003). Agamben's sophisticated pun may ultimately point to ethical indifference, but it chiefly identifies an instability in the primary categorical structures underlying the law. As such, it can be better translated

as "zone of indifferentiation"—the zone that disrupts the structure of difference that makes meaning and ethical differentiation possible.

19. Agamben, *State of Exception*, 85–86.

20. Agamben, *Homo Sacer*, 6.

21. Richard T. Ford, "Law's Territory (A History of Jurisdiction)," *Michigan Law Review* 97 (1999): 852.

22. Pietro Costa, *Iurisdictio: Semantica del potere politico nel pubblicistica medievale (1100–1433)* (1969; Milan: Giuffrè Editore, 2002). I thank Julius Kirshner for pointing me to this study. Costa's analysis of jurisdiction has remained underappreciated by historians of both medieval and early modern literature and culture, having had only slightly more impact in the field of legal history. The 2002 reissue of the original edition (along with two essays by Ovidio Capitani and Bartolomé Clavero) should bring Costa new readers in several fields. Costa's work offers a profound entry into medieval and early modern literary engagements with legal culture, and should be more widely taken up by literary historians. In relation to Dante, for example, Capitani has written of the relevance of Costa's work for the exploration of papal and imperial power in the *De monarchia*, with some attention paid to relevant juridico-political passages in the *Commedia*. See Ovidio Capitani, "Spigolature Minime sul III della *Monarchia*" [1978], in *Chiose minime Dantesche* (Bologna: Pàtron, 1983), 57–82.

23. Paolo Grossi, *L'Ordine giuridico medievale* (Rome-Bari: Laterza Editore, 1995), 131. *"Orbene, se v'è un concetto logicamente estraneo all iurisdictio è la creazione del diritto: 'dire' il diritto significa presupporlo già creato e formato, significa esplicitarlo, renderlo manifesto, applicarlo, non crearlo."* As suggested by the quotation, Grossi's study recuperates a nineteenth-century organic conception of legal, political, and civic development.

24. For a study of medieval jurisdiction in relation to the normativization of power, one deeply grounded in Costa's work but critical of its privileging of jurisdiction as a *hierarchical* process, see Jesús Vallejo, *Ruda equidad, ley consumada: Concepción de la potestad normativa (1250–1350)* (Madrid: Centro de Estudios Constitucionales, 1992); also Vallejo, "Power Hierarchies in Medieval Juridical Thought: An Essay in Reinterpretation," *Ius Commune* 19 (1992): 1–29.

25. Costa, *Iurisdictio*, 139. *"L'imperatore serve l'equità (rude) interpretandola e così traducendola in norma."*

26. Costa, *Iurisdictio*, 142–43. *"La genesi della norma passa per 'iurisdictio.'" "Non si pensava ad una norma creata, ma ad una norma 'raccolta,' riflessa dall'ordine del mondo sullo specchio ('iurisdictio') posseduto in modo eminente dall'imperatore. 'Iurisdictio' non è il luogo simbolico di una norma modificativa dei dati reali, ma recettiva di essi." "'Iurisdictio' non è altro che il luogo in cui un dato informale viene formalizzato: non mutato, ma espresso, non creato, ma rispecchiato."*

27. In respect of its reconfiguration or capture of the real, jurisdiction is thus analogous (and, as this book argues, not only analogous) to literary representation.

28. Foucault, *"Society Must Be Defended,"* 38.

INTRODUCTION

1. On the disruptive temporality of early literature, see Paul Strohm, *Theory and the Premodern Text* (Minneapolis: University of Minnesota Press, 2000), especially chaps. 5–6. Strohm uses Ernst Bloch's concept of "nonsynchronous temporalities" to theorize how, in response to the "complexity of the Now," literature can offer an "imaginative escape from time's apparent dominion" (67).

2. Arnaldo Momigliano, "Historicism Revisited," in Momigliano, *Essays in Ancient and Modern Historiography* (Middletown, Conn.: Wesleyan University Press, 1977), 365–73, at 368.

3. Thomas Wyatt, "Myn Owne John Poyntz," ll. 1–12, as printed in *The Penguin Book of Renaissance Verse*, ed. David Norbrook and H. R. Woudhuysen (Harmondsworth, Middlesex: Penguin, 1992), 487–90. A modern-spelling edition is available in Thomas Wyatt, *The Complete Poems*, ed. R. A. Rebholz (Harmondsworth, Middlesex: Penguin, 1978).

4. H. A. Mason, *Humanism and Poetry in the Early Tudor Period* (London: Routledge and Paul, 1959), 202–6. Cited by Rebholz in Wyatt, *Complete Poems*, 437–38.

5. For the poetics of suspension in Wyatt, see Stephen Greenblatt, "Power, Sexuality, and Inwardness in Wyatt's Poetry," in Greenblatt, *Renaissance Self-Fashioning* (Chicago: University of Chicago Press, 1980), 115–56.

6. Pietro Costa, *Iurisdictio: Semantica del potere politico nel pubblicistica medievale (1100–1433)* (1969; Milan: Giuffrè Editore, 2002), 183.

7. Giorgio Agamben uses the distinction between the topographical relation and the topological relation to specify the relation of sovereignty to the state of exception: "The suspension of the norm does not mean its abolition, and the zone of anomie that it establishes is not (or at least claims not to be) unrelated to the juridical order. Hence the interest of those theories that, like Schmitt's, complicate the topographical opposition [inside/outside] into a more complex topological relation, in which the very limit of the juridical order is at issue" (*State of Exception*, trans. Kevin Attell [Chicago: University of Chicago Press, 2005], 23). As my prologue suggests, I use Agamben's distinction, here and elsewhere in the book, not to subsume jurisdiction under sovereignty, but rather to suggest the value of supplementing the critique of sovereignty with an analysis of jurisdiction.

8. For the ideological configuration of space in the early modern period in relation to literary representations of the land, see, for example, Andrew McRae, *God Speed the Plough* (Cambridge: Cambridge University Press, 1996); Garrett Sullivan, *The Drama of Landscape: Land, Property, and Social Relation on the Early Modern Stage* (Stanford: Stanford University Press, 1998).

9. The antiquarian production of knowledge, in books such as William Lambarde's *Perambulation of Kent* (London, 1576), speaks to the historical emergence of the local in dialectical relation to the national, a point of legal interest in that Elizabethan antiquarianism focused so much of its energies on the excavation of custom within

the growing order of the common law. For a similar argument that legal centralization and local differentiation are complementary aspects of the same development, see Richard T. Ford, "Law's Territory (A History of Jurisdiction)," *Michigan Law Review* 97 (1999): 867.

10. This dynamic between the literary and the political, according to which power articulates its own incompletion, is different from the model of subversion and containment, as seen in the new historicism. There is nothing subversive per se in Wyatt's description of power's processual relation to the production of its own image. Of interest, rather, is the apprehension of power in terms of a relational field and, therefore, according to only contested modes of distribution.

11. On geometry as a melancholy science, see Carla Mazzio, "The Three Dimensional Self: Geometry, Melancholy, Drama," in *The Arts of Calculation: Quantifying Thought in Early Modern Europe*, ed. David Glimp and Michelle Warren (Houndmills: Palgrave, 2004).

12. On the place of the two laws in English legal culture (specifically in relation to sanctuary, compurgation, mortuaries, and civil jurisdiction over the clergy), see R. H. Helmholz, *The Ius Commune in England: Four Studies* (Oxford: Oxford University Press, 2001).

13. On the dialectical process of legal centralization and decentralization, see, for example, T. F. T. Plucknett, "The Courts and the Professions," in *A Concise History of the Common Law*, 5th ed. (Boston: Little Brown, 1956), 79–175. For variations in medieval local jurisdiction, see Frederick Pollock and Frederick W. Maitland, "Jurisdiction and the Communities of the Land," in *The History of English Law*, 2d ed., introduction by S. F. C. Milsom, 2 vols. (1898; Cambridge: Cambridge University Press, 1968), 1:527–688.

14. I take the notion of knotted temporalities from Dipesh Chakrabarty's historiographical analysis of the times of modernity and their disruption of teleological history. See Chakrabarty, *Provincializing Europe: Postcolonial Thought and Historical Difference* (Princeton: Princeton University Press, 2000). J. G. A. Pocock offers a classic account of time and law in the first section of his study of republican virtue. See Pocock, *The Machiavellian Moment: Florentine Political Thought and the Atlantic Republican Tradition* (Princeton: Princeton University Press, 1975), 3–80.

15. It is relevant for Wyatt's analogy that, like the poet's being "emong" the muses (OE *gemangan*, "to mingle"), the "meddling" in Spain speaks, etymologically, to a mixing or mingling (OF *mesler*, "to mix").

16. Seth Lerer, *Courtly Letters in the Age of Henry VIII: Literary Culture and the Arts of Deceit* (Cambridge: Cambridge University Press, 1997), 195.

17. On the hypothesis or cause in classical rhetoric and geometry, and in Aristotelian drama, see Wesley Trimpi, *Muses of One Mind: The Literary Analysis of Experience and Its Continuity* (Princeton: Princeton University Press, 1983), 25–72.

18. [Cicero], *Ad Herennium*, trans. Harry Kaplan, Loeb Classical Library (Cambridge, Mass.: Harvard University Press, 1954).

19. Alongside Trimpi, *Muses of One Mind*, the fullest account of the relation between literary fiction and legal argument is Kathy Eden, *Poetic and Legal Fiction in the Aristotelian Tradition* (Princeton: Princeton University Press, 1986). For Eden, Sir Philip Sidney's defense of the value of the hypothetical fiction he calls poetry is paradigmatic. Sidney argues that the reader "uses the narration but as an imaginative ground-plot of a profitable invention," which is to say that the reader *receives* the poet's elaborated hypothesis as, also, a hypothetical starting point, a "cause" or "plot" for action. For the relevant passage, see *Sidney's* The Defence of Poesy *and Selected Renaissance Literary Criticism*, ed. Gavin Alexander (London: Penguin, 2004), 34–35.

20. In light of the poem's territorial scheme, the "cause" may also be heard as the geometrical hypothesis (in the manner of a groundplot) through which the poet encounters the measurement that both makes him unfree and makes him free.

21. Lerer, *Courtly Letters*, 196.

22. For an extreme account of literature as a legal irrelevance, see Richard Posner, *Law and Literature: A Misunderstood Relation* (Cambridge, Mass.: Harvard University Press, 1988). For a brief reflection on literature's usually subordinate position in the interdisciplinary project, see my review essay, "Practicing Law and Literature in Early Modern Studies," *Modern Philology* 101 (2003): 79–91. In an article with high relevance for my own argument, Bruce Holsinger suggests that the practice of "vernacular legality," especially in relation to medieval jurisdictional discourse, offers a way past the methodological impasse. See Holsinger, "Vernacular Legality: The English Jurisdictions of *The Owl and the Nightingale*," in *The Letter of the Law: Legal Practice and Literary Production in Medieval England*, ed. Emily Steiner and Candace Barrington (Philadelphia: University of Pennsylvania Press, 2002), 154–84, at 157–58n9.

23. Jacques Rancière, *The Names of History: On the Poetics of Knowledge*, trans. Hassan Melehy (Minneapolis: University of Minnesota Press, 1994), 5.

24. On the case as event, see Lauren Berlant, "Introduction: On the Case," *Critical Inquiry* 33, no. 4 (2007). On the subjective and impersonal, see Lauren Berlant, "Two Girls, Fat and Thin," in *Regarding Sedgwick: Essays on Queen Culture and Critical Theory*, ed. Stephen Barber and David Clark (New York: Routledge, 2002), 71–108; and Berlant, "Starved," *South Atlantic Quarterly* 106, no. 3 (2007) (special issue: *After Sex?* ed. Janet Halley and Andrew Parker): 433–44.

25. Rancière, *Names of History*, 8.

26. Work on law and literature that adopts a rhetorical approach has often construed literature as returning law to its disavowed past, to its human rather than scientific origins. Important studies include James Boyd White, *The Legal Imagination* (Boston: Little, Brown, 1973); Richard Weisberg, *Poethics and Other Strategies of Law and Literature* (New York: Columbia University Press, 1992).

27. My argument about jurisdiction differs substantially, therefore, from an adjacent theoretical model in which the distinction between space and time maps onto that between law and literature, as it does in Wai Chee Dimock, "Time against

Territoriality: National Laws and Literary Translations," in *The Place of Law*, ed. Austin Sarat, Lawrence Douglas, and Martha Merrill Umphrey (Ann Arbor: University of Michigan Press, 2003). Working from the case of Osip Mandelstam reading Dante in the early Soviet Union, Dimock proposes that "while law is spatially predicated, most often operating within the limits set by geopolitics, literature is much less so." This is so because, in Mandelstam's case, against the "brute fact of national borders," "the time of literary culture, an extended and continuously evolving duration," constitutes, extraterritorially, "a tribunal that pits the transmission of words against the location of law" (21). This argument that literature is in excess of where and how the law makes its meanings complements Dimock's important earlier thesis, as developed in *Residues of Justice: Literature, Law, Philosophy* (Berkeley: University of California Press, 1996). There, Dimock holds that literature works by carrying forward the "residues of justice" left behind by the law. In both versions of the argument, the binary that Dimock puts in place may actually limit the content of the legal critique that literature can be imagined to do. It does so by downplaying the extent to which law itself becomes "located" through a "transmission of words," the always freighted, ongoing negotiation of the legal present with the history and practice of its language. For a critique of the binaries that influence work in law and literature generally, see Julie Stone Peters, "Law, Literature, and the Vanishing Real: On the Future of an Interdisciplinary Illusion," *PMLA* 120 (2005): 442–53.

28. Ford, "Law's Territory," 856 (emphasis in original). Ford's essay draws on the account of the emergence of territorial jurisdiction in Thongkai Winichakul, *Siam Mapped: A History of the Geo-Body of a Nation* (1994).

29. Ford, "Law's Territory," 867. For the thesis, no longer credited, that the growth of law was from status to contract relations, see Henry Summer Maine, *Ancient Law: Its Connection with the Early History of Society, and Its Relation to Modern Ideas*, 5th ed. (1873; New York: Henry Holt, 1883), especially 164–65.

30. Ford, "Law's Territory," 852.

31. Paul Vinogradoff, "Historical Types of International Law," in *The Collected Papers of Paul Vinogradoff*, 2 vols. (Oxford: Clarendon Press, 1928), 2:288.

32. Pierre Legendre, "The Masters of Law," in Legendre, *Law and the Unconscious: A Legendre Reader*, ed. and trans. Peter Goodrich (New York: St. Martin's, 1997), 132–33. Spiritual jurisdiction, of course, was itself not singular, and the "universal jurisdiction" of the Church was always inflected, from the bottom up, by a de facto territorial organization of episcopal and parochial jurisdiction. In speaking of the universal jurisdiction implied by the competence of the canon law, I do not mean to minimize the plurijurisdictional reality of canonical practice. It may be said, indeed, that the canonical universalism to which Legendre points is, at least in part, a back formation, the historical product of a later secular order that sought there an image of the indivisible sovereignty it looked to claim for itself.

33. In pre-Reformation England, the fourteenth-century statute of *praemunire*, under which Wolsey's fall was managed by his successors at Westminster, became the principal expression of a jurisdictional discourse pitting the temporal authority of the state against the felt intrusiveness of a transnational ecclesiastical authority.

34. For the relevance to English law of the medieval principle adduced by Legendre, see Peter Goodrich, "Specula Laws: Image, Aesthetic and Common Law," *Law and Critique* 2, no. 2 (1991): 233–54, at 240–43. For a recent study of the various modes of representation that contributed to the common law's symbolic order, see Paul Raffield, *Images and Cultures of Law in Early Modern England: Justice and Political Power, 1558–1660* (Cambridge: Cambridge University Press, 2004).

35. An authoritative description of the jurisdictional complexity of English law during the Tudor period, presented as an extended description of the various courts and the continuity of their jurisdictions, is Sir John Baker, *The Oxford History of the Laws of England*, vol. 6: *1483–1558* (Oxford: Oxford University Press, 2003), 117–319.

36. Charles M. Gray, *The Writ of Prohibition: Jurisdiction in Early Modern English Law*, 2 vols. (New York: Oceana Publications, 1994), 1, xiv–xv.

37. For the common law's engagement with threatening discursive orders other than its own, and especially with that of the civil law, see Peter Goodrich, *Languages of Law: From Logics of Memory to Nomadic Masks* (London: Weidenfeld and Nicolson, 1990).

38. For Peter Goodrich's work on the legal shape of an intimate public sphere, see especially his *Law in the Courts of Love: Literature and Other Minor Jurisprudences* (London: Routledge, 1996); and his *Laws of Love: A Brief Historical and Practical Manual* (Houndmills: Palgrave, 2006).

39. For an introduction to Legendre's difficult project, see Legendre, *Law and the Unconscious*; also the critical essays in *Law, Text, Terror: Essays for Pierre Legendre*, ed. Peter Goodrich, Lior Barshack, and Anton Schütz (New York: Routledge-Cavendish, 2006).

40. Marianne Constable identifies in the English medieval mixed jury a concept of law, lost to judicial positivism, rooted in the "principle of personality of law (that one lives and is judged according to one's own law)," rather than in a territorially defined idea of jurisdiction. That is, personal law looked to a person's relationship to a given community among possible communities, rather than to an indifferently constructed state identity. See Constable, *The Law of the Other: The Mixed Jury and Changing Conceptions of Citizenship, Law, and Knowledge* (Chicago: University of Chicago Press, 1994), 1–27, at 1.

41. For copyhold and its movement from manorial jurisdiction to equity jurisdiction and thence to common law, see Charles M. Gray, *Copyhold, Equity, and the Common Law* (Cambridge, Mass.: Harvard University Press, 1963).

42. A. W. B. Simpson, *A History of the Land Law*, 2d ed. (Oxford: Clarendon Press, 1986), 164–65.

43. For the case history, respectively, of evidentiary prohibitions and of the closely related prohibitions on the grounds of self-incrimination, see Gray, *Writ of Prohibition*, 2:207–91, 293–433. See also R. H. Helmholz et al., *The Privilege against Self-Incrimination: Its Origins and Development* (Chicago: University of Chicago Press, 1997).

44. Gray, *Writ of Prohibition*, 2:207–8, 328–30.

45. According to this same pattern of institutional absorption and conquest, Constable notes that the 1353 statute that formalized the unofficial use of mixed juries also marks a shift in the function of the mixed jury and in the meaning of law itself, substituting a central law for personal law by dissociating the jury's *knowledge* from any status as law: "Jurors may still have special knowledge, but it is not that of the law. The common law is distinct from custom and community, that of which and from which the jury speaks. Instead the jury now speaks about facts" (*Law of the Other*, 102). For an account of the literary engagement with the changing construction of legal community analyzed by Constable, see James Landman, "The Laws of Community, Margery Kempe, and the 'Canon's Yeoman's Tale,'" *Journal of Medieval and Early Modern Studies* 28 (1998): 389–425.

46. This is the view of law as practice that Stanley Fish takes as reasonably underpinning the very possibility of law: "'Forgetfulness,' in the sense of not keeping everything in mind at once, is a condition of action, and the difference between activities—between doing judging and doing literary criticism or doing sociology—is a difference between differing species of forgetfulness." See his "Martinez and the Uses of Theory," in Fish, *Doing What Comes Naturally: Change, Rhetoric, and the Practice of Theory in Literary and Legal Studies* (Durham, N.C.: Duke University Press, 1989), 397.

47. Jacques Ehrmann, "The Tragic/Utopian Meaning of History," trans. Jay Caplan, *Yale French Studies* 96 (1999): 225. I thank Lauren Berlant for referring me to this article.

48. Michel Foucault, "Of Other Spaces," trans. Jay Miskowiec, *Diacritics* 16, no. 1 (1986): 24.

49. Ibid., 27.

50. Peter Goodrich, "Law in the Courts of Love: Andreas Capellanus and the Judgments of Love," in Goodrich, *Law in the Courts of Love*, 29–71; Goodrich, "Gay Science and Law," in *Rhetoric and Law in Early Modern Europe*, ed. Lorna Hutson and Victoria Kahn (New Haven: Yale University Press, 2001), 95–124.

51. Richard Firth Green, *A Crisis of Truth: Literature and Law in Ricardian England* (Philadelphia: University of Pennsylvania Press, 1999).

52. Holsinger, "Vernacular Legality," 156–57.

53. James Simpson, *Reform and Cultural Revolution*, vol. 2 of *The Oxford English Literary History* (Oxford: Oxford University Press, 2002), 1.

54. For positive arguments about the shift in jurisdiction that favored the common law over the ecclesiastical law, see, for example, Gray, *Writ of Prohibition*, 1:22;

Lorna Hutson, "From Penitent to Suspect: Reformation and Renaissance Drama," *Huntington Library Quarterly* 65 (2002): 295–319. Hutson's essay takes issue with Stephen Greenblatt's argument concerning drama's relation to Catholicism in *Hamlet in Purgatory* (Princeton: Princeton University Press, 2001), by arguing that post-Reformation drama develops not as ideological compensation but as an epistemological project in which the audience comes to evaluate evidence in the mode of a common-law jury. For a recent reinvigoration of Whig history-making, see Annabel Patterson, *Nobody's Perfect: A New Whig Interpretation of History* (New Haven: Yale University Press, 2002).

55. On the theoretical emergence of judicial interpretation in the wake of the reconfiguration of statutory law, see Samuel E. Thorne, ed., *A Discourse upon the Exposicion & Understandinge of Statutes with Sir Thomas Egerton's Additions* (San Marino: Huntington Library, 1942), 1–100. The principle that the common-law courts alone could interpret statute was itself controversial. The civilians who oversaw the ecclesiastical jurisdiction opposed that view, claiming for themselves the right to interpret statutes affecting the spiritual courts. See R. H. Helmholz, *Roman Canon Law in Reformation England* (Cambridge: Cambridge University Press, 1990), 174–75. In his chap. 5, Helmholz describes the impact of statutory law on the ecclesiastical jurisdiction and the professional authority of the civil lawyer.

56. Robert Weimann, *Authority and Representation in Early Modern Discourse*, ed. David. Hillman (Baltimore: Johns Hopkins University Press, 1996), 5.

57. Christopher St. German, *Doctor and Student*, ed. T. F. T. Plucknett and J. L. Barton, Selden Society 91 (London: Selden Society, 1974). Publications of the Selden Society are hereafter cited as SS with volume number and date of publication. On the importance of St. German's thought for the consolidation of state authority under the early Tudors, see J. A. Guy, *Christopher St. German on Chancery and Statute*, SS supp. ser. 6 (1985); and his introduction to Thomas More, *The Debellation of Salem and Bizance*, ed. John Guy et al., vol. 10 of *The Complete Works of St. Thomas More* (New Haven: Yale University Press, 1987), xvii–lxvii.

58. On the professional life of the early modern common law, see Wilfred Prest, *The Inns of Court under Elizabeth I and the Early Stuarts* (Totowa, N.J.: Rowman and Littlefield, 1972); Wilfred Prest, *The Rise of the Barristers: A Social History of the English Bar 1590–1640* (Oxford: Clarendon Press, 1986).

59. Helmholz, *Roman Canon Law*, 154. The quotation is from *Correspondence of Matthew Parker*, ed. John Bruce and Thomas Perowne (London: Parker Society, 1853), 351–52.

60. L. M. Hill, ed., *The Ancient State Authoritie and Proceedings of the Court of Requests by Sir Julius Caesar* (Cambridge: Cambridge University Press, 1975).

61. William Fulbecke, *A Parallele or Conference of the Civill Law, the Canon Law, and the Common Law of This Realme of England* (London, 1601); William Fulbecke, *The Pandectes of the Law of Nations* (London, 1602). The most ambitious

civilian intervention was probably John Cowell's digest of English laws, published, like Fulbecke's 1602 work, under a title drawn from the Roman tradition: *Institutiones iuris anglicani* (Cambridge, 1605). On the importance of civil-law textuality for the written representation of the common law, see Richard Helgerson, "Writing the Law," in Helgerson, *Forms of Nationhood: The Elizabethan Writing of England* (Chicago: University of Chicago Press, 1992), 63–104. On the influence of civil law and its practitioners on English political thought generally, see Brian P. Levack, *The Civil Lawyers in England 1603–1641: A Political Study* (Oxford: Clarendon Press, 1973); Levack, "Law and Ideology: The Civil Law and Theories of Absolutism in Elizabethan and Jacobean England," in *The Historical Renaissance: New Essays on Tudor and Stuart Literature and Culture*, ed. Heather Dubrow and Richard Strier (Chicago: University of Chicago Press, 1988), 220–41.

62. For the impact on literary production of constitutional debates around royal authority, see, for example, Constance Jordan, *Shakespeare's Monarchies: Ruler and Subject in the Romances* (Ithaca: Cornell University Press, 1997); David Norbrook, *Writing the English Republic: Poetry, Rhetoric and Politics, 1627–1660* (Cambridge: Cambridge University Press, 1999). For the cultural representation of the monarch in terms of the ideology of the *arcana imperii*, see Jonathan Goldberg, *James I and the Politics of Literature: Jonson, Shakespeare, Donne and Their Contemporaries* (Baltimore: Johns Hopkins University Press, 1983).

63. Alan Harding, *Medieval Law and the Foundations of the State* (Oxford: Oxford University Press, 2002), 295.

64. Thomas Ridley, *View of the Civile and Ecclesiastical Law* (London, 1607), *2v.

65. Ibid., *3r.

66. Ibid., 229.

67. Ibid., 120.

68. Relevant here is Jesús Vallejo's extension of Pietro Costa's work, in which he suggests that the latter privileges, within the symbol *iurisdictio*, the image of a hierarchical process of power relative to more horizontal representations of the plurijurisdictional reality. In this context, Vallejo links the ultimate emergence of the prince's uniquely superior jurisdiction with a reshaping of the traditional jurisdictional theory (a genuinely distributive phenomenon) into a set of structures "whose substantial rigidity was not troubled by the accidental variations produced in jurisprudence," with the paradoxical result that the traditional "theory of jurisdiction ... became a factor of stability" in the reproduction of a differently sovereign order ("Power Hierarchies in Medieval Juridical Thought: An Essay in Reinterpretation," *Ius Commune* 19 [1992]: 1–29, at 24). In *Council and Hierarchy: The Political Thought of William Durant the Younger* (Cambridge: Cambridge University Press, 1991), Constantin Fasolt describes for the early fourteenth century the same reconfiguration of jurisdiction—first, in terms of the impact of a distinction between private property and sovereignty on the order of autonomous lordships (106); and second, in terms of

the development of historical attitudes (dating back even to the twelfth-century canon lawyer Gratian) that split the sanction of historical custom from the "unconditional commands" of the pope and thereby supported (alongside the decline of jurisdiction into sovereignty) a "transformation of jurisprudence into legal history" (270).

69. Simpson, *Reform and Cultural Revolution*, 1.

70. Joseph P. Strayer, *On the Medieval Origins of the Modern State* (Princeton: Princeton University Press, 1970), 22.

71. For an account of English law's disavowal of its own religious origins, and of the relation of that dynamic to the emergence of a new casuistry inside the secular state, see Peter Goodrich, "The New Casuistry," *Critical Inquiry* 33, no. 4 (2007) (special issue: *On the Case*, ed. Lauren Berlant).

CHAPTER ONE

1. Greg Walker, *Plays of Persuasion: Drama and Politics at the Court of Henry VIII* (Cambridge: Cambridge University Press, 1991), 60–101; Alistair Fox, *Politics and Literature in the Reigns of Henry VII and Henry VIII* (Oxford: Blackwell, 1989), 236–40; and David Starkey, "Intimacy and Innovation: The Rise of the Privy Chamber, 1485–1547," in *The English Court: From the Wars of the Roses to the Civil War*, ed. Starkey (London: Longman, 1987), 103–4. This interpretation and dating, which my argument substantiates, challenges an earlier orthodoxy that dated the drama to 1515–16 and identified it as Skelton's attack on Wolsey's disastrous foreign and fiscal policies during the French wars. The argument that the play is an anti-Wolsey satire was first developed by R. L. Ramsay in his edition of *Magnyfycence* (London: Early English Text Society, 1908), cvi–cxxviii. David Bevington follows Ramsay's general topical argument, but deftly resists the temptation to identify characters with specific historic figures; see Bevington, *Tudor Drama and Politics: A Critical Approach to Topical Meaning* (Cambridge, Mass.: Harvard University Press, 1967), 54–63. In her edition of *Magnificence* (Manchester: Manchester University Press, 1980), 31–42, Paula Neuss accepts the idea of the play's topical breadth, but thinks the character of Magnyfycence is to be identified principally with Wolsey. That identification, which has not been widely taken up, was first made by E. S. Hopper, "Skelton's *Magnyfycence* and Cardinal Wolsey," *Modern Language Notes* 16 (1901): 426–29. Two recent critics of the play, James Simpson and Jane Griffiths, remain convinced that the play dates to ca. 1516. See Simpson, *Reform and Cultural Revolution: The Oxford English Literary History*, vol. 2: *1350–1547* (Oxford: Oxford University Press, 2002), 543; Griffiths, *John Skelton and Poetic Authority: Defining the Liberty to Speak* (Oxford: Clarendon Press, 2006), 56.

2. Walker, *Plays of Persuasion*, 66.

3. All citations of *Magnyfycence* refer to John Skelton, *The Complete English Poems*, ed. John Scattergood (Harmondsworth, Middlesex: Penguin, 1983).

4. Bevington, *Tudor Drama and Politics*, 25.

5. Aristotle, *Nichomachean Ethics*, ed. H. Rackham, rev. ed., Loeb Classical Library (Cambridge, Mass.: Harvard University Press, 1934). Aristotle's word for "magnificence" (*megaloprepeia*) is connected to the notion of propriety or decorum (*to prepon*), itself closely allied to the concept of the mean. For the argument that the play's action follows a philosophic scheme based on the Aristotelian account of magnificence, appetite, and reason, see Ramsay, ed., *Magnyfycence*, xxviii–xliv. For the position that the greater debt in Skelton was to Cicero's concept of the virtues in *De officiis*, see W. O. Harris, *Skelton's Magnyfycence and the Cardinal Virtue Tradition* (Chapel Hill: University of North Carolina Press, 1965).

6. John Scattergood, "Skelton's *Magnyfycence* and the Tudor Royal Household," *Medieval English Theatre* 15 (1993): 21–48.

7. Ibid., 22.

8. John M. Wallace, "'Examples Are Best Precepts': Readers and Meanings in Seventeenth-Century Poetry," *Critical Inquiry* 1, no. 2 (1974): 285.

9. Seth Lerer, *Courtly Letters in the Age of Henry VIII: Literary Culture and the Arts of Deceit* (Cambridge: Cambridge University Press, 1997), 65.

10. Griffiths, *John Skelton and Poetic Authority*, 4–7, at 6.

11. Ibid., chaps. 3 and 6, at 66 and 135.

12. Maura Nolan, *John Lydgate and the Making of Public Culture* (Cambridge: Cambridge University Press, 2005), 5.

13. For the late medieval nexus of literature and administration, see, for example, Ethan Knapp, *The Bureaucratic Muse: Thomas Hoccleve and the Literature of Late Medieval England* (University Park: Pennsylvania State University Press, 2001).

14. David Starkey, "Court and Government," in *Revolution Reassessed: Revisions in the History of Tudor Government and Administration*, ed. Christopher Coleman and David Starkey (Oxford: Clarendon Press, 1986), 30–32. For the importance of the Privy Chamber to a politics of intimacy, see David Starkey, "Representation through Intimacy: A Study in the Symbolism of Monarchy and Court Office in Early Modern England," in *The Tudor Monarchy*, ed. John Guy (London: Arnold, 1997), 42–77.

15. Starkey, "Court and Government," 34. A correlative to Wolsey's administrative restructuring of Chamber was his reconstitution of Council in the 1520s, a development that directly influenced the creation of the Privy Council under Thomas Cromwell in the 1530s. See J. A. Guy, "The Privy Council: Revolution or Evolution," in *Revolution Reassessed*, ed. Coleman and Starkey, 59–85.

16. Scattergood, "Skelton's *Magnyfycence* and the Tudor Royal Household," 25; Starkey, "Intimacy and Innovation," 72.

17. J. D. Alsop, "The Structure of Early Tudor Finance, c. 1509–1558," in *Revolution Reassessed*, ed. Coleman and Starkey, 133–62, at 159.

18. Alsop, "Structure of Early Tudor Finance," 159–60.

19. Richard Halpern, *The Politics of Primitive Accumulation: English Renaissance Culture and the Genealogy of Capital* (Ithaca: Cornell University Press, 1991), 103–35. See also W. Scott Blanchard, "The Voice of the Mob in Sanctuary," in *Rethinking*

the Henrician Era: Essays on Early Tudor Texts and Contexts, ed. Peter C. Herman (Urbana: University of Illinois Press, 1994), 123–44.

20. Simon Latham, *Lathams Falconry* (London, 1614), ¶3r, as cited by Scattergood in his note to line 1807.

21. J. H. Baker, *An Introduction to English Legal History*, 3d ed. (London: Butterworths, 1990), 430.

22. On the figure of the fool in Skelton's play, see Peter Happé, "Fansy and Foly: The Drama of Fools in *Magnyfycence*," *Comparative Drama* 27, no. 4 (1993–94): 426–52.

23. Halpern, *Poetics of Primitive Accumulation*, 112.

24. Ibid., 108.

25. Scattergood solves the puzzles in his note to the poem in *Complete Poems*, 403–4. I have slightly adapted his translation.

26. For a reading of the priest's failure to decode the puzzle, in relation to Skelton's invitation to his reader to collaborate on the production of meaning, see Griffiths, *John Skelton and Poetic Authority*, 126–27.

27. Notably, Skelton subjects the whole of "Ware the Hauke" to the same process of rhetorical division, breaking the argument into sections with the following Latin headings that, playing on divisions in the art of preaching, index stages in a spiritual meditation and so direct the reader's attention to the idea of order the poem represents as being under threat: *Prologus, Observate, Considerate, Deliberate, Vigilate, Deplorate, Divinitate, Reformate, Pensitate*.

28. The phoenix—which in Skelton's "Phyllyp Sparowe," following traditional iconography, symbolizes the Christian priest (ll. 513–49)—is but one ornithological symbol of vernacular literary authority. On later forms of English literary authority in relation to classical myth and, specifically, the symbol of the nightingale, see Sean Keilen, *Vulgar Eloquence: On the Renaissance Invention of English Literature* (New Haven: Yale University Press, 2006).

29. Sir John Fortescue, *The Governance of England*, ed. Charles Plummer, 2d ed. (Oxford: Oxford University Press, 1926), 95. Fortescue's treatise was not printed until 1714, and it is unlikely that Skelton knew it through manuscript circulation. As an Aristotelian and Ciceronian virtue central to medieval theories of kingship, magnificence had, in any case, a long history on which both English authors could separately draw.

30. Ibid., 124–25.

31. Ibid., 142, 133–34.

32. J. A. Guy, *Tudor England* (Oxford: Oxford University Press, 1988), 12.

33. Fortescue, *Governance of England*, 145–49, 153.

34. A brilliant treatment of this distinction in the medieval context, and of the *status regni* in general, is Gaines Post, *Studies in Medieval Legal Thought: Public Law and the State, 1100–1322* (Princeton: Princeton University Press, 1964).

35. Walker, *Plays of Persuasion*, 88–101.

36. B. P. Wolffe, *The Crown Lands, 1461–1536: An Aspect of Yorkist and Early Tudor Government* (London: Allen and Unwin, 1970), 29–30.

37. The author of a twelfth-century treatise on the Exchequer, the *Dialogus de Scaccario*, "reserved the concept of 'crown lands' for those lands held directly of the king by his tenants-in-chief." See Wolffe, *Crown Lands*, 19.

38. Wolffe, *Crown Lands*, 51–66. From the moment the Duchy of Lancaster came into the royal demesne with the usurpation in 1399, it constituted a model for the private management of Crown land, since both the Lancastrian and Yorkist kings kept its accounts separate from those involving the rest of the royal demesne. The extraordinary success of Chamber under the Tudors was a consequence of Henry VII's extension of the Yorkist methods to a network of Crown lands augmented across his reign through confiscation by attainder, as well as by the fortuitous concentration of royal familial lands in the Crown through the deaths of Prince Arthur in 1502 and of both the queen and the dowager Duchess of York in 1503.

39. Wolffe, *Crown Lands*, 68, 72.

40. Ibid., 22, 41, 42–45.

41. In general, see W. C. Richardson, *Tudor Chamber Administration 1485–1547* (Baton Rouge: Louisiana State University Press, 1952).

42. *Prerogativa Regis: Tertia lectura Roberti Constable de Lyncolnis Inne anno 11 H.7*, ed. Samuel E. Thorne (New Haven: Yale University Press, 1949), xxi.

43. Thorne, ed., *Prerogativa Regis*, xiv. The second point to make in regard to royal wardship is that, after the statute of *Quia Emptores* (1290), which prevented the introduction of any further lords into the ladder of feudal obligation, tenures had the tendency—for example, through escheat—to find their way back to the Crown and thence to capital tenants. It is for this reason that wardship came to be nearly synonymous with a royal privilege rather than a more general feudal one. The history of royal wardship is that of a centuries-long administrative effect.

44. Baker, *Introduction to English Legal History*, 276.

45. Thorne, ed., *Prerogativa Regis*, xiii.

46. Ibid. One more strategy deserves mention: once land had been seized under the prerogative, the Tudors made it more difficult for an heir to retrieve the land. Wards routinely supplemented whatever the king had already taken from their lands "for the privilege of special livery." And when the subject's land had been seized in error, the Crown routinely used a series of writs to delay those proceedings by which the subject might recover his property. See ibid., xix.

47. Richardson, *Tudor Chamber Administration*, 101–3.

48. Ibid., 169.

49. Ibid., 151–53. The functions of these new offices in Chamber frequently overlapped with less specialized commissioners and agents, whose work for the king continued alongside the newer bureaucracy.

50. Ibid., 205. On the surveyor, see also W. C. Richardson, "The Surveyor of the King's Prerogative," *English Historical Review* 56 (1941): 52–75.

51. Edward Hall, *The Union of the Two Noble and Illustrate Famelies of Lancastre & Yorke* (London, 1548), 59r–v.

52. Richardson, *Tudor Chamber Administration*, 214.

53. Ibid.

54. Ibid., 250–51.

55. Ibid., 259–60.

56. Ibid., 289.

57. Understandably, landowners resisted examination of their tenures when they could. In 1504, for example, Henry VII demanded of all his tenants in chief traditional feudal aids for the marriage of Princess Margaret and the knighting of Prince Arthur, who had died in 1502. Rather than lay open their tenures to inspection, members of Parliament asked the king to accept 40,000 pounds in lieu of the feudal payments and, explicitly, to avoid "the gret inquietnes for the serche and non knowledge of their severall tenures and of their londis chargeable" to the ancient feudal aids. Cited in Thorne, ed., *Prerogativa Regis*, xx–xxi.

58. John Fitzherbert speaks about the lord's "demeyne lands" in his *Boke of Surveyinge and Improvmentes* (London, 1523), iir. This volume attests to the rise of the surveyor's general professional status and significance.

59. Fortescue, *Governance of England*, 122, 120.

60. On the literary representation of the classical mean in a later period of English literature, see Joshua Scodel, *Excess and the Mean in Early Modern English Literature* (Princeton: Princeton University Press, 2002).

61. Hall, *Union*, 59v. According to the law Hall criticizes, a respondent in a suit was adjudged outlaw for failing to appear in court even though he might be "ignouraunt of the prosecucion of the cause, and dwell. ii.C. myles from that place." This was, Hall says, no law, but rather the "perverse abuse and disordre of a lawe . . . craftely practised to the utter confusion of many by untrue officiers" (ibid.).

62. Ibid., 57r.

63. Nathaniel Bacon, *Laws and Government of England*, 4th ed., 2 vols. (London, 1739), 2:114. Cited in Thorne, ed., *Prerogativa Regis*, ix.

64. Thorne, ed., *Prerogativa Regis*, vii.

65. For an exemplary study of Inns of Court readings, specifically those on *Prerogativa Regis*, in relation to their institutional and political contexts, see Margaret McGlynn, *The Royal Prerogative and the Learning of the Inns of Court* (Cambridge: Cambridge University Press, 2003).

66. M. T. Clanchy, *From Memory to Written Record: England 1066–1307*, 2d ed. (London: Blackwell, 1993), 294–327; Richard Firth Green, *A Crisis of Truth: Literature and Law in Ricardian England* (Philadelphia: University of Pennsylvania Press, 1999). On late medieval documentary culture, see Emily Steiner, *Documentary Culture and the Making of Medieval English Literature* (Cambridge: Cambridge University Press, 2003).

67. Lerer, *Courtly Letters in the Age of Henry VIII*, 63.

68. Baker, *Introduction to English Legal History*, 67.

69. Ibid., 116.

70. *Registrum omnium brevium tam originalium quam judicialium* (London, 1531), 291v.

71. Ibid., 292r.

72. Simpson, *Reform and Cultural Revolution*, 544–45.

73. For an extended analysis of "trowthe" as a fourteenth-century keyword at the center of the transition to a centralized and increasingly textualized law, see Green, *Crisis of Truth*.

74. When Abusyon, for example, insists that he can procure a mistress for Magnyfycence for less than a thousand pounds, and tells the prince that "for lesse I waraunt you to be sped" (l. 1571), it is only unruly Magnyfycence who does not hear that the warrant is so little a guarantee as to ensure that, by deliberately following his own pleasure, he stands to lose much more than a thousand pounds. Even when a character does live up to his warrant, the guarantee is a sign not of honor, but of the perversity of promising, deliberately, to follow a criminal course. Thus when Abusyon joins his friends' plot against Magnyfycence by saying, "I waraunt you I wyll not go away" (l. 820), his words are at once colloquial and contractual, a promise that can be enacted at Magnyfycence's court only because it is vicious.

75. Paul Strohm, *Social Chaucer* (Cambridge, Mass.: Harvard University Press, 1989), 84–109.

76. The oaths range from "in faythe" (as at lines 2162, 2163, 2169, 2201, 2205) to "By the messe" (as at lines 2175 and 2204) and "by Jesu, that slayne was with Jewes" (l. 2167).

77. John Cowell, "Quo warranto," *The Interpreter* (Cambridge, 1607), Hhh2r.

78. For a contemporary discussion of what constitutes a sufficient warrant, see J. H. Baker, ed., *John Spelman's Reading on Quo Warranto*, SS 113 (1997), 84–90.

79. Harold Garrett-Goodyear, "The Tudor Revival of Quo Warranto and Local Contributions to State Building," in *On the Laws and Customs of England: Essays in Honor of Samuel E. Thorne*, ed. Morris Arnold et al. (Chapel Hill: University of North Carolina Press, 1981), 231–95, at 241.

80. Ibid., 231–32, 274–95.

81. Ibid., 238.

82. J. H. Baker, ed., *Reports of Cases by John Caryll, Part II: 1501–1522*, SS 116 (2000), 703.

83. On sanctuary in the early Tudor period, see Peter Iver Kaufman, "Henry VII and Sanctuary, *Church History* 53, no. 4 (1984): 465–76.

84. On the Savage case, see E. W. Ives, "Crime, Sanctuary, and Royal Authority under Henry VIII: The Exemplary Sufferings of the Savage Family," in *On the Laws and Customs of England*, ed. Arnold et al., 296–320.

85. Baker, ed., *Reports of Cases by John Caryll, Part II*, 707–9.

86. Ibid., 710.
87. Garrett-Goodyear, "Tudor Revival of Quo Warranto," 248.
88. Ibid., 248–49.
89. For the two maxims in the *Corpus iuris civilis*, see *Inst.* 1.2.6, *Dig.*1.4.1, and *Dig.* 1.3.31. For the English reception through Fortescue, see Sir John Fortescue, *De laudibus legum Anglie*, ed. and trans. S. B. Chrimes (Cambridge: Cambridge University Press, 1942), 25–27. Fortescue associates the first saying with a form of government in which the king can change the laws and impose taxes at will, as opposed to English mixed government, in which the king must first consult the representative assembly.
90. Henry de Bracton, *On the Laws and Customs of England*, ed. G. E. Woodbine, trans. S. E. Thorne, 4 vols. (Cambridge, Mass.: Belknap Press, 1968), 2:305. On *Bracton* and kingship, see Ernst Kantorowicz, *The King's Two Bodies: A Study in Mediaeval Political Theology* (Princeton: Princeton University Press, 1957), chap. 4.3.
91. Pierre Legendre investigates the place of law in terms of the absolute "Reference," the symbolic space and source of authority to which judges appeal as "*authorized interpreters* who can stage Reference for the subject." See Legendre, "The Judge amongst Interpreters," in *Law and the Unconscious: A Legendre Reader*, ed. Peter Goodrich, trans. Peter Goodrich, Alain Pottage, and Anton Schütz (London: Macmillan, 1997), 172.
92. *Corpus iuris civilis, Cod.* 6.23.19.
93. The canon-law definition here is taken from the *Summa aurea* of Hostiensis, as quoted in Zofia Reuger, "Gerson's Concept of Equity and Christopher St. German," *History of Political Thought* 3, no. 1 (1982): 11.
94. Christopher St. German, *Doctor and Student*, ed. T. F. T. Plucknett and J. L. Barton, SS 91 (1974), 97. In another formulation from the 1590s, William Lambarde would write concerning the equitable consideration of circumstance that in Chancery the chancellor "doth . . . so *cancell* and *shut up* the *rigour* of the generall *Law*, that it shall not breake forth to the hurt of some one singular Case and Person." See William Lambarde, *Archeion or a Discourse upon the High Courts of Justice in England*, ed. Charles McIlwain and Paul Ward (London, 1635; Cambridge, Mass.: Harvard University Press, 1957), 31–32, 37.
95. St. German, *Doctor and Student*, 95, 97.
96. For a strong reading of Lyberte and Felycyte's debate as an example of inspired, self-energizing speech closely linked to rhetorical and mental *energeia*, see Griffiths, *John Skelton and Poetic Authority*, 139.
97. On the civilian context for the centralization of interpretation in the ruler, see Fritz Pringsheim, "Justinian's Prohibition of Commentaries to the Digest," in Pringsheim, *Gesammelte Abhandlungen*, 2 vols. (Heidelberg: Carl Winter Universitätsverlag, 1961), 2:86–106.

CHAPTER TWO

1. On More's attitudes toward heresy, in relation to *Utopia* and to the work of Tyndale, see Stephen Greenblatt, *Renaissance Self-Fashioning* (Chicago: University of Chicago Press, 1980), chaps. 1 and 2.

2. J. A. Guy, *The Public Career of Sir Thomas More* (New Haven: Yale University Press, 1980), 3. A recent description of the professional shape of More's early legal career is Robert Keane, "Thomas More as a Young Lawyer," *Moreana* 41, no. 160 (2004): 41–71.

3. William Roper, *The Lyfe of Sir Thomas Moore, Knighte*, ed. Elsie V. Hitchcock (Oxford: Early English Text Society, 1935), 9.

4. Guy, *Public Career of Sir Thomas More*, 7; Keane, "Thomas More as a Young Lawyer," 68.

5. G. D. Ramsay, "A Saint in the City: Thomas More at Mercers' Hall, London," *English Historical Review* 97 (1982): 269–88.

6. The quotations are from Roper, *Lyfe of Sir Thomas Moore*, 10. For the case of the pope's ship, see John Guy, *Thomas More* (London: Arnold, 2000), 54–55. This judicious account of More's life and its representation in contemporary and modern historiography is now the standard biography.

7. K. R. Massingham, "Thomas More, 'Laicus,' Gent.," *Moreana* 22 (1985): 22–35. Cited also in Guy, *Thomas More*, 128.

8. Guy, *Public Career of Sir Thomas More*, 6.

9. For More's judicial work under Wolsey, see Guy, *Public Career of Sir Thomas More*, 18–20. On the conciliar jurisdiction later known as the Court of Requests, see I. S. Leadam, *Select Cases in the Court of Requests* A.D. *1497–1569*, SS 12 (1898).

10. Guy, *Public Career of Sir Thomas More*, 27–28.

11. Thomas More, *The Apology*, ed. J. B. Trapp, vol. 9 of *The Complete Works of St. Thomas More* (New Haven: Yale University Press, 1979), xxxiv. The *Complete Works* is hereafter cited as *CW* with the volume number. For More's defense of ecclesiastical jurisdiction generally, as distinct from private Christian charity, see Thomas More, *Responsio ad Lutherum*, I, ed. John Headley, trans. Sister Scholastica Mandeville, *CW* 5, part 1 (New Haven: Yale University Press, 1969), 196–97.

12. Letter 214 in *The Correspondence of Sir Thomas More*, ed. Elizabeth Rogers (Princeton: Princeton University Press, 1947), 552.

13. William Tyndale, trans., *The New Testament*, ed. W. R. Cooper (1526; London: British Library 2000), 200, 435.

14. For other examples of meddling in relation to conscience, see Letters 206 and 208 in *Correspondence*, ed. Rogers, 523, 537.

15. Letter 216 in ibid., 559.

16. G. R. Elton, *The Tudor Constitution: Documents and Commentary* (Cambridge: Cambridge University Press, 1960), 344.

17. Thomas More, *A Dialogue concerning Heresies*, ed. Thomas Lawler et al., *CW* 6, 2 vols. (New Haven: Yale University Press, 1981), 1:333.

18. Ibid., 1:334–35.

19. Thomas More, *The Confutation of Tyndale's Answer*, ed. Louis Schuster et al., *CW* 8, 3 vols. (New Haven: Yale University Press, 1973), 1:64. In a related passage from the *Confutation*, answering Tyndale's slight against his own use of poetic figures, More notoriously wishes, with no apparent irony, that Tyndale for his part "had medled but wyth poetrye in stede of holy scrypture all the dayes of hys lyfe" (1:176).

20. Letter 199 in *Correspondence*, ed. Rogers, 495.

21. Letter 199 in ibid., 497. The letter to Dr. Wilson repeats the claim concerning Clerk's book, in a formulation that gives this chapter its title: "ther upon I sent home ageyne suche bookes as I had savyng that sume I burned by the consent of the owner that was mynded as my selff was no more to medle of the matter." See Letter 208 in ibid., 536.

22. Letter 199 in ibid., 497.

23. Ibid., 500.

24. Letter 197 in ibid., 482.

25. Letter 206 in ibid., 514–32. For an account of the letter as an example of More's artfulness, see Louis Martz's introduction to Thomas More, *A Dialogue of Comfort against Tribulation*, ed. Martz and Frank Manley, *CW* 12 (New Haven: Yale, University Press, 1976), lx–lxv. For the suggestion that the letter is modeled on the *Crito*, see R. W. Chambers, "The Continuity of English Prose," introduction to Nicholas Harpsfield, *The Life and Death of Sir Thomas Moore*, ed. Elsie Vaughan Hitchcock (London: Early English Text Society, 1932), clxii.

26. For the anecdote, see *Correspondence*, ed. Rogers, 521–23. All subsequent page citations are to this edition. Although the letter is well known, the anecdote has received little close attention. For a general account of the story as an expression of More's individualism, see Daniel Sargent, "Singularity," *Moreana* 4, nos. 15–16 (1967): 311–14; for the relation of Company's name to Christian conscience, community, and comfort, see Alvaro de Silva's introduction to *The Last Letters of Thomas More*, ed. Alvaro de Silva (Grand Rapids: Eerdmans, 2000), 8–13. See also Guy, *Thomas More*, 176–77.

27. The letter in which Alice has passed on to Margaret the two fables directed to More by Audley is Letter 205 in *Correspondence*, ed. Rogers.

28. Sir John Baker, *The Oxford History of the Laws of England*, vol. 6: *1483–1558* (Oxford: Oxford University Press, 2003), 312–14.

29. Sir Edward Coke, *The Fourth Part of the Institutes of the Laws of England: Concerning the Jurisdiction of Courts* (London, 1644), 272.

30. Baker, *Oxford History of the Laws of England*, 312. See his note 189 for piepowder courts belonging to priors, including one at Royston in 1530.

31. The phrase comes in this instance from his letter of March 1534 to Thomas Cromwell. See Letter 197 in *Correspondence*, ed. Rogers, 487.

32. In an important essay on More's and St. German's polemical encounter, Lorna Hutson has argued that the relation between purgative and probative procedures associated respectively with ecclesiastical and common-law investigation of fact underwrites the development of early modern theater as a technical form for treating circumstantial evidence. See her "From Penitent to Suspect: Law, Purgatory, and Renaissance Drama," *Huntington Library Quarterly* 65 (2002): 295-319.

33. See More, *Apology,* chaps. 40-41, 129-37; and Thomas More, *The Debellation of Salem and Bizance,* ed. John Guy et al., *CW* 10 (New Haven: Yale University Press, 1987), chaps. 15-16. 120-67.

34. See More, *Apology,* chap. 27, 97-102; and More, *Debellation of Salem and Bizance,* chap. 20, 213-21.

35. On due process as the principle that "individuals must pursue their claims according to law and must not suffer the burdens imposed by law—be punished for instance—except according to law," see Norman Doe, *Fundamental Authority in Late Medieval English Law* (Cambridge: Cambridge University Press, 1990), 30-31.

36. More, *Dialogue concerning Heresies,* 1:43.

37. Ibid., 1:55-56.

38. Alistair Fox, *Thomas More: History and Providence* (Oxford: Blackwell, 1982), 199-205.

39. More, *Confutation of Tyndale's Answer,* 2:794.

40. Fish, *A Supplicacyon for the Beggers,* printed as Appendix B in Thomas More, *The Supplication of Souls,* ed. Germain Marc'Hadour, *CW* 7 (New Haven: Yale University Press, 1990), 420.

41. More, *Supplication of Souls,* 127.

42. Ibid., 130.

43. All page citations are to More's Latin text as printed in Thomas More, *Utopia,* ed. Edward Surtz and J. H. Hexter, *CW* 4 (New Haven: Yale University Press, 1965). The English translations are mine, checked against the translations in both the Yale edition and *Utopia,* ed. George Logan and Robert Adams (Cambridge: Cambridge University Press, 1989).

44. On the medieval development of equity in relation to the common law, see J. B. Post, "Equitable Resorts before 1450," in *Law, Litigants and the Legal Profession,* ed. E. W. Ives and A. H. Manchester (London: Royal Historical Society, 1983), 68-79; and especially Timothy Haskett, "The Medieval English Court of Chancery," *Law and History Review* 14 (1996): 246-313. Two recent studies have focused attention anew on the relation between equity and early English literature. For the cultural breadth of equity, see Mark Fortier, *The Culture of Equity in Early Modern England* (Aldershot, England: Ashgate, 2005). Also relevant for my chapter is Andrew J. Majeske, *Equity in English Renaissance Literature: Thomas More and Edmund Spenser* (New York: Routledge, 2006). Majeske's reading of More's *aequitas* in light of classical concepts of equity intersects with my analysis in several places, but is inevitably more concerned

with doctrine than, as I am, with the procedural implications of More's formalism for his equitable text.

45. Baker, *Oxford History of the Laws of England*, 40–41.

46. J. H. Hexter, *More's Utopia: The Biography of an Idea* (Princeton: Princeton University Press, 1952), 3–30.

47. For the date of More's entry into the Council, as that relates to recent historiography and More's own representation of the decision, see John Guy, *Thomas More* (London: Arnold, 2000), 42–61.

48. Hexter, *More's Utopia,* 99–155; Hexter, introduction to More's *Utopia,* xxxiii–xli, lxxxiv. A subtle account of Book 1 as an expression of the tension between the claims of *otium* and *negotium* is Alistair Fox, *Thomas More: Providence and History* (Oxford: Blackwell, 1982), chap. 2, especially 59–66.

49. Guy, *Public Career of Sir Thomas More,* 8, 11.

50. Quentin Skinner, "Sir Thomas More's *Utopia* and the Language of Renaissance Humanism," in *The Languages of Political Theory in Early-Modern Europe,* ed. Anthony Pagden (Cambridge: Cambridge University Press, 1987), 134–35. On the radical politics of *Utopia,* see also David Norbrook, *Poetry and Politics in the English Renaissance* (London: Routledge, 1984), 18–31.

51. J. A. Guy has argued both for Wolsey's relative merits as chancellor and against the notion that he was responsible for an ideological, as opposed to a professional, breach between Chancery and the common-law courts. In addition to his *Public Career of Sir Thomas More,* 37–49, and *Thomas More,* 130–32, see J. A. Guy, *The Cardinal's Court: The Impact of Thomas Wolsey in Star Chamber* (Hassocks: Harvester, 1977); and Guy, "Thomas More as Successor to Wolsey," *Thought: Fordham University Quarterly* 52 (1977): 275–92.

52. *Doctor and Student* was published in two parts. The First Dialogue appeared in Latin in 1528, in English in 1531; the Second Dialogue appeared in 1530; and a section called *The New Additions,* concerned explicitly with the question of temporal authority over spiritual matters, appeared in 1531. The standard edition of the texts, and the one I cite, is Christopher St. German, *Doctor and Student,* ed. T. F. T. Plucknett and J. L. Barton, SS 91 (1974).

53. St. German, *Doctor and Student,* 97.

54. Ibid., 95.

55. Ibid., 111.

56. J. A. Guy has written the authoritative accounts of the role played by St. German's doctrine in the political and religious controversies of the 1530s. See Guy, *Christopher St. German on Chancery and Statute,* SS suppl. ser. 6 (1985); and his introduction to More, *Debellation of Salem and Bizance,* xvii–lxvii. On St. German's account of the spiritual jurisdiction, see also J. B. Trapp's introduction to More, *Apology,* especially xli–lxvii.

57. Hexter, introduction to More's *Utopia,* cxxiii.

58. For More's engagement with *De officiis* in relation to *honestas* and *utilitas*, see George Logan, *The Meaning of More's Utopia* (Princeton: Princeton University Press, 1983), 51–53, 178–81.

59. Cicero, *De officiis*, trans. Walter Miller, Loeb Classical Library (Cambridge, Mass.: Harvard University Press, 1913). All citations to the Latin text are to this edition. I have adapted the translation.

60. *Diversite de courtz et lour jurisdictions* (London, 1530), c4r. The first edition dates to 1526; for the printing history of this book, once attributed to Sir Anthony Fitzherbert, see J. H. Baker, introduction to *The Reports of Sir John Spelman*, vol. 2, SS 94 (1978), 58n3.

61. Aristotle, *Nicomachean Ethics*, trans. H. Rackham, rev. ed., Loeb Classical Library (Cambridge, Mass.: Harvard University Press, 1934). For an account of John Skelton's "Tunnyng of Elynour Rummynge" (ca. 1517–21) as a critique of the economic person produced in accordance with the Aristotelian construction of proportional value, see Elizabeth Fowler, *Literary Character: The Human Figure in Early English Writing* (Ithaca: Cornell University Press, 2003), 166–73.

62. That the law is published is also important to the argument More gives Hythloday because it underlines the novel, statutory character of the unjust law and so implies a further irony. In England, as Norman Doe explains, even though the publication of enacted law was not a "criterion for validity" (since Parliament was taken automatically to represent the whole realm), publication was nevertheless encouraged as a way justly to "minimize confusion of the part of subjects" (*Fundamental Authority*, 38–39). As Hythloday has it, however, promulgation is only the capping gesture through which law pretends to justice and a respect for the legal subject.

63. Doe, *Fundamental Authority*, 104–6; for the criterion of similarity in relation to the interpretation of common law as opposed to statute, see also 115–17.

64. Sir John Fortescue, *De natura legis naturae*, in *The Works of Sir John Fortescue*, ed. Thomas, Lord Clermont, 2 vols. (London: privately printed, 1869), 1:86. "*Et saepe ea quae legis verba amplectuntur, mens latoris non persensit; quare tunc officium boni principis, quae lex viva dicitur, supplet defectum legis scriptae quae ut mortua semper immobilis perseverat.*" I have adapted the English translation. In his sense of the law as already necessarily full, Fortescue is also exemplifying a medieval jurisprudence that could not imagine law or interpretation as anything other than the revelation of a preexisting order, embodied for the law in the notion of equity itself. Paolo Grossi summarizes the point in his portrait of the medieval juridical mentality: "*lex* is interpretive of *aequitas*, the prince interprets *aequitas*, interpretation is the reduction of the unjust action to *aequitas*, and jurisdiction is the establishment [*instaurazione*] and conservation of *aequitas*." This equity was, in the words of an early glossator Grossi goes on to cite, God: "*Nichil autem est aequitas quam Deus.*" See Grossi, *L'Ordine giuridico medievale* (Rome: Laterza Editore, 1995), 175–76.

65. On the relation between equity, legislative intention, and the public good in early drama, see Lorna Hutson, "Not the King's Two Bodies: Reading the 'Body

Politic' in Shakespeare's *Henry IV*, Parts 1 and 2," in *Rhetoric and Law in Early Modern Europe*, ed. Hutson and Victoria Kahn (New Haven: Yale University Press, 2001), 166-98.

66. For the proverb's legal context, see Guido Kisch, "Summum Ius Summa Iniuria: Basler Humanisten und Juristen über Aequitas und Epieikeia" in *Aequitas und Bona Fides: Festgabe zum 70 Geburtstag von August Simonius* (Basel: Helbing, 1955), 195-211.

67. Erasmus begins his entry on the proverb in this way: "Extreme right is extreme wrong means that men never stray so far from the path of justice as when they adhere most religiously to the letter of the law. They call it 'extreme right' when they wrangle over the words of a statute and pay no heed to the intention of the man who drafted it." See Erasmus, *Adagiorum Chilias Prima, centuriae vi-x,* ed. M. L. van Poll-van de Lisdonk and M. Cytowska (= *Opera omnia* II, 2) (Amsterdam: Elsevier, 1998), 432-34. Of great interest for the English reception of *aequitas* is a passage in the concluding pages of a treatise on the seven penitential psalms written by Bishop John Fisher for Henry VII's mother, Margaret Beaufort, and first published in 1508. In his reading of Psalm 142 concerning God's equitable treatment of the sinner, Fisher links the equity of human law to Cicero's proverb and to Aristotelian *epieikeia*: "*Filius meus mortuus fuerat & reuixit*. My chylde was deed & now is revyved. Now is he revyved, truly by the equyte of his fader. Equitas is called the thynge that phylosophers named epicheia whiche is proprely the mynde of the lawe. A juge ought rather to folowe the mynde of the lawe than the extremyte of the wordes wryten in it. Elles as Cicero sayd. *Summum ius summa iniuria erit.* The lawe if used extremely after the wordes as they be wryten shall be many tymes grete wronge." See J. E. B. Mayor, ed., *The English Works of John Fisher, Part I* (London: Early English Text Society, 1876), 261.

68. Baker, *Oxford History of the Laws of England*, 42.

69. As Hexter points out, the representation of Morton also allowed More the pleasure of giving an "intimate account" of his mentor's household even as he delivered a more public reckoning of recent political history through his "direct and oblique references to Royal policy under Henry VII." See Hexter, *More's Utopia*, 100.

70. Similarly suggestive for the topical resonance of Book 1 is that More takes care to identify Cuthbert Tunstall, the leader of the 1515 embassy, with Chancery, by allusion to Tunstall's appointment in May 1516 as Master of the Rolls, that is, Wolsey's vice-chancellor and the principal clerk in Chancery: "Tunstall, whom the king has recently made master of the royal rolls [*quem sacris scriniis nuper . . . praefecit*]" (46).

71. Hythloday's definition here of inequitable application of law as being "*supra iustum*" (beyond justice) is in interesting tension with the phrasing in Fortescue's account of equity in *De natura legis naturae*, where he says, following Aegidius Romanus, that equity is "*super iustum*" in the sense of being above the law's rigor: "Epieikeia is an indulgence above what is just, for human nature always craves pardon [*Epiches . . . est indulgere super justum, natura namque humana semper supplicat pro venia*]." It is possible, then, that More, even more a formalist than his predecessor,

is directly answering that phrasing, and having Hythloday bring *aequitas* within the law by putting *inequity* beyond it. See Fortescue, *De natura legis naturae*, 1:85.

72. George M. Logan, "*Utopia* and Deliberative Rhetoric," *Moreana* 31, nos. 118-19 (1994): 103-20.

73. Baker, introduction to *Reports of Sir John Spelman*, 2:143. Pleading was originally conducted orally at the bar, but was eventually replaced by an exchange of provisional pleas in writing; as Baker points out, "notwithstanding the increasing (if not by now universal) use of paper drafts, it was still possible in Henry VIII's reign to discuss draft pleas at the bar before they were entered of record" (152). See also 92-100.

74. Ibid., 2:144.

75. Ibid., 2:145-46.

76. Ibid., 2:149.

77. On Utopia in the context of civic humanist arguments around the meaning of a *vera nobilitas*, see Skinner, "Sir Thomas More's *Utopia*," especially 135-47.

78. Baker, introduction to *Reports of Sir John Spelman*, 2:146-49.

79. Cited in Doe, *Fundamental Authority*, 15.

80. The standard form of English statute mirrors this doubled character, with the preface ("Whereas . . .) announcing, forensically, the problem to be met and the declaration ("Be it enacted . . .") deliberatively answering that situation for the future.

81. In the name of uniform justice, interpretive equity could involve an extension of law that went quite squarely against any idea of "mercy."

82. On later sixteenth-century Chancery procedure, see W. J. Jones, *The Elizabethan Court of Chancery* (Oxford: Oxford University Press, 1967). For equity and common law in relation to the 1616 crisis that saw Coke dismissed from the bench over his refusal to countenance interventions from Chancery after judgment given, see Charles M. Gray, "The Boundaries of the Equitable Function," *American Journal of Legal History* 20 (1976): 192-226.

83. *Diversite de courtz et lour jurisdictions*, a5r. On early Chancery procedure, see William Paley Baildon, introduction to *Select Cases in Chancery* A.D. *1364-1471*, SS 10 (1896), xxiv-xxix.

84. *Diversite de courtz et lour jurisdictions*. The association here of equity with an absolute as opposed to ordinary power is found also in Fortescue's description of the king's judicial power in *De natura legis naturae*, 85: "Hence, that superior lord is supposed to have an absolute power, not however so as to undo the effected law, but in order rather to fulfil the law of his kingdom through regard to the law of nature, which is natural equity [*Quo superior ille potestatem censetur habere absolutam, non tamen ut possit solvere legem perfectam; sed ut ratione legis naturae, quae naturalis equitatis est, legem regni sui ipse possit potius adimplere*]."

85. J. H. Baker, *The Order of Serjeants at Law*, SS suppl. ser. 3 (1984), 287. Baker indicates the speech may also be by Robert Brudenell, Chief Justice in Common Pleas.

86. Ibid., 293.

87. Roper, *Lyfe of Sir Thomas Moore*, 44–45.

88. Doe, *Fundamental Authority*, 153.

89. Baker, *Oxford History of the Laws of England*, 46. In his chapter on conscience in the common law, Doe significantly underplays the theoretical significance of St. German's so subordinating conscience to the common law; while St. German looks traditional, his theory is already tilting toward 1566. See Doe, *Fundamental Authority*, 132–54.

90. Baker, *Oxford History of the Laws of England*, 46.

91. For a suggestive critique of the view of Utopia as uniformitarian and destructive of inner life, see Richard Strier, "Identity and Power in Tudor England: Stephen Greenblatt, *Renaissance Self-Fashioning from More to Shakespeare*," boundary 2 82, no. 3 (1982): 383–94, at 387; also Strier, *Resistant Structures: Particularity, Radicalism, and Renaissance Texts* (Berkeley: University of California Press, 1995), 72–73.

92. James Simpson, *Reform and Cultural Revolution: The Oxford English Literary History*, vol. 2: *1350–1547* (Oxford: Oxford University Press, 2002), 229–38.

93. Huntington Library, Ellesmere MS 2655, fol. 10. For a brief treatment of the speech, see Guy, *Cardinals' Court*, 30–31.

94. For More's defense, against Luther, of the utility of human laws, see chapter 18 of More, *Responsio ad Lutherum*, 1:270–83.

95. Earlier readings of *Utopia* have placed interpretive instability at the center of More's project. In relation to rhetoric, see, for example, Andrew Weiner, "Raphael's Eutopia and More's Utopia: Christian Humanism and the Limits of Reason," *Huntington Library Quarterly* 79 (1975): 1–28; David Bevington, "The Dialogue in Utopia: Two Sides to the Question," *Studies in Philology* 58 (1961): 496–509.

96. On the indefinite particular, identifiable in the example and in the *quodlibet* of medieval scholasticism, see Giorgio Agamben, *The Coming Community*, trans. Michael Hardt (Minneapolis: University of Minnesota Press, 1993).

CHAPTER THREE

1. See especially Brian Lockey, "Spenser's Legalization of the Irish Conquest," chap. 4 in *Law and Empire in Renaissance Literature* (Cambridge: Cambridge University Press, 2006), 113–41. Lockey's analysis of natural law in discussions of the Irish legal situation nicely dovetails with my work on the *techne* of common law, especially since he and I share a sense of the tension involved in a given customary law's being applied to a people whose customs are other. On this issue, explored in relation to John Davies's jurisprudence, see also Brian Lockey, "Conquest and English Legal Identity in Renaissance Ireland," *Journal of the History of Ideas* 65, no. 4 (2004): 543–58. For an earlier version of the present chapter, see Bradin Cormack, "A Power to Do Justice: Royal Authority and Jurisdiction in English Law and Literature," Ph.D. diss., Stanford University, 2001.

2. On the project, see Hiram Morgan, "The Colonial Venture of Sir Thomas Smith in Ulster, 1571–1575," *Historical Journal* 28, no. 2 (1985): 261–78.

3. Sir Thomas Smith, *A Letter Sent by I. B. Gentleman unto His Friende Mayster R. C. Esquire* (London, 1572), G2r.

4. Smith, *Letter Sent by I. B. Gentleman*, D1r–v, E3v, E4r.

5. This is laid out in the 1573 broadside "The Offer and Order Given Forth by Sir Thomas Smyth Knyght" (STC 22868.5): "And if any will bear the charges of a Souldier, that cannot goe hymselfe nor send another in his roome, he shall have his part of land allotted to him as wel as though he went himself: but then for a footman he must pay in readie money. xvi pound. xiii.s. iiid. This is one parte."

6. The 1581 *Discourse*, written ca. 1549 and first published by Thomas Marshe under the title *A Compendious or Briefe Examination*, is easily found in *A Discourse of the Commonweal of This Realme of England, Attributed to Sir Thomas Smith*, ed. Mary Dewar (Charlottesville: University of Virginia Press, 1969).

7. Smith, *Letter Sent by I. B. Gentleman*, D1r.

8. Sir Edward Coke, *The Second Part of the Institutes of the Laws of England* (London, 1644), 668.

9. Sir Thomas Smith, *De republica Anglorum*, ed. L. Alston (Cambridge: Cambridge University Press, 1906), 37–38. This text follows the 1583 first edition. An excellent edition based on surviving manuscripts is Smith, *De republica Anglorum*, ed. Mary Dewar (Cambridge: Cambridge University Press, 1982).

10. For the semantic range of the "common," see Raymond Williams, *Keywords: A Vocabulary of Culture and Society* (New York: Oxford University Press, 1976), 61–62.

11. Sir Thomas Elyot, *The Boke Named the Governour,* ed. Donald Rude (New York: Garland, 1992), 15–16.

12. Smith, *De republica Anglorum*, 20.

13. Smith, *Letter Sent by I. B. Gentleman*, D3r.

14. Sir John Davies, *A Discoverie of the True Causes Why Ireland Was Never Entirely Subdued* (London, 1612), 7. A modern-spelling edition has been edited by James P. Myers (Washington, D.C.: Catholic University of America Press, 1988).

15. Ciaran Brady, *The Chief Governors: The Rise and Fall of Reform Government in Tudor Ireland 1536–1588* (Cambridge: Cambridge University Press, 1994), 273–74.

16. The brutal depopulation of Munster, given vivid force in Spenser's account of the famine, certainly supports the narrow association of colonization and conquest. For this aspect of the plantation process, see Willy Maley, *Salvaging Spenser: Colonialism, Culture and Identity* (London: Macmillan, 1997), 49–51, 58–68.

17. Kenneth Nicholls, *Gaelic and Gaelicised Ireland in the Middle Ages* (Dublin: Gill and Macmillan, 1972), especially chaps. 1–3.

18. Ibid., 9, 24.

19. *Tenant at will* and *freeholder* are English terms applied to their rough equivalents within the Gaelic system. The problem of translation emblematizes the substantive

difficulties involved in *systematically* extending English sovereignty into the lordships ordered according to other systems than the common law.

20. Nicholls, *Gaelic and Gaelicised Ireland*, 31, 35, 65–67.

21. Ibid., 26.

22. Ibid., 57–65.

23. Davies, *A Discoverie of the True Causes*, 166.

24. Ibid., 170–71.

25. Edmund Spenser, *A View of the Present State of Ireland*, in *The Works of Edmund Spenser: A Variorum Edition*, ed. E. A. Greenlaw et al., 10 vols. (Baltimore: Johns Hopkins University Press, 1949), 9, 49. All subsequent references are to this edition.

26. Edmund Spenser, *The Faerie Queene*, ed. Thomas P. Roche (London: Penguin, 1978). All subsequent references are to this edition; I have, however, regularized *i/j* and *u/v*.

27. Ovid, *Metamorphoses I–VIII*, trans. F. J. Miller and G. P. Goold, 3d ed., Loeb Classical Library (Cambridge, Mass.: Harvard University Press, 1977). I have adapted this translation.

28. Cicero, *De officiis*, trans. Walter Miller, Loeb Classical Library (Cambridge, Mass.: Harvard University Press, 1913). I have adapted this translation. For Pontanus's citation of Cicero, see Ovid, *Metamorphoseon*, ed. Jacobus Pontanus (Antwerp, 1618; New York: Garland, 1976), 31.

29. Andrew Hadfield, *Edmund Spenser's Irish Experience: Wilde Fruit and Salvage Soyl* (Oxford: Clarendon Press, 1997), 13–16, 174–84.

30. Edmund Spenser, *The Shorter Poems*, ed. William A. Oram et al. (New Haven: Yale University Press, 1989).

31. In line with their bureaucratic origins and aims, many English treatises on Irish policy are designated as "description," "survey," or "view." In addition to Spenser's own *View of the Present State of Ireland*, some examples are Richard Stanyhurst, *A Plain and Perfect Description of Ireland* (published in Holinshed's *Chronicles*); Robert Payne, *A Brief Description of Ireland* (1590); Barnaby Rich, *A Short Survey of Ireland* (1609) and *A New Description of Ireland* (1610); and Peter Walsh, *A Prospect of the State of Ireland* (1652).

32. For the relation of "plot" to the surveying of Ireland, see Julia Reinhard Lupton, "Mapping Mutability: or, Spenser's Irish Plot," in *Representing Ireland*, ed. Andrew Hadfield and Willy Maley (Cambridge: Cambridge University Press, 1993), 116–31.

33. Hadfield, *Edmund Spenser's Irish Experience*, 184.

34. On the Irish savages of Book 6, see ibid., 175–84; Christopher Highley, *Shakespeare, Spenser, and the Crisis in Ireland* (Cambridge: Cambridge University Press, 1997), 126–31; Sheila T. Cavanagh, "'Licentious Barbarism': Spenser's View of the Irish and *The Faerie Queene*," *Irish University Review* 26, no. 2 (1996): 268–80. On Irish incivility in Spenser, see Colin Burrow, "Wild Men and Wild Places," chap. 6

in *Edmund Spenser* (Plymouth: Northcote House, 1996), 72–79; Patricia Coughlan, "'Some Secret Scourge Which Shall by Her Come unto England': Ireland and Incivility in Spenser," in *Spenser and Ireland: An Interdisciplinary Perspective*, ed. Patricia Coughlan (Cork: Cork University Press, 1989), 46–74.

35. For Ireland and cannibalism, see Richard McCabe, *Spenser's Monstrous Regiment: Elizabethan Ireland and the Poetics of Difference* (Oxford: Oxford University Press), 244–45; Robert E. Stillman, "Spenserian Autonomy and the Trial of the New Historicism: Book Six of the Faerie Queene," *English Literary Renaissance* 22 (1992): 309–10; David Norbrook, *Poetry and Politics in the English Renaissance* (London: Routledge and Kegan Paul, 1984), 152. For Serena's plight and the savage's cannibalism as a parody of the Catholic mass, see Highley, *Shakespeare, Spenser, and the Crisis in Ireland*, 130–32.

36. Hadfield, *Edmund Spenser's Irish Experience*, 177–81; Highley, *Shakespeare, Spenser, and the Crisis in Ireland*, 130.

37. For another example of the allegorical representation of a legal question in terms of the objectified female body (fraudulent conveyance allegorized as kidnapping), see Charles Ross, *Elizabethan Literature and the Law of Fraudulent Conveyance: Sidney, Spenser, and Shakespeare* (Aldershot: Ashgate, 2003), especially chaps. 3 and 4.

38. For Sir Bruin's claims in relation to the Fitz-Ursulas ("sons of bears"), see Lockey, *Law and Empire*, 133–39.

39. Edward Coke, *The First Part of the Institutes of the Law of England* (London, 1628), 17r.

40. Ibid., 17v.

41. I take the acreage of Spenser's estate at Kilcolman from Michael MacCarthy-Morrogh, *The Munster Plantation: English Migration to Southern Ireland 1583–1641* (Oxford: Clarendon Press, 1986), 291.

42. Kenneth W. Nicholls, *Land, Law and Society in Sixteenth-Century Ireland: O'Donnell Lecture Delivered at University College, May 1976* (Dublin: National University of Dublin, 1978), 14.

43. Public Record Office: SP/63/121/62. Cited in MacCarthy-Morrogh, *The Munster Plantation*, 71.

44. J. H. Baker, *An Introduction to English Legal History*, 3d ed. (London: Butterworths, 1990), 296.

45. Baker, *Introduction to English Legal History*, 277–78.

46. Nicholls, "Land, Law and Society in Sixteenth-Century Ireland," 20.

47. For the impact of *Quia Emptores* on Irish tenure, see also Hans Pawlisch, *Sir John Davies and the Conquest of Ireland: A Study in Legal Imperialism* (Cambridge: Cambridge University Press, 1985), 12. Pawlisch's argument as a whole is concerned with the early seventeenth-century solution to the legal crux produced by the statute.

48. For an extended analysis of the alternative claims on land in the Munster plantation, see MacCarthy-Morrogh, *Munster Plantation*, 71–106; Anthony J. Sheehan,

"Official Reaction to Native Land Claims in the Munster Plantation," *Irish Historical Studies* 22 (1983): 297–317.

49. Sheehan, "Official Reaction," 307.

50. Nicholas Canny, *From Reformation to Restoration: Ireland, 1534–1600* (Dublin: Criterion, 1987), 122.

51. MacCarthy-Morrogh, *Munster Plantation*, 80.

52. Ibid., 81–82, 84.

53. Sheehan, "Official Reaction," 297; MacCarthy-Morrogh, *Munster Plantation*, 106.

54. Cited in Sheehan, "Official Reaction," 316.

55. Cited in Canny, *From Reformation to Restoration*, 123.

56. Patricia Coughlan relates the Mutability Cantos to the Munster land disputes, and in particular Spenser's quarrel with the Old English Lord Roche. See Coughlan, "The Local Context of Mutabilitie's Plea," *Irish University Review* 26, no. 2 (1996): 320–41.

57. *Commentaires hieroglyphiques ou Images des choses de Ian Pierius Valerian*, trans. Gabriel Chappuys (Lyons, 1576), 428. The Latin text from *Ioannis Pierii Valeriani hieroglyphica* (1614) reads as follows: "*Corvi autem figura hieroglyphicum erat hominis, qui liberos suos exhaeredaret, abdicaretve, aut domo quoque eiiceret modo.*" The association of cormorant and a bad father's expulsion of children from home is surely relevant also to Milton's description of Satan as cormorant (*Paradise Lost* 4.196).

58. Pierre Dinet, *Cinq livres des hieroglyphiques* (Paris, 1614; New York: Garland, 1979), 438.

59. Upton identified Belgard with Belvoir Castle, seat of the Dukes of Rutland, and Sir Bellamour with the dukes' family name of Manners (Moeurs). Later commentators, so far as I can determine, have mainly extended that association. See Ray Heffner's notes in *Works of Edmund Spenser: A Variorum Edition*, ed. Greenlaw et al., 6:262–64. My reading of the episode means to supplement rather than supplant these earlier interpretations.

60. Richard T. Neuse, "Pastorella," in *The Spenser Encyclopedia*, ed. A. C. Hamilton et al. (Toronto: University of Toronto Press, 1990), 533.

61. Artegall is patently another viceregal figure, the male figure who can impose justice to the extent that he moves beyond the feminized policies of his sovereign. For an engaging account of the viceregal system, see Maley, *Salvaging Spenser*, 99–117. For Spenser's gendering of the relationship between the active male reformers in Ireland and the passive female queen "at home," see Hadfield, *Edmund Spenser's Irish Experience*, 146–85; Highley, *Shakespeare, Spenser, and the Crisis in Ireland*, 110–33.

62. I take the phrase from the title of Pawlisch's monograph on Davies.

63. Sir John Davies, *Le Primer report des cases & matters en ley* (Dublin, 1615). All subsequent citations are to this edition.

64. For Pocock's analysis of the "common-law mind" in relation to the insularity of English legal and historiographic method, see J. G. A. Pocock, *The Ancient Constitution and the Feudal Law: A Study of English Historical Thought in the Seventeenth Century, A Reissue with a Retrospect* (1957; Cambridge: Cambridge University Press, 1987). For two responses to Pocock's thesis, see Pawlisch, *Sir John Davies and the Conquest of Ireland*, 161–75; Glenn Burgess, *The Politics of the Ancient Constitution* (University Park: Pennsylvania State University Press, 1992).

65. The relevant cases are the following: the case of customs payable for merchandise; the case of the royal fishery of the *Banne*; the case of mixed money; the case of *praemunire*; the course of trial of legitimation and bastardy. For an extended account of Davies's strategic use of the most important of the eleven cases to centralize English power in Ireland, see Pawlisch, *Sir John Davies and the Conquest of Ireland*, 55–157, where they are grouped as affecting either the native Gaelic population or the Old English colonial community.

66. J. G. A. Pocock, *The Machiavellian Moment: Florentine Political Thought and the Atlantic Republican Tradition* (Princeton: Princeton University Press, 1975), 13.

67. Sir John Fortescue, *De laudibus legum Anglie*, ed. and trans. S. B. Chrimes (Cambridge: Cambridge University Press, 1949), 39–41.

68. Pocock, *Machiavellian Moment*, 15–16.

69. Peter Goodrich, "Critical Legal Studies in England: Prospective Histories," *Oxford Journal of Legal Studies* 12 (1992): 195–236.

70. Goodrich, "Critical Legal Studies," 201.

71. In addition to the article cited, see Goodrich, *Oedipus Lex: Psychoanalysis, History, Law* (Berkeley: University of California Press, 1995); and Goodrich, *Languages of Law: From Logics of Memory to Nomadic Masks* (London: Weidenfeld and Nicolson, 1990).

72. Pawlisch, *Sir John Davies and the Conquest of Ireland*, 34–51.

73. Brendan Bradshaw, *The Irish Constitutional Revolution of the Sixteenth Century* (Cambridge: Cambridge University Press, 1979), 153, 148.

74. Bradshaw, *Irish Constitutional Revolution*, 240.

75. Pawlisch, *Sir John Davies and the Conquest of Ireland*, 35–38. The act known as Poynings' Law, passed in the Irish Parliament of 1494–95, laid out the terms under which Parliament might be summoned and might proceed in its legislative work. Although early on it worked primarily to control the viceregal executive, it later came to symbolize the subordinate status of the Irish Parliament itself. See David B. Quinn, "The Early Interpretation of Poynings' Law, 1494–1534," *Irish Historical Studies* 2 (1941): 241–54; R. Dudley Edwards and T. W. Moody, "The History of Poynings' Law: Part I, 1494–1615," *Irish Historical Studies* 2 (1941): 415–24; Aidan Clark, "The History of Poynings' Law, 1615–41," *Irish Historical Studies* 18 (1972): 207–22.

76. Canny, *From Reformation to Restoration*, 184.

77. Hadfield, *Edmund Spenser's Irish Experience*, 63–64.

78. Cited in Nerys Patterson, "Gaelic Law and the Tudor Conquest of Ireland," *Irish Historical Studies* 28 (1991): 201.

79. Henry F. Berry, ed., *Statutes and Ordinances and Acts of the Parliament of Ireland*, Vol. 1: *King John to Henry V* (Dublin: H.M. Stationery Office, 1907), 436–37. The English text of the Statutes of Kilkenny, although not the law French text, is available in *Irish Historical Documents 1172–1922*, ed. Edmund Curtis and R. B. McDowell (London: Methuen, 1943).

80. Davies, *Discoverie of the True Causes*, 123; Hiram Morgan, ed., "'Lawes of Irelande': A Tract by Sir John Davies," *Irish Jurist* 30 (1995): 310.

81. Nicholas Canny, ed., "Rowland White's 'The Dysorders of the Irisshery', 1571," *Studia Hibernica* 19 (1979): 154.

82. Richard Becon, *Solon His Follie or a Politique Discourse, Touching the Reformation of Common-weales Conquered, Declined or Corrupted* (Oxford, 1594), 21.

83. Nicholas Canny, ed., "Rowland White's 'Discors Touching Ireland,' c. 1569," *Irish Historical Studies* 20 (1977): 452.

84. Brady, *Chief Governors*, 245.

85. An excellent account of the shift in England from a private to a public construction of the law, and one responsive to the development of parliamentary omnicompetence under Henry VIII, is Samuel E. Thorne, ed., *A Discourse upon the Exposicion & Understandinge of Statutes* (San Marino, Calif.: Huntington Library, 1942), 3–100.

86. On Spenser's *View* and attitudes toward the common law in Ireland and England, see David J. Baker, "'Some Quirk, Some Subtle Evasion': Legal Subversion in Spenser's *A View of the Present State of Ireland*," *Spenser Studies* 6 (1986): 157–63. On the *View* in relation to Spenser's interest in antiquarianism, including legal antiquarianism, see Bart van Es, "Discourses of Conquest: *The Faerie Queene*, the Society of Antiquaries, and *A View of the Present State of Ireland*," *English Literary Renaissance* 32, no. 1 (2002): 118–51.

87. Christopher Hill, "The Norman Yoke," chap. 3 in *Puritanism and Revolution: Studies in Interpretation of the English Revolution of the Seventeenth Century* (London: Secker and Warburg, 1958), 61–62. Hill popularized "Norman Yoke" as the name for a constitutive constitutional theory. The designation is potentially confusing in that it can be taken to refer both to the theories of the ancient constitution that sought in pre-Conquest society precedents for a mixed polity, and to those theories, associated with absolutism, that saw the Conquest as determinative of the law that followed from it. J. G. A. Pocock recommends that the "Norman Yoke" be used only in reference to the latter, with the "ancient constitution" reserved for the former. Although I see the problem of nomenclature, for reasons developed in chapter 4, I prefer to retain the term "Norman Yoke" as potentially determining both positions, since both looked to that crisis as the starting point, or the scene, of their respective theories. See Pocock's retrospective essay in the reissue of *Ancient Constitution and the Feudal Law*, 318–19.

88. Diana Parkin-Speer, "Allegorical Legal Trials in Spenser's *The Faerie Queene*," *Sixteenth Century England* 23, no. 3 (1992): 495.

89. Pauline Henley, *Spenser in Ireland* (Cork: Cork University Press, 1928), 127.

90. On Spenser's treatment of "Folkmotes" or place of assembly, see Annabel Patterson, "The Egalitarian Giant: Representations of Justice in History/Literature," *Journal of British Studies* 31 (1992): 116–17.

91. Through a slippage between the "hair" she exacts from passers-by and the "heir" violated by tanistry, Briana's exaction may correspond to that custom in particular.

92. For the Pollente episode as a critique of monopolies and historical tolls on bridges in England and Ireland, see Merlin L. Neff, "Spenser's Allegory of the Toll Bridge," *Philological Quarterly* 13 (1934): 159–67.

93. Elizabeth Fowler, "The Failure of Moral Philosophy in the Work of Edmund Spenser," *Representations* 51 (1995): 47–76, at 51. More generally, Fowler's article offers an incisive analysis of legal representations in *The Faerie Queene* in terms of the dangerous gap between the ethical and political virtues.

94. Brady, *Chief Governors*, 273–78.

95. Ibid., 278.

96. For an analysis of composition in one province, see Bernadette Cunningham, "The Composition of Connacht in the Lordships of Clanricard and Thomond, 1577–1641," *Irish Historical Studies* 24 (1984): 1–14.

97. The connection between the two episodes is noted by Frederick M. Padelford, "Spenser's Arraignment of the Anabaptists," *Journal of English and German Philology* 12 (1913): 434.

98. Patterson, "Egalitarian Giant," 116.

99. Ibid., 113.

100. Fowler, "Failure of Moral Philosophy," 63–64.

101. For Spenser's view of judicial pronouncement, the precise relationship between the common-law courts and the equity courts such as Chancery is of secondary importance. As a theoretical matter, there was general agreement that, as St. German had argued, equity was integral to the law as a supplementary principle of justice.

102. Fowler, "Failure of Moral Philosophy," 64; Patterson, "Egalitarian Giant," 113.

103. On the temporal and spatial register of Spenser's allusion to the Lee, in relation to Derricke's exemplary poetry, see McCabe, *Spenser's Monstrous Regiment*, 70–72.

104. John Derricke, *The Image of Irelande* (London, 1581), K4v.

105. The letter to Ralegh, which was published as an appendix to the 1590 *Faerie Queene*, but omitted in 1596, is reprinted in Roche's edition of *The Faerie Queene*, 15–18. The better known instance of Spenser's allegorization of allegory is Britomart's interpretation of her dream in the Isis Church (5.7). The religious rites of ancient Egypt provided from an early date a site for the theorization of allegorical reading. Spenser's chief source for the Isis episode is Plutarch's essay on Isis and Osiris in the *Moralia* (351C–384C), in which Plutarch interprets Isis' search for Osiris as an allegory for allegorical reading. See David Dawson, *Allegorical Readers and Cultural*

Revision in Ancient Alexandria (Berkeley: University of California Press, 1992), 58–61.

106. On the transmission of the classical theory of equity in the rhetorical tradition, see Wesley Trimpi, *Muses of One Mind: The Literary Analysis of Experience and Its Continuity* (Princeton: Princeton University Press, 1983), especially 247–74.

107. Edmund Plowden, *Les Comentaries ou les reportes* (London, 1571), 363r. Cited in Thorne, ed., *Discourse*, 63n132.

108. Cited in Thorne, ed., *Discourse*, 77n162.

109. Ibid., 140.

110. For the transmission of the classical tradition of *interpretatio scripti*, and the connection articulated there between equity and interpretation, see Kathy Eden, *Hermeneutics and the Rhetorical Tradition: Chapters in the Ancient Legacy and Its Humanist Reception* (New Haven: Yale University Press, 1997).

111. Michael Murrin, *The Allegorical Epic: Essays in Its Rise and Decline* (Chicago: University of Chicago Press, 1980), 126.

112. J. H. Baker, *Manual of Law French* (Amersham: Avebury Publishing, 1979), 77, 97.

113. This is the implication of a medieval definition that finds a judicial decision inconvenient: "issint serrvit *le jugement repugnaunt a un aultre, quod esset* inconveniens." See John P. Collas, ed., *Year Books of Edward II, Vol. XXV, 12 Edward II Part of Easter and Trinity, 1319*, SS 81 (1964), cix.

114. Ibid.

115. F. W. Maitland, ed., *Year Books of Edward II, vol. 1, 1 & 2 Edward II* A.D. *1307–1309*, SS 17 (1903), xviii–xix.

116. This later, and too narrow, version of the distinction is cited in reference to Spenser by Patterson, "Egalitarian Giant," 120n48.

117. Thorne, ed., *Discourse*, 30, 35.

118. Ibid., 40.

119. Ibid., 71–74.

CHAPTER FOUR

1. Claudius Holyband, *The Frenche Littelton* (London, 1576 [1566]). A scholarly edition of the 1609 printing is easily available: Claudius Holyband, *The French Littelton: The Edition of 1609*, ed. M. St. Clare Byrne (Cambridge: Cambridge University Press, 1953). See Byrne's Appendix A for the dating of the first edition to 1576.

2. Holyband, *French Littelton* (1576), B5v–B6r. From 1578 on, perhaps also for reasons of marketing, the dialogue "Des Escholiers et Eschole" is given first in the sequence. From 1581 the address on the title page becomes "Paules Churchyarde at the signe of the golden Ball," translated in the French dialogue as "à l'enseigne de la boule d'or."

3. Holyband, *French Littelton* (1576), *ii r–v.

4. For the literary milieu of the Inns, see Philip J. Finklepearl, *John Marston of the Middle Temple: An Elizabethan Dramatist in His Social Setting* (Cambridge, Mass.: Harvard University Press, 1969).

5. John Rastell published the first translation of Littleton in 1525. According to the STC, twenty-two editions of the Englished *Tenures* had been printed by 1576, thirty-two by 1609. The effort involved all the great legal publishers, including Rastell, Berthelet, Redman, Tottel, Marsh, and Wight.

6. Holyband, *French Littelton* (1576), *iiii v. "Englishman, you have been separated from the French, and Frenchman, you from the Englishman who kisses you in greeting—by a difference in language longer than by blood; you have been separated by faith, and for a while by laws. Laws, Frenchman, did not prevent the English from having already welcomed you, for faith has put you in grace, the faith that gathers all the elect children of God in one body with Christ, eternal king of kings. Thus there remains only a difference in language, but here now is Holyband, who weds the two. Rise then and read him in one voice, so that, united in language, blood, faith, and laws, you might live in a double peace, fashioned of true love, and so conquer the world, sin, Satan and death."

7. See W. B. Patterson, *King James VI and I and the Reunion of Christendom* (Cambridge: Cambridge University Press, 1997), especially chaps. 2–4.

8. Cited from Sir Edward Coke, *The First Part of the Institutes of the Lawes of England* (London, 1628), 1r.

9. Sir Edward Coke, *La Unzieme part des reports* (London, 1615), 87v.

10. Abraham Fraunce, *The Lawiers Logike, Exemplifying the Praecepts of Logike by the Practise of the Common Lawe* (London, 1588). Reprinted in facsimile as *The Lawiers Logike* (Menston: Scolar Press, 1969).

11. On the Norman Yoke and Ancient Constitution, see Christopher Hill, "The Norman Yoke," chap. 3 in *Puritanism and Revolution* (London: Secker and Warburg, 1958), 50–122; Johann P. Sommerville, "The Ancient Constitution," chap. 3 in *Politics and Ideology in England, 1603–1640* (London: Longman, 1986); Glenn Burgess, *The Politics of the Ancient Constitution: An Introduction to English Political Thought 1603–1642* (University Park: Pennsylvania State University Press, 1992).

12. Steven Mullaney, "Strange Things, Gross Terms, Curious Customs: The Rehearsal of Cultures in the Late Renaissance," *Representations* 3 (1983): 40–67.

13. F. W. Maitland, "Of the Anglo-French Language in the Early Year Books," in *Year Books of Edward II*, Vol. 1: *1 & 2 Edward II*, SS 17 (1903), xxxiii–lxxxi, at xxxvi.

14. For a compact account of the impact of the Conquest on linguistic practice in England from the eleventh through the twelfth centuries, and for a picture of the gradual assimilation of even the Norman French ruling class into an English-speaking paradigm, see Rolf Berndt, "The Linguistic Situation in England from the Norman Conquest to the Loss of Normandy (1066–1204)," *Philologica Pragensia* 8 (1965): 145–63. In addition to Maitland's excellent "Of the Anglo-French Language in the

Early Year Books," I have drawn on three discussions of the early history of law's languages: Frederick Pollock and Frederick W. Maitland, *The History of English Law*, 2d ed., introd. S. F. C. Milsom, 2 vols. (1898; Cambridge: Cambridge University Press, 1968), 1:79–87; George E. Woodbine, "The Language of English Law," *Speculum* 18, no. 4 (1943): 395–436; Peter Goodrich, "Literacy and the Languages of the Early Common Law," *Journal of Law and Society* 14 (1987): 422–44.

15. Pollock and Maitland, *History of English Law*, 1:79–80.

16. Law French was, with Latin, abolished as a written language in the law only in 1731 (Statute 4 George II, c.26). For the place of the legal report in English law, see J. H. Baker, "Records, Reports and the Origins of Case-law in England," in *Judicial Records, Law Reports and the Growth of Case Law*, ed. Baker (Berlin: Duncker and Humblot, 1989), 15–46.

17. French proved more tenacious for moots than in any other context, law French being retained even during the Interregnum when, from 1650, it was banned from the courtroom and records. Since the lawyers valued the language for its theoretical precision, it is unsurprising that their institutionalized pedagogy should have so efficiently encouraged and perpetuated its use.

18. Woodbine, "Language of English Law," 400.

19. Pollock and Maitland, *History of English Law*, 1:83–84; Woodbine, "Language of English Law," 425–26.

20. Pollock and Maitland, *History of English Law*, 1:84.

21. Woodbine, "Language of English Law," 426–27.

22. Ibid., 425.

23. Sir John Fortescue, *De laudibus legum Anglie*, ed. and trans. S. B. Chrimes (Cambridge: Cambridge University Press, 1942), 114–17. As Chrimes points out, Fortescue in addition to being styled chancellor in the Lancastrian court in exile may have been named to that office in the weeks following the battle of St. Albans in February 1461 (145–46).

24. *The Whole Volume of Statutes at Large* (London: C. Barker, 1587), 143–44. The French quoted parenthetically I take from an earlier Tudor printing: *Nova statuta* (London: Richard Pynson, 1505?).

25. Goodrich, "Literacy and the Languages of the Early Common Law," 434. The counts ("stories") were collected from the thirteenth century in the *Narrationes* and *Novae narrationes*. For an account of counts and pleading in general, see J. H. Baker, *An Introduction to English Legal History*, 3d ed. (London: Butterworths, 1990), 84–110.

26. Goodrich, "Literacy and the Languages of the Early Common Law," 435.

27. On the shift from oral to written pleading and the related decline of the (medieval) common-law system, see Baker, *Introduction to English Legal History*, 97–110; and J. H. Baker, introduction to *The Reports of Sir John Spelman*, vol. 2, SS 94 (1978), 152–63.

28. Coke, *First Part of the Institutes*, ¶¶2v.

29. Sir Edward Coke, *Le Tierce part des reports* (London, 1602), E1r. Cited hereafter as *3 Reports*.

30. One part of the history that Coke obscures in his evocation of Edward III's claims in France is the fate of that "lawfull right" once Henry IV came to the throne, since the claims on France through Edward, pertaining to a familial line rather than the Crown, descended not to Henry IV and Henry V (whatever his use of them to buttress his military invasion), but, through the Yorkist line, to Edmund Mortimer.

31. It is probable that Coke formulated his theory of a secret or private law French as a version of another linguistic hermeticism recorded earlier in the preface to *3 Reports*. To show that the ancient inhabitants of Britain wrote their laws in the Greek tongue, Coke recalls Julius Caesar's testimony that the Druids in ancient France, whom Coke designates as "but a verie Colony" of Britain's Druids, wrote the "mysteries of their Religion . . . in the Greeke tongue, to the end that their disciplines might not be made common among the vulgar" (C4v).

32. J. G. A. Pocock, *The Ancient Constitution and the Feudal Law* (Cambridge: Cambridge University Press, 1957). The various responses and emendations to Pocock's account of the common law's historical insularity by and large argue that Coke is anomalous.

33. See Hill, "Norman Yoke," 50–67; Burgess, *Politics of the Ancient Constitution*, 37–78, 139–78.

34. Sir John Davies, *Le Primer report des cases & matters en ley* (Dublin, 1615), *2r. All page citations are to this edition.

35. The classic statement here is Pocock's paradox: "If the idea that law is custom implies anything, it is that law is in constant change and adaptation, altered to meet each new experience in the life of the people; and it might seem that there was no theory more likely to lead to a historical conception of the nature of law. Yet the fact is that the common lawyers, holding that law was custom, came to believe that the common law, and with it the constitution, had always been exactly what they now were, that they were immemorial." See Pocock, *Ancient Constitution*, 36. My reading of Davies on law French suggests that the contemporary construction of custom did not in fact compass Pocock's "exactly."

36. Even Coke adapts to a less anxious nationalism than Davies expresses. In 1628, in the *First Part of the Institutes*, presented as a *Commentarie upon Littleton*, Coke defends his presentation of Littleton's fifteenth-century text in a bilingual edition, a textual emblem of the vernacular conflict marked by the 1362 Statute of Pleadings. As opposed to his position in 1602, Coke's defense of his format accommodates two alternative legal nationalisms: while the English vernacular now stands for the common law's jurisdictional scope over all English subjects and the need for the laws to be "reasonably perceived and knowne" by all, Littleton's "owne" language—that is, law French—identifies a fully confident and unembarrassed *institutional* nationalism, in that the French terms, "so apt and significant," are wholly necessary "to expresse the true sence of the Laws" (¶¶2v). This confidence belongs to the book as a whole: unlike

his *Reports*, which for all the claims that they textually represent the English legal tradition are haunted by the recognition that English case law is one alternative among other legal methods, Coke's 1628 volume asserts full English legal automony. As the *Institutes*, it claims the status of Roman and continental law, and as *A Commentarie upon Littleton* it remains rooted in a peculiarly English authority. Coke's commentary has absorbed the trope of conquest, and the vexed national identity it produces, into a single, domestic, institutional body.

37. Sir Thomas Smith, *De Republica Anglorum: A Discourse on the Commonwealth of England*, ed. L. Alston (Cambridge: Cambridge University Press, 1906), 65–66. This is an edition of the 1583 first edition.

38. Ibid., 67.

39. Coke, 3 *Reports*, D1r.

40. Sir Thomas Elyot, *The Boke Named the Governour*, ed. Donald Rude (New York: Garland, 1992), 66.

41. Ibid., 67–68, 70.

42. Thomas Wilson, *Arte of Rhetorique*, ed. G. H. Mair (London, 1560; Oxford: Clarendon Press, 1909), 2.

43. Thomas Starkey, *A Dialogue between Reginald Pole and Thomas Lupset*, ed. Kathleen M. Burton (London: Chatto and Windus, 1948), 117.

44. Ibid., 174, 110–11.

45. Ibid., 175.

46. John Rastell, *An Abridgment of the Statutes*, also catalogued under the title *The Statutes Prohemium Iohannis Rastell* (London, 1519), A1r. I cite from the 1527 edition. Using an alphabetical organization, the French and English Abridgments guided their readers to relevant statutes for various legal categories and penalties (*atteynder, corne, damage, kynge, juror*). For an account of Rastell's nationalist construction of the Norman Conquest, see Amos Lee Laine, "John Rastell and the Norman Conquest," in *The Rusted Hauberk: Feudal Ideas of Order and Their Decline*, ed. Liam O. Purdon and Cindy L. Vitto (Gainesville: University Press of Florida, 1994), 299–308. But note Amos's attribution of Rastell's 1519 preface to Robert Redman's later *Great Boke of Statutes* (1530–33), a book that translated, in chronological sequence, the statutes themselves. On Redman's signal contribution to early Tudor legal translation and publishing, see Howard Jay Graham, "'Our Tong Maternal Marvellously Amendyd and Augmentyd': The First Englishing and Printing of the Medieval Statutes at Large, 1530–1533," *UCLA Law Review* 13 (1965): 58–98.

47. Rastell, *An Abridgment of the Statutes*, A1r-v.

48. Ibid., A1v–A2r.

49. Citations to Shakespeare's plays are to the following editions: *Henry IV Part I*, ed. David Bevington (Oxford: Oxford University Press, 1987); *Henry IV Part II*, ed. René Weis (Oxford: Oxford University Press, 1997); *Henry V*, ed. Gary Taylor (Oxford: Oxford University Press, 1982); *The Tragedy of King Richard III*, ed. John Jowett (Oxford: Oxford University Press, 2000); *Henry VI, Part Three*,

ed. Randall Martin (Oxford: Oxford University Press, 2001); *Cymbeline*, ed. Roger Warren (Oxford: Oxford University Press, 1998).

50. Christopher Highley, *Shakespeare, Spenser and the Crisis in Ireland* (Cambridge: Cambridge University Press, 1997), 143.

51. Philip Schwyzer, *Literature, Nationalism and Memory in Early Modern England and Wales* (Cambridge: Cambridge University Press, 2004), 126–50.

52. Leah Marcus, *Puzzling Shakespeare: Local Reading and Its Discontents* (Berkeley: University of California Press, 1988), 51–105; David Womersly, "France in Shakespeare's *Henry V*," *Renaissance Studies* 9, no. 4 (1995): 442–59; Deanne Williams, *The French Fetish from Chaucer to Shakespeare* (Cambridge: Cambridge University Press, 2004), 181–226.

53. On the ambivalence of nationalism, see Homi K. Bhabha, *Nation and Narration* (New York: Routledge, 1990).

54. Reinforcing the importance of the fourteenth-century context for the second tetralogy is the striking similarity between the narrative treatments of Anglo-French relations in *Henry V* and the anonymous *Edward III* from the early 1590s. For the argument, not widely accepted, that the play is by Shakespeare, see Eric Sams, ed., *Shakespeare's Edward III* (New Haven: Yale University Press, 1996).

55. The trope of reversing the conquest is used by Christopher Highley in *Shakespeare, Spenser and the Crisis in Ireland* in a chapter that accounts for 2 *Henry VI* as a reversal of the English conquest of Ireland. Deanne Williams's argument that *Henry V* stages, in reverse, England's long cultural engagement with and resistance to Frenchness similarly dovetails with my analysis of the play's legal and linguistic politics as a reversal of Conquest. See Williams, *French Fetish*, 217–26. For an earlier version of my argument, see Bradin Cormack, "A Power to Do Justice: Royal Authority and Jurisdiction in English Law and Literature," Ph.D. diss., Stanford University, 2001.

56. Richard Dutton, "'Methinks the Truth Should Live from Age to Age': The Dating and Contexts of *Henry V*," *Huntington Library Quarterly* 68, nos. 1–2 (2005): 173–204, at 194–200.

57. On skepticism and the crisis of early modern exemplarity, see Timothy Hampton, *Writing from History: The Rhetoric of Exemplarity in Renaissance Literature* (Ithaca: Cornell University Press, 1990).

58. As David Quint has argued, the Welshman's substitution of one consonant for another undermines any possible attempt, including Fluellen's own, to justify Henry's order to kill the French prisoners (4.6.35–39). I would add that this is an action the play asks us to evaluate according to the pun itself, whether the action falls within the norms of military justice or not. See David Quint, "'Alexander the Pig': Shakespeare on History and Poetry," *boundary 2* 10, no. 3 (1982): 49–67.

59. In 2 *Henry IV*, Falstaff parodically anticipates Henry's program of becoming Caesar in France when he boasts to Prince John that he took Sir John Colville in battle in Gaultres Forest: "He saw me, and yielded, that I may justly say, with the hook-nosed fellow of Rome, three words, 'I came, saw, and overcame'" (4.2.39–41).

60. Highley, following the usual identification of Henry with Essex, notes the ambivalence of the allusion, linking it to the fear that a returning Essex might play conqueror in London. See Highley, *Shakespeare, Spenser and the Crisis in Ireland*, 158.

61. For a skeptical analysis of the value of the exemplary model, see Montaigne's *Essais*. Among others, the following essays explicitly treat the problem of exemplary imitation: "Of Cato the Younger," "Of the Education of Children," "Of Experience." For an analysis of Montaigne's skeptical exemplarity, see Hampton, *Writing from History*, chap. 4.

62. Jowett prints the relevant lines from the Folio under M in Appendix A, 365. For the passage in context, see *King Richard III*, ed. Antony Hammond, Arden edition (London: Methuen, 1981), 4.4.334–36.

63. Joseph Hall, *Virgidemiarum* 4.2.135–36, in *Works of Joseph Hall*, 12 vols. (Oxford: Talboys, 1837–39), 12:223.

64. Following other editions, Hammond's Arden edition emends "our mother's cost" at 5.5.53 (5.3.325 in the Arden) to the more historically accurate "our brother's cost." Jowett (in his gloss) convincingly argues for retaining "mother's" since the error originates in Holinshed.

65. In the early seventeenth century, too, it is striking that Henry, Prince of Wales should have fashioned himself as conqueror through association with Brutus, Alexander, and Caesar, with Arthur and Richard I, but not, so far as I can determine, even once with William. For Henry's self-fashioning, see Roy Strong, *Henry, Prince of Wales and England's Lost Renaissance* (London: Thames and Hudson, 1986), especially 222; and Barbara N. Lindsay and J. W. Williamson, "Myth of the Conqueror: Prince Henry Stuart and Protestant Militancy," *Journal of Medieval and Renaissance Studies* 5 (1975): 203–22.

66. John Rastell, *The Pastyme of People* (London, 1529), in Rastell, *The Pastyme of People and A New Boke of Purgatory*, ed Albert J. Geritz (New York: Garland, 1985), 201.

67. Rastell, *Pastyme of People*, A1r, B1v, B3r, B6v, C5r, E1v, F2v.

68. In a valuable article on Rastell's book as dissenting history, Peter C. Herman identifies the portrait of Henry V, with "broken nose, an aggressive posture, and a raised sword," as iconographically emphasizing "Henry's brutality." See Herman, "Rastell's *Pastyme of People*: Monarchy and the Law in Early Modern Historiography," *Journal of Medieval and Early Modern Studies* 30, no. 2 (2000): 275–308, at 283.

69. Rastell, *Pastyme of People*, E6v.

70. Anon., *A Breviat Cronicle Contaynynge All the Kinges from Brute to This Daye* (Canterbury: John Mychell, 1552), A3r–v.

71. Gordon Kipling, *The Triumph of Honour: Burgundian Origins of the Elizabethan Renaissance* (Leiden: Leiden University Press, 1977), 61.

72. Rastell, *Pastyme of People*, A2v.

73. Thomas Talbot, *A Booke, Containing the True Portraiture of the Countenances and Attires of the Kings of England* (London, 1597), A2r, A3r; Anon., *To the Reader. Beholde Here (Gentle Reader) a Brief Abstract of the Genealogie of All the Kynges of England* (London: Gyles Godet, 1560). The latter text is cited hereafter as *Brief Abstract*. I am grateful to Sean Keilen for these references.

74. Anon., *Breviat Cronicle*, A5v.

75. Ibid., A3v.

76. Anon., *Brief Abstract*.

77. On the Salic Law in the French religious controversy of the 1590s, see Womersly, "France in Shakespeare's *Henry V*," 454–57, who shows that a change in English attitudes to Henri IV across the 1590s was marked by a discursive shift from support for the Salic Law to a rejection of it.

78. A moment of syllabic oddness at the end of the anonymous *Edward III* (ca. 1592) similarly represents Crécy as a structural iteration of Conquest. Lord Salisbury has received in Act 4 the assurance of "Lord Mountford," now in possession of Brittany, that he will swear allegiance to Edward (ll. 1693–1701). In Act 5, to the victorious Edward's question, "what news from Brittaine?" Salisbury answers, "this, might king, the country we have won" (ll. 2450–51). "Country" here means a region but also, in the now more usual sense, a national territory. That ambiguity reinforces the unsteadiness of "Brittaine." Syllabically, the exchange between Edward and Salisbury remembers the Norman conquest of "Britain" as the tropological origin of this English, and reiterative, conquest of Brittany.

79. Rowland Cotterill, "The Structural Role of France in Shakespeare's First and Second Historical Tetralogies," *Renaissance Studies* 9, no. 4 (1995): 460–76, at 476. The passages Cotterill includes from Derrida are from Jacques Derrida, "Structure, Sign, and Play in the Discourse of the Human Sciences," in *The Structuralist Controversy: The Languages of Criticism and the Sciences of Man*, ed. R. Macksey and E. Donato (Baltimore: Johns Hopkins University Press, 1972), 247–49.

80. Cotterill, "Structural Role of France," 475.

81. For an account of linguistic negotiation in *Henry V* that emphasizes an English triumphalism in relation to the French vernacular, see David Steinsaltz, "The Politics of French Language in Shakespeare's History Plays," *Studies in English Literature* 42, no. 2 (2002): 317–34. A briefer consideration of Shakespeare as theorist/eulogist of the English vernacular is George Watson, "Shakespeare and the Norman Conquest: English in the Elizabethan Theatre," *Virginia Quarterly Review* 66, no. 4 (1990): 613–28.

82. The Folio prints Pistol's question as "Che vous la?" The quarto gives "Ke ve la," which J. W. Lever explains not as French, but as "thieves' argot." See J. W. Lever, "Shakespeare's French Fruits," *Shakespeare Survey* 6 (1953): 79–90.

83. Shakespeare, *Henry V*, 262. In the anonymous *Brief Abstract*, Godet prints the following text after the portrait of Cadwallader: "Here endeth the raignes of the Britaines, from the time of Brute to Cadwallader, and then this realme being in

great misery, the English Saxons invaded it, and so raigned untill the comming in of Willyam Conquerour." For his part, Rastell surmises that Cadwallader, who follows "Cadwall kynge of britteyns" was "both kyng of brittons & of west saxons." See Rastell, *Pastyme of People*, 265–69.

84. Shakespeare, *Henry V*, 234–35.

85. Paola Pugliatti, *Shakespeare the Historian* (London: Macmillan, 1996), 143. More generally, Pugliatti provides a useful analysis of *Henry V* in terms of the play's heteroglossia.

86. Edmund Plowden, *Les Comentaries ou les reportes* (London, 1571).

87. On Catherine's earlier language lesson (3.4) in relation to the gendered and eroticized teaching of French, see Juliet Fleming, "*The French Garden*: An Introduction to Women's French," *English Literary History* 56, no. 1 (1989): 19–51.

88. For an account of how Shakespeare punningly exploits Latin to hypothesize a way around the distance between lover and beloved, see Bradin Cormack, "Tender Distance: Latinity and Desire in Shakespeare's Sonnets," in *A Companion to Shakespeare's Sonnets*, ed. Michael Schoenfeldt (Malden, Mass.: Blackwell, 2006), 242–60.

89. Shakespeare, *Henry V*, 119.

90. For the argument that Henry's army becomes effective by becoming an audience, see also Schwyzer, *Literature, Nationalism and Memory*, 135–47, especially 146, where he similarly speaks of "a past which must be iterated in the present."

91. This is also the strategy in Act 2.2, where Henry traps the conspirators into condemning themselves according to the authority they themselves attribute to the king.

92. On the early modern practice of commonplacing, see especially Ann Moss, *Printed Commonplace-Books and the Structuring of Renaissance Thought* (Oxford: Clarendon Press, 1996). For a brief account of commonplacing in relation to the material book as a usable object that is, however, vulnerable to abuse, see Bradin Cormack and Carla Mazzio, *Book Use, Book Theory: 1500–1700* (Chicago: University of Chicago Library, 2005), 12–13, 70–73.

CHAPTER FIVE

1. David Bergeron, *Shakespeare's Romances and the Royal Family* (Lawrence: University Press of Kansas, 1985); Jonathan Goldberg, *James I and the Politics of Literature: Jonson, Shakespeare, Donne and Their Contemporaries* (Baltimore: Johns Hopkins University Press, 1983).

2. Constance Jordan, *Shakespeare's Monarchies: Ruler and Subject in the Romances* (Ithaca: Cornell University Press, 1997).

3. Brian Lockey places *Cymbeline* in the context of the early Jacobean constitutional debates around *praemunire* and the relation of common law to other laws. His focus on the tensions that led to Coke's dismissal from the Bench in 1616 thus complements my argument for *Cymbeline*'s relation to international jurisdiction. See Lockey, "Roman

Conquest and English Legal Identity in Cymbeline," chap. 6 in *Law and Empire in English Renaissance Literature* (Cambridge: Cambridge University Press, 2006), 160–86.

4. James Larkin and Paul Hughes, eds., *Stuart Royal Proclamations*, 2 vols. (Oxford: Clarendon Press, 1973), 1:1–2.

5. Ibid., 1:18, 95.

6. For the differences between the personal (regal, dynastic) and constitutional unions, as well as the seventeenth- and early eighteenth-century history of the relationship between the two, see Brian Levack, *The Formation of the British State* (Oxford: Oxford University Press, 1987). The most detailed account of the project for union, particularly useful for its analysis of parliamentary opposition to James's plans, is Bruce Galloway, *The Union of England and Scotland 1603–1608* (Edinburgh: Donald, 1986).

7. David Armitage, *The Ideological Origins of the British Empire* (Cambridge: Cambridge University Press, 2000), 30.

8. G. R. Elton, *The Tudor Constitution: Documents and Commentary* (Cambridge: Cambridge University Press, 1960), 344.

9. Walter Ullmann, "'This Realm of England Is an Empire,'" *Journal of Ecclesiastical History* 30 (1979): 175–203.

10. Armitage, *Ideological Origins of the British Empire*, 33. Citing Robert Folz, *The Concept of Empire in Western Europe from the Fifth to the Fourteenth Century*, trans. Sheila Ann Ogilvie (London: Edward Arnold, 1969), 7.

11. Armitage, *Ideological Origins of the British Empire*, 32.

12. Ibid., 31.

13. J. H. Burns, *Lordship, Kingship and Empire: The Idea of Monarchy 1400–1525* (Oxford: Clarendon Press, 1992), 99.

14. Anthony Pagden, *Lords of All the World: Ideologies of Empire in Spain, Britain and France c. 1500–c. 1800* (New Haven: Yale University Press, 1995), 31–32.

15. Ibid., 32.

16. The point is also that the prestige of *imperium* did not derive principally from its constitutional implications, since *regnum* expressed the more highly organized political entity. On this distinction in the Stuart period, but most particularly in the American revolutionary context, see J. G. A. Pocock, "The Politics of Extent and the Problems of Freedom," *Colorado College Studies* 25 (Colorado Springs: Colorado College, 1988), especially 9–13.

17. Levack, *Formation of the British State*, 2. See Thomas Dekker, *The Magnificent Entertainment* (London, 1604), Iir; and John Thornborough, *The Joieful and Blessed Reuniting the Two Mighty and Famous Kingdomes, England & Scotland into Their Ancient Name of Great Brittaine* (Oxford, 1604), 7. Elsewhere, Thornborough alludes to James's monarchy as "an Empire of many kingdomes thus reduced into one." See his *Discourse Plainely Proving the Evident Utilitie and Urgent Necessitie of the Desired Happie Union* (London, 1604), 11.

18. All political readings of *Cymbeline* are indebted to Emrys Jones's groundbreaking review article, "Stuart Cymbeline," *Essays in Criticism* 11 (1961): 84–89.

19. William Shakespeare, *Cymbeline*, ed. Roger Warren (Oxford: Oxford University Press, 1998). All citations to the play are to this edition; I have, however, reversed Warren's decision to change the Folio's "Imogen" to "Innogen" (the version of the name recorded in Simon Forman's 1611 account of a performance) and "Iachimo" to Giacomo. For Warren's argument concerning the emendations, see Appendix A of his edition. Given the absence of any other copy text, I preserve the Folio's version of the names as part of the play's textual and material history. For the cost and gain of refusing to emend the text in such cases, see Stephen Orgel, "What Is an Editor?" *Shakespeare Studies* 24 (1996): 25.

20. The phrase comes from a 1469 act of the Scottish Parliament concerning the authority of James III. Cited in J. H. Burns, *The True Law of Kingship: Concepts of Monarchy in Early-Modern Scotland* (Oxford: Clarendon Press, 1996), 5–6. See also Burns, *Lordship, Kingship and Empire*, 99; Armitage, *Ideological Origins of the British Empire*, 36.

21. For the thematization of interpretation and its relation to the politics of union, see Leah Marcus, *Puzzling Shakespeare: Local Reading and Its Discontents* (Berkeley: University of California Press, 1989), 106–48.

22. On James's diplomatic ambitions, see W. B. Patterson, *King James VI and I and the Reunion of Christendom* (Cambridge: Cambridge University Press, 1997).

23. In the edition of *Cymbeline* used in this chapter, Roger Warren consolidates Folio's 5.3 and 5.4. His 5.4 thus designates the final scene in the play.

24. Philip Edwards argues that in ultimately representing Britain and Rome as partners, Shakespseare's concern is "not . . . the succession of empires but . . . the only true form of empire, which is when vassalage is removed, and union is a contract freely entered into." See Edwards, *Threshold of a Nation: A Study in English and Irish Drama* (Cambridge: Cambridge University Press, 1979), 93.

25. For the play's identification of Imogen and Britain, see, for example, 1.3.5, where Posthumus is reported as calling her "his queen, his queen," even though Cymbeline's wife formally carries that name to the exclusion of all others. Posthumus speaks of Britain as "my lady's kingdom" and of Imogen as its "mistress" (5.1.19–20). And Imogen herself responds to Iachimo's slanderous reports of her husband's sexual infidelity by saying, "My lord, I fear, / Has forgot Britain" (1.6.112–13). On Imogen as heir, see Ann Thompson, "Person and Office: The Case of Imogen, Princess of Britain," in *Literature and Nationalism*, ed. Vincent Newby and Ann Thompson (Liverpool: Liverpool University Press, 1991), 76–87.

26. Aristotle, *The Art of Rhetoric*, trans. J. H. Freese, Loeb Classical Library (Cambridge, Mass.: Harvard University Press, 1926).

27. St. Augustine, *The Confessions*, Book 11, chap. 28; trans. R. S. Pine-Coffin (Harmondsworth, Middlesex: Penguin, 1961), 277. "But how can the future be diminished or absorbed when it does not yet exist? And how can the past increase when

it no longer exists? It can only be that the mind, which regulates this process, performs three functions, those of expectation, attention, and memory. The future, which it expects, passes through the present, to which it attends, into the past, which it remembers. No one would deny that the future does not yet exist or that the past no longer exists. Yet in the mind there is both expectation of the future and remembrance of the past. Again, no one would deny that the present has no duration, since it exists only for the instant of its passage. Yet the mind's attention persists, and through it that which is to be passes towards the state in which it is to be no more."

28. For an analysis of *Cymbeline* in terms of alternatively ideological meanings of landscapes (and of the competing roads that signify these), see Garrett Sullivan, "Civilizing Wales: Cymbeline, Roads, and the Landscapes of Early Modern Britain," chap. 4 in *The Drama of Landscape: Land, Property, and Social Relations on the Early Modern Stage* (Stanford: Stanford University Press, 1998), 127–58.

29. In addition to the warning that he and the boys ("we") will turn Roman against the other Britons, Belarius's language probably hides the implication for the audience in 1610 that only standing can *prevent* Britain from turning Roman, now in the subversive sense of the alternative religious identity represented by Catholic Rome.

30. John Donne, "A Valediction: Forbidding Mourning," in *The Complete Poems*, ed. A. J. Smith (Harmondsworth, Middlesex: Penguin, 1971), 84–85.

31. Marcus, *Puzzling Shakespeare,* 124–25.

32. *A Complete Collection of State Trials,* ed. T. B. Howell, 33 vols. (London: Longman, 1809–26), 2:609.

33. Ibid., 2:636.

34. Ibid., 2:563.

35. Ibid., 2:577.

36. I thank Allan Macinnes for suggesting this point to me. For the king as lord, see James VI and I, *The Trew Law of Free Monarchies,* in *Political Writings,* ed. Johann P. Sommerville (Cambridge: Cambridge University Press, 1994), 73–74. On the structure of state power in early modern Scotland, in relation to lordship, see Julian Goodare, *State and Society in Early Modern Scotland* (Oxford: Oxford University Press), especially 38–65. On Scottish clanship in relation to central government, see Allan I. Macinnes, *Clanship, Commerce, and the House of Stuart, 1603–1788* (East Linton: Tuckwell, 1996), 30–87. For the Scottish reaction to Union, see the essays collected in *Scots and Britons: Scottish Political Thought and the Union of 1603,* ed. R. A. Mason (Cambridge: Cambridge University Press, 1994).

37. *State Trials,* 2:575.

38. Louis Knafla, ed., *Law and Politics in Jacobean England: The Tracts of Lord Chancellor Ellesmere* (Cambridge: Cambridge University Press, 1977), 246.

39. *State Trials,* 2:570.

40. Ibid., 2:579–80.

41. Ibid., 2:570.

42. Ibid., 2:656.

43. Ibid., 2:570.

44. Ibid.

45. Ibid., 2:614.

46. This vision of the state would receive its most striking representation in the frontispiece to Hobbes's *Leviathan*, where the monarch's body is made up of the natural bodies of his subjects. It is also present in an earlier iconography of the king as head and the country as body, an image that equally eschews the corporate in favor of the personal.

47. Knafla, *Law and Politics in Jacobean England*, 245-46.

48. See Ernst Kantorowicz, *The King's Two Bodies: A Study in Medieval Political Theology* (Princeton: Princeton University Press, 1957).

49. *State Trials*, 2:589, 576.

50. Ibid., 2:589, 597.

51. Ibid., 2:597.

52. Ibid., 2:597-98.

53. Ibid., 2:598.

54. Ibid., 2:630.

55. Ibid., 2:631.

56. Ibid., 2:564.

57. Ibid., 2:639.

58. Ibid., 2:640.

59. Ibid., 2:583.

60. Ibid., 2:656.

61. With respect to time, Coke posits, natural allegiance differs from denizenship or "acquired allegiance," as, for example, in relation to the impact of conquest on the conquering (though not the conquered) people: "as if the king and his subjects should conquer another kingdom or dominion, as well Antenati as Postnati, as well they which fought in the field, as they which remained at home, for defence of their country, or employed elsewhere, are all denizens of the kingdom or dominion conquered." Where a natural alien was made denizen, the distinction between before and after was absorbed as a distinction internal to his legal capacity: "To this person," Bacon argued, "the law giveth an ability and capacity abridged, not in matter, but in time. And as there was a time when he was not subject, so the law doth not acknowledge him before that time.... So as he is but privileged *a parte post,* as the schoolmen say, and not *a parte ante*." See *State Trials*, 2:616, 582.

62. Thomas Hobbes, *Leviathan*, ed. Richard Tuck (Cambridge: Cambridge University Press, 1996), 135.

63. Ibid., 134.

64. Giorgio Agamben, *The Coming Community*, trans. Michael Hardt (Minneapolis: University of Minnesota Press, 1993), 1-2. See also Agamben, "On Potentiality," in *Potentialities*, trans. Daniel Heller-Roazen (Stanford: Stanford University Press, 1999), 177-84.

65. Heather James, *Shakespeare's Troy: Drama, Politics, and the Translation of Empire* (Cambridge: Cambridge University Press, 1997), 151–52.

66. Patricia Parker, "Romance and Empire: Anachronistic *Cymbeline*," in *Unfolded Tales: Essays on Renaissance Romance*, ed. Gordon Logan and Gordon Teskey (Ithaca: Cornell University Press, 1989), 204–5.

67. J. G. A. Pocock: "Virtues, Rights and Manners: A Model for Historians of Political Thought," *Political Theory* 9, no. 3 (1981): 12.

68. Jordan, *Shakespeare's Monarchies*, 89–92, also 104.

69. *State Trials*, 2:382.

70. Ibid., 2:479. The speech in which this sentence appears is given in *State Trials* as Yelverton's, but this seems to be an error. A digest of Yelverton's speech is printed in *Parliamentary Debates in 1610*, ed. S. L. Gardiner, Camden Society 81 (Westminster: Camden Society, 1862), 85–88.

71. *State Trials*, 2:382.

72. Glenn Burgess, *The Politics of the Ancient Constitution: An Introduction to English Political Thought 1603–1642* (University Park: Pennsylvania State University Press, 1992), 141.

73. *State Trials*, 2:395.

74. Gardiner, ed., *Parliamentary Debates in 1610*, 71.

75. *State Trials*, 2:390.

76. Ibid., 2:387.

77. Ibid., 2:385–86.

78. Ibid., 2:389.

79. Gardiner, ed., *Parliamentary Debates in 1610*, 87.

80. For an account of the exchange between Grotius and Welwood, see T. W. Fulton, *The Sovereignty of the Sea* (London: Blackwood, 1911), 338–58. See also Armitage, *Ideological Origins of the British Empire*, 108–13.

81. William Welwood, *An Abridgement of All Sea-Lawes* (London, 1613), 68. The passage from Grotius quoted by Welwood can be found in Hugo Grotius, *Mare Liberum / The Freedom of the Seas*, ed. Ralph Van Deman Magoffin (New York: Oxford University Press, 1916), 39.

82. Welwood, *Abridgement of All Sea-Lawes*, 68.

83. Ibid., 67.

84. Fulton, *Sovereignty of the Sea*, 356, 349. For the date of Grotius's response to Welwood, the *Defensio capitis quinti maris liberi*, see Fulton, *Sovereignty of the Sea*, 343. For an account of the development of Grotius's thought that takes full account of the *Defensio*, see J. K. Oudendijk, *Status and Extent of Adjacent Waters: A Historical Orientation* (Leiden: Sijthoff, 1970), 15–33.

85. Welwood, *Abridgement of All Sea-Lawes*, 69.

86. "A Proclamation for Revocation of Mariners from Forreine Services," in *Stuart Royal Proclamations*, ed. Larkin and Hughes, 1:108–11. For an extended account

of the implications for marine sovereignty of the proclamations I discuss here, see Fulton, *Sovereignty of the Seas*, 118–64.

87. Larkin and Hughes, eds., *Stuart Royal Proclamations*, 1:109.

88. Fulton, *Sovereignty of the Sea*, 119.

89. [*A Note*] *of the Head-lands of England* (London, 1605). See Fulton, *Sovereignty of the Seas*, 120–21. But note that Fulton's date of 4 March 1604 is a year off, since the printer followed the Julian calendar, which dated the year from 25 March.

90. John Selden, *Mare clausum seu de dominio maris* (London, 1635). For the date of Selden's text, see Fulton, *Sovereignty of the Sea*, 288, 366–67; and Richard Tuck, *Philosophy and Government 1572–1651* (Cambridge: Cambridge University Press, 1993), 212. Tuck gives the publication date as 1636; I have retained the traditional date of 1635.

91. John Selden, *Of the Dominion, or Ownership of the Sea*, trans. Marchamount Nedham (1652; New York: Arno, 1972), 365. Where the Latin term is important, I have given in square brackets the Latin from 1635.

92. Selden, *Of the Dominion, or Ownership of the Sea*, 365–67.

93. Fulton, *Sovereignty of the Sea*, 373. An excellent account of the late medieval construction of *dominium* is Burns, *Lordship, Kingship, and Empire*. For the relationship between *dominium* and *ius* (right), see also Richard Tuck, *Natural Rights Theories: Their Origin and Development* (Cambridge: Cambridge University Press, 1979).

94. Larkin and Hughes, eds., *Stuart Royal Proclamations*, 1:109.

95. Ibid., 1:218–19.

96. Fulton, *Sovereignty of the Seas*, 124, 148–53.

97. Larkin and Hughes, eds., *Stuart Royal Proclamations*, 1:217–18.

98. Ibid., 1:219.

99. Ibid., 1:109.

100. Oudendijk, *Status and Extent of Adjacent Waters*, 27–31.

101. British Library, Lansdowne MS 142, 379r–v. For a brief description of the document, see Fulton, *Sovereignty of the Sea*, 148.

102. Ibid., 148.

103. It is impossible to say with certainty that the corrections were all made at the same time. It is arguable that the document was twice revised: the words to be omitted from the first draft of the first article have been struck out in a browned ink that is also used for most of the emendations to the second article, but some corrections to the latter article have been made in a thicker, black ink.

104. Larkin and Hughes, eds., *Stuart Royal Proclamations*, 1:218–19.

105. Richard Helgerson, *Forms of Nationhood* (Chicago: University of Chicago Press, 1992), chap. 3.

106. Armitage, *Ideological Origins of the British Empire*, 100.

107. David A. Waters, *The Art of Navigation in England in Elizabethan and Early Stuart Times*, 2 vols., 2d ed. (Greenwich: Maritime Museum, 1978), 1:63. Waters

has an excellent description of how the central or "mother" compass on a chart was related to the sixteen or thirty-two subsidiary compasses.

108. Thornborough, *Joieful and Blessed Reuniting*, 18–19.

109. Ben Jonson, *The Complete Poems*, ed. George Parfitt (New Haven: Yale University Press, 1975), 336. *Hymenaei*, Jonson's 1606 masque of Union, variously uses the image of the sun's rays as exemplifying the king's ability to effect union. On *Hymenaei* and the political metaphysics of Union, see D. J. Gordon, "*Hymenaei*: Ben Jonson's Masque of Union," in Gordon, *The Renaissance Imagination*, ed. Stephen Orgel (Berkeley: University of California Press, 1975), 185–93.

110. Thornborough, *Discourse*, 14.

111. The table, printed opposite Speed's dedication to James, is entitled "The Achievement of our soveraigne King Iames as he nowe beareth With the Armes of the Severall kings that have aunciently raigned within his nowe Dominions."

112. Exceptionally, in 1613, James claimed in support of the Muscovy Company that Spitzbergen was, by reason of discovery, English *dominium*, arguing thence for an English monopoly on whaling in the seas around that distant island. See Fulton, *Sovereignty of the Sea*, 181–83; Oudendijk, *Status and Extent of Adjacent Waters*, 36–37.

113. William Shakespeare, *Pericles*, ed. Suzanne Gossett, Arden edition (London: Thomson Learning, 2004). All references to the play are to this edition. For the textual history of the play and evidence of Wilkins's and Shakespeare's collaboration, see Gossett's introduction; Stephen Orgel, introduction to *Pericles Prince of Tyre*, in William Shakespeare, *The Complete Works*, ed. Orgel and A. R. Braunmuller (New York: Penguin, 2002), 604–9; Brian Vickers, *Shakespeare Co-Author* (Oxford: Oxford University Press, 2002); and especially MacDonald P. Jackson, *Defining Shakespeare: Pericles as a Test Case* (Oxford: Oxford University Press, 2003). For an earlier argument that the play is all Shakespeare's, see F. D. Hoeniger, introduction to *Pericles*, ed. Hoeniger, Arden edition (London: Methuen, 1963).

114. On the play's popularity, see Gossett, introduction to *Pericles*, 2–7.

115. For the argument that the play posits the various eastern Mediterranean locales as politically and ethically liminal in relation to Europe, see Constance C. Relihan, "Liminal Geography: *Pericles* and the Politics of Place," *Philological Quarterly* 71, no. 3 (1992): 281–99.

116. Lisa Hopkins rightly notes how little realized the play's geographical locales are, but goes too far, I think, in saying that the play's "true borders and the true journeys are of the mind." See Hopkins, "'The Shores of My Mortality': Pericles' Greece of the Mind," in *Pericles: Critical Essays*, ed. David Skeele (New York: Garland, 2000), 228.

117. M. P. Jackson, "North's Plutarch and the Name 'Escanes' in Shakespeare's *Pericles*," *Notes and Queries*, n.s. 22 (1975): 174.

118. J. M. S. Tompkins, "Why Pericles?" *Review of English Studies*, n.s. 3 (1952): 315–24. Tompkins and Jackson thus downplay the alternative linking of Shakespeare's play and Sidney's *Arcadia*, of Pericles and Pyrocles.

119. John Dee, *General and Rare Memorials Pertayning to the Perfect Arte of*

Navigation (London, 1577), 3-4. For Dee's relationship to early English conceptions of marine empire, see William H. Sherman, *John Dee: The Politics of Reading and Writing in the English Renaissance* (Amherst: University of Massachusetts Press, 1995), especially chap. 7. Dee's theoretical arguments for English sovereignty in the northern seas were influential in the early seventeenth century, almost certainly helping to shape claims for English marine jurisdiction made by John Selden in *Mare clausum* and by Alberico Gentili in "De marino territorio tuendo," chap. 8 in *Hispanicae advocationis libri duo* (London, 1612), a treatise that records Admiralty cases in which Gentili had acted as advocate for the Spanish embassy in London.

120. Dee, *General and Rare Memorials*, 11.

121. Ibid., 12.

122. Ibid., 37. In a marginal note on the phrase "Brytish, or English Pericles," however, Dee expresses his pessimism about England, and offers an exemplary figure alternative to Pericles: "Yf Pereles *Pericles* be dead, pore *Pletho* (as a Passager in the Ship of the Common-welth) By leave, doth utter his Faithfull Care, to the Helm-man." The reference is to the fifteenth-century Byzantine Gemisthus Plethon, whose orations on maintaining imperial power in the Peloponnesus Dee appends to his treatise. For Dee's use of Plethon's orations, see Frances Yates, *Astraea: The Imperial Theme in the Sixteenth Century* (1975; London: Ark, 1985), 48-50; and Sherman, *John Dee*, 161-62.

123. Fulton, *Sovereignty of the Sea*, 105.

124. *State Trials*, 2:598.

125. Richard Halpern, *Shakespeare among the Moderns* (Ithaca: Cornell University Press, 1997), 153.

126. Virgil, *Eclogues, Georgics, Aeneid 1-6*, trans. H. R. Fairclough, rev. ed., Loeb Classical Library (Cambridge, Mass.: Harvard University Press, 1935).

127. Grotius, *Mare liberum*, 9.

128. On Pericles's abandonment of Marina as irresponsible governance and "the inverse of Antiochus's complete domination of his Daughter," see Jordan, *Shakespeare's Monarchies*, 61-63.

129. Laurence Twine, *The Patterne of Painefull Adventures* (London, 1607), C2r.

130. Ibid.

131. Steven Mullaney, *The Place of the Stage: License, Play, and Power in Renaissance England* (Chicago: University of Chicago Press, 1988), 138.

132. Twine, *Patterne of Painefull Adventures*, C2r.

133. Mullaney, *Place of the Stage*, 139.

134. On the place of Diana and Ephesus in relation to the play's treatment of the maternal body, see Caroline Bicks, "Backsliding at Ephesus: Shakespeare's Diana and the Churching of Women," in *Pericles: Critical Essays*, ed. Skeele, 205-27.

135. In Twine's version, Apollonius even receives Antioch, whose crown is "reserved" to him, presumably by election. See Twine, *Patterne of Painefull Adventures*, E2v.

136. Following the Oxford edition, Gossett transposes 5.3.73 to read "At Pentapolis shall marry her" to produce a more regular iambic line. I have retained the Quarto word order.

137. As Stephen Orgel notes in his edition (introduction to *Pericles*, 606n), the story of Lysimachus's names may take us even further into the play's politics: in changing Gower's Athenagoras to Lysimachus, Shakespeare chose the name of "one of Alexander's generals, who became the ruler of Macedonia and was notorious for his tyranny and cruelty. Perhaps this is another case in which Pericles fails to see beyond the surface—and perhaps Jacobean audiences with classical educations did not foresee a happy future for Marina."

138. G. N. Clark and W. J. M. Van Eysinga, *The Colonial Conferences between England and the Netherlands in 1613 and 1615, Part II* (Leiden: E. J. Brill, 1951), 59–81. See also Oudendijk, *Status and Extent of Adjacent Waters*, 37–40.

139. IR [Robert Keale], *The Trades Increase* (London, 1615), 48. Captain Best had returned in 1614 from the tenth voyage undertaken by the East India Company. See *The Voyage of Thomas Best to the East Indies, 1612–1614*, ed. William Foster, Hakluyt Society, 2d ser., 85 (London: Hakluyt Society, 1934).

140. George Birdwood and William Foster, eds., *The First Letter Book of the East India Company* (London: Quaritch, 1893), 103–10.

141. Ibid., 48.

142. The critical word for my argument is a widely accepted emendation from Q, which prints "sea marre it."

143. John Cowell, "Wreck," *The Interpreter* (Cambridge, 1607), Cccc2v.

144. Sir Edward Coke, *Quinta pars relationum* (London, 1605), 106r–v.

145. Ibid., 107v.

146. Ibid., 107r.

147. Mullaney, *Place of the Stage*, 147–48.

148. Jeffrey Masten, *Textual Intercourse: Collaboration, Authorship, and Sexualities in Renaissance Drama* (Cambridge: Cambridge University Press, 1997), chap. 3, especially 75–93.

CHAPTER SIX

1. On the extreme case, see J. V. Cunningham, "Ideal Fiction: *The Clerk's Tale*," in Cunningham, *The Collected Essays* (Chicago: Swallow Press, 1976), 277–81.

2. For the dating of the play, see *The Works of John Webster: An Old-Spelling Critical Edition*, ed. David Gunby, David Carnegie, and MacDonald P. Jackson, 2 vols. (Cambridge: Cambridge University Press, 2003), 2:263. All citations to the play are to this edition.

3. On the representation of illegitimacy on the early modern stage, see J. W. Draper, "Bastardy in Shakespeare's Plays," *Shakespeare Jahrbuch* 74 (1938): 123–36;

Alison Findlay, *Illegitimate Power: Bastardy in English Renaissance Drama* (Manchester: Manchester University Press, 1994); Michael Neill, "'In Everything Illegitimate': Imagining the Bastard in Renaissance Drama," in Neill, *Putting History to the Question: Power, Politics, and Society in English Renaissance Drama* (New York: Columbia University Press, 2000), 127–47; Michael Neill, "Bastardy, Counterfeiting, and Misogyny in *The Revenger's Tragedy*," in Neill, *Putting History to the Question*, 149–65; B. J. Sokol and Mary Sokol, *Shakespeare, Law, and Marriage* (Cambridge: Cambridge University Press, 2003), 157–63.

4. R. H. Helmholz, "Bastardy Litigation in Medieval England," *American Journal of Legal History* 13 (1969): 360–83, at 370.

5. John Brydall, *Lex Spuriorum: or the Law Relating to Bastardy* (London, 1703; New York: Garland, 1978), 58.

6. Ibid.

7. Ibid., 50–51.

8. Helmholz, "Bastardy Litigation," 370.

9. Relevant too is that, as Keith Wrightson has emphasized, in matters of human behavior, including sexual conduct, the law's construction of legitimacy operated always in relation to social norms that differently construed what was and was not acceptable. See Wrightson, "Two Concepts of Order: Justices, Constables, and Jurymen in Seventeenth-Century England," in *An Ungovernable People: The English and Their Law in the Seventeenth and Eighteenth Centuries*, ed. John Brewer and John Styles (New Brunswick: Rutgers University Press, 1980), 21–46. On the implications of social history for the legal-historical representation of the past, see David Cohen, "The Church Courts and the Enforcement of Morals: Public Order in England 1580–1640," *Ius Commune* 18 (1991): 17–35.

10. William Shakespeare, *King John*, ed. A. R. Braunmuller (Oxford: Oxford University Press, 1989). I follow Braunmuller's dating of the play.

11. Sir Edward Coke, *The First Part of the Institutes of the Lawes of England* (London, 1628), 244.

12. Helmholz, "Bastardy Litigation," 370. See also Sokol and Sokol, *Shakespeare, Law, and Marriage*, 158.

13. Sir Harris Nicolas, *A Treatise on the Law of Adulterine Bastardy* (London: Pickering, 1836), 29.

14. Ibid., 53–54.

15. Ibid., 72. Cited from the similarly ungrammatical entry in Henry Rolle, *Un Abridgment des Plusieurs Cases*, 2 vols. (London, 1668), 1:358. *"Si le feme dun home qui ad estre oustre le mer per tant de temps devant le nestre del issue que le feme ad en son absence que le issue ne poet estre son issue, ceo est un bastard."*

16. In their summary of *King John*, the Sokols rightly find the four-seas rule to be irrelevant to the Faulconbridge case, since Sir Robert was at home during some— which is to say, any—part of the pregnancy. See Sokol and Sokol, *Shakespeare, Law, and Marriage*, 160–61.

17. David Gunby, critical introduction to *A Cure for a Cuckold*, in *Works of John Webster*, 2:264–81, at 277.

18. For the representation of abduction as the literary reconfiguration of the laws of fraudulent conveyance, see Charles Ross, *Elizabethan Literature and the Law of Fraudulent Conveyance: Sidney, Spenser and Shakespeare* (Aldershot: Ashgate, 2003).

19. Thomas Powell, *Tom of All Trades: or the Plaine Path-way to Preferment* (London, 1631). Of relevance, too, is the proliferating textual culture of the how-to book, books of didactic instruction that promised to transform their readers into new kinds of agents, whose authority would ultimately be grounded in their own experience and practice. See in general the essays collected in *Didactic Literature in England, 1500–1800*, ed. Natasha Glaisyer and Sara Pennell (Aldershot: Ashgate, 2003).

20. On the relation of literary character to social persona, see Elizabeth Fowler, *Literary Character: The Human Figure in Early English Writing* (Ithaca: Cornell University, Press, 2003).

21. Luke Wilson, *Theaters of Intention: Drama and Law in Early Modern England* (Stanford: Stanford University Press, 2000).

22. The interpretation of Clare's letter is closely related to the equitable interpretation of statute. As Lorna Hutson has pointed out, in looking to the idea of legislative intention, equity had to figure that intention as being directed necessarily to the public good. Where drama asked an audience to participate in the equitable construction of intention, it thus promoted a new form of political consciousness. See Hutson, "Not the King's Two Bodies: Reading the 'Body Politic' in Shakespeare's *Henry IV*, Parts I and 2," in *Rhetoric and Law in Early Modern Europe*, ed. Lorna Hutson and Victoria Kahn (New Haven: Yale University Press, 2001), 166–98.

23. Gunby, critical introduction to *A Cure for a Cuckold*, 278.

24. W. S. Holdsworth, *A History of English Law*, 16 vols. (London: Methuen, 1922–66), 5:118, 140. For a general overview of legal fictions, see Lon Fuller, *Legal Fictions* (Stanford: Stanford University Press, 1967).

25. For the place of *status* in classical rhetoric, and in relation to the literary exploration of circumstance, see Wesley Trimpi, *Muses of One Mind: The Literary Analysis of Experience and Its Continuity* (Princeton: Princeton University Press, 1983), 245–84.

26. Sir John Baker, *The Oxford History of the Laws of England*, vol. 6: *1483–1558* (Oxford: Oxford University Press, 2003), 574.

27. The parodic proliferation of familial relations that accompanies the comic peace between the two fathers further marks their legal accommodation to one another by turning the names' potentially tragic implications to good. For Compass's statement—"And I am his son, sir, and all the sons he has; and this is his Grand-Childe, and my elder brother, you'll think this strange now"—poses a riddle whose solution is incest, and it is only Franckford's supplementary paternity that makes licit the apparently illicit and Oedipal relation by which Compass can be both father and brother to his son. At the same time as Franckford complicates the story of paternity that can be told

in relation to the baby, the play ends up needing him in order comically to remake tragedy's family. And it does this by pressing on a familiar and disquieting relation to the proper name within all families: to be a father or mother is to possess, in "father" or "mother," a name that belongs absolutely also to others. In the drama's accounting of this conventional instability among name and category and referent, Compass's paternity becomes, instead, something that allows another father in, with the effect that his family can stand, at a crossroads intersecting with other relations, as one family comically with others.

28. A. W. B. Simpson, *A History of the Land Law*, 2d ed. (Oxford: Clarendon Press, 1986), 173.

29. Paul Clarkson and Clyde Warren, *The Law of Property in Shakespeare and the Elizabethan Drama* (Baltimore: Johns Hopkins University Press, 1942), 43-44.

30. The play mobilizes a third kind of landholding in reference to the child when Urse says of Franckford that she (and Compass) are beholden to him "in better courtesies" than his role in the child's begetting, a formula that causes Compass to exclaim that "Ile acknowledge no other courtesies: for this I am beholding to him" (2.3.137-40). This is probably a punning reference to tenure "by curtesy" or "by the curtesy of England," whereby, until its abolition in 1925, as J. H. Baker explains, the widower of a woman possessed of land was seised "of his wife's land after her death for the rest of his own life," so long as "a child of the marriage should have been born." Especially in light of Compass's requiring his wife fictively to die so he can remarry her as widower, Compass can be seen, in the "this" for which he is "beholding," to be formulating a claim by "curtesy" on his wife's son: Franckford's "courteous" action, which would appear to give him a right to possession, is transformed into the legal basis for Compass's own tenure or holding. See Baker, *An Introduction to English Legal History*, 3d ed. (London: Butterworths, 1990), 310.

31. Ibid., 349. On copyhold, see Charles M. Gray, *Copyhold, Equity and the Common Law* (Cambridge, Mass.: Harvard University Press, 1963). On the fate of the manorial jurisdiction, see W. J. Jones, "A Note on the Demise of Manorial Jurisdiction: The Impact of Chancery," *American Journal of Legal History* 10 (1966): 297-318.

32. Simpson, *History of the Land Law*, 164-65.

33. For the historical context of the legislation, see E. W. Ives, "The Genesis of the Statute of Uses," *English Historical Review* 82 (1967): 673-97.

34. Francis Bacon, *Reading on the Statute of Uses* (New York: Garland, 1979, 408-9.) Reprinted from *The Works of Francis Bacon*, ed. James Spedding et al., 14 vols. (London: Longmans, 1857-74), 7:391-450.

35. Webster, *Cure for a Cuckold*, in *Works of John Webster*, 423.

36. Ibid., 421. Note, however, that where legitimacy was at issue, the subject of infidelity was, of course, very much a matter for the common law, even to the exclusion of other laws.

37. Holdsworth, *History of English Law*, 1:218-21.

38. Ibid., 1:220.

39. If the defendant appeared before the court and gave "sureties for his future appearance he was sufficiently in the custody of the Marshal to give jurisdiction to the court [over the real rather than fictitious action]." Where the defendant did not appear, the plaintiff could himself give "as sureties for his [the defendant's] appearance his friends John Doe and Richard Roe," and thereby—once again, wholly fictitiously—bring the defendant into the marshal's custody and thus under the court's jurisdiction. See Holdsworth, *History of English Law*, 1:220.

40. Baker, *Introduction to English Legal History*, 48.

41. John Cowell, "Latitat," *The Interpreter* (Cambridge, 1607), Rr1v.

INDEX

Page numbers in italics refer to illustrations.

absolutism: and France, in Fortescue, 194, 349n89; and Norman Yoke, 162–63, 180; and royal interpretation, 80–84; and royal prerogative, 35–37, 111–12, 227; and Tudor centralization, 126
absque hoc clause, 119–20
action, theatrical representation of, 307–9
Ad Herennium (Pseudo-Cicero), 20
Admiralty, High Court of, 2–3, 34, 259, 320
adultery, 128, 292–95, 299, 328
aesthetics, politics and, 4–5
Agamben, Giorgio, 6–7, 9–10, 253, 335n7, 357n96
agency: of accessory and principal, 316; in bureaucratic distribution, 56, 59, 61–66, 73; collaborative, 313–15; under coverture, 305–6; and legal subjection, 2; of ocean, 285, 313–14; royal, 59, 275–76, 288–90; and subjection, in *Cure for a Cuckold*, 293–94, 307, 309–18, 324, 328–29; and subjection, in Wyatt, 13–21
Agincourt, Battle of, 200–202, 205, 213–16, 220–21
Alemanni, Luigi, 13
Alexander the Great, 204
allegiance: as amatory dynamic, 246–48, 252; and conquest, 377n61; and distance, 242–49, 297; and dynamics of vision, 248–49; and international law, 262–66, 279–80
allegory, 41; of allegory, 171–73, 363n105; and Egypt, 364n105; and exemplarity, 170–72; and inexpressibility, 173; of legal centralization, 92–100; and statute, 170–76. *See also* Spenser, Edmund
Allington, Alice, 92–93, 98
Alsop, J. D., 344nn17–18
Ancient Constitution. *See* Norman Yoke
ante-nati, 245, 249–53. See also *Calvin's Case* (1608)
Appeals, Act in Restraint of (1533), 89, 228

arbitration, 324, 328–29
Arendt, Hannah, 331n2
Aristotle: on *energeia*, 234; on equity (*epieikeia*), 83, 105, 109–11, 127–28, 355n67; on the just, 108; on magnificence, 48, 55, 344n5. Works: *Nichomachean Ethics*, 48, 108, 110; *Rhetoric*, 234
Armitage, David, 228–29, 266, 375n20
Arthur (king of Britain), 210
assistants, court of, 325
assizes, courts of, 326
assumpsit, action of, 307, 332n6
Audley, Sir Thomas, 92
Augustine, St.: on present as threshold (*Confessions*), 237, 375n27; and time, 17
Auvergne, Martial d', 31

Bacon, Francis: on allegiance, 244–47, 250, 279, 377n61; on impositions, 254; on uses and copyhold, 323; and Yoke, 162
Bacon, Nathaniel, 67, 71
Baildon, William P., 356n83
Baker, David J., 363n86
Baker, J. H., 116–19, 339n35, 345n21, 346n44, 348nn68–69, 348n78, 354n60, 356n73, 356n85, 357nn89–90, 365n112, 367n16, 367n25, 367n27, 384n26, 385n31, 386n40; on courts of piepowder, 93–94; on meaning of equity, 103, 106, 110, 113–14; on More and equity, 125; on ownership and seisin, 148; on pleading, 119; on tenancy by the curtesy, 385n30
Baldwin, William, *Mirror for Magistrates*, 170
Baron, Jane, 331n1
bastardy. *See* illegitimacy
Bate's Case (1606), 254–56, 262, 282, 287
Becon, Richard, *Solon His Follie*, 161
Belknap, Edward, 61

Benjamin, Walter, 6
Bergeron, David, 373n1
Berlant, Lauren, 23, 337n24
Berndt, Rolf, 366n14
Bevington, David, 48, 343n1, 357n95
Bhabha, Homi K., 370n53
Bicks, Caroline, 381n134
biopolitics, 6–10
Black Book of the Household of Edward IV, 48
Blackstone, Sir William, 27
Blanchard, W. Scott, 344n19
Bloch, Ernst, 335n1
Blount, Charles (Lord Mountjoy), 202
Boccaccio, Giovanni, 230, 233, 253
Bodin, Jean, 333n14
Boleyn, Ann, 90
Bracton, Henry de, treatise attributed to, 32, 80
Bradshaw, Brendan, 158
Brady, Ciaran, 161, 166, 358n15
Brehon law, 41, 133; allegorical representation of, 164–70; English attitudes toward, 160–61. *See also* gavelkind (Ireland); tanistry
Breviat Cronicle (1552), 209, 211
Brief Abstract (ca. 1560). *See* Godet, Gyles
Britain, idea of, 228–31, 266–75
Brittany, England in relation to, 204–5, 215, 372n78
Brooks, Peter, 331n1
Brutus (founder of Britain), 210
Brydall, John, *Lex Spuriorum*, 293
Budé, Guillaume, 127
Burgess, Glenn, 254, 362n64, 366n11, 368n33
Burnham, Daniel, 331n4
Burns, J. H., 229, 375n20, 379n93
Burrow, Colin, 359n34

Cadwallader (Welsh king), 216
Caesar, Julius, 201–3, 233
Caesar, Sir Julius, 34, 259, 263–66, 264, 341n60

Calais, England in relation to, 63, 201, 298–300, 306
Calvin's Case (1608), 242–55, 262, 279
Camden, William, *Britannia*, 266, 267, 275, 276
Canny, Nicholas, 361n50, 361n55, 362n76
canon law, 2, 32, 40, 341n55; and break with Rome, 33–34; in conflict with common law, 85, 88, 93, 95–102, 105–6, 292–97; and conscience, 25–26, 105–6; and heresy, 85, 88, 93, 97–100; and illegitimacy, 292–97; and More, 85, 90–91, 93–102; and territoriality, in Wyatt, 16–17
Capellanus, Andreas, 31
Capitani, Ovidio, 334n22
Cardiganshire, map of, 272, 274
Caryll, John, 78
case jurisprudence, statutory character of, 153–59
Catherine of Aragon, 90
causa (in rhetoric), 20
Cavanagh, Sheila T., 359n34
Cecil, Sir William, 34
centralization, legal: and bureaucratic development, 39–40, 57–62; and conscience, 105–6; and contingency, 28–30; and *Cure for a Cuckold*, 293–94, 317, 323–29; as desire or fantasy at law, 18, 39; in dialectical relation to the local, 15, 27; and documentary culture, 66–71; and interpretation, 33–34; and legal normativity, 40, 43, 86, 94, 100–102, 128–29, 293–94, 318–29; and legal profession, 67, 76–78, 123–25; and literary authority, 18–21, 30–32, 43, 53–54, 72; and local law, 15, 18, 27–28; in More, 92–102; and *quo warranto*, 75–79; without rationalization, 29, 39, 321–22; and royal justice, 35–38, 94–95, 99–102; in Skelton, 53–54, 67–72, 74–79; and symbolic order of the state, 26; in Wyatt, 13–21

ceremony, legal procedure as, 97–98
Chakrabarty, Dipesh, 336n14
Chamber, 50–51, 75; crown lands as managed in, 58–62; legal documents and, 68–72; officers pertaining to, 58–59, 61–63; Skelton on, 50–51, 56–57, 62–72, 74–76
Chambers, R. W., 351n25
Chancery: and Chamber, 68; and crown lands, 60; and original writs, 69–72
Chancery, High Court of, 84, 103, 113; common-law courts and, 34, 105, 122–23; copyhold and, 322; topical meaning of *Utopia* and, 103–6, 115, 128, 355n70; uses and, 322–23; *Utopia* on, 116, 121–25; Wolsey and, 82, 104–6, 115
chargeable land (Ireland), 147
Charlemagne, 213
Charles I, 261, 275
Chaucer, Geoffrey, 20, 49, 53, 74
Chichester, Sir Arthur, 158
children, legal conveyance of, 150, 320–21
Chudleigh's Case (1594), 323
Cicero: and civic humanism, 104, 107; on conquest, 141; on equity (*aequitas*), 107–9, 112–13, 128, 141, 355n67; on private ownership, 107, 141, 145; and Skelton, 344n5; and *Utopia*, 107–13. Works: *De officiis*, 107–8, 112, 141, 344n5, 354n59. See also *Ad Herennium* (Pseudo-Cicero)
civil law, 2, 157, 331n2; and absolutism, 80–81; in conflict with common law, 34–35, 292, 319–21, 327; and *imperium*, 228–29 and *iurisdictio*, 8; as linguistic model in English law, 194–99; and marine jurisdiction, 257–58, 266; and More, 87, 94; and piepowder procedure, 94; in theatrical representation, 319–21, 327

Clanchy, M. T., 69
Clark, Aidan, 362n75
Clark, G. N., 382n138
Clarkson, Paul, 321
Clavero, Bartolomé, 334n22
Clerk, John (Dean of the Chapel Royal), 90
Clerkenwell, theater in, 311
Cohen, David, 383n9
Coke, Sir Edward: on allegiance, 246–48; on courts of piepowder, 94; on denizenship, 377n61; on law French, 187–93, 195, 199–201, 219; on presumption of legitimacy, 295–96; and prohibitions, 29; as reporter, 154, 158, 217; on status of esquire, 135; on *ut* as adverb, 146–47. Works: *Institutes*, 94, 135, 146–47, 188, 295, 368n36; *Reports*, 180, 188–91, 243, 246–48, 250, 286–87, 368n36, 377n61
Collas, John P., 174, 365n113
comity, 165–66
commonness: in Cicero, 141; and commonweal, 135–36, 143; and English law, in Ireland, 41, 133–40, 158, 162–63; in *Faerie Queene*, 139–53, 167–70; in Ovid, 140–41; as source of juridical insight, 92, 95–96, 329
commonplacing, 222
Common Pleas, Court of, 2, 84, 87; King's Bench in relation to, 326–27
commonwealth (*respublica*), 135–36, 143, 153, 158
compass rose: in cartography, 266–69; as jurisdictional symbol, *260*, 267–68, 269–75, *270–76*, 284
composition (in Ireland), 166–67
confession and avoidance (in pleading), 116–17
conquest: and allegiance, 377n61; in Cicero, 141; as counter-conquest, in France, 41, 181, 188–92, 202–3, 212–14, 222–23; of England, by English, 203–10; of England, by Rome, 201–3, 213, 230–33, 235, 239–42; in *Faerie Queene*, 142–53, 163–70; of France, by English, 188–89, 200–202, 205; of Ireland, by law, 41, 133, 137–40; 147–49; 153–63; 166; of Ireland, by military force, 137, 147, 159; in Shakespeare, 181–82, 199–214, 222–23, 230–35, 239–42; in visual representation, 206–12, 216; of Wales, 212. *See also* Norman Conquest
conscience: at common law, 89, 91, 96, 102, 125; and ecclesiastical jurisdiction, 25–26, 34. *See also* equity; St. German, Christopher
consent, 80–82, 141, 143; jurisdiction as an effect of, 311–12, 317–18; theatrical audience in relation to, 220–21, 311
Constable, Case of Sir Henry (1601), 286–87
Constable, Marianne, 339n40, 340n45
Constable, Robert, 67, 76
constitutionalism, 33–38, 227
contract, 283–85, 304–5
copyhold, 29, 320–24
Cormack, Bradin, 337n22, 373n88, 373n92
cormorant. *See* disinheritance
Cornwall, France in relation to, 215
Costa, Pietro, 8–9, 14, 38, 334n22, 342n68
Cotterill, Rowland, 214
Coughlan, Patricia, 360n34, 361n56
courts. *See* Admiralty, High Court of; assistants, court of; assizes, courts of; Chancery, High Court of; Common Pleas, Court of; *curia regis*; ecclesiastical courts; Exchequer, Court of; Exchequer Chamber (est. 1585); General Surveyors, Court of; King's Bench, Court of; Lancaster, Duchy Chamber of; love, courts of; manorial courts; municipal courts; piepowder, courts of; Requests, Court of; Star

Chamber; Wards and Liveries, Court of
coverture, 306
Cowell, John, *The Interpreter*, 5, 75, 157, 327, 332n10
coyne and livery, 138
Crécy, Battle of, 200, 213, 372n78
Cromwell, Thomas, 88–91, 93–94, 158, 162, 228
Crown: and common-law tenure, 140, 147–50, 152; economic stability of, 35, 55–56; and evolution of prerogative, 35, 55–63; and jurisdictional centralization, 76–79, 166–67; and jurisdictional variegation, 36–38, 92–102; and parliament, 18, 35, 80; and person of king, 222, 246–53; and state, 35–38, 49, 56; in time, 55–56, 152–53
crown land, 51, 55–63, 66–67, 70–71; private estate management and, 58
Cuffe, Hugh, 149
Cunningham, Bernadette, 364n96
Cunningham, J. V., 382n1
Cunningham, Karen, 332n5
Cunobilis (king of Britain), 269
Cure for a Cuckold (Webster, Rowley, Heywood), 42; coverture in, 305–6; doubleness of names in, 303–9; empire in, 309–11; English Channel as jurisdictional marker in, 300; geography disrupted in, 310–14; illegitimacy and, 292–97; on jurisdiction as theatrical effect, 311–12, 317–18; jurisdictional conflict in, 292–93, 318–29; jurisdiction privatized in, 294; on labor, 315–16; legal fictions in, 311–12, 326–27; on legal normativity, 294, 312–13, 317–18, 324, 329; legal pleading in, 319–21; on legal rationalization, 313–15, 318–29; legal satire in, 324–29; on legal subjection, 293–94, 310–18, 324, 328–29; on marriage, 304–6, 312, 316–18; on normative resistance, 294, 298, 324, 328; paternity as landholding in, 322–23; 385n30; on patriarchy, 292, 304–5, 329; on professional mobility, 301–2; on rationalization of action, 307–9; on rationalization of agency, 313–17; suspension of time in, 305–6, 310–11; theater's authority in, 298, 307, 311–12, 316–18; on time of jurisdiction, 318
curia regis, 184
custom (at law): in England, 18, 75, 368n35; and Ireland, 41, 153–58, 160–63; in Spenser, 163–70

Dante, 334n22
Darcy v. Allen (1602), 255
Davies, Sir John: on Brehon law, 161; and Coke, 154; on custom, 139, 154, 161; on English sovereignty in Ireland, 137; on Irish landscape, 139; on Norman Conquest, 191–93, 199; as reporter, 153–59. Works: *A Discoverie of the True Causes Why Ireland Was Never Entirely Subdued*, 137, 139; "Lawes of Irelande," 161; *Reports*, 153–58, 191–93
Dawson, David, 364n105
decorum, 108–9, 113
Dee, John, *General and Rare Memorials*, 278–79
Derricke, John, *Image of Irelande*, 170
Derrida, Jacques, 6–7, 214, 372n79
de Silva, Alvaro, 351n26
deterritorialization: and allegiance, 242–49, 297; and conscience, 16–17, 25–26, 338n32; and legal subjectivity, 256, 285–90, 313–14; and mercantilism, 243–56; and ocean, 256–66; and sovereignty, 275–85; and theatrical treatment of space, 42, 219–23, 248–49, 275–90, 310–14
diem clausit extremum, writ of, 70–71
dignitas, 332n10

Dimock, Wai Chee, 337–38n27
Dinet, Pierre, 150
Discourse on the Exposicion and Understandinge of Statutes, 172–73
discretion, judicial, 315
disinheritance, 150–51
dispensation, royal, 120–21
displacement: and *imperium*, in *Pericles*, 275–83, 287–90; and Irish labor, 136; and thieving, 117, 121–22, 301–4; and university study, 331n2. *See also* Munster plantation (1585–98); Ulster plantation (1608–)
Doctors' Commons, 87
documentary culture, 66–79, 81
Doe, Norman, 125, 352n35, 354nn62–63
dominium: of conscience, 89; and *imperium*, 137, 149, 261–66, 275; in Ireland, 137, 141–42, 149; in ocean, 259–61, 263, 275; in Scotland, 244; in Spitzbergen, 380n112
Donation of Constantine, 229
Done and Egerton v. Hinton and Starkey (1617), 296
Donne, John, 376n30
dramatic authority: in *Cure for a Cuckold*, 298, 307, 311–12, 316–18; in Shakespeare, 201, 215–23, 290; in Skelton, 57, 72
Draper, J. W., 382n3
Drayton, Michael, *Poly-Olbion*, 266
Drobak, John N., 332n11
druids, 368n31
Dudley, Edmund, 61, 65, 76
Dudley, Robert (Earl of Essex), 199, 202
duo jura rule, 246–47
Dutton, Richard, 202

East India Company (Dutch), 257, 283
East India Company (English), 284–85, 301, 311
ecclesiastical courts, 2–3, 34, 36–38, 88, 91–93, 95–101, 292–93, 327

Eden, Kathy, 337n19, 365n110
Edward (the Black Prince), 213
Edward I, 76, 184, 212; Coke on, 188–89; visual representation of, 206
Edward II, 174
Edward III, 183, 200, 213; Coke on, 188–90, 200; Shakespeare on, 213; visual representation of, 206, *207*, 208–9
Edward IV, 50, 55, 58, 210; visual representation of, 206, *208*
Edwards, Philip, 375n24
Edwards, R. Dudley, 362n75
Egerton, Thomas (Baron Ellesmere), 154, 244, 246, 250
Ehrmann, Jacques, 30–31
Eleanor of Provence, 184
Elizabeth I, 217, 250, 321; and centralization, 15; and colonization of Ireland, 134, 137, 149; in Ditchley portrait, 266; and marine *imperium*, 275, 277, 278–79; in Spenser, 145, 151–53
Elyot, Sir Thomas, *Boke Named the Governour*, 135–36, 194–99
empire: in Britain, 24, 42, 89, 228–33, 243; of the ocean, 257–66, 275–85; and *regnum*, 253; symbolic representation of, 266–75; in urban comedy, 42, 291–92, 309–11. See also *imperium*
Empson, Richard, 61, 65
enactment, concept of, 181, 199–201, 214, 223
enclosures, 117, 123
energeia, 49, 234–35, 349n96
English Channel: in cartography, *260*, *268*; as jurisdictional threshold, 201, 205, 300
English Headlands, chart of, 259, *260*
equality (*aequalitas*), 106–7
equity, 4, 40; in Aristotle, 105, 110; and circumstantiality, 103, 113–14, 125–29; and conscience, 40, 105–6, 125; and decorum, 108–9; definitions of,

103; and equality, 106–9; as ethical principle, 34, 82–83, 103–6; in Fisher, 355n67; as interpretive principle, 34, 103, 105, 109–13; and juridical irony, 103, 128–29; and justice, 87, 101–3, 110, 113–15, 125–27; and law, 105–6; 123–25; and norm, in glossators, 8; and public interest, 109–13; of the statute, 110; and topical meaning of *Utopia*, 103–6, 115, 128, 355n70
Erasmus, *Adagia*, 112–13
escheator, 94–96, 99
esquire, status of, 134–35
estate in land, 55, 148, 152. *See also* copyhold; fee; fee farm; lease for years; tenancy at will
event, representation of, 47–49, 78–79, 179–81, 190–91, 200–201, 214, 223
Evesham, Battle of, 184
example: and allegory, 170–72; and historical topicality, in Skelton, 48–50; and humanism, in *Henry V*, 201–3; and legal humanism, 194–99
exception, legal character of, 6–10
Exchequer, 58–59, 67–68
Exchequer, Court of, 2
Exchequer Chamber (est. 1585), 243
Exeter Rebellion, 211
ex officio jurisdiction, 96
ex officio oath, 29

Fasolt, Constantin, 332n10, 342n68
fear, 235–36
fee: as heritable estate, 146–49; and jurisdiction over land, 321–22
fee farm, 58
fiction, truth status of, 100–101. *See also* hypothesis; legal fiction
Findlay, Alison, 382n3
Fineux, Sir John, 76–78, 121, 123
Finklepearl, Philip J., 366n4
fiscal feudalism, 4, 35, 39–40, 57–62, 67, 70
Fish, Simon, 100, 102

Fish, Stanley, 340n46
Fisher, John (Bishop of Rochester), 355n67
Fitzgerald, Gerald (Earl of Desmond), 147, 149
Fitzherbert, John, *Boke of Surveyinge and Improvmentes*, 347n58
Fleming, Juliet, 373n87
Fleming, Thomas (Chief Baron of the Exchequer), 254–55
Ford, Richard T., 7, 24–26, 336n9
Fortescue, Sir John: on absolutism, 194, 349n89; on equitable interpretation, 110–11, 355n71, 356n84; on law French and Conquest, 185–87; and legal nationalism, 187–93, 201; on maintenance of estate royal, 55; and Skelton, 55–57, 66. Works: *De laudibus legum Anglie*, 157, 185–87, 349n89; *De natura legis naturae* 111; 355n71, 356n84; *On the Governance of England*, 55, 63
Fortier, Mark, 352n44
fortune, 12–13, 56; romance plot and, 276, 285
Foucault, Michel, 4, 6–7, 9–10, 31
four-seas rule, 295
Fowler, Elizabeth, 165, 168–69, 354n61, 384n20
Fox, Alistair, 47, 99, 343n1, 353n48
France: and counter-conquest, 181, 188, 192–93, 200–206, 212; as England, 180–81, 194, 199–201, 205, 214; English conquest of, 189, 199–206, 212–14; as Ireland, 199; and jurisdictional production of English sovereignty, 3, 41–42, 219–23; in Shakespeare, 181, 199–206, 212–23; as Wales, 212; in Wyatt, 16, 19. *See also* French language; law French (Norman French); Norman Conquest
Fraunce, Abraham, *Lawiers Logike*, 157, 180

French language, 41; hybridity and, 178–80, 215–19; teaching of, 177–80. *See also* law
French (Norman French)
Frith, John, 85
Frowyk, Thomas, 67
Fulbecke, William, 35
Fuller, Lon, 384n24
Fulton, T. W., 259, 263, 378n80, 379nn89–90, 379n96, 380n112, 381n123
Fumerton, Patricia, 331n2
Furnivall's Inn, 86

Gaelic law (Ireland). *See* Brehon Law
Galloway, Bruce, 374n6
Garrett-Goodyear, Harold, 76–78
Gascoigne, George, 178–79
gavelkind (Ireland), 138–40, 156; allegory of, 144–46, 150–51
gavelkind (Kent), 18, 139
General Surveyors, Court of, 62
geographic irony, 203, 219–23, 310–11
Gerson, Jean, 105
Glaisyer, Natasha, 384n19
Glanvill, Sir Ranulf de, treatise attributed to, 188
Globe Theater, 222, 311
Godet, Gyles, *A Brief Abstract,* 210–12, 216, 372–73n83
Goldberg, Jonathan, 342n62, 373n1
Goodare, Julian, 376n36
Goodrich, Peter, 339n34, 339nn37–38, 343n71, 367n14; on jurisdiction as liberating force, 28, 31; on law French, 187; on positive unconscious of law, 157–58
Gordon, D. J., 380n109
Gossett, Suzanne, 380nn113–14, 383n136
Gower, John, *Confessio amantis,* 278, 290
Graham, Howard Jay, 369n46

Gray, Charles, 2, 27, 29, 339n41, 340n54, 356n82, 385n31
Greek, English vernacular and, 195, 199
Green, Richard Firth, 32, 69
Greenblatt, Stephen, 335n5, 341n54, 350n1
Griffiths, Jane, 49, 343n1, 345n26, 349n96
Grossi, Paolo, 8, 354n64
Grotius, Hugo, *Mare liberum,* 257–58, 263, 266, 275, 281–84, 378n81
Guernsey, 257
Guildhall, 300, 325–26
Gunby, David, 300, 384n23
Guy, John A., 34, 55, 104, 341n57, 344n14, 350n2, 350n4, 350nn6–10, 353n47, 353n51, 353n56, 357n93

Hadfield, Andrew, 142, 144, 160, 361n61
Hall, Edward, 61, 65
Hall, Joseph, 204
Halpern, Richard, 51, 53, 381n125
Hampton, Timothy, 370n57, 371n61
Hanson, Elizabeth, 332n5
Happé, Peter, 345n22
Harding, Alan, 35, 37–38
Harfleur: in *Henry V,* 220–21; in legal fiction, 312
Harris, W. O., 344n5
Haskett, Timothy, 352n44
Hastings, Battle of, 209
Hatton, Christopher, 278
hawking, 51–54
Heffner, Ray, 361n59
heir, status of: in Coke, 248; in Shakespeare, 251–53; in Spenser, 143
Helgerson, Richard, 266, 342n61
Helmholz, R. H., 34, 293, 295, 336n12, 340n43, 341n55
Henley, Pauline, 364n89
Henry I, *211*
Henry II, 156
Henry III, 184

Henri IV, 200
Henry IV: in Shakespeare, 212–14, 219–21; in visual representation, 206, *208*
Henry V: in Shakespeare, 41–42, 181, 201–3, 205–6, 212–23; in visual representation, 206, *207*, 208
Henry VI, Shakespeare on, 203, 212, 214
Henry VII, 114–15: and Chamber bureaucracy, 50, 58–61; and law French, 183, 192; as model for James I, 269; and *Prerogativa Regis*, 67; and *Quo Warranto*, 76; and Richmond portraits, 209–12; in Shakespeare, 203–6, 212
Henry VIII: and break with Rome, 33–34, 67, 89–91, 228; and bureaucratic centralization, 50–51, 58–62, 69; and evolution of prerogative, 52, 58–62; and expulsion of the minions, 47, 79; and Ireland, 151, 158, 160; and legal centralization, 15–17, 38, 76–79, 84, 93–94, 96, 99–102; and legal Normanism, 196; and More, 104; and Wyatt, 12–16
heresy, 85, 88, 97–99
Herman, Peter C., 371n68
herring, rights over, 24, 262–66
heterotopia, 31
Hexter, J. H., 103, 107, 355n69
Heywood, John. See *Cure for a Cuckold* (Webster, Rowley, Heywood)
Highley, Christopher, 145, 199, 359n34, 361n61, 370n55
Hill, Christopher, 363n87, 366n11, 368n33
Hobbes, Thomas, *Leviathan*, 251, 377n46
Hoeniger, F. D., 380n113
Holdsworth, W. S., 327, 384n24
Holinshed, Raphael, *Chronicles*, 213, 217, 219, 230, 359n31
Holsinger, Bruce, 32, 337n22

Holyband, Claudius, *French Littelton*, 177–80, 217
Homer, *Odyssey*, 171–72
Hood, Thomas. *See* English Headlands, chart of
Hopkins, Lisa, 380n116
Hopper, E. S., 343n1
Household, 50
Howell, T. B., 376n32
Hundred Years War, 189
Hutson, Lorna, 111, 341n54, 352n32, 354–55n65, 384n22
hypothesis: in common-law pleading, 116–19; in drama, 79, 215, 219–23, 311–12; and fiction of intention, 110–11, 307–8; in geometry, 337n20; in legal fiction, 311–12; in poetic fiction, 337n19; in rhetoric, 20

illegitimacy: at canon law, 292–93; at common law, 42–43, 292–97, 318–21; in Irish jurisprudence, 156; and William I, in *Richard III*, 205
imperium: as crisis event, in *Cymbeline*, 230–35; as distinct from *dominium*, 137, 149, 261–66; and Henry VIII, 89, 228; in Ireland, 137, 149; and James I, 257–66, 275; as jurisdictional principle, 18, 26, 137, 149, 228–30, 243; over ocean, 257–66; in Scotland, 375n20; symbolic representation of, 266–75
impositions. See *Bate's Case* (1606)
incest: in comedy, 384n27; in tragicomedy, 283
inconvenience, statutory, 112, 160, 173–76
inheritance: as legal principle, in Ireland, 149, 156; in Spenser, 142–43, 150–53, 364n91. *See also* heir, status of
Inns of Court, 178, 292, 319; readings and moots at, 67, 76, 183, 323, 367n17

intention: and consequentialism, 308–9; of king, 79–84; of legislator, 103, 110–12, 356n80; in theatrical representation, 307–9
interpretation: as coercion, 168–70, 174–76; and documentary culture, 67–73; and equity, 8–9, 34, 103, 105, 109–13; and evolving role of judiciary, 124–25, 169–70, 174–75; and sovereignty, 79–84, 222; and tyranny, 80–81, 111–12
Investiture Conflict, 43–44
Ireland, 4, 41; case-law in, 153–58; colonization of, 134–36, 141, 147–53, 159; legal coercion in, 24, 41, 153–63, 168–70; statute in, 158–60, 172–76; traditional landholding in, 138–40, 144–49, 152–53, 156. *See also* Davies, Sir John; Spenser, Edmund
issue (in pleading), 116–19, 315–16
ius commune, 16, 292
ius gentium. *See* law of nations (*ius gentium*)
Ives, E. W., 348n84, 385n33

Jackson, Macdonald P., 278, 380n113
James, Heather, 253
James I: and *ante-nati*, 249–53; and colonization of Ireland, 153, 159; and East India Company, 283–85; and ecumenism, 179; and idea of Britain, 227–30, 266, 267, 269; and imperial cartography, 269–75; and impositions, 254–56; and marine *imperium*, 257–69, 278–79, 282–83, 291; and minor jurisdictions, 36–38; and Norman Yoke, 162; as peacemaker, 232, 269, 270; and *post-nati*, 243–47; and royal prerogative, 35–38, 254–56; and Scottish dominion, 244, 376n36
Jerusalem Chamber, 219, 222
John (king of England), 156; visual representation of, 206

Jones, Emrys, 375n18
Jones, W. J., 356n82, 385n31
Jonson, Ben, 229, 269, 312
Jordan, Constance, 254, 342n62, 373n2, 381n128
judges, role of, 124–25, 169–70, 174–75, 315
jurisdiction, concept of: as administrative-legal principle, 1, 3; and conscience, 25; as counter-site (heterotopia), 31; and disorientation, 44; and displacement, 2–5, 9, 21, 121–22, 136, 287–90, 331n2; as distributive process, 8, 14, 38, 342n68; as dramatic projection, in theater, 219–23, 298, 312, 316–18; as interpretation, 8; in its plurality, 1–6, 24–31, 36–38, 91–92, 128–29, 292–94, 324, 329; as law's speaking (*iuris dictio*), 8, 298, 312, 317–18; and legal centralization, 18, 26–30, 32–33, 53–54, 59, 67, 75–79; and legal ideology, 4, 12, 24–30; and legal normativity, 1, 5–10, 91–92, 100–102, 128–29, 312–13, 319, 324, 329; and legal subjectivity, 15, 17–18, 21, 25, 121, 253–56, 287–90, 293–94, 324, 329; and literary production, 1–5, 30–33, 38–39, 43–44; as mirror, 8–9; and particularity, 91–92, 126–29; and political accommodation, 220–23, 232, 235, 275, 279–85; as potentiality in law, 1–5, 8–10, 43–44, 293–94, 329; as practice, 14, 19–20, 24–25; and privacy, 19, 89, 289–90, 294; and royal authority, 35–38; and sovereignty, 5–10, 36–38, 221–23, 275–85, 329, 342n68; and spatialization, 30–31; and state formation, 26, 33–38, 44; as symbolized by digestion, 220–23; as symbolized by translation, 215–19; and territorialization, 14–17, 25–26; and time, 17–18, 23, 30–31, 318

jurisdiction, historical: over bastardy, 292–97; and bureaucratic delegation, 51–54, 57; in cartographic representation, 267–68, 270–74, 276–77; and conscience, 25, 34, 83, 89, 105–6; and dueling, 300; and Investiture Conflict, 43–44; over Ireland, 136–40, 147–49, 153–63; over land not held by common-law seisin, 138–40, 147–49, 321–23; and letters of Marque, 299, 301; over liminal shore; 258–59, 260, 285–87; over ocean, 37, 42, 256–66, 278–79; and piracy, 287, 299; over *post-nati*, 242–53; of Roman Church, 17, 25–26, 44, 85, 89–91, 339n33; and royal authority, 35–38, 96, 99–102; and sanctuary, 77–79, 121; and sovereignty, 36–38, 342n68; over spiritual matters, 16–17, 25–26, 33–34, 36, 39–40, 53–54, 77–79, 93–102, 121, 292–93; and state formation, 26, 33–38, 44; over travelers, 248–49, 253–56, 295–97, 331n2; over wreck, 286–87. *See also specific courts; specific laws*
jury trial, 95–98
Justinian, *Corpus iuris civilis*, 35. *See also* civil law
Juvenal, 195

Kantorowicz, Ernst, 349n90, 377n48
Kaufman, Peter Iver, 348n83
Keane, Robert, 350n2
Keilen, Sean, 345n28
Kent: and customary law, 12, 16–18, 139; and local identity, 14–16, 20; as threshold, 300
King's Bench, Court of, 2, 76; Common Pleas in conflict with, 326–27; conscience and, 125
King's chambers (coastal waters), 259–61
King's Council, 58–59, 97, 103–4
king's two bodies, theory of, 246–48

Kinsale, Battle of, 202
Kipling, Gordon, 209
Kirshner, Julius, 331n2
Kisch, Guido, 355n66
Knapp, Ethan, 344n13
Knolles, Richard, 333n14

labor, 117, 136; legal character of, 315–16; poetry as, 19–21
Laine, Amos Lee, 369n46
Lambarde, William, works: *Archeion*, 349n94; *Perambulation of Kent*, 335n9
Lancashire, map of, 269, 270, 275, 276, 277
Lancaster, Duchy Chamber of, 87
Landman, James, 340n45
Latham, Simon, 345n20
Latin: and English vernacular, 53–54, 69–71, 88, 102, 116, 180–94, 217–19; and law French, 183, 187, 194, 198, 217–19
latitat, writ of, 326–27
law and literature (subfield), 2–5, 10, 21–23, 30–31
law French (Norman French), 41, 178; Coke on, 187–91, 368n36; Davies on, 191–93; Elyot on, 195–96; English characterization of, 197–98; Fortescue on, 185–87; Holyband in relation to, 177–80, 217; national identity and, 182–85; Norman Conquest and, 179–87; Rastell on, 197–98; Shakespeare's invocation of, 217–19; Smith on, 194–95; Starkey on, 196–99
law merchant, 94
law of nations (*ius gentium*), 231, 256, 280–81, 287
law of reason, 105
laws. *See* Brehon law; canon law; civil law; custom (at law); *ius commune*; law merchant; law of nations (*ius gentium*); law of reason; *leges terrae*; natural law

Leadam, I. S., 350n9
lease for years, 58
legal antiquarianism, 335n9
legal fiction, 295, 311–12, 326–27
legal formalism, 86, 111, 114–25
legal nationalism: in Ireland, 133, 154–58, 161; and law French, 40–41, 185–99; in legal historiography, 182–85
legal profession: as audience for theater, 292, 318–19; and counter-professionalization, 301, 328–29; and education, 67, 76, 178, 185–86, 217–18; and jurisdictional conflict, 34–36, 40; and More, 86–88, 124–25; and nationalism, 40, 133, 182; satire of, 324–29
legal realism, 86
legal reason, 30, 105, 176, 182, 368n36
legal satire, 324–28
legal subjectivity: and impersonality, 23, 252–53; in Ireland, 136, 149; and jurisdictional heterogeneity, 14–17, 293–94, 324; in sanctuary, 121; in territorial regime, 25; and transnational *imperium*, 253–56, 287–90
Legendre, Pierre, 26, 28, 339n39, 349n91
leges terrae, 18
legitimacy, presumption of, 293–97, 309–10, 329
Lemon, Rebecca, 332n5
Leo X, 87
Lerer, Seth, 19–20, 48–49, 69
Levack, Brian, 229, 342n61, 374n6
Lever, J. W., 372n82
liberty, 2, 13–21, 29, 32; equitable procedure and, 122–23; royal identity and, 79–84
Lincoln's Inn, 67, 86
Lindsay, Barbara, 371n65
literary authority, 2–5, 22–23, 30–33, 38–39, 43, 345n28. *See also* dramatic authority

Littleton, Sir Thomas, *Tenures*, 146, 178, 180, 368n36
livery of seisin, 150
Livy, 113
local law, 15–16, 18, 27, 32
Lockey, Brian, 357n1, 360n38, 373n3
Logan, George, 115, 354n58
London, 87, 103–4, 177, 201–2, 249, 300; East India Company and, 301; legal activity in, 39, 42, 325–26; market court in, 94–95; north of England in relation to, 99; ocean in relation to, 292, 309–11, 313; and *quo warranto*, 76–77
love, courts of, 31
Lupset, Thomas, 127, 196–97
Lupton, Julia Reinhard, 333n17, 359n32
Luther, Martin, 85, 90
Lydgate, John, 49

MacCarthy-Mor, Donal (Earl of Clancare), 149
MacCarthy-Morragh, Michael, 149, 360n41
Macinnes, Allan I., 376n36
Macrobius, 107
MacShane, James, 149
Maine, Henry Summer, 25, 338n29
Maitland, F. W., 174, 182, 184–85, 336n13, 367nn14–15, 367nn19–20
Majeske, Andrew J., 352n44
Maley, Willy, 358n16, 361n61
Mandelstam, Osip, 338n27
Manlian laws, 113–14
manorial courts, 3, 321–23
Marcus, Leah, 200, 243, 375n21
Markham, John, 296
marque, letters of, 299, 301
marriage: in city comedy, 298, 304–6, 316–18; in *Cymbeline*, 252; in dynastic negotiation, 217–19, 279, 283; in *Henry V*, 217–19; in *Pericles*, 279, 283
Marshall, William, 76
Marshalsea prison, 326

martial law, 166
Martz, Louis, 351n25
Mason, H. A., 13
Mason, R. A., 376n36
Massingham, K. R., 350n7
Masten, Jeffrey, 290
Mazzio, Carla, 336n11, 373n92
McCabe, Richard, 360n35, 364n103
McGlynn, Margaret, 347n65
McRae, Andrew, 335n8
McVeigh, Sean, 331n4
Mediterranean Sea, 275; jurisdictional complexity of, 257, 277, 282
merchants, 253–56, 281–85, 297, 299, 301
mesne tenure, 148
Middlesex, 75–78; bill of, 326–27
Milton, John, *Paradise Lost*, 361n57
mischief, inconvenience in relation to, 174
Momigliano, Arnaldo, 11
Montaigne, Michel de, 145, 371n61
Moody, T. W., 362n75
More, Sir Thomas: and Cicero, 107–9, 112–13; and common-law forms, in *Utopia*, 115–21; on courts of piepowder, 92–102; and equitable jurisdictions, 87–88, 124–25; on equity, 102–14, 121–25; on fiction, in relation to truth, 86, 100–102, 125–29; on law's relation to the real, 100–101, 125–29; legal career of, 86–88; on legal interpretation, 109–12; on legal proceduralism, 114–24; and legal realism, 86; on meddling, 88–92; on particularity, 125–29; and Plato, 90, 92, 104; and Shakespeare's *Richard III*, 201; and spiritual jurisdiction, 17, 85, 89, 90, 93–102. Works: *Apology*, 88, 93, 97; *Confutation of Tyndale's Answer*, 88, 90, 99; *Debellation of Salem and Bizance*, 88, 93, 97, 341n57; *Dialogue concerning Heresies*, 88–89, 98;

History of King Richard III, 85, 201; legal parable in letter from Margaret Roper, 92–102; *Utopia*, 22, 40, 43, 85–86, 91, 102–29
Morgan, Hiram, 358n2
Mortimer, Edmund, 213
Morton, John (Archbishop of York), 114–25, 128
Moss, Ann, 373n92
Mullaney, Steven, 181, 200, 281–82, 290
municipal courts, 3, 325
Munster plantation (1585–98), 133, 137, 141–42, 147–50, 159
Murrin, Michael, 173

name: and contract, 305; and empire, 283–85; in family, 384–85n27; in law, 298, 318, 329; and logic of categorization, 302–4, in marriage, 304–5; potential in doubleness of, 303–9; and professional vocation, 302–5; as source of action, in theater, 305–7, 309; as source of judgment, 309
narratio (in pleading), 116
nationalism, English: and hybridity, 178–79; in Ireland, 161; and James VI, 244, 266; and mercantilism, 284–85; and militarism, 193; in Shakespeare, 199–200, 214–17; in Wyatt, 16. *See also* legal nationalism
natural law, 141, 145, 247–48, 280–81, 292, 320–21
Neff, Merlin L., 364n92
Neill, Michael, 383n3
Neuse, Richard, 151
Neuss, Paula, 70, 343n1
new historicism, 336n10
New Inn, 86
Nicholls, Kenneth, 138–39, 148
Nicolas, Sir Harris, 296
nightingale, 345n28
Nine Years War, 144, 159
nisi prius, 325–26
Nolan, Maura, 49

Norbrook, David, 342n62, 353n50, 360n35
norm, legal, 27; jurisdictional disruption of, 1, 5–10, 12, 30–31, 40, 91–92, 100–102, 128–29, 291, 294, 319, 324, 329; poetic norms and, 20–21; social norm and, 332n11, 383n9; theatrical production of, 312, 316–18; time's disruption of, 17–18, 30–31, 318
Norman Conquest: and conquest of France, 41, 205, 212–23; as crisis event, 181, 184–85; and dynastic legitimization, 206–12; in *Henry V*, 42, 212–23; and hybrid identity, 179, 181–82, 214; as iterative structure, 181, 188–91, 199–23; and law French, 41, 182–93; in legal humanism, 194–99; in legal nationalism, 185–93; and linguistic hybridity, 215–19; in *Richard III*, 41–42, 203–6, 212; and Saxon England, 209, 216. *See also* law French (Norman French); Norman Yoke; William I
Normandy, England in relation to, 205
Norman Yoke, 154, 162–63, 180–81, 191–92; historiography of, 363n87
Northamptonshire, map of, 271
North Sea, jurisdiction over, 24, 262–66, 278–79
novel disseisin, writ of, 184

oaths, 73–76
O'More, Rory Og, 170
O'Neill, Hugh, 144, 159
Ordinances at Eltham for Henry VIII, 48
ordo, jurisdiction in relation to, 332n10
Orgel, Stephen, 375n19, 380n113, 382n137
Oudendijk, J. K., 378n84, 380n112, 382n138
outlawry, 94–95, 236, 239, 247–48
Ovid, *Metamorphoses*, 140–41, 144
Owl and the Nightingale, 32

Padelford, Frederick M., 364n97
Pagden, Anthony, 229
Pale (Ireland), 136, 158, 160
Parker, Matthew (Archbishop of Canterbury), 34
Parker, Patricia, 253
Parkin-Speer, Diana, 363n88
Parliament (English), 87, 101, 143, 244, 250, 254; crown and, 18, 35, 38, 94; customs of, 192; omnicompetence of, 162, 174–75, statute and, 162
Parliament (Irish), 136, 158–59, 162, 363n75
pastoral: vs. epic, 153; as imperial genre 134, 141, 144, 153; and property, 41, 133, 142–43, 152
Patterson, Annabel, 167–69, 341n54, 364n90
Patterson, Nerys, 363n78
Patterson, W. B., 366n7, 375n22
Pawlisch, Hans, 159, 360n47, 362nn64–65, 362n72, 362n75
Payne, Robert, 359n31
Pennell, Sara, 384n19
Peters, Julie Stone, 2, 338n27
piepowder, courts of, 92–102
piracy, 135, 287, 299
pleading: as legal form, 116–20, 356n73; as literary form, 115–20, 316, 319–21
Pleadings, Statute of (1362), 186–87
Plowden, Edmund, *Reports*, 172, 217–18
Plucknett, T. F. T., 336n13
Plutarch, 278–79, 364n105
Pocock, J. G. A., 154, 157, 190, 253, 336n14, 362n64, 363n87; poetic authority, 49, 53–54
Pollock, Frederick, 336n13, 367nn14–15, 367nn19–20
Polydore Vergil, 191
Pontanus, Jacobus, 141, 358n28
Portugal, 257, 283–84
Posner, Richard, 337n22
Post, Gaines, 345n34

Post, J. B., 352n44
post-nati. See *Calvin's Case* (1608)
Powell, Thomas, *Tom of All Trades*, 302
Poyning's law, 362n75
Poyntz, John, 12–14, 17–20
praemunire, writ of, 89, 91, 155–56
Prerogativa Regis (ca. 1324), 67, 76, 80, 84
Prest, Wilfred, 341n58
primer seisin, 60
Pringsheim, Fritz, 349n97
Priory of St. John of Jerusalem, 77–78
Privy Chamber, 47, 50–51
prize, 135, 287, 299
prohibitions, 2, 34–38, 293
Pugliatti, Paola, 373n85

Quia Emptores, Statute of (1290), 148, 346n43
Quinn, David B., 362n75
Quint, David, 370n58
quodlibet being, 129, 252–53
Quo Warranto, Statute of (1290), 76, 78
quo warranto, writ of, 75–79

Racine, Jean, *Phèdre,* 30
Raffield, Paul, 339n34
Ralegh, Sir Walter, 172
Ramsay, R. L., 343n1, 344n5
Rancière, Jacques, 4–5, 23
Rastell, John, works: *Abridgement of the Statutes,* 197–98; *Pastyme of People,* 206, 207–8, 209–10, 210
rationalization, legal: and bureaucratic culture, 55, 57–62, 66–71; through case law, in Ireland, 153–58; and centralization, 1, 29; and conscience, 40, 83, 105–6, 124–25; and contingency, 28–30, 157; and France, at common law, 182–93; and illegitimacy, 292–97; incompleteness of, 5, 29, 39, 318–29; and institutional reason, 175–76; and legal humanism, 194–99; and legal intentionalism, 307–9; and legal reason, 294, 309–18; through natural law, in relation to Scotland, 242–53; obstacles to, in Ireland, 137–40, 147–49; through royal prerogative, on ocean, 257–66; in Spenser, 139–53, 162–76; through statute, in Ireland, 158–63; and statutory convenience, 173–75; and territorialization, 26
readings, 67, 76
Redman, Robert, 369n46
Relihan, Constance, 380n115
reports of cases: in Ireland, 153–58; and law French, 183, 188–93; as linguistic model, in theater, 217–19
republicanism, 284
repugnancy, 174
Requests, Court of, 34
Reuger, Zofia, 349n93
rhetoric: and *energeia,* 49, 234–35, 349n96; and legal reform, 195–96; and time, 115–16
Rich, Barnaby, 359n31
Richard I: and prescription or customary use, 75–76; in Shakespeare, 213; in visual representation, 206, *207,* 209–10
Richard II, 188; deposition of, 208, 212, 214
Richard III: and law French, 183; and legitimization of Tudor dynasty, 210; in More, 201; in Shakespeare, 201, 203–6; 210
Richardson, W. C., 61, 346n41, 346nn47–50, 347nn52–56
Ridley, Thomas, 36–38
Rockhill, Gabriel, 332n9
Roman law. *See* civil law
Rome, 16, 19, 33, 40, 99, 202, 222, 228–35
Roper, Margaret, 88, 92–100
Roper, William, 86–87, 124–25
Ross, Charles, 332n5, 360n37, 384n18

Rowley, William. See *Cure for a Cuckold* (Webster, Rowley, Heywood)
royal dispensation, 120–21
royal household, 39, 48. *See also* Chamber; Household; Privy Chamber
royal prerogative, 35–38; animal life and, 24, 52, 155, 262–66; documentary culture and, 67–73; evolution of, 57–62, 66–67; impositions and, 254–56, 282; legal interpretation and, 112; liberty and, 80–84; Nathaniel Bacon on, 67; Skelton on, 51–54, 57–66
Rutlandshire, map of, 271, 272

Sackville, Robert, 177
Salic law, 212–13, 218–19
sanctuary, 77–78, 121
Sandys, Sir Edwin, 244, 249–50
Sargent, Daniel, 351n26
Sassoferrato, Bartolo da (Bartolus), 266
Savage, Sir John, 77
Saxon kings, 208–9, 213, 216
Saxton, Christopher, 275, 277
Scattergood, John, 48, 345n25
Schmitt, Carl, 7
Schwyzer, Philip, 199, 373n90
Scodel, Joshua, 347n60
Scotland, 36–37, 42, 375n20; James VI and I and, 228–30, 242–53, 262, 269; Spenser on, 151–52; symbolic representation of Britain and, 266–68
seisin, 146–53
Selden, John, *Mare clausum*, 259, 261, 275, 381n119
seneschal (in Ireland), 137, 165–66
serjeant at law, status of, 87, 327
Shakespeare, William: on allegiance, 42, 242–43, 248–49, 256; on crisis in relation to jurisdictional limit, 230–35, 291; and enactment, as historical concept, 181, 199–201, 214, 223; and exemplarity, 201–3; on France as shadow jurisdiction, 41–42, 214, 222–23; and historical drama, 181–82, 214, 220–21; and languages of case law, 217–19; on linguistic interference as source of meaning, 215–19; on marine jurisdiction, 42, 275–78, 285–90; on Norman conquest, 181–82, 199–214, 223; and rehearsal, as cultural concept, 181, 200; on reiterative conquest, 181, 199–206, 212–14, 222–23; on Roman conquest of England, 201–3, 213, 230–33, 235, 239–42; on royal authority, 42, 201, 219–23, 275–83, 285–90; and sources, 217–19, 278–79, 281; on Stuart *imperium*, 42, 227, 230–33, 242–43, 248–49, 251–57, 275–85; on temporal threshold, 42, 236–42, 251–53; on territorial threshold, 42, 219–23, 235–40, 248–49, 285–91; and theater's authority, 201, 215–23, 290; on theatre's disruption of jurisdictional space, 219–23, 290; on William I as bastard, 204–5; on wreck, 286–87. Works: *Cymbeline*, 22, 42, 202, 227, 230–44, 248–56, 279, 289, 375n19; *Edward III*, 372n78; 1 *Henry VI*, 200; 3 *Henry VI*, 212; 1 *Henry IV*, 181; 2 *Henry IV*, 181, 213–15, 219, 370n59; *Henry V*, 199–203, 205, 212–23; *King John*, 294–97, 383n10; *Pericles*, 42, 227, 256–57, 275–90, 380n113; *Richard III*, 41, 85, 200, 203–6, 212; *The Tempest*, 227; *The Winter's Tale*, 227
Sheehan, Anthony, 149
Sherman, William H., 381n119, 381n122
Shuger, Deborah, 333n17
Sidney, Sir Philip, 337n19; 380n118
Simpson, A. W. B., 320, 339n42, 385n32
Simpson, James, 32–33, 43, 72, 126, 343n1
Skelton, John: on conscience, 72, 79–82; on equity, 82–84; on evolving

prerogative, 51–54, 62–84; on legal centralization, 39–40, 51–57, 75–79; and literary topicality, 47–50, 78–79; on oaths, 73–75; and poetic authority, 49, 53–54; and *quo warranto*, 73–79; and sanctuary, 4, 51, 76–77; and time, 54–55, 62–64, 70–72, 79; on writing, 66–72, 81, 84. Works: *Magnyfycence*, 39, 47–56, 62–84; *Ware the Hauke*, 53–54

Skinner, Quentin, 104, 333n14, 356n77

Smith, Sir Thomas, works: *De republica Anglorum*, 134–35, 194–98; *Discourse of the Commonweal*, 134; *Letter sent by I. B. Gentleman*, 134

Sokol, B. J., and Mary, 383n3, 383n16

Sommerville, Johann P., 366n11

Sophocles, *Oedipus Rex*, 30

sovereignty: and alternative sovereignty, 40–42, 275–85; as conceptual trap, 2, 9; as decline from jurisdiction, 37–38, 99–100, 329, 342n68; and discipline, 6; as fantasy of centralized power, in Wyatt, 15–16; as fantasy of personal power, 33, 214, 221–23; as *imperium*, in Britain, 228–30; as indivisible power, 6, 37, 222; and intention, in Skelton, 79–82; and juridical exception (Agamben), 6–7, 9; and jurisdiction in Ireland, 137, 151; and jurisdiction over France, 192; jurisdiction's disruption of, 6–10, 9, 44, 222–23, 275–85, 329

Spain, 19, 229, 258, 261, 285

Speed, John, *Theatre of the Empire of Great Britaine*, 268, 269, 270–71, 272, 272, 273, 274

Spelman, Sir John, 76

Spenser, Edmund: on allegorical interpretation 170–76; on custom, 160–70; on Elizabeth as queen of Ireland, 145–46, 151–53; and epic, 153; and exemplarity, 170–71; and Homer, 171–72; on inconvenience, 160, 173–76; on inheritance, 142, 150–53; on kin ownership in Ireland, 140–53; on legal conquest, in Ireland, 41, 140–53, 159–60, 162–76; and natural law, 145; on Norman Yoke, 162–63; and Ovid, 140–41, 144; and pastoral, in Ireland, 140–53; on seisin, 146–47, 150, 151–53; and statute, 159–63, 170–76; on statutory interpretation, 167–70, 172–76; on tanistry, 139–40. Works: *Colin Clouts Come Home Againe*, 142; *Faerie Queene*, 22, 41, 133, 140–48, 150–53, 163–74, 359n26; *View of the Present State of Ireland*, 139, 159–60, 162–65, 173–75, 359n25

Stanyhurst, Richard, 359n31

Star Chamber, 87, 104

Starkey, David, 47, 50, 343n1

Starkey, Thomas, *Dialogue between Reginald Pole and Thomas Lupset*, 194, 196–99

state, concept of, 32–38, 43–44

state of exception, 6–10

status regis, 55–57

status regni, 56–57

statute: and allegory, 170–76; and case-law, in Ireland, 153–58; and common law, 154, 158; and inconvenience, 174–75; interpretation of, 33, 110–13, 121–23, 172–73, 341n55; as judgment, 121; and legal reform, in Ireland, 158–63; in linguistic relation to case reports, 183, 186–88, 197–98

Statutes of Kilkenny, 160

Steiner, Emily, 347n66

Steinsaltz, David, 372n81

St. German, Christopher: on conscience as equity, 34, 40, 82–83, 105–6, 125; and More, 85, 88, 93–99; on spiritual and temporal authority, 93–97, 99, 102, 106. Works: *Doctor and Student*, 34, 40, 82–83, 105–6, 125, 353n52

Stillman, Robert E., 360n35
St. Leger, Warham, 149, 158–59
St. Martin's-le-Grand, 78
Strayer, Joseph, 43–44
Strier, Richard, 357n91
Strohm, Paul, 74, 335n1
Strong, Roy, 371n65
subinfeudation, 148
Succession, Act of (1534), 91
Sullivan, Garrett, 335n8, 376n28
Surat (India), 311, 313
surrender and regrant, 137–40
surrogacy, 292
swans, 51–52

Talbot, Thomas, 210
tanistry, 138–40, 156, 164; allegory of, 144–46
Taylor, Gary, 216
tenancy at will, 147, 149
tenancy in chief (*in capite*), 51, 58, 60–62, 70–71
tenure, English: and feudalism, 148; in Ireland, 137–38, 146–53; as metaphor for holding children, 150–51, 321–23; and uses, 320–24. *See also* Ireland: traditional landholding in
territorialization, 14–17, 25–26, 52–54; surveying and, 15, 64
Thomas Aquinas, 105
Thomas Dekker, 229
Thompson, Ann, 375n25
Thornborough, John, 229, 374n17
Thorne, Samuel, 67, 174–75, 341n55, 346nn42–43, 346nn45–46, 347n57, 363n85
threshold, temporal: in Augustine, 237, 375n27; in *Calvin's Case*, 243, 249–51, 253; in *Cymbeline*, 42, 227–28, 230–31, 235–42, 251–53, 291; and political crisis, 230–31, 237–38, 241–42; and presumption of legitimacy, 296–97; and *quodlibet* subjectivity, 252–53
threshold, territorial: in *Bate's Case*, 255; in *Calvin's Case*, 243–45; in *Cure for a Cuckold*, 300, 309–11; in *Cymbeline*, 42, 230–35, 238–40, 242–43, 248–49, 291; and estrangement of identity, 287–90; in *Henry V*, 215, 219–23; and jurisdictional elasticity of shore, 257–66, 260, 285–87, 300; and jurisdictional hybridity, 215, 285–91; and limits of centralization, 14–19; as marker of law's reason, 309–11; in *Pericles*, 275–77, 285–91; and political crisis, 230–35, 238–49; and presumption of legitimacy, 295–97; and property, 285–87; and split subjectivity, 255–56; in Wyatt, 14–19
Tierney, Brian, 332n10
time: and bureaucratic action, 62; and fear, 235–36; and intention, in theater, 307–9; and jurisdiction, 17–18, 30–31, 54–55, 64, 317–18; in land, 55, 148, 152; and law, 337n27; of legal judgment, 121; and literary topicality, 47–48; and literature, 11–12; and presumption of legitimacy, 295–97; and rhetorical *topoi*, 115–16; and social forms, 11–12; and its suspension, in theater, 305–6; and virtue, 236–42
Tompkins, J. M. S., 380n118
topicality: and allegory, 363n105; and event, 47–49, 52, 78–80; and interpretation, 41, 170, 173–76; and time, 47–48
Tottel, Richard, 13
Tower of London, 12, 40, 88, 114
translatio imperii, 230–33
Trapp, J. B., 88, 353n56
Treaty of London (1604), 258
trial, form of, 94–102
Trimpi, Wesley, 336n17, 365n106, 384n25

Tuck, Richard, 379n90, 379n93
Tunstall, Cuthbert, 355n70
Twine, Laurence, *Patterne of Painefull Adventures*, 278, 281
Tyndale, William: and More, 89–90; *New Testament*, 88

Ullman, Walter, 374n9
Ulster, colonization of, 134–36
Ulster plantation (1608–), 159
uniformity (*aequabilitas*): and equity, 106–9, 167–68; and particularity, 126–29; and Wolsey's justice, 127
Union, Act of (1536), 212
Union, politics of, 228–30, 243. See also *Calvin's Case* (1608)
Union of the Crowns (1603), 42, 228
United Provinces, 258–59, 261–63, 283
uses, 320–24
Uses, Statute of (1536), 322

Valeriano, Piero, *Hieroglyphica*, 150
Vallejo, Jesús, 334n24, 342n68
van Es, Bart, 363n86
van Eysinga, W. J. M., 382n138
Venice, 254–56
verdict, truth status of, 100–102
viceregal authority (Ireland), 152, 362n75
Vickers, Brian, 380n113
Vinogradoff, Paul, 25
violence: interpretive; 6–7, 109–13, 160–63, 167–76; military, 159–60, 165, 168, 170–71, 202, 208–9, 216, 221
Virgil, *Aeneid*, 153, 253, 280–81

Wales: and absorption of Conquest, 212; in cartographic representation, 266, 273, 274, 274; in *Cymbeline*, 236; in *Henry V*, 199, 215–16, 230; as France, 212
Walker, Greg, 47–48, 57, 343n1
Wallace, John, 48

Walsh, Peter, 359n31
Wards and Liveries, Court of, 62
wardship, 60–62, 346n43
warrant, 73–75. See also *Quo Warranto*, Statute of (1290); *quo warranto*, writ of Warren, Clyde, 321
Warwickshire, map of, 269, 271
Waters, David A., 267–69
Watson, George, 372n81
Webster, John. See *Cure for a Cuckold* (Webster, Rowley, Heywood)
Weimann, Robert, 33
Weiner, Andrew, 357n95
Weisberg, Richard, 337n26
Welwood, William, *Abridgement of All Sea-Lawes*, 257–59
West, William, 172
Westminster: as legal center, 18, 87; as sanctuary, 76–78
whiggism, 32, 35–37, 340n54
White, James Boyd, 337n26
White, Rowland, works: "Discors Touching Ireland," 161; "The Dysorders of the Irisshery," 161
Wilkins, George, *The Painefull Adventures of Pericles Prince of Tyre*, 275
William I: in Coke, 190–91; in Davies, 191–92; in Fortescue, 185–86; as present absence in dynastic representation, 209–12; in Rastell, 197; in rhetorical exercise (Wilson), 196; in Shakespeare, 204–6, 213, 216; in Spenser, 162–63; in visual representation, 206, 207, 208–9, 211. See also Norman Conquest
William II: and accommodation of Conquest, 209–13, 215; in visual representation, 209–12, 210, 211
Williams, Deanne, 200, 370n55
Williams, Raymond, 358n10
Williamson, J. W., 371n65
Wilson, Luke, 307, 332n6

Wilson, Thomas, *Arte of Rhetorique*, 196–97
Wiseman, Sir Robert, 157
Wolffe, B. P., 58, 346nn37–40
Wolsey, Thomas (Archbishop of Canterbury), 47, 51, 62, 82–83, 90–91, 103–6, 115, 123–24, 127
Womersly, David, 200, 372n77
Woodbine, George E., 184, 367n14, 367n18
wreck (*wreccum maris*), 286–87
Wrightson, Keith, 383n9

Writ, original, 69–70; poetry as, 72
Wyatt, Sir Thomas: and Alemanni, 13; and local identity, 15–16, 18, 27; and poetic authority, 18–21; and spiritual jurisdiction, 16–17; and territoriality, 14–21, 26, 36; and time as jurisdiction, 17–18

Yates, Frances, 381n122
year-books, 183, 188, 192–93
Yelverton, 255
Ymage of Love, 98

www.ingramcontent.com/pod-product-compliance
Lightning Source LLC
Chambersburg PA
CBHW021928290426
44108CB00012B/764